Egypt
& the Sudan
a travel survival kit

Scott Wayne

Egypt & the Sudan - a travel survival kit
   1st edition

Published by
   Lonely Planet Publications
   Head Office: PO Box 88, South Yarra, Victoria 3134, Australia
   Also: PO Box 2001A, Berkeley, California 94702, USA

Printed by
   Colorcraft, Hong Kong

Photographs
   Scott Wayne (SW)
   Hugh Finlay (HF)
   Linda Henderson: front cover
   Richard Everist: back cover

Cartoons
   Tony Jenkins

Published
   November 1987

National Library of Australia
Cataloguing in Publication Data

Wayne, Scott
Egypt & the Sudan, a travel survival kit

   Includes index.
   ISBN 0 86442 001 3.

   1. Egypt – Description and travel – 1945 – Guide-books.
   2. Sudan – Description and travel – Guide-books. I. Title.

916.2'04
© Lonely Planet Publications 1987

Scott Wayne

Scott Wayne is an American who has lived, studied and travelled throughout the Middle East, Africa and Europe. He graduated from Georgetown University's School of Foreign Service with a degree in International Relations. He also did graduate studies at the Royal Institute of International Affairs in London and the University of Southern California. His studies at Georgetown included a long stint at the American University in Cairo and many adventures up and down the Nile. He later returned to Egypt and the Sudan to write this guide. Scott is also author of Lonely Planet's forthcoming *Baja – a travel survival kit*.

Lonely Planet Credits

Editor	Lindy Cameron
Maps, design, cover design & illustrations	Graham Imeson
Typesetting	Ann Jeffree

Thanks also to: Sue Mitra for proof-reading and copious corrections; Peter Turner for proofing; Debbie Lustig for the index, contents and glossary; Hugh Finlay and Geoff Crowther for additional information; Lindy Cameron for additional research; and Peter Flavelle and Chris Lee-Ack for paste-up corrections.

Acknowledgements

I am grateful to many organisations and individuals for help given in my research.

For the Sudan section many thanks to Mrs Sitana Agarib and Mr Salah Hamad, of the Ministry of Tourism; Andrew Pugh of CARE, Sudan; Jacques Morand (France); Terry Underhill (UK); Paul Chadwick (UK); Marcel Verhaag (Netherlands); Estelle Mason (UK); Adam Storey (UK); and Mark Jones (Australia). Special thanks must also be extended to the people of LALMBA, the Colorado-based relief organisation; Tom and Merissa Rogers of the American Refugee Committee in Kassala; and Pata and Allister Villiers of BANDAID, Sudan.

In Egypt the Ministry of Tourism people were helpful with many details. Thanks also to Dirk and Erika Knip (Netherlands); Claudine Guy (Switzerland); Bill Eldridge (UK); Claude Antoine of the Aquamarine Dive Shop, Na'ama Bay, Sinai; and a long list of extremely hospitable Egyptians.

On the home front, a thousand-and-one thanks go to Shirley who helped tremendously with several parts of the guide. If this book were to be dedicated to a single person, it would be her. Also at home, or at least nearby, pharaonic thanks to my father, Janet and my mentor Clancy Sigal, whose invaluable words of advice have continually guided me.

A Request

All travel guides rely on new information to stay up to date and one of the best sources of this information is travellers on the road. At Lonely Planet we get a constant stream of letters and postcards that keep us in contact with the latest travel developments. So if you find that things have changed, write to us and let us know. Corrections and suggestions are greatly appreciated and the best letters will get a free copy of the next edition or another Lonely Planet guide of your choice.

Contents

THE SUDAN

EGYPT

EGYPT

Introduction

Ever since Herodotus, the ancient Greek historian and traveller, first described Egypt as a 'gift of the river' the Land of the Nile has been capturing the imagination of all who visit her.

The awe-inspiring monuments, that were the legacy of the ancient pharaohs, Greeks and Romans as well as the early Christians and Muslims, attract thousands of visitors every year but the pyramids, temples, tombs, monasteries and mosques of Egypt are just part of this country's fascination.

Modern Egypt – where mud-brick villages stand beside pharaonic ruins surrounded by towering steel, stone and glass buildings – stands at the cultural crossroads of east and west, ancient and modern. While TV antennae decorate rooftops everywhere, from the crowded apartment blocks of Cairo to the mud homes of farming villages and the goatskin tents of the Bedouins, the *fellahin* throughout the Nile's fertile valley still tend their fields with the archaic tools of their ancestors.

In the gargantuan city of Cairo the sound of the muezzin beckoning the faithful to prayer or the mesmerising voice of Om Kalthum, the 'Mother of Egypt', compete with the pop music of ghetto blasters and the screech of car horns. And everywhere there are people, swathed in long flowing robes or western-style clothes, hanging from buses, weaving through an obstacle course of animals and exhaust-spewing traffic or spilling from hive-like buildings.

Spectacular edifices aside, the attraction of this country lies also in its incredible natural beauty and in the overwhelming hospitality of the Egyptian people. Through all this the Nile River flows serene and majestic, the lifeblood of Egypt, as it has been since the beginning of history.

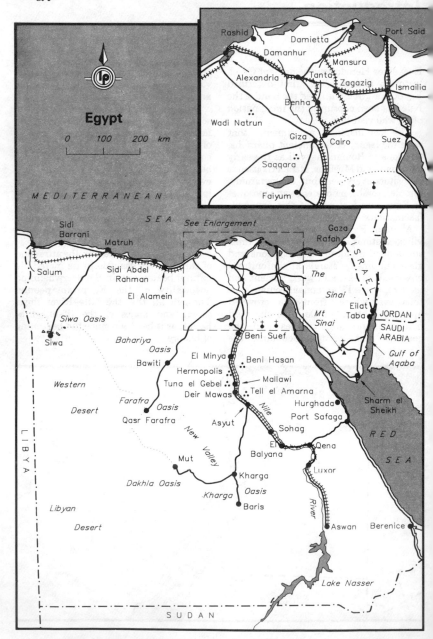

Egypt

0   100   200 km

Facts about the Country

HISTORY

About 5000 years ago an Egyptian king named Menes unified Upper and Lower Egypt for the first time. No one is quite sure how he did this, but it is known that his action gave rise to Egypt's first relatively stable dynasty of kings. While little is known of Egypt prior to the dynastic rule of the pharaohs, it can be assumed that for the powerful and civilised reign of Menes to be at all possible, a unique and definite civilisation must have been developing in the Nile Valley for centuries.

The history of Egypt is inextricably linked to the Nile. Ever since the earliest-known communities settled the Nile Valley, the river has inspired and controlled the religious, economic, social and political life of Egyptians. For many centuries the narrow, elongated character of its fertile lands hampered the fusion of those early settlements which held fast to their local independence. But once again it was the river, this time as a common highway, which broke the barriers by providing an avenue for commercial traffic and communication. The small kingdoms eventually developed into two important states, one covering the valley as far as the delta, the other consisting of the delta itself. The unification of these two states, by Menes in about 3000 BC, set the scene for the greatest era of ancient Egyptian civilisation. More than 30 dynasties, 50 rulers and 2300 years of native rule passed before Alexander the Great ushered in a long period of foreign rule.

Fifty centuries of history! Obviously, it is not within the scope of this book to cover it in great detail. To give some idea of the major events in Egypt's history, the last 5000 years, from the time of Menes, can be divided roughly into seven periods:

Pharaonic times (3000-341 BC)

Greek rule (332-30 BC)
Roman & Byzantine rule (30 BC-638 AD)
The Rise of Islam, Arabs & Mamelukes (640-1517)
Turkish rule (1517-1882)
British rule (1882-1952)
Independent Egypt (1952-today)

Pharaonic Times (3000-341 BC)

Little is known of the immediate successors of Menes except that, attributed with divine ancestry, they promoted the development of a highly stratified society, patronised the arts and built many temples and public works.

In approximately 2640 BC, Egypt's pyramids began to appear. King Zoser and his architect Imhotep built one of the first, the Step Pyramid of Saqqara, and ruled from the nearby capital of Memphis. Until the reign of Zoser, the royal tombs had been built, rather modestly by comparison, of sun-dried bricks. The construction of Zoser's massive stone mausoleum therefore was not only a striking testimony to his power and the prosperity of the period but the start of a whole new trend. It was also during this period that the sun god *Ra* became the most important Egyptian deity.

For the next three dynasties and 500 years – a period called the Old Kingdom – the power of Egypt's pharaohs and the size of their pyramids and temples greatly increased. Some Egyptologists speculate that the pyramids rose as Egypt's power rose in the world. As the vast majority of the population was put to work on these great tombs, their size also symbolised the pharaoh's importance and power over his own people. The pyramid also gave the pharaoh steps to the heavens and the ceremonial wooden barques buried with them were their symbolic vehicles to the next life.

11

Not long after Zoser's pyramid was completed, 4th dynasty pharaohs built several more pyramids in the relatively short period between 2650 and 2500 BC.

Pharaoh Sneferu built the pyramid of Meidum in the Faiyum and the Red Pyramid of Dahshur near Saqqara and took royal power and the accompanying artistic and commercial development of Egypt to even greater heights. During his time trading vessels nearly six metres long began plying the waters of the Nile; he brought back thousands of prisoners from successful campaigns against the Nubians in the south; and defeated all enemies who threatened the country.

The last three pharaohs of the 4th dynasty, Cheops, Chephren, and Mycerinus, built the three great pyramids of Giza. Cheops took the throne when the pharaonic era was reaching the apex of its prosperity and culture, and if his colossal pyramid is any indication he must have been one of the greatest pharaohs of all the Egyptian line. Not only is its sheer size and mathematical precision a monument to the incredible development of Egyptian architecture but many Egyptologists credit the era of Cheops with the emergence, for the first time in human history, of an organisational principle.

Under Cheops' rule and through the enormous labour and incredible discipline involved in the construction of the pyramid, the organisation of Egypt as a state was complete.

As the centuries passed and the 5th dynasty began (circa 2490-2330 BC), changes in the power and rule of pharaohs appeared. One of the first indications of this was the comparatively small pyramids constructed at Abu Sir, 12 km south of Giza. The kings had begun to share power with various high officials and nobles in the vast bureaucracies they had created, so unlike their pharaonic predecessors, they were no longer absolute monarchs and did not have the resources at their disposal for the construction of immense funerary monuments.

As control became even more diffused throughout the 6th and 7th dynasties, (circa 2330-2170 BC), a number of small local principalities popped up around the country and a second capital was established at Heracleopolis (near present-day

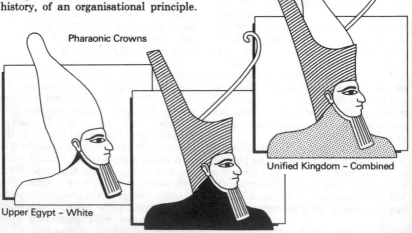

Pharaonic Crowns

Upper Egypt – White

Lower Egypt – Red

Unified Kingdom – Combined

Beni Suef). The princes of these small dynasties ruled Egypt for many years but their feudal struggles, from one end of the country to the other, prevented any possibility of economic or artistic development. With the collapse of the Old Kingdom a state of anarchy succeeded the unparalleled grandeur of the early pharaonic dynasties.

Civil war at the beginning of the 11th dynasty (circa 2045-1991 BC) finally put an end to the squabbling. An enterprising member of the Intef family had rallied all the principalities of the south in a rebellion against the weakness of Heracleopolis and established an independent kingdom with Thebes as its capital. Under Menuhotep II the north and south was again united under the leadership of a single pharaoh. The princes of Thebes (present-day Luxor) became rulers of all Egypt and the Middle Kingdom period began.

With political order came economic stability, social and artistic development. Thebes prospered for about 250 years. Tombs and temples were built throughout Egypt – the remains of which can be seen today in almost every Egyptian town. The Pharaohs Mentuhotpe, Amenemhet and Sesostris built monuments at Lisht, Dahshur, Hawara and Lahun – all of which are near the Faiyum and Saqqara. Their building frenzy diminished as the governors and nobles of the nomarchs (provinces) once again began squabbling among themselves and demanding more control (around 1780-1660 BC). Royal power weakened as anarchy once again took the reins; the empire was divided and ripe for conquest by an outside power.

Those invaders came from the northeast and called themselves the Hyksos – Princes of the Foreign Lands. They ruled Egypt for more than a century but are remembered for little more than having introduced the horse-drawn chariot and the scarab to Egypt. By about 1550 BC, however, the Egyptians had routed and expelled the Hyksos from the power struggle. A new kingdom with its capital at Thebes was established and Egypt truly entered the ranks of the great powers.

The New Kingdom represented, perhaps, the blossoming of culture and empire in Pharaonic Egypt. For almost 400 years, from the 18th to the 20th dynasties (1550-1150 BC), Egypt reigned supreme in north-east Africa and the eastern Mediterranean. Renowned kings and queens ruled an expanding empire from Thebes and built monuments which even today are unique in their immensity and beauty.

The temple complex of Karnak at Thebes became an important symbolic power centre for the empire. The temple seemed to grow as the empire expanded. Each successive pharaoh of the 18th and 19th dynasties added a room, hall, or pylon with intricately carved hieroglyphic inscriptions on every wall and pillar. Much of what is known about Egyptian life during this time comes from the stories told by these inscriptions.

Significant expansion of the empire began with the reign of Tuthmosis I in 1528 BC. He grabbed Upper Nubia and became the first pharaoh to be entombed in the Valley of the Kings on the west bank across from Thebes. After a relatively brief power struggle, his daughter, Hatshepsut became one of Egypt's few female rulers. A spectacular mortuary temple was built for her at Deir el Bahri on the west bank.

Tuthmosis III, Hatshepsut's nephew, followed and became Egypt's greatest conqueror. He expanded the empire past Syria and into western Asia. He built and contributed to temples throughout Egypt at Thebes, Buhen, Amada and other locales.

Empire expansion and temple/tomb building continued under the next three pharaohs: Amenophis II, Tuthmosis IV and Amenophis III. The empire reached its peak in 1417 BC under Amenophis III.

He built the Luxor Temple and a massive mortuary. Only the Colossi of Memnon on the west bank remain of the mortuary temple. The country was relatively prosperous and stable; governing became easier.

Amenophis IV realised this and began to pay less attention to governing the empire. He chose, instead, to quarrel with the priesthood of the god *Amun* – the leading god of Thebes – and took the name Akhenaten in honour of *Aten*, the Sun God. Akhenaten and his wife Nefertiti were so obsessed with the worship of Aten that they established a new capital called Akhetaten devoted solely to the worship of the Sun God. Their actions were particularly significant because they represented the first organised form of monotheism. Today, the scant remains of their capital and innovative religious thought can be seen at Tell el Amarna near the town of Minya.

After Akhenaten's death, the priests of Thebes went on a rampage and destroyed any signs of his rule and his monotheism. This included the Temple of the Sun at Karnak Temple. Recently, an American archaeological team photographed the hieroglyphic inscriptions on more than 35,000 stone blocks from that temple which had been scattered around the world. Through the photographs, the archaeologists were able to reconstruct the temple and learn more about the lives of Akhenaten and Nefertiti.

The priests took control and ruled Egypt through Akhenaten's young son-in-law Tutankhamun. The boy-king only ruled for about 10 years and died just before reaching manhood. His tomb was discovered in 1922 with almost all of its treasures untouched.

For the next few centuries Egypt was ruled by generals: Ramses I, II and III, and Seti I. Like good pharaohs and military leaders they built massive monuments, such as the temples at Abydos and Abu Simbel, and waged war against the Hittites and Libyans. However, by the time Ramses III had come to power, as the second king of the 20th dynasty in 1198 BC, Egypt was on a losing streak; a streak

Queen Nefertiti & Pharaoh Akhenaten

which lasted ostensibly until Alexander the Great arrived in the 4th century BC.

Greek Rule (332-30 BC)

Egypt was a mess when Alexander arrived in 332 BC. Over the previous several centuries the country had been sacked by Libyans, Ethiopians, Persians and Assyrians. Alexander promptly established a new capital which he named after himself – Alexandria, and then created a new ruling dynasty over Egypt with his friends, the Ptolemy family of Macedonia, as sovereigns.

The Ptolemies ruled Egypt for 300 years. Alexandria became a great Greek city and a museum and library were built. The temples of Dendara, Philae and Edfu, which were built further south, are still in excellent shape with most of their walls and roofs extant. There was a melding of the Greek and Egyptian religions, which can be seen in the hieroglyphics on those walls, and the Greek gods, *Zeus* and *Aphrodite*, were compared to the Egyptian deities *Amun* and *Hathor*.

Despite the prosperity, however, the Ptolemies' rule was not without its share of murder, intrigue and threats from abroad. While they bickered, expelled and assassinated one another, the overall weakness and instability of their reign attracted the interest of the rulers of the expanding Roman Empire. For awhile, the Romans supported various Ptolemies, but this seemed to lead to more rivalry and assassination rather than peace and stability. The litany of events leading to complete Roman rule over Egypt reads like a bloody soap opera.

From 51 to 48 BC Cleopatra VII co-ruled Egypt, under Roman protection, with her younger brother Ptolemy XIII Philopator Philadelphus. Pompei, one of Julius Caesar's rivals, was sent from Rome to watch over them. Ptolemy had Pompei killed and Cleopatra banished. However, in the same year (48 BC),

Caesar gave his all to Cleopatra and on arrival in Egypt threw Ptolemy in the Nile, appointing another of her brothers, Ptolemy XIV as co-ruler. Cleopatra gave birth to Caesar's son in 47 BC and had her brother killed in 45 BC. A year later Caesar was also assassinated. (Are you lost yet?) Marc Antony arrived from Rome, fell in love with Cleopatra, and moved in with her for 10 years of bliss, an arrangement the Roman Senate wasn't too thrilled about. They declared Antony persona non grata – enemy of the people – and sent Octavia to deal with him. Antony and Cleopatra preferred bliss to strife. They both committed suicide in 30 BC and Egypt became a Roman province.

Roman & Byzantine Rule (30 BC-638 AD)

Octavia was one of the first Roman rulers of Egypt. He ruled as Emperor Augustus for a few years and made Egypt the granary of the Roman empire. Except for a brief invasion from Ethiopia in 24 BC, Egypt was basically stable and peaceful for about 30 years. Then Mary, Joseph and their young baby fled to Egypt from Bethlehem where King Herod was running amok, slaughtering children in order to remove the threat of a future new king – the prophesied Messiah.

Jesus grew up in Egypt before returning to Palestine to spread the word of God but it was not until St Mark started preaching the gospel, around 40 AD, that Egyptians began converting to Christianity. Emperor Nero capitalised on this renewed sense of religious unity by developing Egypt as a trade centre between Rome and India in 54 AD. A few architectural marvels were built such as parts of temples at Esna, Philae and Dendara.

The founding of a national Egyptian, or Coptic, Church took place despite the persecution of Christians throughout the Roman Empire during the following centuries. Egypt prospered, but by the 3rd century the Roman Empire had begun to succumb to war, famine and power struggles. In the 4th century, not long after Christianity was declared the state religion, the Roman Empire cracked in half. The eastern half became part of the Byzantine empire ruled from Byzantium (now Istanbul) and the Western Roman Empire was ruled by Rome.

The empire was too weak to effectively rule its dominions, so Egypt was left to invaders – Nubians from the south and North Africans from the west. She was also left to develop the Coptic Church independently of the Byzantines. The Copts' adoption of a monophysitic doctrine, (the belief that Christ is primarily divine with human attributes), was deemed heretical by the Byzantine and Roman orthodoxy, so they expelled the Coptic Church from the main body of Christianity. That doctrine however, and a tradition of monasticism, greatly influenced later developments in European Christianity and is still an integral part of the Christian church in Egypt.

Aside from a few wars with Nubians and Blemmyes, a famine, and a couple of Persian invasions, life in 'Byzantine' Egypt was relatively sedate during this period. Then, in 640 AD, the Arabs arrived.

The Rise of Islam, Arabs & Mamelukes (640-1517)

The Arabs brought Islam and armies of Muslims determined to convert the infidels. By 642 Fustat was established as a military base and seat of government – the precursor of Cairo. The ruins of Fustat can still be seen just south of Cairo and although it didn't last long as the seat of government, it grew quickly as a city of Muslims.

In 658 the Omayyads, an Arab dynasty based in Damascus, snatched control of Egypt and stayed until 750. During those 92 years of rule, Islam and the Omayyad empire extended from Spain all the way to central Asia. Theological splits were inevitable in such a large empire. One of the main splits concerned the spiritual leadership of the descendents of Ali, the Prophet Mohammed's son-in-law. Two groups – the Sunni and the Shiite – evolved because of this dispute and conflict between them continues even today (see the Religion section). More than 1200 years ago though, this conflict led to the downfall of the Omayyad dynasty and the decapitation of Marwan, the last Omayyad caliph (ruler). Persian troops paraded his head around the burnt remains of Fustat. For the next 108 years Egypt was ruled by the Abbasid dynasty of Baghdad.

The Abbasids ruled Egypt a little differently from their predecessors. They brought in outsiders, Turkish-speaking soldier slaves, to protect their interests throughout the empire. One of these fighting nomads, Bayikbey, eventually gained enough power and influence to become a threat to the caliph. The caliph gave him Egypt before killing him. Bayikbey's son-in-law, Ibn Tulun (son of Tulun) was sent as governor instead.

Ibn Tulun wanted Egypt as an independent state, not a Persian province, so he fought and defeated the Abbasids and established a dynasty. A new capital arose, along with one of the largest mosques in the Middle East (even today). The Mosque of Ibn Tulun was large enough to accommodate all of his cavalry – both horses and men.

After Ibn Tulun's death, Egypt was unable to keep its independence. Various leaders and invaders followed including the Abbasids, Byzantines, Ikhshids and finally the Fatimids. The Fatimids came from a kingdom of rulers in north-west Africa who claimed descent from Mohammed's daughter Fatima and Ali. They quickly established a dynasty of independent caliphs which lasted for approximately 200 years (968-1169).

Egypt flourished under the first Fatimid rulers. At the behest of the mysterious Caliph al-Móizz, a Greek named Gohar spent four years building the new city of Cairo. Desmond Stewart wrote in his book, *Great Cairo, Mother of the World*, that al-Móizz:

was to rule mysteriously, as befitted an imam, from behind the curtain of awe. For Fatimid power was based on an idea: the sense that God allows an aspect of himself to be incarnate in an infallible ruler.

Gohar's construction work in Cairo befitted an imam imbued with godliness and his greatest work was the Al-Azhar mosque. This immense structure, which resembles a fortress, became one of the world's greatest centres of Islamic studies. Today it continues to function as both a mosque and major university. After al-Móizz's death, Egypt continued to flourish under his son, al-Aziz, but the good times ended with the rule of al-Aziz's crazy son, al-Hakim (996-1021).

At first, al-Hakim ruled Egypt as an absolute monarch of beneficence and grace. A magnificent mosque was built at the northern wall of Cairo between the gates of al-Futuh and al-Nasr. He began to share his rule with a council of advisers and also attempted to understand the problems of Cairenes by touring the city on a mule and talking to his people. All of this paled into insignificance however, as the young al-Hakim began ruling like a lunatic.

At the age of 15 he murdered his tutor. He then decided he didn't like his advisers anymore so he murdered them too. He loved the night and took to riding after dark, on *moon* his pet mule, so it became illegal and punishable by death to work during the day and sleep at night. Al-Hakim also hated merchants who cheated their customers so if he found one during his nightly mule rides, he would have his big black slave Masoud sodomise the merchant. Sometimes al-Hakim would help by standing on the merchant's head.

Al-Hakim also hated women. He tried to impose a 24-hour curfew on them but when that didn't work, he imposed a ban on the manufacture of women's shoes. He figured that without shoes women would not want to plod through the manure and open sewers on the streets.

This lunacy continued until one day in 1021 al-Hakim mounted *moon* and rode off into the Moqattam hills near Cairo. The mule was found but al-Hakim had disappeared, never to be heard from again. In his wake, he left a group of disciples who maintained the mystical belief that al-Hakim was divine. This group became the Druzes and although they still exist in Lebanon, Syria, Jordan and Israel, very little is known of their beliefs and practices as it is blasphemous for a Druze to reveal his peoples' secrets to outsiders.

Over the next 150 years several Fatimid caliphs ruled Egypt. Aside from a relatively brief spate of plague and famine and a few power squabbles, battles and wars, Egypt was prosperous. Food was plentiful in the markets, or *souks*, and apartment buildings with as many as 10 floors (sometimes more) rose in Cairo. This prosperity, however, could not be maintained in those parts of the empire outside Egypt. At the same time the Christians of western Europe had begun a crusade to spread Christianity and rescue the Holy City from the Muslims.

The Crusaders seized Jerusalem from the Fatimids in 1099. Tripoli, in Lebanon, fell in 1109 and so did several other parts of the Fatimid empire. By 1153 all of Palestine was under their control and rather than suffer a similar fate the weakened Fatimid state decided to co-operate with the Crusaders. The Islamic Seljuk dynasty of Syria was not happy about this, as the balance of power was upset; a balance which had begun to tip increasingly in their favour. To correct the imbalance, the Syrians sent an army led by a Kurdish warrior named Shirkoh and his nephew Salah al-Din.

Salah al-Din eventually gained control of Egypt and founded his own dynasty, the Ayyubid dynasty in 1171. The Crusaders attacked and partly burned Cairo in 1176 so Salah al-Din immediately began fortifying the city. He built part of the city walls and the Citadel, which became a small town of shops, stables and workshops. Salah al-Din's reign was not only the heyday of medieval Egypt but in 1187 he also drove the Crusaders from Jerusalem.

Above all, Salah al-Din sought power. He purchased *Mamelukes*, an Arabic word for 'owned' or 'held', to assist him. Most Mamelukes were Turkish mercenaries, sold by their parents when they were boys to be trained solely to fight for the sultan. In his book, *Travels through Syria & Egypt in the Years 1783, 1784 & 1785*, M Volney described the Mamelukes as:

Strangers among themselves .... Without parents ... the past has done nothing for them; they do nothing for the future. Ignorant and superstitious by upbringing, they become fierce through murders, mutinous through tumults, deceitful through intrigues ... corrupt through every species of debauch. Above all they are addicts of that shameful custom ... it is the first lesson they learn from their master of arms.

The 'shameful custom' or 'lesson' referred to, was sodomy with young boys. After a certain period of servitude and military service, many Mamelukes were free to own land and raise families. Yes, despite their violent nature and diverse sexual proclivities, some did choose to settle down quietly. Other Mamelukes however, began to seek positions of power and influence within the state. Their efforts brought about the demise of Shagarat al-Durr, making her the last Ayyubid ruler and the first woman to rule Egypt since Cleopatra, and ushered in more than two and a half centuries of Mameluke rule.

Two dynasties of Mamelukes ruled Egypt. The Bahri Mamelukes were the first and, in their 132 years of rule, there were more than 25 sultans. Murder, intrigue and war were rife. In between fighting and conspiring, however, the Mamelukes developed a distinctive style of architecture and several mosques were built including the Mosques of Sultan Hassan, El-Zahir and Qalaun.

The sultans of the next dynasty were equally constructive. This dynasty began when a Circassian slave named Barquq seized power from the Bahri ruler, a six-year-old Mameluke (not difficult!). More than 21 Circassian Mamelukes became sultan before Egypt fell to the Turks in 1517.

Turkish Rule (1517-1882)

Since most of the Mamelukes were either of Turkish descent or from Turkey and the surrounding areas, rule over Egypt by the Ottoman sultans of Constantinople was not difficult. In fact, their rule basically consisted of collecting taxes from Egypt, while the rest of the governing business was left to the Mamelukes. This continued until Napoleon came to Egypt in 1798.

Napoleon and his army routed the Mameluke army supposedly as a show of support for the Ottoman sultan. In reality, Napoleon wanted to eventually strike a blow at British trade in the Indian Ocean by gaining control of the land and sea routes to India. Napoleon was also keen to 'civilise' Egypt.

He established a French-style government; the tax system was revamped; and public works projects were implemented – canals were cleared, streets were cleaned of garbage and temporary bridges spanned the Nile. Through his 'Institut d'Egypte' he put a variety of French intellectuals to work on a history of ancient Egypt and a record of Egypt's ancient monuments. They were also responsible for the planting of new crops, establishing a new system of weights and measures, and reorganising the hospitals. However, as Alan Moorehead indicated in his book *The Blue Nile*:

Everything these new conquerors proposed was a strain; it was a strain *not* to throw rubbish in the streets, *not* to bribe witnesses and officials, and it was upsetting to be obliged to undergo medical treatment where prayers had always served in the past. They had been getting on very well, they felt, as they were before. They had no need for new canals, new weights and measures, and new schools ... They did not believe Bonaparte's protestations of his respect for Muhammad, nor were they much impressed by his dressings-up in turban and caftan ...

Napoleon's Egyptian adventure seemed doomed from the beginning. Less than a month after he arrived, the British navy, under Admiral Nelson, appeared off the coast of Alexandria. Nelson quickly destroyed the French fleet and cut off Napoleon's forces from France. A year later the Turks sent an army to expel the French from Egypt. The resulting battle at Abu Qir was a victory for the French; 15,000 Turks were killed, captured or drowned. Nevertheless, the British returned in 1801 and compelled the French to leave.

Egypt's next ruler was a headstrong Albanian named Mohammed Ali. Mohammed quickly rose to power by first expelling the Turkish governor of Egypt and then, with Mameluke help, the British. The Mameluke leaders however, also posed a threat to Mohammed Ali, so he invited them to a sumptuous banquet and then had them massacred on their way home. A charming host!

Mohammed was power-hungry. He sent his troops on successful forays into the Sudan, Greece, Syria and Arabia and by 1839 he controlled most of the Ottoman Empire. However the British intervened again and forced him into sharing power with the Sultan in Istanbul. Mohammed died in 1848 and was succeeded by his grandson Abbas and then his son Said.

Said began implementing many government reforms and projects, foremost of which was the establishment of the railway system and the digging of the Suez Canal.

Pasha Ismail followed in Said's path by establishing factories, a telegraph and postal system, canals and bridges. The fledgling cotton industry of Egypt pros-

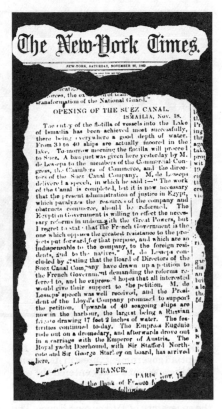

pered as the American Civil War disrupted cotton production in the southern US. He opened the Suez Canal in 1869 and achieved political independence for Egypt in 1873. With independence, Ismail confidently spent more state money than he had. The national debt became so great that he was forced to abdicate in 1879.

British Rule (1882-1952)

The debt and abdication brought greater British control over Egyptian affairs. With pressure from the British, Ismail's son Tawfiq reorganised Egypt's finances and British and French controllers installed themselves in the government.

Allied soldiers – WW I

With the outbreak of WW I the Egyptian government threw in its lot with the Allies. When Turkey entered the war, Britain placed Egypt 'under the protection of His Majesty' effectively terminating the suzerainty of Turkey over Egypt. The Khedive was deposed for his Turkish sympathies, Prince Hassain Kamil became sultan and martial law was proclaimed.

During this time several groups in Egypt, particularly the *Ulama* or Muslim elite, and Egyptian civil servants, military officers and landowners, were disturbed by the increase in foreign influence within the Egyptian government and civil service. A movement to expel Europeans from these areas evolved from a coalition of these groups but the plan backfired and the British remained in those positions until 1952.

The British did eventually allow the formation of a nationalist political party, called the *Wafd*, and a monarchist party.

The first elections were held in 1922, independence was granted and King Fuad I was elected to head a constitutional monarchy. For the next 30 years the British, monarchists and Wafdists jockeyed for power. WW II (see the El Alamein section) and defeat in Israel's 1948 war of independence left Egypt in chaos. By 1952 only a group of dissident military officers had the wherewithal to take over the government.

Independent Egypt (1952-1981)

The Free Officers, led by Colonel Gamal Abdel Nasser, overthrew King Farouk, Fuad's son, in a bloodless coup. The coup was quickly dubbed the *Revolution of 1952*. The first independent Arab Republic of Egypt was formed and Nasser, as head of state, wasted no time in getting embroiled in international politics. He became one of the architects of the non-aligned movement, a movement of countries which sought closer relations with the Soviet Union and the People's Republic of China and more distant relations with the west. Through his role in the movement Nasser criticised the west which cost him assistance in building the Aswan High Dam, so he turned to the Soviets instead. In 1956, Nasser also nationalised the Suez Canal Company. The British, French and Israelis promptly invaded. The United Nations successfully urged the invaders to leave and installed a UN peace-keeping force to guarantee safe passage through the canal. Nasser was a hero, especially in the Arab world.

The Suez Crisis of 1956 made Nasser head of a Pan-Arab Nationalist movement which emphasised Arab unity. Unsuccessful attempts were made to unite Egypt, Syria and Yemen in a United Arab Republic. As Egypt's economy worsened, under Nasser's *Arab Socialist* policies of nationalisation, he began diverting attention from the internal problems by emphasising Arab Unity and making Israel a scapegoat. He asked the UN force to leave the Sinai and then closed the Straits of Tiran, Israel's only outlet to the Indian Ocean. On 5 June 1967 Israel attacked and in only six days destroyed the Egyptian air force, captured the Sinai and closed the Suez Canal. Despite this devastating defeat, the Egyptian people insisted that Nasser remain in power, which he did until his death in 1970. Arabs continue to revere him and his photograph can still be found in many homes and shops.

Anwar el-Sadat succeeded Nasser and attempted to repair Egypt's economy by becoming friendlier with the west, particularly the USA, at the expense of relations with the Soviets. Sadat also realised that to truly revitalise Egypt's economy he would have to deal with Israel, but first he needed bargaining power, a basis for negotiations. So, on the Jewish holiday of Yom Kippur on 6 October 1973, he launched a surprise attack across the Suez Canal. Although Egypt actually lost the war, Sadat's negotiating strategy succeeded.

On 19 November 1977 Sadat travelled

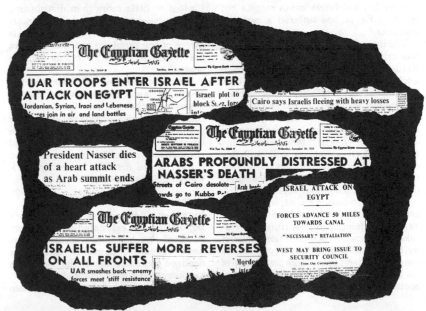

to Jerusalem to begin making peace with Israel. A peace treaty based on the Camp David Accords was signed. The Sinai was returned by 1982 and relations between Egypt and Israel were normalised. Egypt was immediately ostracised by the rest of the Arab world and most socialist and developing countries. But for most Egyptians the treaty promised future peace and prosperity. However, radical groups of Fundamentalist Muslims were opposed to the price of peace: normalisation of relations with Israel and alignment with the west. One such group assassinated Sadat during a military parade on 6 October 1981.

Egypt Today

Hosni Mubarak, Sadat's Vice President since 1974, was sworn in as president and has had his hands full of problems ever since. The prosperity promised by the treaty has been difficult to obtain. Western investment has been encouraged at the expense of a drastic increase in imports. More than US$2 billion in annual US aid offers some respite but recently Egypt has suffered a series of setbacks.

The low price of oil on the world market has crippled the fledgling Egyptian oil industry, once a major source of foreign exchange. Another major source has been tourism but the sensational media coverage of terrorist incidents in other countries and a rebellion by a small group of disgruntled conscripts in the internal security forces has frightened away many tourists. Both situations will probably change in Egypt's favour, but the advantages gained will be drastically outweighed by her other domestic problems.

Egypt's population has exploded and is estimated to be as high as 50 million. The expanding population continually overtakes any increases in production achieved by imports of technology. Egypt can no longer feed itself and a large proportion of its food is now imported. Birth control seems to be one answer but Muslim

President Hosni Mubarak

fundamentalists have seen to it that government efforts in this area are limited to little more than distributing multi-colored condoms and simple informational posters. The government is aware of the problems but will they act before Egypt literally bursts at the seams?

The people are equally aware of the problems and don't always regard Mubarak as the right man for the job. For many Egyptians Mubarak personifies the popular symbol of a French cheese company whose billboards are found throughout Egypt. The company is called *La Vache Qui Rit* (The Laughing Cow). Its symbol is self-evident.

POPULATION

In the last official census, in 1981, Egypt's population was estimated at 41 million. Medical care has improved, birth rates have increased, mortality rates have declined and consequently the population has increased almost five-fold since 1907. Today, it is estimated there are more than

51 million people in Egypt, nearly 25% of whom live in Cairo.

Until this past decade Egypt had the agricultural resources to support its burgeoning population, however, with a growth rate of almost 2.7% Egypt can no longer feed itself. The population is too large for the mere 4% of the country which is cultivatable so to feed the people almost all of Egypt's foreign exchange reserves is now spent on food imports, especially cereals. Normally these reserves would be used for long term investments, in projects like new industrial plants and improved transportation, but capital works have taken a back seat to the basic task of providing enough food. If the money was not spent on food imports the potential for civil strife and political upheaval would be very great.

Potential religious conflict is another problem resulting from Egypt's economic troubles. As the economy worsens, more Egyptians are beginning to look to Islamic fundamentalism for answers to the country's woes. The *fellahin*, the peasant farmers who form Egypt's largest economic group, have been most affected by the economic climate and many want to establish a theocratic state similar to Iran. The Copts, who comprise only about 10% of the total population, are understandably threatened by this rise in fundamentalism because the establishment of an Islamic state in Egypt would make life even more difficult for Egypt's Christians.

Ironically, the Egyptians whose lives would be least affected by economic changes are the Bedouins of the Sinai and Eastern and Western Deserts. Nearly 500,000 Bedouins survive in the harshest, most isolated environment leading a life which, by its very nature, has made them a self-sufficient and independent people.

PEOPLE

Egyptians are fond of telling jokes about the government, about other Arabs and, most of all, about themselves. Every other Egyptian man on the street seems to be a walking encyclopedia of jokes. One of the most common quips about themselves concerns IBM's control of Egypt.

An Egyptian taxi driver once told me, 'Hey, you know, Egypt controlled by IBM. You know, big company, IBM.'

'What do you mean?' I asked since, in all my time in Egypt, I had seen only one IBM electric typewriter.

'I for *insha-allah*; B for *bukra*; M for *malaysh*,' he chortled and quickly swerved to the left to avoid clipping a donkey cart full of garbage. A banana peel slid across the hood. The driver knew he was right.

Although these three words can't completely sum up life in Egypt, they tell a lot about Egyptians: *insha-allah* means if God wills it; *bukra* means tomorrow; and *malaysh* means never mind, it doesn't matter. You will probably hear them used like this:

You are walking down Shari'a Talaat Harb, one of Cairo's main streets. An Egyptian with an ear-to-ear smile and an outstanding American accent begins walking and talking next to you. You are in an adventurous mood.

Egyptian: Hello, hello. Welcome to Egypt. Change money, change money?
Traveller: No.
Egyptian: You have girlfriend? Yes? Good, then come to my bazaar and perfume shop. Many things there.
Traveller: OK, but I don't have any money. I just want to look.
Egyptian: Fine. No problem. Here is bazaar.

By now you know that the guy's name is Mohammed (every other Egyptian seems to be named Mohammed). Mohammed sits you down on a couple of big velvet cushions and takes a vial of purple liquid from a glass case.

Egyptian: You want perfume for girlfriend, yes? (Mohammed's smile seems even bigger now.)
Traveller: No, actually I need a money pouch. I was on the bus to the pyramids yesterday and mine was taken. My passport was in it. Can you get me another?

Egyptian: Yes, yes. I get money pouch. *Bukra, bukra* I get money pouch. Tomorrow. Now, perfume for your girlfriend.

Yes is a favourite response. Mohammed doesn't really know if he can get the pouch but, like many Egyptians, he won't say *no* because it looks bad to say *no*. This can cause a lot of problems, especially when you ask for directions. Back to Mohammed and the perfume.

Before you know it, he is dabbing purple perfume on your arm, wheezing and saying 'Smell, smell; smell the essences of jasmine.' With fat fingers clutching the open vial, Mohammed pushes it up to your nose. Purple perfume splashes on your tan shirt.

Traveller: (Jumping to his feet.) Hey, you got the stuff all over my shirt.
Egyptian: (As if nothing happened.) Ach, *malaysh*. Don't worry. *Malaysh*.
Traveller: (Fuming.) What do you mean, don't worry? Will this stuff come out?
Egyptian: (Looking to the ceiling with an open palm as if expecting rain.) *Insha-allah, insha-allah*. It is how Allah wants it. Here, have some mint tea.

hello excuse me, m'sieur!
m'sieur!
excuse me, excuse me, hello!

tourist trinkets

HOT ON THE TRAIL OF THE TOURIST DOLLAR...

It's hot, smoggy and dusty outside, but the sweet mint tea cools your temper and temperature. And, even though you smell like a field of jasmine, you're again ready for Egypt and the Egyptians.

This nonchalance, fatalism, apathy – call it what you wish – comes from the Nile. Well, not exactly. Like the Nile, life in Egypt has flowed with relatively few interruptions. Life is simpler here, living is not. The main events of life – birth, marriage and death; and the main concerns of daily life – family, friends and food, are most important. The future is not important because it has not been and will not be much different than the past or present. Life goes on in Egypt irrespective of lost money pouches, spilled perfume or a thousand and one other mishaps and inefficiencies which you might encounter. However, this is all beginning to change.

Western technology and lifestyles have come to Egypt. The *fellahin* (peasants) in the countryside, who make up the majority of Egypt's population, have begun using tractors and diesel-powered irrigation pumps in place of ploughs and ancient ox-driven water wheels. Despite these innovations, however, Egypt can no longer feed itself and great quantities of food must be imported. Along with the food and agricultural machines, other imports have arrived which have significantly affected life in Egypt.

Television programmes from the west, particularly the USA, have had an incredible impact. At the flick of a switch, a family of *fellahin* in their home of mud and straw are transported from their Upper Egypt village to places like the streets of San Francisco or the living rooms of the Ewing family in Dallas. A lifestyle of previously unimaginable luxury suddenly comes alive on a little screen in front of them and the seed of possibility, the chance of living a better life, is planted.

The impact is at least twofold. First, young people have begun to realise that life doesn't have to be limited to the village and the farm. They can go to the city, earn more money, and live better lives; thus the second major impact.

Egyptian cities like Cairo, Alexandria and Aswan are all experiencing population explosions. Population growth is sky-rocketing because people are generally healthier and living longer. But the increase is straining public services such as housing construction, transportation, water supplies and sewerage. Industrial growth can't keep up and unemployment and under-employment are becoming more common.

Television and tractors aren't the only western imports which have affected Egyptian society. Egypt is gradually being 'Coca-Cola-ised' by the trappings of western life. Things such as Coca-Cola, cassette players and blue jeans are quite popular, not only for what they are, but more importantly for what they symbolise. For the man on the street these things that he can buy over the counter are a slice of the better life – life at the Ewing's ranch or even life among the relatively few upper-crust Egyptians. That man will either be motivated to try and go beyond these small things to a bigger and better life or become frustrated in the attempt. The ranks of both frustrated *and* motivated people are growing.

Egypt's Coptic Christians, estimated at nearly 15% of the population, seem to be one of the most motivated groups in the country. Perhaps this is because Coptic Christianity is more similar to western religion and more amenable to change than Islam. For whatever reasons, Coptic Christians seem to have welcomed the 'Coca-Cola-isation' of Egypt and become an economically powerful minority.

Some Egyptian Muslims have also welcomed the country's modernisation but the vast majority, the Muslim *fellahin*, are frustrated by the possibility of sudden change to a way of life which has remained virtually unchanged for so

many centuries. A few Muslim funda-mentalist groups feel that traditional Egypt is threatened by the 'Coca-Cola and blue jeans revolution'. As the economy worsens, they argue that the answers to Egypt's problems do not lie outside in the import of western technology and lifestyles but rather, they lie inside, with a return to traditional Islam and culture. The funda-mentalists, however, are perhaps over-estimating the impact of the west on life in Egypt. Like the Nile, life flows practically unchanged here and many things, such as music and dance, have changed very little over the centuries.

Music & Dance

It's 5 pm. Radios throughout Egypt are turned up. A female voice is heard. At first it is soft and quiet, like a mother whispering and humming a bedtime story; then come the flutes, a gentle wailing which induces you to breathe and gyrate in time with the music, like a mesmerized snake. The rest of the orchestra picks up – the violins, drums, organs and traditional flute and string instruments. You inhale deeply as the drums beat faster and the violins resound in powerful unison. The voice returns with a clear booming resonance. The voice of Om Khalthum – the 'Mother of Egypt' – has got you by the ears.

Om Kalthum died in 1975 but her music lives on. For western ears it epitomises and simplifies the mystery and complexity of Arabic music. As you walk down a street in Cairo or any other Egyptian city, the music lends a certain mystique to the street life. It's then, when it begins clawing at your ears, that you really know you haven't accidentally landed in the backlot of a Hollywood movie studio. You have, in a sense, landed back in time.

Dance in Egypt is equally alluring. However, unlike the music, it is a bit more difficult to see the 'real' thing. Although belly-dancing shows can be seen in most of Cairo's major hotels that is when you *will* think you have landed on that Hollywood set. Most of the dancers will be European or American because it is not considered proper for an Arab woman to dance in public. Although the performances are usually full of Hollywood glitter and hype, the dancing is often quite authentic. A talented dancer, even if she is American, will capture your eyes with her alluring gyrations and flowing silk scarves.

Thanks to Islam, dancing among the Egyptians is generally considered promiscuous. Nevertheless, there are a few Egyptian dance troupes of both men and women who perform in Cairo, Luxor and Aswan during the winter and in Alexandria during the summer. Egyptians also dance among themselves at weddings, private parties and other family gatherings. Get yourself invited to an Egyptian wedding (which is not difficult) and you will experience Egypt and Egyptians at their best.

GEOGRAPHY
Egypt is practically a square-shaped country. The distance from north to south is 1030 km (640 miles); and from east to west is 965 km (600 miles). For most Egyptians the Nile Valley is Egypt. To the east of the valley there is the Eastern (Arabian) Desert – a barren plateau bounded on its eastern edge by a high ridge of mountains. To the west there is the Western (Libyan) Desert – a plateau punctuated by huge clumps of bizarre geological formations and luxuriant oases.

North of Cairo the Nile splits into several tributaries; the main two being the Rosetta and the Damietta branches. The valley becomes a delta, a wide green fan of fertile countryside, and the tributaries eventually flow into the Mediterranean.

Along the north coast to the west of Alexandria there are hundreds of km of brilliant white-sand beaches. Some have been, or are being, developed as resorts but most parts are still fairly isolated. If you're a sun-worshipper in search of the perfect beach, be careful about wandering off the beaten track. The coast from El Alamein to the Libyan border was the scene of the WW II stand-off between Generals Rommel and Montgomery. Land mines were laid throughout this area and many have still not been recovered.

To the east across the Suez Canal there is another ex-battlefield – the Sinai. Terrain in the Sinai varies from Mt Sinai in the south to desert coastal plains and lagoons in the north. The jagged mountains and wadis around Mt Sinai appear to change shape and colour as the sun passes overhead and a climb to the top offers a commanding view of this spectacle. Moses certainly chose the right mountain to climb.

CLIMATE
Egypt's climate is easy to summarise. Most of the year, except for the winter months of December, January and February, it is hot and dry. Temperatures increase as you travel south from Alexandria. Alexandria receives the most rain – approximately 19 cm a year – while far to the south in Aswan any rain at all is rare.

Summer temperatures range from a scorching 50°C (122°F) in Aswan to 31°C (87°F) on the Mediterranean coast. At night the temperatures sometimes plummet to as low as 8°C.

Be prepared for the temperature extremes. Sweaters are useful in the evenings throughout the country, all year around. Evenings will tend to be warmer the farther south you go. It can also be a bit cool all day in the winter, especially in Cairo and Alexandria.

The Sinai has somewhat unique weather. The desert is typically hot during the day and cold at night. However, the mountains can be freezing, even during the day. See the Sinai section for further information.

RELIGION
Islam

Thousands of thin towering minarets, some as high as 80 metres, are one of the first things people notice in Egypt. Five times a day *muezzins* (Muslim criers) bellow out the call to prayer through speakers atop the minarets. Faithful Muslims follow the call and fill the mosques below for several minutes of elaborate prayers. With these prayers an Egyptian reaffirms his or her faith in Islam, the predominant religion of Egypt.

Islam shares its roots with two of the world's other major religions – Judaism and Christianity. Adam, Abraham, Noah, Moses and Jesus are all accepted as Muslim prophets, although Jesus is not recognised as the son of God. Muslim teachings correspond closely with the Torah, the Old Testament and the Gospels but the essence of Islam is the Qur'an and the Prophet Mohammed.

Islam means submission to Allah (God). Mohammed was the last and truest prophet to deliver this and other messages from Allah to the people. He was born in 570 AD in Mecca (now in Saudi Arabia) and had his first revelation from Allah in 610. He began to preach against the idolatry that was rampant in the region, particularly in Mecca, and proved to be a powerful and persuasive speaker. He quickly gained a fanatical following.

The Muslim faith was more than just a religion as it also called on its followers to spread the word – by the sword if necessary. Within two decades of the Prophet's death, most of Arabia had converted to Islam and in succeeding centuries it spread over three continents. Mecca became their holiest city because it was there that Ibrahim (Abraham) built the first shrine to Allah. The building, known as the *Kabah*, is still the holiest pilgrim shrine in Islam and contains the black stone given to Abraham by the angel Gabriel.

More than 10 years after Mohammed's

Mosque of Mohammed Ali

death in 632 AD, his messages and revelations were compiled into the Muslim holy book, the Qur'an (Koran). No changes to that text have been permitted since 651 AD.

According to the Qur'an, faithful Muslims must carry out five acts known formally as the Five Pillars of Faith:

Publicly declare that 'There is no God but Allah and Mohammed is his Prophet'.
Pray five times a day: sunrise, noon, afternoon, sunset and night.
Pay zakah or charity for the propagation of Islam and for help to the needy.
Fast during the day for the month of Ramadan.
Make the haj or pilgrimage to Mecca.

The first pillar is accomplished through prayer, thus the second pillar. As you'll probably see a lot of praying whilst travelling through Egypt and the Sudan, here is a brief description of what happens:

As a Muslim enters the mosque he takes off his shoes and carries them, sole to sole, in his left hand. It is considered offensive to wear shoes in the House of God. He then washes himself in a certain way before proceeding to pray.

Prayers are done in one to two minute cycles called rek'ah. Each worshipper faces the mihrab or pulpit which is always directed toward Mecca. In fact, the entire mosque is built so that it too points toward Mecca. Then he prays silently, and bows his head a number of times. This is followed by certain actions and prayers said aloud:

Alla-hu Akbar
– which means Allah is great.
The first chapter of the Qur'an.
Verses from another chapter.
Alla-hu Akbar

Then he bows, kneels and places his palms on the ground, followed by his nose and forehead. (The foreheads of the most faithful Muslims have a slight but noticeable indentation created by this genuflection).

I extoll the perfection of Allah the Great (three times, then he stands).
Alla-hu Akbar

Back to the ground saying the same thing as before.

That is one rek'ah, and a good Muslim performs several in a single prayer session. The rek'ah requires a lot of concentration. To create the right condition for this, the interior of most mosques is simple and devoid of elaborate decoration.

Visiting Mosques Before traipsing through mosques there are a few 'rules' you should be aware of. You cannot visit during prayer time but any other time is fine. You must dress modestly. For men that means no shorts; for women that means no shorts, tight pants or anything else even remotely suggestive. Just use common sense. Lastly you must take off your shoes or use the shoe coverings available, for a few piastres, at most mosques.

Egyptian Coptic Christianity
Before the arrival of Islam, Christianity was the predominant religion in Egypt. St Mark, one of the 12 apostles of Jesus, began preaching Christianity in Egypt in 35 AD, although it didn't become the official religion of the country until the 4th century.

By the 5th century Egyptian Christianity had developed an identity independent of that of both the Eastern and Western Roman Empires. Egyptian Christians split from the orthodox church of the Eastern, or Byzantine, Empire which ruled it, after the main body of the Christian Church decided that Christ was both human and divine. The Copts believed and still believe that to consider Christ human is demeaning. A Coptic language is still used in religious ceremonies.

Today, the Copts comprise between 10 and 15% of Egypt's population, although their actual number has been a subject of much controversy. The Muslims and the Copts have each done a census and come up with very different figures. Muslim extremists have continuously harassed the Copts and in the late 1970s the government further Islamicised the legal system. This move infuriated the Copts, but pleased the Muslim extremists. By 1981 relations between the two were very tense. A Coptic church in Cairo was bombed and to avoid further conflict Sadat sent Coptic Pope Shenuda III into internal exile. He stayed at one of the monasteries of Wadi Natrun until Mubarak allowed him to return in early 1985.

Egyptian Jews

Until 1948 more than 80,000 Jews lived in Egypt. However, with the independence of Israel and subsequent wars, many of them had to leave. Today, there are fewer than 500 Jews, mostly elderly, scattered through Alexandria, Cairo and Minya. The marble-pillared synagogues of Alexandria and Cairo are open to the public and are an interesting vestige of what must have once been a thriving community.

Ancient Egyptian Religion

The religion of pharaonic Egypt is difficult to describe because so much is still unknown. The stories behind the many gods and goddesses depicted in hieroglyphics tell more about how, rather than what, ancient Egyptians actually worshipped. Egyptologists have been able to solve a few of the mysteries and at the very least, it is known what most of the ancient deities symbolised.

The sun shines through cloudless skies during the day almost always in Egypt. Thus, it is no surprise that a sun god became one of Egypt's most important deities. The sun god has been known most often by the names of *Ra* and *Amun*. *Ra* was the creator and ruler of other deified elements of nature. There was *Nut*, the sky goddess; *Shu*, the god of air; and *Geb*, the earth god.

Nut was a noticeably interesting goddess. She was always depicted, either as a woman or a cow, stretched across the ceilings of tombs, swallowing the sun and creating night. The next morning she would give birth to the sun.

Animals were another element of nature which was important to the ancient Egyptians. Several animals were considered sacred, especially the Apis bulls of Memphis, the cats of Beni Hasan, the rams of Elephantine (part of ancient Aswan), and the crocodiles of Kom

Nut, Shu & Geb

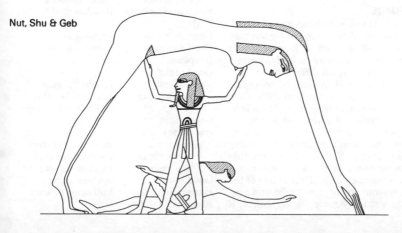

Ombo. Animals were also often associated with various gods and goddesses and eventually, many deities were portrayed in a combined animal-human form.

The human aspects of the gods were often presented like ancient soap operas. Only a few of these 'soaps' have endured Egypt's long past. One of the most celebrated, starred the godly heavyweights of *Osiris, Isis* and *Horus*.

Osiris was the benevolent 'ruler' of Egypt. His brother *Seth*, the epitome of evil, talked him into testing the inside of a crate by laying in it. Once *Osiris* was in the crate, evil *Seth* promptly locked it and tossed it into the Nile. *Isis, Osiris's* sister and wife, searched all over the world until she found the crate and smuggled it back to Egypt. *Seth* discovered the crate, cut *Osiris* into 14 pieces and distributed the bits throughout the country. Loyal *Isis* managed to find all the pieces, built temples dedicated to *Osiris*, and put him back together again. *Isis* and *Osiris* than begat *Horus* who then slew *Seth*. End of story.

Throughout this book there will be other stories recounted and gods described. However, if you wish to learn more about religion in ancient Egypt, refer to the section on Books in the Facts for the Visitor chapter.

LANGUAGE

Arabic is the official language of Egypt. However, the Arabic spoken by the man in the street, written in newspapers or spoken on the radio and recited in prayers at the mosque are all different.

Egyptian street Arabic – colloquial Egyptian Arabic – is fun, but difficult to learn. Unlike most languages, there is no written version of colloquial Arabic. In other words, the Arabic which you learn to speak, you won't be able to write using written Arabic. You will have to either devise your own system of transliteration or use someone else's. That is one of the main reasons so few non-Arabs and non-Muslims study Arabic. Nevertheless, if you take the time to learn even a few words and phrases, you will discover and experience much more while travelling through the country.

Greetings

For every Egyptian greeting there is a certain way to respond. It is more formal than English. There are also different ways to address men and women; and different words to use when referring to yourself, which also depend on your sex.

If you can say just a few of the following greetings and responses, you will have Egyptians saying 'You speak Arabic better than I do'. They are very eager to help you learn their language.

Hello (Peace upon you)	*salaam alake-koom*
Hello or How do you do?	*ahlan-wi-sahlan*
Hello (response)	
– to a man	*ahlan-beek*
– to a woman	*ahlan-bee-kee*
Pleased to meet you.	*tah-sha-raf-na*
Nice meeting you (when leaving)	*fursa sa'eeda*
How are you?	
– to a man	*izzay-yak?*
– to a woman	*izzay-yik?*
– to a group	*izzay-yukoom*
Fine (thanks be to God)	*il-hahm-deel-lee-lah*
Good morning	*sabah il xeer*
Good morning (response)	*sabah il nuur*
Good night	
– to a man	*tiss-bah il xeer*
– to a woman	*tiss-bah-hee il xeer*
– to a group	*tiss-bah-hoo il xeer*
Good night (response)	
– to a man	*wenta min-il xeer*
– to a woman	*wentee min-il xeer*
– to a group	*wentoo min-il xeer*
Good bye	*ma'asalaama*
Happy Birthday/ season's greetings	*kull sana wi enta tiyyib*

General Expressions

The following are a few words and phrases to help you get around.

yes	aywa, naam (aywa is more common)
no	la

There are three forms of please; each is used differently:

1) When asking for something from, for example, a shop.
2) The next is more formal but used in the same circumstances.
3) The last form is used when offering something to somebody.

1)	– to a man	minfadlak
	– to a woman	minfadlik
	– to a group	minfadluku
2)	– to a man	lao-sah-maht
	– to a woman	lao-sah-mahtee
	– to a group	lao-sah-mahtu
3)	– to a man	it'fahdel
	– to a woman	it'fahdeli
	– to a group	it'fahdelu

thank you	shuke-rahn
thank you very much	shuke-rahn gazeelan
you are welcome	afwan or el-affw
excuse me	
– to a man	aan-iznak or ehs-Mah-lee
– to a woman	aan-iznik or ehs-mah-Hee-lee
– to a group	aan-iznuku or ehs-mah-Hoo-lee
excellent	mumtaz
good	kwayyis
bad	meesh kwayyis
how much?	bee-kam?
how many?	kam?

What do you want?	
– to a man	ayiz eh?
– to a woman	ayza eh?
– to a group	ayzeen eh?

I/me	ana

you	
– to a man	enta
– to a woman	entee
– to a group	entu
he/him	huwwa
she/her	hiyya
we/us	ehna
they/them	humma

my wife	meh-Rah-tee
my husband	go-zee
my sister	ukh-tee
my brother	ach-khoo-ya

I am . . .	ana . . .
a student (m)	talib
a student (f)	taliba
American (m)	am-ree-kah-nee
American (f)	am-ree-kah-niyya
British (m)	bree-to-nee
British (f)	bree-to-niyya
Australian (m)	austrah-lee
Australian (f)	austrah-liyya
Canadian (m)	canadee
Canadian (f)	cana-diyya

I speak . . .	ana bi-Kal-lim . . .
English	in-glee-zee
French	fran-sa-wee
German	al-man-nee

I understand you.	ana fah-hemt
I did not understand.	mah-fah-hem-tish
Do you understand me?	
– to a man	fah-hemt-nee?
– to a woman	fah-hem-tee-nee?

What does this mean?	yah-nee ay?
We need an interpreter.	ehna ayzeen moo-tar-gim

Allah

Finding Your Way Around

The following words should help you get from place to place.

here	*henna*
there	*hennak*
left	*shimmel*
right	*yi-mean*
straight ahead	*a-la-tuul*
at the corner	*il-lee gayyah*

Where?	*fayn?*
Where is . . .?	*fayn . . .?*
the police station?	*is-meh el-bo-lees?*
the men's room?	*mir-hahd ir-reh-gel?*

men

the ladies' room?	*twah-let iss-yeh-daht?*

women

the ticket window	*il shibbak it-ta-za-keer?*
train station	*mah-hattit il-atr*
bus station	*mah-hattit it otobees*
airport	*mah-tar*

Give me a ticket to . . .	*id-dee-nee tahz-karrah lee . . .*
1st class	*dah-rah-gah oo-lah*
2nd class	*dah-rah-gah tan-yah*
What bus goes to . . .?	*oto-bees nim-rah kam bi-rooh . . .?*
Where can I rent a bicycle?	*ah-dahr ah-oog-gahr ah-gah-lah?*

Do you speak English?	
– to a man	*enta bit-Kal-lim in-glee-zee?*
– to a woman	*enti bit-Kal-lim-tee in glee-zee?*
Does anyone here speak English?	*fee hahd henna bi-yit-Kal-lim in-glee-zee?*

In the Hotel

Now that you have found your way to wherever you were going, here are a few words to help you find a place to stay.

hotel	*fawn-duke* or *lakonda*
Do you have a room?	*fee odah fahd-yah?*
a double room	*fee odah lit-nayn*
I want a room (m)	*ana ayiz odah*
I want a room (f)	*ana ayza odah*
with double bed	*bis-reer doob-leh*
with bath	*bi-hahm-Mam*
with shower	*bi-doosh*
with hot water	*bi-miyyah sukhnah*
cheaper	*ar-khas*

Miscellaneous Essentials

customs	*goon-ruke*
post office	*el-bohs-stah*
I want to send this by . . .	*ana ayiz ah-baht dee bil . . .*
surface mail	*ba-reed el-Ah-dee*
air mail	*ba-reed gow-wee*
soap	*sah-boon*
toilet paper	*wara twah-let*
I am busy (m)	*ana mash-rool*
I am busy (f)	*ana mash-rool-la*

Compliment to a beautiful girl (slang); literal translation is 'cream'	ishta
fluent (slang)	lib lib
not fluent	meesh lib lib
OK	tiyyib
flirt	el-ah
insult	afeeya
foreigner (slightly derogatory)	kchah-wag-ah
thief!	hah-rah-mee

Numbers

English	Arabic	Pronunciation
0	•	sif-re
1	١	wahid
2	٢	it-nane
3	٣	talata
4	٤	ahr-bah-ah
5	٥	kham-sah
6	٦	sitta
7	٧	saba'a
8	٨	tamanyah
9	٩	tisa'a
10	١٠	ashara
11		hidasher
12		it-nasher
13		talatash-er
14		arba'a-tahsh-er
15		khammahstahsh-er
16		sitt-tah-sher
17		saba'a-tah-sher
18		taman-tah-sher
19		tissa'a-tah-sher
20		aysh-reen
21		wahid-wi-ayshreen
30		talateen
40		arba'aeen
50		kham-seen
60		sitt-teen
70		saba'aeen
80		taman-neen
90		tisa'aeen
100		may-yah
101		may-yah wi-wahid
110		may-yah wi-ashahrah

1000	alf
2000	al-fayn
3000	talat-talaf
4000	arba'a-talaf
5000	khamas-talaf

HOLIDAYS & FESTIVALS

Egypt's holidays and festivals are primarily Coptic and Islamic religious celebrations. On the western calendar the Islamic calendar moves up 11 days each year so if you're calculating by a western calendar, holiday dates will seem to change each year. The Islamic calendar has 12 lunar months:

1st	Moharram
2nd	Safar
3rd	Rabei El Awal
4th	Rabei El Tani
5th	Gamada El Awal
6th	Gamada El Taniyya
7th	Ragab
8th	Shaaban
9th	Ramadan
10th	Shawal
11th	Zuu'l Qeda
12th	Zuu'l Hagga

Islamic Holidays

Ras al Sana
New Year's Day, celebrated on 1 Moharram.

Mulid al Nabi
Birthday of the Prophet Mohammed; celebrated on 12 Rabei El Awal. The streets of Cairo are a feast of lights and food.

Ramadan
The ninth month of the Islamic calendar, Ramadan is considered the fourth of Islam's five fundamental pillars of faith. For the entire month, faithful Muslims fast from dawn to sunset in order to gain strength against evil spirits. No food and water are allowed until sunset. The *feteer* or breaking of the fast occurs the moment the sun has set. Try to attend a *feteer*

at an Egyptian family's home. Everyone counts the minutes and seconds until feast time and when it's time to eat, chicken bones, bread scraps and vegetable pieces fly as the family descends upon the feast dish. You need to be quick! A feast for 10 is consumed in less than 10 minutes.

Eed al Fitr

The end of Ramadan fasting. The celebration lasts from 1-3 Shawal.

Eed al Adhah

The time for Muslims to fulfill the fifth pillar of Islam, the *haj* or pilgrimage to Mecca. Every Muslim is supposed to make the *haj* at least once in his lifetime. This special period for making the *haj* lasts from 10-13 Zuu'l Hagga.

Coptic Christian Holidays

Christmas

7 January

Epiphany

19 January

Annunciation

23 March

Easter

Celebrated on different dates each year.

Sham el Nessim (Sniffing the Breeze)

A special Coptic holiday with Pharaonic origins. It falls on the first Monday after Easter and is celebrated by all Egyptians with family picnics and outings.

Other holidays

1 January

New Year's Day

28 February

Union Day

18 June

Evacuation Day; the day the British left Egypt.

23 July

Revolution Day

6 October

National Day; a day of military parades and air displays.

23 October

Suez National Day; commemoration of the Suez crisis.

23 December

Victory Day.

Facts for the Visitor

VISAS & REGISTRATION

All foreigners entering Egypt, except nationals of Malta and Arab countries other than Libya, must obtain visas from Egyptian consulates overseas or at the airport or port upon arrival. A three month multiple-entry Tourist Visa from the consulate costs US$11 for US passport holders, US$23 for West German passport holders and US$20 for others. Processing of your visa application takes 48 hours if you drop it off in person or about 10 days if you mail it. Be sure to include one passport-sized photograph, a money order or certified cheque (not a personal cheque), a stamped self-addressed envelope with enough postage to send it registered (if you are mailing it) and, of course, your passport with the application.

If you wait until you get to the airport or port, processing supposedly takes only 30 minutes, a photograph is not required and the visa will cost US$20. Try to avoid doing this as it could actually take much longer.

Most people are given a three month tourist visa with either single or multiple entries. If you plan to return to Egypt after, for example, visiting Israel, Jordan or the Sudan, then you should request the multiple entry visa.

Warning Don't be duped by the fact that your visa is valid for 'three months'. All it means, is that you have three months from the time the visa was issued to actually enter Egypt. Upon arrival you will be required to exchange US$150 and, within one week, register with the government. You will then be issued a permit which is valid for a one month stay.

If you are coming from Israel, you can't get a visa at the border. Your passport will be stamped with the name of the Egyptian border post. If the stamp is legible (not smeared), then you will not be permitted to enter Jordan, Syria, the Sudan or other Arab countries.

Embassies

Following are the addresses and telephone numbers of Egyptian embassies in major cities around the world:

Australia
125 Monaro Crescent, Red Hill, Canberra, ACT 2603 (tel (062) 950394)
Canada
3754 Cote des Neiges, Montreal, Quebec H3H 7V6 (tel 514-9367781)
454 Laurier Avenue, Ottawa, Ontario K1N 6R3 (tel 613-2344931)
Greece
3 Avenue Cassilissi Sosias, Athens (tel 612954)
Sudan
Sharia El Gamaa, El Mogran, Khartoum (tel 72836)
UK
South Audley St, London W1 (tel 01-2913209)
USA
1110 2nd Avenue, New York, NY 10022 (tel 212-7577120)
2300 Decatur Palace NW, Washington DC 20008 (tel 202-2343903)
3001 Pacific Avenue, San Francisco, CA 94415 (tel 415-3469700)
2000 West Loop South, Houston, TX 77027 (tel 713-9614915)
505 North Shore Lake Drive, Chicago, IL 60611 (tel 312-6702633)

There are also Egyptian consulates in Australia (Melbourne), West Germany, France, Italy, Kenya, Jordan, Turkey and Israel (Tel Aviv and Eilat).

In Tel Aviv the embassy is at 50 Rehov Basel; take bus No 5 from Tel Aviv central bus station. If you get there before 9 am you can probably beat the long queues and pick up your passport at noon. If you don't have any passport-size photos (you need two for the visa) you can have your photograph taken just outside the embassy for a couple of dollars. Visa fees also vary; it will cost at least US$20 plus varying amounts of shekels.

The Egyptian consulate in Eilat issues visas in 20 minutes for about US$20. The consulate (tel 059-76115) is at No 34, The Moore Centre, near the Melony Tower. Bring spare photographs with you.

There is also an Egyptian consulate in Aqaba, Jordan. Visas cost seven dinar and take 1½ hours. One photograph is required.

Vaccination Certificate

A vaccination certificate proving that you have been vaccinated for yellow fever and/or cholera is only necessary if you are coming from an infected area. However, I've never heard of any travellers – even those coming from infected areas such as the Sudan – ever being asked for their certificate. To be on the safe side though, it is still a good idea to have these vaccinations. See the section on health in this chapter for more information.

Registration

You must register with the police within one week of your arrival in Egypt. Most hotels will take care of this for a small fee. It's worth paying the fee unless you are really anxious to have the cultural experience of dealing with the bureaucracy of Cairo's dreaded *Mogamma*.

The *Mogamma* is a mammoth government building on Tahrir Square in central Cairo. If you have to go there, enter through the right side of the main entrance, not the left, or you will be stampeded by the exiting herd. Climb the stairs on your right and follow the signs to the Passport Department, Room 48. It is near there that you also go for re-entry visas and visa extensions.

In Alexandria the Passport Registration office is on Talaat Harb St. Both offices are open from 8.30 am to 2 pm.

Visa Extensions

Extensions can be obtained for periods of from one to four weeks. Normally, you must show bank receipts proving that you changed another US$150 for the second month. The amount remains at US$150 even if you're only getting an extension for an extra week or two. They keep the bank receipts – something which can be a nuisance when you need the receipts to buy a plane ticket. (For details on how to evade this requirement, refer to the Money section later in this chapter.) You also need one photograph, E£2 for each two-week period and the usual amount of patience.

CUSTOMS

The Egyptian government issues a list of articles which are duty-free, dutiable, prohibited or restricted. The following information comes from that list:

Duty Free Articles The following articles can be brought into Egypt without duty being charged: personal clothing and toiletries, equipment and tools for use during work, one bottle of liquor and 100 cigarettes.

Dutiable Articles Customs duty will be levied on articles in excess of the duty free allowance. Duty will have to be paid on the following items regardless of whether or not they have been used previously: automobiles, motorcycles and video-cameras.

Prohibited & Restricted Articles Books, printed matter, motion pictures, phonographs and materials that are considered subversive or constituting a national risk or incompatible with the public interest. (Obviously, this is censorship.)

Articles for espionage or intelligence activities. (They didn't specifically say what they meant by this).

Explosives (to blow up buses and things like that).

Sometimes, *Customs Declaration Form D* is given to arriving tourists to fill out. You are supposed to to list all cameras, jewellery, cash, travellers' cheques and electronics (Walkman, radios, video recorders, etc). I have never heard of anyone ever being asked for this form upon departure.

WORKING IN EGYPT

More than 40,000 foreigners already live and work in Egypt. That figure alone should give you some idea of the immense presence foreign companies have in the country. It is possible to find work with one of these companies if you are committed and motivated. Begin your research before you leave home. *Cairo, A Practical Guide* published by the American University in Cairo Press has a relatively up-to-date list of all foreign companies

Re-entry Visas

Patience is also required when obtaining a re-entry visa. If you have a multiple entry visa, you should not need a re-entry visa but double-check on this. This can get a bit tricky. A re-entry visa will definitely exempt you from having to change money again whereas a multiple entry visa might not. In Cairo re-entry visas are obtained from rooms 1 and 17 in the Mogamma building.

Transit & Temporary Visas

Transit and temporary visas, valid for 48 hours, are issued at the airport, free of charge. You are not required to change money. However, if you decide to stay longer, then you must change US$150 and obtain a visa by presenting bank receipts at the Mogamma. If you stay longer than one week, then you must register with the police before the end of the week.

operating in Egypt. If you know some Arabic, you will definitely be in an advantageous position. Once you have an employer, securing a work permit through an Egyptian Consulate or in Egypt, from the Ministry of Interior, should not be difficult.

In addition to working for foreign companies, there are also many opportunities for teaching English as a second language. The Institute of International Education has information on teaching opportunities abroad. Contact them at 809 United Nations Plaza, New York, NY 10017 (tel 212-8888200).

If you just want to earn a few extra pounds in Egypt while you're travelling, you can appear in Egyptian television commercials, as the local advertising agencies are always looking for western faces. A Dutch traveller appeared in a shaving cream commercial and the advertising people dressed him up as a cowboy and had him get on and off a horse at the pyramids. It took about three hours and he received E£60. Not bad! To arrange something like this, you might try calling the following agencies:

AMA – Leo Burnett, No 49 Sharia Shahab, Mohandiseen (tel 807891 or 805570).
Americana, 32H Radwan Ibn El Talib, Giza (tel 725020 or 720707).
Arab Graphic Center, 4 Molla, Matria.
Intermarkets, 17 Gamal al-Din Abdul Mahassen, Garden City (tel 31138).

STUDYING IN EGYPT
The American University in Cairo AUC is one of the premier universities in the Middle East. The campus is in the heart of Cairo on Midan Tahrir. The curriculum and half the faculty, of 160, are American and accredited in the US. Four types of programmes are offered.

AUC offers non-degree and summer school programmes. The non-degree programmes are primarily designed for American university students who wish to take their third year of studies in Egypt. Any of the regular courses offered

can be taken. Popular subjects include Arabic Language, Arab History and Culture, Egyptology, Middle East studies and social science courses on the Arab world. Up to 15 unit hours can be taken per semester at the undergraduate level.

Summer programmes offer similar courses. The term lasts from mid-June to July. Two three-unit courses can be taken and several well-guided field trips throughout Egypt are usually included.

The largest programmes at AUC are for bachelor's and master's degrees in more than 20 subjects ranging from Anthropology to Teaching English as a Foreign Language.

AUC is also home to the Center for Arabic Studies. This independent wing of the university offers intensive instruction in Arabic language at beginning, intermediate and advanced levels. There are courses on both colloquial Egyptian Arabic and modern standard Arabic.

Applications for programmes with the Center for Arabic Studies and courses with the university are separate. Specify which you want when requesting an application. A current catalogue and programme information can be obtained from:

The Office of Admissions
The American University in Cairo
    866 United Nations Plaza, New York, NY 10017-1889
or
    PO Box 2511, Cairo, Egypt (tel no 22962, ext 115 or 255)

Tuition in 1986 was US$5000 for the year. The summer session cost US$1400 for two courses.

Egyptian Universities It is also possible to study at Egyptian universities such as Al Azhar, Alexandria, Ein Shams and Cairo. Courses offered to foreign students include Arabic Language, Islamic History, Islamic Religion and Egyptology. For information on courses, tuition fees and applications, contact:

The Cultural Counselor
  The Egyptian Educational Bureau, 2200 Kalorama Rd NW, Washington DC 20008

Other Programmes Short intensive programmes in Arabic language are offered through several language institutes in Cairo. The *Berlitz School* (tel 915096), 165 Mohammed Farid St, offers personalised colloquial Arabic courses. The *Egyptian Center for International Cooperation* (tel 815419), 11 Shagaret El Dor in Zamalek, offers courses in classical Arabic. The *International Language Institute* (tel 803087), 3 Mahmoud Azmy St, Medinat al-Sahafeyeen, offers a variety of courses at all levels.

MONEY

The official currency of Egypt is called the pound (E£). In Arabic it is pronounced *guinay*. A pound = 100 piastres (pt – sometimes indicated by ‿). The Arabic word for piastre is *irsh* or *girsh*. There are notes in denominations of 5, 10, 25 and 50 pt and E£1, 5, 10, 20 and 50. Avoid the 50 pound notes. (A couple of years ago Egyptian police discovered a lot of counterfeit E£50 notes in circulation.) Although new notes have been issued for most denominations because so much of the money was literally falling apart, you will still come across bills held together by cheap bits of packing tape.

The E£1 note is being phased out in favour of a E£1 coin. Other coins in circulation are for denominations of ½ pt (5 millims), 1, 5 and 10 pt.

The low values of both coins and notes are one of the first signs that prices in Egypt are relatively low. Prices can be written with or without a decimal point. For example, E£3.33 can also be written as 333 pt.

Official Exchange Rates These are fixed by the government at over-valued rates. There are two rates: an official and a tourist rate. Current tourist exchange rates are approximately:

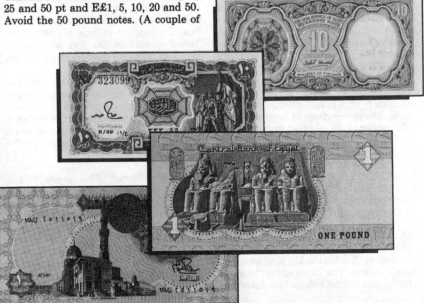

```
US$1 = E£2.19
 A$1 = E£1.56
UK£1 = E£3.54
 C$1 = E£1.65
 DM1 = E£1.19
```

The Exchange Game One of the arrival hassles which many travellers complain about is the exchange requirement. Everybody entering Egypt on a tourist visa must exchange US$150, or the equivalent in another hard currency, at the port of entry. With a black market exchange rate of about US$1 = E£1.75, nobody likes to exchange at the official or tourist rates.

Don't forget to claim how much money you're carrying if you plan to leave Egypt with most of it. Once in awhile the Egyptian customs people will confiscate unclaimed currency as a traveller is leaving the country, though this is very rare.

There are ways around the exchange requirement but it's a hit and miss affair. If you are coming from Israel, Masada Tours and Galilee Tours offer inexpensive travel packages which include transportation to Cairo, three nights in a decent hotel and exemption from the exchange requirement. See the Getting There chapter for more information.

We've heard of a few people who told customs officials on arrival that they had no money, only postal cheques or credit cards. They were given 48-hour visas and told to change the required money within that period. They then checked into a hotel and paid one of the staff to register their arrival at the *Mogamma*. (Most hotels do this for their guests for a small fee; see the section on Registration). Their passports were registered and they received one-month visas.

Official Exchanges Money can be officially changed at American Express offices, commercial banks, the US Embassy and hotel cashiers. The latter offers the worst official and tourist rates while American Express and the US Embassy offer the best. Banks are open from 9 am to 1.30 pm everyday except Fridays, Sundays and public holidays. On Sundays banks are usually open from 10 am to 1.30 pm. Banking services are available 24 hours a day at the airport and major luxury hotels.

Official Re-exchange Excess pounds can be exchanged into hard currency at the end of your stay, if you can show bank receipts which indicate that you spent the equivalent of US$30 per day. It is a big hassle, so avoid it if possible.

Carrying Money Pickpockets like money. In fact, some like it so much they are brave and deft enough to search your pockets while standing in front of you on a crowded bus – and you probably won't even realise what's happening until it's too late. I write from personal experience.

Be careful about carrying money and valuables in a day pack or hand bag. Razor blades work wonders on bags when the dastardly perpetrator is standing behind you in a queue or on a crowded bus. Passengers on bus No 900 from Tahrir Square to the Pyramids are a favourite target for these fingers of stealth and stickiness.

Money belts and pouches around your neck keep your money where it belongs. Another protective measure is to carry travellers' cheques; they can be replaced if stolen or lost. However, cheques are a bit more difficult to exchange on the black market than cash.

The Black Market The words 'black market' conjure up images of dark alleyways where mumbling, shifty-eyed characters count wads of notes. Well, in Egypt that's a fairly accurate image. The characters do have shifty-eyes and mumble, but they also bumble. Most of the action takes place on the street and in bazaars full of papyrus paintings and fake antiquities. The bumblers will constantly approach you chanting 'change money, change money.' Ignore them. When you want to change money, compare the rates yourself at a few bazaars. Large amounts of hard currency, and cash rather than travellers' cheques, bring higher rates.

After the black market transaction has been made, always sit down and count the money yourself directly in front of the person who did the exchange. Changing money on the black market is officially illegal but relatively small transactions are unofficially tolerated. Nevertheless, exercise caution.

It is also illegal to import or export any more than E£20. Even so a lot still ends up overseas; it sells for slightly less than the current black market rate. If you have more than E£20 when entering the country, there is a risk – albeit slim – of having the excess confiscated.

If you have an American Express card and travellers' cheques or personal cheques, you can exchange or cash them for hard currency at American Express offices. American Express charges a 2% commission and writes the amount obtained in the back of your passport.

Money from Home There are two convenient ways to receive money from home. If you have an American Express card and personal cheques, American Express will cash your cheques. If you have an American Express green card though, you are not permitted to cash more than US$400 each 21 days without authorisation from their offices in London or the US. If you have a Visa or Mastercard, you can get a cash advance from the Bank of America in Cairo or the Commercial Bank of Egypt.

It is also possible to have money wired from home through American Express, the Bank of America and the following banks:

Manufacturers Hanover, 3 Ahmed Nessim, Giza (tel 988266)
Chase Manhattan, 9 Gamal al-Din Abdul Mahassen, Garden City, Cairo (tel 26111)

Chemical Bank, 14 Talaat Harb, 2nd floor, Cairo (tel 740707)
Citibank, 4 Ahmed Pasha, Garden City (tel 272 46)

COSTS

Travel in Egypt is cheap. It is easily possible to get by on US$10 a day or even less if you're willing to endure certain inconveniences. Forgoing hot water or showers and taking 3rd class trains packed to the hilt with screaming babies, chicken cages and half the Egyptian army, will save you quite a bit in daily expenses. For the most part, the amount of convenience and comfort varies according to how much you are willing to pay. Yet, even at the 1st class level, Egypt is cheap compared to similar travel amenities in western countries.

TIPPING

Tipping in Egypt is called *baksheesh*, although it is more than just a reward for having done a service properly. *Baksheesh* is sort of a bribe, a way to persuade someone to do a service the way you want it done. It keeps palms greased and some Egyptians happy. For western travellers who are not used to this, demands for *baksheesh* for doing anything from opening a door to being unwillingly guided through an ancient site can be quite irritating. But it is the accepted way of getting things done in Egypt. Don't be intimidated into paying *baksheesh* when you don't think the service warrants it, but remember that more things warrant *baksheesh* here than anywhere in the west.

Services such as opening a door or carrying your bags warrant 10 pt to 25 pt. A personal guide to, for example, the Egyptian Museum costs about E£5 per hour in *baksheesh*. A guard who shows you something off the beaten track at an ancient site should receive about 50 piastres to E£1. *Baksheesh* is not necessary when asking for directions.

A last tip on tipping: carry lots of small change with you.

INFORMATION

The Egyptian government has tourist information offices in nine countries and throughout Egypt. The tourist offices outside Egypt, with the exception of the head office in Cairo, are more helpful than the ones within Egypt. At the head office several languages including English and French are spoken by the very helpful staff. If they don't know the answer to a question they will call someone who does. They have maps of Cairo and Egypt, as well as brochures on various sites around the country. The information tends to be a bit faulty, but the photographs should give you a better idea of what you might visit.

Egyptian Tourist Offices

Cairo
   Head office, 5 Adly St (tel 923000)
   Airport office (tel 966475)
   Pyramids office, Pyramids Rd, near the Mena House (tel 850259)
Luxor
   Tourist Bazaar, across from the Luxor Temple (tel 2215)
Aswan
   Corniche al-Nil, two blocks north of the Abu Simbel Hotel behind a small park (tel 23297)
Alexandria
   Nabi Danial St, just off Saad Zaghloul Square (tel 807611)
Marsa Matruh
   The corner of Alexandria St & the Corniche
Port Said
   No 43 Palestine St (tel 23868)
Ismailia
   Governorate building
Suez
   16 al-Shohadaa St (tel 2389)

Overseas Offices

Canada
   Egyptian Tourist Authority, Place Bonaventure, 40 Frontenac, Montreal, Quebec H5A 1V4 (tel 514-861-4420)
   PO Box 304, Montreal, H5A 1V4
France
   Bureau de Tourisme, Ambassade de la RAE, 90 Avenue Des Champs Elysees, Paris (tel 5629442)
Germany
   Aegyptisches Frem Denverkehrsamt, 641 Kaiser Strasse, Frankfurt, West Germany (tel 252319)
Greece
   Egyptian State Tourist Office, 10 Amerikas St, 6th floor, Athens 134 (tel 3606906)
Italy
   Ufficio Informazioni Turistiche, 19 Via Bissolati, 00187 Roma (tel 475-1985)
Japan
   The Egyptian State Tourist Office, Akasaka 2-Chome Annex, 19-18 Akasaka 2 Chome Minato Ku, Tokyo (tel 58906531)
Switzerland
   Office du Tourisme d'Egypte, 11 Rue de Chantepoulet, 1211 Geneve (tel 022-329132)
UK
   The Egyptian State Tourist Office, 168 Piccadilly St, London W1 (tel 01-4935282)
USA
   The Egyptian Tourist Authority, 630 5th Avenue, New York, NY 10020 (tel 212-246-6960)
   Egyptian General Authority for the Promotion of Tourism, 323 Geary St, Suite 608, San Francisco, CA 94102 (tel 415-433-7562)

GENERAL INFORMATION

Post

The Egyptian postal system is slow but eventually most mail gets to its destination. Letters are slow in coming and going; post cards are even slower; and packages ... well, bring out the Camel Express, it may be faster. Receiving and sending packages through customs can cause tremendous headaches, but I've sent many letters and postcards from Egypt to the USA, Australia, Singapore and Great Britain without any problems; they took about three weeks to get through. It takes about the same time for a letter to arrive from the US and one to two weeks from Europe.

Postal Rates Airmail letters cost 6 pt to Arab countries and 23 pt to all other countries. Postcards to non-Arab countries cost 18 pt. Postage for packages is relatively inexpensive. Stamps are available at souvenir kiosks, reception desks of major hotels, some shops, news stands, and of course post offices.

Sending Mail Post offices in Egypt are open from 8.30 am to 3 pm everyday except Fridays. The Central Post Office in Cairo at Ataba Square is open 24 hours. Sending mail from the post boxes at major hotels instead of from the post offices seems to be quicker.

If you have American postage, you might consider sending your mail through the American University in Cairo Student Affairs Office. You should have a foreign student at the university arrange this for you. The Student Affairs Office regularly sends out mail to the US with people who are on their way there.

Packages will probably have to be sent via the Central Post Office with an export license. Most curio shops will send your packages for a fee. See the Cairo information section for details about the formalities.

Receiving Mail Mail can be received at American Express offices, the Poste Restante in most Egyptian cities, and at some consulates.

Receiving mail at your country's consulate is probably the fastest and most efficient way. The envelopes should be marked *Visitors' Mail* and *Please hold for arrival* and sent to you c/o the embassy or consulate. A few embassy and consulate addresses are listed in the Cairo information section.

American Express offices are the next best option for receiving mail. Have it sent to the American Express office in central Cairo. The address is: 15 Sharia Kasr el Nil, Cairo, Egypt. Sending mail to other American Express offices is less reliable because it's often forwarded to the central office anyway.

I have never met any travellers who have received mail through the Poste Restante in Egypt, but supposedly it does function throughout the country. If you plan to pick up mail there, have the clerk

check under Mr/Ms/Mrs in addition to your first and last names. The main Poste Restante is at the Central Post Office in Ataba Square in Cairo.

Supposedly, the Royal Bank of Canada at No 3 Abu El Feda, The Abu El Feda Building, 10th floor, Cairo will also hold mail for travellers. However, you should double-check this.

Telephones, Telex & Telegraph

Telephones The phones in Egypt are a test of one's patience and sense of humour. If you're lacking in either, then be prepared for frustration. Making long-distance or international telephone calls is often easier than ringing locally. Fortunately, this is changing.

In 1986 the Egyptian government was in the process of revamping the system. Lines and connections are being upgraded. Most importantly, *telephone numbers are being changed*. For those Cairo numbers listed in this book which do not function, first try dialing a 3, 5 or 7 and then the number. If that doesn't work, consult a copy of the 5th edition of *Cairo, A Practical Guide* which lists many updated telephone numbers. There's also a Cairo 'yellow pages' telephone directory, available at most of the major hotels, published by Hawk Publishing, 23A Ismail Mohd St, Zamalek, Cairo (tel 698818).

Local telephone calls cost 10 pt. Calls can be made from cigarette kiosks, major hotels and telephone offices. There are a few pay phones in the lobby of the Nile Hilton. Telephone office locations are mentioned throughout the book.

International calls must be made from a hotel or telephone office. At the telephone office you pay for the call in advance. You can either use one of the booths in the office or have the operator call you at a private number. A few private lines (very few) have direct connections to international lines.

Three minute calls to North America cost approximately E£12; to Australia and New Zealand, E£18; Great Britain, E£11; and Canada, E£14. Collect calls cannot be made from Egypt.

In Cairo, the Central Telephone & Telegraph Offices at Sharia Adly, Midan Tahrir, Sharia Ramses and Sharia El Alfy are open 24 hours a day. Other telephone offices are open from 7 am to 9 pm.

Telegraph Telegrams in English or French can be sent from the Central Telephone & Telegraph Offices. The rate to North America is 60 piastres per word.

Telex Machines are available at the Central Telephone and Telegraph Offices on Sharia Adly and Sharia El Alfy and at major hotels. Rates vary.

Permits & Student Identification Cards

An antiquities permit is a useful thing to have as it allows you easier access to many of Egypt's archaeological sites. To get the permit, from the Department of Antiquities in Abbassiya, you might need a letter from the Archaeology Department of any university. The manager in Abbassiya, Ahmed Idri, can sometimes give you special permission to visit certain royal tombs.

Travel permits are still required for trips to certain parts of Egypt. They are needed for travel westward past Marsa Matruh, for Siwa Oasis and for some parts of the Nile Delta. Check with the main tourist office at No 5 Adly St in Cairo for the latest details.

Legitimate student identification cards are available for E£10 from Cairo University's Faculty of Medicine building near Manyal Palace (after 12.30 pm). Proof of student status is never requested but you need a photograph.

It's also easy to obtain student identification cards in Turkey and Greece.

Some travellers who have written to Lonely Planet claim that sometimes they also received student discounts by showing their International Youth Hostel cards. Discounts were received on trains and entry fees to temples and tombs.

A Dutch traveller said he took a photocopy of a student identification card and placed his own photograph on the copy. He never had any problems obtaining student discounts.

Another source of identity is a business card. A card can give you a certain degree of credibility in Egypt and depending what's on it, can be a great help in obtaining assistance.

Electricity

Electric current is 220 volts AC, 50 cycles everywhere except Alexandria and the Cairo suburbs of Maadi and Heliopolis, where the current is 110 to 120 volts, 50 cycles. Wall plugs are the round, two prong European type. Bring adapter plugs and transformers if necessary.

Time

Egypt is two hours ahead of Greenwich Mean Time and daylight saving time is observed. So allowing for variations due to daylight saving, when it's 12 noon in Cairo it is: 10 am in London; 5 am in New York and Montreal; 2 am in Los Angeles; 1 pm in Moscow; and 7.30 pm in Melbourne and Sydney.

Laundry

There are a few self-service laundries around Cairo. Their addresses are listed in the Cairo information section.

Another option is to take your clothes to one of Egypt's many 'hole-in-the-wall' laundries where they wash and iron your clothes by hand. The process is fascinating and entertaining to watch. The ironing man takes an ancient iron, which opens at the top, places hot coals inside and then fills his mouth with water from a bottle on the table. The water is sprayed from his mouth over the clothes as he vigorously irons.

Your last option, and the most common, is to do your own laundry. You can buy powdered laundry soap throughout Egypt. Bring a nail brush for scrubbing and some nylon cord for hanging your wet clothes.

Business Hours

Banks They're open daily except Fridays. Hours are from 10 am to 12 noon on Sundays and from 8.30 am to 1.30 pm on other days. Bank Misr at the Nile Hilton is open 24 hours.

Shops Generally they keep different hours at different times of the year. In summer most shops are open from 9 am to 1 pm and from 5 to 8 pm. Winter hours are from 10 am to 6 pm. Hours during Ramadan are from 9.30 am to 3.30 pm and from 8 to 10 pm.

Weights & Measurements

Egypt is on the metric system. Following, are basic conversion and equivalency charts:

To Convert	Multiply by
inches to centimetres	2.540
centimetres to inches	0.3937
feet to metres	0.3048
metres to feet	3.281
yards to metres	0.9144
metres to yards	1.094
miles to kilometres	1.609
kilometres to miles	0.6214

Episode in a laundry — fellow takes a mouthful of water and spits it out as a fine mist over your laundry, then he irons this to perfection using a massive two handed hot plate heated over glowing coals.

THE IRON

imperial gallons to litres	4.546
litres to imperial gallons	0.22
ounces to grams	28.35
grams to ounces	0.03527
pounds to kilograms	0.4536
kilograms to pounds	2.205

Temperature Conversion

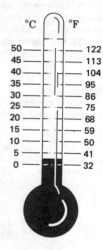

°C		°F
50	—	122
45	—	113
40	—	104
35	—	95
30	—	86
25	—	75
20	—	68
15	—	59
10	—	50
5	—	41
0	—	32

MEDIA
Newspapers & Magazines
The Egyptian Gazette is Egypt's daily English language newspaper. It is difficult to find outside of Cairo and Alexandria and the news coverage is mediocre. That is due, in part, to government censorship. At the very least though, it gives you some idea of what is happening in the Egyptian government. The Saturday issue is called *The Egyptian Mail*.

Cairo Today, another English language publication, is a monthly magazine which covers a variety of subjects including the arts and sport in Egypt. Every issue has a guide to nightlife in Cairo.

Almost every major western newspaper and news magazine can be found in Cairo and Alexandria, including *Newsweek* and *Time*. They're available in major hotels and a few newstands and bookstores.

For the latest international news there are wire service teletype machines in the lobby of the Cairo Sheraton. It's on the opposite bank of the Nile from Tahrir Square. The news printouts are hung on a bulletin board next to the machines.

Radio & Television
There are daily English language pro-grammes on radio and television. Check the *Egyptian Gazette* for the latest programme information. Normally, the news can be heard in English on a radio frequency of 557 kHz at 7.30 am, 2.30 pm and 8 pm. On 640 kHz news from the BBC World Service can be heard at 8 am in winter and 9 am in summer. The Voice of America can also be heard in Egypt. For full schedules see the media section for the Sudan.

Television news in English is usually shown at 7.30 pm. Several American and British television series appear on Egyptian television. Sometimes the programmes are shown with Arabic sub-titles, other

Four page

The Egyptian Gazette

ذى اچبشـيان جازيــت

No. 28064 ✷   Tuesday, June 6. 196

times they're dubbed. J R Ewing speaking Arabic needs to be seen to be believed!

HEALTH

Vaccinations

These should be obtained before you arrive in Egypt. However, if you have to get a vaccination in Egypt, buy a sterilised syringe at a pharmacy and go to the government Public Health Unit, at the back of the lobby of the Continental Savoy Hotel in Opera Square.

The recommended vaccinations are cholera, typhoid, yellow fever and tetanus. You should also consider gamma globulin for protection against infectious hepatitis.

Travel Insurance

Get some! You may never need it, but if you do you'll be very glad you got it. There are many different travel insurance policies available which cover medical costs for illness or injury, the cost of getting home for medical treatment, life insurance and baggage insurance. Some protect you against cancellation penalties on advance purchase tickets should you have to change travel plans because of illness. Any travel agent should be able to recommend one but check the fine print, especially regarding baggage insurance.

Medical Kit

It is always a good idea to travel with a small first aid kit. Some of the items which should be included are: bandaids, a sterilised gauze bandage, elastoplast, cotton wool, a thermometer, tweezers, scissors, antibiotic cream or ointment, an antiseptic agent (dettol or betadine), burn cream (Caladryl is good for sunburn, minor burns and itchy bites), insect repellent and multi vitamins.

Don't forget water sterilisation tablets or iodine; anti-malarial tablets; any medication you're already taking; and contraceptives, if necessary.

Recommended traveller's medications include diarrhoea tablets, such as Lomotil or Imodium; paracetamol (Panadol) for pain and fever; and a course of antibiotics (check with your doctor). *Erythromycin* is recommended for respiratory, teeth and skin infections and is a safe alternative to penicillin. *Tinidazole* (Fasigyn) is recommended for the treatment of amoebic dysentery and giardia.

Food & Water

Tap water in Egypt's cities is generally safe to drink. It is so heavily chlorinated that most microbes and other little beasties are annihilated. Unfortunately, the excessive chlorination can sometimes be hard on your stomach. If the tap water makes you feel sick it is possible to buy bottled water. Make sure that the bottles have been properly sealed before you pay for them, as there used to be a scam of refilling them with tap water.

In the countryside the water is not so safe. You should only drink tap water which has been boiled, filtered or treated with tincture of iodine or purification tablets. You should also be sure that clean water is used for brushing your teeth and rinsing your mouth. Bottled water is safe for this.

There are also a few common sense precautions to take with food in Egypt. You should always wash and peel fruits and vegetables and avoid salads. Egyptians sometimes fertilise their fields with human excrement and this waste has a way of sticking to the produce. The food is seldom washed before it reaches your plate. If you can't wash or peel it, don't eat it.

Meat is safe as long as it has been thoroughly cooked. If you favour raw meat, keep in mind that conditions in Egypt can make the meat a nice and tasty home for worms. Your stomach and intestines are an even better habitat. Similar precautions should be taken with fish.

Avoid milk and cream which have not at least been boiled. Milk in sealed cartons is usually imported and safe to drink because it has been pasteurised and homogenised. Ice cream is also to be avoided.

Avoid anything raw, especially shellfish.

Contaminated food or water can cause dysentery, giardia, hepatitis A, cholera polio and typhoid – all of which are best avoided!

Health Precautions
Common Ailments Almost every traveller who stays in Egypt for more than a week seems to be hit with *Pharaoh's Revenge*, more commonly known as diarrhoea. There is usually nothing you can do to prevent the onslaught; it is simply your system trying to adjust to a different environment. It can happen anywhere. There is no 'cure' but following certain regimens will eventually eliminate or suppress it. Avoid taking drugs if possible, it is much better to let it run its course.

The regimen to follow is fairly basic: drink plenty of fluids but not milk, coffee, strong tea, soft drinks or cocoa. Avoid eating anything other than dried toast or fresh yogurt. Yogurt is recommended by Egyptians, but I'm not absolutely convinced about it as a remedy.

If you are travelling, it may be difficult to follow this path. That is when Lomotil, codeine phosphate tablets, a liquid derivative of opium prescribed by the doctor, or a medicine with pectin (like *kaopectate*) can be useful. Lomotil is convenient because the pills are tiny. If you are still ailing after all of this, then you might have dysentery. See a doctor.

Dysentery This is, unfortunately, quite common among travellers. There are two types of dysentery, characterised by diarrhoea containing blood and lots of mucus.

Bacillary dysentery, the most common variety, is short, sharp and nasty but rarely persistent. It hits suddenly and lays you out with fever, nausea, cramps and diarrhoea but, as it's caused by bacteria, it responds well to antibiotics.

Amoebic dysentery which, as its name suggests is caused by amoebic parasites, is much more difficult to treat, is often persistent and is more dangerous. It builds up more slowly, cannot be starved out and if untreated, it will get worse and permanently damage your intestines. *Tinidazole* (Fasigyn) is the recommended drug for the treatment of amoebic dysentery.

Hepatitis This is a liver disease caused by a virus. There are two types – infectious hepatitis (Type A) and serum hepatitis (Type B). Type A, the most common, can be caught from eating food, drinking water or using cutlery or crockery contaminated by an infected person. Type B can only be contracted by having sex with an infected person or by using the same syringe. Symptoms appear 15 to 50 days after infection (generally around 25 days) and consist of fever, loss of appetite, nausea, depression, lack of energy and pains around the base of the rib-cage. Your skin turns yellow, the whites of your eyes yellow to orange and your urine will be deep orange or brown. Do *not* take antibiotics. There is no cure for hepatitis except complete rest and good food. You should be over the worst in about 10 days but continue to take it easy after that. A gamma globulin injection provides protection against Type A for three to six months but its effectiveness is still debatable.

Cholera This can be extremely dangerous as it is very contagious and usually occurs in epidemics. The symptoms are: very bad but painless, watery diarrhoea (commonly known as 'rice-water shits'), vomiting, quick shallow breathing, fast but faint heart beat, wrinkled skin, stomach cramps and severe dehydration. Do not attempt to treat cholera yourself, see a doctor immediately. Cholera vaccinations are valid for six months and if you're re-vaccinated before the expiry date it is immediately valid. The vaccine doesn't give 100% protection but if you take the usual precautions about food and water as well you should be safe.

Polio This is another disease spread by insanitation and found more frequently in hot climates. There is an oral vaccine against polio – three doses of drops taken at four to eight week intervals. If you were vaccinated as a child you may only need a booster. Once again take care with food and drink while travelling.

Typhoid Fever This is a dangerous infection which starts in the gut and spreads to the whole body. It can be caught from contaminated food, water or milk and, as its name suggests, the main feature is a high temperature. Another characteristic is rose coloured spots on the chest and abdomen which may appear after about a week. Two vaccinations, a month apart, provide protection against typhoid for three years.

Malaria Malaria is spread by mosquitoes and the disease has a nasty habit of coming back in later years – and it can be fatal. Protection is simple – a daily or weekly anti-malarial tablet which you start taking before you travel. Although malaria is uncommon in Egypt you should exercise caution in rural areas of the Nile Delta, the Faiyum area, the Nile Valley and the Western Oases. The disease is common in the Sudan and becomes more so the further south you travel. Common symptoms are: headache, fever, chills and sweats.

Following, is an excerpt from a leaflet issued by The British Airways Medical Service, entitled *Guidelines for Malaria Prophylaxis.*

No tablet will completely prevent malaria, however the tablets recommended will provide a useful degree of protection in addition to the following precautions. Malaria mosquitoes bite after dark. Exposure outdoors can be reduced by wearing clothing that adequately covers your arms and legs. Repellent creams and lotions can be applied to exposed skin. Indoors, aerosol knockdown spray can be used and, where there is no air conditioning, window screens and mosquito nets are advised. If none of this is available then at least try to sleep under or next to a fan.

Remember to take the tablets whilst you are in the malarial area and for at least six weeks afterwards.

Malaria prevention drugs:

Paludrine – two tablets daily after same meal each day
Daraprim – one tablet weekly. Start one week prior to travel.
Nivaquine or Avloclor (Chloroquine) – two tablets weekly, best taken after food starting one week prior to travel. Use for southern Sudan.
Maloprim – one tablet weekly for adults starting one week before travel.
Fansidar – one tablet weekly starting one week before travel.

When two, weekly tablets are to be taken concurrently, for example, Maloprim and Nivaquine, they should be taken on different days of the week so that protection overlaps.

Yellow Fever A serious, often fatal disease, transmitted by the mosquito. It is caused by a virus that produces severe inflamation of the liver. Yellow fever is entirely preventable. It requires one injection, at least 10 days before departure, which is valid for 10 years.

Bilharzia Or *Schistosomiasis* is prevalent in Egypt. The Nile and Nile Delta are infested with the bilharzia parasite and microscopic snail which carries them; both prefer warm stagnant pools of water. Do not drink, wash, swim, paddle or even stand in water that may be infected. The parasites, minute worms, enter humans by burrowing through the skin. They inhabit and breed in the blood vessels of the abdomen, pelvis and sometimes the lungs and liver. The disease is painful and causes persistent and cumulative damage by repeated deposits of eggs. The main symptom is blood in the urine, and sometimes in the faeces. The victim may suffer weakness, loss of appetite, sweating at night and afternoon fevers. See a doctor.

Rabies If you are bitten, scratched or even licked by a rabid animal and do not start treatment within a few days, you may die. Rabies affects the central nervous system and is certainly an unpleasant way to go. Typical signs of a rabid animal are: mad or uncontrolled behaviour, inability to eat; biting at anything; frothing at the mouth. If you are bitten by an animal, react as if it has rabies – there are no second chances. Get to a doctor and begin the course of injections that will prevent the disease from developing.

Tetanus This is a killer disease but it can easily be prevented by immunisation. It is caught by cuts and breaks in the skin caused by rusty or dirty objects, animal bites or contaminated wounds. Even if you have been vaccinated wash the wound thoroughly.

Taking the Heat
Protect yourself against the heat of the sun in Egypt and the Sudan. It is difficult, especially in Egypt, to gauge how quickly you are losing body water, because the climate is dry. Headaches, dizziness and nausea are signs that you have lost too much water and might have heat exhaustion. To prevent this, take a bit of extra salt with your food, drink plenty of fluids and wear a hat and sunglasses. The salt helps keep you from getting dehydrated. Incidentally, the caffeine in coffee and tea also contribute to dehydration. Sunscreen will prevent the sun from frying your skin. Wearing pants and long sleeves is cooler than shorts and short sleeves because your body moisture stays closer to your skin. Lastly, the sunshine on the beach and in the water is deceiving and will burn you quite quickly, so wear a shirt while snorkelling or swimming.

Doctors & Hospitals
There are hospitals throughout Egypt. Addresses will be listed in the relevant sections. Most of the doctors are well trained and often have to deal with a greater variety of diseases and ailments than their western counterparts. On the other hand most medical facilities are *not* well equipped and consequently, it is not unusual for diagnoses to be inaccurate. If you need an operation don't have it here. London is only a few hours away by plane.

Before you leave for Egypt or the Sudan it is worthwhile writing to the *International Association for Medical Assistance to Travellers (IAMAT)* for their worldwide directory of English-speaking doctors. Doctors who belong to this organisation charge standard fees for their services which are fair and reasonable. The fees are set by IAMAT. Their address is 736 Center St, Lewiston, NY 14092, USA.

The British, Canadian and American embassies can also help you find a doctor.

General Thoughts
Make sure your teeth are in good shape before you leave home. If you have an emergency, however, there are dentists in most of Egypt's cities and towns who speak English. In Cairo, consult your embassy.

If you wear eyeglasses, carry a second pair or at least a copy of your prescription in case of loss or breakage.

Public toilets are bad news. Fly-infested, dirty and stinky. Some toilets are still of the squat-over-a-hole-in-a-little-room variety. Always carry a roll of toilet paper with you.

FILM & PHOTOGRAPHY
Film This generally costs more in Egypt than in the west. For example, the price for a 36-exposure colour print film at an ASA of 200 or 400 is E£12. The same film costs less than US$5 in the US. Processing is quite cheap however, but it's not always good.

Photography Egypt is full of opportunities for great photography. Early morning and late afternoon are the best times to take photographs. During the rest of the day, the sunlight can be too bright and the sky too hazy and your photos will look washed-out. There are a few remedies for this though: a polarisation filter will cut glare and reflection off sand and water; a lens hood will cut some of the glare; and Kodachrome film, with an ASA of 64 or 25, is good slide film to use when the sun is bright.

Cameras and lenses collect dust quickly in Egypt. Lens paper and cleaner are difficult to find, so bring your own. A dust brush is also useful.

Be careful when taking photos of anything other than tourist sites, the Nile, the Suez Canal and beaches. It is forbidden to photograph bridges, train stations, anything military, airports and other public works. You can take photos of the interior of mosques, temples and some tombs though at some sites the government now charges E£10 for the privilege.

It can sometimes be a bit tricky taking photos of people, so it's always better to ask first. Children will almost always say yes but their parents or other adults might say no. Some superstitious Muslims believe that by taking photos of children you might be casting an 'evil eye' upon them. Similar attitudes sometimes apply to taking photos of women, especially in the countryside. Egyptians are also sensitive about the negative aspects of their country. It is not uncommon for someone to yell at you when you're trying to take photos of things like a crowded bus, a donkey cart full of garbage or a beggar – so exercise discretion.

WOMEN

Egyptians are conservative, especially about matters concerning sex and women; Egyptian women that is, not foreign women.

Unlike many Middle Eastern Muslims, the majority of Egyptian women don't wear veils but they are still, for the most part, quite restricted in what they can do with their lives. They do not have the same degree of freedom, if any at all, that western women have. Egyptian men see this not as restraint and control, but as protection and security – they don't want their wives to *have* to work. For many Egyptians, both men and women, the role of a woman is specifically defined; she is simply mother and matron of the household, and it is this which the men seek to protect. Ironically, in maintaining this position a woman actually works very hard. Even if she can afford domestic help and doesn't do any household work herself, her husband's view is still that she doesn't have to do anything. It is *his* role to provide for the family.

There is obviously a consideration lacking here, that maybe some women want to do more than play the dutiful mother and wife. While this may be so in a few cases, most Egyptian women are still raised by their mothers to want or expect nothing else. Consequently, very few have broken away from the house and family. The traditional role is still taken very seriously by the women themselves as well as their men.

Premarital sex is considered a violation of this role – for women that is. So, enter the foreign woman. In western television programmes and films shown in Egypt, she is presented, by Egyptian standards, as a walking billboard for sex of all kinds. By their standards however, it doesn't actually take much in the way of presentation to promote and perpetuate this belief – bare shoulders or shorts on a woman are proof enough.

For the woman traveller from the west, this could mean harassment, even if she is dressed in jeans and a long-sleeved shirt. Although Cairo is becoming a bit more liberal about westerners' dress habits, most of the rest of the country is not. And as far as many Egyptian men are concerned, the misconception about the sexual availability of foreign women seems to be something they'd rather *not* have disproved. The two go together – western women and sex.

I say 'could mean harassment' because it all depends on how the woman carries herself. Physical harassment and rape are not significant threats in Egypt. A woman can travel independently in Egypt if she follows a few tips: avoid direct eye contact with an Egyptian man unless you know him; try not to respond to an obnoxious comment from a man – act as if you didn't hear it; be careful in crowds where you are crammed between people as it is not unusual for crude things to happen behind you; if you're in the countryside it's often a good idea to wear a scarf in your hair; and most of all be careful about behaving in a flirtatious manner – it could create more problems than you ever imagined.

A more positive way to avoid trouble is to befriend an Egyptian girl. Apart from being with someone totally non-threatening, you will probably also learn much more about life in Egypt from her.

Lastly, if you need any more information, refer to an article by Ludmilla Tüting titled *The Woman Traveller*, which has appeared in both the *The Globetrotters Handbook* and *The Traveller's Handbook*.

ACCOMMODATION

Accommodation in Egypt ranges from cheap to expensive and rough to luxurious. There are hotels, pensions, youth hostels and a few camping grounds.

Hotels

At the five star end of the price range there are hotels representing most of the world's major chains: Hilton, Sheraton, Holiday Inn, Marriott, Jolie Ville and the Meridien. Prices at these hotels typically start at about US$65 per night, not including a 14% service charge and tax. There are also a few Egyptian hotels in this range.

At the next price range – four stars – there are mostly Egyptian hotels managed and owned by a government organisation, the Egyptian Hotels Company. These hotels range upwards in price from US$30 per night and also charge the 14% tax and service charge. Standards are still fairly high at this price.

Next come the three star hotels. They are clean, comfortable and good for someone who wants most of the comforts of the fancier hotels but doesn't want to spend as much money. Rooms cost from US$15 to US$30 per night. Taxes and service charges are added on.

The two, one and no star hotels form the budget group. Often the ratings mean nothing at all, as a hotel without a star can be equally as good as a two star hotel, only cheaper. You can spend as little as E£4 per night for a clean room with hot water and a shower or as much as as E£10 for a dirty room without a shower. Pensions are in this range and tend to be fairly good. No extra charges and taxes are levied by the hotels in this range.

For the purposes of this book, middle range hotels are listed at an approximate price range of E£8 to E£18. That will vary somewhat from place to place.

Youth Hostels

Hostels are cheaper than the cheapest hotels in Egypt. They are located in Cairo, Alexandria, Port Said, Aswan, Asyut, Damanhur, Marsa Matruh, Sohag and Suez and range in price from 40 pt to 80 pt. The youth hostel at Sharm el Sheikh, in the Sinai, charges E£2 per night because it is nicer and has air-conditioning. Having an International Youth Hostel card is not absolutely necessary as non-members are admitted. A card will save you about 10 pt to 20 pt. The youth hostels tend to get noisy, crowded and a bit grimy. Reservations are not usually needed.

The Egyptian Youth Hostel Association office (tel 758099) is at 7 Dr Abdel Hamid St (near Cinema Odeon), Cairo.

Camping

Officially, camping is allowed at only a few places around Egypt: in Cairo, at Giza near the pyramids; on the Mediterranean coast at Sidi Abdel Rahman; and at Marsa Matruh, Luxor and Aswan. Outside the plots specifically set aside for camping, almost all of the land is either harsh desert or cultivated fields. And even at the official sites, with a few exceptions, facilities tend to be rudimentary.

FOOD

Egyptian food varies from exotic to mundane and you can have a uniquely great meal here for very little money. Sampling the various types of Egyptian food should be part of the adventure of your visit. Be open-minded and don't look at the kitchens.

Appetisers & Fast Food

Fuul and *ta'amiyya* are unofficially the national staples of Egypt. *Fuul* is fava beans, with a variety of things such as oil, lemon, salt, meat, eggs and onions added to spice it up. *Ta'amiyya* is a concoction of mashed chickpeas and spices fried into little balls, similar to *felafel*. A *fuul* and *ta'amiyya* sandwich on pita bread with a bit of tomato makes a tasty snack or light lunch. It's also popular to substitute *tahina* for *fuul* in pita bread sandwiches.

Tahina, another national staple, is a delicious sesame spread spiced with oil, garlic and lemon. In addition to putting it on *ta'amiyya*, you can also order a plate of *tahina* to eat as a dip with pita bread. With a couple of sandwiches, pita bread, a plate of *tahina* and some fruit from the market, you have a decent meal for about 50 pt.

Hoummus and *baba ghanough* are two other popular spreads which can be eaten in the same way as *tahina*. *Hoummus* is a chickpea spread which is especially tasty with a bit of oil and a few pinenuts on top. *Baba ghanough* is a mix of mashed eggplant and *tahina*.

Sandwich stands also serve – you guessed it – the *sand-weech*. However, they aren't quite sandwiches as you and I know them. Most Egyptian sandweeches are small rolls with an equally small piece of meat, cheese or *basturma*, a smoked meat which resembles pastrami. Nothing else. Add some mustard to perk it up.

Shwarma is also good for sandwiches and is the Egyptian equivalent of the Greek *gyros* sandwich. Throughout Egypt you will see the *shwarma* spits with rotating legs of lamb. Hot strips of lamb are cut from the spit and placed in a pocket of pita with tomatoes to make a sandwich fit for 'pigging out.'

Another appetiser which you will often be served is *Torshi* which are mixed, pickled vegetables such as radishes, carrots and cucumbers. They look somewhat strange and discoloured but taste great if they're pickled properly.

There are several other quick, cheap dishes available, such as *fiteer, shakshooka, makarone* and *mahshi*.

Fiteer is a cross between pizza and pastry and is served at a place called a *Fataran*. It's flat and flaky and contains sweet things like raisins and powdered sugar or something spicy like white cheese, ground meat or eggs. One *fiteer* is almost filling enough to be an entire meal.

Shakshooka is a mixture of chopped meat and tomato sauce with an egg tossed on top. You must taste this; the combination is delicious.

Makarone is a clump of macaroni baked into a cake with ground meat and sauce or gravy. It is very filling and costs from 25 pt to 50 pt.

Mahshi are vine leaves usually stuffed with meat and rice.

For those who find themselves on long train or bus rides, it is essential to also know about bread and cheese – the easily transportable staple of the traveller. Bread, including pita, is called *aysh*. In Egypt *aysh* also means 'life'. Egyptians say that life without *aysh* isn't life. Most of the *aysh* which you'll see and eat is *aysh baladi*, also called country bread or pita. The other main type is called *aysh fransawi* or 'French bread' (for obvious reasons).

There are also two main types of cheese: *gibna beyda* or white cheese, which tastes like Greek *feta* cheese; and *gibna rumi* or Roman cheese, which is a hard and sharp, yellow-white cheese.

Main Dishes

Kufta and *kebab* are two of the most popular dishes in Egypt. *Kufta* is ground meat peppered with spices, skewered and grilled over a fire just like shish-kebab. *Kebab* is similar, but the meat isn't ground. Grilled tomatoes and onions are also served. Both dishes are ordered in Egyptian restaurants by weight.

Molokhiyya is also very popular and is one of the few truly Egyptian dishes. It's a green, slimy, delicious soup made by stewing a strange leafy vegetable, rice and garlic together in chicken or beef broth.

Firakh, or chicken, is something you'll probably be eating quite often. It is usually grilled or stewed and served with a vegetable.

Grilled *samak* (fish) is tasty. The best fish comes from the Mediterranean and south Sinai coasts. The restaurants along the Mediterranean serve their fish by the kilo. You choose it yourself from a large ice tray near the kitchen and the price usually includes a salad, bread and dips like tahina and hoummus. Along the Sinai coast eat at one of the Bedouin fish restaurants in Nuweiba. See the Nuweiba section for more information.

Another grilled dish is *hamam*, or pigeon. Pronounce the word carefully because another 'm' makes the word *hammam* which means bathroom.

Here are some more food words which could be helpful as you eat your way around Egypt:

Soup

soups	*shurba*
lentil soup	*shurba 'aads*

Fish

fish	*samak*
Nile perch (try it grilled)	*Ishr Bayadee*
flat fish	*samak musa*
red mullet	*mourgan*
prawns	*gambari*

Vegetables

vegetables	*khudrawat*
potatoes	*batatas*
green beans	*fasulya*
lentils	*'aads*
peas	*baseelah*
cauliflower	*anabeet*
cabbage	*kharoum*
carrots	*gazar*
turnips	*lift*
okra	*ba'amiyya*
maize	*durra*
green wheat	*fareek*
aubergine	*badingan*

Salads

salad	*salata*

cigarette behind one ear
pencil behind other

A waiter appears bearing the requisites of an evenings enjoyment in the café.

lettuce	*kahss*
tomato	*tamatim* or *uta*
onion	*bassal*
garlic	*tum*
cucumber	*xiyaar*
sweet pepper	*filfil*
hot pepper	*shattah*

Meat

meat	*al-luhum*
lamb	*lahma danee*
veal	*lahma bateelu*
beef	*lahma kanduz*
camel meat	*lahma gamali*
chicken	*firaq*
turkey	*deek roumee*
liver	*kibda*
kidney	*kelawwi*

Desserts

mahalabiyya	a type of cornflour pudding
bilaylah	a milk dish with nuts, raisins and wheat
ays krim/gelati	ice cream
baklawah	flaky pastry and nuts drenched in honey
atayf	shredded wheat pastry with nuts
zalabiyyah	pastries dipped in rosewater
malban	Turkish delight
Basboosah	semolina cake

Fruit

fruit	*fawakah*
apricots	*meesh-meesh*
peaches	*kukh*
pears	*kumitrah*
apples	*toofa*
orange	*burtuaan*
tangerines	*yusuf Affandi*
lime	*limuun*
mango	*manga*
guava	*guafa*
banana	*mohz*
strawberries	*farawleh*
dates	*tamr*
grapes	*einab*
figs	*tiin*
pomegranate	*ruman*
watermelon	*bateeq*

Miscellaneous Foods

salt	*mahal*

bread	*aysh* or *khobz*
eggs	*bayd*
jam	*murabbah*
honey	*asal*
cheese	*gibna*
mint	*nannah*
sugar	*sukur*
yogurt	*zabadi*
butter	*zibda*
cream	*Ishta*
watermelon seeds roasted, a national passion	*lib*

DRINKS – *Shirbat*
Tea & Coffee

Shy and *Ahwa* – tea and coffee – head the list of things to drink in Egypt. Both are usually made strong enough to be major contenders for the title of most caffeinated drink in the world.

Tea is served in glasses at traditional Egyptian cafés and in teacups at western-style restaurants. At cafés, the tea leaves are boiled with the water. If you don't tell the café-man how much sugar you want,

SANDWICH VENDORS CART – any street corner in Egypt.

two or three big teaspoons of sugar will be automatically plopped into your glass. If you only want a bit of sugar in your tea, ask for *shy ma'ah shwayya sukur*. If you don't want any sugar at all ask for *shy meen reer sukur*. Egyptians are always amazed that westerners don't like as much sugar as they do. Unless you enjoy chomping on tea leaves, wait until they settle back down to the bottom. Tea bags are appearing in the western-style places. Try *shy bi-nannah* (mint tea) or *shy bil-lehben* (tea with milk).

If you ask for coffee, you will probably get *ahwa turki*, Turkish coffee, which is served throughout the Middle East. It bears a strong resemblance to mud and it's quite a surprise to find your spoon doesn't actually stand up in it. Don't be deceived by the size of the tiny porcelain cups; this coffee is *very* strong. Let the grains settle before drinking it, in small sips. As with tea, you have to specify how much sugar you want if you don't want to suffer an overdose. *Ahwa ziyadda* is for those who seek the ultimate sugar and caffeine high – it is extra sweet; *ahwa mazboota* is with a moderate amount of sugar but still fairly sweet and *ahwa saada* is without sugar. Egyptians drink the latter when a relative or close friend has died.

Western-style instant coffee is called *Nescafe*. It comes in a small packet with a cup of hot water. There's not much adventure in drinking this.

Juice – *Asiir*

On practically every street corner in every town throughout Egypt there is a juice stand, where you can get a drink squeezed out of just about any fruit or vegetable you want. The standard fare includes:

banana – *mohz*
guava – *guafa*
lime – *limuun*
mango – *manga*
orange – *burtuaan*
pomegranate – *ruman*
hibiscus – *karkaday*

strawberries – *farawleh*
sugar cane – *asiir asab*
tangerines – *yusuf affandi*
tamarind seeds – *tamr hindi*

Other Drinks

Soft drinks are extremely popular in Egypt and most major brands are sold here including *Coca-Cola, Sport Cola, Seven-up* and *Pepsi*. If you drink at the soda vendor's stand, you won't have to pay a deposit on the bottle. Soft drinks are cheap – only 15 pt to 35 pt per bottle. Cans of drink can cost as much as 75 pt each though because the can isn't reusable. Diet soft drinks are just beginning to appear in Egypt but they are still expensive. There is also a variety of 'indigenous' soft drinks with names like *Si-Cola* and *Spathis*. Remember that when it's hot, a soft drink will not quench your thirst. In fact, if anything, the sugar in it will make you more thirsty.

Egypt also has several indigenous alcoholic beverages. The beer, which can be excellent, is called *Stella Beer* and is served in huge one litre bottles. There is also *Stella Export* which comes in smaller bottles, has double the alcohol content of regular *Stella* and also costs more. Few things can beat a cold bottle of Stella on a hot day. It has a rich, smooth taste which makes it easy to drink a lot in a short amount of time.

Try the Egyptian wines too. One of the best white wines is called *Cru des Ptolemees* and the better red is called *Omar Khayyam*. They don't exactly compare with the wines of the west, but they aren't bad.

A few other drinks which you might encounter are:

carob	*carob*
cocoa	*kakaw*
aniseed	*yansun*
licorice	*arasus*
caraway seed	*karawiyya*
milk	*laban*
water	*miyya*

BOOKS

The following is a short list of books which can further introduce you to Egypt and the Egyptians. Most can be found at bookshops in Egypt or in the library of the American University in Cairo. Outside Egypt, many of them can be ordered through local bookshops.

People & Society

Shahhat: An Egyptian, Richard Critchfield (Syracuse University Press, 1978). Critchfield lived and worked for an extended period in a west bank village near Luxor to write this in-depth portrait of a young man named Shahhat and his life in an Egyptian village.

Egypt: Burdens of the Past, Options for the Future, John Waterbury (Indiana University Press, 1978). An excellent portrayal of Egyptian society.

An Account of the Manners & Customs of the Modern Egyptians, Edward Lane (first published 1839). Lane's wonderful classic continues to offer insight into the traditional Arab culture of Egypt.

Journey to the Orient by Gerard de Nerval will prime you for exploration of the mysteries of Egypt. It was first published in the 19th century.

Midaq Alley, Children of Jebelawi and *Miramar*, Naguib Mahfouz (American University in Cairo Press). These three novels, by one of Egypt's foremost contemporary authors, provide insightful perspectives of life in impoverished parts of Cairo and Alexandria.

History

The Penguin Guide to Ancient Egypt, William J Murnane (Penguin Books 1983). Murnane has given us one of the best overall books on the life and monuments of ancient Egypt. There are plenty of illustrations and descriptions of almost every major monument in the country.

The Ancient Egyptians - Religious Beliefs & Practices, Rosalie David (Routledge & Kegan Paul, 1982). This is one of the first books to trace the evolution of religious beliefs and practices in ancient Egypt. It's a thorough and comprehensive study of a complex subject.

The Gods & Symbols of Ancient Egypt, Manfred Lurker (Thames & Hudson 1984). This is an illustrated dictionary which offers brief explanations and descriptions of the most important aspects of ancient Egypt. It can be helpful in understanding some of the hieroglyphics.

The Blue Nile and *The White Nile*, Alan Moorehead (New English Library, 1982 and Penguin Books). Both books are classics which cover the history of the Nile during the 19th century. *The Blue Nile* deals with the years 1798 to 1856; and *The White Nile* is concerned with events from 1856 to the end of the century. Moorehead's detailed descriptions of events and personalities are superb. These two should definitely be read.

In Search of Identity, Anwar Sadat (Harper & Row, 1977). Sadat's autobiography is a good introduction to the events leading up to and following Egypt's revolution in 1952.

Great Cairo - Mother of the World, Desmond Stewart (The American University in Cairo Press, 1981). This covers 55 centuries of Cairo's history and the descriptions of the many diabolical rulers are wonderful.

Nagel's Encyclopedia Guide to Egypt is an expensive, but extremely thorough guide to Egypt's ancient monuments.

Travel Guides

The Blue Guide, Veronica Seton-Williams and Peter Stocks (W W Norton, 1984). This massive tome is one of the most comprehensive guides to Egypt. It describes every place of even the slightest historical interest and has excellent sections on Egypt's natural history. However, it is a bit heavy to lug around in a backpack.

Alexandria: A History & a Guide, E M Forster (Michael Haag Limited, 1985). First published in 1922, this is still one of the best guides to the sights and history of Alexandria.

Cairo – A Practical Guide, Deborah Cowley and Aleya Serour, editors (The American Univeristy in Cairo Press, 1986). Almost every bit of practical information from auctions to toy shops is contained in this annual guide. The maps are some of the best you will find.

Guide to Egypt, Michael von Haag (Travelaid Publishing). A fairly comprehensive guide with plenty of detail about the monuments and their place in history, as well as practical information for getting around.

Let's Go Israel & Egypt (St Martins Press). Put together by Harvard Uni students, the Let's Go series provide plenty of background info, things to see, places to stay, etc and is updated annually. This one also covers Jordan.

Language
For those who are serious about learning to speak colloquial Egyptian Arabic check at the American University in Cairo bookstore for the latest textbooks. Otherwise, *Say it in Arabic*, Farouk el-Baz (Dover Publications) should be sufficient. It's small enough to easily fit in your pocket.

Bookshops
Cairo and Alexandria both have several English language bookshops where you can find most of the books mentioned here. For addresses refer to the Cairo and Alexandria sections. In Cairo there are also several excellent second-hand book-stalls in Ezbekiah Gardens selling some of the most unlikely books and magazines, including three-year-old copies of *Time*.

MAPS
Michelin map No 154 covers Egypt, the Sudan and the Sinai. The Sudan section is excellent but there are better maps on Egypt and the Sinai. The best is published by Kummerly & Frey, a Swiss company. It covers all of Egypt and the Sinai, on a scale of 1:750,000, and sells for US$6.95.

Another map publisher, by the name of Freytag & Berndt, publishes a map which includes a plan of the pyramids and covers all of Egypt except the western quarter. The scale is 1:1,000,000 and it sells for US$5.95.

The Bartholomew World Travel Map of Egypt is another good map. The scale is 1:1,000,000; it costs US$6.95.

THINGS TO BUY
Egypt is a budget souvenir shopper's paradise. Hieroglyphic drawings of pharaohs, queens, gods and goddesses embellish and blemish everything from ashtrays to engraved brass tables. Brass plates engraved with various pharaonic scenes are well done and sometimes cost no more than E£5. Similar scenes are precisely and colourfully painted on cotton wall-hangings.

Since cotton is one of Egypt's major crops it is, therefore, no surprise that cotton clothing is very popular. Cotton shirts, pants and *galabiyyas* (the loose, gowns worn by many Egyptians) can be made to your specifications. Many Cairene tailors can work from photographs of the clothing. Gold and silver jewellery can also be made to specification for not much more than the cost of the metal. Cartouches with the name of a friend or relative spelled in hieroglyphics make great gifts.

The best thing about souvenir hunting in Egypt is not, however, the souvenirs. They are secondary to the excitement of the expedition up and down the back alleyways of the bazaars, past pungent barrels of basil and garlic and through medieval caravanserais. Take your sense of humour and curiosity with you and if you want to buy something, be prepared to bargain for it; it is expected.

Everyone seems to have a different bargaining strategy. I have found that one of the best is to not show too much interest in the thing that you want to buy. Start the bargaining with a price which is much lower than what you really want to pay and then banter up to that point.

When you state your first price the shopkeeper will inevitably huff about how absurd that is and then tell you his 'lowest' price. If it is still not low enough, then be insistent and keep smiling. Tea might be served as part of the bargaining ritual and accepting it doesn't place you under obligation to buy. If you still can't get your price, then just walk away. There are hundreds of shops in the bazaars.

It would be impossible to list everything that you can buy in Egypt but the specialities of a few regions are: The Faiyum – baskets of all sizes; the Sinai, especially around El Arish – colourfully embroidered Bedouin dresses; Port Said – duty free electronic goods from Japan; Giza, at the village of Kerdassa – tapestries; and Aswan – camels and spices.

WHAT TO BRING

Sunglasses, flashlight, a collapsible drinking cup, a water bottle/canteen, sun screen, a hat, a flat drain stopper (not a plug), pocket knife, two to three metres of nylon cord, a day pack, a small sewing kit and a money belt or pouch (leather pouches can be made to order in the bazaars).

Certain toiletries can be expensive or difficult to find in Egypt. You should bring your own contact lens solution, tampons, contraceptives, shaving cream in a can (in a tube it's readily available), any favourite brand of shampoo and deodorant (which is expensive).

Duty Free It's easy to make a little profit on duty free liquor. If you haven't already bought some, drop into the Duty Free shop when you arrive at the Cairo airport, (it's just off to the left before you walk down the last hallway). A 750 ml or one litre bottle of Johnny Walker Red will cost about US$5 and you can sell it to one of the hustlers in front of the Egyptian Museum for at least E£18 to E£20. Some travellers report that Johnny Walker Black is easier to sell. Bottles of Chivas Regal, White House and Cognac are also popular.

Anubis

Getting There

If you're heading to Egypt or the Sudan from Europe you have the choice of either flying direct or going overland to one of the Mediterranean ports and taking a ferry to North Africa. If you're coming from any other continent it can also sometimes be cheaper to fly first to Europe and then make your way to Egypt, than it is to fly direct. There are also of course the overland combinations of bus, taxi and ferry from other countries in Africa, from Jordan, Kuwait, Saudi Arabia and Israel.

Whichever route you take there is always the inescapable search for the cheapest ticket and the certainty that no matter how great the deal you got, there's always someone out there who got a better one.

AIR

Egypt has several airports but only three are international ports of entry: Cairo, Alexandria and, occasionally, the Aswan and Luxor 'International' Airport. Most air travellers enter Egypt through Cairo.

Cairo The airport is 25 km, or a 45 to 60 minute drive, from central Cairo. Most of the world's major airlines fly through Cairo. Check out the duty free stores on your arrival or departure as they supposedly offer some the best deals in the world on perfumes and liquor.

Alexandria The international airport in Alexandria is much smaller than Cairo's. A few flights to and from North Africa and southern Europe are serviced there.
Aswan Sudan Airways is the only international carrier that uses Aswan Airport. Every Tuesday a wild flight arrives from and goes to Khartoum.
Luxor Occasionally, charter planes fly directly from Europe to Luxor International Airport. A couple of charter companies associated with the Jolie Ville/Movenpick hotel chain do this.

With flying there are a bewildering number of possibilities, ticket types and jargon to get used to. The best thing to do first is arm yourself with as much general info and fare details as you can. One of the best sources of information about cheap fares all over the world is the monthly magazine *Business Traveller*. It's available from most newsstands or direct from: 60/61 Fleet St, London EC4 & ILA, UK; or 13th floor, 200 Lockhart Rd, Hong Kong. Other very useful magazines are: *Trailfinder* from Trailfinders Travel Centre, 46 Earls Court Rd, London W8 6EJ, UK; and *Time Out*, London's weekly entertainment guide available direct from the publisher at Tower House, Southampton St, London WC2E 8QW, UK.

The main terms you need to know are:
APEX (and Super-APEX) This means Advance Purchase Excursion and these tickets must be bought from 14 days to two months in advance. They're usually only available on a return basis, have minimum and maximum stay requirements, no stopovers are allowed and there are cancellation charges.
Excursion Fares These are priced midway between APEX and full economy class. There are no advance booking requirements

077 4406 831 518 5

PASSENGER TICKET AND BAGGAGE CHECK
ISSUED BY

EGYPTAIR

MEMBER OF INTERNATIONAL AIR TRANSPORT ASSOCIATION
EACH PASSENGER SHOULD CAREFULLY EXAMINE THIS TICKET
PARTICULARLY THE CONDITIONS INSIDE

but a minimum stay abroad is often mandatory. Their advantage over APEX is that you can change your bookings and/or stopover without surcharge.

Point-to-Point This is a discount ticket which can be bought on some routes in return for passengers waiving their rights to stopover.

ITX An Independent Inclusive Tour Excursion is often available on tickets to popular holiday destinations. It's officially only a package deal, combined with hotel accommodation, but many agents will sell you one of these for the flight only. They'll give you phoney hotel vouchers in the unlikely event you're challenged at the airport.

Economy Class Symbolised by 'Y' on the airline ticket, this is the full economy fare. Tickets are valid for 12 months.

Budget Fare These can be booked at least three weeks in advance but the actual travel date is not confirmed until seven days prior to travel. There are cancellation charges.

MCO A Miscellaneous Charge Order is a voucher which looks just like an airline ticket but without the destination or date on it. It is exchangeable with any IATA airline for a ticket on specific flight. Its principal use for travellers is as an alternative to an onward ticket in those

countries which demand them and it's much more flexible than an ordinary ticket if you're not sure of your route.

Round-the-World An RTW ticket is just that. You have a limited period in which to circumnavigate the globe and you can go anywhere the carrying airlines go, as long as you don't backtrack. These tickets are usually valid for one year, the number of stopovers or total number of separate flights is worked out before you set off and they often don't cost much more than a basic return flight.

Standby This is one of the cheapest ways of flying. You simply turn up at the airport – or sometimes the airport's city terminal – without a ticket and take your chances on an available seat on the flight you want. The discount is quite considerable, but get there early as it's first come, first served.

FARES

Fares change everyday, so those given here are simply an indication of what was available at the time of writing. The types of discounted tickets already mentioned are those which the airlines officially sanction. There are, however, unofficially discounted tickets available through certain travel agents around the world. The cheapest fares are always those offered by these so-called 'bucket shops' who sell an airline's unsold tickets at discounts of up to 50% off the 'official' fares. Despite the airlines' protestations to the contrary these tickets are actually released by them to selected travel agents. After all it's better to fill all the seats even if some of the passengers are only paying half price.

Most of the bucket shops are well established and reputable but there are exceptions so you need to exercise a little caution. When you pay your deposit make sure you get all the details of the flight in writing and never hand over the full amount until you have the ticket in your hand. If you change the flight, also get the changes in writing. Ask about any refund restrictions on the ticket, such as getting your money back or a new ticket if you change your plans.

The best places in the world for bucket shops are London, Amsterdam and Hong Kong. They can also be found in other European cities, the USA and most places where no-one with any sense buys their ticket direct from the airline. Use the airline price as a guide and shop around for something cheaper.

When booking your flight consider using an American Express card as they have a special travel plan called 'Sign and Travel' which allows you to charge airline tickets and pay for them over a period of 20 months. The bad news is that they also charge a whopping 18% annual interest.

FROM THE UK

London is one of the best centres in the world for discounted air tickets. The price of Round-the-World tickets especially, is about the best available anywhere. An RTW ticket on TWA, Singapore Airlines or Japan Airlines will take you via Cairo for £1028. That's about US$600 less than the price for the same ticket bought in the US.

For the latest fares, check out the travel page ads of *Time Out*; *LAM*; or *The News & Travel Magazine (TNT)*. All are available from most London newsstands.

Following are a few sample fares and agencies which offer them. Two of the most reliable London agents are *STA*, 74 Old Brompton Rd, London SW7, or 117 Euston Rd, London NW1; and *Trailfinders*, 46 Earls Court Rd, London W8. Two others are *World-Wide Flights*, 93 Regent St, London W1; and *Sun'n'Sand*, 21 Swallow St, London W1.

STA (tel 01-5811022) were offering a London to Cairo ticket for £238 return or £119 one-way. *World-Wide Flights* (tel 01-4396561) were quoting £190 return; and with *Sun 'n' Sand* (tel 01-4370537) the return fare to Cairo was £205.

Another possibility from London is to buy a return ticket to Eilat, Israel for £45. A bucket shop in London called *FLAIR* sells these tickets for flights on Monarch Airways, a subsidiary of British Airtours. These flights, however, aren't regularly scheduled.

FROM EUROPE

Amsterdam is another popular departure point. Some of the best fares are offered by the student travel agency *NBBS Reiswinkels*, Dam No 17, Amsterdam (tel 020-237686). With them a return fare from Amsterdam to Nairobi with a stopover in Cairo costs about fl1882. For another 200 guilders you can fly to Bombay via Cairo return. Another possibility is Amsterdam to Cairo via Brussels for fl998 on EgyptAir. RTW fares, which include Cairo, cost about fl4099, or US$2128, on Singapore Airlines, TWA, Japan Airlines or Qantas.

Brussels From Brussels you can fly to Cairo for 795 guilders or to Khartoum via Cairo for 1428 guilders. A flight to Bangkok via Cairo is offered for 1650 guilders one-way. These tickets can be purchased from *NBBS Reiswinkels*. Also check prices with *Acotra*, 38 rue de la Montagne, Brussels (tel 5134480).

Athens Bucket shop agencies around the Plaka and Syntagma Square in Athens charge about 10,500 drachmas, or US$80, for a one-way student fare from Athens to

Cairo. *Fantasy Travel* at 10 Xenofontas St (near Syntagma Square) and the *Speedy Ways Travel Agency* have also been recommended by some travellers.

Standard excursion fares are available with airlines such as TWA for US$234 return. This fare requires a stay of at least 10 days.

An Egyptian visa can be obtained in one day from the Egyptian Embassy in Athens for 2650 drachmas (US$20); one photograph is required.

FROM AUSTRALIA

Some of the best fares from Australia to Cairo are offered by Student Travel. Fares are A$795 one-way or A$1430 return from Melbourne or Sydney; and A$710 one-way, A$1335 return from Perth. RTW fares, which include a stop-over in Cairo, cost approximately A$1600. Student Travel has offices throughout Australia and also in Auckland, New Zealand.

FROM ASIA

Cheap tickets to Cairo are available in Hong Kong and Singapore usually as part of an RTW ticket. From Hong Kong an RTW ticket on Singapore Airlines, Japan Airlines or Qantas costs approximately HK$12,900 or US$1655.

FROM THE USA

A return fare from Los Angeles to London and then London to Cairo on a bucket shop ticket costs about US$900.

An RTW ticket which includes a stop-over in Cairo is another possibility. If your trip originates in the USA, the ticket will cost about US$2090 on TWA, Singapore Airlines or Japan Airlines. Check the travel sections of Sunday newspapers for the latest deals.

TWA flies from New York and Los Angeles to Cairo. APEX and youth fares are available. An APEX ticket must be booked at least 14 days in advance. You must stay in Egypt a minimum of six days and no more than two months. The youth fare is valid all year, but you must be between 12 and 24-years-old and book at least 72 hours in advance. The following prices are, respectively, for APEX high and low season fares and youth fares: from New York – US$999, $799, $599; from Los Angeles – US$1182, $1056 and $796. The high season is from May 15 to September 14 and the low season is the rest of the year.

FROM ISRAEL

Air Sinai and El Al regularly fly between Cairo and Tel Aviv for about US$120 one-way. El Al offers a 'Cairo extension' fare for half the regular price if you fly into Tel Aviv with them from somewhere else, like London. If you have the time, however, travelling overland between Egypt and Israel is much cheaper and more adventurous.

FROM THE SUDAN

Flights on a variety of airlines leave Khartoum everyday for Cairo and once a week for Aswan. Sudan Airways flies from Khartoum to Aswan and Cairo. The one-way flight costs US$200 to Aswan and US$300 to Cairo. The Aswan flight is quite an experience – rather like an airborne caravan without the camels. See the 'Getting There' section for the Sudan.

FROM TUNISIA

Tunis Air and EgyptAir offer student discounts on flights between Cairo and Tunis. Consult the offices of each airline for the latest information.

OVERLAND
From Israel

Egypt can be entered from two points in Israel. If you are crossing from the town of Eilat, you will go through the Egyptian borderpost in Taba. From Taba there are buses and collective, or service (pronounced ser-vees), taxis which go south to Nuweiba, Dahab and Sharm el Shaykh. The four-hour bus ride to Sharm costs E£4.

The other entry-point is through the

border-post at Rafah in the south-western section of the Gaza Strip. *Sheruts*, the Israeli version of a service taxi, will take you and seven others to Rafah. Public buses also travel to the border, though changing buses could be a bit of a hassle.

Several Israeli tour operators offer bus transportation from Tel Aviv or Jerusalem to Cairo with relatively quick processing through Customs. Tickets cost from about US$41 and some of the agents offer packages which include a few nights in a clean and comfortable Cairo hotel. There are a few agents near the Egyptian Embassy in Tel Aviv which have been recommended, including: *Neot Hakahor*, 252 Hayarkon St (tel 03-403111); *Masada Tours*, Ibn Givirol St, (if you get a group together for the trip, you'll receive a discount); *Galilee Tours*, 142 Hayarkon St, offer a package for US$60 return, including three nights at a Cairo hotel; *VIP Tours*, 130 Hayarkon St, Tel Aviv (tel 03-244181); and *Egged*, the national bus company of Israel, which also puts together travel packages to Cairo.

If you plan to return to Israel, buy an open return ticket before you travel to Egypt. Don't forget the Israeli exit fee of US$15 and the Egyptian entry fee US$5, both of which can be paid either in the local or a western currency.

Egyptian visas can be obtained from the embassy in Tel Aviv or the consular office in Eilat. For more information see the section on Visas in the Facts for the Visitor chapter.

To Israel There are several possibilities for travel to Israel from Cairo. With *Emeco Travel*, 2 Talaat Harb St, Cairo (tel 747398) you can reserve a place over the telephone between 9 am and 7 pm. The bus leaves from in front of the Egyptian Museum in Tahrir Square at 5 am. They charge US$24 one-way and the Egyptian government charges E£10.50 as an exit tax.

Eastern Delta Transportation Company, Travco, and *Holy Land Tours* also arrange transport to Israel. See the Cairo section for more information. *Travco* is at 3 Ishak Yacomb St, Zamalek, Cairo (tel 803448).

The cheapest way to go between Egypt and Israel is to take service taxis or *sheruts* and buses. From Egypt, take a service taxi from Midan Ulali (Ulali Square, behind Ramses Station) between 4.30 and 6 am to El Qantara. It should cost about E£3 and takes two hours. At El Qantara a ferry takes you across the Suez Canal (free) and on the east bank another service taxi will take you to the border at Rafah, for about E£4. That trip takes about 2½ hours. A bus takes you between the Egyptian and Israeli border posts and after going through Israeli customs you have a choice of shared taxi (about US$7) or public bus (US$4). Buses depart at 12.30 and 3 pm to Ashkelon, where you can change for Tel Aviv or Jerusalem.

From the Sudan

There are three ways to travel from the Sudan to Egypt, but only one is practical for foreign travellers – unless you're already a practised camel herder or have your own four-wheel drive vehicle.

The camel herders, following an age-old caravan route known as *Darb al Arba'een* or 'The 40 Day Road', bring their camels up from western Sudan through the Sahara desert to Aswan where they sell them. With a bit of negotiation and an adventurous spirit, you might be able to join a caravan.

If you have a tough four-wheel drive vehicle, it is possible to drive up from the Sudan along the Red Sea coast. The border is seldom crossed though because the roads are very rough.

The most common way of going overland from the Sudan is by train to Wadi Halfa in the Sudan and then by steamer up Lake Nasser to Aswan. For more details on this refer to the sections on Wadi Halfa and Aswan.

Another way to enter Egypt overland is

from Libya. However, at the time of writing, political tensions between Egypt and Libya had closed the border indefinitely.

BOAT
From Europe
Adriatica Lines operates a weekly ferry between Venice, Piraeus (Greece) and Alexandria. Their Venice office can be contacted through Adriatica di Navigazione, 1412 Zattere (tel 29133). Other agents for Adriatica Lines include: Extra Value Travel, 437 Madison Avenue, New York, NY 10022 (tel 212-75-8800); Gilnavi Agencies, Akti Miaouli, 97, Piraeus (tel4524517); Mena tours, 14 Talaat Harb St, Cairo (tel 740864); and Mena tours, Saad Zaghloul St, Alexandria (tel 809676).

The Maritime Company of Lesvos operates a weekly ferry between Piraeus, Rhodes, Limassol (Cyprus) and Alexandria. There are also bi-monthly boats to and from Corfu, Odessa (Soviet Union), Varna (Bulgaria), Istanbul, Latakia (Syria) and Larnaca (Cyprus). For fare information see the Alexandria getting there section.

From Jordan & Saudi Arabia
Two ferry services operate between Suez and Aqaba in Jordan. For one of the services, contact Utopia Travel, 18 Talaat Harb St, Cairo (tel 767412). The other service operates the ferry boats *El-Arish* and *El Tor* between Suez, Aqaba and Jeddah (Saudi). For details on those boats contact Mena Tours, 14 Talaat Harb St, Cairo (tel 750775). Twice a week there is also a ferry from Aqaba to Nuweiba (in the Sinai). Refer to the Sinai and Alexandria chapters for more information.

From Kuwait
A bus travels from Kuwait across Saudi Arabia to Aqaba, Jordan. From Aqaba you can take a boat to Nuweiba and then a bus to Cairo. The bus leaves Kuwait on Thursdays and Mondays at 1.30 pm and arrives in Aqaba at 11 am on Saturdays and Wednesdays. You're allowed 70 kg of luggage per person and this is checked thoroughly by the customs officials when you cross the Saudi border. The bus only takes 15 people, stops every four hours for a break and costs US$100.

Getting Around

Egypt has a very extensive public and private transport system. If you don't suffer from claustrophobia, have plenty of patience and a tough stomach you can travel just about anywhere in Egypt for relatively little money.

AIR

In Egypt, air fares are expensive and definitely out of the budget travel range. For example the air fare from Cairo to Luxor is E£51. In general, it is only worth flying if your time is very limited.

If you do have to go by plane, EgyptAir flies from Cairo to Hurghada, Sharm el Shaykh, St Catherine's Monastery, Luxor, the Oasis of Kharga (called the New Valley) and Aswan.

TRAIN

Trains travel to almost every major city and town in Egypt from Aswan to Alexandria. Services range from relatively inexpensive first class *Wagon-Lits* – cars with sleeper compartments, to ridiculously cheap 3rd class cars. Student discounts as high as 50% are granted with an International Student Identification Card (ISIC) on all fares except *Wagons-Lits* fares. It is possible to travel from Cairo to Aswan for less than US$1 if you have an ISIC and are willing to take a bit of a beating in the 3rd class cars.

Wagon-Lits Trains with Wagon-Lits cars are the best and fastest in Egypt. The cars are the same ones used by trains in Europe and only sleeper compartments are available. Two 'Wagon-Lits' trains travel between Cairo, Luxor and Aswan everyday. Both are express trains. The schedule is:

Cairo	Luxor	Luxor	Aswan
Depart	*Arrive*	*Depart*	*Arrive*
7 pm	5.38 am	6.06 am	10 am
7.35 pm	7.38 am	8.30 am	12.35 pm

Aswan	Luxor	Luxor	Cairo
Depart	*Arrive*	*Depart*	*Arrive*
2 pm	5.50 pm	7.30 pm	6.40 am
5.45 pm	9.35 pm	10.35 pm	9.50 am

Wagon-Lits trains are air-conditioned and each compartment has hot and cold water. There are lounge cars and dinner and breakfast are served in the compartments. A double compartment costs about US$46 one-way, per person including the sleeping-rail ticket, meals, service and taxes.

Reservations can be made at the Wagon-Lits Central Reservation office, 48 Giza St, Cairo (tel 842367).

Other Trains There are other trains which travel to Luxor and Aswan. Regular night trains with sleeper compartments leave everyday. Second class fare is E£12.95 to Luxor and E£14.55 to Aswan with meals included. Reservations must be made in advance at Ramses Station in Cairo.

Night trains without sleepers also go to Luxor and Aswan. The 1st class fare is E£11 to Luxor and E£13.75 to Aswan; and 2nd class is E£5.05 to Luxor and E£6.10 to Aswan.

Schedules for most of these and other trains throughout Egypt are in the Cairo getting there section.

BUS

Buses service just about every city, town and village in Egypt where the railway does and doesn't go and on average they're also cheaper than the trains. Intercity buses tend to become quite crowded though and even if you are lucky enough to get a seat in the first place, you'll probably end up with something or somebody on your lap. It's a great way to meet Egyptians!

There are also buses and motorcoaches, which are less crowded, that travel between a few of Egypt's main cities. A super-deluxe coach runs hourly throughout the day and night between Cairo and Alexandria. Cool, comfortable coaches with a few less amenities also run between Cairo, Ismailia, Port Said, Suez, Saint Catherine's monastery, Luxor and Hurghada (Ghardaka). Tickets cost a bit more but they're still cheap. Information about these buses will be given in the appropriate sections.

Tickets can be bought at windows at the bus stations or, sometimes, on the bus. Hang on to your ticket until you get off as controllers sometimes board the bus to check fares.

SERVICE TAXIS

Travelling by *ser-vees* taxi is the fastest way to go from city to city. In most places the service taxis and their drivers congregate in lots, usually near bus and train stations. Each driver waits with his Peugeot taxi until he has six or seven passengers; he won't leave before his car is full. If you want to go somewhere these taxis don't usually go, you can either hire a whole taxi for yourself or coax other travellers into joining you.

On the other hand service taxi rides are really only for those with strong stomachs and blind faith in a driver who might have no more than a camel's brains and a geriatric's eyes. Most of Egypt's main Nile road is only two lanes, so one ambling donkey cart can cause an immense traffic jam. This prompts everyone else to try to pass each other even though the oncoming traffic usually prevents a clean, smooth pass. It's a modern joust where, fortunately, the jousters usually miss each other. Occasionally they don't however, and the metal scraps of past accidents litter the roadside all over the country.

CAMELS

Yes, it is actually possible to travel around Egypt by camel. While the more intrepid travellers will probably want to buy their own 'ship of the desert' there are easier and less costly alternatives.

Camels are brought, in caravans, from the Sudan to Egypt's two main camel markets at Daraw, near Kom Ombo, and Imbaba, near Cairo. If you're serious about owning your own, then the camels are cheaper at Daraw as it's closer to the end of the caravan route. They cost about US$200 there while in Imbaba the price rises to more than US$1000 per animal. Once you've purchased your camel you then have to buy a proper saddle and appropriate kit bags. It all gets somewhat costly and complicated. It would be a good idea to try and get hold of an article by René Dee called *Travel by Camel*, which appeared in *The Traveller's Handbook*.

If you're less adventurous (or more sensible!) there are easier ways to realise your camel fantasies which aren't so physically and financially draining. The easiest way is to hire a camel for a couple of hours and take a tour around the pyramids at Giza or the temple complex at Saqqara. A guide usually accompanies you. It is also easy to arrange a camel safari in the Sinai from near Nuweiba. More information about those treks are given in the Nuweiba section.

DONKEYS

Donkeys are a very popular means of transport and you'll see them everywhere in Egypt except, perhaps, in restaurants. *Don't* buy one of these critters. They are cheap enough to rent for a couple of hours or a few days to get you around some of Egypt's ancient sites.

LOCAL TRANSPORT

Bus

Cairo and Alexandria are the only cities in Egypt with their own bus systems, although neither ever seem to have enough vehicles. If this is your first visit to a 3rd world country, it will probably be the first time you have ever seen buses as crowded as these. The typical city bus has had its windows popped out and doors yanked off so that passengers can make use of the extra space by hanging from the door and window frames.

Tram

Cairo and Alexandria are also the only two cities with tram systems. Alexandria's trams are relatively efficient and go all over the city but they also get quite crowded. Cairo's trams are similar but as Cairo's subway system nears completion, they're gradually being phased out. The trams are as cheap and sometimes cheaper than the buses.

Taxis

There are taxis in most cities in Egypt. The most common and cheapest are the black and white taxis in Cairo and the black and orange ones in Alexandria. Almost all of them have meters but most of the meters don't work, so basically you have to pay what you think is right and be prepared to argue and bargain. If you really feel cheated then just mention the police and the taxi driver will probably accept your price to avoid any hassle. However, if he agrees with you about seeing the police then the fare you offered is probably too low. A few sample fares are listed in the Cairo section.

The taxis marked *special* charge more than other taxis. Although their meters usually work, it makes little difference to the price because the fares are so inflated. The advantage of these taxis though, is

that you can get a group together and commandeer one for a trip to the pyramids or Saqqara for less than a black-and-white might charge. They often also make the trip from the airport to downtown Cairo for about E£8 plus E£3 for each extra passenger.

Whatever type of taxi you choose, if you're uncertain about the fare, then negotiate it before you get in. The best strategy, however, is to pretend that you know the fare and pay just before leaving the taxi.

When you want a taxi, stand where a driver can see you and wave your arm. When he slows down, yell out your destination so that, if he feels like it, he can stop for you. It's quite common to share a taxi with other passengers.

Feluccas

These ancient sailboats of the Nile are still the most common means of transport up and down the river. Sunset is one of the best times to take a *felucca* ride but you can arrange a few hours peaceful sailing at any time from just about anywhere on the Nile. *The* trip to make however is the three to five-day journey between Luxor and Aswan.

DRIVING

Several car rental agencies have offices in Egypt, including Avis, Hertz, Budget and Bita. Their rates are similar to American rates and you need an international driving license. Drivers in Egypt are complete maniacs so think seriously before you decide to rent a car there. Refer to the 'Getting Around' section in the Cairo chapter for rental costs.

BICYCLES

Bicycles are a practical way of getting around a town and its surrounding sites. In most places, particularly Luxor, you can rent a bicycle quite cheaply for a few days.

Bicycles are, however, somewhat impractical for travelling long distances. The biggest problem is the possibility of getting flattened by one of Egypt's crazy drivers as they're not the slightest bit accustomed to cyclists on the roads.

HITCHING

It is easy to hitch in Egypt, but drivers are used to being paid for giving you a ride. You probably wouldn't save very much money by hitching but it's a good way to meet people.

MOTORCYCLES

Motorcycles would be an ideal way to travel around Egypt. The only snag is that you have to bring your own and the red tape involved is extensive. Ask your country's automobile association and the Egyptian consulate about regulations.

Cairo

Cairo is a seething, breathing monster of a city that swallows new arrivals and consumes those who return. All are destined to be captured and captivated in some small way by its incredible past and vibrant present. There are few, if any, cities in the world where the clash between old and new, modern and traditional, and east and west is more evident. Tall, gleaming hotels and office buildings overlook streets where cars and buses rumble and weave past donkey carts and their stubborn drivers. Less than a km from a computer store and supermarket in central Cairo there are mud brick houses where goats still wander through 'living rooms' and water is obtained from spigots down the street.

Cairo is still the heart of Egypt and, somewhat allegorically, the 'Mother of the World.' Since its rise in the 10th century, under Ibn Tulun, Egyptians have called Cairo *al-Qahira*, which means 'the victorious'. They also call it *al-Misr* which means Egypt. For Egyptians this is the centre of their country; a centre which has been attracting them in ever-increasing numbers for centuries. No-one is quite sure just how many people have been drawn in from the countryside, even over the last few years, but the city has

grown to mammoth proportions. Estimates of Cairo's population range from 11 to 14 million – roughly one quarter of Egypt's total.

The massive and continual increase in the number of people has overwhelmed the city. Housing shortages are rife; buses are packed to the hilt; snarled traffic paralyses life in the city; and broken pipes spew water and sewerage into the streets. Everything is discoloured – buildings, buses and footpaths are brown and grey from smog and desert dust.

Amidst this chaos, the city government is trying to do what it can. A subway line, between Ramses Station and Midan Tahrir, is being built to alleviate some of the traffic problems. It is supposed to be completed in 1987. (The broken pipes are, in part, a result of this construction.) Satellite suburbs such as Nasser City have been, or are being, built to alleviate housing shortages and there have been attempts to ban donkey carts from the city streets.

Finding your way through this chaos is, remarkably, not as complicated as you may first think and Cairo is a great city for walking around because it's not too spread out.

Orientation

Almost all travellers find themselves in Midan Tahrir at the beginning of their trip through Egypt. From Midan Tahrir eastward to Midan Talaat Harb and Ezbekiya Gardens you will find most of Egypt's western-style shops and many of the budget hotels.

Further east there are Cairo's poorest districts, the market and medieval neighbourhoods of Muski and Darb al-Ahmar. South of Darb al-Ahmar there is the City of the Dead and the Citadel. Continuing even farther east towards the airport you will enter *Masr Gidida* or New Cairo,

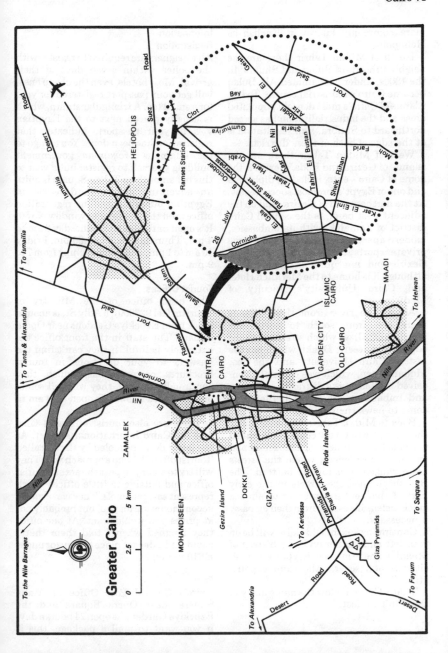

Greater Cairo

0   2.5   5 km

To the Nile Barrages

To Ismailia

To Tanta & Alexandria

To Alexandria

To Kerdassa

To Fayum

To Saqqara

To Helwan

Suez Road

Desert Road

Ismailia

Salah Salem

Port Said

Ramses

Corniche

El Nil River

HELIOPOLIS

ZAMALEK

MOHANDISEEN

Gezira Island

DOKKI

GIZA

CENTRAL CAIRO

ISLAMIC CAIRO

GARDEN CITY

OLD CAIRO

MAADI

Roda Island

Nile River

Giza Pyramids

Sharia al-Ahram

Pyramids Road

Desert Road

(Central Cairo inset)

Geish

El Said

Port Said

Bey

El Nil

Abdel Aziz

Sharia Gumhuriya

El Bustan

Mohamed Farid

Sheikh Rihan

Tahrir

Kasr El Eini

Talaat Harb

Orabi

Ramses Street

6 October

26 July

8 & El Gala

Corniche

Clot

Ramses Station

more commonly known in English as Heliopolis.

North of Midan Tahrir there are the neighbourhoods of Bulaq and Shubra. In the 1800s, under Mohammed Ali, Bulaq became Cairo's industrial centre. Today, it's one of Cairo's most densely populated areas and the industrialisation has spread northward to Shubra. Ramses Station is at the edge of both of these districts.

West of Midan Tahrir there are the islands of Gezira and Roda. Gezira is the home of Cairo's elite, including diplomats and one of Egypt's foremost soccer teams. At the northern end of Gezira, and on the adjacent west bank, is the central Cairo district of Zamalek, with its embassies, modern apartment buildings and a large private sports club. Roda is south of Gezira and not quite as fashionable, although it is home to the Meridien Hotel and Cairo University's Faculty of Medicine.

Across the river from these islands there are, from south to north, the districts of: Giza, which stretches to the edge of the desert; Dokki, which has the rest of Cairo University and the zoo; Mohandiseen, which was originally conceived by Nasser as a district of engineers; and Imbaba, where camel herders still come to hawk their wares.

Back to Midan Tahrir. Heading south, the first district you come to is called Garden City, an area of embassies and expensive residences, where the streets are arranged in a unique pattern. The British planned the streets in the early part of this century in order to allow a quick, defensible escape from their embassy if necessary.

Continuing south, Old Cairo will be on your left and further on is the district of Maadi, home to many of Egypt's wealthiest citizens and several thousand expatriates.

That's Cairo. Follow the maps and you shouldn't get lost.

Information

Registration

All foreigners are required to register with the police within seven days of their arrival. Most hotels, even the cheap ones, will get your passport registered for you, for a small fee. A triangular stamp, which is usually placed next to the Egyptian visa in your passport, indicates that registration has been done. You *can* go to the infamous *Mogamma* government building yourself to register but a visit to this behemouth on Tahrir Square is quite an adventure and a hard lesson in Egyptian bureaucracy. The registration office is on the 2nd floor at window No 50. It's open Saturday to Wednesday 8 am to 4 pm; Thursday 8 am to 1.30 pm, Friday 10 am to 1 pm, and every evening from 7 to 9 pm.

Tourist Offices

The head office of the Ministry of Tourism (tel 923000), 5 Adly St, is about a block from Ezbekiya Gardens near Opera Square. The staff in the front office are extremely helpful. If they can't find the answers to your questions in tourist brochures or notebooks, which they continually update, they will call someone who does know. It's open 8.30 am to 7 pm.

There are also tourist offices at Giza and the Cairo International Airport. At the latter don't be fooled by the so-called 'tourist officials' who approach you. They will try to steer you past the actual tourist office and outside to little offices which represent several hotels. They can arrange accommodation for you, but probably not at prices you would want. At one office they laughed when I told them that I could find a decent place to stay for under E£10 per night.

Post

Cairo's Central Post Office in Ataba Square, near Opera Square and the Ezbekiya Gardens, is open 24 hours a day. If you want to mail a package, this is where you must go but be prepared for a potentially time-consuming process. Do not seal your package before letting a customs official see the contents. First, go to the Ataba Post Office Parcel and Customs area (there is a sign in English outside the door) and pay 40 pt to an official to complete the necessary forms for you. Someone behind the counter will approve the forms and slap on a few stamps. Then the package is weighed and sewn up for E£2.50. A 4½ kg package will cost about E£48 airmail or E£23 surface to the US.

The easiest way to send a package is to pay someone else a small fee and have them do it for you. A shopkeeper, especially if you've bought the article in his bazaar, would provide this service, which should include obtaining an export license, packaging and sending it.

There are branch post offices throughout Cairo: at the airport, downstairs from the first waiting room; on Midan Falaki; and in the grounds of the Egyptian Museum. You can send packages from the airport branch, but not from the others. Hours are 8.30 am to 3 pm.

The branches tend to be crowded most of the day, so it's much easier to buy stamps from hotel bookstores or cigarette/postcard kiosks. They charge about 5 pt more than the post office. Airmail postage to the US or Europe is 30 pt for a letter, and 25 pt for a postcard. The Arabic word for stamp is *busta*.

Letters deposited in the reception desk mail box at the Nile Hilton, or any other major hotel, seem to take less time to arrive at an overseas destination than if they were sent directly through the post office.

Mail can be received at the Poste Restante counter in the Ataba Central Post Office, the central American Express office or hotels. The American Express office seems to be the most reliable.

Telephone & Telegraph

Local telephone calls can be made for 10 pt from pay phones at telephone offices and major hotels. Many kiosks and small shops also have telephones for public use for 15 pt per call.

In 1986 Cairo was in the process of revamping its telephone system. All phone numbers were going to gain another digit at the beginning – either a 3, 5 or 7.

Direct long distance calls can be made from some home phones. However, most long distance calls must be made from hotels or telephone offices. Most hotels (except for the very cheap ones) have direct international lines, but they'll charge more than the telephone offices. At either place the connections are usually quite good. Collect calls from Egypt are impossible.

Calls booked at telephone offices must be paid for in advance. They can either be taken in a booth at the office or directed to an outside number (such as a private home or hotel). If you opt for the latter, keep the receipt just in case you need a refund for an uncompleted call.

There are telephone offices in several places around Cairo, just look for the sign with a telephone dial on it. There's an office on the north side of Midan Tahrir; in Adly St, near the Tourist Information office; and in Mohammed Mahmud St, in the new telecommunications building. All main telephone offices are open 24 hours a day. Branch offices are open from 7 am to 9 pm.

Telegrams can be sent from most of the telephone offices. The charge for a telegram to the US is 60 pt per word. Each word in an address is also counted.

American Express

American Express has seven offices in Cairo. The central office (tel 753142), 15 Kasr El Nil St, between Midan Tahrir and Midan Talaat Harb, is open from 8 am to 4.30 pm; and 9 am to 3.30 pm during Ramadan. The client letter service is closed on Fridays. This is one of the best places in Cairo to receive mail and to have

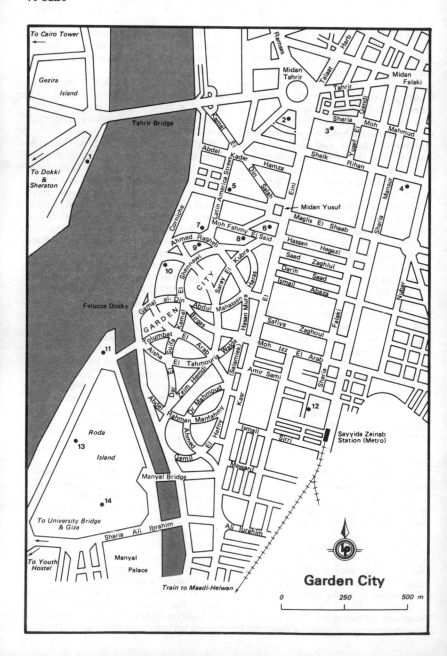

Garden City

To Cairo Tower

Gezira Island

Tahrir Bridge

To Dokki & Sheraton

Midan Tahrir

Midan Falaki

Ramses

Talaat Harb

Tahrir

Abdel Kader

Kamel

Latin America Street

Din Salah

Hamza

Eini

Sheik Rihan

Sharia

Moh Mahmud

Yusef El Gendi

Mansur

Sharia

Midan Yusuf

Maglis El Shaab

Corniche

Moh Fahmy

El Said

Ahmed Ragheb

Saray El Hares

Kubra

Hassan Hegazi

Saad Zaghlul

Darih Saad

Ismail Abaza

Nubar

GARDEN CITY

Shennawi

Gamal al-Din El

Abdul Mahassen

Hasan Mura

El

Safiya Zaghoul

Falaki

Tolumbat

Sufia Kamel

El Arab

Birqas

Aisha

El Tahmouria

Walda

Salamliek

Moh Izz El Arab

Sharia

Dar El

Zeim Hemdi

Dr Mahmoud

Kasr

Amir Sami

Abdel Rahman Mantahmy

Ahmed

El Herny

Ismail

Sirri

Felucca Docks

Roda Island

13

14

To University Bridge & Giza

Sharia Ali Ibrahim

Manyal Bridge

Manyal Palace

To Youth Hostel

Train to Maadi-Helwan

Ali Ibrahim

Hawari

Sayyida Zeinab Station (Metro)

0   250   500 m

1 Nile Casino Cafe
2 Bus Terminus
3 American University in Cairo
4 Ministry of the Interior
5 US Embassy
6 Sudan Embassy
7 UK Embassy
8 Canadian Embassy
9 US Cultural Centre
10 Australian Embassy
11 Meridien Hotel
12 French Cultural Centre
13 Hospital
14 Cairo University Medical Faculty

money wired from overseas. To qualify for the mail service you should have an American Express card or travellers' cheques.

All American Express offices offer financial services such as providing US$ cash for US$ travellers' cheques, exchanging money, cashing personal cheques or selling travellers' cheques. An American Express card is necessary for cashing personal cheques and purchasing travellers' cheques. Money which must be changed for a visa extension should be done at a commercial bank. This rule, however, is subject to change. Also, if you're exchanging money at an American Express office for the purchase of an airline ticket, be sure that they don't invalidate your exchange receipt with an Arabic stamp that translates as 'Not for airline tickets'.

There are American Express offices at the Nile Hilton (tel 743383); Cairo Marriott (698840); Cairo International Airport; Meridien Hotel (tel 844017); the Ramses Hilton (tel 744400); and the Sheraton Hotel (tel 988000). The Nile Hilton office is open from 8 am to 10 pm. The airport branch will only cash travellers' cheques.

Banks

Most of the world's major banks have branches in Cairo. Cash advances in US dollars are definitely available at the Bank of America and Citibank if you have a Visa or Master Card. Advances might also be available with the same cards through Chase Manhattan, Chemical Bank and Manufacturer's Hanover. Money can be wired through all of these banks. Their addresses in Cairo are:

The Bank of America, 106 Kasr El Eini St, Garden City (tel 27500)
Barclays International, 1 Latin America St, Garden City (tel 26992)
Lloyds Bank International, 44 Mohammed Mazhar St, Zamalek (tel 698366)
Manufacturer's Hanover, 3 Ahmed Nessim, Giza (tel 988266)
Chase Manhattan, 9 Gamal al-Din Abdul Mahassen, Garden City (tel 26111)
Chemical Bank, 14 Talaat Harb St (tel 740707)
Citibank, 4 Ahmed Pasha, Garden City (tel 27246)
The Royal Bank of Canada, 10th floor, Abu el Feda Building, 3 Abu el Feda, Zamalek (tel 698128)
Misr America International Bank, 8 Ibrahim Neguib St, Garden City (tel 756341). This is the head office of an Egyptian bank, affiliated with the Bank of America.

Bank hours are: Monday to Thursday from 8.30 am to 1.30 pm; Sunday from 10 am to noon. Most Egyptian banks are also open on Saturdays. *Bank Misr* at the Nile Hilton is open 24 hours a day.

Bookstores & Newsstands

The Readers' Corner Bookshop, 33 Abdel Khaliq Sarwat St, near Sherif St and Mustafa Kamel St, have a fairly good selection of English language books and newspapers. There's also a branch in the Nile Hilton.

The American University in Cairo Bookstore (tel 722969), Mohammed Mahmud St and Yusuf el Gendi St, carries an excellent selection of books in English. The AUC Press publishes a wide range of books and guides about life in Egypt. Their *Cairo Guide* is sold here and has information on almost every service and consumer item in Cairo. The bookstore also carries several periodicals and newspapers from Europe and the US.

In front of *Groppi's* on Midan Talaat Harb is the best newspaper and magazine stand in Cairo. They carry the most recent editions of major newspapers and magazines from around the world, including *Time, Newsweek, The Times* and the *International Herald Tribune*.

Across the street *L'Orientaliste*, at 15 Kasr El Nil, is one of only three bookstores in the world which specialises in Egyptology. (The others are in Geneva, Switzerland and Westwood, California.) *L'Orientaliste* has an excellent collection of antiquarian books and prints of 19th century Egypt.

Nearby in Midan Talaat Harb, *Madbouly* bookstore has an extensive collection of books in English, French and German. Anything you can't find in the other bookstores, you should be able to find here.

A few other good bookstores around Cairo are:

The Garden City Bookstore, 1103 Corniche el Nil, between the British Embassy and the Shepeard's Hotel (tel 33906)

Lehnert & Landrock, 44 Sherif St, (tel 747606)

Al Ahram Bookstore, the Nile Hilton, (in the outside arcade)

The Anglo-Egyptian Bookshop, 165 Imad el Din St (tel 914337)

There are also bookstores in most of the major hotels.

For the latest wire service news reports, check out the telex machines in the lobby of the Sheraton Hotel in Giza.

Look around the bookstalls at Ezbekiyya Gardens. Their collections of second-hand books and magazines in English are remarkable. You will find some of the most unlikely books here – everything from Dickens to Plato.

Books

The American University in Cairo Press publishes a few books about Cairo which can be very helpful. Their *Cairo, A Practical Guide* has already been mentioned. They also publish a *Guide to the Islamic Monuments of Cairo* which is probably one of the best of its kind available. *The Blue Guide to Egypt* describes almost everything in Cairo and the rest of Egypt in more detail than you probably want, though it's useful for finding some of Cairo's lesser known monuments.

For a perceptive look into life on Cairo's backstreets, read the short novel *Midaq Alley* by Naguib Mahfouz, one of Egypt's foremost authors. It was written in the 1940s, but much of what is portrayed about life on a small street near Khan el Khalili is still relevant.

Airline Offices

Most airlines which operate in and out of Egypt will only sell you air tickets if you can show them bank receipts which prove that you officially changed enough money for the ticket. They will also keep the receipts so you can't reuse them for visa extensions. Airlines which are not part of IATA (the International Airlines Transport Association) usually *don't* require receipts, so you can buy a ticket through them, at discounts of up to 30%, with black market money. Some of these airlines also offer discounts for students and youths but this changes quite often, so you'll have to check for yourself. Most of the Eastern European airlines, such as Yugoslav Airlines (JAT), Polish Airlines (LOT) and Balkan Airlines, don't belong to IATA.

The addresses of airlines which operate in and out of Cairo are:

Air France
    2 Midan Talaat Harb (tel 743300)
Air India
    1 Talaat Harb (tel 744976)
Air Sinai
    Nile Hilton Hotel (tel 760948)

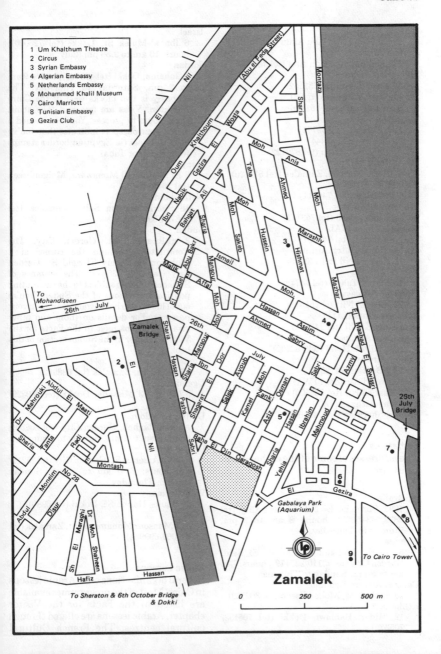

1 Um Khalthum Theatre
2 Circus
3 Syrian Embassy
4 Algerian Embassy
5 Netherlands Embassy
6 Mohammed Khalil Museum
7 Cairo Marriott
8 Tunisian Embassy
9 Gezira Club

To Mohandiseen

Zamalek Bridge

25th July Bridge

Gabalaya Park (Aquarium)

To Cairo Tower

Zamalek

0   250   500 m

To Sheraton & 6th October Bridge & Dokki

Balkan Airlines
    13 Sh Moh Sabri Abu Alam (tel 751211)
British Airways
    1 Abdel Salaam Moh Aref (tel 759977)
Bulgarian Airlines
    17 Kasr El Nil (tel 751152)
Czechoslovak Airlines (CAS)
    9 Talaat Harb (tel 751416)
Egypt Air
    Nile Hilton (tel 759771)
    6 Adly St (tel 922444)
    Flight information (tel 872122)
El Al Israel Airlines
    5 Sharia Mazriki, Zamalek (tel 811620)
Ethiopian Airlines
    Nile Hilton (tel 740911)
Hungarian Airlines
    12 Talaat Harb (tel 753111)
Japan Airlines (JAL)
    Nile Hilton (tel 740621)
KLM (Royal Dutch Airlines)
    11 Kasr El Nil (tel 740648)
Kenya Airways
    15 Midan Tahrir (tel 747428)
Olympic Airways
    23 Kasr El Nil (tel 751318)
Polish Airlines (LOT)
    1 Kasr El Nil (tel 747312)
Singapore Airlines
    Nile Hilton Hotel (tel 762702)
Sudan Airways
    1 El Bustan (747251)
Trans World Airlines (TWA)
    1 Kasr El Nil (tel 666500)
Yugoslav Airlines (JAT)
    9 El Sherifien (tel 742166)

Embassies

The addresses of some of the embassies in Cairo are:

Australia
    1097 Corniche El Nil, Garden City (tel 983939/845205); hours: 8 am to 3 pm, Sunday to Thursday.
Canada
    6 Sharia Mohammed Fahmy El Said, Garden City (tel 23110/233119); hours: 7.30 am to 3 pm, Sunday to Thursday.
Central African Republic
    13 Shehab St, Mohandiseen (tel 802523)
Ethiopia
    12 Midan Bahlawi, Dokki (tel 705133/705372)

Israel
    6 Ibn al-Malek St, Dokki (tel 726000); hours: 10 am to 2.30 pm daily.
Jordan
    6 Gohaina, Dokki (tel 485566); hours: 9 am to 2 pm, Saturday to Thursday. The embassy is two blocks west of the Cairo Sheraton. Visas are free and take about three hours to process. You'll be denied a visa if your passport indicates that you've been to Israel (ie Egyptian border stamps from Rafah or Taba).
Kenya
    8 El Medina El Monawara, Mohandiseen (tel 704455)
Netherlands
    18 Sharia Hassan Sabri, Zamalek (tel 698744/698936)
Sudan
    3 al-Ibrahimi St, Garden City. The Consulate is around the corner at 1 Mohammed Fahmy El Said St, Garden City (tel 25043/25658). The issuance of Sudanese visas is subject to the fluctuating political conditions of the Sudan. You're out of luck if you have Israeli stamps in your passport. For details on those and other visa restrictions refer to the Facts for the Visitor chapter in the Sudan section of this book.
Tunisia
    26 El Gezira, Zamalek (tel 698962)
Uganda
    9 Midan El Missaha, Dokki (tel 980329/981945)
United Kingdom
    Ahmed Ragheb, Garden City (tel 20850); hours: 8 am to 1 pm, Sunday to Thursday.
United States
    5 Latin America St, Garden City (tel 28211/-9); hours: 8.30 am to 2 pm, Sunday through Thursday.
West Germany
    20 Boulos Hanna St, Dokki (tel 698016)
Zaire
    5 El Mansour Mohammed St, Zamalek (tel 699069/699954)

Arabic Lessons

Several organisations offer Arabic lessons in Cairo. Most of the programmes available are listed in the Facts for the Visitor chapter. Arabic lessons are offered through cultural centres. The French Cultural

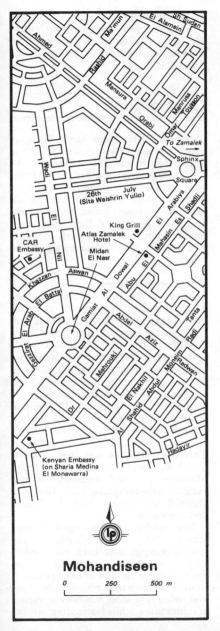

Mohandiseen

0   250   500 m

Center offers a nine month course for E£1000. Classes are for four hours daily, Monday through Friday. In the winter the class is held for one month at a ramshackle hotel on the west bank of Luxor. The Goethe Institute (the German centre) also offers relatively inexpensive Arabic lessons. Check the *Cairo Today* magazine for a listing of other organisations which occasionally offer Arabic courses.

Cultural Centres

There are several cultural centres in Cairo sponsored by other countries. Most have libraries, present films and sponsor various lectures, exhibits and performances. They are great places to get caught up on the latest news from home or to watch a free movie or video.

The American Cultural Center, 4 Ahmed Ragheb, Garden City, is opposite the British Embassy. The library holds more than 200 periodicals and 10,000 books and also shows video-taped news, from the ABC *Nightline* programme, twice a week. You can arrange to see a videotape on your own when the facilities are not being used for public presentations. The reading rooms are open from 10 am to 8 pm on Mondays, Wednesdays and Fridays; from 10 am to 4 pm on Tuesdays and Thursdays; and they're closed on Saturdays, Sundays and on American and Egyptian holidays.

The British Council Library is in a villa near the Circus grounds at 192 Sharia el Nil, Zamalek. They carry most major daily and weekly newspapers. They have more than 30,000 books and 120 periodicals and the reading rooms are open daily, except Sundays, from 9 am to 1 pm and from 5 to 8 pm.

If you speak German, the *Goethe Institute* (tel 759877), 5 Abdel Salam Aref, near the Cleopatra Hotel and Midan Tahrir, presents interesting seminars and lectures on Egyptology and other topics. They also sponsor performances by visiting music groups and special art exhibits. The library has rather erratic hours so phone first.

Other cultural centres include:

The Canadian Cultural Center, The Canadian Embassy, Garden City (tel 23110)
The French Cultural Center, Madrasat El Houquq al Fransiyya, Mounira (tel 27679)
The Italian Cultural Institute, 3 Sharia El Sheikh Marasfy, Zamalek (tel 808791)
Japanese Cultural Center, 10 Sharia Ibrahim Neguib, Garden City (tel 339624)
Information Service of India, 37 Talaat Harb (tel 747702). If you don't have Lonely Planet's India book, this is the next best source of information on India.

Medical

Hospitals There are three hospitals in Cairo with more modern facilities than most of Egypt's other hospitals: *The Cairo Medical Center* in Heliopolis (tel 695168); *The Anglo-American Hospital*, next to Cairo Tower in Zamalek (tel 806163); and *Al Salaam International Hospital*, Corniche el Nil, Maadi (tel 506050). The latter has 24-hour facilities.

24-Hour Pharmacies There are a number of pharmacies in Cairo that operate day and night including: *Gomhuriyya*, at 3 Shagarat El Dor, Zamalek (tel 816424), on Sharia Mazloum, Bab el Louk (tel 748835), and on the corner of Ramses and Sharia July 26th; and *Abul Ezz* (tel 843772), 49 Kasr El Eini.

Most things can be bought without a prescription in Egypt's pharmacies.

Doctors & Dentists Enquire at your embassy for the latest list of recommended doctors and dentists or consult *Cairo, A Practical Guide* published by AUC Press.

Important Numbers

Ambulance: tel 123 (possibly time-consuming)
Police: Emergency – tel 122; Garden City – tel 20781; Zamalek – tel 80179
Fire: tel 125

Diving Equipment

Diving equipment is available in Cairo at 'Bas Khalides' on Sharia Champolion. They sell masks, snorkels, scuba gear and fishing tackle.

Central Cairo

Most travellers begin their Egyptian experience somewhere in the vicinity of Tahrir Square and Talaat Harb St. It's the bustling, noisy centre of central Cairo where you'll find an amazing variety of shops as well as most of the budget hotels and eating places, banks, travel agents and cinemas. Central Cairo also has a number of museums, art galleries, markets and gardens and scenic views of the Nile.

The Egyptian Museum

Also called the Cairo Museum or the Museum of Egyptian Antiquities, this is one of the greatest museums you will ever see; it should not be missed. In fact, it's a good idea to visit this place at least twice – at the beginning of your visit, to familiarise yourself with Egypt's ancient history and at the end, to better understand all you have seen throughout the country.

More than 100,000 relics and antiquities, from almost every period of ancient Egyptian history, are housed in the huge warehouse-like building in Midan Tahrir. This vast collection was first gathered under one roof in 1858 by Auguste Mariette, a French archaeologist who excavated the temples of Edfu, Dendara, Deir el Bahri, Amun (at Karnak in Luxor) and a few others.

The exhibits are arranged chronologically from the Old Kingdom to the Roman Empire and each room could easily be a museum in its own right. If you spent only one minute at each exhibit it would take more than nine months to see everything. The sheer number and variety of things to see, while fascinating, is quite

Top: Cairo from the tower (SW)
Left: Cairo backstreets (SW)
Right: Mosque of al-Hakim, Islamic Cairo (SW)

Top: Garlic sellers, Cairo (SW)
Bottom: Ta'amita (felafel) stand, Cairo (SW)

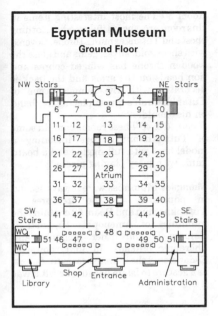

Egyptian Museum
Ground Floor

tively insignificant New Kingdom pharaoh, Tutankhamun.

The tomb and treasures of this boy-king, who ruled for only nine years during the 14th century BC, was discovered in 1922 by Howard Carter. Its well-hidden location in the Valley of the Kings, below the much grander but ransacked tomb of Ramses VI, had prevented tomb-robbers, and later archaeologists, from finding it any earlier. The incredible contents of his rather modest tomb can only make one wonder about the fabulous wealth looted from the tombs of pharaohs far greater than Tutankhamun.

The kings's decaying, mummified body, the outer of three mummiform coffins and the huge stone sarcophagus are all that remain in his tomb. The rest of his funerary treasures, about 1700 items, are spread throughout 12 rooms on the 1st floor of the museum. The rooms and the best relics are:

Room 4 Gold is the glittering attraction of

overwhelming. To help you deal with this labyrinth there are a couple of guidebooks available.

A Guide to the Egyptian Museum is available at the museum's ticket window or the gift shop for E£3. It's basically just a 300-page list of the museum's artefacts, organised by catalogue number not by room, with relatively little description of each item. The *Blue Guide*, published by A & C Black, is a costlier alternative but it describes the museum room by room in excellent detail.

The following is an abbreviated guide to some of the most popular exhibits. If you wish to learn more about a particular period or set of antiquities, check out the selection of Egyptology books in the library of the American University in Cairo.

Tutankhamun Without doubt, the exhibit that outshines everything else in the museum is the treasure of the compara-

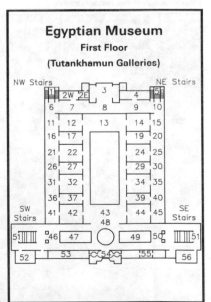

Egyptian Museum
First Floor
(Tutankhamun Galleries)

this room which features an astounding collection of jewels, including the 143 amulets and pieces of jewellery found amongst the wrappings on the king's body; a pair of gold sandals, which were on the feet of the mummy; and the two innermost coffins, one gilded wood and the other solid gold. The centrepiece of the room is Tutankhamun's legendary and exquisite mask of beaten gold inlaid with lapis lazuli and other gems.

Rooms 7, 8 & 9 The gilded wooden shrines, which fitted inside each other and held the gold sarcophagus of Tutankhamun at their centre, are in these rooms.

Room 15 King Tutankhamun's bed befits a pharaoh. It is covered with sheet gold with string stretched across the frame.

Room 20 A gilded copper trumpet is the feature of this room. It was once 'played' in 1939.

Room 30 The most interesting items in this room are a beautiful wooden clothing chest and Tutankhamun's throne. Covered with sheet gold, silver, gems and glass the wooden throne has winged cobras and lion heads on the arms and the back is decorated with the famous scene of Tutankhamun's queen placing her hand on his shoulder.

Room 40 & 45 These rooms contain some of Tutankhamun's toys including a model boat with full rigging and a board game with ivory playing pieces.

Mummies Mummies were always second in popularity to the treasures of Tutankhamun and Room 52 contains the mummies of Amenophis III, Seti I, Ramses II and other pharaohs and pharaonic officials. In 1981, however, Sadat closed the mummy room to visitors, as a gesture to Islam because he felt it was

Tutankhamun & his sister/Queen

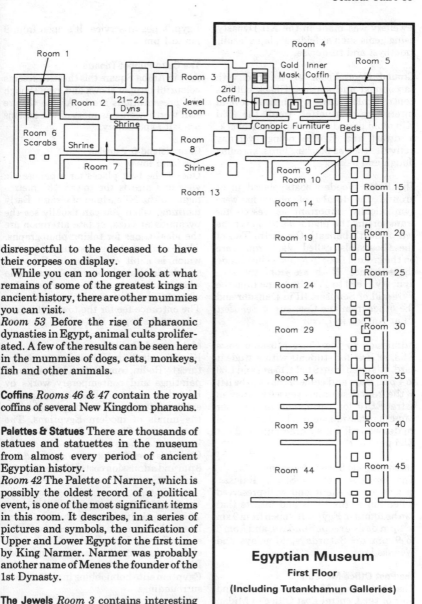

Egyptian Museum

First Floor

(Including Tutankhamun Galleries)

Room 1

Room 2

21–22 Dyns

Room 6 Scarabs

Shrine

Room 7

Shrine

Room 3

Jewel Room

Room 8

Shrines

Room 13

Room 4

Gold Mask | Inner Coffin

2nd Coffin

Canopic | Furniture

Beds

Room 5

Room 9
Room 10

Room 14

Room 19

Room 24

Room 29

Room 34

Room 39

Room 44

Room 15

Room 20

Room 25

Room 30

Room 35

Room 40

Room 45

disrespectful to the deceased to have their corpses on display.

While you can no longer look at what remains of some of the greatest kings in ancient history, there are other mummies you can visit.

Room 53 Before the rise of pharaonic dynasties in Egypt, animal cults proliferated. A few of the results can be seen here in the mummies of dogs, cats, monkeys, fish and other animals.

Coffins *Rooms 46 & 47* contain the royal coffins of several New Kingdom pharaohs.

Palettes & Statues There are thousands of statues and statuettes in the museum from almost every period of ancient Egyptian history.

Room 42 The Palette of Narmer, which is possibly the oldest record of a political event, is one of the most significant items in this room. It describes, in a series of pictures and symbols, the unification of Upper and Lower Egypt for the first time by King Narmer. Narmer was probably another name of Menes the founder of the 1st Dynasty.

The Jewels *Room 3* contains interesting jewellery from the 1st Dynasty to the Byzantine period. Some of the best jewellery was made in the XII Dynasty using gems such as feldspar, lapis lazuli, amethyst and turquoise.

Ground Floor *Room 47* is lined with sarcophagi and statues. Check out the centre exhibit cases which have several interesting statuettes from the Old Kingdom period including a hunchback, a dwarf and figures doing everyday activities such as plucking birds, kneading dough and baking.

The Boats Wooden boats placed in or around the tombs of pharaohs were symbolically important as vessels for transporting the pharaoh's soul over the sea of death beneath the earth. Two of these boats, also called solar barques, are on the ground floor in *Room 43* just inside the entrance. Both are from the 12th dynasty (1990 to 1780 BC); one from the Pyramid of Senusert III in Dahshur and the other from the Colossus of Senusert III at Karnak in Luxor.

Admission to the Cairo Museum costs E£3, or E£1 for students with a student card. It's open from 9 to 11.15 am and 1.30 to 4 pm. Bags and cameras have to be left at the front desk unless you wish to pay an extra E£10 for permission to use your camera in the museum. There are official guides who will take you around for about E£5 per hour.

Entomological Society Museum
This museum, at 14 Sharia Ramses, houses an excellent and well-preserved collection of the birds and insects that can be found in Egypt. It's open from 9 am to 1 pm daily except Sundays, and from 6 to 9 pm on Saturdays, Mondays and Wednesdays.

The Post Office Museum
The Post Office Museum is on the 2nd floor of the Central Post Office in Midan Ataba. There are collections of old stamps and displays show the history of Egypt's postal service. It's open from 9 am to 1 pm.

The Cairo Puppet Theatre
Also in Ataba Square this theatre presents colourful puppet shows and even though the presentations are in Arabic they're still worth seeing as most of the actions are self-explanatory.

Gezira Island & Zamalek
The Cairo Tower
One of the best places for a panoramic view of Cairo is the tower, 185 metres high, on the Nile island of Gezira. Early morning, when you can usually see the pyramids at Giza, or late afternoon are the ideal times for taking photographs. There's a revolving restaurant on top which is a bit expensive by Egyptian standards, but there's also a cafeteria where you can have the same revolving view of Cairo, with much cheaper drinks. The entrance fee for the tower, if you're going to the top, is E£1.

Mohammed Khalil Museum
Khalil's collection includes several sculptures by Rodin, some French Impressionist paintings and contemporary works by Egyptian artists. The contemporary exhibits offer an interesting insight into the minds of modern Egyptians. The museum, at 1 Sharia El Sheikh Marsafy, is opposite the entrance to the Gezira Club. It's open from 9 am to 3 pm and 5 to 8 pm and admission costs E£1, or 50 pt for students.

The Gezira Club
This is a private sporting club on Gezira Island but for E£2 you can use the swimming pool for the day or eat in the club restaurant which serves good food. It's also a good place to watch the Egyptian elite hobnobbing in glamourous surroundings.

Aquarium Park
This cute place, where the fish inhabit

aquariums built into tunnels that look they were once bomb shelters, seems to be practically unknown to foreigners. The aquarium is in Gabalaya Park, near Sharia El Gezira. Even if fish don't interest you, the park is still worth a visit for the respite it offers from the chaos of Cairo.

The Museum of Sculptor M Moukhtar (1891-1934)

Moukhtar was the sculptor-laureate of Egypt and this museum contains most of his major works. Also known as the National Center for Fine Arts it is open from 9 am to 1.30 pm daily except Mondays. The entrance fee is E£2, or E£1 for students. The museum is on the left side of Sharia al Tahrir on Gezira just before you cross al-Galaa Bridge to Dokki.

Roda Island

Roda Island is south of Gezira in the Nile. In the 13th century Sultan al-Salih Ayyub built an immense fortress here for his army of Mamelukes. The fortress had barracks, palaces, mosques and more than 50 towers. Various sultans used the facilities until the 18th century, by which time other, stronger fortresses in Egypt had replaced this one. Today, the island is home to an eclectic palace built in the early 20th century, the Nilometer, a small art museum and several thousand Cairene apartment dwellers.

Manyal Palace Museum

The Manyal Palace was built in the early part of this century as a residence for Prince Mohammed Ali Tewfik. The government converted it into a museum in 1955. Apparently Tewfik couldn't decide which architectural style he preferred for the palace so each of the five main buildings are different. The styles include Persian, Syrian, Moorish and Ottoman.

After you enter the palace grounds, walk along the path on the right to Mohammed Ali's mosque and the hunting museum of the royal family. The hunting museum was added to the complex in 1962 to house King Farouk's huge collection of stuffed animal trophies. The heads of several hundred gazelles line the walls along with a variety of other animals shot by the royal family and there's also a strange table constructed from elephant's ears. This is not a place for animal lovers.

Return to the path leading from the palace entrance and follow it to the other buildings. The Residence Palace is the next one you will see. Each room is ornately decorated with hand-painted geometric shapes – a traditional design of Islamic art; several of the doors are inlaid with carved pieces of ivory; and the windows feature intricate *mashrabiyya* screens, which are carved wooden panels.

There is rather an odd view from one of the bedroom windows on the 2nd floor. You can see over the fence into the swimming pool area of the Club Mediterranean which now occupies half of the palace grounds. It's a bit of a surprise, while touring rooms steeped in the art, history and conservative traditions of Islam, to be suddenly yanked back to the 20th century with views of scantily clad Club Med vacationers!

The largest museum contains Mohammed Ali's fascinating collection of manuscripts, clothing, silver objects, furniture, writing implements and other items dating from medieval times to the 19th century. A self-appointed guide likes to show you around this part of the museum object by object. If you don't want him to follow you, or vice versa, let him know.

The Manyal Palace is on your left as you cross the canal to Roda Island on Ali Ibrahim St (near the youth hostel). It's open daily from 9 am to 3 pm and admission costs E£1, or 50 pt for students.

The Nilometer

Built in the 9th century to measure the

rise and fall of the Nile, which in turn helped predict the state of the annual harvest, this interesting ancient monument is on the southern tip of Roda Island. When the Nile rose to 16 cubits, approximately equal to the length of a forearm, it would hold great promise for the crops and the people would celebrate.

The conical dome was added when the Nilometer was restored in the 19th century. The actual measuring device, a graduated column, is well below the level of the Nile in a paved area at the bottom of a flight of steps. The structure is often locked but the caretaker lives in a small house on the left side of the building and there are usually lots of kids around who'll get him for you. The admission fee is 25 pt.

The Center for Art & Life

This small, but interesting art and crafts museum, next to the Nilometer, occupies a former palace. Every form of local art from batik, ceramics, glass, pottery, textiles and handicrafts to photography is on display. There are also more formal Persian, Islamic and Coptic art objects.

Dokki, Mohandiseen & Imbaba
The Museum of Modern Art

This museum in Dokki will give you some idea of the contemporary culture and changing life in Egypt. The watercolour room is especially good; check out the painting of the temple complex at Philae by an artist named Zaky. To find the room look for the stone crocodile on the floor and go in the direction of its big nose. The garden in front is overgrown with weeds and dotted with statues, some of which are quite unique. The museum, at 18 Ismail Abou Foutuh St, around the corner from the Indiana Hotel, is open from 9 am to 2 pm, Sundays to Thursdays; and 9 am to 1 pm on Fridays. Admission costs E£1, or 50 pt for students.

The Agricultural Museum/Cotton Museum

This complex in Dokki is off Sharia Wisaret El Ziraa, at the foot of the overpass on Sharia 6th October. The Agricultural Museum contains lots of stuffed animals and exhibits showing life in Egyptian villages and the Cotton Museum has displays of the history of cotton production in Egypt. In winter it's open from 9 am to 4 pm, Sundays to Thursdays; and from 9 to 11.30 am and 1 to 4 pm on Fridays. There's a small entrance fee.

The Cairo Circus

This small big top is at the foot of the Zamalek Bridge, off Sharia 26th of July in Zamalek. Check with the Tourist Office for a schedule of performances.

The Camel Market

The *Souk el Gahmell*, or camel market, in Imbaba is the largest of its kind in the country. Despite the fact that, amongst the growing urban sprawl, the market looks rather like a mirage it's probably, for that very reason, one of the most interesting things to see in this part of Cairo. It is north of Mohandiseen, near the Imbaba airport and just off Sharia Sudan.

The camels are brought up the *40 Day Road* from the Sudan to Aswan by camel-herders from Western Sudan. (Refer to the section on Western Sudan). In Aswan the camels are crammed into trucks for the 24-hour journey to Imbaba, where they're traded and/or sold for other livestock such as goats, sheep and horses. Early Friday morning, between about 6.30 and 8 am is the best time to visit.

Getting to the market is as much of an adventure as the market itself. The easiest way is to take a taxi, but the more scenic route is a 45-minute walk from central Cairo. Take the 6th October Bridge through Zamalek to Sharia 26th of July which, after about three blocks, opens into Midan 26th of July (also known as Sphinx Square). Bear right, off the traffic circle, and walk up Sharia Ahmed Orabi all the way to the end, then

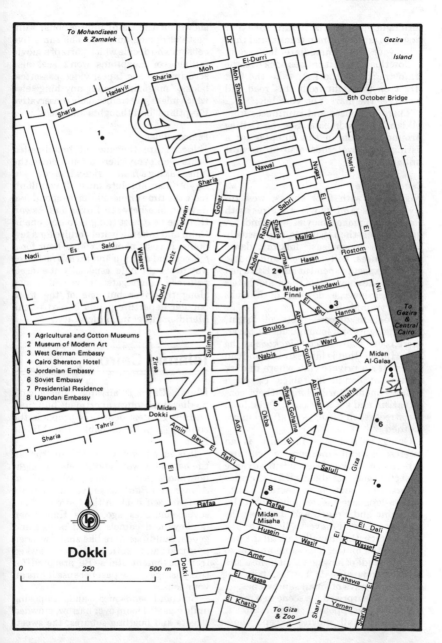

1 Agricultural and Cotton Museums
2 Museum of Modern Art
3 West German Embassy
4 Cairo Sheraton Hotel
5 Jordanian Embassy
6 Soviet Embussy
7 Presidential Residence
8 Ugandan Embassy

Dokki

0   250   500 m

turn right on to Sharia Sudan. Take your first left, cross the train tracks, and then take your first immediate left again. Follow this road as it crosses back over the train tracks on the left; take the first street on the right from this road and you'll see the market on your left.

There are buses and minibuses from Midan Tahrir to Imbaba. See the 'Getting Around' section in this chapter for a listing. The waterbus also stops near Imbaba.

Cairo Nightlife

Nightclubs with floor shows, western-style discos and movie theatres with English-language movies abound. A night out on the town in a club usually includes a lavish feast, folkloric dance performances, belly dancers and Arabic music. Expect to spend at least E£10 just to watch the show. All of the major hotels have floor shows, as do many of the clubs along Pyramids Rd.

Discos are discos – lots of bright, twirling lights and loud music. However, there is one Cairo disco – *Jackie's* at the Nile Hilton – that is interesting if you can get in. It's a private club where in dark corners at candle-lit tables Egyptian couples momentarily forget their conservatism and get a bit cozy. Outside on the street, such displays of affection are scorned.

Going to a movie in Cairo is an interesting and inexpensive cultural experience. Tickets are sold in advance by section and cost about a E£1; the price differs from section to section. Most foreign-language movies have sub-titles in Arabic and French and, because the audience doesn't have to listen to the sound-track, they usually talk all the way through the movie. The same applies to the multitude of hawkers plying the aisles with buckets of soda bottles, boxes of candy and trays of small sandwiches.

Don't be surprised if a scene in a movie suddenly disappears. Censorship is common for all movies except those shown for the Cairo International Film Festival during autumn. The same five censors who decide which parts of a movie millions of Egyptians won't see, also scrutinise music tapes, video cassettes, books, magazines and anything else which might give traditionally conservative Egyptians 'bad thoughts and ideas'.

Felucca Rides

Feluccas are the ancient broad-sailed boats seen everywhere up and down the Nile. Taking a *felucca* ride while you're in Egypt is an absolute must. If you don't have the time or inclination to spend five days on one between Luxor and Aswan then the next best thing is to hire one in Cairo and take a leisurely cruise for a few hours. It costs about E£6 per hour for a *felucca* and captain and there's no better way to see the Nile, especially at sunset. *Feluccas* congregate at several quays along the river but one of the most popular departure points is next to the Meridien Hotel in Garden City.

Islamic Cairo

Islamic Cairo is an area replete with medieval mosques, apartment buildings and the greatest density of people in the country – and probably the Middle East.

It is easy to get lost in this district. In the back alleyways and streets, of neighbourhoods with names like *Darb al Ahmar* and *Baatiniyya*, you'll suddenly find yourself back in the Cairo of six or seven centuries ago; in a time when donkeys and camels towed people and goods, buildings were like shaky wooden pyramids and exotic foods were hawked from pavement stalls. Be prepared for this passage to the past because it hits all your senses.

Splendid mosques and imposing buildings still loom over narrow, crowded streets and bustling squares; the sweet, pungent aromas of turmeric, basil and cumin drift from open barrels, mix with the offensive odours of livestock and grab at your nose like invisible fingers; and people go about their daily business as they have done, it seems, forever. This *could* be the medieval Cairo of Ibn Tulun or Salah al-Din except that the age-old aromas now mingle with petrol fumes as donkeys and camels compete with cars for space; and an awful lot of poverty offsets the grandeur of the architecture throughout what was once the intellectual and cultural centre of the Arab world.

Your passage can begin anywhere in the area, but the following describes two possible sets of independent walking tours. Before you begin, you may want to buy a specialised guide to the monuments in the area. Parker and Sabin's *A Practical Guide to Islamic Monuments in Cairo* is packed with detailed explanations and maps of the monuments and is available at the American University in Cairo bookstore.

As you begin your exploration of this part of Cairo, carry lots of small change for *baksheesh*. You'll need it for tipping guards and caretakers, who will expect *baksheesh* if you ask to see something special, such as a minaret.

One set of walking tours begins at Midan Salah al-Din at the foot of the Citadel and in front of the mosques of Sultan Hassan and Rifa'i. To get there, take bus No 72 (usually extremely crowded) or minibus No 54 (not crowded) from Midan Tahrir, or walk there (it will take about 45 minutes).

There are several interesting monuments to visit in the area. On this five or six-hour walk, en route to the Citadel, you can visit the Sultan Hassan Mosque, Rifa'i Mosque, an open-air market, the Ibn Tulun Mosque, Gayer-Anderson House, the Tomb of Shagarat al-Durr and the Mausoleum of Imam al-Shafi'i.

Sultan Hassan Mosque

The mosque is to your left, if the Citadel is behind you. It was built during the time of Mameluke rule, from 1356 to 363 AD with stones, historians believe, that were taken from one of the Great Pyramids of Giza. Originally the mosque was a *madrasa* or theological school and each of the four vaulted halls, or *liwan*, surrounding the central court served as classrooms for each main school of Sunni Islam. The interior is typically devoid of decoration to make it easier for worshippers to concentrate on prayers. Hundreds of chains, which once held oil lamps, still hang from the ceiling of each *liwan*. Try to visit this place in the morning when the sun lights up the mausoleum portion of the mosque; the effect is quite eerie.

The Rifa'i Mosque

Just across the street from the Sultan Hassan, this is a 19th century imitation of a Mameluke-style mosque. The Princess Dowager Khushyar, mother of the Khedive (viceroy) Ismail, had the mosque built in 1869 to serve as tomb for herself, her descendants and future khedives. Members of the late royal family, including King Farouk, are buried here as is the Shah of Iran. His casket was paraded through the streets of Cairo in 1980, from Abdin Palace to the mosque, with President Sadat, the Shah's family and Richard Nixon leading the cortège. Opening hours are 8 am to 6 pm and admission is E£1.

After visiting these two mosques, walk down Sharia al-Salibah away from the Citadel. Turn left at the next major street, Sharia al-Khalifa, and walk through the open-air fruit and vegetable market. You may get a lot of stares because very few foreigners wander through there. Turn right at the next street, Sharia Tulun, and the mosque of Ibn Tulun will be ahead of you on your right.

Ibn Tulun Mosque

This is one of the largest mosques in the world. Ibn Tulun was sent to rule Cairo in the 9th century by the Abbasid Caliph of

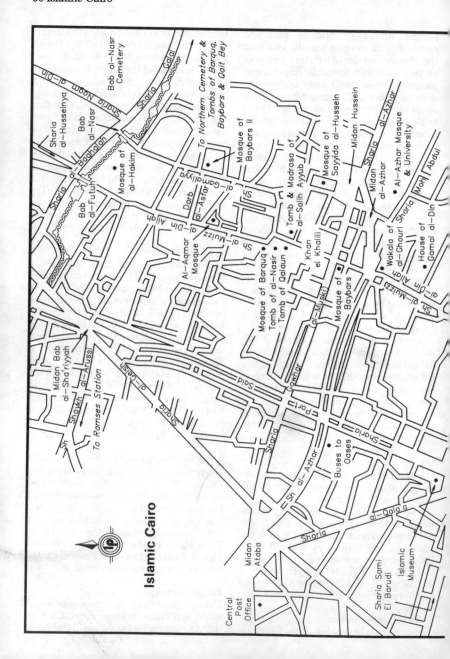

Islamic Cairo

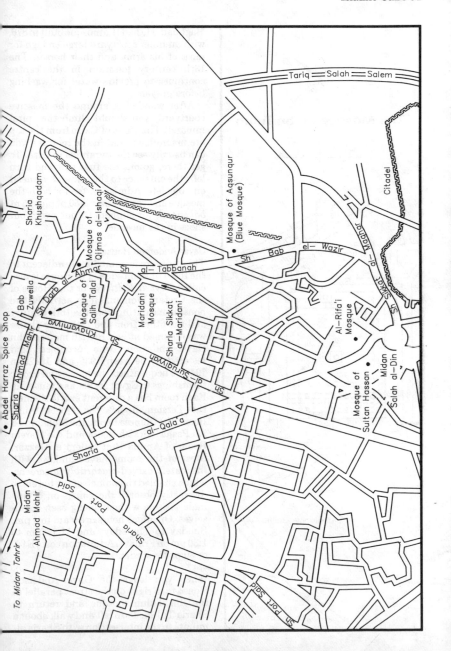

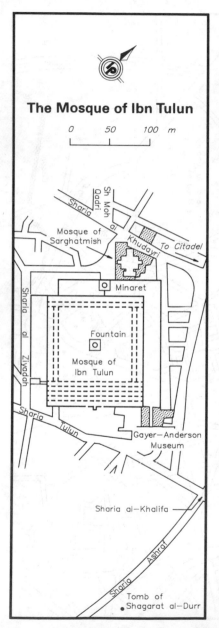

The Mosque of Ibn Tulun

0   50   100 m

Baghdad. He had the mosque built in 876, with an inner courtyard large enough for most of his army and their horses. The 13th century fountain in the centre continues to provide water for washing before prayers.

After wandering around the massive courtyard, you should climb the spiral minaret. The views of Cairo from the top are magnificent and in the morning you can usually see the pyramids in Giza. To get there, go out the first exit and turn left; the entrance to the minaret is ahead on your left. Admission fee for both the mosque and the minaret is 50 pt plus 25 pt *baksheesh* for slippers to put over your shoes in the mosque.

Gayer-Anderson House

This museum is immediately adjacent to the Ibn Tulun mosque. The House is also called *Bayt al-Kritliyya* or the 'House of the Cretan Woman.' It is actually two houses, one dating from the 16th century and the other from the 18th. The House was renamed after a British major, John Gayer-Anderson, who occupied and restored it, between 1935 and 1942. In 1942 he bequeathed the house and exotic furnishings to Egypt for use as a museum. Each room has a different exotic theme – the Persian Room, the Queen Anne Room, the Chinese Room, the Mohammed Ali Pasha Turkish Room and the Harem Room of Amina Bint Salem el Gazzar. Most of the rooms have windows with intricately carved *mashrabiyya* screens, which enabled the women of the harem to discreetly observe the goings-on of any male visitors without being seen themselves. Openings hours are 9 am to 4 pm, Sunday to Thursday; and 11.15 am to 1.30 pm on Fridays. Admission costs E£1, or 50 pt for students.

When you leave the Gayer-Anderson House turn right on the street parallel to the Ibn Tulun mosque and return to Sharia Tulun. Turn left and walk about a minute to the intersection with Sharia al-

Khalifa, then turn right. Sharia al-Khalifa becomes Sharia al-Ashraf and you continue walking down this street into a district called the Southern Cemetery. This is the beginning of a vast Muslim necropolis which stretches all the way to the suburb of Maadi, about five km south. At about 250 metres on the left you will find the Tomb of Shagarat al-Durr.

Tomb of Shagarat al-Durr

Built in 1250 this is a small and simple tomb which has Byzantine glass mosaics gracing the prayer niche. The most interesting thing about it though is the story of the woman whose remains are entombed here.

Shagarat al-Durr was a slave from a nomadic tribe who managed, albeit briefly, to become the only female Muslim sovereign in history. She secured this position fairly easily but behaved irresponsibly, for a woman, came to a very nasty end and, in the process, instigated Mameluke rule which was to last for the next 200 years.

Salih Ayyub, the last ruler of the Ayyubid dynasty, married Shagarat al-Durr at a time when the soldiers of the Seventh Crusade had taken control of Damietta, in the Nile Delta. Knowing that Ayyub was sick and dying the Crusaders were prepared to wait out his death and attack Cairo when the government collapsed. So when he died in 1249, Shagarat al-Durr hid his corpse and for three months managed to pretend that he was still alive and passing on orders to his generals through her while she was waiting for her son to come back from Mesopotamia and take control. But when he did return he proved to be a weak ruler, so she had him killed.

She then openly declared herself Sultana of Egypt and ruled for 80 days – the only woman to rule over Muslims until Queen Victoria. The Abbasid Caliph of Baghdad refused to recognise her position however, so she married a Mameluke, the leader of her slave-warriors, and ruled through him. When he decided that he needed an extra wife, Shagarat al-Durr had him killed and his second wife thrown into prison. When his Mameluke warriors discovered Shagarat al-Durr's part in the assassination, she offered to marry their new leader but was imprisoned instead. She was eventually turned over to her husband's second wife who, along with several other women, beat Shagarat al-Durr to death with wooden clogs. They hung her body from the side of the Citadel as food for the dogs. What was left of her, was saved and entombed.

Tomb of Imam al-Shafi'i

An easy side-trip from Midan Salah al-Din, this mausoleum is two km south of the square, in the Southern Cemetery. Imam al-Shafi'i, a descendent of an uncle of the Prophet, was the founder of *Shafi'ite*, one of the four major schools of Sunni Islamic thought. Regarded as one of the great Muslim saints, he died in 820 and his mausoleum, the largest Islamic tomb in Egypt, is the centre of a great annual *moulid*, or birthday festival, held in his honour.

In the 12th century Salah al-Din founded the first *madrasa* (theological school) on the same site, to counter the influence of the Shi'ite Muslim sect of the Fatimid dynasty he had overthrown. It became a centre of Shafi'ite missionary work. Today most Muslims in Cairo are Shafi'ite, and Shafi'ite Sunni Islam is also predominant in much of the Saudi peninsula, Malaysia and East Africa.

To get to the mausoleum, you can walk south from the Citadel to Tariq Salah Salem, turn right and then left off the square into Sharia al-Qadiriyyah which becomes Sharia Imam al-Shafi'i. You can also take bus No 405 from Midan Salah al-Din and get off before it turns left towards the Moqattam Hills; the tomb is a little further down Sharia Imam al-Shafi'i. Another way from Midan Salah al-Din is the tram, which stops almost directly in front of the mosque. You can't miss the building as it has a large red, blue and gold dome topped by a bronze boat.

The Citadel

A spectacular medieval fortress of crenel-

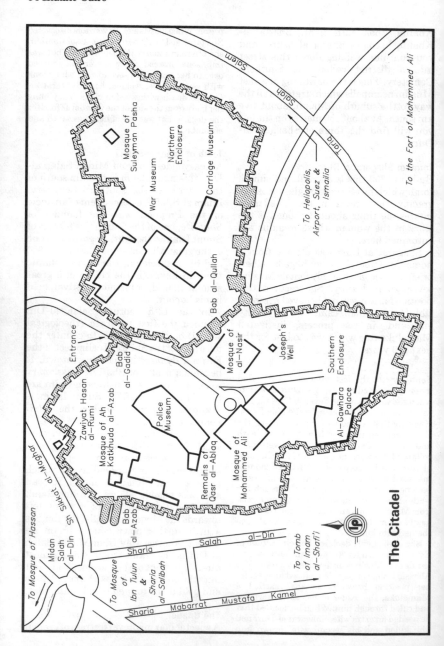

The Citadel

lated walls and towers perched on a hill above Midan Salah al-Din, the Citadel was home to most of Egypt's rulers for about 700 years.

Salah al-Din began building the Citadel in 1176, to fortify the city against the Crusaders, and over the centuries it has been modified and enlarged with the palaces and buildings of subsequent rulers and governments.

Mohammed Ali, one of the last rulers to reside in the Citadel, actually levelled most of the buildings of the Mameluke period to build his own mosque and palace. And, it was in a narrow rock-hewn passage near one of the Citadel's front gates, that he sealed his control over Egypt with the massacre of the Mamelukes.

On 1 March 1811, he treated the Mameluke leaders to a day of feasting and revelry, at the end of which they were escorted from the Citadel through a narrow laneway. Mohammed Ali's troops sealed both ends of the passage, trapping all 470 dinner guests. All but one, who managed to escape, were massacred from the wall above.

Today, the Citadel is a complex of three mosques and four museums. From Midan Salah al-Din the entrance is up the hill to the left and you can also enter from the Heliopolis and airport road on the far side. Admission costs E£2, or E£1 for students, and it's open from 9 am to 5 pm daily. The following are most of the main sights in the Citadel.

Mosque of al-Nasir As you enter the main complex, the mosque will be in front of you to your left. It was built in 1318 by Sultan al-Nasir Mohammed with marble panels on the floor and walls. The Ottoman ruler Selim I, later instructed his troops to strip the mosque of its marble. Outside to the right and behind the mosque lies Joseph's Well.

Joseph's Well A tower stands over Joseph's (or Yusef's) Well, which is also called the

Well of the Snail because of the spiral staircase which leads 88 metres down a shaft to the level of the Nile. Yusef was one of Salah al-Din's names and the well was named after him, not the biblical Joseph, as it was built in the 1180's by Crusaders who were imprisoned by him in the Citadel. The prisoners were attempting to escape, or at least ensure a secure water supply in the event of a siege.

Be careful when descending the stairs as there is no railing at the bottom to keep you from falling down the well.

Return to the front of al-Nasir Mosque. The National Police Museum is straight ahead and the Mosque of Mohammed Ali is the large building on your left. Walk to your left and then between the two mosques and across the parapet to the edge, where all of Islamic Cairo is beneath you – the medieval mosques and minarets, winding alleyways and countless shaky, ramshackle buildings. In the distance you can see the tall buildings of downtown Cairo and, sometimes, the Great Pyramids.

Al Gawhara Palace/Museum With the view behind you, the palace is on your right. It was built in 1814 by Mohammed Ali and after the 1952 Revolution was used as a museum for the jewels of the khedives. In 1972 thieves attempted to make off with that valuable collection and in doing so set part of the palace on fire. Today, the museum contains a diorama of palace life.

Mosque of Mohammed Ali Also known as the *Alabaster Mosque*, this mosque/mausoleum was built by Mohammed Ali between 1830 and 1848. His gilt tomb is on the right as you enter and although the interior is vast, it is badly decorated. The 'ginger bread' clock in the central court, which has never worked, was given to Mohammed Ali by King Louis-Philippe of France, in return for the gift of a pharaonic obelisk from Luxor, that still stands in the Place de la Concorde in

Paris. The most spectacular features of the mosque are outside – its huge dome and half-domes and tall, slim minarets are very impressive.

The National Police Museum This museum has an interesting collection of exhibits covering such subjects as the 'Police Struggle', 'Police in Islamic and Pharaonic Times' and the 'Confiscations of Antiquities.' There is also an Assassination Room where descriptions and photographs tell the stories of the attempted assassination of Nasser and the successful assassination of Sir Lee Stack.

There are three sights worth seeing in the northern enclosure of the Citadel. With the Police Museum behind you, the entrance gate to the enclosure faces the left side of the Mosque of al-Nasir.

The Archaeological Garden Museum While it's really neither a garden nor a museum this area does have an interesting collection

of statues and pieces of monuments spread out among the park benches. Just follow the signs.

The Royal Carriage Museum Next to the garden, this museum contains a small, but interesting collection of 19th century horse-drawn carriages and painted wooden horses.

The War Museum There are lots of swords, rifles, military uniforms and cannons in the various exhibits detailing Egypt's military history from pharaonic times, through the Graeco-Roman and Islamic periods to the present. The museum is open from 9 am to 2 pm daily except Tuesday.

Leaving the Citadel If you've had enough sight-seeing for the day, you can take a bus or minibus back to the city centre from Midan Salah al-Din. Minibus No 54 goes to Midan Tahrir; and buses 81, 83, 84 and 604 go to Midan Opera.

The Citadel

Top: View over Islamic Cairo (SW)
Left: Apartment pigeon coop, Cairo (SW)
Right: Bazaar street in Khan el Khalili, Cairo (SW)

Top: The fellahin farmers of the Delta (SW)
Bottom: Carting sugar cane by camel, El Faiyum (SW)

From the Citadel to al-Azhar

This second set of walking tours takes you through one of Cairo's oldest and poorest districts. It is called *Darb al Ahmar*, which means 'the Red Road', and it almost seems like time stopped here completely several centuries ago. Poverty and conservatism have kept this district isolated from many of the changes, both good and bad, that other parts of Cairo have experienced.

I recommend that you begin your exploration at either the Citadel or al-Azhar Mosque. The following section describes some of the main sights with the Citadel as your departure point.

Leave the Citadel by the main entrance, go downhill and left into Sharia Sikkat al-Maghar. Take the first right, onto Sharia Bab el-Wazir, the Street of the Gate of the Vizier, and about 550 metres up the street on the right side there is a unique mosque.

The Mosque of Aqsunqur

The *Blue Mosque* was first built in 1347 and then rebuilt in 1652 by a Turkish governor named Ibrahim Agha who added the blue tiles on the walls. Agha imported the decorated tiles from Damascus but, apart from making the mosque rather unique in Egypt, they do little for the aesthetics of the place.

Behind the mosque you can see part of Salah al-Din's city walls which ran from north to south. Across the street from the mosque there is a Turkish apartment building which dates from 1625 and is still inhabited. However, unless by some strange stroke of luck you happen to know one of the inhabitants, this building is not open to curious visitors.

Maridani Mosque

Continue walking up Sharia Bab el-Wazir another 350 metres; the street is now called Sharia al-Tabbanah. The Maridani Mosque will be on your left where a small street, Sikkat al-Maridani, meets Sharia al-Tabbanah. Built in 1339, the mosque is one of the oldest buildings in the area. Several styles of architecture were used in its construction. Eight granite columns were taken from a pharaonic monument and placed here; the arches were made from Roman, Christian and Islamic designs; and the Ottomans added a fountain and wooden housing. There are several other decorative details inside. There won't be any hands thrust at you for *baksheesh* here because very few foreigners visit the mosque.

Mosque of Qijmas al-Ishaqi

Sharia al-Tabbanah changes name again and becomes Sharia Darb al-Ahmar (the Red Road), and this beautiful little mosque is about 200 metres up the street from the Maridani. Qijmas was Master of the Sultan's horses and officer-in-charge of the annual pilgrimage to Mecca and his mosque is one of the best examples of architecture from the 15th century Burgi Mameluke period. The plain exterior of the building is quite deceiving as inside there are beautiful stained glass windows, inlaid marble floors and stucco walls. Under the prayer mats in the east *liwan* (vaulted hall), the floor is a fantastic, marble mosaic. Ask the guard to lift the mat for you.

Mosque of Salih Talai

This small but intriguing building, 150 metres further up on the left, is one of the best examples of the Fatimid style of architecture, with strange-shaped arches, classical columns and wooden beams. The mosque is directly opposite Bab Zuweila, one of the original city gates. Ask the guard to show you up to the roof as the views of the surrounding neighbourhood are great. The guard will expect some *baksheesh*; 25 pt should be appropriate.

Sharia Khayamiyya

This is the *Street of the Tentmakers* which intersects Sharia Darb al-Ahmar at the Mosque of Salih Talai. About 400 metres further on, it becomes Sharia al-

Surugiyyah, the *Street of the Saddle-makers*. Part of this thoroughfare is a wooden arcade and has been covered for several centuries. Medieval apartments, with *mashrabiyya* screens on the windows, jut out over the street. The Tentmakers here make the applique panels used throughout Egypt on the ceremonial tents that are set up for funerals, wakes, weddings, and holiday celebrations.

Bab Zuweila

Of the original 60 gates of the medieval city of Cairo, Bab Zuweila, built in 1092, is one of only three that remain. The other two, Bab al-Nasr and Bab al-Futuh, were built at about the same time and even as recently as the late 19th century they were used to close off the city. Bab Zuweila, the southern gate, was also often the site of public executions. The last Mameluke Sultan, Tumanbay, was hanged here three times – he survived the first two attempts! You can climb up to the top of the gate through the adjoining Mosque of Sultan Mu'ayyad Shaykh.

Mosque of Sultan Mu'ayyad Shaykh

This was built between 1416 and 1420 by the Burgi Mameluke, Mu'ayyad Shaykh, a freed Circassian slave who eventually rose through the ranks of the Mamelukes to become Sultan of Egypt. Mu'ayyad had a drinking problem before becoming Sultan and his fellow Mamelukes considered beatings and incarceration just therapy for such a weakness. Mu'ayyad was imprisoned on this site and vowed to one day have that prison replaced by a mosque. His wish came true and although it's not a terribly impressive building there is a magnificent view of Cairo from its minaret – which is actually on top of Bab Zuweila, not the mosque.

If you climb the minaret, be careful on the first set of stairs where the wooden railing is very shaky, and the second set which is steep and very dark in parts. The guard will insist on giving you a tour and showing you the entrance to the minaret.

This is not necessary, but be careful if you refuse his offers of assistance and don't give him *baksheesh*. I made this mistake, found the entrance myself and mounted the stairs to the roof. When I returned to the door at the bottom of the stairs, it was locked. Believe me, being trapped in a medieval minaret is not all that much fun; so watch out!

The entrance fee is 50 pt, or 25 pt for students with an additional 50 pt of *baksheesh* to the guard for showing you the minaret.

Turkish Baths

In front of the Mosque of Mu'ayyad Shaykh there is a small door which leads to the *Old Turkish Baths*. There is no sign, you just have to guess which door is the entrance. The admission fee is E£2, for which you'll get a massage and traditional Turkish-style steam bath.

The Abdel Rahman M Harraz Spice & Herb Shop

For another change from mosques and minarets, go back through Bab Zuweila onto Sharia Darb al-Ahmar and turn right and walk another 400 metres. The street changes name again, to Sharia Ahmad Mahir. On the right side, one block before the Museum of Islamic Art, there is a very special shop which has everything imaginable in the way of herbs, spices and exotic concoctions. In the store window there is even a jar of dessicated crocodiles for use by people who are over-sexed. The crocodiles are ground up, boiled into a potion and then drunk.

Islamic Museum

With the treasures of the pharaohs being the main objective of most tourists to Cairo this museum, which has one of the world's finest collections of Islamic art, is rarely crowded.

The exhibits are arranged either chronologically, showing the influence of various eras, such as the Fatimid, Ayyubid or

Mameluke periods, on Islamic art in Egypt, or in special displays of a particular subject. The latter includes collections of textiles, glassware, calligraphy, tapestries and pottery from throughout the Islamic world. The intricate woodwork in the collection of *mashrabiyya* window screens, for instance, is the best you will see in Egypt; there is one room of inlaid metalwork; another with a collection of magnificent Oriental carpets; and a wonderful exhibit of medieval weapons and suits of armour. There is also a collection of superb illluminated books and ancient Qur'anic manuscripts.

The museum is on Midan Ahmad Mahir, where Sharia al-Qala'a, Sharia Port Said and Sharia Ahmad Mahir all meet. Admission costs E£2, or E£1 for students, and it's open Saturdays to Thursdays from 9 am to 4 pm and on Fridays from 11.15 am to 1.30 pm.

Second Departure Point
The second departure point for walking tours around Islamic Cairo is from the al-Azhar Mosque and University. The first set of things to see is south of al-Azhar back towards Bab Zuweila; and the second set begins across the street in the bazaar area of Khan el Khalili.

Al-Azhar Mosque & University
The oldest university in the world, and one of the first mosques, al-Azhar was built in 970 AD for the study of Qur'anic law and doctrine. There are more than 80,000 Islamic manuscripts in its libraries. While the basic curriculum in theology has changed very little since the time of the Mamelukes, the university has expanded to cover subjects such as medicine, physics and foreign languages. Courses in Islamic theology sometimes last as long as 15 years and the traditional Socratic method of teaching, with one tutor and a small group of students is still practiced. Over 4000 students from all over Islam receive free board and tuition and live all year on mats around the courtyard of the mosque. On the eastern side there is also a Chapel of the Blind which accommodates blind students.

The university is open Sundays to Thursdays and Saturdays from 9 am to 3 pm; and on Fridays from 9 to 11 am and 1 to 3 pm. Admission costs E£1 and for an extra 50 pt the guard will show you up the minaret for a great view of the complex. Women are required to cover their heads with scarves.

Wakala of al-Ghouri
This ancient caravanserai, at 3 Sharia al-Sheikh Mohammed Abdul, is excellently preserved and now serves as a cultural centre. It was built in 1505 and served as a merchants' hotel. The merchants would sleep in the rooms above where their animals were stabled and business would be carried out in the courtyard around the fountain. The courtyard now serves as a theatre and concert hall and the hotel rooms house a permanent exhibition of peasant and Bedouin crafts and host workshops for teaching traditional crafts. The wakala is around the corner from al-Azhar mosque and is open from 9 am to 5 pm daily except during Ramadan, when it's 9 to 11 am and 2 to 4 pm. Entrance fee is E£2.

Madrasa & Mausoleum of al-Ghouri
Opposite each other, at the intersection of Sharia al-Muizz al-Din Allah and Sharia al-Azhar are two of the last great Mameluke structures built before the Ottomans took control of Egypt. Al-Ghouri was the penultimate Mameluke Sultan who went all-out to ensure that he left his architectural mark on the city. During his 16 years of rule he managed, quite well, to perpetuate the Mamelukes' reputation for being thieves, murderers and tyrants. His *madrasa*, though elegant and peaceful, was apparently partly built from materials extorted or just simply stolen from other buildings.

However al-Ghouri, who was killed in a battle against the Turks near Aleppo in

Syria when he was well into his 70s, is not actually entombed in his mausoleum. The body there is that of his successor, the almost-lucky Sultan Tumanbay who was hanged three times from Bab Zuweila before the rope held together long enough to kill him.

Both monuments can be visited anytime the doors are open. Inside the *madrasa* there is a library, with a beautifully carved dome, and a community centre. In the 16th century, one part of the library was used as a bedroom; it's now a centre for typing lessons.

House of Gamal al-Din

This restored upper class 16th century merchant's house, at 6 Sharia Khush-qadam is worth visiting. Enter through the mammoth wooden door, continue through the foyer, where horses used to be tied up, and into the courtyard. Then call out for the guard who will show you around. Don't miss the beautiful *mashrabiyya* and stained glass windows of the 'business room'; when the sun shines through these, the effect is brilliant. The house is open from 9 am to 2 pm and admission costs 50 pt, or 25 pt for students.

Khan el Khalili to Bab el Futuh

This is the last set of the recommended things to see in Islamic Cairo, beginning at Khan el Khalili.

Khan el Khalili

The Khan is one of the largest bazaars in the Middle East, if not the world. It stretches from Sharia al-Muski, between Sharia Port Said and Midan Hussein, and up Sharia al-Muizz al-Din Allah or Sharia al-Gamaliyya to the Mosque of al-Hakim.

The bazaar began as a caravanserai, built in 1382 by Garkas el Khalili, Sultan Barquq's Master of Horse. When the Ottomans gained control of Egypt, the caravanserai changed from a fairly simple inn, where caravans rested and a little trade was carried out, to a fully-fledged Turkish bazaar which attracted traders and customers from throughout the world.

Today, the Khan is an immense conglomeration of shops and markets. As you wander through the labyrinth of narrow streets you'll find craftsmen building, dyeing, carving and sewing as well as shop after shop selling all manner of things from woodwork, glassware, leather goods, perfumes and fabrics to souvenirs and 'authentic' pharaonic antiques.

Some parts of the Khan are just tourist traps with anxious and aggressive shop-keepers eagerly rubbing their palms in anticipation of getting as many of your dollars as they can. These people are some of the greatest con-artists, salesmen and all-around smooth-talkers you will ever meet. Almost anything can be bought in the Khan and if one merchant doesn't have what you're looking for, then he'll find somebody who does.

Bargaining is the rule here but don't start haggling until you have an idea of the true price and never quote a price you're not prepared to pay. Most of all, take your time, have some fun, accept the tea or coffee they offer and play along with them. You're not obligated to buy and they won't be offended if you don't – though no doubt they'll keep up the sales pitch.

After you have finished roaming through the bazaar, stop at the famous *Fishawi's* café on Sharia Khan-il-Khalili. It's a colourful place where you can chat with the locals, puff on a *sheesha* (water pipe), or just sit and soak up the atmosphere.

Mosque of Sayyida al-Hussein

One of the most sacred places of Muslim worship in Cairo this mosque, opposite the al-Azhar Mosque and next to the bazaar, is revered as the final resting place of the head of al-Hussein, grandson of the Prophet. In 1153, almost 500 years after his death, al-Hussein's head was

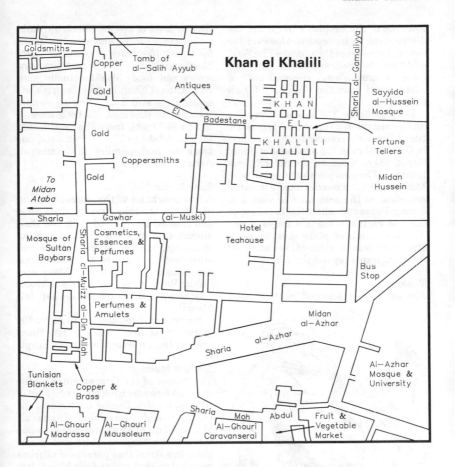

brought to Cairo in a green silk bag and placed in the Fatimid mosque which preceeded this more modern structure.

The powerful Umayyad family of Mecca, who were supported by the Prophet's favourite wife, had assumed control of the Caliphate after Mohammed had died without naming a successor. As Islam began to spread and gain more power in the world, the tribal tensions over the rights of succession to the position of the 'Apostle of God' also grew. Ali, who was the husband of Mohammed's daughter Fatima, put himself forward as the natural successor, claiming right by marriage. When he was passed over he took up arms against the Umayyads but was assassinated. His son Hussein, an actual blood-relative of the Prophet, then led a revolt but was killed in battle.

Their deaths resulted in the schism which still exists in Islam today. The followers of Hussein and Ali became *Shia*, or 'partisans of Ali' and refuse to acknowledge as Caliph anyone but descendants of Mohammed, believing only someone of the Prophet's blood has the divine right to succession. However the Sunni, followers of the *sunna* – The Way, still have the power and the majority and have banned any descendents of Mohammed from the Caliphate for all time.

Despite being the mausoleum of a Shi'ite martyr, the shrine of al-Hussein is one of the main congregational mosques in Cairo and even the president of Sunni Egypt prays there on special religious holidays. The mosque is not open to non-Muslims, though you can look in from the entrance, so the best time to visit it is during Ramadan when the breaking of the fast each evening is a major event. The square in front of the mosque comes alive with festive celebrations when all the restaurants lay out their food.

Muski

Almost always jammed with a solid

Street
Coffee Vendor

moving mass of people, Sharia al-Muski is the bazaar avenue where the locals shop for things like bolts of colourful cloth, plastic furniture, wedding portraits, toys, spices and food. Muski actually joins with Khan el Khalili, and though it's less exotic it is still interesting to wander through. It stretches, on both sides of Sharia al-Muski, from Sharia al-Muizz (al-Din Allah) to Sharia Port Said, one block in and parallel to Sharia al-Azhar.

Spice Bazaar

A true delight for all the senses is the *Suq al Attarin*, the spice bazaar, where dried and crushed flowers and fruit, add their aromas to that of the bags of saffron, cinnamon, ginger, pepper, cloves and other exotic or easily recognisable spices. The bazaar is next to the Mosque of Sultan Baybars, just off Sharia al-Muizz and down from Sharia Gawhar (al-Muski).

It would cost you about E£1.50 for 100 grams of saffron – easily 100 times cheaper than it would be outside Egypt.

Sharia al Muizz

The 'Street of the Coppersmiths' is the thoroughfare which takes you north out of Khan el Khalili. During the times of the Fatimids and Mamelukes Sharia al-Muizz al-Din Allah was the major avenue through the heart of Cairo and it was along this street that parades of pilgrims marched on their return from Mecca. It is still easy to imagine how life may have been here several centuries ago.

Mausoleum & Madrasa of al-Salih Ayyub

These were built in the 13th century by the last sultan of Salah al-Din's Ayyubid dynasty. Al-Salih Ayyub died before his complex was finished so it was completed by his wife, Shagarat al-Durr, who became one of Egypt's few female rulers. During the following Mameluke period the complex became Cairo's central court and executions were conveniently carried out just outside the doors on Sharia al-Muizz.

The *madrasa* is just off of Sharia al-Muizz on a small alley about 125 metres from Sharia al-Muski. The entrance is marked by an arch but there is not much left to see. The mausoleum can be entered by going back to Sharia al-Muizz and turning right. The door, below the dome on your right, will probably be locked but there will be someone around who can find the keeper.

The Mausoleum of Qalaun

There is actually a hospital, *madrasa* and mausoleum in this late 14th century complex opposite the tomb of al-Salih Ayyub. Qalaun, one of the most successful Mameluke Sultans, was also one of the longest-living (1220 to 1290) and founded a dynasty which lasted nearly a century.

A *maristan*, or hospital and insane asylum, has stood on this site for more than 700 years and a new modern facility has been built within the boundaries of the original. At a time when Christian Europe was locking up its sick and insane, Islam was providing enlightened medical care and sultans, like Qalaun, were building the facilities that enabled that care. Hospitals and separate clinics were established and even delicate surgery, such as the removal of cataracts, was done here.

The interior of Qalaun's mausoleum, especially near the entrance, is beautifully decorated and once your eyes become accustomed to the soft rainbow effect of sunlight through the stained-glass windows the tomb seems to be much larger than it actually is. *Mashrabiyya* screens, inlaid stone and carved stucco add to the overall feeling of peace and tranquillity that, in fact, pervades the entire Qalaun complex.

Mausoleum of al-Nasir Mohammed

Except for the facade, doorway and courtyard, there is very little left of this 14th century tomb which was one of several public works projects undertaken by Qalaun's son, al-Nasir Mohammed. He also built the mosque on the Citadel and the aqueduct from the Nile and his 40-year reign marked the pinnacle of Egyptian culture and prosperity under the Mamelukes.

The Gothic doorway was taken from a church in Acre (Israel) when al-Nasir and his Mameluke army ended Crusader domination there in 1290. Not many people visit the mausoleum and al-Nasir is actually buried in his father's tomb next door.

House of Uthman Katkhuda

Katkhuda was an 18th century city official who built his house from a 14th century palace. Despite his renovations it is still a fine example of Mameluke domestic architecture and what's left of the decor of the spacious interior shows the influences of both the 14th and 18th centuries. One of the best things about the house is that there won't be hordes of tourists around, in fact you may be the only one there, and the view from the roof is fantastic. Katkhuda's house is opposite the tomb of Qalaun, on a small street which runs east from Sharia al-Muizz. The doorway is about half-way down on the left side and you either knock or go upstairs and ask for someone to show you around. *Baksheesh* is expected, but wait until you have seen all you want to see.

Mosque of Barquq

Barquq was the first Burgi Mameluke Sultan and came to power, as did most of the Mamelukes, through a series of plots and murders. His beautifully restored mosque, with its black and white marble entrance way and silver-inlaid bronze door was built in 1386 as a *madrasa*. The colourful ceiling over part of the inner courtyard is supported by four pharaonic columns made of porphry quarried from near the Red Sea coast. Barquq's daughter is buried in the splendid domed tomb chamber, which is decorated with marble walls and floors and stained-glass windows, while the Sultan himself rests in his mausoleum in the Northern Cemetery.

Qasr Beshtak

Only a small part of this splendid 14th century palace remains. It's on Sharia al-Muizz just north of the Mosque of Barquq, on the right side, and was built on the foundations of an earlier Fatimid palace. The Emir Beshtak was a very wealthy man who was married to the daughter of Sultan al-Nasir. When he built this palace, in 1334, it had five storeys with running water on all floors.

The Sabil Kuttab of Abdul Katkhuda

Further down Sharia al-Muizz, where the street forks, is a *sabil kuttab* built in 1744 by Uthman Katkhuda's son, Abdul. The porches of the *kuttab*, a Qur'anic school for children, overhang the street on both sides of the fork and the remains of the great *sabil*, a covered, public drinking fountain, are underneath. The *kuttab* is still used as a local school and behind it is a 14th century apartment building.

Bayt al-Suhaymi

This superb merchant's house, built in the 16th and 17th century, is one of Cairo's greatest houses. It is excellently preserved, fully furnished and has a peaceful and elegant atmosphere that invites you to linger as long as possible. *Mashrabiyya* screens, latticed windows, beautiful tiling and arched galleries abound. Ask the self-appointed guides to show you the womens' bedroom and the harem reception room which overlooks the garden courtyard.

To find the house turn right on Darb al-Asfar, one block after the Mosque of Aqmar on Sharia al-Muizz, and it's No 19 on the left-hand side. Just knock on the big wooden door. Admission costs E£1, or 50 pt for students.

Bab al-Futuh

One of the original 60 gates of medieval Cairo, Bab al-Futuh is at the end of Sharia al-Muizz. Built in 1087 AD, and often called the Gate of Conquests, it was through this entrance that thousands of pilgrims returned from Mecca. Of the three remaining gates of Cairo, Bab al-Futuh has the most interesting interior. Wide stone-cut stairs lead to a large room with a high ceiling and there are narrow slits, just wide enough for arrows, cut in the sides of the room and along the tunnel which leads to Bab al-Nasr. Soldiers were once housed in this tunnel while awaiting their next battle. There's a wonderful view of the Fatimid wall, Bab al-Futuh, Bab al-Nasr and the minarets of al-Hakim. You can walk either through the tunnel or along the wall linking the two gates. Admission is 50 pt, or 25 pt for students. The caretaker usually sits in front of a café opposite the gate.

Bab al-Nasr

Still attached to Bab al-Futuh by a tunnel inside the old wall, this is the 'Gate of Victory'. If you're in the tunnel above this gate, look for the hole over the entrance. Boiling oil was poured through this aperture to discourage unwelcome visitors from entering the city. Wandering through the passageways between the gates is quite an eerie experience. Climb the stairs to the roof and the minaret of the adjoining Mosque of al-Hakim. Outside the gate and walls you can see the vast 'City of the Dead' with its tombs stretching for several km across the horizon. On the other side, walk across the roof to the Mosque of al-Hakim.

The Mosque of al-Hakim

The almost haunting mosque of the ruthless al-Hakim, has rarely been used as a mosque. Completed in 1010 it has, however, been used as a prison for Crusaders, as one of Salah al-Din's stables and as a warehouse by Napoleon. It's currently being repaired by members of the Ismaili sect of Shi'ite Islam, who claim the Fatimids as their religious ancestors and the Aga Khan as their spiritual leader.

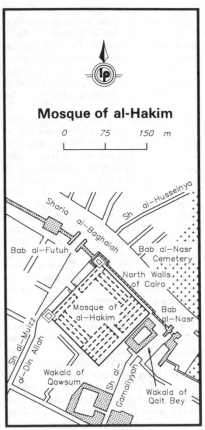

Mosque of al-Hakim

0   75   150   m

Sharia al-Baghalah

Sh al-Husseinya

Bab al-Futuh

Bab al-Nasr
Cemetery

North Walls
of Cairo

Mosque of
al-Hakim

Bab
al-Nasr

Sh al-Muizz al-Din Allah

Wakala of
Qawsum

Sh al-Gamaliyyah

Wakala of
Qait Bey

time riding around the streets of Cairo after dark on a donkey called Moon. On one such nightly jaunt he headed into the Moqattam hills, where he often went looking for portents from the stars, and was never seen again. Some believe he was murdered by his sister, whom he planned to marry; the Copts believe he had a visitation from Christ; while others, later to become the Druse, believe he formulated his own version of tolerant religion akin to Islam.

The Northern Cemetery

The 'City of the Dead' is a vast Mameluke necropolis inhabited by hundreds of thousands of Cairenes – both dead and alive. The dead are still buried there, in tombs which date from the 12th century, while the living exist, in what amounts to little more than a huge shanty town, amongst the impressive marble tombs of Mameluke sultans and nobles. On Fridays and holidays visitors flock to the 'city' to picnic and pay their respects to the dead. Sometimes you can see an entire family feasting atop a tomb and, wandering around this area, you often have to remind yourself that, yes, you really *are* in a cemetery. The city of the dead begins outside and to the right of Bab al-Nasr and Bab al-Futuh. As you leave Bab al Nasr turn right down Sharia Galal and walk about 1½ km; you'll cross Tariq Salah Salem (Rd) before entering the cemetery.

The Mausoleum of Barquq You will be able to see the minarets of this mausoleum, 1½ km from Bab al-Nasr, long before you cross into the City of the Dead. From the outside, the effect of its domes is reduced by the surrounding architecture but the interior of these high vaulted structures is quite splendid. The building was completed in 1411 and the tomb chambers contain the bodies of Barquq, who was moved from his mosque, his sons and the women of the family. Don't miss the beautiful marble *minbar*, or pulpit, and for a little

Al-Hakim was the third of the Fatimid caliphs, who ruled with absolute political, religious and military authority. His name means 'he who rules at the command of God', which was something he did with complete disregard for anyone but himself, and he's ranked close to the infamous Caligula in the dreadful treatment of his subjects. He restricted the free movement, around the city, of women, Jews and Christians; ordered decapitations for the slightest offences, sometimes out of mere personal dislike; incited riots which resulted in huge sections of the city being burnt; and spent an inordinate amount of *baksheesh* the caretaker will take you up the northern minaret. There is a magnificent view of Cairo, including the necropolis. Admission fee is 50 pt.

The Mausoleum of Sultan Baybars The interior of the decorated dome and the mosaics on the floor and *minbar* are the highlights of this mausoleum which was built in 1432. It is 50 metres down the road from Barquq's tomb, on the left side. Look for the guard, or have one of the children in the area find him, and he'll let you in for a bit of *baksheesh*.

The Mausoleum of Qait Bey Completed in 1474 and rated as one of the greatest buildings in Cairo, Qait Bey's tomb is also featured on the Egyptian one-pound note. The finely tapered minaret, which has three intricately decorated tiers, and its exquisite dome, stand out among the mausolea in the area. The splendid, refined interior is equally beautiful.

Sultan Qait Bey, a prolific builder, was the last Mameluke leader with any real power in Egypt. He ruled for 28 years and though he was as ruthless as the Mameluke sultans before him, he also had a reputation for fairness and a great love of beautiful architecture. The tomb contains the cenotaphs of Quait Bey and his two sisters, as well as two stones which supposedly bear the footprints of the Prophet.

Old Cairo

Originally a Roman fortress town called Babylon, this part of Cairo was of great importance to the early Christians. Egypt was one of the first countries to embrace the new Christian faith in the 1st century AD and the fortress was built, about 900 years before the Fatimids founded Cairo, on a then strategic point of the Nile. (The river has since shifted its course about 400 metres to the west.)

While the development of Coptic Christianity, and the monastic tradition it adopted after Paul of Thebes (St Paul) chose a life of solitude in the Egyptian desert, greatly influenced early European Christianity, for Egypt the Christian epoch was, in a sense, merely a period of transition from pharaonic times to the Islamic era.

However, during the several centuries that Christianity did predominate in Egypt this town, only five km south of where the Muslims would later build their city, became quite a metropolis. It was considered a holy place not only by the Copts but by the Jews and later the Muslims who lived in the area and, at one time, there were 20 churches and a synagogue there. The Christian monuments of Old Cairo, or Babylon, that have survived the centuries are still very important to the Copts. There are also several mosques in the area and Cairo's small Jewish population continues to worship at the ancient synagogue.

Old Cairo is 5½ km south of central Cairo. You can take either a bus; a taxi – ask for *Masr Qadima*; or the metro from Sayyida Zeinab Station, getting off at the second stop, Mari Girgis. Sayyida Zeinab Station is just over one km directly south of the Bab el Louk market. The metro only costs 10 pt, but it's usually crowded to the point where you could be risking your personal well-being by travelling on it.

The easiest bus to take is a water bus from the Radio & Television building just north of the Nile Hilton and Midan Tahrir. Get off at the Mari Girgis stop and walk the rest of the way. The 'land' bus is easier to take from, rather than to, Old Cairo as it's usually empty when it makes the return trip to Midan Tahrir. The Old Cairo terminus is north of the Coptic Museum, on the main street.

The Fortress of Babylon
The only remaining part of the fortress, built in 30 AD by the Emperor Augustus,

is a tower that was part of the waterside Roman battlements. The tower originally overlooked an important port on the Nile, before the river shifted course, and excavations directly below the tower have revealed part of the ancient quay, several metres below street level.

The Coptic Museum

The fortress's tower now marks the entrance to the tranquil courtyards and gardens of the Coptic Museum. The museum building itself, which is paved with mosaics and decorated with elegant *mashrabiyya* screens from old Coptic houses, is bright and airy. Its exhibits cover Egypt's Christian era from 300 to 1000 AD, showing the pharaonic, Graeco-Roman and Islamic influences on the artistic development of the Copts. It is the world's finest collection of Coptic religious and secular art and there are splendid examples of stonework, manuscripts, woodwork, metalwork, glass, paintings and pottery. The icons and textiles are particularly interesting.

The museum is open from 9 am to 4 pm, Sundays to Thursdays; and from 9 to 11 am and 1 to 4 pm on Fridays. Admission costs E£2, or E£1 for students.

The Church of al-Muallaqa

Dubbed the 'Hanging Church', it's one of the oldest Christian places of worship in Egypt. It was built atop one of the old fortress gatehouses with its nave suspended over the passage. Dedicated to the Virgin and properly known as Sitt Mariam, or St Mary, Al-Muallaqa is also one of Cairo's most beautiful churches.

Just inside the entrance, via a doorway in the walls just south of the Coptic Museum, there is an interesting 10th century icon of the Virgin and the Child. The inner courtyard is adorned with icons and the interior of the church, renovated many times over the centuries, is quite beautiful. In the centre, standing on 13 slender pillars representing Christ and his disciples, is a beautiful pulpit which is used only on Palm Sunday every year.

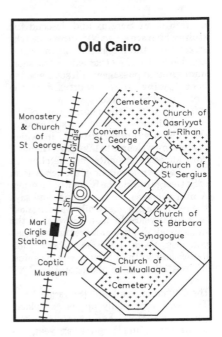

There is no admission fee because the church is still in use. Coptic Mass is held on Fridays from 8 to 11 am and on Sundays from 7 to 10 am. The ancient liturgical Coptic language is still used in part of the services.

Church & Monastery of St George

When you leave al-Muallaqa head back towards the train tracks and turn right on Sharia Mari Girgis, the street in front of the station. You will pass the Church of St George, one of the few remaining circular churches in the Middle East. The interior is a bit gutted from past fires, but the stained glass windows are bright and colourful. The monastery next door is closed to the public.

The Coptic Convent of St George

This is an especially interesting place to visit because of a rather strange ritual that is practised there. To get there follow the sign, on Sharia Mari Girgis, for the

Church of St Sergius and descend the stairs which are about 50 metres down the street from the monastery on the right-hand side. On the other side of the short underground passage you'll see a wooden door leading to the courtyard of the Convent of St George.

To the left of the church part of the convent there is a small room still used for the 'chain-wrapping ritual', in which visitors are welcome to take part. (Remove your shoes before entering the church.) The chains are symbolic of the persecution of St George during the Roman occupation. A nun oversees the 'wrapping' and says the requisite prayers, while standing next to a 1000-year-old icon. Several of the nuns speak English and are thrilled when you ask them questions about their beliefs and will gladly wrap you in chains. It's possible to take photographs.

The Church of Abu Serga (St Sergius)

This was supposedly one of the places where the Holy Family rested after fleeing from King Herod. Every year, on 1 June, a special mass is held here to commemorate the event. At the turn of the century this little church, which dates from the 10th century, was *the* most important pilgrimage spot in Old Cairo for visiting Christian tourists. There are 24 marble columns lining the central court and a series of 12th century icons above the *iconostasis* (a partition screen, bearing icons), which depict the 12 Apostles.

To get to St Sergius, leave the Convent of St George by the same door you entered, turn left and walk down the lane to the end. Pass under the low archway on the right and enter the church on the left side.

The Church of Sitt Barbara

This church is dedicated to St Barbara, who was beaten to death by her father for trying to convert him to Christianity. The church is similar to St Sergius and was restored during the Fatimid era. St Barbara's relics supposedly rest in a small chapel to the right of the nave and the remains of St Catherine, after whom the famous monastery in the Sinai was named, are also said to be here. To get there you turn right as you leave St Sergius; when you get to the end of the alley turn left and the Church of St Barbara is in front of you.

The Ben Ezra Synagogue

This is the oldest synagogue in Egypt and although there is no rabbi and services are rarely held, it is used by the 42 Jewish families that reside in the area. Set in a shady garden, it was built on the site of a 4th century Christian church which the Copts had to sell, in the 9th century, to enable them to pay taxes to Ibn Tulun for the construction of his mosque. The synagogue was named after a 12th century Rabbi of Jerusalem, Abraham Ben Ezra, and was severely damaged by Arabs after the 1967 war with Israel. It is still being repaired.

There are also many legends about the synagogue. It is said that the temple of the prophet Jeremiah once stood on the same spot and that Jeremiah is actually buried under a 'Miracle Rock' in the grounds. There is also a spring which is supposed to mark the place where the Pharaoh's daughter found Moses in the reeds *and* where Mary drew water to wash Jesus. The synagogue is a few metres south of the Church of St Barbara. Turn left when leaving the church and enter the first gate on your left; it's marked by a Star of David.

Fustat

Fustat was where Cairo first rose as a city. The area, behind Old Cairo, is being excavated by an American University in Cairo archaeological team and although the remains are scanty you can make out traces of alleyways, houses, wells and water pipe systems surrounded by a low wall. The entire area is covered with shards of pottery.

Fustat started out, in about 640 AD, as a tent city, a garrison town for the conquering Muslim army. It became the first Islamic capital in Egypt and for three centuries it continued to grow and prosper. At the height of its glory, before the conquering Fatimids founded the neighbouring city of Cairo in 969 AD, Fustat had a water supply, sewerage and sanitation facilities far superior to anything that was known in Europe before the 18th century. The city was destroyed and abandoned in 1168 to prevent it falling into the hands of the invading Crusader, King Amalric of Jerusalem.

To get to Fustat from Coptic Cairo head north up Sharia Mari Girgis till you see the Mosque of Amr on the right. Take Sharia Ain al-Sira, just south of the mosque, over a crossroad and then go left along a short lane to the Fustat site.

The Mosque of Amr

The original mosque, of which nothing remains, was the first place of Muslim worship built in Egypt. It was constructed in 642 AD by the victorious invader Amr, the same general who founded Fustat, it is said, on the site where he had pitched his tent. The present mosque structure probably dates back to 827. It's a few blocks north of the fortress but not all that interesting. Admission costs E£1 or 50 pt for students.

The Pottery District

Behind the mosque and nestled beneath smouldering mounds that are actually workshop roofs and kilns is a community of potters. You can wander around and watch the artisans at work, making and firing pottery vessels and utensils.

Giza

Giza is a district of Cairo which begins opposite the west side of Roda Island and stretches 18 km westward to the Great Pyramids. Most of the things of interest are either near the Nile or on the outskirts, at the end of Sharia al-Ahram (Pyramids Rd). All of the following sights are accessible by bus, minibus or taxi.

The Great Pyramids of Giza

The ancient Greeks ranked them one of the Seven Wonders of the World; they are Egypt's most visited monuments and one of the world's greatest tourist attractions. For centuries the Great Pyramids of Giza have intrigued and puzzled visitors and even now, in the space-age of the 20th century, it would be difficult to stand before them and not be completely overwhelmed. For 4½ millenia, surviving the rise and fall of great dynasties and outlasting Egypt's many conquerors, they have shared the desert plateau of Giza with smaller attendant pyramids, some for royal wives; rows of *mastabas*, the tombs of 4th and 5th dynasty princes and nobles; and of course the imposing, enigmatic figure of the Sphinx.

It was not an obsession with death, or a fear of it, on the part of the ancient Egyptians that led to the construction of these incredible mausolea. It was rather, a belief in life, eternal life and the desire to ultimately be one with the immense, timeless cosmos that transformed their tombs from underground crypts into monuments that, by their very design, were reaching for the heavens. There was also the fact that a pharaoh was the son of a god and sole receiver of the *ka*, the life force that emanated from the god. The pharaoh, in turn, was the conduit of this vital force to his people, so in life and death he was worshiped as a god.

The pyramid then, was not just an indestructible sanctum for the preservation of the pharaoh's *ka*; nor simply an incredible, geometrically designed pile of stones raised over the mummified remains of a vain king, and his treasures, to ensure his immortality. It was actually the apex of a much larger funerary complex, that provided a place of worship for his

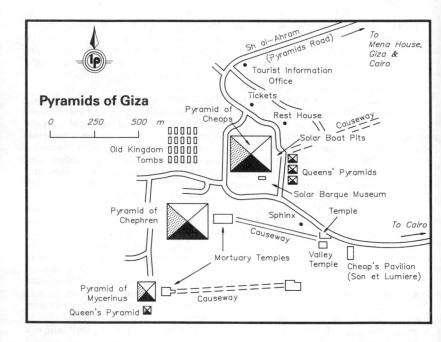

Pyramids of Giza

Sh al–Ahram (Pyramids Road)

To Mena House, Giza & Cairo

Tourist Information Office

Tickets

Rest House

Pyramid of Cheops

Causeway

0   250   500   m

Old Kingdom Tombs

Solar Boat Pits

Queens' Pyramids

Solar Barque Museum

Pyramid of Chephren

Sphinx

Temple

To Cairo

Causeway

Mortuary Temples

Valley Temple

Cheop's Pavilion (Son et Lumiere)

Pyramid of Mycerinus

Causeway

Queen's Pyramid

subjects, as well as a visible, inescapable reminder of the absolute and eternal power of the gods and their universe.

Egypt's first pyramid, in Pharaoh Zoser's mortuary complex at Saqqara, was a 62-metre-high marvel of masonry; a product of the technical brilliance of Imhotep, the pharaoh's grand vizier and high priest. Built around 2670 BC it was the first time stone had been used to such an extent and with such artistry and precision. Imhotep's architectural genius changed the face of Egypt but it was his skill in supervising such a grand project and his recognition that organisation was a vital key in the development of a new civilisation that had far more lasting implications. The age of the pyramids lasted only 200 years but less than one century after Imhotep's tribute to his pharaoh there arose from the sands of Giza the perfection and enormity of the Great Pyramid of Cheops. In mastering the formidable logistics involved in its construction the ancient Egyptians stumbled on the principle of the organised state.

The mortuary complexes of Cheops, Chephren and Mycerinus, who were father, son and grandson, included a pyramid – the pharaohs' tomb, which was also a repository for all his household goods, clothes and treasure; a funerary temple on the east side of the pyramid; pits for the storage of the pharaoh's *solar boats* – his mode of transport in the afterlife; a valley temple on the banks of the Nile; and a causeway from the river to the pyramid. The entrance passageways, as with all 80 royal pyramids found in Egypt, face north towards the polar star; the tomb chambers inside face west, towards the location of the Kingdom of the Dead; and the mortuary temples outside face east, towards the rising sun.

The pyramids and temples at Giza were built from stone quarried locally and from the Moqqatam Hills. Napoleon estimated that there would be enough stones in the three main pyramids alone to build a wall, three metres high, all around France.

Every visit to the Great Pyramids includes a stroll, or sometimes a run, through a veritable obstacle course of hustlers, con artists, souvenir shops, alabaster factories, papyrus museums and self-appointed, and usually unwanted, guides. However, don't despair; escape from this maddening onslaught is possible.

The best strategy is to just ignore them, though this is not always easy. An alternative is to rent a horse or camel and gallop or flow or get jolted through the desert around the pyramids. There are stables just up from the tourist office on Pyramids Rd. You can also try approaching one of the many camel and horse owners around the pyramids. It is better to approach them first rather than vice versa because then you have more chance of being the one who determines what will be negotiated. Once you set off, if you haven't already set a price the camel driver will begin doing 'special' things for you, like taking a more scenic route to an extra tomb or two, and at the end of your ride he'll list all the extra charges. So set a price before you even touch the animal and if your guide offers extra things en route find out the price. It should cost about E£4 an hour and the best time to go for a ride is at sunset, ending at Cheops' Pavilion just as the Sound and Light show illuminates the pyramids and Sphinx.

There is no admission charge for the site at Giza so you can roam around the outside of the pyramids and the Sphinx. However, there is an entry fee of E£5 (E£3 for students) to climb up the inside

The Sphinx

of the pyramids and a separate charge of E£4 to enter the Solar Boat museum next to the pyramid of Cheops.

Plan on spending at least half a day around the pyramids. The site is open from 8 am to 4.30 pm daily, though the interior chambers usually close at about 3.30 pm. The best times to visit are at sunrise, sunset, and night. During the day it can get very hot and crowded and the hazy sky makes it difficult to take photographs.

Ride to Saqqara Another adventurous possibility is to rent a camel, donkey or horse for the three-hour ride, each way, across the desert to Saqqara. The cost is approximately E£15 for a horse and E£20 for a camel. Don't forget that a camel can carry two people. This trip is not really for inexperienced riders. By the end of the day you will have spent about six or seven hours atop a horse or camel and a few more hours roaming around the sites at Saqqara.

The Pyramid of Cheops
The Great Pyramid, the oldest at Giza and the largest in Egypt, stood 146.5 metres high when it was completed in 2690 BC. After 45 centuries its height has only been reduced by nine metres. Approximately 2,500,000 limestone blocks, weighing six million tons, were used in the construction and, it supposedly took 10 years to build the causeway and the massive earth ramps used as a form of scaffolding, and 20 years to raise the pyramid itself. The job was done by a highly skilled corps of masons, mathematicians, surveyors and stone cutters as well as about 100,000 men who carried out the back-breaking task of moving and laying the stones. The blocks had to be exactly placed to prevent excess pressure building up on any one point and causing the collapse of the whole structure.

Although there is not much to see inside the pyramid of Cheops, the experience of climbing through such an ancient structure is unforgettable. The entrance, on the north face, leads to a descending passage which ends in an unfinished tomb (usually closed) about 100 metres along and 30 metres below the pyramid. About 20 metres from the entrance, however, there is an ascending passage, 1.3 metres high and one metre wide, which continues for about 40 metres before opening into the Great Gallery, which is 47 metres long and 8.5 metres high. There is also a smaller horizontal passage leading into the so-called Queen's Chamber. As you ascend the Great Gallery to the King's Chamber at the top notice how precisely the blocks were fitted together. Unlike the rest of the pyramid, the main tomb chamber, which is just over five metres wide and 10 metres long, was built of red granite blocks. The roof, which weighs more than 400 tons, is formed of nine huge, slabs of granite, above which are another four slabs separated by chambers designed to distribute the enormous weight away from the chamber. There is plenty of oxygen in this room as Cheops had it built so that fresh air flowed in from two shafts on the north and south walls.

Climbing the outside of the Great Pyramid has been a popular adventure for centuries and although it's officially forbidden, and guards will do what they can to stop you, it is still possible. But be careful, especially coming down again. There are plenty of 'guides' to show you the way and it's recommended to follow one as each year a few people fall off and die. It takes about 20 minutes to get to the top and it's quite a climb as many of the blocks will be taller than you are. The view of Cairo and the surrounding desert from the summit is magnificent.

Back on the ground around the Great Pyramid are five long pits which once contained the pharaoh's boats. These *solar barques* possibly brought the mummy of the dead pharaoh across the Nile from the valley temple, from where it was brought up the causeway and placed in the tomb

Top: The pyramids at Giza (HF)
Bottom: The Sphinx & the Pyramid of Cheops, Giza (SW)

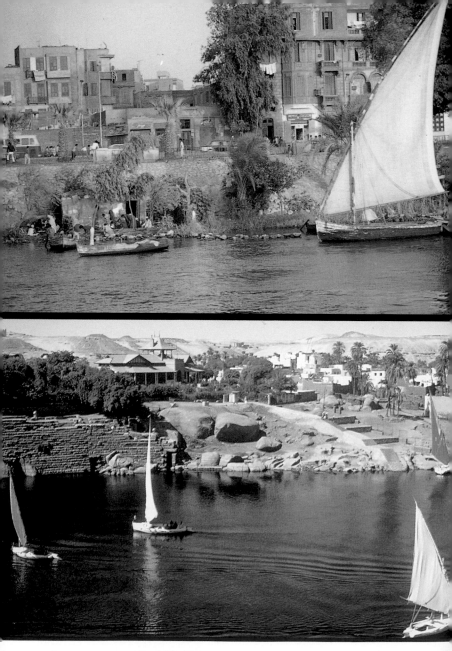

Top: Felucca on the Nile, Cairo (SW)
Bottom: The Nile at Aswan (HF)

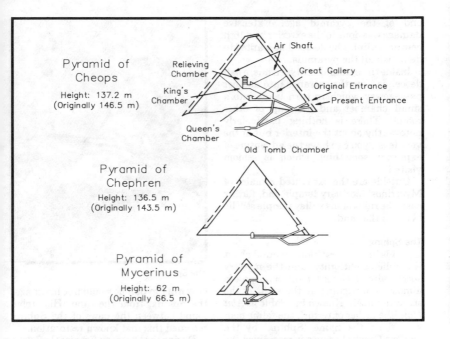

Pyramid of
Cheops

Height: 137.2 m
(Originally 146.5 m)

Air Shaft

Relieving
Chamber

Great Gallery

King's
Chamber

Original Entrance

Present Entrance

Queen's
Chamber

Old Tomb Chamber

Pyramid of
Chephren

Height: 136.5 m
(Originally 143.5 m)

Pyramid of
Mycerinus

Height: 62 m
(Originally 66.5 m)

chamber. The boats were then buried around the pyramid to provide transport for the king in the next world. One of these ancient wooden vessels, possibly the oldest boat in existence, was unearthed in the 1950s. The sacred barge was restored and a glass museum built over it to protect it from damage from the elements.

On the east side of the pyramid are the Queens' Pyramids, three small structures about 20 metres high, which resemble little more than pyramid-shaped piles of rubble. They were the tombs of Cheops' wives or sisters.

The Pyramid of Chephren

South-west of the Great Pyramid and almost the same dimensions, Chephren's pyramid at first seems larger than that of his father's because it stands on higher ground and its peak still retains part of the original limestone casing which once

covered the whole structure. It is 136.5 metres high (originally 143.5 metres) and although the chambers and passageways are less elaborate than the ones in Cheops' pyramid they are also less claustrophobic. The entrance leads down into a passage and then across to the burial chamber which still contains the large granite sarcophagus of Chephren.

One of the most interesting features of this pyramid are the substantial remains of Chephren's mortuary temple outside to the east. Several rooms can be visited and the causeway, which originally provided access from the Nile to the tomb, still leads from the main temple to the valley temple.

The Pyramid of Mycerinus

At a height of 62 metres (originally 66.5 metres), this is the smallest pyramid of the three and its construction, between 2525 and 2500 BC, effectively marked the end of the pyramid age. Extensive damage was done to the exterior by a 16th century caliph who decided he wanted to demolish all the pyramids.

Inside the pyramid of Mycerinus, a hall descends from the entrance into another passageway which in turn leads into a small chamber and a group of other rooms. There is nothing particularly noteworthy about the interior but at the very least, you can have the adventure of exploring something which is seldom visited.

Outside are the excavated remains of Mycerinus' mortuary temple and, further east, the ruins of his valley temple still lie beneath the sand.

The Sphinx
Legends and superstitions abound about this relic of antiquity, and the mystery surrounding its long-forgotten purpose is almost as intriguing as the sight of the structure itself. Known in Arabic as *Abu Hol*, 'the father of terror', the feline man was given the name 'Sphinx' by the ancient Greeks because it resembled the mythical winged monster with a woman's head and lion's body, who proposed a riddle to the Thebans and killed all who could not guess the answer.

Carved almost entirely from one huge, solid piece of limestone left standing in the quarry from which Cheops cut the stones for his pyramid, the Sphinx is about 50 metres long and 22 metres high. It is not known when it was carved but one theory is that it was Chephren who thought of shaping the rock into a lion's body with a god's face, wearing the royal headress of Egypt. Another theory is that it is the likeness of Chephren himself that has been staring out over the desert sands for so many centuries.

One legend about the Sphinx is associated with the fact that it was engulfed by sand and hidden completely for several hundred years. The sun god *Ra-Harakhte* appeared to the man who was to become Tuthmosis IV and promised him the

The Sphinx

crown of Egypt if he would free his image, the Sphinx, from the sand. His stelae found between the paws of the Sphinx recorded this first known restoration.

During the Ottoman Empire the Turks used the Sphinx for target practice and its nose and beard, which are now in the British Museum, fell off. A team of American and Egyptian archaeologists is currently restoring parts of the Sphinx and negotiations are underway to have his nose and beard returned.

The Tomb of Khenthawes
This imposing structure, opposite the Great Pyramid and north of Mycerinus' causeway, is the tomb of Khenthawes, daughter of Pharaoh Mycerinus and, eventually, Queen of Userkaf and founder of the 5th Dynasty. The tomb is a rectangular building cut into a small hill and you can go down a corridor at the back of the chapel room to the burial chambers. The descent is a bit tricky and could be hazardous, so be careful when exploring this rarely visited site.

Cemeteries

Around the pyramids there are private cemeteries with several rows of tombs, most of which are closed to the public, organised in a sort of grid pattern. The tombs of *Qar, Idu and Queen Mersyankh III*, in the eastern cemetery, are accessible but it's sometimes difficult to find the guard who has the keys. The *tomb of Iasen* in the western cemetery contains interesting inscriptions and wall paintings which show life and work 2500 years ago during the Old Kingdom.

Sound & Light Show

The Sphinx takes the role of the narrator in this show which, though designed with the tourist in mind, is definitely worth seeing. The booming narrative and all-around sound which accompanies the colourful illumination of the pyramids and Sphinx is an entertaining way to learn a little of Egypt's ancient history.

The are two *son et lumiere* shows every evening with various languages scheduled for different nights of the week. There is open air seating on the terrace of Cheops Pavilion, near the Sphinx and facing Chephren's valley temple. Admission costs E£4, but if you go beyond the pavilion and sit on the wall (watch out for the guards) you can see almost as much as when you pay for a seat.

The following is a schedule of performances.

Day	1st show (sunset)	2nd show (7.30 pm)
Monday	English	French
Tuesday	French	German
Wednesday	English	French
Thursday	Arabic	English
Friday	English	French
Saturday	English	French
Sunday	French	German

During summer, the sunset show has the same schedule but there is no second show, except on Fridays (in French) and Sundays (in German). During Ramadan the first show starts at 8.30 pm.

Getting There For the mere pittance of 10 pt you can have the bone-crushing

MINISTRY OF CULTURE
SOUND AND LIGHT
SPECTACLE
PYRAMIDS AND SPHINX
(SON ET LUMIERE)

P. T. 500

№ 188820

experience of riding bus No 8, 9 or 900 almost all the way to the pyramids. All three leave from the terminal in front of the *Mogamma* on Midan Tahrir and drop you at the Mena House Hotel on Sharia al-Ahram.

A much more practical and comfortable alternative is to take a minibus. Most of the minibuses are converted Volkswagen or Toyota vans and it costs 25 pt for the trip to the pyramids. They leave when full (not jammed to the hilt though), from in front of the *Mogamma*. You will hear the drivers calling out *ahram, ahram* – which means 'pyramids'. The minibuses will drop you off at the corner of Pyramids Rd and a canal road.

Another way to get through Giza and out to the pyramids is to take a taxi which should cost about E£5. However, you may have to bargain and argue with the driver to get this price.

Pyramids Road

The road to the pyramids is called Sharia al-Ahram or Pyramids Rd, and was built in the 1860s so that Empress Eugenie could travel the 11 km from Cairo in her carriage. The road was another in a long list of public works projects initiated by Khedive Ismail. He also had a palace built for the Empress, so that she would have a place to stay while attending the ceremonies for the opening of the Suez Canal. The Pyramids Rd intersects Sharia El Giza about 500 metres south of the Zoo.

Before you go to the pyramids, you might want to first turn left at Midan al-Galaa, from Tahrir St, on to Sharia El Giza to see a couple of interesting buildings. The first big building on your left after you pass the Cairo Sheraton is the *Soviet Embassy*. Ironically, or perhaps strangely, the *Official Residence of the President of the Republic* is next to it. About one km further south along Sharia El Giza you will see the entrance to the zoo. The buses to the pyramids pass by here.

The Cairo Zoological Gardens

The zoo, near Cairo University between Gamiat El Qahira (Cairo University St) and Sharia El Giza, is worth a visit especially if you've had an overdose of ancient tombs and medieval mosques. The animals aren't the healthiest, but it's still pleasant to get away from the Cairo chaos, walk around the grounds and toss a few peanuts to the beasts. Avoid the place on holidays, Fridays and Saturdays though as it becomes extremely crowded. There's a restaurant on an island in the centre of the park. Opening hours are 9 am to 5 pm and admission costs 10 pt.

Faculty of Agriculture

Just south of the zoo before Midan Giza, one of Mohammed Ali's palaces is still being used – as the home of the Cairo University Faculty of Agriculture. The palace/faculty is worth visiting if you can get permission from the Tourist Police. The large swimming pool was used by Mohammed Ali's harem, and downstairs in the basement, the remnants of his torture chambers are still visible.

Kerdassa

Many of the *galabiyyas*, scarves, rugs and weavings sold in the bazaars and shops of Cairo are made in this village near Giza. To get there, head down Sharia al-Ahram towards the pyramids and turn right at the second canal and follow the road to the village of Kerdassa. The minibus begins and ends its trips at the junction of this canal and Sharia al-Ahram. Many tourists now visit this village in search of bargains, so it's probably no longer the great place it once was for special deals.

The camel trail across the Western Desert to Libya begins in Kerdassa. If you're looking for an incredibly challenging adventure (only for the initiated!) join a caravan here.

Places to Stay – bottom end

Cairo is full of inexpensive hotels and pensiones. The prices can be deceiving

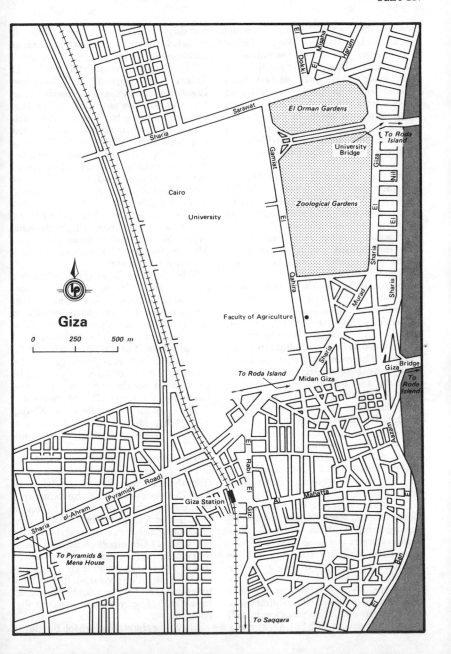

Giza

0   250   500 m

because they aren't always accurate indicators of the hotel's quality, or lack of it. Prices are also sometimes subject to individual negotiation. So consider the room rates given here as estimates because although they were obtained directly from the hotels, travellers have reported paying more, or less, for the same accommodation. The Youth Hostel is the cheapest place to stay in Cairo; see the Roda Island section following.

Central The *Golden Hotel* (tel 742659), 13 Talaat Harb, Cairo is between Midan Tahrir and Midan Talaat Harb – a great location. It was once somewhat of an institution among travellers, but it has deteriorated over the years and gets few recommendations. Bed bugs are rife. A double with shower costs E£6, a single E£3 and a mattress on the floor in a common room is E£2. Use of a refrigerator and stove is included and bottles of mineral water are on sale.

The *Tulip Hotel* (tel 758433), 3rd floor, 3 Midan Talaat Harb, is right on the Midan (also known as Suleiman Pasha Square). The rooms are a bit dark and bleak, but otherwise OK. The bathrooms are dirty and not all rooms have hot water. You can ask one of the staff to fire up the hot water heater and water pump on the 4th floor for a nice steamy shower. It costs E£8.65 for a single, E£12 for a double with shower, E£13.25 for a double with bath. For 50 pt one of the hotel clerks will register your passport for you at the *Mogamma* government building.

The *Hotel Beau Site* (tel 749877), 5th floor, 27 Talaat Harb St, is down a small alley just off of Talaat Harb St. Five flights of stairs is a long way to carry a heavy pack. Many travellers say that this is an interesting place to stay and more than one 'star' has been discovered here by Cairene advertising men on the hunt for foreign faces for local TV commercials. Other reports about this place are mixed. Rooms range from OK but dark, dusty and dirty to darker, dustier and dirtier. It costs E£4 for singles and E£7 for doubles including breakfast.

The *Oxford Pensione* (tel 758172), 32 Talaat Harb, opposite the Hotel des Roses, has been another long-time favourite way-station. You've heard of five star ratings, well this hotel gets a five roach rating. However, despite the roaches, bed bugs and dirty bathrooms the Oxford is still popular with a lot of hard-core trans-Africa travellers. A variety of activities can be arranged and things obtained here, especially information. There are 32 rooms and prices vary, but average about E£2.50 a single, E£5 a double or E£1 for a mattress on the floor. All prices seem negotiable, but don't consider this a rule. Most rooms have three to four beds and sometimes hot water.

The *Hotel des Roses* (tel 758022), 4th floor, 33 Talaat Harb, near the junction with Abdel Khaliq Sarwat St, has singles for E£4.40 and doubles with showers for up to E£6.60. This is probably one of the best deals in town. The bathrooms are usually clean. The dining room is well-lit so you can see your breakfast in the mornings (if you really want to). Try to get a room on the top floor along the balcony as the views of Cairo are great.

The *Pensione de Famille*, Abdel Khaliq Sarwat St, just off Talaat Harb, is a pleasant place with singles for about E£2.50.

The *Hotel Select*, 8th floor, 19 Adly St, is next to the synagogue. It's clean and friendly and costs E£2.40 a single and E£4.75 a double including breakfast and hot water. It's also possible to get a mattress on the floor here for E£2.

The *Anglo-Swiss Pensione* (tel 759191), 6th floor, 14 Champollion St, is a clean and comfortable favourite among travellers. A few rooms are a bit grimy but for the most part it's a good deal. It costs E£5 for a single and E£8 for a double including breakfast. The elevator occasionally conks out.

The *Swiss Hotel*, Sharia Moh Bassiuni,

down the street from Midan Talaat Harb has small singles for E£3 and doubles for E£5.50, including breakfast. This is a good place to meet other travellers. Try and stay on the 6th floor as there have been reports of things getting ripped off on the 5th floor.

The *Pensione Roma* (tel 911088), 169 Imad El Din (the extension of Mohammed Farid St), near the junction with Adly St, is definitely one of the best of the budget hotels. Every traveller I've met who has stayed here highly recommends it. Doubles are E£9.50 with breakfast included. The entrance is opposite the El Walid clothing store.

The *Luna Park* (tel 918626), 65 El Gumhuriya St, is a good clean place for the budget traveller. Each room comes with soap, towels, toilet paper and a sink with hot and cold water. A small café and bar are attached to the hotel. Singles are E£5, doubles are E£10. It is between Midan Ramses and Midan Opera.

The *Plaza Hotel*, 8th floor, 32 Kasr El Nil St, is next to the Galion children's store near Mustafa Kamel Square. It's a good clean place with hot water and costs E£3 a single and E£6 a double including breakfast.

Around Ramses Square The *Everest Hotel*

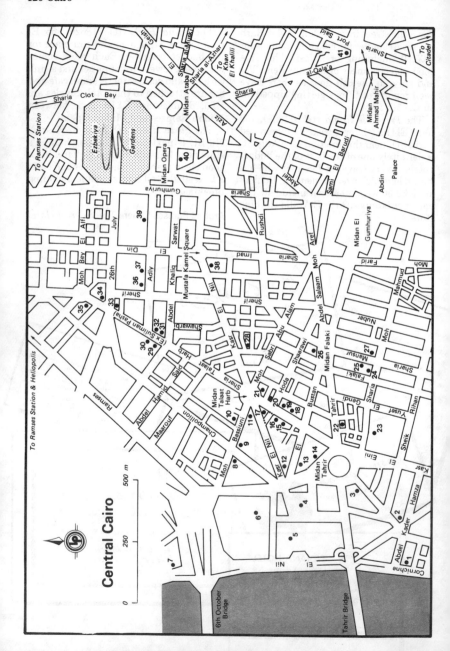

Central Cairo

(tel 74270...
tallest buil...
station. It ha...
and 16th floc...
restaurant and...
floor. The room...
otherwise clean...
showers or E£6...
doubles with or wi...   ...cost E£6
or E£7.25. Breakfa...   ...s E£1.25, lunch
is E£3.95 and dinner E£4.05. All of the
people on the reception desk claim to be
doctors and say they make more money
working at the desk than as doctors for the
government at E£60 per month. The low
prices, nearness to the train station and
fantastic views from the balcony have
made this a popular place.

Roda Island The *Manyal Youth Hostel*
(tel 840729), 135 Abdel Aziz al-Saud St, is
near Manyal Palace. It used to be a dump,
but has now been cleaned up and there
are meals, locks on the doors and clean
bathrooms. It's a good place to pick up
information from other travellers and the
mosquitoes and cats are plentiful enough
to ensure constant companionship (of a
sort). This is definitely the cheapest place
to stay in the city and is only 30 minutes
from Midan Tahrir. It costs 60 pt for
members under 21 years and 80 pt for
members over 21 and non-members.
Hostel membership costs E£12. To get
there you take bus No 8 or 900 from Midan
Tahrir and get off at the University
Bridge; or bus No 95 from Ramses
Station.

Giza The *Tiba House Hotel*, 6 Aly
Mohammed St (corner of King Faisal Rd)
is 10 minutes walk from the pyramids and
nine km from Tahrir Square. The hotel is
relatively new, has 40 rooms and each
floor has its own toilets and showers. The
rooms are all very clean and some have
views of the pyramids. There's a small
restaurant attached to the hotel where
you can get a sandwich at any time of the
day or night. Singles cost E£5 and

...8.90, including breakfast. ...longer than one week, you can ...tiate the price.

Places to Stay – middle

Central *The Garden City House* (tel 3544969), 23 Kamel El Din Salah St, Garden City, is around the corner from the American Embassy. Look for the small sign outside the 3rd floor and the bronze plaque at the front of the building. The American University in Cairo and the American Embassy send a lot of people here. Rooms are medium sized without bath, large without bath or large with bath and cost, respectively, E£14, E£16 and E£19 for singles; or E£22, E£24 or E£28 for doubles. All prices include compulsory half-board, taxes and breakfast. Reservations are recommended.

The *Lotus Hotel* (tel 750627), 12 Talaat Harb St opposite Felfelas, is one of the best deals in this price range. The elevator to the reception desk is through an arcade which almost faces Hoda Shaarawi St. The rooms are clean and comfortable and range in price from E£14.31 for a single without bath to E£17.45 for a single with a bath and air conditioning. Doubles with and without bathrooms are about E£18 to E£21. There's also a restaurant, bar and sundeck on the top floor.

The *Hotel Viennoise* (tel 743103), 11 Mohammed Bassiuni St, is down the street from the Swiss Hotel (going away from Midan Talaat Harb). Big dusty single rooms with hot water, televisions, and telephones are E£15.30 and doubles are E£20. This place is over priced at any price. There are much better deals.

The *National Hotel* (tel 745625), 30 Talaat Harb St, is past Midan Talaat Harb away from Midan Tahrir. The hotel is large and busy with a loud disco in front and a much quieter café behind. Single rooms with baths are E£10 per night and doubles with baths are E£12. These prices are reputedly negotiable. Avoid the restaurant which faces the street as their prices are absurd and their service dreadful.

The *Claridge Hotel*, near the corner of Talaat Harb and 26th July streets, is a place to stay away from. For E£11.80 a double you get a dirty room and a lousy breakfast.

The *Grand Hotel* (tel 757509), 17 26th July St, on the intersection with Talaat Harb St, is definitely one of the best deals in town. Singles cost E£15.50 with a shower or E£9.30 without; while doubles with or without a shower are E£21.15 or E£14.30. The rooms are some of the cleanest and most comfortable I have seen in Egypt (especially at these prices), and all have sinks, dressers and clothing stands. Breakfast is included; lunch costs E£4 and dinner E£4.50.

The *New Riche Hotel* (tel 900145), 47 Sharia Abdel Aziz, near Midan Ataba, is a new hotel with singles for E£22 including a shower and air conditioning.

The *Hotel Montana*, 7th floor, 23-25 Sherif St, was being renovated at the time of writing. Sparkling new showers were being installed and the management expected prices to be about E£11 a single and E£15 a double.

The *Windsor Hotel* (tel 915277), 19 Moh Bey El Alfi St near Ezbekiya Gardens, is great if you want lots of class and comfort. It's a bit more costly here but worth it and the Windsor has an interesting history. During the Ottoman Empire, it was the private bathhouse of the Turkish leaders; it was used to house Russian engineers during the construction of the Aswan Dam; and because it served as the British Officers Club it was set on fire during the 1952 revolution. The lounge/bar is a great place to read newspapers or write letters. Rooms with showers cost E£16/20 for singles/doubles; or with a shower and toilet they're E£24/ 30. Air conditioning, TVs, fans and heaters are available for a small extra charge. Breakfast costs E£1.85, lunch is E£5 and dinner E£5.50. Add 14% taxes and service charges.

Around Ramses Square The *Fontana Hotel* (tel 922321), Ramses Square, is on your left as you leave the train station. There are clean double rooms for E£18 or singles for E£12. Even the sheets are clean and towels are provided. There are also fans in all rooms or air conditioning is available for E£3. There's a swimming pool and disco on the 8th floor.

Islamic Cairo The *Hotel el Hussein* (tel 918089), in El Hussein Square, is about as close to the centre of Islamic Cairo and the Khan el Khalili bazaar as you can get in a hotel. The rooms are clean and well-maintained and the restaurant on the roof has a fantastic view of medieval Cairo. Singles with bathrooms cost E£11.50 or E£9 without; and doubles with bathrooms cost E£16.40 or E£12.40 without. Air conditioning, a telephone and hot water are included; a TV or fan and the 14% service and taxes are extra.

Dokki *The Indiana Hotel* (tel 714503), 16 Hasan Rostom St, around the corner from the Museum of Modern Art, has very clean singles for E£33.76 and doubles for E£43.36. Some rooms have televisions and refrigerators.

Places to Stay – top end
Almost all of the world's major hotel chains have hotels in Cairo. Their prices, standards and amenities are on a par with others overseas. Prices are sometimes a bit lower, but they are still out of the range of the budget traveller, unless you're treating yourself to a big splurge. A few of the 'top end' hotels are interesting to visit and pleasant places to seek refuge from the chaos and cacophony of Cairo's streets.

The *Cairo Mariott* (tel 408888) Saray el Gezira St, Zamalek, is in a palace built by Khedive Ismail in 1869 to accommodate Empress Eugenie while she attended the opening ceremonies of the Suez Canal. It is 19th century elegance at its best with polished marble floors, engraved brass lamps and ornately carved *mashrabiyya* screens. Have a *Stella* beer in the garden next to the swimming pool.

The *Meridien Hotel – Le Caire* (tel 845444), Corniche el-Nil, Roda Island, is right on the river and the views are magnificent. Drop in to take photos, or for E£7 you can partake of an all-you-can-eat breakfast buffet by the Nile.

The *Cosmopolitan Hotel* (tel 743956), Ibn Taalab St is just off of Kasr El Nil St. It costs much less than the big name hotels and could, perhaps, be a manageable final splurge. It has beautifully plush old rooms with lacquered cabinets. Doubles cost E£31.25, singles are E£25; breakfast is E£2.20, lunch E£5.50 and dinner E£6.90, with the 14% service charge and taxes extra.

Camping
There are camping facilities in Giza, with a view of the pyramids from the rear of the grounds, owned by an Egyptian with a Swiss-German education. *Camping Salome* is next to a carpet school called the Wissa Wassef School and camping costs E£1 per person. There are 12 toilets and cold showers and the one hot shower costs 50 pt per person. There's a bar where you can get meals of grilled pigeon, kufta and kebab. To get there, head down Sharia al-Ahram toward the pyramids and turn left at the Mariouteh Canal which you follow until you see signs for the campgrounds on your left.

Places to Eat
Eating in Cairo is a real treat. There are thousands of cafés, teahouses and market stalls where you can find exotic or plain food and where it's easy to have a very filling meal for less than E£1. On the more expensive front there are plenty of restaurants serving European dishes and places where you can get a hamburger or other western imports.

Cheaper Restaurants
Central – Between Midan Tahrir & Midan Talaat Harb *Felfelas* (tel 752751), 15 Hoda Shaarawi St, near Talaat Harb St, is the best all-round restaurant in Cairo.

It's a favourite among Egyptians and foreigners alike, and a great many cats (who ensure that mice and rats don't make it their favourite place too). Your dinner of fuul, ta'amiyya, stuffed vine leaves, tahina, pigeon and tea can cost as little as E£1 to E£2. Try the desserts: *Om Ali* is a pastry baked with milk, raisins and nuts; and there's *baked rice and milk* and the *Felfela cocktail* of ice cream, rice pudding and nuts. Check out the tiny crocodiles and turtles in the aquariums.

Felfela Sandwich Take-Away is just around the corner from the main restaurant. They have excellent ta'amiyya sandwiches for 7 pt to 10 pt. A couple of these make a satisfying light lunch.

Abu Aly, in the courtyard of the Nile Hilton on Midan Tahrir, has some of the best fuul, ta'amiyya, kushari and shwarma around, served from the fanciest carts you'll see in Egypt. The prices are double the street prices but still relatively cheap. Fuul and ta'amiyya sandwiches cost 50 pt. It's open from 10 am to 11 pm but the carts only operate until 5 pm.

Pizzeria (tel 750651) in the Nile Hilton serves pizza and various Italian dishes for about E£4 to E£5. It's open from noon to 2 am.

The *Café Riche*, 17 Sharia Talaat Harb is around the corner from Felfelas just before the square. Supposedly, this was a favourite hang-out for Nasser and other military officers while they planned the 1952 Revolution. Today, it's a popular place to get a cheap meal inside or sip a *Stella* beer while people-watching outside. Their E£1 breakfast special includes an omelette, bread, honey and cheese. For lunch or dinner there is soup for about 60 pt, spaghetti with a bizarre bolognaise sauce for E£1, an omelette for E£1, and tahina.

Near Midan Tahrir on Sharia Mohammed Mahmud there's a *24-hour sandwich shop*. (The now-defunct Bab el Louk station and the new telecommuni-

cations centre are across the street). Sandwiches of basturma, cheese and olives or egg cost 15 pt to 20 pt. They also serve macaroni and turshi.

There's a *bakery* a couple of doors down from the sandwich shop where you can get small steaming loaves of French bread or hot pieces of pita right out of the oven for about 15 pt. The almond cookies are also good, but the pastries are only for those looking for intense sugar highs.

Along Sharia Mansur, between Sharia Moh Mahmud and Midan Falaki, there are several small, nameless restaurants and an interesting market. This area is a great place to orient yourself to Egyptian food and shopping strategies.

On your left, with the old Bab el Louk station behind you, there is a *juice stand* and *fiteer* restaurant. At the juice stand you can get a freshly squeezed drink from almost any kind of fruit or vegetable for 10 pt to 25 pt. Pay the cashier first and he'll hand you a token which you give to the juice-squeezer. This may sound a bit fastidious, but having stood next to a toothless old guy with a hacking cough who sucked on his glass as he drank, I recommend that you bring your own drinking vessel as the glasses here are only rinsed. At the restaurant, for about 75 pt, you can get sweet and savoury fiteers – with either raisins, nuts, coconut and powdered sugar or with cheese, tomatoes and onions. Just one fiteer is plenty for a meal or big dessert.

Further along the street there's a *kushari* restaurant where you can fill up on carbohydrates. A very filling bowl of this dish of lentils, rice, noodles and fried onions only costs 25 pt. You may need to ask for extra onions. You'll recognise the place by the mounds of kushari in the front window waiting to be consumed. Pay at the cashier on your way out.

Next to the kushari place there is a *fuul and ta'amiyya stand*. Try the fuul in a bowl or throw it together with the small balls of ta'amiyya (similar to felafel) and pita bread for a great sandwich. Macaroni is also served and all these dishes cost about 25 pt.

A few more doors up the street on your left is the entrance to the open market, which is not all that open considering it's in a converted warehouse just off the street. Each stall and shop in the market specialises in something different like eggs or fruit or flowers. Watch out for the meat man! He hangs huge dripping hunks of meat on high hooks which you probably won't see until something wet and red lands on your shirt. Most prices are posted, but it's not uncommon to bargain. Go early in the morning before the stench of old meat and chicken gets too strong. Shopping or, at least, a look around here is an adventure which everyone should have at least once, if only to get a taste of daily life in Cairo.

If you return to Sharia Mansur and turn left towards Midan Falaki there is another cheap restaurant, called *El Doumyati*, straight ahead on Tahrir St. Look across the tram tracks for the pale orange awning at the foot of the blue pedestrian overpass. They serve an incredible amount of food for 50 pt; you get a plate of fuul, a few patties or balls of ta'amiyya, pickled vegetables and tahina.

To your left down Tahrir St before you cross the tram tracks, there's another quite good kushari place, called *LUX*.

Another block down on the left, at 166 Tahrir St, there is *Fataran el Tahrir*, an excellent place for fiteer.

You can get barbecued hamburgers and hot dogs at *TGIT – Thank God It's Thursday*, the Marine House in the American Embassy compound. On Thursdays, a huge dose of Americana is unofficially available for homesick Americans; just take your passport and tell the guard you're desperate for a taste of home. It's open from 4 pm to 10 pm.

Take Away Restaurant (tel 554341), 1 Latin America St, Garden City, serves cheap sandwiches, hamburgers and other main dishes and is open 8 am to midnight.

From Midan Talaat Harb to 26th of July St
The *Casablanca*, opposite the Grand
Hotel on Sharia Talaat Harb, does good
chicken, chips, tahina, tomatoes and
pickled vegetables for E£3.80.

The *Rex*, 33 Abdel Khaliq Sarwat St, is
a small restaurant which serves good
oriental, Lebanese and European food.
It's open from 12.30 to 4 pm and 6.30 to
10.30 pm.

Zeina Restaurant, 34 Talaat Harb, is
next to the Oxford Pensione. You can get a
simple meal of chicken, vegetables, rice
and bread for under E£2. Eating at the
counter is cheaper. The food is on display
so all you need to do is point. There's also
an English menu on the wall. Sometimes
the meat dishes are a bit greasy but the
macaroni is fairly good and filling. One
serve, for about 60 pt, makes a great
lunch. The 35 pt shwarma sandwiches
are also good.

A COMMON SIGHT —
TEA HOUSE DELIVERY
BOY ON THE CITY
SIDEWALKS.

Fu Shing (tel 756184), 28 Talaat Harb
is in a laneway off Talaat Harb St; look for
the sign on the main street. It is one of
Cairo's few Chinese restaurants and costs
from E£5 to E£7 for a full meal.

The *Kebab Coin* (or Kebab Corner) 28
Talaat Harb St is actually about one
block off the main street. It's just past the
Fu Shing, in the same laneway. The *Coin*
serves excellent kebab and tahina for
about E£4.

Ali Hassan El Hatti (tel 918829), 8
Midan Halim (off 26th of July St) is yet
another kebab and kufta place. Try their
speciality called moza, which is roast
lamb on rice. A meal of moza costs about
E£5. Other prices are comparable to
other cheap kebab restaurants.

Other Parts of Cairo *Abou Shakra*, 69 Kasr
El Eini in Garden City, is near the bridge
across the Nile to Roda Island about 1½
km south of Tahrir Square. They serve
some of the best kufta and kebab in Cairo.
A half order is plenty of food for one
person and costs E£2.40. Another
speciality, pigeon and rice, costs E£3.75.
There are seven types of salads and each
costs 25 pt. A 12% service charge is added.
It's open from 1 to 5 pm and 7 to 11 pm;
take-away is possible. To get there from
Midan Tahrir, either walk or take bus No
8 or 900 and get off when it turns right.

El Hussein Restaurant, in Islamic
Cairo, is a roof-top restaurant near the
mosque and in the hotel of the same
name. The views of the Citadel and
surrounding area are great and the kebab
is delicious. A full meal of kebab and
kufta costs from E£3.50 to E£5. During
Ramadan this is one of the most popular
places in the area. It's open from 8 am to
midnight.

Ahzab's Place is close to Bab Zuweila,
just off the main drag near the El Ganabki
Mosque. It's a hole-in-the-wall sort of
place with a painting of Mickey Mouse on
the wall and cheap *Stellas* in the cooler.
Mickey is pointing to the menu and a
couple of sayings from Mohammed which

translate as 'By the name of Allah, Allah is merciful and generous. Eat what Allah gives to you.' Allah, Mickey and Ahzab the cook, serve cheap juicy kebab right from the grill. This is a fantastic place to do lots of people-watching.

For pizza with a Middle Eastern flavour try the *Il Capo* (tel 3413870), 22 Taha Hussein St in Zamalek, next to the President Hotel. This place used to be called Pizza Buffo and is relatively expensive. Their pizza and pasta dishes cost from E£3.50 to E£5.50.

The *Tandoori*, 11 Shelab Street, just off Gamiat Al Dowal El Arabiya, in Mohandiseen serves tandoori chicken for E£4; kema curry of minced lamb with potatoes and peas for E£3.50; and jhinga curry prawns cooked in a special sauce for E£9. It's open from 12.30 to 4.30 pm and from 7.30 to 11.30 pm.

The King Grill is opposite the Atlas Zamalek Hotel on Gamiat Al Dowal El Arabiya. Their speciality is tasty grilled chicken with 15 different spices, all of which affect your stomach in strange and mysterious ways. It's a bit overpriced at E£4 per dish.

More Expensive Restaurants

Central *Taverne du Champs de Mars* (tel 740777), on the ground floor of the Nile Hilton, is a great bar and good for lunch and dinner. The entire interior was transported from Belgium and reassembled. It's not in the budget range.

Arabesque Restaurant, 6 Kasr El Nil St, between Midan Talaat Harb and Midan Tahrir, is the only restaurant in Egypt which is also an art gallery. The atmosphere is great but the European food is very expensive. Even if you don't eat there take a look at the gallery. Some of the artwork is interesting.

Le Grillon (tel 743114), 8 Kasr El Nil St, specialises in French food.

The *Caroll* (tel 246434), 12 Kasr El Nil St, is a popular place for both European and Egyptian food. It's opposite the American Express office.

Estoril, 12 Talaat Harb Street is in a laneway next to the Amex Office. Meals are a combination of French and Middle Eastern food and cost about E£6 to E£8. It's open from noon to 3.15 pm and 7.15 to 10.15 pm.

Paprika (tel 749744), 1129 Corniche el Nil, just south of the Radio & Television building serves various European dishes including pizza. Prices start at about E£6 for a meal and it's open from noon to midnight.

The *Peking* (tel 912381), 14 Saray El Ezbekiya, near Sharia Mohammed Farid, serves Cantonese-style food for about E£7.

The New Borsalino, 1 Latin America St, Garden City, one block from the US Embassy, is a Mexican restaurant. It's one of the few places in Cairo where you can get a real margarita and nachos. They also have take-away sandwiches and are open from noon to 2 am.

The oven was made of rusty tin and stoked with scraps of firewood. The purpose of this piece eluded me.

Sweet potatoes warming →

HOT SWEET POTATO VENDOR — Cairo

The *Kowloon* (tel 550629), in the Garden Palace Hotel, Garden City, serves Korean food.

Other Parts of Cairo The *Four Seasons*, 12 Mustafa Kamel St in Maadi, is a Korean/Chinese restaurant which serves several exotic dishes such as shark's fin soup and sauteed kimchi. It's open from noon to midnight everyday.

The Seahorse (tel 988499), Corniche el Nil opposite El Salam Hospital in Maadi, is a seafood restaurant right by the Nile. It's open from 12.30 pm to 1.30 am.

In Giza the *Andrea Chicken Restaurant & Andreana Fish Restaurant* (tel 851133), 60 Maryutia St, is one km from Pyramids Rd opposite the road to Saqqara. A full meal of chicken, fish or kebab, served with salads, dips and fruit costs about E£8. It is usually a bit over-run by tour groups.

Felfela Village (tel 854209), also in Giza, is down the road and across the canal from *Andrea's*. If you're after a packaged Middle Eastern atmosphere with everything that is supposedly exotic, then this is the place. This restaurant/circus has everything including dancing horses, camel rides, a playground and small zoo for the kids, acrobats and snake charmers.

Auberge Des Pyramids, 325 Pyramids Rd is one of Cairo's most popular tourist nightclubs and restaurants. Western and Middle Eastern entertainment shows which include music and belly dancing start at 11 pm.

Hotel Buffets
Almost all the major hotels offer all-you-can-eat breakfast buffets which are fairly good deals.

The Nile Hilton has a buffet from 6 to 10.30 am for E£7.50.

The Meridien Hotel buffet, from 7 to 10 am, is great value for E£7.50 and is a favourite among expatriate students. The views of the Nile are incredible from the dining room, the chocolate croissants are great and free newspapers in French or English are available.

There is also a buffet at the *Jolie Ville Hotel* near the pyramids.

Cafes, Tea Rooms & Juice Bars
Groppi's, on Midan Talaat Harb, is one of the most popular places in Cairo for sipping coffee, munching on baklava and watching a unique assortment of people troop in and out. If you want to have a pastry with your coffee, order and pay for it at the bakery in front. The *café au lait* is superb and they also serve *prix fixe* meals: lunch for E£5.75 and dinner for E£6.35 plus 12% for service. There is also a *Garden Groppi's* on Adly St opposite the tourist office.

Lappas on Kasr El Nil St is similar to Groppi's, but the atmosphere isn't quite as intriguing; not as many people flow in and out of here.

The *Brazilian Coffee House* is at two locations: 38 Talaat Harb St and 12 26th of July St (below the Grand Hotel). They have great café au lait for 30 pt and also serve Ovaltine milkshakes, capuccino, black espresso, hot chocolate, iced tea and iced coffee. It's probably the only place in Cairo where you can get the latter two.

One of the greatest juice stands in Cairo is on Midan Dokki on the side where Tahrir and Amin Bey El Rafi'i streets meet. Next door, there is a cheap fish restaurant. While you're there, check out the mausoleum for saints across the street.

The Floating Restaurants of Cairo
The Omar Khayyam Restaurant is aboard a houseboat on the Nile opposite the Gezira club in Zamalek. It's a fairly formal place with a full oriental grill.

The Scarabee is moored on the Corniche next to the Shepheard's Hotel. It sails twice a day, at 2.30 pm for lunch and 9.30 pm for dinner. The Scarabee is affiliated with the French-based Wagon-Lits company.

The *Kamar El Zaman* is moored just south of the El Gama'a Bridge on the east bank. It costs E£15 for dinner and a short cruise on the Nile. It is possible to just take the boat trip.

The *Pharaoh* is moored on the opposite side of the river and is a bit jazzier and more expensive than the others. The dinner and Nile cruise cost E£23 and it departs at 8 pm and 10 pm.

The Western Contingent
There are several *Wimpy* bars in Cairo where you can partake of the Egyptianised version of these very British hamburgers. The combinations are a little weird, such as hamburgers with strange ice cream concoctions and hot dogs wrapped in fried eggs! If you really can't live without a Wimpy burger, you can find them in Taha Hussein St in Zamalek, Medinat Mohandiseen in Dokki, Pyramids Rd in Giza, Hoda Shaarawi St near Felfelas, and Talaat Harb St opposite Felfelas.

There's a few *Kentucky Fried Chicken* places in Cairo offering the Colonel's usual menu. There's one in El Vatal Ahmed Abdel Aziz St in Mohandiseen.

Getting There
Air EgyptAir flies between Cairo and several places within Egypt including Hurghada, Sharm el Shaykh, St Catherine's, Luxor, Kharga Oasis and Aswan. Fares are not exactly in the budget travel range. A one-way ticket to Luxor costs E£51 so unless you're in a big hurry, it's not worth flying.

A taxi from the Cairo airport to central Cairo costs E£4. It's best not to travel by bus if they're crowded because it is too difficult to get off.

Train Ramses Station, on Midan Ramses, is Cairo's main train station. Everything and everyone seems to be moving all at once and at first it can be a bit confusing trying to buy tickets from the right window. The Tourist Police have an office just inside the entrance and the officer on

duty usually speaks some English and can be very helpful. Sometimes, representatives of the Tourist Friends Association roam around the station, and they will help you buy tickets. The 'friends' will probably find you before you find them if you look lost enough and they're quite sincere when they say they only want to help you and practice their English.

Most tickets for destinations south of Cairo, including Luxor and Aswan, are bought on the far side of the station, not in the main building near the Tourist Police office. To get there, follow the crowd towards the outside tracks, turn left and go through the tunnel under the tracks. The ticket windows are on the other side. Windows No 2 & 3 sell 1st class tickets. Many of the south-bound trains also depart from this side of the station.

Remember that if you have an International Student Identity Card, you are eligible for 50% discounts on the tickets. Other forms of student or quasi-student identification have sometimes been used by travellers.

Following are some schedules for Egypt's major rail routes. Not all trains have 1st and 2nd class air-conditioned carriages but basically there are six classes – 1st and 2nd class deluxe, 1st and 2nd class air-con, 2nd class and 3rd class. The fare examples given in this section are for 3rd class and 1st class deluxe, in order to give an indication of the lowest and highest fares for each journey.

The overnight trains to Luxor and Aswan are the ones usually taken by foreigners and are some of the best in Egypt.

In the following schedule the express trains, Nos 84 and 86, from Cairo to Luxor and Luxor to Aswan, have sleepers and a dining car. Train No 88 has sleepers, a dining car, buffet and air-con; and No 868 has 2nd class and air-con.

The 3rd/1st class fares are: 75 pt/E£5.80 to Minya; E£1.05/8.15 to Asyut; E£1.45/11.65 to Qena; E£1.50/12.55 to Luxor; E£1.60/13.30 to Isna; E£1.65/14.05 to Idfu; E£1.75/14.85

to Kom Ombo; and E£1.80/15.50 to Aswan.

Except for the time of departure from Cairo all times given are arrival times. Trains 88 and 868 stop for five to 45 minutes at stations en route.

	No 84	No 86	No 88	No 868
Cairo	18.45	19.20	20.00	20.30
Minya			23.39	00.08
Asyut			01.29	02.00
Qena		06.06	06.37	07.55
Luxor	05.38	07.30	08.10	09.15
Isna			10.14	10.50
Idfu			11.20	11.51
Kom Ombo			12.33	13.16
Aswan	10.00	12.35	13.30	14.12

Trains from Cairo to Alexandria, via Tanta and Damanhur, depart at least every hour, almost 24 hours a day. The 3rd/1st class fares from Cairo are 30 pt/ E£2.25 to Tanta; 45 pt/E£3.60 to Damanhur; and 65 pt/E£5.05 to Alexandria.

From Cairo to Port Said the fares range from 60 pt in 3rd class to E£5.50 in 1st class deluxe. The train goes via Zagazig – 30 pt to E£2.15; Ismailia – 50 pt to E£3.95; and Qantara.

There are two train routes to Suez, one via Zagazig and Ismailia, and the other via Qubba Palace. The latter costs 35 pt in 3rd class and 70 pt in 2nd class.

Train No 7, in the following schedule of departure times, has a buffet and the other three have air-con.

	No 7	No 61	No 941	No 27
Cairo	06.25	09.55	15.30	18.45
Zagazig	07.56	11.15	17.00	20.15
Ismailia	09.12	12.25	18.25	21.27
Suez			22.05	
Qantara	10.02			22.17
Port Said	10.55			23.10

	No 311	No 313	No 315
Cairo	10.00	15.35	19.35
Qubba Palace	10.12	15.47	19.47
Suez	13.05	18.20	22.40

While you are at Ramses Station, visit the military surplus market next door, on the far side of the station. They sell an interesting assortment of surplus military boots, pants, shirts, blankets and other items.

Bus Cairo has several long distance bus stations. The principal departure points are:

To Alexandria and the Mediterranean Coast – from Midan Tahrir. The office for buses to Marsa Matruh is next to the telephone office on the east side of Midan Tahrir. Kiosks for buses to Alexandria are opposite the Hilton and behind the main terminus.

To the Delta, Suez Canal, Red Sea and Upper Egypt – from Midan Ulali and Midan Ahmed Hilmi behind Ramses Station. You will see the big yellow buses.

To the Sinai – from the Abbassiya Station just off Midan Abbassiya.

To the Western Oases – from a station near Midan Ataba.

For information about fares and locations of the stations see the relevant regional section.

Taxi Cairo's service taxis depart from various station lots around the city. For destinations in the Delta and on the Suez Canal most taxis leave from Midan Ahmed Hilmi behind Ramses Station. Following are a few sample fares.

To	Fare
Alexandria	E£3
Port Said	E£3
Qantara	E£1.50
Ismailia	E£1.80
Suez	E£1.80
Tanta	E£2
Damanhur	E£2.25
Zagazig	E£1.25
El Arish	E£3.75

Service taxis for Alexandria also leave from in front of Ramses Station and the Nile Hilton.

Taxis for destinations in and around the Faiyum leave from Midan Giza in Giza. Taxis for Helwan leave from Bab el Louk station opposite the Telecommunications building.

Getting Around

Getting around Cairo can be a confusing and frustrating experience but there are several options. Buses are the most common form of transportation for the majority of Cairenes; minibuses are equally popular, but not as prevalent; taxis are everywhere at any time of the day or night; there's a suburban train service to and from the southern suburbs; and a 'riverbus' travels the Nile from Maadi, south of Cairo, to Qanater in the north. Private donkey carts and horse-drawn wagons continue to weave through the streets and alleyways, along with an occasional camel laden with goods for the market. A subway system is also being built.

Bus If you're really planning on squeezing in and out of Cairo's crowded buses, then buy the small datebook which lists all the city's bus and minibus routes. The datebook is sold at some newsstands including the one directly opposite the American University in Cairo campus on Sharia Mohammed Mahmud. Although this little book is all in Arabic, you can easily find someone to translate the routes for you.

Riding a bus in Cairo requires more than just the slippery eel-like qualities necessary for staking out your space. Route numbers are usually indicated in Arabic numerals on small signs behind the windshield. You have to be able to recognise the numerals quickly because the buses never really stop. They roll into the station sometimes already full and a few seconds later roll out the other side with even more passengers and less space. If there are lots of people waiting for the bus, the strategy for boarding is to push, shove and grunt. Watch your wallets and money pouches because it is during this crunch that a lot of things tend to disappear. Once you're on the bus, try to squeeze your way up towards the front door, which is the exit. At some point during the trip, a little man with a long wooden box will slither by you to collect the 10 pt fare.

There are two parts to Cairo's main bus terminal, which is in the area around Midan Tahrir. Directly in front of the Nile Hilton there are buses and minibuses which go eastward to Islamic Cairo, Heliopolis, the airport and Shubra. Taking a minibus, easily recognised by its smaller size and orange and white stripes, is one of the best ways to travel. It costs only 20 pt for a seat, passengers are not allowed to stand and crowd each other and they leave when every seat is taken.

The other part of the terminal is in front of the *Mogamma*. Most of the buses from there go across the river to Giza, Mohandiseen and Imbaba.

Following is a list of some of the bus numbers and their destinations.

From the Nile Hilton terminal
No 400
    Cairo Airport
No 510
    Heliopolis
Nos 173 & 403
    The Citadel and Mosque of Sultan Hassan
No 75
    The Islamic Museum and Bab Zuweila
No 63
    Mosque of al-Azhar & Khan el Khalili
Nos 170 & 95
    Ramses Station & Zamalek
No 500
    Masr Gidida (Heliopolis)
Nos 44, 128 & 350
    Ain Shams
No 330
    Medinat Issalam
No 302
    Shubra
No 99
    Midan Lubman
No 60
    Aguza

Minibus No 24
    Roxy & Masr Gidida
Minibus No 2
    Shubra

From the Mogamma terminal
No 900
    Kasr El Eini, Manyal Palace, Cairo
    University, Giza & the Pyramids
No 8
    Kasr El Eini, Manyal Palace, Giza & the
    Pyramids
No 174
    Sayyida Zeinab, the Mosques of Ibn Tulun
    and Sultan Hassan & the Citadel
Nos 83, 86 & 182
    Mausoleum of Shafi'i in the Southern
    Cemetery
No 140
    Midan Ramses & Ramses Station
Nos 6 & 803
    Giza Square
No 166
    Ula Daqar

There are also private minibuses which go
to Giza and the pyramids for 25 pt. Other
minibuses run between Midans Tahrir
and Ramses – Nos 70 and 95; Midans
Ramses and Ataba – Nos 65 and 80;
Midans Ataba and Ramses – Nos 24 and
25; Midan Tahrir and Old Cairo – No 92;
Midan Tahrir and the Citadel – No 173.

You can also catch a bus No 3 from Giza
Square to the Great Pyramids; a minibus
for 50 pt from Bab el Louk, on Sharia Moh
Mahmud to Old Cairo, Maadi and
Helwan; a bus No 69 from Opera Square
to Abbassiya Sinai Terminal; or from
Ramses Station a bus No 9 to Giza or
No 444 to Helwan.

Riverbus Two riverbuses leave from
Maspero, directly in front of the big round
Radio & Television building, and go north
as far as the Nile barrages and Qanater.
Others go south and stop near Cairo
University, Old Cairo and Maadi.

Taxis A taxi is one of the most convenient

ways of getting around Cairo. Fares
should be about E£1 for a ride of
approximately five km or 45 minutes; so,
for example, a ride from Midan Tahrir to
Ramses Station should cost about 50 pt.
For more information on the different
sorts of taxis and how to flag them down
see the Getting Around chapter.

Renting a Car If you're crazy enough to
want to battle the traffic in Cairo, there
are several car rental agencies in the city,
including the 'big three' – Avis, Hertz and
Budget. Their rates and terms vary and
change often but the following, quoted in
US dollars, should give you an idea of the
prices.

Avis rents a Fiat 128 at a daily rate of
$16.25 plus 16 cents per km and a 12% tax
on the total. At least 100 km per day is
required. They also offer a weekly rate of
$294 (plus 12% tax) for a period of five to
seven days with unlimited kms. Insurance
is included but a Collision Damage
Waiver of $3.75 per day is required.

Hertz rents the same car for $10 per day
plus 11 cents per km and 12% tax. At least
100 km per day and a daily $5 Collision
Damage Waiver is also required. Insurance
is included. They offer a weekly rate of
$72 plus 11 cents per km. Hertz has offices
at the Ramses Hilton, the President
Hotel, the Sonestra Hotel, Maadi Hotel
and the airport.

Budget rents a Fiat 127 for three to six
days with unlimited km, at a daily rate of
E£30. For one to two days the daily rate is
E£13 plus 13 pt per km. They also offer a
seven-day minimum weekly rate of
E£200. If you book 21 days in advance
and prepay in dollars, you will be
guaranteed a weekly rate of $193 with
unlimited km. A 12% tax is added to the
final total of all rentals. Insurance is
included, but a Collision Damage Waiver
of E£5 per day is required.

All car rental agencies require an
International Driving Permit.

Around Cairo

The region around Cairo offers some of Egypt's most interesting attractions including the ancient tombs and pyramids of Saqqara; the Faiyum – one of the world's largest oases; and the medieval monasteries of Wadi Natrun. Most of the destinations described in this chapter can be visited on day trips from Cairo.

MEMPHIS

Memphis, once the glorious Old Kingdom capital of Egypt, has all but completely vanished. It is believed the city was founded around 3100 BC, probably by King Menes, at the time when Upper and Lower Egypt were first united. It grew quickly, with many splendid palaces and gardens, and was one of the most renowned and populous cities of the ancient world. Like most Egyptian cities with any degree of importance Memphis also had its own deity, the all-powerful creator god *Ptah*, who formed the world with words from his tongue and heart.

Even as late as the 5th century BC, long after Thebes had taken over as capital of Egypt, Memphis was described by the Greek historian Herodotus as a 'prosperous city and cosmopolitan centre'. Its enduring importance, even then, was reflected in the size of its cemetery on the west bank of the Nile, an area replete with royal pyramids, private tombs and sacred animal necropolises. This city of the dead, centred at Saqqara, covers a 30 km stretch on the edge of the desert, from Dahshur to Giza.

Centuries of annual floods, however, have inundated the city with Nile mud, while other ancient buildings and monuments have long since been ploughed over and cultivated by the *fellahin*. Today there are few signs of the grandeur of Memphis, in fact it's extremely difficult to imagine that a city once stood where there is now only a small museum and some statues in a garden. The museum contains one relic – the limestone Colossus of Ramses II, similar to the one which stands at the centre of Midan Ramses in Cairo. This one however is a lot more neglected and minus a few limbs.

In the garden, there are other statues of Ramses II, an eight-ton alabaster sphinx, the sarcophagus of Amenhotep and the alabaster beds on which the sacred Apis bulls were mummified before being placed in the Serapeum at Saqqara.

Getting There

Memphis is 24 km south of Cairo and three km from Saqqara. The cheapest way to get there from Cairo is to take the metro from Sayyida Zeinab Station to Helwan, the last stop, and then take a taxi to Memphis. The metro starts running at 5 am and continues throughout the day at 15 minute intervals. An alternative is to take a local train from Ramses station to the village of El Bedrashein, from where you can either walk or take a taxi. The most common way of getting there is to get a group of six or seven people together and hire a taxi for about E£15 to E£20 for the day.

Saqqara

When Memphis was the capital of Egypt, during the Old Kingdom period, Saqqara was its necropolis. Deceased pharaohs, family members and sacred animals were ceremoniously transported from Memphis to be buried and permanently enshrined in a myriad of temples, pyramids and tombs at Saqqara.

In the 3000 years between the foundation of Memphis and the end of Greek rule under the Ptolemies the necropolis grew till it covered a seven km stretch of the

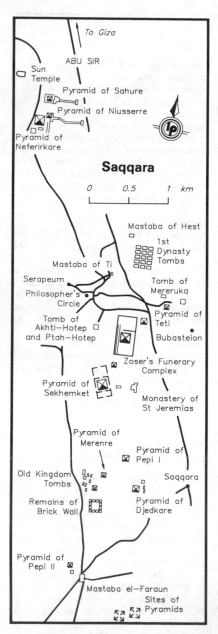

To Giza

ABU SIR

Sun Temple

Pyramid of Sahure

Pyramid of Niusserre

Pyramid of Neferirkare

Saqqara

0   0.5   1 km

Mastaba of Hest

1st Dynasty Tombs

Mastaba of Ti

Serapeum

Philosopher's Circle

Tomb of Mereruka

Tomb of Akhti–Hotep and Ptah–Hotep

Pyramid of Teti

Bubasteion

Zoser's Funerary Complex

Pyramid of Sekhemket

Monastery of St Jeremias

Pyramid of Merenre

Pyramid of Pepi I

Old Kingdom Tombs

Saqqara

Remains of Brick Wall

Pyramid of Djedkare

Pyramid of Pepi II

Mastaba el–Faraun

Sites of Pyramids

Western Desert. The Step Pyramid Egypt's first and the oldest stone structure of its size in the world, was just one of the many funerary monuments and temples built in the area. In terms of the value of what has been, and has yet to be uncovered there are few archaeological sites in the world that compare with Saqqara. However, apart from the Step Pyramid, the necropolis was virtually ignored by archaeologists until the mid 19th century when Auguste Mariette found the Serapeum. Even Zoser's massive mortuary complex, surrounding his pyramid, wasn't discovered and reclaimed from the sand until 1924, and it is still being restored.

A worthwhile visit to Saqqara will take more than one day and because of its size, apart from the organised tour groups which are rushed through in the mornings, it seems that other visitors are few and far between. You'll find here, in the middle of the desert, a peaceful quality rarely found at other ancient sites in Egypt.

The main places of interest are in North Saqqara, with other sites spread between South Saqqara, Dahshur and Abu Sir. If you don't have a vehicle or animal it's best to start your visit in North Saqqara, from where it's easy to walk to either Abu Sir or South Saqqara, especially between November and February when it's not quite so hot. Both hikes take about 1½ hours through a fantastic desert landscape and there's no chance of getting lost as you can see both sets of pyramids from the Serapeum in North Saqqara. (See the Getting Around section.)

The pyramids and tombs at Saqqara can be 'officially' visited between 9 am and 4 pm. The guards start locking the doors of monuments at about 3.30 pm. Admission fee for all Saqqara sights is E£3, or E£1.50 for students and the ticket office is at the base of the plateau of North Saqqara.

ABU SIR

The three pyramids of Abu Sir, at the edge of the desert surrounded by a sea of sand dunes, formed part of a 5th Dynasty necropolis. There were originally 14 pyramids at Abu Sir and those that remain are mostly just mounds of rubble, though at least one can still be entered.

The Pyramid of Neferirkare

Neferirkare's tomb is one of the best in the area and stands 45 metres high. It now resembles Zoser's step pyramid but originally had an outer casing of stone, like the Giza pyramids once had.

The Pyramid of Niuserre

Though the most dilapidated of the three, Niuserre's pyramid features the causeway which runs to what's left of his mortuary temple to the south-east.

The Pyramid of Sahure

This is the most complete and northern-most of the group. The entrance is open but it's only half a metre high and you have to crawl along for about two metres through pharaonic dust and spider webs to get into the pharaoh's tomb. The

remains of Sahure's mortuary temple still stands nearby and from his pyramid, on a clear day, you can see anything up to 10 pyramids stretching out before you to the horizon.

North of the temple there are several interesting things including several *mastabas* and the tomb of Ptahshepses, who was a court official and relative of King Niuserre. If you happen to be going to Abu Sir by camel, horse or donkey across the desert from Giza then stop off at the 5th Dynasty **Sun Temple of Abu Ghorab**. It was built by King Niuserre in honor of the sun god *Ra*. The huge altar is made from five big blocks of alabaster and once served as the base of a large Solar Obelisk. Very few travellers ever make it this far off the beaten track.

Abu Sir is open from 9 am to 4 pm and admission costs E£3 or E£1 for students.

NORTH SAQQARA
The Step Pyramid

When it was constructed by Imhotep, the pharaoh's chief architect, in the 27th century BC, the Step Pyramid of King Zoser was the largest stone structure ever

The Step Pyramid, Saqqara

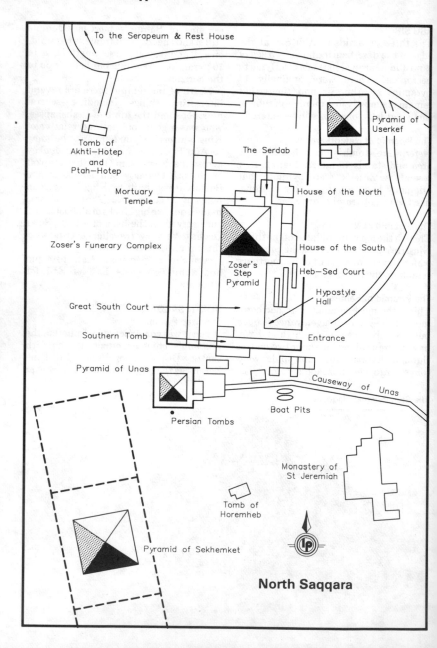

To the Serapeum & Rest House

Pyramid of
Userkef

Tomb of
Akhti—Hotep
and
Ptah—Hotep

The Serdab

Mortuary
Temple

House of the North

Zoser's Funerary Complex

House of the South

Zoser's
Step
Pyramid

Heb—Sed Court

Hypostyle
Hall

Great South Court

Southern Tomb

Entrance

Pyramid of Unas

Causeway of Unas

Boat Pits

Persian Tombs

Monastery of
St Jeremiah

Tomb of
Horemheb

Pyramid of Sekhemket

North Saqqara

built. It is still the most noticeable feature of Saqqara. Imhotep's brilliant use of stone and his daring break with the tradition of building royal tombs as underground rooms with the occasional mud brick *mastaba* was the inspiration for Egypt's future architectural achievements.

The pyramid began as a simple *mastaba* (which means 'bench'), the flat tomb superstructure common at the time, but Imhotep added to it five times. With each new level of stone he gained confidence in his use of the new medium and mastered the techniques required to move, place and secure the huge blocks. This first pyramid rose to over 62 metres, in six steps, before it was sheathed in fine limestone.

The Step Pyramid dominates Zoser's mortuary complex, which is 544 metres long and 277 metres wide and was once surrounded by a magnificent bastioned and panelled limestone wall. The enclosure wall survives, in part, to a height of over 4.5 metres and a section near the south-east corner has been restored, with stones found in the desert, to its original 10-metre elevation. The many false doors in the enclosure wall, carved and painted to resemble real wood with hinges and sockets, allowed the pharaoh's *ka* to come and go at will.

For the living there is only one entrance, on the south-east corner, via a vestibule and along a colonnaded corridor into the broad **Hypostyle Hall**. The 40 pillars in the corridor are the original 'bundle columns', ribbed to resemble a bundle of palm stems, and the walls have been restored but the protective ceiling is modern concrete. The roof of the Hypostyle Hall is supported by four impressive bundle columns and there's a large false half-open *ka* door.

The Hall leads into the **Great South Court** a huge open area, flanking the south side of the pyramid, with a rebuilt section of wall featuring a frieze of cobras. The cobra, or *uraeus*, was a symbol of

Egyptian royalty, a fire-spitting agent of destruction and protector of the King. A rearing cobra, its hood inflated, always formed part of a pharaoh's headdress.

Near the frieze is a shaft which plunges 28 metres to the floor of Zoser's **Southern Tomb**, which is similar in decoration to the main tomb beneath the Step Pyramid. Originally it probably stored the canopic jars containing the pharaoh's preserved internal organs.

In the centre of the Great Court there are two stone altars representing the thrones of Upper and Lower Egypt. During the 30th year of a pharaoh's reign it was traditional for him to renew his rule by re-enacting his coronation. In a ritual called the *Heb-Sed race* he would sit first on one throne and then on the other to symbolise the unification of Egypt. He would also, during the five-day jubilee, present all the provincial priests with gifts, obliging them to recognise his supremacy over their local gods. The jubilee would actually have been held in Memphis while these altars in the Great Court perpetuated in stone the cosmic regeneration of the pharaoh's power and *ka*.

On the eastern side of the pyramid are two 'houses' which symbolise the unity of the country by representing the shrines of Upper and Lower Egypt. **The House of the South**, which is faced with proto-Doric columns, features the oldest-known examples of tourist graffiti. The 'vandalism' of visiting 12th century BC Theban scribes, who scrawled their admiration for Zoser on the wall in a cursive style of hieroglyphics, is now protected under a piece of plexi-glass just inside the entrance. **The House of the North** is similar to its southern counterpart, except that sculpted papyrus flowers grace the capitals of its columns.

The Serdab, a stone structure right in front of the Pyramid, contains a slightly tilted wooden box with two holes drilled into its north face. Look through these 'windows' and you'll have the eerie experience of coming face to face with the *immortal* Pharaoh Zoser himself. Inside is a life-size, lifelike painted statue of the long dead king gazing stonily out towards the stars. Although it's only a copy (the original is in the Egyptian Museum), it is still quite haunting. Serdabs were designed so the pharaoh's *ka* could communicate with the outside world. The original entrance to the Step Pyramid is directly behind the Serdab but is closed to the public.

The Pyramid of Unas

What appears to be a big mound of rubble to the south-west of the Zoser's tomb is actually the pyramid of Unas, the last pharaoh of the 5th Dynasty. It was only 350 years from the inspired creation of the Step Pyramid, through the perfection of the Great Pyramids to the raising of this unassuming pile of loose blocks and dirt. Mycerinus' pyramid at Giza effectively marked the end of the Pyramid Age but the tomb of this king, who reigned 150 years later, revealed the beginning of a whole new trend in design. Until the time of Unas, pyramid interiors had been unadorned so while the outside of his tomb looks more like Zoser's than Cheops', the inside is of immense historical importance.

In 1881 Thomas Cook & Sons sponsored the excavation of the tomb by Gaston Maspero, who found the walls covered in hieroglyphs. Carved into the huge slabs of white alabaster these so-called *Pyramid Texts* are the earliest known examples of decorative writing in a pharaonic tomb chamber. The texts record the rituals, prayers and hymns that accompanied the pharaoh's burial to enable the release of his *ka*, and list the articles, like food and clothing, necessary for his existence in the afterlife.

This is one of the easiest pyramids to visit at Saqqara, which means if there's a tour group in the area it will probably be crowded. The entrance is on the north face along a 1.4-metre-high passage.

Part of the one km causeway, which ran from the east side of the Pyramid of Unas, has been restored. On either side of it more than 200 *mastabas* have been excavated and there are several well-preserved tombs, some of which can be visited. The beautiful tomb of the 5th Dynasty princess **Idut**, who was probably a daughter of Pharaoh Unas, is next to the southern wall of Zoser's complex. The walls of its 10 chambers feature colourful scenes of oxen, gazelle, ibex, hippos and other animals. The **Mastaba of Queen Nebet** and the **Mastaba of Mehu** are also beautifully decorated; and the **Tomb of Nebkau-her**, which may be closed, is worth visiting if you can gain access.

Egyptologists debate whether the huge sculpted-stone **Boat Pits**, south of the causeway, actually held the royal barges which took the pharaoh on his journey to the afterlife, or whether they merely represented these solar boats. Nothing was found when the 40-metre-long, crescent-shaped trenches were excavated.

The Persian Tombs

The tombs of three Persian noblemen, just south of Unas' pyramid, are some of the deepest subterranean burial chambers in Egypt. The entrance is covered by a small inconspicuous wooden hut, to which a guard in the area has the key. If you don't have your own torch he will lead you the 25 metres down the winding staircase to the vaulted tombs of Psamtik, Zenhebu and Pelese. According to the ancient wall drawings, which are colourful and fantastic, Zenhebu was a famous Persian admiral and Psamtik was chief physician of the pharaoh's court. The tombs were built to prevent grave-robbers from stealing the contents. It didn't work; it was thieves who cut the spiral entrance passage.

The Monastery of Saint Jeremiah

The half-buried remains of this 5th century AD monastery are up the hill from Unas' causeway and south-east of the boat pits. There's not much left of the structure because it was ransacked by invading Arabs in 950 AD and more recently the Egyptian Antiquities Department took all the wall paintings and carvings to the Coptic Museum in Cairo.

The Pyramid of Sekhemket

Sekhemket was one of Zoser's successors and his unfinished pyramid is a short distance to the west of the ruined monastery. It was abandoned before completion, for unknown reasons, when it was only three metres high. There's an unused alabaster sarcophagus in one of the underground passageways but no one is permitted to enter this pile of rubble because of the danger of cave-ins.

The Tomb of Akhti-Hotep & Ptah-Hotep

Akhti-Hotep and Ptah-Hotep, who were father and son officials during the reign of Djedkare, designed their own tomb complex which consists of two burial chambers, a chapel and a hall of pillars. The Hotep duo were judges, overseers of the priests of the pyramids and chiefs of the granary and treasury. The reliefs in their chambers are some of the best at Saqqara and depict everyday life during the 5th Dynasty. There is Akhti-Hotep in the marshes building boats, fighting enemies and crossing rivers; a splendid scene of wild animals with Ptah-Hotep and other hunters in hot pursuit; people playing games, collecting food and eating; and Ptah-Hotep having a manicure while being entertained by musicians. The dual tomb is south of the main road between the Step Pyramid and the Rest House.

The Philosopher's Circle

Down the slope in front of the Rest House there are several statues of Greek philosophers arranged in a circle beneath a protective roof. From left to right the statues are Plato (standing), Heraclitus (seated), Thales (standing), Protagoras (seated), Homer (seated), Hesiod (seated), Demetrius of Phalerum (standing against a bust of Serapis) and Pindar. The Circle was set up, during the Ptolemaic period at the eastern end of a long avenue of sphinxes which ran from the temple, where a live Apis bull was worshipped, to the *Serapeum* where the bulls of this strange animal cult were buried.

The Serapeum

The sacred Apis bulls were by far the most important of the cult animals entombed at Saqqara. The Apis, it was believed, was an incarnation of *Ptah* the god of Memphis and was the calf of a cow struck by lightning from heaven. Once divinely impregnated, the cow would never again give birth and her calf was kept in the temple of *Ptah* and worshipped as a god. The Apis, always portrayed with a sun disc between its horns, was black with a distinctive white diamond on its forehead, the image of an eagle on its back and a scarab on its tongue. On its death the bull was mummified, on an alabaster bed, then carried to the subterranean galleries of the Serapeum at Saqqara and placed in a huge sarcophagus.

The Apis catacombs date from the 13th century BC when Ramses II began the first gallery which reached a length of 68 metres. In the 7th century BC Psammetichus I cut a new gallery which was extended by the Ptolemies, to a length of 198 metres, and used till around 30 BC. Twenty-five Apis were embalmed and stabled in perpetuity here in monolithic granite coffins weighing up to 70 tons each. Only one mummified bull, now in the Cairo Agricultural Museum, was found when the Serapeum was excavated.

Until 1851 the existence of the sacred Apis tombs was known only from classical references. Having found a half-buried sphinx at Saqqara, and following the description given by Strabo in 24 BC, the French archaeologist Auguste Mariette began digging and uncovered the avenue of sphinxes leading to the Serapeum. His great discovery sparked the extensive and ongoing excavation of Saqqara. In 1856 Mariette wrote that he'd been so profoundly struck with astonishment on first gaining access to the Apis vaults, five years before, that the feeling was still fresh in his mind. Only one chamber, walled up during the reign of Ramses II, had escaped the notice of tomb robbers. Of finding it intact, Mariette wrote:

The finger marks of the Egyptian who had inserted the last stone in the wall built to conceal the doorway were still recognisable on the lime. There were also the marks of naked feet imprinted on the sand which lay in one corner of the tomb chamber. Everything was in its original condition in this tomb where the embalmed remains of the bull had lain undisturbed for 37 centuries.

The entrance to the Serapeum is near the Rest House, on the main road, west of the Philosopher's circle. It's very likely you'll experience the same feeling as Mariette for this place is definitely weird and gets stranger still as you wander along galleries, lit only by tiny lanterns that cast a murky light over the vaults and the enormous, macabre black sarcophagi they contain. The largest sarcophagus, at the end of the main gallery, is carved from a single piece of black granite and is covered in hieroglyphs.

The Mastaba/Tomb of Ti

This tomb is one of the main sources of knowledge about life in Egypt towards the end of the Old Kingdom. Ti, an important court official who served under three pharaohs, collected titles like his kings collected slaves. He was Lord of Secrets, Superintendent of Works, Overseer of the Pyramids of Abu Sir, Counsellor to the Pharaoh and even royal hairdresser. He married a woman of royal blood and the inscriptions on the walls of his tomb reveal that his children were rated as royalty. One of the best reliefs depicts Ti standing regally on a boat sailing through papyrus marshes, while others show men and women at various jobs like ploughing, ship-building, reaping grain and feeding cranes. The tomb, discovered by Mariette in 1865, is a few hundred metres north of the Philosopher's Circle.

Tombs of Teti, Mereruka & Ankhma-Hor

The Avenue of Sphinxes excavated by Mariette in the 1850s has been engulfed by desert sands again, but it once extended as far east as the Pyramid of Teti. To get to this somewhat weathered tomb now, you must follow the road from the Rest House heading a little to the north once you've passed the Step Pyramid. The interior is often closed to the public but is worth seeing if you can get in.

Nearby is the Tomb of Mereruka which has 30 rooms, many of which have magnificent wall inscriptions. Egyptologists have learned a great deal about the wildlife of ancient Egypt from these drawings. As you enter the tomb, notice the big-mouthed hippopotamuses with sharp tusks on one of the walls.

The Tomb of Ankhma-Hor, a little further east, contains some very interesting scenes depicting 6th Dynasty surgical operations, including toe surgery and a circumcision.

Excavations in this area have also uncovered several temples including the **Anubieion**, which was sacred to the jackal-headed *Anubis*, god of embalming and the dead, with a gallery for dogs; the **Bubasteion**, sacred to the cat goddess *Bastet*, and filled with mummified cats; and other galleries with thousands of mummified birds and monkeys.

SOUTH SAQQARA

The pyramids of the 6th Dynasty pharaohs Pepi I, Merenre and Pepi II, who made the move to South Saqqara, have been cleared of sand and feature some interesting hieroglyphic texts. The oldest structure in this area however, is the unusual mortuary complex of the 4th

Dynasty king Shepseskaf. The crumbling southernmost pyramids, built of sun-dried bricks, belong to 13th Dynasty pharaohs.

The Mastabat el-Faraun

The tomb of Shepseskaf, believed to be a son of Mycerinus, is neither a *mastaba* nor a pyramid. The Mastabat el-Faraun, or *Pharaoh's Bench*, is an enormous stone structure that resembles a sarcophagus topped with a rounded lid. The complex once covered 700 square metres and the interior consists of long passageways and a burial chamber. It is possible to enter the tomb if you can find a guard.

The Pyramid of Pepi II

A little north of the Mastabat el-Faraun is the pyramid of this 6th Dynasty pharaoh who supposedly ruled for 94 years. Pepi II's tomb contains some fine hieroglyphs and the ruins of his mortuary temple, which was once connected to the pyramid by a causeway, can also be explored. Nearby, to the west, are the remains of the pyramids of Queen Apuit and Queen Neith.

The Pyramid of Djedkare

North of what's left of Pepi II's valley temple, is the tomb of Djedkare a 5th Dynasty pharaoh. Known as *Ahram esh-Shawaf*, or Pyramid of the Sentinel, it stands 25 metres high and can be entered through a tunnel on the north side.

DAHSHUR

The southern extension of the necropolis of Memphis is a field of royal tombs, about 3.5 km long, just west of the village of Dahshur. The Bent and Red pyramids were both built by Pharaoh Sneferu, the father of Cheops and founder of the 4th Dynasty. That Sneferu had two pyramids, and possibly a third at Meidum, is a mystery that has not been altogether solved by Egyptologists, because if the purpose of a pyramid was to be a container for the pharaoh's *ka* then why

would one pharaoh with one *ka* need more than one tomb?

The Bent Pyramid

This is the most conspicuous of the four pyramids at Dahshur and although its rather strange shape seems to suggest otherwise this tomb, and the Pyramid of Meidum also built (or at least completed) by Sneferu, demonstrates the design transition from step pyramid to true pyramid.

For some reason though, just a little over half way up its 105 metre height, the angle of its exterior was reduced from 52° to 43.5° giving it its distinctive blunt shape. The reason for the change in design is not known except that perhaps it was believed the initial angle was too steep to be stable. If it was considered unsafe it could explain why Sneferu built another tomb, the so-called Red Pyramid which rises at a constant angle of 43.5°, only two km away.

Most of the Bent Pyramid's outer casing is still intact and it is unique in having two entrances. Nearby are the remains of the mortuary temple and further north the ruins of Sneferu's valley temple which yielded some interesting reliefs.

The other two dilapidated pyramids at Dahshur, which belong to 12th Dynasty pharaohs Amenemhat III and Sesostris III are less interesting and really only for those with pyramid fever. Around all the pyramids there are also the customary tombs of the members of the royal families, court officials and priests.

If you want to go to Dahshur, you must first check with the Tourist Office in Cairo to see if you still need permission from the Ministry of Interior as Dahshur was considered a military zone.

Getting to Saqqara

Saqqara is about 32 km south of Cairo and three km west of Memphis. If you are coming from Memphis, take the Giza road north, then turn west and Saqqara will be straight ahead. If you're coming from Cairo or Giza, you have several options. Refer to the Memphis getting there section for details on the train, metro and taxi services from Cairo. The train from Cairo to the village El Bedrashein also goes to Dahshur. A taxi from either to North Saqqara should cost about 50 pt. A taxi from Giza to Saqqara should cost about E£5 and there are plenty of taxis available for the return journey.

One of the cheapest ways of getting to Saqqara without going via Memphis is to take bus No 8, which starts running at 6 am, from Midan Tahrir to Midan Giza and then a minibus from there to the village of Abu Sir. The minibus costs 25 pt and can drop you off before it turns off the paved road towards Abu Sir. It's usually quite easy to hitch the six km from there to the main entrance to North Saqqara. If it's too hot and you don't feel like hitching, then stay on the bus until you get to Abu Sir, from where it's about a three km walk through the desert to North Saqqara. Refer to the following getting around Saqqara section for directions.

The most adventurous, though physically strenuous, option is to hire a camel, donkey or horse and cross the desert from the pyramids of Giza to Saqqara. This takes at least eight hours for a round-trip so make sure you're prepared for it. That amount of time spent on an animal will make it rather difficult for you to sit anywhere for a few days.

Animals can be rented from the stables near the Mena House Hotel and the Giza Pyramids.

Getting Around Saqqara

If you haven't already crossed the desert from Giza on your own beast of burden then the ideal visit would be to first rent an animal at North Saqqara and take a return ride to South Saqqara, then hike through the desert to the pyramids of Abu

Sir. From there it's only two km to the village of Abu Sir, where you can get a minibus to Giza and back to Cairo.

To make the hike from North Saqqara to Abu Sir, walk straight towards the green fields, then go to the right, heading for the grove of palm trees, until you reach the canal. You then turn right, along the canal, and follow it until you reach the canal village. There is very little chance of getting lost as you can clearly see the pyramids of Abu Sir from North Saqqara.

If you want an animal, it is possible to hire one at the Rest House near the Serapeum in North Saqqara. A round-trip between North Saqqara and Abu Sir should cost, after bargaining, E£2.50 to E£3.50 for a donkey; E£6 for a camel; or E£7 to E£8 for a horse. Prices to South Saqqara are about the same, sometimes a bit less; and to Dahshur are almost double but should include South Saqqara.

HELWAN

Helwan, an industrial suburb of some 40,000 people, is about 25 km south of Cairo. At one time this was probably quite a pleasant place but as a factory city it grew quickly and is now probably the most polluted area in Egypt. There are, however, a few unique things that are worth seeing.

Japanese Gardens

Strange as it may seem, Helwan is home to the only Japanese gardens in the Middle East. Although most of the garden is scruffy and overgrown with weeds and the once grand duck ponds now have more squawking human bathers than quacking ducks, it is still obvious that it was once a magnificent place. It's worth seeing if only to check out the row of disfigured red Buddhas – probably one of the last things you expect to see in Egypt. The gardens are close to the centre of town, down the

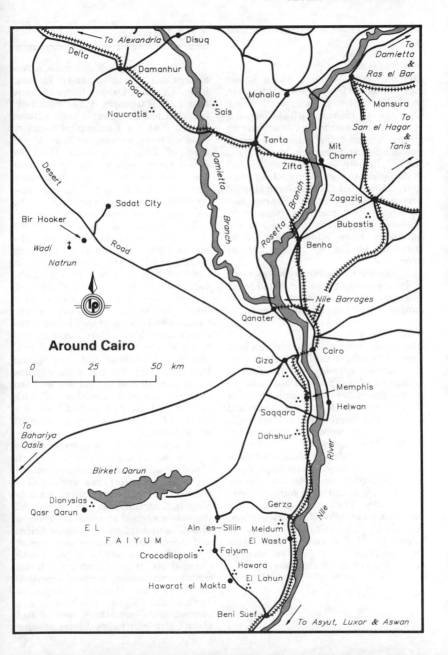

Around Cairo

0   25   50 km

street to your right as you leave the train station.

Wax Museum

Helwan's Wax Museum, which depicts Egypt's history from Ramses II to Nasser, in life-like tableaus, is also worth seeing. Displays include the death of Cleopatra, Roman soldiers stabbing Christians with spears, a man being hanged, scenes of peasant life and Nasser's leadership of the 1952 Revolution. Fans whir at the feet of the figures to keep them cool, although most of them look they've already melted once and been re-moulded. The caretaker usually insists on guiding you through the museum. It's open from 9 am to 5 pm and admission costs E£1, or 50 pt for students, plus a 40 pt tip for the caretaker.

If you don't feel like walking around Helwan you can take a horse and buggy ride from the train station to both the Japanese Gardens and the museum.

Getting There

The easiest way to get to Helwan from Cairo is to take a minibus from Bab el-Louk market, opposite the telecommunications building. You can also take the metro commuter train from Sayyida Zeinab station to Helwan which is the end of the line. However, the train is usually so packed with workers that this might not be a viable option.

To get from Helwan to Saqqara you can take a taxi to a ferry boat for 50 pt. There is also a minibus which leaves from the Helwan station and takes you to the ferry boat for 10 pt. The boat is a green, donkey ferry/motorboat called *Markib Bedrashein*. It costs 10 pt to cross the Nile to the village of El Bedrashein, from where there are taxis and micro-buses which go to Abu Sir and Kerdassa (near Giza).

The Faiyum

The Faiyum, Egypt's largest oasis, covers an area about 70 km wide and 60 km long, including Lake Qarun. Home to more than 1,300,000 people, it is an intricately irrigated, extremely fertile basin watered by the Nile via hundreds of capillary canals. The entire area, just 90 km south-west of Cairo, was once filled by Birket Qarun, which is fed by the Bahr Yusef (River of Josef) a tributary which leaves the Nile at Dairut. The lake now occupies only about one fifth of the Faiyum, on the north-western edge.

The pharaohs of the 12th Dynasty reduced the inflow of water into the lake and reclaimed the land for cultivation thereby regulating the annual flooding of the Nile. The oasis became a favourite vacation spot for pharaohs of the 13th Dynasty and many fine palaces were built. The Greeks later called the area Crocodilopolis because they believed the crocodiles in Birket Qarun were sacred. A temple was built in honour of *Sobek*, the crocodile-headed god, and during Ptolemaic and Roman times pilgrims came from all over the ancient world to feed the sacred beasts. By the 13th century AD the Faiyum had become a centre of Christianity, with over 30 monasteries.

Though not a true oasis, because of its link to the Nile, the Faiyum has been called the garden of Egypt. Lush fields of vegetables and sugar cane, and groves of citrus fruits, nuts and olives produce abundant harvests; the lake, canals and vegetation support an amazing variety of bird life; and the customs, living conditions and agricultural practices in the mud brick villages throughout the oasis have changed very little in centuries. All this tradition and fertility however, surrounds the rather grimy Medinet el Faiyum, or Town of the Faiyum, which sadly is a microcosm of everything that is bad about Cairo: horn happy drivers, choking

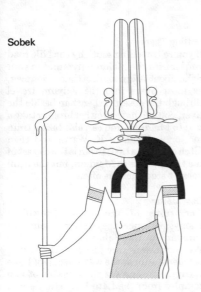

Sobek

fumes and dust, crowded streets and a population of more than 350,000.

MEDINET EL FAIYUM
Information
There are tourist offices in Faiyum opposite the water wheels, at the lake and at Ain es-Siliin. The people in the office near the wheel don't speak much English, so they aren't too helpful, though they can direct you to the train, bus or service taxi station.

There is a police station on Midan Qa'oun; a post office on Sharia Saad Zaghloul; and a telephone office on Sharia Hurriya.

The Water Wheels
Three functioning models of the actual water wheels still in use around the Faiyum can be seen opposite the tourist office. Irrigation water has to be obtained from the Nile, not from Birket Qarun, as the lake is salty.

The Faiyum Market
This is an interesting local market which sells fruits, vegetables, and houseware such as huge aluminum pots and copper

pans. You won't get hassled here because no one speaks English.

The Hawara Pyramid & Labyrinth
About 10 km south-east of Faiyum, on the road to Beni Suef, is the dilapidated 58-metre mud-brick pyramid of Amenemhat III. What was his vast mortuary complex is now nothing but mounds of rubble and even his temple, which had quite a reputation in ancient times, has suffered at the hands of stone robbers. Herodotus said the temple was a labyrinth of 3000 rooms, that surpassed even the pyramids; while Strabo claimed there were as many rooms as there were provinces so that all the pharaoh's subjects could be represented by their local officials in the offering of sacrifices. In 24 BC, Strabo wrote:

. . . there are long and numerous covered ways, with winding passages communicating with each other, so that no stranger could find his way in or out of them without a guide. The roofs of these dwellings consist of a single stone each, and the covered ways are roofed in the same manner with single slabs of stone of extraordinary size, without the intermixture of timber or any other material.

The area was also used as a cemetery by the Greeks and Romans, who here adopted the Egyptian practice of mummification. Now, all that remains are pieces of mummy cloth and human bones sticking through the mounds of rubble. There's also a crocodile cemetery north-east of the pyramid.

The buses between Beni Suef and Faiyum pass through Hawarat el Makta from where it's a short walk to the pyramid. Just ask the driver to let you off.

The Pyramid of Lahun
About 10 km south-east of Hawara, on the Nile side of the narrow fertile passage through the desert that connects the Faiyum to the river, is the ruins of a small mud-brick pyramid. Once cased in

limestone it was built by Senusert II back in the Middle Kingdom period, around 1885 BC. This monument is definitely off the beaten track and although there's not much of it left you can climb to the top for a great view of the surrounding area. The locals will probably be so surprised to see you that they'll invite you to tour their fields and houses.

You can probably hitch from Beni Suef or Faiyum to the dirt road which leads to the village of El Lahun; or take the local bus between the two cities and tell the driver where you want to stop.

The Pyramid of Meidum

Standing beyond the vegetation belt, about 32 km north-east of Faiyum is the ruin of the first real pyramid attempted by the ancient Egyptians. The Pyramid of Meidum is impressive, although rising abruptly as it does from a large hill of rubble, it looks more like a stone tower than a pyramid. This is one case, however, where the apparent state of disrepair was not caused by time or centuries of stone robbers, but was actually the result of one instantaneous accident. The pyramid began as an eight-stepped structure, the steps were then filled in and the outer casing was added, forming the first true pyramid shell. However, there were serious design flaws and sometime after completion the pyramid's own weight caused the sides to collapse, leaving just the core that still stands today.

The pyramid was started by King Huni, but completed by his son Sneferu, the founder of the 4th Dynasty. Sneferu's architects obviously learnt well from the disaster of Meidum as he also built the more successful Bent and Red pyramids at Dahshur and it was his son Cheops who built the Great Pyramid at Giza.

Ask the guard at the nearby house to unlock the entrance of the pyramid for you. You have to descend a shaky ladder and then follow a passageway to the empty underground burial chamber.

Getting There

If you're travelling south by the Nile road you can see the Meidum pyramid to your right, about 70 km south of Cairo. However, as most buses into the Faiyum travel through the desert rather than beside the river, you will have to either hitch or take a taxi to Meidum. You can also take a train to Gerza, Ifwah or El Wasta and then hitch or catch a taxi. Ifwah is the closest of the three towns to Meidum, but the train doesn't stop there as often.

Qasr Qarun

The ruins of the ancient town of Dionysias, once the starting point for caravans to the Bahariyya Oasis in the Western Desert, are just near the village of Qasr Qarun at the western end of Lake Qarun. You can see the remains of two temples from the Late Dynastic Period, circa 1090 to 332 BC, (the larger temple once had two storeys), and what's left of the municipal baths and a Roman fortress.

To get to Qasr Qarun you'll either have to hitch or take a taxi.

Places to Stay

There is a dearth of places to stay in the Faiyum. There's a *Youth Hostel* in the city itself, on Sharia el Hurriya. At 80 pt per night it's cheap but a bit decrepit.

The *Ain es-Siliin Hotel* has dusty and musty singles and doubles for E£5 to E£7 with showers. Hot water is sometimes available, breakfast costs E£1 and there's a restaurant attached to the hotel. It's a fair place to stay, if a little run down, but its best features are the surrounding gardens and mineral springs. Ain es-Siliin, which means 'the Springs of Siliin', is about half way between the city of Faiyum and Lake Qarun. Buses which run between the town and the lake pass right by Ain es-Siliin and there are also collective taxis.

The *Auberge Fayyoum Oberoi* is a new five-star hotel on the site of the original Auberge du Lac on Lake Qarun. Winston

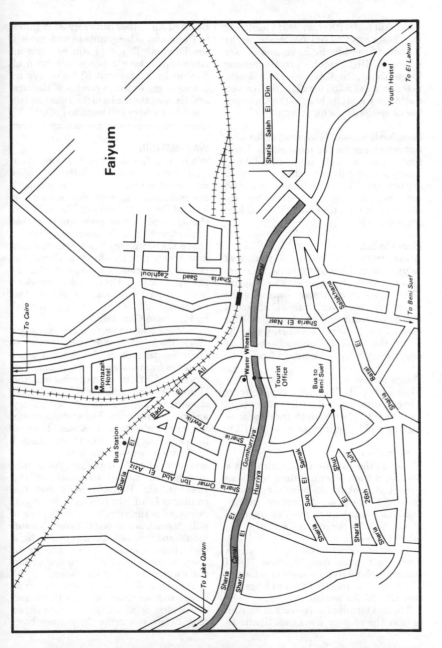

Faiyum

To El Lahun
Youth Hostel

Sharia Salah El Din

Sharia Saad Zaghloul

To Cairo

Canal

To Beni Suef

Sharia El Nasr

El Salakhana

Montazah Hotel

Water Wheels

Sharia El Bahr

Tourist Office

Bus to Beni Suef

El Badr

Sharia Tewfik

El Ali

Bus Station

Sharia El Aziz

Abd El Ibn Omar

Sharia El Gomhurriya

Sharia El Hurriya

Suq El Samak

El Shut

July

26th

Sharia El

Sharia El

Sharia El Canal

Sharia El Canal

To Lake Qarun

Churchill met with other world leaders at this hotel after WW I to decide on the borders of the Middle East; and it later served as King Farouk's private hunting lodge. Today, the Auberge is an expensive place to stay (E£60 for a single), but you could have a Stella beer in the Churchill bar or splurge on a big lunch.

Camping It is possible to camp at the lake, but watch out for the mosquitoes. Don't forget your malaria tablets and bring mosquito repellent as the nasty little critters get a bit thick sometimes. Also prepare your nose for the slightly offensive smell of the lake; it is possible to get used to it.

Places to Eat
Aside from the standard *fuul and ta'amiyya* and *kushari* stands, there are also a couple of restaurants in Faiyum. The *Cafeteria al Medina* opposite the water wheels serves shish-kebab and a few other meat and chicken dishes for about E£3. Near the Montazah (see the map), the *Nadi el Muhavsa* serves just about every type of Egyptian food.

Things to Buy
Throughout the Faiyum, especially at Ain es-Siliin, you will see lots of colourful basketwork. There's all shapes and sizes for sale and lot of it costs less than E£1.

Getting There
To get to the Faiyum from Cairo take a bus No 8 from Midan Tahrir to Midan Giza, then look for the minibus terminal near the overpass. A service taxi or minibus from there to the Faiyum costs about E£1.50 per person and the trip takes 1½ hours.

There are other buses to the Faiyum every half hour from Ahmed Helmi station (behind Ramses station in Cairo). The buses run from 6.30 am to 6 pm and cost E£1.25 per person.

The bus terminal in the city of Faiyum is near the railway tracks on Sharia El

Badd El Ali. Buses run every 30 minutes to Cairo and other points in and around the Faiyum. To get to Ain es-Siliin or Lake Qarun take a bus to the town of Sanhur from Mahattit El Ba'udiyya in town. To get to the pyramids of Hawara and Lahun take the Beni Suef bus and tell the driver where you want to get off.

WADI NATRUN
While the Coptic churches and their collections of macabre religious relics may seem a little incongruous amongst the minarets and muezzins of Cairo, a visit to the monasteries of Wadi Natrun should explain the endurance of this ancient sect. It is the desert, in a sense, that is the protector of the Coptic faith for it was there that thousands of Christians retreated to escape Roman persecution in the 4th century. They lived in caves or built monasteries and developed the monastic tradition that was later adopted by European Christians.

In Wadi Natrun alone there were once more than 50 monasteries, built as fortresses to protect the isolated communities from marauding Bedouins. The focal point of the monasteries was the church, around which was built a well, storerooms, a dining hall, kitchen, bakery and the monks' cells. The whole complex was surrounded by walls, about 14 metres high and four metres thick, and guarded by the keep – a tower which also served as an internal fort during sieges. While only four of the monasteries survived the Romans, the Bedouin raids and the coming of Islam, the religious life they all protected is thriving. The Coptic pope is still chosen from among the Wadi Natrun monks and monasticism is experiencing a revival as younger Copts are again donning the hooded robes to live within these ancient walls in the desert.

You can visit the monasteries either as a side trip en route between Cairo and Alexandria or as a day tour from either city. Before you make the journey however you should check with the Coptic Orthodox Patriarchate. In Cairo the Patriarchate is next to St Mark's Church, 222 Ramses St, Abbassiya (tel 825863/ 821274); and in Alexandria it's on Nebi Daniel St. You also need written permission from either of these offices if you wish to spend the night at one of the monasteries. The latter only applies to men; women are not allowed to stay overnight at all.

Wadi Natrun itself is a partly cultivated valley, about 100 km north-west of Cairo, that was important to the Egyptians long before the Copts took refuge there. The natron used in the mummification process came from the large deposits of sodium carbonate left after the valley's salt lakes dried up every summer.

Deir Amba Bishoi
St Bishoi founded two monasteries in Wadi Natrun, this one bearing his name, and the nearby Deir el Suriani. The Monastery of St Bishoi, which is a great place to watch a desert sunset, contains the body of St Bishoi, supposedly perfectly preserved under a red cloth, and the remains of Paul of Tamweh who made quite a name for himself by committing suicide seven times. The monks there claim it is not uncommon for St Bishoi to perform miracles for true believers.

Deir el Suriani
The Monastery of the Syrians, so-named for the many Syrian monks that once lived there, is about 500 metres north-west of Deir Amba Bishoi. There are several domed churches amongst the gardens and courtyards of this tranquil monastery. Ask the monks to show you St Bishoi's private cell where he stood for nights on end with his hair attached to a chain dangling from the ceiling. It was during one of these marathon prayer vigils that Christ appeared and allowed Bishoi to wash His feet and then drink the water.

Deir Abu Makar
Though structurely it has suffered a greater beating at the hands of raiding Bedouins, the Monastery of St Makarus is perhaps the most renowned of the four because over the centuries most of the Coptic popes have been selected from among its monks. The monastery, which is south-east of Deir Amba Bishoi, is the last resting place of many of those popes and also contains the remains of the '49 Martyrs', a group of monks killed by Bedouins in 444 AD.

Deir el Baramus
The most isolated of the Wadi Natrun monasteries is that of St Baramus, which is across the desert to the north. It's probably the best one to stay at if you can get to it, and have permission, as it's a little less austere than the others. The feature of its church is a superb *iconostasis* of inlaid ivory.

Places to Stay
If you can't stay at one of the monasteries then try the resthouse in nearby Bir Hooker. You pass through this village, which is three km off the Cairo-Alexandria road, en route to Deir Amba Bishoi. Singles cost E£9 and doubles are E£10 and there's a restaurant with meals for about E£2.

Getting There
Getting to Wadi Natrun may be difficult if you don't have your own transportation. You can take one of the regular buses which run between Cairo and Alexandria, via the Desert road, and ask the driver to drop you off at the resthouse by the roadside, about 95 km from Cairo. From there you can try to find a private taxi or minibus to take you out to Deir Amba Bishoi. At the very least you should be able to get a ride to the village of Bir Hooker and arrange for additional transportation from there.

If you do happen to have your own vehicle, and you're coming from Cairo, you take Sharia al-Ahram (Pyramids Rd) through Giza and turn onto the Desert road just before the Mena House Hotel. At about 95 km from Cairo (just after the resthouse) you turn left into the wadi, go through the village of Bir Hooker and continue on, following the signs indicating the monasteries. The first one you come to is Deir Amba Bishoi; Deir el Suriani is about half a km to the west; Deir Abu Makar is a few km via a paved road to the east; and Deir el Baramus is quite a hike through the sands to the north-west.

The Nile Delta

If you have the time it's well worth the effort to explore the lush fan-shaped Delta of Egypt between Cairo and Alexandria. This is where the Nile divides in half to flow north into the sea at the Mediterranean ports of Damietta and Rosetta (Rashid). The Delta is also laced with several smaller tributaries and is reputedly one of the most fertile and, not surprisingly, most cultivated regions in the world.

The Delta region played just as important a part in the early history of the country as Upper Egypt did, though there are few archaeological remains that record this. While the desert and dryness of the south were conducive to the preservation of pharaonic sites the amazing fertility of the Delta region had the opposite effect. Over the centuries when the ancient cities, temples and palaces of the Delta were left to ruin they were literally ploughed into oblivion by the *fellahin*. The attraction in this area then is the chance of coming across communities rarely visited by foreigners, where you can gain a little insight into the way of life of Egypt's peasant farmers.

Though service taxis and buses criss-cross the region from town to town, the best way to get off the beaten track and wander this incredibly green countryside

is to hire a car. By travelling the backroads and along the canals under your own steam you can visit the quaint farming villages that thrive amongst the fields of cotton, maize and rice. Theoretically, you're not supposed to leave the main roads, but in the unlikely event that you get hassled by the police, you can always say you're lost.

THE NILE BARRAGES & QANATER

The Nile Barrages and the city of Qanater lie 16 km north of Cairo where the Nile splits into the eastern Damietta Branch and the western Rosetta Branch. The Barrages were begun in the early 19th century and after several decades of trial and error the series of basins and locks on both main branches of the Nile and two side canals were successfully completed, ensuring the vital large scale regulation of the Nile into the Delta region. Almost immediately there was a great increase in cotton production.

The Damietta Barrage consists of 71 sluices stretching 521 metres across the river; the Rosetta Barrage is 438 metres long with 61 sluices; and between the two is an area, one km wide, filled with beautiful gardens and cafés. It's a superb place to rent a bicycle or a *felucca* and take a relaxing tour. The town of Qanater, at the fork of the river, is officially the start of the Delta region.

Getting There

To get to the Barrages from Cairo you can take a ferry for 50 pt from the water-taxi station in front of the Television building (Maspero station), just north of the Ramses Hilton. The trip takes about two hours. There is a bus to Qanater which leaves from in front of the Nile Hilton, on the Midan Tahrir side.

ZAGAZIG

Just outside this town, founded in the 19th century, are the ruins of **Bubastis**, one of the most ancient cities in Egypt. There's not much to see in Zagazig itself but as it's only 80 km north-east of Cairo it's an easy day trip to the ruins. You can take any train heading for Port Said from Cairo and the trip will take about 1½ hours. A service taxi to Zagazig takes about one hour.

Bubastis

The great deity of the ancient city of Bubastis was the elegant cat-goddess *Bastet*. Incredible festivals held in her honour supposedly attracted more than 700,000 revellers who would sing, dance, feast, consume great quantities of wine and offer sacrifices to the goddess. The architectural gem of Bubastis was the Temple of Bastet, sited between two canals, surrounded by trees and encircled by the city which was built at a higher level so as to look down on it. The temple was begun by Cheops and Chephren during the 4th Dynasty and pharaohs of the 6th, 12th 18th, 19th and 22nd Dynasties, covering about 17 centuries, made their additions. Herodotus gave this description:

Although other Egyptian cities were carried to a great height, in my opinion the greatest

Bastet

mounds were thrown up about the city of Bubastis, in which is a temple of Bastet well worthy of mention; for though other temples may be larger and more costly, none is more pleasing to look at than this.

The temple is now mostly just a pile of rubble and the most interesting site at Bubastis is the *Cat Cemetery* 200 metres down the road. The series of underground galleries, where many bronze statues of cats were found, is perfect for a bit of exploration.

TANIS

Just outside the village of San el Hagar, 70 km north-east of Zagazig, are the ruins of ancient Tanis which many believe to be the Biblical city where the Hebrews were persecuted by the Egyptians before fleeing through the Red Sea in search of the Promised Land. It was certainly of great importance to a succession of powerful pharaohs, all of whom left their mark on the extraordinary buildings or statues they commissioned, and for several centuries was one of the largest cities in the Delta.

Tanis covers an area of about four square km, only a small part of which has been excavated. The monuments uncovered date from as early as the 6th Dynasty reign of Pepi I, around 2330 BC, through to the time of the Ptolemies in the 1st century BC. The city so far has revealed sacred lakes, the foundations of many temples, a royal necropolis and a multitude of statues and carvings.

TANTA

The largest city in the Delta, Tanta is 90 km from Cairo and 110 km from Alexandria. There's nothing much of interest there, though it is a centre for Sufism, a form of Islamic mysticism. A mosque in Tanta is dedicated to Said Badawi, a Moroccan Sufi, who fought the Crusaders from there in the 13th century and then went on to assist in the defeat of Louis IX at Damietta.

In this area of the western Delta, though there are no actual structural remains, there are the sites of three ancient cities. North-west of Tanta on the east bank of the Nile was **Sais**, Egypt's 26th Dynasty capital. Sais, sacred to *Neith* the goddess of war and hunting and protector of embalmed bodies, dates back to the start of Egyptian history and once had palaces, temples and royal tombs.

West of Tanta, about half-way along the road to Damanhur, is the site of **Naucratis**, an ancient city where the Greeks were allowed to settle and trade during the 7th century BC. The city of **Buto**, east of Damanhur and north of Tanta, was the cult-centre of *Edjo*, the cobra goddess of Lower Egypt, always represented on a pharaoh's crown as a uraeus.

MANSURA

As the centre of Egypt's cotton industry Mansura is one of the most important cities in the Delta. The best thing about a visit to Mansura is the chance to taste the city's delicacy – buffalo milk ice cream.

Known as the 'city of victory', Mansura also played quite a part in Egypt's early Islamic history. In 1249 the Egyptians retreated from the coast and set up camp at Mansura after the Crusader forces, under Louis IX of France, had captured the Mediterranean port town of Damietta. When the Crusaders decided to make their push inland they charged straight through the Muslim camp only to be cut down on the other side of Mansura by 10,000 Mameluke warriors. Louis himself was captured and ransomed for the return of Damietta.

DAMIETTA

Once a prosperous Arab trading port, Damietta's fortunes suffered greatly with the construction of the Suez Canal and the subsequent development of Port Said. During the Middle Ages, its strategic position on the north coast of Egypt, at the mouth of the Nile, meant it was regularly being threatened by foreign armies. Over the centuries it was taken by the Germans, English and French and defended by, among others, Salah al-Din and Mohammed Ali. When it wasn't being attacked by marauding Crusaders Damietta was doing a roaring trade in coffee, linen, oil and dates and was a port of call for ships from all over the known world.

RAS EL BAR

The small town of Ras el Bar, north of Damietta, is right at the point where the eastern branch of the Nile meets the sea, 120 km north-east of Cairo. It is a pleasant beach resort with several hotels and restaurants and if you're planning on staying anywhere in the Delta region this would be the best choice.

There are other quiet little beach resorts to the west of Ras el Bar at **Gamasa**, **Baltim** and **El Burg**.

A most common sight...

Places to Stay

Abou Tabl, 4 Sharia 17, is a basic hotel with singles for E£12 and doubles for E£15, plus 20% tax. Its restaurant is well known for its fiteer and other types of oriental food.

Other OK hotels are the *Marine Fouad*, the *Marine el Nil* and the *Marine Ras el Bar*.

Getting There

Buses leave Cairo every hour, from 7.15 am to 5.15 pm, and travel direct to Ras el Bar. They leave from Qali station, which is near Ramses station. During summer you need to book at least one day in advance. The trip takes 3½ hours and costs E£3.50 on an air-conditioned bus.

The Nile Valley

The ancient Greek traveller and writer Herodotus described Egypt as 'a gift of the river'; the ancient Egyptians likened their land to a lotus – the Delta being the flower, the oasis of Faiyum the bud and the river and its valley the stem. Whichever way you look at it, Egypt is the Nile. The river is the life-blood of the country and the fertile Nile Valley is its heart. And whether you journey down the valley by *felucca*, train, bus or plane you'll discover that even an outsider cannot ignore the power of the Nile and the hold it has always had over Egyptian life.

Rain seldom falls in the Nile Valley so the verdant stretch of land, ranging from a couple of metres to a few kms wide on either side of the river, is rendered fertile only by the long winding blue of the Nile as it makes its way through the barren desert. The countryside is dotted with thousands of simple, rustic villages where people toil, day in day out, using tools and machinery modelled on designs 1000 years old. Even the region's large towns and cities, like Minya, Asyut, Luxor and Aswan, are in some ways merely modernised extensions of these villages.

Travelling south from Cairo you pass through a world where ancient and medieval monuments almost seem to be part of the present. From Saqqara to Luxor, while you marvel at the remarkable history of the pharaonic tombs and their builders, you'll realise that the daily labour and recreation of the *fellahin* in the 20th century differs very little from the images depicted in the wall paintings of the ancient monuments. The colourful scenes of Egyptians building, hunting, fighting, feasting, harvesting and fishing more than 2500 years ago, are repeated daily before your very eyes on the banks of the Nile and in the valley's fertile fields.

BENI SUEF

Beni Suef is a provincial capital 130 km south of Cairo. Even with a population of 150,000 and a few multi-storeyed buildings, it isn't exactly what you'd call a big town. It is, however, typical of the large Egyptian country towns which are basically overgrown farming villages. There are more donkey carts and *hantours* (horse-drawn carriages) in the streets than cars and buses and while there's nothing of particular interest in Beni Suef itself, it is a good base for visiting the Faiyum.

Places to Stay

The *Semiramis Hotel* is really the only hotel in town worth mentioning. It has six singles and 24 doubles. Two of the singles have bathrooms and cost E£6; the other four cost E£4. Of the doubles, 20 have bathrooms and cost E£10; the rest cost E£7.50. Hot water and televisions are included, the 12% service charge is not and a continental breakfast costs an extra E£1. The hotel faces the train tracks and is opposite the post office.

There is also a *Teacher's Club* down the street toward the Nile (refer to the map) which has a few cheap rooms. It's a bit run-down but you're bound to meet some interesting characters there who speak some English.

Places to Eat

Aside from the usual assortment of *fuul* and *ta'amiyya* stands, there is the *Nadi Shurta* on the Corniche along the Nile. Meals of fish and typical Egyptian fare cost about E£4.

Getting There

There are frequent buses, trains and service taxis to Beni Suef from Cairo and Helwan. From Beni Suef there are buses to Cairo for E£1.50, to Medinet el Faiyum

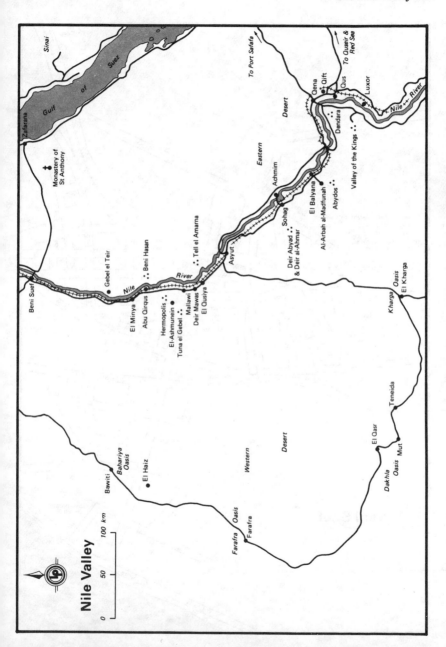

Nile Valley

0   50   100 km

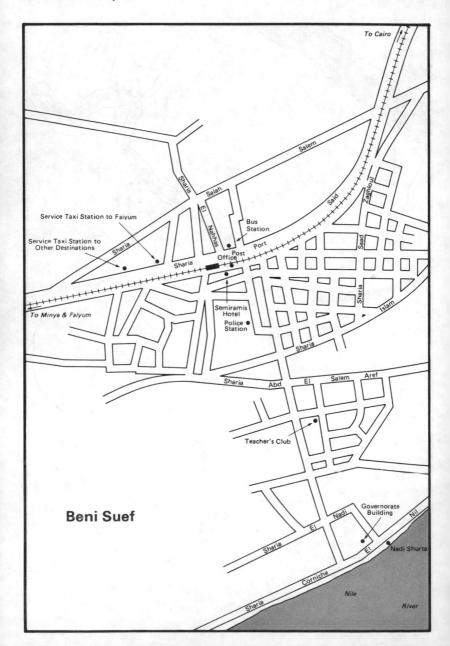

To Cairo

Salem

Sharia

Salah

El Nahhas

Said

Zaghloul

Service Taxi Station to Faiyum

Bus
Station

Port

Saad

Service Taxi Station to
Other Destinations

Sharia

Sharia

Post
Office

To Minya & Faiyum

Semiramis
Hotel

Police
Station

Sharia

Sharia

Islam

Sharia

Abd

El

Salem

Aref

Teacher's Club

Beni Suef

El

Nadi

Governorate
Building

Nil

Sharia

El

Nadi Shurta

Corniche

Nile

Sharia

River

for 40 pt and to Minya for E£1.25. Service taxis for the same locations cost E£2.50 pt and E£1.50. The Beni Suef bus station is opposite the post office and the service taxi station is a little further down Sharia Port Said.

The buses tend to be quite crowded and often the best 'seats' are on the roof. While travelling atop one of these buses a couple of 19-year-old soldiers from the countryside told me why they were already married, or rather their graphic gestures and ear-to-ear grins explained why. I asked them how many kids they planned to have. 'Six or seven', they said. 'And how will you feed all of these kids?' I asked. *Allah, Allah, Allah hu-akbar*, they said. That means 'God, God, God is Great'. Hmmm!

Beni Suef is also a departure point for the track and trek across the desert to St Antony's Monastery, which is about 150 km east, near the Red Sea. You'd really need your own truck or four-wheel drive vehicle to make this journey as it might be difficult to hire a service taxi in Beni Suef for the whole trip.

GEBEL EL TEIR

The main feature of this small Christian hamlet, 93 km south of Beni Suef, is **Deir el Adhra** – the Monastery of the Virgin. Established as a church/monastery in the 4th century AD by Empress Helena it was built on one of the sites where the Holy Family supposedly rested while fleeing Palestine. Gebel el Teir and its church are perched on a hill 130 metres above the east bank of the Nile.

Getting from the main Nile road to the east side of the river is definitely an adventure. In the west bank village opposite Gebel el Teir you ask for *il markib li Gebel el Teir* – the boat to Gebel el Teir. You then walk to the Nile and wait for a shaky little canoe to appear and ferry you to the other side. Once across you walk through a field to the stairs cut into the side of the cliff that go up to the hamlet. Someone will probably lead you

to the priest but if not just ask for the *kineesa* or church. The priest speaks some English and can give you a short tour of the monastery and the hamlet.

There's a guest house which provides accommodation. Back down at the foot of the stairs you can hitch a ride either north or south to a bigger ferry crossing. There's a ferry boat 24 km south of Gebel el Teir which crosses the river to El Minya.

EL MINYA

A semi-industrial provincial capital 247 km south of Cairo with a population of about 160,000, Minya is a centre for sugar processing and the manufacture of soap and perfume. There are several hotels which make this a convenient place to base yourself for day trips to the pharaonic tombs and temples of Beni Hasan, Tuna el Gebel and Hermopolis.

There is not much to see or do in town, except just walk around and meet some of the friendly local people, most of whom will be extremely interested in whether or not you're married. The tree-lined Corniche along the Nile is a pleasant place for a picnic or a ride in a *hantour*.

The Ministry of Tourism (tel 2044 & 2155), has an office in the Minya Governorate building on the Corniche, north of the main street, Sharia el Mahattit.

Zawiyet el Mayyiteen

This is a large Muslim and Christian cemetery across the river from Minya, near the ferry landing. Translated it means 'Corner of the Dead'. The corner consists of several hundred mud-brick mausolea stretching for four km from the road to the hills. It is, supposedly, one of the largest cemeteries in the world.

Places to Stay

The *Ibn Khassib Hotel* is an old building on Sharia Adly Yakan, about a block from the Minya train station. It has plenty of rooms both old, with high ceilings, and

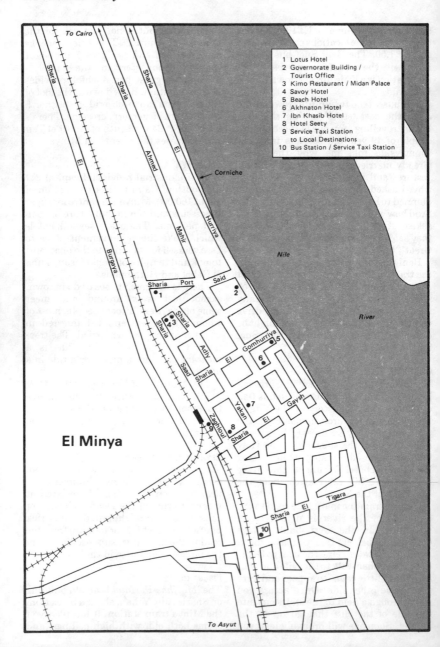

To Cairo

Sharia

Sharia

Sharia El

Sharia Ahmed Mahir

Sharia El Hurriya

Sharia Burgaya

Corniche

Nile

River

Sharia Port Said

Sharia

Sharia Saad

Sharia Adly

Sharia El

Sharia Gomhurriya

Sharia El Gaysh

Sharia Yakan

Sharia Zaghloul

Sharia

El Minya

Sharia El Tigara

Sharia El

To Asyut

1 Lotus Hotel
2 Governorate Building /
  Tourist Office
3 Kimo Restaurant / Midan Palace
4 Savoy Hotel
5 Beach Hotel
6 Akhnaton Hotel
7 Ibn Khasib Hotel
8 Hotel Seety
9 Service Taxi Station
  to Local Destinations
10 Bus Station / Service Taxi Station

new. Singles/doubles with bathrooms cost E£8.50/10, or without bathrooms cost E£7/8.50. Breakfast is included and other meals are available. A lunch of chicken, kufta, rice, vegetables, salad and dessert costs about E£4. A 12% tax and service charge is added to everything. Tour groups use this hotel and it's often easy to get a ride with them to some of the local attractions.

The *Beach Hotel* (tel 22307), is a clean pleasant place three blocks from the train station and overlooking the river. Singles with or without bath cost from E£7 to E£15. If possible try to avoid the crooked-toothed, cantankerous old grouch at the reception desk; you'll save a lot of time.

The *Hotel Seety*, 71 Sharia Saad Zaghloul, is opposite the station. It's a bit antiquated and dusty but reasonable value. A double room with/without bath costs E£7/5. Sometimes there is hot water.

The *Savoy Hotel*, on Midan Palace north of the station off Sharia Saad Zaghloul, has large rooms and an eclectic combination of lamps and wall hangings. Singles/doubles with showers cost E£4.10/5.45; or without showers cost E£3.10/4.30. The bathrooms smell but the showers are OK.

The *Lotus Hotel* is on Sharia Port Said. It's a modern pink structure with a restaurant on top which serves delicious meals for E£5. Singles cost E£9, doubles E£12 and triples E£15; all have air-conditioning and include breakfast.

The *Akhnaton Hotel*, on the Corniche near the Beach Hotel, has clean rooms on the 3rd and 4th floors. It has 21 rooms, some with spectacular views of the Nile, and hot water is available. Doubles with/without bath cost E£6.75/5, plus 12% taxes. Continental breakfast costs 75 pt plus 12% tax.

Camping It's possible to pitch a tent at the Minya Stadium, which is north of the station directly up the tracks.

Places to Eat
The restaurant and cafeteria on top of the Lotus Hotel serves full meals for E£3 to E£5. The views of the Nile and surrounding fields are fantastic.

Kimo is a small restaurant at the

corner of Midan Palace opposite the petrol station. They serve kufta, kebab and sometimes chicken.

AROUND EL MINYA
Beni Hasan
Beni Hasan is a necropolis on the east bank of the Nile about 20 km south of Minya. More than 30 distinctive Middle Kingdom tombs of varying sizes are carved into a limestone cliff. Only a few of them are accessible.

To get to Beni Hasan from Minya, or from Mallawi which is further south, you take a minibus or service taxi to Abu Qirqus for about 20 pt. From there you can walk the 2½ km to the Nile or take a taxi/pick-up truck for 10 pt. You then cross the Ibrahimiya canal and then take the 50 pt boat across the river. From the

east side you can walk or rent a donkey (50 pt), to the rest-house at the foot of the hill. There's a great view of the Nile from the tombs further up the slope. The tombs which you can see at Beni Hasan are:

No 17 *The Tomb of Kheti.* Kheti was a governor of the *Nome*, or district, of Oryx during Egypt's 11th Dynasty (circa 2000 BC). Wall scenes in his tomb show daily life in the Middle Kingdom as well as an attack on a fort and two copulating cows.

No 15 *The Tomb of Baqet.* Baqet was the father of Kheti and his tomb has some strange wall paintings. There are wrestlers doing more than just wrestling with each other, gazelles doing the same and a hunt for unicorns and winged monsters.

No 3 *The Tomb of Khnumhotep* is a beautiful tomb. Khnumhotep served as a

Entrance to Beni Hasan

Top: Pyramid of Meidum, El Faiyum (SW)
Bottom: Columns of the Basilica of Hermopolis, near Mallawi (SW)

Top: Temple of Dendara (SW)
Left: Temple of Abydos, near El Balyana (SW)
Right: Baboon god Thoth, Hermopolis (SW)

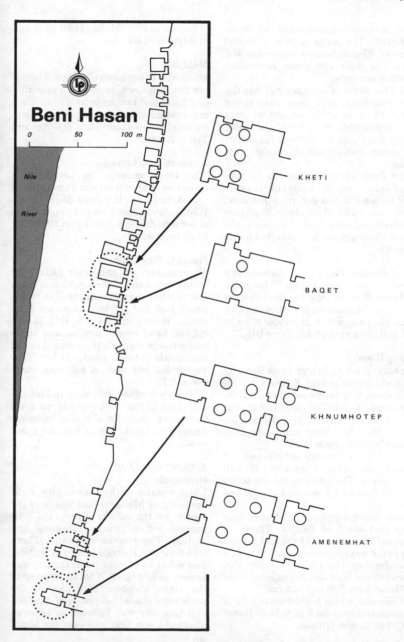

Beni Hasan

0   50   100 m

Nile

River

KHETI

BAQET

KHNUMHOTEP

AMENEMHAT

governor under Amenemhat III (circa 1820 BC). The walls feature colourful scenes of Khnumhotep's family life and above the door are some interesting scenes of acrobats.

No 2 *The Tomb of Amenemhat* has the unique addition of a false door facing west. The dead are supposed to enter the underworld only from the west. Amenemhat was a *nomarch* (governor) and commander-in-chief of the Oryx Nome.

The Beni Hasan necropolis is open from 6 am to 7 pm. It's a good idea to start early because it can get quite hot here. Admission is E£1.50, students 75 pt, plus *baksheesh* for the guard who unlocks the tombs. Photography is prohibited inside the tombs.

Tell el Amarna The site of Akhenaten's ruined city and necropolis is 73 km south of Minya. It is described in the following section on Mallawi as it's closer to that town. Minya however, is a nicer place to stay and close enough for a day trip.

Getting There
It is easy to get to Minya from Cairo by bus, train or service taxi. By train the trip takes about four hours and costs E£1.35 in 1st class, 90 pt in 2nd class and 45 pt in 3rd class. By service taxi from Giza station the three-hour trip costs E£3. Buses also leave from Giza.

From Minya there are 2nd class air-con trains to Cairo at 10.30 am and 1.30, 4.10 and 7.30 pm. The 1st class air-con trains leave at 7.30 and 8 am and 1, 4.50 and 8 pm.

Buses leave regularly for destinations north and south of Minya. There are buses to Cairo at 8 and 11 am and 1, 5 and 5.30 pm. Fares range from E£2.15 to E£6 depending on the quality of the bus. Buses to Beni Suef and Asyut leave every half hour from 7.30 am to 5 pm.

Minibuses, which leave from in front of the train station, cost 5 pt to Beni Hasan and 20 pt to Abu Qirqus.

Service taxis to Mallawi cost 50 pt and to Asyut cost E£1.50.

MALLAWI
Mallawi is 48 km south of Minya. There is not much in town, except for a museum, one hotel and two restaurants but it's a convenient departure point for the ancient sights of Hermopolis, Tuna el Gebel and Tell el Amarna.

Archaeological Museum
The small museum in town has a collection of artefacts from Tuna el Gebel and Hermopolis. It is open daily, except Wednesdays, from 9 am to 1 pm. It closes at noon on Fridays. Admission is 50 pt, or 25 pt for students.

Places to Stay & Eat
There is only one – the *Samir Amis Hotel* on the west bank of the Ibrahimiya canal just north of the train station. The rooms aren't bad, but the bathrooms are a bit grimy. Rooms are E£1.35, E£2.20 and E£2.90 for a single, double, and triple respectively. Samir's restaurant has the best meals in town: meat, chicken, rice, vegetables and beer. A full meal costs about E£2.

There's another restaurant in Mallawi called the *El Hourriya* which is just down the street; look for the cow carcasses hanging in front. It cost E£2 for a full meal.

AROUND MALLAWI
Hermopolis
Little remains of the ancient city, eight km north of Mallawi, that was once the centre for the cult of *Thoth*, the ibis-headed god of wisdom, healing and writing. The Greeks associated Thoth with their own Hermes, hence the Hellenic name, but in ancient times the city was known as Khmunu. *Khmun* was one of the eight all-powerful deities of the primordial chaos that preceded creation, and this city was believed to be sited where the sun first rose over the earth.

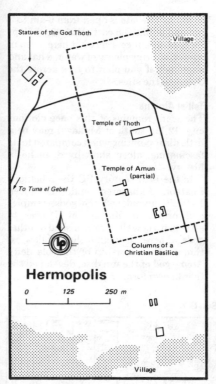

Statues of the God Thoth

Village

Temple of Thoth

Temple of Amun
(partial)

To Tuna el Gebel

Columns of a
Christian Basilica

Hermopolis

0   125   250 m

Village

The Arabic name for the present-day village and the area surrounding the ruined city of Hermopolis, is **el-Ashmunein** – a derivation of Khmun.

Apart from a few Middle and New Kingdom remains the only real monument at Hermopolis is the ruins of a Roman *agora* and its early Christian basilica – the largest of its type still standing in Egypt. A museum is being built near two large sandstone statues of *Thoth* unearthed in the area.

To get to Hermopolis from Mallawi you need to take a local bus or taxi to the village of el-Ashmunein; the turn-off to the site is one km from the main road. From the junction you can either walk the short distance to Hermopolis or coax your driver to go a bit further. Hitching around the area shouldn't be a problem as the sight of a foreigner walking down the road is bound to attract quite a lot of attention.

Tuna el Gebel
Apart from bordering the edge of *Akhetaten*, Pharaoh Akhenaten's short-lived capital, Tuna el Gebel was also the necropolis of Hermopolis. The oldest monument in the area is one of the six stelae which marked the boundary of *Akhetaten*; in this case the western perimeter of the city's farm lands and associated villages. The stela, a rock-hewn shrine and some statues show Akhenaten and Nefertiti in various poses.

To the south of the stela, which is about five km past the village of Tuna el Gebel, are the catacombs and tombs of the residents and sacred animals of Hermopolis. Cairo University has an archaeological team at Tuna el Gebel excavating the complex.

The most interesting things to see there are the dark catacomb galleries filled with thousands of mummified baboons, ibises and ibis eggs – the animals sacred to *Thoth*. Most of the mummification was done in the Ptolemaic and Roman periods. The subterranean cemetery extends for at least three km, though Egyptologists suspect it may stretch all the way to Hermopolis. You definitely need a torch if you're going to explore the galleries.

The Tomb of Petosiris is an interesting Ptolemaic tomb-chapel; a sign directs the way. Petosiris was a high priest of *Thoth* and his family tomb, in the design of a temple, is entered through a columned vestibule. The tomb paintings show a mixture of two cultures for although they depict typical Egyptian farming scenes, the figures are wearing Greek dress.

The Mummy of Isadora In a small building

behind the Tomb of Petosiris, is the extremely well-preserved mummy of a woman who drowned in the Nile in about 150 AD. Isadora's teeth, hair and fingernails are clearly visible. You'll need to give the guard a bit of *baksheesh* to see her though.

The Well, or *al-Sakiya*, has a water wheel next to it which once brought water up from its depths. The well was the sole source of water for the priests, workers and sacred baboons of Tuna el Gebel. For a bit more *baksheesh* the guard will unlock the door and let you walk down to the bottom of the well. Watch out for the bats!

Getting There Tuna el Gebel is seven km from Hermopolis. There's a fair amount of traffic between the Hermopolis junction and the village so it should be fairly easy to hitch. The site is open from 6 am to 5 pm and admission costs E£1.25, or 50 pt for students. It gets very hot here, even in winter, so bring plenty of water, a hat and sunscreen if you plan to trek across the desert to the sites.

Tell el Amarna
The scant remains of this once glorious city, 12 km south of Mallawi, may be a little disappointing when compared to its fascinating, albeit short-lived, niche in history.

In the 14th century BC the rebellious Pharaoh Akhenaten and his queen Nefertiti abandoned the gods, temples and priests of Karnak at Thebes to establish a new city, untarnished by other gods. There they and their followers, through their worship of the sole deity *Aten* – god of the sun disc, developed the first known form of monotheism.

Pharaoh & his Queen making offerings to the Sun God

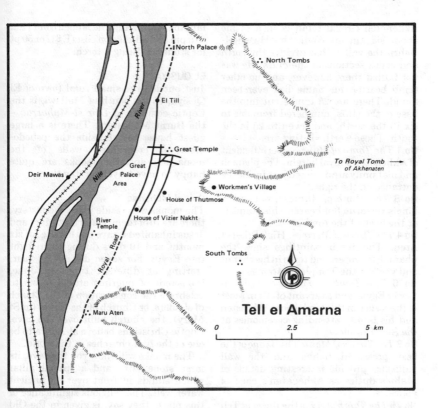

Tell el Amarna

North Palace

North Tombs

El Till

River

Nile

Great Temple

To Royal Tomb
of Akhenaten →

Deir Mawas

Great
Palace
Area

Workmen's Village

House of Thutmose

Royal Road

House of Vizier Nakht

River
Temple

South Tombs

Maru Aten

0   2.5   5 km

The city, in the area now known as Tell el Amarna, was built on the east bank of the Nile on a beautiful, yet solitary, crescent-shaped plain, extending about 12 km from north to south. Except for the side bounded by the river the palaces, temples and residences of the city were surrounded by high cliffs, broken here and there by wadis. The royal couple named their city *Akhetaten*, or 'Horizon of the Sun Disc', and it served as the capital of Egypt for about 14 years.

It was abandoned for all time shortly after Akhenaten's death, when the priests of Karnak managed to regain their religious control. They desecrated the temples of *Aten* and generally did their best to obliterate all record of the heretic

pharaoh's objectionable new religion. Polytheism was again predominant throughout the land as the Karnak priests persuaded Akhenaten's son-in-law and successor Tutankaten, or Tutankhamun as he became known, to re-establish the cult of *Amun* at Thebes. *Akhetaten* fell into ruin and the stones of its palaces and temples were used for buildings in Hermopolis and other cities.

The Tell el Amarna necropolis, comprised of two groups of cliff tombs at both ends of the city, feature colourful wall paintings of life during the *Aten* revolution. Many of the tombs, due to the city's sudden demise, were never finished and very few were actually used.

Akhenaten's royal tomb is in a ravine about six km up Wadi Abu Hasah el-Bahri, the valley that divides the north and south sections of the cliffs. He was not buried there however, and no other tomb bearing his name has ever been found. There are 25 tombs cut into the base of the cliffs, numbered from one to six in the north, and seven to 25 in the south. Those worth visiting are:

No 1 *The Tomb of Huya*, superintendent of Akhenaten's royal harem. The pharaoh and his family are depicted just inside the entrance on the right.

No 3 *The Tomb of Ahmose*, one of the king's versatile fan-bearers; his statue is at the back of the tomb.

No 4 *The Tomb of Merirye*, High Priest of Aten. The tomb paintings show the pharaoh riding around town in his chariot and visiting the Temple of *Aten*.

No 6 *The Tomb of Panehse*, vizier of Lower Egypt and a servant of *Aten*. Most of the scenes in this tomb show Akhenaten and his family attending ceremonies at the Sun Temple.

No 9 *The Tomb of Mahu* This is one of the best preserved tombs and the wall paintings provide interesting details of Mahu's duties as Akhenaten's chief of police.

No 25 *The Tomb of Ay* is the finest at Tell el Amarna. The wall paintings show street and palace scenes, and one depicts Akhenaten and Nefertiti presenting Ay and his wife with golden collars.

Getting There To get to Tell el Amarna from Mallawi, take a service taxi, from the south depot, or a local train to Deir Mawas from where you can walk or take a pick-up truck to the Nile boat landing. There you can try talking a *felucca* captain into ferrying you across, for 25 pt, or take the overpriced motorboat for E£2. Once on the other side, you have the choice of renting a donkey or taking a tractor ride for the five km trek across the desert to the northern tombs. The other tombs are about 10 km south of the ferry

landing. Tell el Amarna is open from 7 am to 5 pm and admission costs E£1, or 50 pt for students. Bring a torch.

EL QUSIYA

Just outside the small rural town of El Qusiya, 35 km south of Mallawi, is the Coptic complex of *Deir el-Muharraq* – the Burnt Monastery. There is a large guest house just outside the psuedo-medieval crenellated walls of the monastery and the monks are quite happy to have travellers stay there.

Deir el-Muharraq

The monks who reside in the monastery, there are 70 of them, claim that Mary and Jesus inhabited a cave on this site for six months and 10 days during their flight into Egypt. For seven days every year, starting at different times in June, thousands of pilgrims attend feasts to celebrate the consecration of the **Church of al-Adhra**, or Church of the Virgin (or St Mary), the church built over the cave. Coptic Christians believe al-Adhra to be one of the first churches in the world.

The monks will show you the cave, its large stone altar and a special pillar which stands in front over an ancient water well. The religious significance of this place, they say, is given in the Old Testament – Isaiah Chapter 19, verse 19:

In that day there will be an altar to the Lord in the midst of the land of Egypt, and a pillar to the Lord at its border. It will be a sign and a witness to the Lord of Host in the land of Egypt; when they cry to the Lord because of oppressors he will send them a saviour, and will defend and deliver them. And the Lord will make himself known to the Egyptians; and the Egyptians will know the Lord in that day and worship with sacrifice and burnt offering, and they will make vows to the Lord and perform them.

Other buildings in the monastery complex include **The Tower**, a 5th century structure built for the monks to use as added protection in case of attack. It has four floors and a church inside and is right next to al-Adhra.

The **Church of St George**, built in 1880, is lavishly decorated with paintings of the 12 apostles, each one with a wooden frame of inlaid ivory. The painting of St Markus with the lion is particularly interesting. Mark is always represented with a lion at his feet because one once attacked his father and when Mark ordered the lion to go away, the great beast lay down at his feet instead.

Getting There A service taxi will take you from Asyut or Mallawi to El Qusiya for about 60 pt and there are occasionally minibuses between there and Deir el Muharraq.

ASYUT

Asyut, settled during pharaonic times on a broad fertile plain on the west bank of the Nile, is unofficially the point where Upper (southern) and Lower (northern) Egypt meet. These days it's the largest town in Upper Egypt and the chief agricultural centre, dealing in things such as camels, cotton, grain and its local specialty – carpets.

It has been an important trading town since ancient times and was once head of the great caravan route to the Western Desert oases and across the Sahara. For several centuries, the camel caravans which travelled up the *40 Day Road* from Darfur province in the Sudan ended their trip in Asyut and as recently as 150 years ago the town boasted the largest slave market in Egypt.

Though never really politically important, Asyut was once the capital of the 13th Nome – the Sycamore province, and cult centre of the wolf god *Wepwawet*, the avenger of *Osiris* (god of the dead). In the 4th century AD Christianity became the dominant religion and today there are often confrontations in the city between the large communities of Copts and Muslim fundamentalists.

The Asyut barrage was built across the Nile in the late 19th century, under British supervision, to regulate the flow of water into the Ibrahimiya Canal and assist in the irrigation of the Valley as far north as Beni Suef. Asyut is still a major departure point for trips to the Western Oases, or the New Valley as it is now known.

Information

There is a Tourist Office (tel 322400), on Sharia El Mohafaza in the Governorate building.

The Post Office is next to the Asyut Tourist Hotel facing the train station and the telephone office is inside the station.

Things to See

There is a small **museum** of pharaonic and Coptic artefacts in the American College on Sharia Gomhurriya. The museum, which includes a mummy display, was being renovated in 1986.

On the way to the museum you'll pass a Coca-Cola bottling plant. It's a bit strange to watch the mechanised bottling process through one of the front windows and then turn around and watch the donkey carts pass by.

Gezira il Moz, or 'Banana Island', is in the Nile at the end of Sharia Salah Salem. The island's lush tropical forest is a very pleasant place to have a picnic or even camp. A *felucca* ride to the island quay costs 10 pt.

Places to Stay

The *Youth Hostel* (tel 324846), is at Lux Houses, 503 Sharia El Walidiya. It costs 60 pt to 80 pt a night.

The *Zamzam Hotel*, a cheap and basically clean place, is around the corner from the train station on Sharia Salah Salem. It costs E£2 per person a single or double and includes hot showers.

The *Lotus Hotel* is down the street from the Zamzam. Rooms cost from E£1.50 to E£2.50, but stay there only if the Zamzam is full.

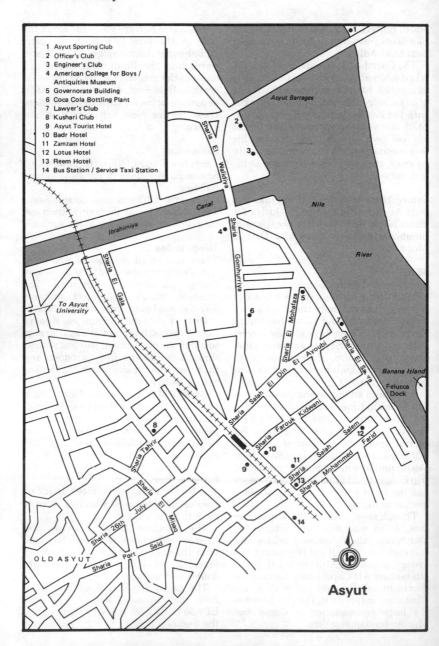

1 Asyut Sporting Club
2 Officer's Club
3 Engineer's Club
4 American College for Boys /
  Antiquities Museum
5 Governorate Building
6 Coca Cola Bottling Plant
7 Lawyer's Club
8 Kushari Club
9 Asyut Tourist Hotel
10 Badr Hotel
11 Zamzam Hotel
12 Lotus Hotel
13 Reem Hotel
14 Bus Station / Service Taxi Station

Asyut Barrages

Sharia El Walidiya

Canal

Ibrahimiya

Nile

River

To Asyut University

Sharia El Gala

Sharia Gomhurriya

Sharia El Mohafaza

Banana Island

Felucca Dock

Sharia El Sayra

Sharia El Ayoubi

Sharia Salah El Din

Sharia Farouk Kidwani

Salem

Salah

Sharia Farid

Sharia Tahrir

Sharia 26th July

Sharia El Misaq

Sharia Mohammed

OLD ASYUT

Sharia Port Said

Asyut

The *Reem Hotel*, also on Sharia Salah Salem, is a medium priced place with singles for E£14.05 and doubles ranging from E£19 to E£24.31. Towels, breakfast, a colour television, bathrooms and air conditioners are included in most of the rooms.

The *Badr Hotel* is the deluxe, western-style hotel of Asyut and an expatriate hang-out. Room rates are E£21 for a single and E£25 for a double plus 17% tax. There's a restaurant with an a la carte menu. The hotel was started by a Horatio Alger sort of Egyptian – a poor man who became extremely rich and then spread his money around town. The *Badr* is behind the train station.

Camping It's possible to camp at the Asyut Sporting Club, the Officers' Club and on Banana Island. The clubs have bathrooms and food available but there's nothing on the island except refreshing peace and quiet.

Places to Eat

The *Asyut Sporting Club* (tel 322139), next to the barrage/bridge, serves simple meals. Also known as the Public Works Club it is on the east bank of Sharia El Khazan.

The *Officers' Club* (tel 322134), also on Sharia El Khazan (west bank) has a restaurant and casino.

The *Engineers' Club* (tel 325302), is similar to the other two clubs and is located near the latter.

The *El Nil Café & Restaurant*, opposite the train station, serves good cheap meals of chicken and rice (among other things) from about E£2.

Getting There

Asyut, which is 378 km south of Cairo, 142 km north of Qena and 240 km east of Kharga (the nearest Western Desert oasis), is a major terminus for all forms of transport.

Trains arrive and depart for destinations north and south of Asyut almost every half hour. The 1st class air-con trains to Asyut leave Cairo at 8 pm and 8.30 pm. A 1st class ticket for the trip, which takes about 5½ hours, costs E£7.05, or E£3.60 for students. The 3rd class fare is £1.05. The train to or from Mallawi, 80 km north, takes two hours; and its another 6½ hours south to Luxor.

Buses leave Cairo for Asyut and the Western Desert oases from a station near Midan Ataba. From Asyut they depart for Cairo at 8 and 10 am, noon and 2 pm and cost E£3.60. The evening buses, which leave at 9.30 and 10.30 pm, cost E£5.10. Buses from Asyut to Sohag leave every half hour from 6 am to 6 pm. From Asyut to Kharga oasis the buses take four hours, cost E£2 and leave at 7 am and 2 pm. It costs E£3.50 to Dakhla oasis and the buses depart at 6 and 9 am.

A service taxi to Mallawi costs E£1.50 and takes one hour; to El Minya costs E£2 and takes two hours; and to El Qusiya costs 60 pt.

The Western Oases

About 90% of Egypt is barren desert, lying relentlessly hot, unproductive and uninhabited on both sides of the fertile Nile Valley and Delta, all the way from the Mediterranean to the Sudan border. Only about 1% of Egypt's total population lives in this wasteland and most of them reside in the five isolated, yet thriving, oases of the Western Desert.

Since the late 1950s, in an attempt to make use of all this spare land, the Egyptian government has been investing heavily in development projects in and around these oases. At the same time, to relieve the pressures of overpopulation, landless *fellahin* and families from crowded towns in the Nile Valley have been encouraged to resettle in this so-called 'New Valley Frontier District', a region centred on the Kharga Oasis and covering about 376,000 square km.

Although the oases are attracting more and more travellers their increased popularity has not diminished the adventure of exploring this remote region. It is recommended that you visit the area during winter as in summer the temperature soars as high as 52°C (125°F). You have to register with the police at each oasis. Permission used to be needed to visit Farafra and Dakhla, but lately this hasn't been necessary. You should double-check with the tourist office in Cairo though; they're quite well informed.

The Kharga and Dakhla oases are easily visited from Asyut; the oases of Farafra and Bahariya are best visited from Cairo though it is possible to get there via Asyut and Dakhla; and access to Siwa Oasis, in the north-west of Egypt, is via Marsa Matruh. The latter is described in the Alexandria section.

If you want in depth information on the history and archaeological sites of the oases, there is a three-volume publication, by the American University in Cairo Press, that is available at the AUC bookstore and most hotel bookshops.

KHARGA OASIS

Kharga, the largest and most developed of the oases, lies in a desert depression which is about 30 km wide and 200 km long. The chief town of El Kharga, which is 230 km from Asyut, is a boom town with a population of about 90,000. Most of these people are Nubians resettled from the Nubian lands inundated by the creation of Lake Nasser after the construction of the Aswan Dam. The present day community of Berbers however, whose ancestors were Kharga's original inhabitants, can trace their roots back to when the oasis was a way station on the *40 Day Road* caravan route between the Sudan and Asyut.

The Temple of Hibis

This 6th century BC structure dedicated to the god *Amun* was built mostly by the

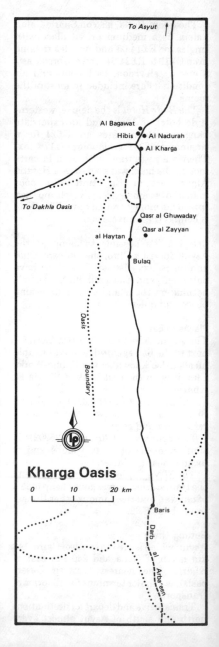

Kharga Oasis

Persian Emperor Darius I. The temple, a few km north of town near the road, has been reconstructed and there's a great view of the surrounding palm groves from the roof.

The Necropolis of al-Bagawat

Most of the several hundred mud-brick tombs in this Christian cemetery date from the 4th to the 6th centuries AD. They are traditional Coptic tombs with domes on top, some of which have interesting wall paintings of biblical scenes. Ask the caretaker, who will expect *baksheesh*, to unlock the doors of the most colourful tombs. The cemetery is half a km past the Temple of Hibis on the road to Asyut.

The Temple of Nadura

This small temple, to the south-east of the town, was built by the Roman Emperor Antonius Pius in 138 AD. Look out for Kharga's duck farms nearby.

Also near the temple are the ruins of a 9th century Islamic mud-brick town, most of which was built underground so the inhabitants could escape the intense desert heat. Some of the buildings are still inhabited and the locals will gladly show you around and probably even invite you to their homes for tea.

Places to Stay

The *New Valley Tourist Home* (tel 3728), near the Cinema Hibis, has cheap accommodation available. Singles cost E£3.50 and doubles are E£5. Fans are available and breakfast is served in the hotel's cafeteria.

The *Hotel 'Mut Balad el Shendi'* has singles for E£13 and doubles for E£16.

The *Kharga Hotel* is the best hotel in town. It's in a modern building at the north end of town and has 30 rooms, each with a bathroom. Singles cost E£20 and doubles are E£26. The hotel restaurant offers meals for E£2 to E£5. Room reservations can be made from Cairo through the Victoria Hotel (tel 918766).

Camping You can camp in the grounds of the Oasis Hotel for E£3 per person including access to showers.

Places to Eat

The best places to eat are the hotels or you can shop for your own food in the town *souk* or market.

Getting There

Two buses a day run between Kharga and Cairo via Asyut. Both leave Cairo from the al-Azhar bus station near Midan Ataba and continue on to Farafra oasis from Kharga. The air-con bus leaves at 7 am, takes anywhere from eight to 12 hours and costs E£7. The ordinary bus leaves at 10 am, takes about 10 hours and costs E£5. The 7 am bus requires reservations at least one day in advance.

From Asyut there are buses to Kharga at 6 am and 2 pm. Hitching from Asyut shouldn't be too difficult if you get to the road junction, which is 12 km north of the city, early enough.

From Kharga there are four buses a day to Asyut at 7 am and 2 pm. The trip takes five hours and costs E£2.

A service taxi is a convenient way to travel from Asyut. The trip takes from three to four hours. Service taxis will also occasionally go to Dakhla oasis.

EgyptAir flights stop at Kharga en route between Cairo and Aswan on Wednesdays and Saturdays.

DAKHLA OASIS

Dakhla, about 200 km west of Kharga, was created from more than 600 natural springs and ponds in the area. The bus from Asyut and Kharga drops you off at Mut, which is the largest town in the oasis, from where you can take a service taxi to El Qasr, the other town of interest in the area. The bus trip between El Kharga and Mut should take from three to four hours; and by taxi, the 30 km to El Qasr, takes about 40 minutes.

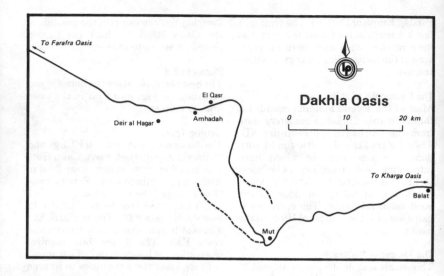

Dakhla Oasis

0   10   20 km

To Farafra Oasis

El Qasr

Amhadah

Deir al Hagar

To Kharga Oasis

Balat

Mut

Things to See

One of the dubious attractions of Dakhla are the hot sulphur pools to the west of the main road between Mut and El Qasr. The pools smell like rotten eggs and look like bubbling mud holes with brown nodules floating on the surface but are supposedly quite salubrious. An irrigation ditch near the pools has clean, clear water where you can rinse off the brown stuff afterwards.

The area just north of El Qasr is full of lush vegetation. The town itself, which is a charming little place, seems to have hardly been touched by the development projects in other parts of the New Valley. The people are still so unaccustomed to foreigners that you'll probably find their hospitality overwhelming. In the town centre you can watch the women doing laundry at the communal well.

There are several pharaonic sites south-west of El Qasr. Near the village of **Amhadah** there are several tombs which date from the 22nd century BC. A few km down the road there's a **Roman Cemetery** with several colourful tombs; and a little further west at **Deir al-Hagar** there's an intriguing sandstone temple.

Places to Stay

There are two *resthouses* in Mut. The one next to the football field is clean and has doubles for E£3. Meals there cost 40 pt for breakfast; E£1.50 for lunch; and 50 pt for dinner. The other resthouse is next to the tourist information office but should be avoided as several travellers have reported that the tourist office made them pay a E£4.60 tax for each day they stayed there.

Camping It's possible to camp in El Qasr, on a desert plateau just north of town, where the night sky is a spectacular field of stars. Be discreet though and try not to attract too much attention. You can also camp at the sulphur springs near Mut, but the smell might be a bit much there.

Places to Eat

There are several cafés in Mut. Food supplies are sometimes quite limited although bread and a few other basics are usually available. Bring your own drinking water.

Getting There

There are two buses a day between Cairo and Dakhla that go via Asyut and Kharga. The air-conditioned bus costs E£10 a ticket in either direction. The bus leaves Mut at 6 am and arrives in Cairo at 9 pm. There is also a daily bus that does the run between Mut, Kharga and Asyut.

As of late 1986 there was still no public transport between Dakhla and Farafra, however hitching a ride with the occasional commercial truck might be possible.

FARAFRA OASIS

The main town of Farafra, which is the smallest oasis in the Western Desert, is Qasr al Farafra. Despite the recent construction of a 310 km macadamised road linking it to Dakhla, the 1500 people of this oasis are still quite isolated from most of the world. There is no public transport in or out of the area so foreigners especially are a very rare sight. If you thought the hospitality of the locals in Dakhla was magnificent then wait till you get here. You'll be such a novelty to the people of Farafra that just about everyone will want to take you home with them.

Many of the people are Bedouin and still adhere to many of the age-old traditions of their culture. The small mud-brick houses of the town all have wooden doorways with medieval peg locks and the walls are painted with murals. The Bedouin women of Farafra produce beautifully embroidered dresses and shirts, though most of the work is for their own personal use and not for sale. Olives and olive oil are a speciality of the region.

Places to Stay

The *resthouse* in Qasr al Farafra has clean rooms for E£2.15 per person. It's the red building on the right as you enter town. Bring your own sheets or a sleeping bag and drinking water. There is electricity from 7 pm to midnight. There is another resthouse of similarly basic standards near the checkpoint.

Camping It's possible to pitch a tent at 'Well No Six', which is four km west of the town. You can also go swimming there.

Places to Eat

There is one café in Qasr al-Farafra which serves meals; just look for the place with the green and blue walls. Ahmed, the owner, can help you arrange transport to Mut, in Dakhla.

There are two shops in town which sell canned food and other staples.

Getting There

If you can find someone to give you a ride to Farafra then be prepared for a *long* seven-hour trip across the desert. The landscape is interesting but that many hours can seem like an eternity in the heat and dust. Buses never travel this far so

Farafra Oasis

0   25   50 km

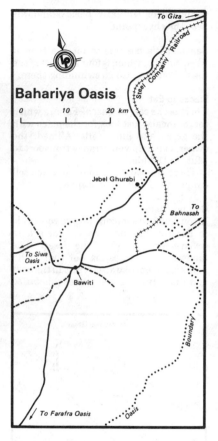

Bahariya Oasis

0   10   20 km

To Giza

Steel Company Railroad

Jebel Ghurabi

To
Bahnasah

To Siwa
Oasis

Bawiti

To Farafra Oasis

Oasis

Boundary

Things to See

Bahariya is not renowned for its ancient sites, although in Bawiti there are the remains of a temple and settlement dating back to the 17th dynasty. There is also a special hill, south-west of the town, known as **Qarat al-Firaki**, or Ridge of the Chicken Merchant. The hill features several underground galleries containing signs of bird burials.

Three km north of town are some sulphur hot springs called *Bir al-Sukhna*; and at **Bir al-Mattar**, 10 km south-west of Bawiti, hot springs pour into a viaduct and then down into a concrete swimming pool.

Places to Stay

The *Hotel Alpenblick*, which sits on a small hill (you can't miss it) is one of the few places to stay in this oasis. The hotel has a little restaurant where you can buy basic meals or cook your own food. Salah Sherif, the owner, can take you in his jeep to the nearby hot springs for 30 pt and also offers overnight stays in the desert, near the springs, for E£4 to E£5 including food.

There are two other hotels in town, but no one recommends them.

Getting There

There is a daily bus which makes the five hour trip to Cairo.

Twice a week a jeep makes the long trip to Farafra; you camp in the desert along the way.

check with the locals about transportation out again.

BAHARIYA OASIS

Bahariya is 330 km south of Cairo and is linked to the capital by a paved road across the desert. There are several little villages spread throughout the oasis but the main one, with a population of 25,000, is Bawiti. The oasis is renowned for its dates, olives and turkeys. Try the date wine.

SOHAG

The city of Sohag, 93 km south of Asyut is an administrative centre for the governorate of Girga and one of the major Coptic Christian areas of Upper Egypt. The only real reason to stop off there, however, is to see the White and Red Monasteries just outside Sohag and to visit the town of **Achmim** across the river.

Things to See

Deir Abyad, was built in 400 AD by the Coptic saint Shenouda, with chunks of white limestone pilfered from a pharaonic temple. The so-called White Monastery once supported a community of 2000 monks. Its fortress walls still stand but most of the interior is in ruins, though you can see the several types of arches used in its construction. The monastery is 12 km north-west of Sohag; there's a cafeteria across the road.

Deir al-Ahmar, the Red Monastery, was founded by Bishoi, a thief who converted to Christianity, built this and two monasteries in Wadi Natrun and eventually became a Coptic saint. There are two chapels on the grounds, **Santa Maria Chapel** and the **St Bishoi Chapel**. Be sure to see the remains of a 10th century fresco on the central altar, it contains a 1000-year-old icon. There are interesting though fading frescoes on the walls, unusual pillars and old wooden peg locks on the doors.

Unless you visit during the first two weeks of July, when you can catch a bus to the monasteries for 40 pt with thousands of other pilgrims, your only option is to take a taxi, which should cost about E£4.

The town of **Achmim**, on the east bank of the Nile, is renowned for its unique woven carpets and wall hangings. Though little of its past glory remains, except for an extensive, unexcavated cemetery, Achmim was once a flourishing provincial centre. There are several rock-cut tombs in the area and a rock chapel dedicated to the local deity *Min*, the ithyphallic god of fertility. There's a bus across the river to Achmim from Sohag which takes 15 minutes and costs 10 pt.

Places to Stay

There is a *Youth Hostel* at 5 Sharia Port Said in Achmim.

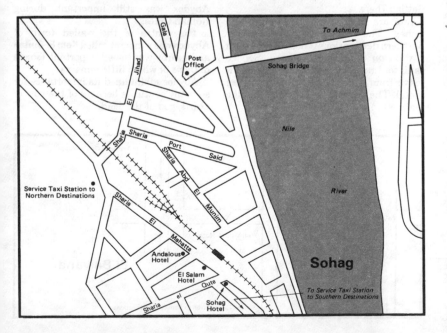

The *Sohag Hotel* is a dirty place with singles for E£2 and doubles for E£4. Each room has three beds and a shower, supposedly with hot water.

The *El Salam Hotel* is directly in front of the train station. It has basic singles for E£2 and doubles for E£4. The place was being renovated and hot water heaters were being installed.

The *Andalous Hotel* is also opposite the train station. Singles are E£3.50 and doubles are E£5.85 including breakfast. Most of the rooms have fans and small tables. The bathrooms are basically clean and there's hot water.

Places to Eat

Other than the usual fruit and vegetable stands, there are also a few fuul and ta'amiyya places near the train station. There are no restaurants in Sohag, at least not in the western sense of the word.

Getting There

There are two service taxi stations in Sohag. The one for Asyut and other northern destinations is north of the train station on Sharia El Mahatta. Service taxis for Luxor, Qena and Nag Hammadi leave from a depot south of the Sohag Hotel. The bus station is nearby and the train often stops at Sohag.

EL BALYANA

The only reason to go to this town is to visit the necropolis of Abydos and the magnificent Temple of the Seti, in the nearby village of Al-Arbah al-Madfunah.

If you really want to stay in El Balyana, there's the *Wadi Melouk Hotel* which looks like it's suffered greatly from its position right next to the train tracks.

It's easy to get away from this place as the bus, train and service taxi stations are all conveniently close to each other. Service taxis and minibuses both go to the temple complex; the former costs 25 pt.

Abydos

The temples at Abydos served several dynasties of live Egyptians and its huge necropolis was, for a long time, *the* place to be buried. Excavations indicate that it was a burial place of the last pre-dynastic kings, before 3100 BC; Seti I and Ramses II built the most important temples of the complex in the 13th century BC; and Abydos was still important during Roman times.

The centre of the walled town of Abydos was a mound called **Kom El-Sultan** and nearby was the all important **Temple of Osiris** of which little remains.

Abydos maintained its importance for so many centuries because of the cult of *Osiris*, god of the dead.

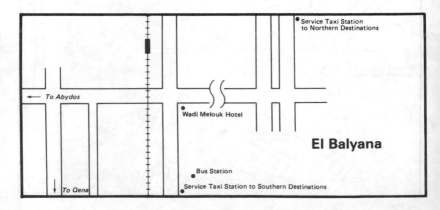

To Abydos

Service Taxi Station
to Northern Destinations

Wadi Melouk Hotel

Bus Station

Service Taxi Station to Southern Destinations

To Qena

El Balyana

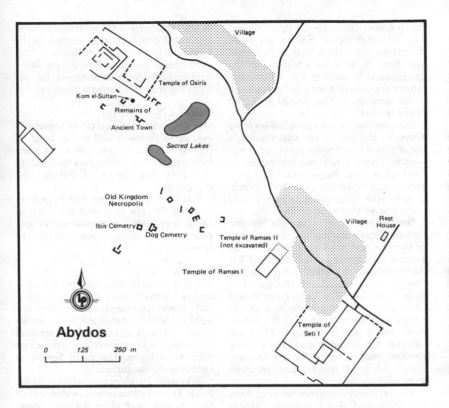

Abydos

0   125   250 m

The area was a natural shrine for the worship of this 'ruler of the netherworld' because, according to mythology, it was here that the head of *Osiris* was buried after his brother *Seth* had murdered him, cut his body into several pieces and scattered the bits all over Egypt. *Osiris'* wife and sister, the goddess *Isis*, searched for and found all the pieces and put him back together again, building temples wherever she found the dissected parts. *Osiris* and *Isis* then begat *Horus*, the falcon god, who killed his uncle *Seth*. The temple at Abydos was the most important shrine to *Osiris* and became a place of pilgrimage. Most Egyptians do make a journey there at least once in their lifetime or between death and burial.

The Cenotaph Temple of Seti I The first structure you'll see at Abydos is one of Egypt's most complete temples. A cenotaph temple was a secondary mortuary temple dedicated to one or more gods and honouring the deified, deceased pharaoh who built it. Pharaoh Seti's splendid temple honours seven gods: *Osiris, Isis, Horus, Amun, Re-Harakhty, Ptah* and *Seti I* himself. The *Osiris* sanctuary was especially important and opens into an area, extending the width of the temple, with two halls and two sets of three chapels dedicated to *Osiris, Isis* and *Horus*.

As you roam through Seti's dark halls and sanctuaries a definite air of mystery, an almost tangible impression of ancient pomp and circumstance, surrounds you. The colourful hieroglyphs on the walls, describing the rituals that were carried out there, make it easy to imagine the ceremonies honouring the death and rebirth of *Osiris* and the great processions of cult worshippers that passed in and out of the temple.

In a corridor known as the **Gallery of the Kings**, to the left of the sanctuaries, a list of Egypt's pharaohs up to Seti I was found. Though not complete the 76 cartouches, oval rings containing each king's name, greatly assisted archaeologists in unravelling Egypt's long history from Menes onwards.

North-west of Seti's temple his son, Ramses II, built another temple dedicated to *Osiris* – and himself. The roof of the Temple of Ramses II has collapsed but the hieroglyphs on the walls are interesting, though you have to get the guard to unlock the gate. The local villagers will let him know that a *xawaga*, a not so complimentary way of saying 'foreigner', wants to get into the temple. The same villagers will probably also send a young stranger bearing 'gifts' for the *xawaga*. Watch out; you'll quickly discover these 'gifts' cost money.

The extensive cemetery between Kom El-Sultan and Seti's temple includes burials of dogs, falcons and ibises as well

as the cenotaphs or actual graves of those ancient Egyptians who wanted to lie forever in the company of *Osiris*.

Abydos is open from 9 am to 5 pm daily. Admission fee for both temples is E£1, or 50 pt for students. Bring a torch.

QENA

Qena, a provincial capital 91 km southeast of El Balyana and 62 km north of Luxor, is at the intersection of the main Nile road and the road across the desert to the Red Sea towns of Safaga and Hurghada.

Unless you're on your way to or from the Red Sea the only reason to stop in Qena is to visit the spectacular temple complex at Dendara, just outside the town.

Dendara

Though it indicates the decline of a purely Egyptian style of art, the wonderfully preserved complex at Dendara is a sight to behold. Complete with a massive stone roof, dark chambers, underground passages and towering columns inscribed with hieroglyphs, the main **Temple of Hathor** is almost intact.

While the Dendara necropolis includes Early Dynasty tombs and evidence that Cheops and later pharaohs built there, the temple complex, as it stands today,

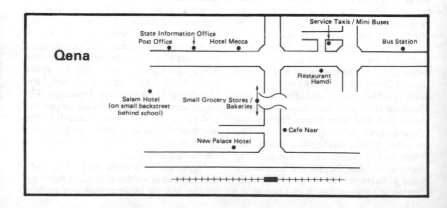

Temple complex at Dendara

was built by the Greek/Egyptian Ptolemies and the Romans. Its very design, however, suggests it was built on the site of an older temple and, as was the custom of the day, reproduces the character and mythology of the original. So despite the apparent short-comings in the quality of its design and decoration and the fact that it was raised during foreign occupation, it is an impressive, beautiful monument to an ancient goddess of great renown.

Hathor was the goddess of pleasure and love, represented as a cow, or a woman with a cow's head, or as a woman whose headdress was a sun disk fixed between the horns of a cow. She was the benificent deity of maternal and family love, of beauty and light, whom the Greeks associated with *Aphrodite*.

Hathor was also the wet-nurse of *Horus*, before becoming his mate and bearing *Ihy*, the youthful aspect of the creator gods. Since the earliest times it was important for a pharaoh to trace his ancestry back to *Horus*, so it was there-

fore politically sensible for the Ptolemies and the Romans to claim the same divine link with the triad of *Osiris, Isis* and *Horus*. As the suckler of the young *Horus*, and thereby the living pharaoh, *Hathor* had a special relevance to successive dynasties of kings. Dendara was the ritual location where *Hathor* gave birth to the child of *Horus* and her temple stands on the edge of the desert as if waiting for her return.

Hathor's head forms the capital of all 24 columns in the temple's **Outer Hypostyle Hall**. On the walls, there are strange scenes showing the Roman Emperors Augustus, Tiberius, Caligula, Claudius and Nero as pharaohs, making offerings to *Hathor*. The ceiling shows vultures flying amongst the sun, moon and stars of the Egyptian zodiac with the sky goddess *Nut* and other deities sailing their solar boats across the heavens.

The hieroglyphs in the **Inner Hypostyle Hall** deal with the temple's foundation. Beyond is the Offering Hall and Sanctuary of the temple proper, surrounded by a gallery of chapels and the east and west staircases to the roof.

The **Hall of Offerings**, where the daily rituals of the cult were carried out, shows the king and others making offerings to *Hathor*. During the New Year festival images of the goddess were carried from here to the roof to be looked on by *Ra*, the sun god. The views of the surrounding countryside from the roof are magnificent. The graffiti on the edge of the temple was left by Napoleon's commander Desaix and other French soldiers in 1799.

The **Sanctuary** was usually kept bolted and only the pharaoh or priests acting on his behalf could enter. Reliefs on the walls show the special rituals of the pharaoh entering the Sanctuary to show his adoration for the goddess.

From the **Chapel** behind the sanctuary *Hathor* would embark each New Year on her annual journey to Edfu where she would lie in blissful union with *Horus*.

The reliefs on the exterior of the temple's south wall show various Roman emperors such as Nero and Caesarian, son of Julius and Cleopatra, and the great Egyptian queen herself making offerings to the head of *Hathor*.

Behind the main temple is the smaller **Temple of the Birth of Isis** built by Emperor Augustus; and in front, to the north, the second structure on your left is a Roman **mammisi**, or birth-house, dedicated to *Hathor* and her son *Ihy*.

A 5th century Coptic Basilica is squeezed in between the mammisi, the court of *Hathor's* temple and another birth-house. The latter was begun by Nectanebo, a 30th dynasty pharaoh, and completed by the Ptolemies.

Getting There Dendara is four km west of Qena along the Nile and there are local buses and service taxis, which cost 15 pt to 25 pt, which run there from the town. From the road you can either walk, or hitch a ride with peasants from the village next to the temple.

The Dendara complex is open from 6 am to 6 pm and admission costs E£2, or E£1 for students.

Places to Stay

The *El Salam Hotel* is a quiet place behind the school and around the corner from the post office. The bathrooms are dreary but the prices are rockbottom. It costs E£1 for a single and E£2 for a double without bath.

The *New Palace Hotel* is just off Midan Mahattat opposite the train station. A double with/without bath is E£6/4. The place is a bit drab but basically clean; there's no hot water.

There is supposedly a *Youth Hostel* on Sharia Shuban Muslimeen, but no one seemed to know where this street was.

Places to Eat

The *Café Nasr* has backgammon, tea and lots of Egyptians who stare at you because there's nothing else to do in Qena.

The *Restaurant Hamdi* serves full meals of chicken, rice, pudding, tea, bread and beans for E£1.60.

Along the main street there are also several kushari, kufta and ta'amiyya places.

Things to Buy

Pottery, particularly water jugs, is the speciality in Qena; though it's probably a difficult purchase to carry around in your backpack.

Getting There

The bus station is behind the central mosque. From the train station you walk down the main street towards the Nile, turn right at the large intersection and you'll see the minaret of the mosque ahead of you. Walk past it and the station is on your left.

There are buses to Cairo every hour from 5 am to 3 pm. Tickets cost E£6 and the trip takes 10 to 11 hours. On the buses that leave from 3 pm to 9 pm the tickets cost E£8.

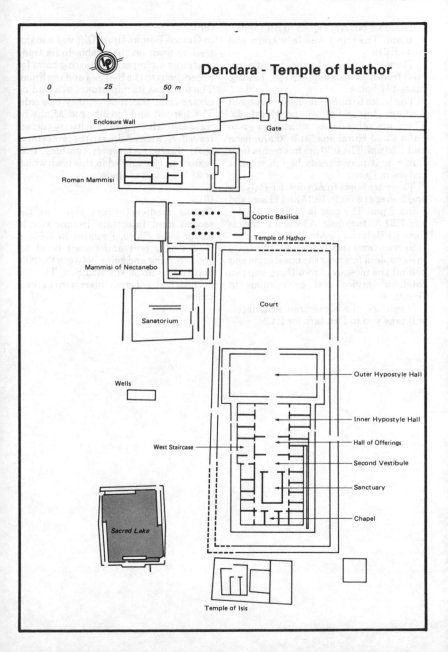

Dendara - Temple of Hathor

0   25   50 m

Enclosure Wall

Gate

Roman Mammisi

Coptic Basilica

Temple of Hathor

Mammisi of Nectanebo

Sanatorium

Court

Wells

Outer Hypostyle Hall

Inner Hypostyle Hall

West Staircase

Hall of Offerings

Second Vestibule

Sanctuary

Chapel

Sacred Lake

Temple of Isis

There's a bus from Qena to Alexandria at 6 am. The trip takes 13½ hours and costs E£10.

There are buses to Luxor almost every hour from 6 am to 9 pm for 75 pt. The trip takes 1¼ hours.

The buses to Suez which leave at 6 and 6.30 am stop at Safaga and Hurghada. There are other buses which just go to Safaga and Hurghada, at 9.30 am, noon and 1.30 pm. The 1.30 pm bus comes from Luxor so it may already be full when it arrives in Qena.

There are buses to Abydos, El-Balyana and Sohag at 6.30, 9, 10.15 and 11 am; and 1 and 2 pm. The cost is 75 pt to Abydos and E£1.50 to Sohag. A local bus travels from El-Balyana to Abydos.

Service taxis and local taxis congregate in a couple of lots near the bus station and behind the mosque. From there you can catch a service taxi or minibus to Dendara.

Hantours, the horse-drawn carriages, will take you to Dendara for E£2.

QIFT

In Graeco-Roman times Qift was a major trading town on the Arabia-India trade route and an important starting point for expeditions to the Red Sea and the Sinai. The town lost its importance as a trading centre from the 10th century onwards. The harvest and fertility god *Min*, who was also the patron deity of desert travellers, was considered the protector of Qift. There is however, nothing that really can't be missed in this town which is 23 km south of Qena.

QUS

During medieval times this was the second most important Islamic city in Egypt after Cairo. Founded in 1083, it served as a port and transit point for goods coming and going between the Nile and El Quseir on the Red Sea. There is nothing really of great interest in the town today.

Luxor

The sheer grandeur of Luxor's monumental architecture, and its excellent state of preservation, have made this village-city one of Egypt's greatest tourist attractions. Built on and around the 4000-year-old site of ancient Thebes, Luxor is an extraordinary mixture of exotic history and modern commercialism. Here the *fellahin* work the fields as they have done since time immemorial; mundane daily business is carried on as if there weren't hordes of foreigners walking the streets; modern hotels are full of westerners; the bazaars are full of fake antiquities made just for the tourists; and modern Egyptians make a fine living out of the legacy of their ancestors. It is one of the world's greatest open air museums, a time capsule of a glorious long-gone era. Yet at the same time this over-grown village, with a population exceeding 100,000, thrives and bustles with life.

The attraction for tourists is by no means a recent phenomenon, in fact travellers have been visiting Thebes for centuries, marvelling at the splendid temples of Luxor, Karnak, Ramses II and Hatshepsut. As far back as Graeco-Roman times visitors would wait in the desert to hear the mysterious voice of Memnon emanating from the colossal statues of Amenophis III; and in the past 100 years or so, since archaeology became a respectable science, curious travellers have been following the footsteps of the excavators into the famous tombs of the Valley of the Kings.

What most visitors today know as Luxor is actually three separate areas, the city of Luxor itself, the village of Karnak a couple of km to the north-east and the monuments and necropolis of ancient Thebes on the west bank of the Nile. Along the river, which for some reason seems even more majestic here, the rows of *feluccas* and antiquated barges share the east bank quays with the posh hotel/ships of the Hilton and Sheraton. Behind the tourist facade the dirt streets are crowded with mud-brick tenements, pocked with mud puddles and filled with ordinary, friendly people. Luxor is definitely one of the highlights of a visit to Egypt.

Orientation
There are only three main thoroughfares in Luxor so it's easy to find your way around – as long as you don't ask for street names. Some streets have signs, some have names but no signs and some have no names at all. If you ask the locals what the name of a particular street is they're quite likely to make one up on the spot, which is why nearly every map of Luxor is different. So, it's best to ask directions to a specific location rather than to the street or road it's on. The three main roads are Sharia El Mahatta, Sharia El Karnak and Sharia El Bahr.

Sharia El Mahatta – the street directly in front of the train station – runs perpendicular to the Nile all the way to the gardens of Luxor Temple. Sharia El Karnak runs one block in and parallel to the river, from Luxor Temple to Karnak Temple. Sharia El Karnak meets Sharia El Mahatta and runs around the southern end of Luxor Temple, which overlooks the Nile, to the corniche road, Sharia El Bahr. To confuse matters Sharia El Karnak, where it meets Sharia El Mahatta, is also known as Sharia El Markaz and to the south, around the temple to the river, it's known as Sharia El Lokanda. The corniche road is known variously as Sharia El Bahr, Sharia Bahr El Nil or simply the Corniche.

Information
The Tourist Office and the State Information Office are in the tourist

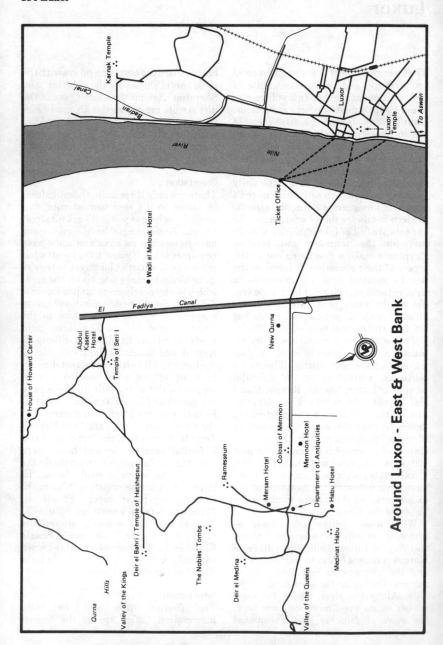

Around Luxor – East & West Bank

Karnak Temple

Badran Canal

River

Nile

Luxor

To Aswan

Luxor Temple

Ticket Office

Wadi el Melouk Hotel

House of Howard Carter

Abdul Kasem Hotel

Temple of Seti I

El Fadlya Canal

New Qurna

Colossi of Memnon

Memnon Hotel

Department of Antiquities

Ramesseum

Mersam Hotel

Habu Hotel

Deir el Bahri / Temple of Hatshepsut

The Nobles' Tombs

Deir el Medina

Medinat Habu

Valley of the Kings

Qurna Hills

Valley of the Queens

bazaar on Sharia El Bahr, next to the New Winter Palace. They're open from 8 am to 8 pm and the staff can fill you in on what the official prices for various services should be. They also have a handy booklet titled *Upper Egypt by Night & Day*.

Maps, guidebooks to the monuments, and aerogrammes embellished with mug shots of Tutankhamun can be bought at the *A A Gaddis Bookstore* also on the Corniche south of Luxor Temple, two doors down from the Information Office.

The Telephone Office is at the resplendent entrance of the Winter Palace Hotel. Three minute telephone calls cost E£11 to the US and West Germany, E£9 to Great Britain and E£12.50 to Canada.

The American Express Office is next door to the Winter Palace Hotel and is open from 8 am to 9 pm. All of the usual services are available. If you are heading south, this is the last American Express office where you can cash personal cheques and buy travellers' cheques until you get to Nairobi.

The Post Office is half way down Sharia El Mahatta and there's a branch office in the tourist bazaar.

Things to See

Following the collapse of centralised power at the end of the Old Kingdom period the small village of Thebes, under the 11th and 12th Dynasty pharaohs, emerged as the main power in Upper Egypt. Rising against the northern capital of Heracleopolis, Thebes reunited the country under its political, religious and administrative control and ushered in the Middle Kingdom period. The strength of its government also enabled it to re-establish control after a second period of decline, liberate the country from foreign rule and bring in the New Kingdom dynasties. At the height of its glory and opulence, from 1570 BC to 1090 BC, the new kingdom pharaohs made Thebes their permanent residence, the city had a population of nearly one million and the architectural activity was astounding.

Because so many kings left their mark at Thebes it can quickly become very confusing trying to keep track of who built what temples or tombs and when they did so. The following chronology may help you to muddle through about seven centuries of Theban extravagance.

The Old Kingdom (2600 BC to 2100 BC) Memphis was the capital of Egypt and during the first two dynasties most of the major pyramids were constructed; not much was happening in Thebes.

Middle Kingdom (2000 BC to 1800 BC) During the 12th Dynasty, around 1930 BC, Sesostris I built part of the first stages of Karnak's Great Temple of *Amun* and designed the central court.

Second Intermediate Period (1786 BC to 1567 BC) This period of unrest, during the 13th to 17th Dynasties, included about a century of foreign Hyksos rule.

New Kingdom (1567 BC to 1085 BC) The majority of the tombs and temples of Thebes were built by the pharaohs of the 18th to 20th Dynasties.

1525 BC to 1504 BC – Tuthmosis I and II built the 4th and 5th Pylons of Karnak Temple. This period also marked the first royal burials in the Valley of the Kings.

1503 BC to 1482 BC – Queen Hatshepsut built her spectacular mortuary temple at Deir el Bahri, the 8th Pylon and two obelisks at Karnak and a small temple at Medinat Habu.

1504 BC to 1450 BC – Tuthmosis III, Egypt's great warrior built the Festival Hall and the 6th Pylon of Karnak Temple, a tomb in the Valley of the Kings and a temple at Medinat Habu.

1450 BC to 1425 BC – Amenophis II built his own temple at Karnak.

1417 BC to 1379 BC – Amenophis III ruled Egypt at its zenith of empire-building. He oversaw the initial construction of the Luxor Temple, built the 3rd Pylon at Karnak and his own mortuary temple, on the west bank, of which only the Colossi of Memnon remain.

1379 BC to 1362 BC – Amenophis IV re-named himself Akhenaten and moved his temples and palaces to Tell el Amarna.

1361 BC to 1352 BC – Tutankhamun, Akhenaten's successor, returned to Thebes and reinstated the cult of *Amun*. The discovery of his intact tomb in the Valley of the Kings was one of the greatest archaeological finds of this century.

1318 BC to 1304 BC – Seti I built Karnak's immense Hypostyle Hall, his own temple on the west bank and his tomb in the Valley of the Kings.

1304 BC to 1237 BC – Ramses II built the 1st Pylon and Court of Luxor Temple, the colossal statues and obelisks in front of Karnak and part of that temple's Hypostyle Hall, as well as the Ramesseum, his own mortuary temple on the west bank.

Many other pharaohs including Seti II, Horemheb, Tuthmosis IV and Ramses I and III, contributed pylons or extensions to the temples of Karnak and Luxor as well as building their own temples, tombs or both, on the west bank.

EAST BANK
Luxor Museum

This wonderful little museum on the Corniche, about half way between Luxor and Karnak temples, has a small but well chosen collection of relics from the Theban temples and necropolis. The displays which include pottery, jewellery, furniture, statues and stelae, were arranged by the Brooklyn Museum of New York. The most interesting exhibit is the **Wall of Akhenaten**, which is actually a set of 283 sandstone blocks found within the 9th Pylon of Karnak Temple. The reliefs show the rebel pharaoh and his queen, Nefertiti, making offerings to *Aten*.

On the 2nd floor check out the canopic jars which once contained the internal organs of the priest of the god *Montu*. There are a few other relics in the small garden outside. The museum is open from 4 to 9 pm in winter, 5 to 8 pm in summer, 10 am to 2 pm during Ramadan and admission costs E£2, or E£1 for students.

Luxor Temple

Amun, one of the gods of creation, was the most important god of Thebes and head of the local triad. As *Amun-Ra*, the fusion of *Amun* and the sun god *Ra*, he was also a state deity worshipped in many parts of the country. Once a year from his Great Temple at Karnak the images of *Amun* and the rest of the triad – his wife, the war goddess *Mut*, and their son, the moon god *Khons* – would journey down the Nile to Luxor Temple for the *Opet festival*, a celebration held during the inundation season.

Built by the New Kingdom pharaoh Amenophis III, on the site of an older sanctuary dedicated to the Theban triad, Luxor Temple is a strikingly graceful piece of architecture on the banks of the Nile. Amenophis re-dedicated the massive temple as *Amun's* sacred 'Harem of the South', and retained what was left of the original sanctuary built by Tuthmosis III and Hatshepsut 100 years earlier.

Luxor Temple was added to over the centuries by Tutankhamun, Ramses II, Nectanebo, Alexander the Great and various Romans. The Muslims built a mosque in one of the interior courts and there was also once a village within the temple walls. Excavation work has been going on since 1885 and has included removing the village and clearing the forecourt and 1st Pylon of debris which exposed part of the **Avenue of Sphinxes** leading to Karnak.

Fronting the entrance to the temple is the enormous **1st Pylon**, about 24 metres high, in front of which are some colossal statues of Ramses II and a pink granite obelisk. There were originally six statues, four seated and two standing, but only two of the seated figures and the westernmost standing one remain. The obelisk too was part of a pair; its towering counterpart now stands in the Place de la Concorde in Paris. Behind the pylon, which is decorated with Ramses' victorious exploits in battle, is another of his additions to the main complex. The **Great**

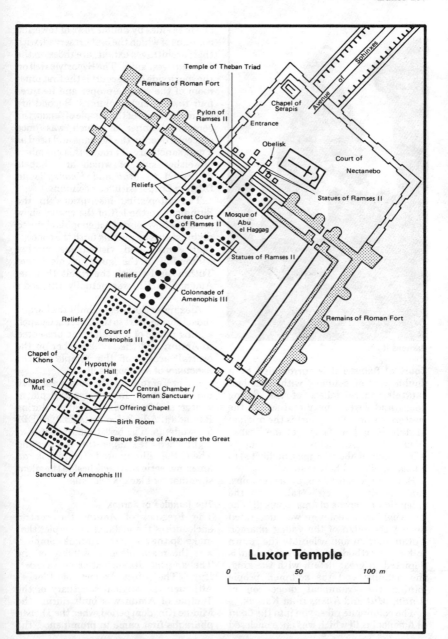

Luxor Temple

0   50   100 m

Ramses II

Court of Ramses II is surrounded by a double row of columns with lotus-bud capitals, more reliefs of his daring deeds and several huge statues. In the western corner of the court is the original Middle Kingdom **Temple of the Theban Triad** and south of that is the 13th century AD **Mosque of Abu el Haggag**, dedicated to a local sheik and holy man.

Beyond the court 14 papyrus columns, each nearly 16 metres tall, form the splendid **Colonnade of Amenophis III**. The walls behind the columns were decorated during the reign of the young pharaoh Tutankhamun and celebrate the return to Theban orthodoxy. The *Opet festival* is depicted in great detail, with the king, the nobility and the common people joining the triumphal procession of *Amun, Mut* and *Khons* from Karnak.

The colonnade takes you into the **Court of Amenophis III** which was once enclosed on three sides by double rows of towering columns of which the best preserved, with their architraves extant, are those on the east and west sides. The **Hypostyle Hall** on the south side of the court is the first inner room of the temple proper and features four rows of eight columns. Beyond are the main rooms of the **Temple of Amun**, the central chamber of which was once stuccoed over by the Romans and used as a cult sanctuary. Through this chamber, on either side of which are chapels dedicated to *Mut* and *Khons*, is an **Offering Chapel** with four columns.

The interesting inscriptions in the **Birthroom**, to the left of the chapel show scenes of how mortal Amenophis claimed divine status by putting forth the concept that *Amun* had visited his mother Mutemuia in the 'guise' of his father Tuthmosis IV with the result that he, Amenophis III, was actually the god's son.

Alexander the Great rebuilt the barque (boat) shrine, next to the Offering Chapel, adding reliefs of himself being presented to *Amun*; and the last chamber on the central access of the temple is the **Sanctuary of Amenophis III**.

Luxor Temple is open from 6 am to 10 pm in summer; from 7 am to 9 pm in winter; and from 6 am to 6.30 pm during Ramadan. Admission costs E£2, or E£1 for students. The best time to visit is at night when the temperature is lower and when the illuminated temple is an amazing, eerie spectacle beside the silent shimmering black of the Nile.

The Temples of Karnak

The Precinct of *Amun*, the central enclosure of the melange of temples that make up the enormous Karnak complex, was the main place of worship of the Theban triad. Its ancient name was *Ipet-Isut*, 'The Most Perfect of Places'. Although the original sanctuary of the Temple of Amun was built during the Middle Kingdom period, when the Theban pharaohs first came to prominence, the rest of the temples, pylons, courts, columns and reliefs were the work of New Kingdom rulers. Karnak was built, added to, dismantled, restored, enlarged and decorated over a period of nearly 1500 years and during the height of Theban power and prosperity it was the most important temple in all Egypt.

The complex can be divided into three distinct areas: the Great Temple of *Amun*, which is the largest enclosure; the precinct of *Mut*, on the south side, once linked to the main temple by an avenue of ram-headed sphinxes; and the precinct of *Montu*, to the north, honouring the original local god of Thebes. A canal once connected the temples of *Amun* and *Montu* with the Nile providing access for the sacred boats in the journey to Luxor Temple for the *Opet festival*. A paved avenue of human-headed sphinxes also once linked Karnak, from Euergetes' Gate on the south side of the precinct of *Amun*, with Luxor Temple. Only a small section of this sacred way, where it leaves *Amun's* Great Temple and enters the forecourt of his Southern Harem, has been excavated. The rest of the three km avenue lies beneath the city and paved roads of modern Luxor.

The Karnak site measures about 1.5 km by 0.8 km, which is large enough to hold about 10 Christian cathedrals, and the 1st Pylon, at the entrance, is twice the size of the 1st Pylon at Luxor Temple. As you venture further into the complex, the further back in time you go.

The oldest part of the complex is the **White Pavilion of Sesostris I** and the 12th Dynasty foundations of what became the most sacred part of the extended temple, the **Sanctuary** and **Central Court of Amun**, which is behind the 6th Pylon. The limestone fragments of the demolished pavilion, or chapel, were recovered from the foundations of the 3rd Pylon, built five centuries after Sesostris' reign, and expertly reconstructed in the Open Museum to the north of the Great Court.

The major additions to the complex were constructed by pharaohs of the 18th to 20th dynasties, between 1570 BC and 1090 BC. Kings of the later dynasties, 1090 BC to 670 BC, extended and rebuilt and the Ptolemies and early Christians also left their marks. The following were the main contributors to Karnak, moving forward in time from *Amun's* Central Court and Sanctuary to the construction of the 1st Pylon.

Amenophis I and his son Tuthmosis I built chapels around the central temple; the latter also built the 4th and 5th Pylons; Queen Hatshepsut initiated the south axis of the temple, Tuthmosis III raised the 7th and 8th Pylons on that axis and built the Great Festival Hall; Amenophis III built the 3rd Pylon and started the Great Hypostyle Hall which was completed by Seti I and Ramses II; Ramses III built his own temple on the

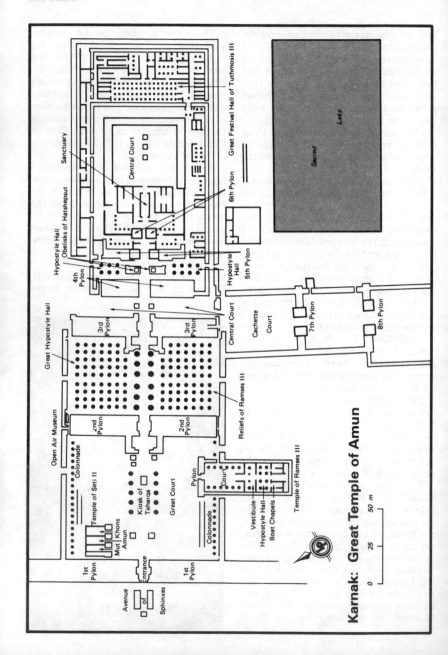

Karnak: Great Temple of Amun

south-west side of the enclosure; Horemheb built the 2nd, 9th and 10th Pylons; pharaohs of the 22nd Dynasty constructed the massive Great Court; and though the date of the 1st Pylon is not known for sure it's thought to be either of the 25th or 30th dynasties or a Ptolemaic construction.

You'll need to visit Karnak at least twice to fully appreciate the full enormity and magnificence of the complex and a return visit in the evening for the *son et lumiere* would complete the picture.

From the entrance you pass down the processional avenue of ram-headed sphinxes, which once led to the Nile, to the massive **1st Pylon**. It measures about 115 metres wide and 45 metres high though it was never actually completed. You can climb the stairs on your left to the top of the pylon's north tower, from where you'll get an amazing perspective of Karnak and the surrounding country.

Back on the ground you emerge from the 1st Pylon into the **Great Court**, the largest single area of the Karnak complex. To the left is the **Temple of Seti II**, dedicated to the Theban triad. The three small chapels held the sacred barques of *Amun*, *Mut* and *Khons* during the lead-up to the *Opet festival*.

The north and south walls of the court, which measures about 100 by 120 metres, are lined with columns with papyrus bud capitals and the south wall is intersected by the earlier built **Temple of Ramses III**. Obligatory scenes of the pharaoh as glorious conqueror adorn the pylon of this 60 metre long temple which also features an open court, a vestibule with four columns, a hypostyle hall of eight columns and three barque chapels.

In the centre of the Great Court is the one remaining column of the **Kiosk of Taharqa**. A 25th Dynasty Ethiopian pharaoh, Taharqa built his open-sided pavilion of 10 columns, each rising 21 metres and topped with papyrus form capitals.

The **2nd Pylon** was built by Horemheb,

an 18th Dynasty general who headed a military dictatorship and became the last pharaoh of his dynasty. Ramses I and II added their names and deeds to the pylon above that of Horemheb and Ramses II raised two colossal pink granite statues of himself on either side of the entrance.

Beyond the 2nd Pylon is the awesome **Great Hypostyle Hall** begun by Amenophis III while he was also building Luxor Temple, continued by Seti I and finished by Ramses II. Covering an area of 6000 square metres, large enough to contain Notre Dame Cathedral, the hall is an unforgettable forest of towering stone pillars. The 134 lavishly decorated monstrous columns, which once supported the roof, are arranged in 16 rows. The 12 central aisle columns, which rise 23 metres from the ground, are 10 metres taller than the 122 columns in the wings. The circumference of each is about 15 metres and the tops are large enough to hold about 50 people. It is impossible to

Amun

get an overall idea of this court; there is nothing to do but stand and stare up at the dizzying spectacle, up to where the papyrus-form capitals seem to sway and jostle each other for space.

Between the **3rd Pylon**, built by Amenophis III, and the **4th Pylon**, raised by Tuthmosis I, is a narrow court. Tuthmosis I and III raised two pairs of obelisks before the 4th Pylon which was, during their reign, the entrance to the temple proper. Only one of the four is still standing but parts of the others lie in the court.

Beyond the 4th Pylon is the oldest preserved part of the complex, its 14 columns suggests that it was originally a small hypostyle hall. It was constructed by Tuthmosis III in his attempt to eradicate or hide all signs of the reign of his step-mother Queen Hatshepsut. (See the section Deir el Bahri.) In this court, around the two magnificent **Obelisks of Hatshepsut**, the vengeful king built a 25-metre high sandstone structure. Although the upper shaft of one of the obelisks, which she raised to the glory of her 'father' *Amun*, lies on the ground by the Sacred Lake the other still stands, reclaimed from the sandstone, before the 5th Pylon. It is the tallest obelisk in Egypt, standing 29.5 metres high, and was originally covered in electrum from its pyramidal peak to half way down the shaft.

The **5th Pylon** was constructed by Tuthmosis I, with little space between it and the later built, now ruined **6th Pylon**. The latter, the smallest pylon at Karnak, was raised by his son Tuthmosis II who was Hatshepsut's husband and half-brother. In the small vestibule beyond the 6th Pylon are two pink granite columns on which the emblems of Egypt are carved in high relief – the lily of Upper Egypt on the north pillar and the papyrus flower of Lower Egypt on the south pillar. Two huge statues of *Amun* and his female counterpart *Amunet* dated from the reign of Tutankhamun are nearby.

Also amongst the ruins of this area around the temple's original **Central Court** are a **Sacred Barque Sanctuary** and at least two well-preserved walls.

Hatshepsut's wall and its colourful reliefs survived the years well because once again Tuthmosis III chose to cover hers with a structure of his own rather than destroy the offending piece once and for all. Although the king was no match for his powerful, though peace loving, step-mother he made up for Hatshepsut's domination of him during his teenage years by setting out, almost immediately after her death, to conquer the known world. His reputation as a great hero and empire builder was justly deserved as the relief work on what is known as the **Wall of Records** demonstrates. Though unrelenting in his bid for power he had a penchant for being fairly just in his treatment of the people he conquered. This wall was a running tally of the organised tribute he exacted in honour of *Amun* from his subjugated lands.

East of the foundations of the original Temple of *Amun* stands the **Great Festival Temple of Tuthmosis III** which contains several fine reliefs of plants and animals in the so-called **Botanic Garden** and many columns, 20 of which are unique in Egypt in that they are larger at their peak than their base.

Between the end of the Festival Temple and the eastern gate of the enclosure are the ruins of two other structures, a portico built by Taharqa and another smaller temple of Tuthmosis III. The world's largest obelisk once stood on the base in front of this temple. The so-called **Lateran Obelisk**, which was 32.2 metres high, was removed from Karnak in 357 AD on the orders of the Roman Emperor Constantine. Although it was bound for Constantinople it ended up in the Circus Maximus in Rome and finally, in the 1580s, was re-erected in the Piazza San Giovanni in Laterano.

Against the northern enclosure wall of the precinct of *Amun* is the cult **Temple of**

Top: A felucca crew on the river near Luxor (HF)
Left: Feluccas moored in Luxor (HF)
Right: A peasant girl minding sheep by the river (HF)

Top: The Colossi of Memnon, Luxor (HF)
Left: Columns in the Karnak Temple, Luxor (HF)
Right: Statue of Ramses II in Karnak Temple, Luxor (HF)

Ptah, started by Tuthmosis III and finished by the Ptolemies. Access to the inner chambers is through a series of five doorways which lead you to two of the temple's original statues. The headless figure of *Ptah*, the creator-god of Memphis, is in the middle chapel and to his left is the eerily beautiful, bare-breasted and lioness-headed, black granite statue of his goddess-wife *Sekhmet*, the 'spreader of terror'.

A usually locked gate on the wall near this temple leads to the northern enclosure of the precinct of *Montu* the falcon-headed warrior god and the original deity of Thebes. The main temple was built by Amenophis III and modified by others but the complex is very dilapidated.

The secondary axis of the extended Great Temple of *Amun* runs south from the 3rd and 4th Pylons and is basically a processional way, bounded on the east and west sides by walls, and sectioned off by a number of pylons which create a series of courts. In front of the **7th Pylon**, built by Tuthmosis III, is the **Cachette Court** so named because of the thousands of stone and bronze statues discovered there during excavation work in 1903. Seven of the statues, of Middle Kingdom pharaohs, stand before the pylon and nearby are the remains of two colossal statues of Tuthmosis III.

The well-preserved **8th Pylon**, built by Queen Hatshepsut, is the oldest part of the north-south axis of the temple. Four of the original six colossi are still standing; the most complete being the one of Amenophis I.

The **9th & 10th Pylons** were built by Horemheb who used some of the stones of a demolished temple that had been built to the east by Akhenaten, before he decamped to Tell el Amarna.

To the east of the 7th and 8th pylons is the **Sacred Lake** where the priests of *Amun* would purify themselves before performing ceremonies in the temple. On the north-west side of the lake is the top half of Hatshepsut's fallen obelisk and a huge

statue of a *scarab* beetle dedicated by Amenophis III to the god of the rising sun, *Atum*.

There are the ruins or remains of about 20 other chapels within the main enclosure. In a fairly good state of repair in the south-west corner, is the **Temple of Khons**, god of the moon and time and son of *Amun* and *Mut*. The pylon faces Euergetes' Gate and the avenue of sphinxes to Luxor Temple and provides access to a small hypostyle hall and ruined sanctuary. The temple was started by Ramses III, added to by other Ramessids, Ptolemies and Herihor. The latter, like Horemheb, had pushed his way up through the ranks of the army to claim power, declaring himself not only pharaoh but High Priest of *Amun* as well.

Nearby is the small finely decorated **Temple of Opet**, dedicated to the hippo-potamus goddess *Opet*, who was the mother of *Osiris*.

From the 10th Pylon an avenue of sphinxes leads to the partly excavated southern enclosure – the precinct of *Mut*. The badly ruined **Temple of Mut** was built by Amenophis III and consists of a sanctuary, a hypostyle hall and two courts. The **Temple of Ramses III** stands south-west of the crescent-shaped lake which partly surrounds the main temple and all throughout the area are granite statues of *Sekhmet*, with her leonine head crowned by a solar disk.

Sound & Light Show Karnak Temple's *son et lumiere* easily rivals the one at the Great Pyramids. The 90 minute show recounts the history of Thebes and the lives of the many pharaohs who built the sanctuaries, courts, statues or obelisks in honour of *Amun*. The show starts at the avenue of ram-headed sphinxes, passes through the 1st Pylon to the Great Court and on through Great Hypostyle Hall to the Sacred Lake where there's a grand-stand for the show's finale.

There are two performances a night, in

either English, French, German or Arabic and the show costs E£5. The first show is at sunset (around 6 pm) and the second is at 8 pm. The following is the language schedule:

	1st show	2nd show
Monday	English	French
Tuesday	French	English
Wednesday	English	German
Thursday	Arabic	English
Friday	French	English
Saturday	English	French
Sunday	French	German

General admission to the temples of Karnak is between 7 am and 5.30 pm and tickets cost E£3, or E£1.50 for students. To get to Karnak you can take a local bus from Luxor station for 5 pt or hire a *hantour* for E£3 per hour. Give the driver a bit of *baksheesh* if you want him to wait.

THE WEST BANK

The west bank of Luxor was the necropolis of ancient Thebes, a vast City of the Dead where magnificent temples were raised to honour the cults of pharaohs entombed in the nearby cliffs and where queens, royal children, nobles, priests, artisans and even workers built tombs which ranged, in the quality of their design and decor, from the spectacular to the ordinary.

During the New Kingdom the necropolis also supported a large living population. In an attempt to protect the valuable tombs from robbers the artisans, labourers, temple priests and guards lived permanently in the City of the Dead, their lives devoted to its construction and maintenance. They perfected the techniques of tomb building, decoration and concealment and passed the secrets down through their own families.

The desire for secrecy greatly affected tomb design. Instead of a single mortuary monument like a pyramid, that was both a venue to worship the immortal pharaoh and the resting place of his mummified remains, the New Kingdom Theban rulers commissioned their funerary monuments in pairs. Magnificent mortuary temples were built on the plains, where the delusion of the pharaoh's immortality could be perpetuated by the devotions of his priests and subjects, while the king's body and worldly wealth were laid in secret tombs excavated and splendidly decorated in the hills. The prime location for the latter was an isolated canyon to the north-west, surrounded on three sides by high rugged cliffs. However, even though there was only one way into the Valley of the Kings and the tombs were well hidden, very few escaped the vandalism of the grave robbers.

It's unrealistic to attempt to explore all of the attractions of the west bank in one day. The incredible heat and the desolate and mountainous landscape make it an expedition not to be taken lightly. The ideal time to visit is between sunrise and 1 pm, so a series of morning trips is the best way to go about it. Take a torch and, more importantly, your own water because although drinks are available at some sites they're incredibly expensive.

Tickets for the sites must be bought at either the kiosk at the downstream 'tourist ferry landing' or at the General Inspectorate office (for student discounts), which is three km inland from the local ferry landing. You cannot pay for admission at the sites and individual tickets are required for each tomb, temple or group of sites, so you need to know just what you want to see before you set off. Tickets are valid only for the day of purchase and no refunds are given.

The Valley of the Kings costs E£5, or E£2.50 for students and the following cost E£1, or 50 pt for students: Deir el Bahri – the Temple of Hatshepsut; Medinat Habu – the Temple of Ramses III; the Ramesseum; the Tombs of Nakht & Menna; the Tombs of Rekhmire & Sennofer; the Tombs of Ramose, Userhet & Khaemet; Deir el Medina; the Valley of the Queens; and the Temple of Seti I.

Once you have your tickets you have the choice of getting around by bicycle, donkey, taxi or your own feet. The most practical and economical way is to rent a bicycle which can be done on the east or west bank (see the Getting Around Luxor section).

Special collective taxis for seven to eight people cost E£12.50 for a five to six hour tour. The taxi will wait for you. A donkey will cost about E£2.25 per day, plus the same for a guide, but remember they are not as easy to ride as they seem to be. You can hire them from the town landing.

From the canal junction it is two km to the Valley of the Queens, seven km to the Valley of the Kings, and one km straight to the student ticket office, past the Colossi of Memnon.

The Temple of Seti I

Seti I, the father of Ramses II, expanded the Egyptian empire to include Cyprus and parts of Mesopotamia. His imposing mortuary temple, dedicated to *Amun*, was an inspiring place of worship for his own cult and also served as a treasure house for some of the spoils of his military ventures. Though the first two pylons and courts are in ruins the temple itself is in reasonable repair and the surviving reliefs, in the hypostyle hall, chapels and sanctuary, are superbly executed and some of the finest examples of New Kingdom art. This temple, just off Sharia Wadi el Melouk (the road to the Valley of the Kings), is seldom visited by tourists so is well worth the effort.

On a barren hill, where the road from Deir el Bahri to the Valley of the Kings meets the road from Seti's temple, there is a domed house where Howard Carter lived during his search for the tomb of Tutankhamun.

The Valley of the Kings

Once called the 'Gates of the Kings' or 'the Place of Truth', the canyon now known as the Valley of the Kings is at once

a place of death, for nothing grows on its steep, scorching cliffs, and a majestic domain befitting the mighty kings who once lay there in great stone sarcophagi, awaiting immortality. The isolated valley, behind Deir el Bahri, is dominated by the natural pyramid-shaped mountain peak of El Qurn, 'the horn', and consists of two branches, the east and west valleys, with the former containing most of the royal burial sites.

All of the tombs followed a similar design, deviating only because of structural difficulties or the length of time spent on their construction. The longer the reign of the pharaoh, the larger and more magnificent his tomb. Two groups of workers and artisans would live, in alternating shifts, in the valley itself for the duration of the work, which usually took many years.

The tombs were designed to resemble the underworld with a long, inclined rock-hewn corridor descending into an ante-chamber, or series of sometimes pillared halls, and ending in the burial chamber. Once the tomb was cut its decoration was started, the themes almost exclusively concerned with the afterlife and the pharaoh's existence in it.

The colourful paintings and reliefs are extracts from ancient theological compositions, or 'books', and were incorporated in the tomb to assist the pharaoh into the next life. Texts were taken from the *Book of Amduat* – 'the book of him who is in the netherworld'; the *Book of Gates* which charted the king's course through the underworld; and the *Book of the Litany of Ra*, believed to be the words spoken by *Ra*, the sun god, on his own journey through the caverns of death.

The worshippers of *Amun* or *Amun-Ra* (the fusion of the two deities and king of the gods) believed that the Valley of the Kings was traversed each night by *Ra* and it was the aim of those who had been buried that day to secure passage on his sacred barque. To do this they had to be

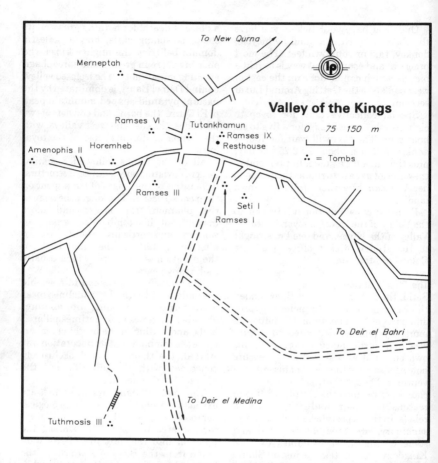

Valley of the Kings

0   75   150   m

∴ = Tombs

To New Qurna

Merneptah

Ramses VI

Tutankhamun

∴Ramses IX

●Resthouse

Amenophis II

Horemheb

Ramses III

Ramses I

Seti I

To Deir el Bahri

To Deir el Medina

Tuthmosis III

well equipped with a knowledge of the magic texts, hence the tomb decorations, before they could enter the boat of the god. Once aboard, they were brought to the kingdom of *Osiris*, god of the dead, where they were judged. Those kings who passed the ordeal would then board a second sacred barque for the journey to the east, where having overcome the powers of darkness and death, they would live again, immortal in the company of *Amun-Ra*.

Tuthmosis I was the first pharaoh to have his tomb cut in the barren cliffs,

around 1495 BC, and in all 62 tombs have been excavated in the valley, though not all belong to pharaohs. Each tomb is numbered in order of discovery but only 10 of them – Nos 6, 8, 9, 11, 15, 16, 17, 35, 57 and 62 – are open to the public. No 15 is the only one without electric lighting but you should take a torch anyway. The guards have the most endearing habit of switching off the lights if you won't give them *baksheesh* – and they wait till you're half way in to leave you in the pitch dark.

The road into the Valley of the Kings is

steep and dry and hot, so be prepared. There is a resthouse in the valley but they charge E£1 for a 50 pt bottle of mineral water. It's also usually crowded and closes at 2 pm so it's best to bring your own supplies, especially water.

The Tomb of Tutankhamun (No 62) The story behind the celebrated discovery of this, the most famous tomb in the Valley of the Kings, and the fabulous treasures it contained, far outshines its actual appearance. Tutankhamun's tomb is neither large nor impressive and bears all the signs of a rather hasty completion and inglorious burial. The extraordinary contents of this rather modest tomb built for a fairly insignificant boy-king, however, can only make you guess at the immense wealth that must have been laid to rest with the likes of the powerful Seti I or Ramses II.

For years archaeologists believed that, if in fact Tutankhamun was buried in the valley, his tomb would contain little of interest. The nephew of Akhenaten, he was merely a puppet pharaoh of the priests of *Amun*, supporting their counter-revolution against the parvenus of the late rebel king's desertion from Thebes. During his brief reign Tutankhamun was seen to re-embrace the cult of *Amun*, restoring its popularity with the people, and then he died, young, with no great battles or buildings to his credit.

The English Egyptologist Howard Carter, however, believed he would find the young pharaoh buried amongst his ancestors with his treasures intact. He toiled for six seasons in 'the Place of Truth', excavating thousands and thousands of tons of sand and rubble from possible sites, until even his wealthy patron Lord Carnarvon tired of the obsession. With his funding about to be cut off Carter made one last attempt at the only unexplored area that was left – a site covered by workers huts just under the already excavated tomb of Ramses VI.

On 4 November 1922 he uncovered steps and then a door, its seals untouched, and wired Lord Carnarvon to join him immediately for the opening of what he believed was the intact tomb of Tutankhamun. The discovery proved his sceptics wrong and the tomb's priceless cache of pharaonic treasures, which had remained undisturbed by robbers, vindicated Carter's dream beyond even his wildest imaginings. Sadly, in perhaps the last great irony in the history of tomb robbing in the Valley of the Kings, evidence came to light some years later that prior to the tomb being officially opened in the presence of experts from the Metropolitan Museum of Art, it seems that Carter and Carnarvon themselves broke in, stole several articles and resealed the door.

The tomb, opposite the resthouse, is small and for the most part undecorated. Three small chambers were crammed

Tutankhamun sarcophagus

with furniture, statues, chariots, musical instruments, weapons, boxes, jars and food, all of which is now in the Cairo Museum. The second coffin of gilded wood, the solid gold mummy case and of course the magnificent funerary mask, found on the king's body, are also in Cairo. The innermost coffin of gilded wood containing the decaying, mummified body of Tutankhamun, lies *in situ* within the carved granite sarcophagus in the burial chamber of his tomb, the walls of which are decorated with texts from the *Book of the Dead*.

The Tomb of Ramses VI (No 9) The early excavation of this tomb forestalled the discovery of Tutankhamun's tomb below it. Originally built for Ramses V but usurped by his successor, who saved time and money by appropriating the site, this tomb extends 83 metres into the mountain. It is best known for its beautiful and unusual ceiling which details the *Book of Day & Night* and

features the goddess *Nut* twice, stretched across the morning and evening sky. The passageway is decorated with scenes from the books of the Dead, of the Caverns and the complete text of the *Book of Gates*. Ramses VI's smashed sarcophagus lies in the pillared burial chamber at the end of the corridor.

The Tomb of Merneptah (No 8) Reliefs of *Isis*, the wife of *Osiris* and divine mourner of the dead, and *Nepthys*, the sister of *Isis* and guardian of coffins, adorn the entrance to this tomb north-west of the resthouse. Merneptah was the son of Ramses II and the pharaoh of the biblical *Exodus*. The walls of the steep corridor, which descends 80 metres to his burial chamber, are decorated with texts from the *Book of Gates*.

The Tomb of Ramses IX (No 6) The first on the left as you enter the Valley of the Kings, just before the resthouse, this tomb consists of a long, sloping corridor,

Wall paintings in the tomb of Horemheb

a large antechamber decorated with animals, serpents and demons, then a pillared hall and short hallway before the burial chamber. The goddess *Nut* is the feature of the ceiling painting, surrounded by sacred barques full of stars.

The Tomb of Horemheb (No 57) Horemheb, a general of the Egyptian army in about 1320 BC, became military dictator and eventually last pharaoh of the 18th Dynasty. A chamber just inside the entrance, which has fine festive reliefs, leads into a false burial chamber supported by two pillars. This attempt to fool any potential grave robbers didn't work as ancient thieves managed to find and uncover the stairway which leads steeply down to the real tomb, leaving nothing but Horemheb's red granite sarcophagus. The murals in the burial chamber were never finished, indicating an untimely death, but they're interesting because they reveal the different stages of decoration.

The Tomb of Amenophis II (No 35) One of the deepest structures in the valley, this tomb has more than 90 steps which take you down to a modern gangway built over a deep pit designed to protect the inner, lower chambers from thieves. The huge burial chamber is a beautifully decorated room where stars cover the entire ceiling and the walls feature, as if on a giant painted scroll, the entire text of the *Book of Amduat*. This was indeed the final resting place of Amenophis II, for although thieves did manage to make off with everything of value, they did no damage to the interior and left the king himself undisturbed. When the huge tomb was excavated, by the French in 1898, 13 mummies were found, including that of Amenophis lying *in situ* in his sarcophagus, a garland of flowers still around his neck. Nine of the other mummies were also of royal blood, hidden there by priests, and included the bodies of Tuthmosis IV, Seti II, Amenophis III and his wife Queen Tiy.

The Tomb of Ramses III (No 11) The burial chamber of this tomb, which is one of the largest in the valley (south-west of the resthouse) remains unexcavated and is closed to the public. There is, however, plenty to see in the three passageways and 10 side-chambers in the first part of the tomb. Also known as the Tomb of the Harpers, because of the painting of two musicians playing to the gods in a room off the second passage, it is interesting because the colouring of its sunken reliefs is still quite vivid. The side-chambers are decorated with pictures of their former contents and other walls depict daily happenings.

The Tomb of Tuthmosis III (No 34) Hidden in the hills between high limestone cliffs and reached only via a steep staircase that crosses an even steeper ravine, this tomb demonstrates the length that the ancient pharaohs went to to thwart the cunning of the ancient thieves. Tuthmosis III was one of the first to build his tomb in the Valley of the Kings and with secrecy his utmost concern, he chose the most inaccessible spot and designed his burial place with a series of passages at haphazard angles and a deep well to mislead or catch potential robbers – all to no avail, of course.

The shaft, now traversed by a narrow gangway, leads to a hall supported by two pillars, the walls of which are adorned with a list of over 700 gods and demi-gods. The burial chamber, which is oval-shaped like a cartouche, is decorated in a fairly restrained manner. The roof is supported by two pillars between which is the king's empty red sandstone sarcophagus; his mummy was found at Deir el Bahri.

The Tomb of Seti I (No 17) The longest, most splendid and best preserved tomb of the Theban necropolis is the burial site of Seti I which plunges over 100 metres down into the hillside. The detail of the enchanting, finely executed reliefs rivals even the much renowned decorations in his Cenotaph Temple at Abydos. Three long passages, intersected by decorated chambers culminate in the large, two part burial chamber. Colourful scenes include Seti appearing before *Ra-Harakhty*, god of the morning sun, beneath a ceiling of flying vultures and texts from the *Litany of Ra*. In the first chamber Seti is shown in the presence of deities and in another passage the walls feature the *Opening of the Mouth* ritual which ensured the mummy's organs were functioning. The first section of the burial chamber is a pillared hall decorated with texts from the *Book of Gates* and the second part, which contained Seti's magnificent alabaster sarcophagus, features texts from the *Amduat* and an astronomical ceiling. The tomb is east of the resthouse.

The Tomb of Ramses I (No 16) Although the tomb next to Seti's belongs to the founder of the 19th Dynasty it is a very simple affair because Ramses I only ruled for a couple of years. The tomb, which has the shortest entrance corridor of all the royal resting places in the valley, has a single almost square burial chamber, containing the king's open, pink granite sarcophagus. The chamber is the only part of the tomb that is decorated and features the pharaoh in the presence of deities such as *Osiris, Ptah, Anubis* and *Maat*.

From the tomb's of Seti I and Ramses I you can continue south-east and hike over the hills to Deir el Bahri, or vice versa of course. The walk takes about 45 minutes through an amazing lunar-type landscape, offering various perspectives of Hatshepsut's temple in the amphitheatre setting of Deir el Bahri below and excellent views across the plain towards the Nile. In summer you should start this hike at about 5.30 or 6 am, partly to catch the changing colours of the barren hills as the sun rises, but also because it gets mighty hot there later in the day. There's also a much longer trail from the Valley of the Kings to the Valley of the Queens via Deir el Medina.

Deir el Bahri/Temple of Hatshepsut

Rising out of the desert plain, in a series of terraces, the Mortuary Temple of Queen Hatshepsut merges with the sheer limestone cliffs of the eastern face of the Theban Mountain as if nature herself had built this extraordinary monument. The partly rock-cut, partly free-standing structure is one of the finest monuments of ancient Egypt though its original appearance, surrounded by myrrh trees, garden beds and approached by a grand sphinx-lined causeway, must have been even more spectacular.

Discovered in the mid 19th century by Auguste Mariette it wasn't completely excavated till 1896 and is still being restored. The third terrace is currently closed to the public while a team of Polish archaeologists clear and repair it. Unfortunately over the centuries the temple has been vandalised, mostly it seems, by one religious group or another. Akhenaten removed all references to *Amun*, before taking his court off to Tell el Amarna; and the early Christians who took it over as a monastery, hence the name Deir el Bahri (Monastery of the North), also defaced the pagan reliefs. The worst damage, however, was done out of pure spite by Hatshepsut's successor Tuthmosis III, who developed a fairly strong hatred for the queen in the 20 years he waited to ascend the throne of Egypt. Within weeks of her death he had obliterated or covered her name or image wherever he found it. Even in her own mortuary temple where he and Hatshepsut were always represented together, as co-rulers, he hacked out her likeness, leaving only his own.

Following the death of Tuthmosis I in 1495 BC, a great controversy arose, between the late pharaoh's daughter Hatshepsut and his grandson Tuthmosis III, over the rights of succession. The struggle for ultimate control was eventually won by the formidable Hatshepsut who, as if it wasn't enough to be only the third queen to ever rule ancient Egypt, declared herself pharaoh, which made her the first woman to ever reign as king.

Hatshepsut had married her father's son, her own half-brother Tuthmosis II, and she held many titles including 'pharaoh's wife and daughter' and of course 'queen'. She failed, however, to bear any sons so it was Tuthmosis III, the son of one of the king's concubines, who became heir presumptive. Following the death of her sibling/husband Hatshepsut became regent to the new pharaoh Tuthmosis III, but such was her power that the young boy had little chance of ruling in his own right. Despite the backing of the army Tuthmosis was no match for his aunt/step-mother/co-ruler and Hatshepsut eventually overshadowed him enough to proclaim herself absolute monarch, both queen and king. She still, however, had to win over the priesthood and this she managed by claiming divine birth, as most pharaohs did, by assuming the dress and manner of a man and, in reliefs, had herself depicted wearing the traditional pharaonic beard.

Hatshepsut ruled for 20 years and for Egypt it was a time of peace and internal development. It is not known how she died, whether it was from natural causes or something more sinister, but almost as soon as Tuthmosis III finally took his place on the throne, he led his country into war with Palestine.

The temple's 37-metre wide causeway led onto the three huge terraced courts, which are each approached by ramps and separated by colonnades. The renowned delicate relief work of the lower terrace features scenes of birds being caught in nets and the transport to Thebes of a pair of obelisks commissioned by Hatshepsut from the Aswan quarries.

The central court contains the best preserved reliefs. There Queen Hatshepsut recorded her divine birth and told the story of an expedition to the Land of Punt to collect live myrrh trees needed for the precious myrrh incense used in temple ceremonies. There are also two chapels at either end of the colonnade. At the northern end the colourful reliefs in the

Chapel of Anubis show the co-rulers, Hatshepsut and Tuthmosis III, with the queen's image again disfigured by her nephew, in the presence of *Anubis*, the god of embalming, *Ra-Harakhty*, the falcon-headed sun god, and his wife *Hathor*. In the Chapel of Hathor you can see (if you have a torch) an untouched figure of Hatshepsut worshipping the cow-headed goddess.

Although the third terrace is out of bounds you can see the pink granite doorway leading into the Sanctuary of Amun which is hewn out of the cliff.

In 1876 the greatest mummy find in history was made just north of Hatshepsut's temple. After many antiquities began showing up in the marketplace the authorities realised someone had found, and was plundering, an unknown tomb. After investigations they discovered a massive shaft at the foot of the cliffs which contained the mummies of 40 pharaohs, queens and nobles. It seems the New Kingdom priests realised the bodies of their kings would never be safe from violation in their own tombs, no matter what precautions were taken against grave robbers, so they moved them to this communal grave. The mummies included those of Amenophis I, Tuthmosis II and III, Seti I and Ramses I and III.

Tombs of the Nobles

The Tombs of the Nobles are one of the best though least visited attractions on the west bank. Nestled in the foothills and amongst the houses of the old village of Qurna (Sheikh Abd el-Qurna) are at least 400 tombs which date from the 6th Dynasty to the Graeco-Roman period. The tomb-chapels in the area date from the 18th to the 20th Dynasties.

Of the 100 or so tombs that have something of interest, seven are highly recommended. They have been numbered and divided into three groups, each requiring a separate ticket, as follows: Nakht and Menna (now possibly closed);

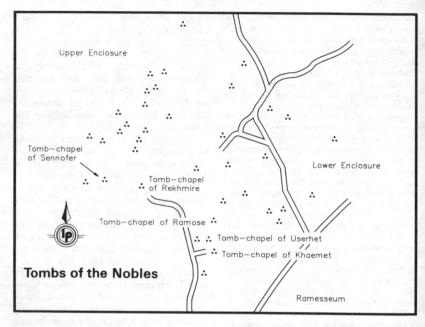

Tombs of the Nobles

Ramose, Userhet and Khaemet; and Rekhmire and Sennofer.

You'll see signs leading to the tombs leading off the main road, opposite the Ramesseum.

No 55 This is the tomb-chapel of Ramose who was a governor of Thebes during the reigns of Amenhophis III and Akhenaten. It's a fascinating tomb and one of the few monuments dating from that time, when the cult power of the priests of Karnak was usurped by the new monotheistic worship of *Aten*. Exquisite paintings grace the walls, showing scenes from the reigns of both kings and the transition between the two forms of religious worship. The tomb was never actually finished because Ramose deserted Thebes to follow the rebel Pharaoh Akhenaten to his new city at Tell el Amarna.

No 56 The tomb of Userhet, who was one of Amenhophis II's royal scribes, is right next to Ramose's tomb. Its most distinctive features are the wall paintings depicting daily life in ancient Egypt. Userhet is shown presenting gifts to Amenhophis II; there's a barber busy cutting hair on another wall; and there are men shown making wine and hunting gazelles from a chariot.

No 57 This fine tomb belonged to Khaemet, who was Amenhophis III's royal inspector of the granaries and court scribe. Scenes on the walls show Khaemet offering sacrifices; the pharaoh depicted as a sphinx; the funeral ritual of *Osiris*; and images of daily country life and official business.

No 100 The tomb of Rekhmire, a governor during the reigns of Tuthmosis III and Amenhophis II, is one of the best preserved in the area. In the main chamber, just inside on the right, are scenes of Rekhmire receiving gifts from foreign lands. The panther and giraffe are gifts from Nubia; the elephant, horses and chariot come from Syria; and the expensive vases come from Crete and the Aegean Islands.

No 96 Prince Sennofer of Thebes worked for Amenhophis II as a supervisor of the *Gardens of the Temple of Amun*. The most interesting parts of his tomb are deep underground in the main chamber. The ceiling there is covered with paintings of grapes and vines and most of the scenes on the surrounding walls and columns depict Sennofer with his sister.

Nos 52 & 69 The wall paintings in the tombs of Menna and Nakht, which may now be closed to the public, both emphasise rural life in the 18th Dynasty. Menna was an estate inspector and Nakht was an astronomer of *Amun* and their finely detailed tombs show scenes of farming, hunting, fishing and feasting.

The Ramesseum

The Ramesseum is yet another monument raised by Ramses II for the ultimate glory of himself. The massive temple was built to impress his priests, his subjects, his successors and of course the gods so that he, the great warrior king, could live forever. Many of his other works were rather crudely constructed but in this, his mortuary temple, he demanded perfection in the workmanship so that it would stand as an eternal testimony to his greatness.

Sadly the Ramesseum, which was dedicated to *Amun*, is mostly in ruins. This fact no doubt disappoints Ramses II more than it does modern-day visitors to the site because he had dared all those who questioned his greatness in the centuries to come, to simply gaze on the magnificence of his monuments to understand his power over life and death. How the mighty fall! The scattered remains of the colossal statue of the king and the ruins of his temple prompted the English poet Shelley to cut this presumptuous pharaoh down to size by using the undeniable fact of Ramses' mortality to ridicule his immortal aspirations. In the early 19th century Shelley wrote *Ozymandias*:

I met a traveller from an antique land
Who said: Two vast and trunkless legs of stone
Stand in the desert ... Near them, on the sand,
Half sunk, a shattered visage lies, whose frown,
And wrinkled lip, and sneer of cold command,
Tell that its sculptor well those passions read
Which yet survive, stamped on these lifeless things,
The hand that mocked them, and the heart that fed:
And on the pedestal these words appear:
'My name is Ozymandias, king of kings:
Look on my works, ye Mighty, and despair!'
Nothing beside remains. Round the decay
Of that colossal wreck, boundless and bare
The lone and level sands stretch far away.

Although a little more elaborate than other temples, the fairly orthodox layout of the Ramesseum, with its two courts, hypostyle hall, sanctuary, accompanying chambers and storerooms is unusual in that it is a parallelogram. The usual rectangular floor plan was altered to incorporate the orientation of an older, smaller temple – that of Ramses' mother Tuya, which is off to one side.

The 1st and 2nd pylons measure more than 60 metres across and feature reliefs of Ramses' military exploits. Between them the ruins of the huge 1st Court include the double colonnade which fronted the royal palace. Near the western stairs is part of the **Colossus of Ramses II**, the 'Ozymandias' of Shelley's poem, lying somewhat forlornly on the ground. When it stood, it was 17.5 metres tall. The head of another granite statue of Ramses, one of a pair, lies in the 2nd Court. Twenty-nine of the original 48 columns of the Great Hypostyle Hall are

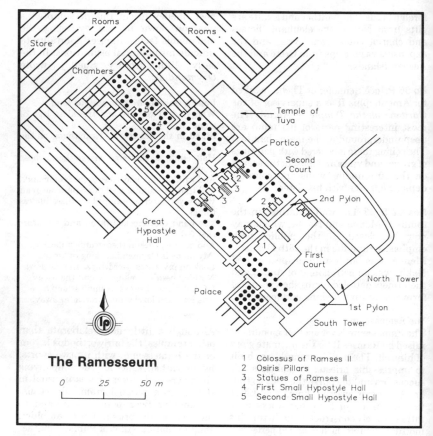

The Ramesseum

0   25   50 m

1 Colossus of Ramses II
2 Osiris Pillars
3 Statues of Ramses II
4 First Small Hypostyle Hall
5 Second Small Hypostyle Hall

still standing and in the smaller hall behind it, the roof which features astronomical hieroglyphs, is still in place.

There is a resthouse/restaurant next to the temple which is called, not surprisingly, the *Ramesseum Resthouse*. It is owned by Sayed Hussain, whose father discovered the Tomb of Hatshepsut and was a friend of Howard Carter. The resthouse is a great place to relax and have a cool drink or something cheap to eat.

Deir el Medina

The small Ptolemaic temple of Deir el Medina is one km off the road to the Valley of the Queens. The temple was built between 221 BC and 116 BC by Philopator, Philometer and Euergetes II. It was dedicated to *Hathor*, the goddess of pleasure and love, and to *Maat*, the goddess of truth and the personification of cosmic order. However, the temple is called Deir el Medina, which means 'monastery of the town', because it was occupied by early Christian monks.

If you have the energy and the inclination, hike southward a short distance to see the remains of a New Kingdom settlement occupied by the artists and workmen who built some of the tombs in the area. Archaeologists have been excavating this settlement for most of this century and at least 70 houses have been uncovered.

One of the tombs in this area which is definitely worth visiting is the **Tomb of Sennedjem** (No 1). Sennedjem was a 19th Dynasty (1303 BC to 1200 BC) servant in the 'Place of Truth' – the Valley of the Kings. The tomb has only one chamber, but the wall paintings are magnificent. One of the most famous scenes shows a cat killing a snake. There is no light but the guard has a lantern if you haven't brought your own torch.

Most of the other tombs in the area belonged to the servants, foremen and labourers who worked in the 'Place of Truth'.

The Valley of the Queens

There are at least 75 tombs in *Biban el-Harim*, the Valley of the Queens, belonging to queens of the 19th and 20th Dynasties and other members of the royal families including princesses and the Ramessid princes. Only tomb Nos 43, 44, 52 and 55 are open.

The top attraction here is No 55, the **Tomb of Amunherkhepshep** who was the son of Ramses III. Amun was nine years old when he died and the scenes on the tomb walls show his father grooming him to be pharaoh by introducing him to various gods. Amun's mother was pregnant at the time of his death and in her grief she aborted the child and entombed it with Amun. A five-month-old mummified fetus was discovered there. Wall paintings also show Ramses leading his son to *Anubis*, the jackal-headed god of the dead, who then takes the young Prince Amun down to the entrance of the Passage of the Dead.

The **Tomb of Queen Titi** (No 52), who was wife and consort to one of the Ramses, is also interesting.

Medinat Habu

The temple complex of Medinat Habu was one of the first places in Thebes to be closely associated with the local god *Amun*. Hatshepsut, Tuthmosis III and Ramses III constructed the main buildings of the complex, which is second only to the Temples of Karnak in size and complexity, but Medinat Habu was added to and altered by a succession of rulers right through to the Ptolemies. At its height there were temples, workshops, storage rooms, administrative buildings and accommodation for the priests and officials. It was the centre of the economic life of Thebes for several centuries and was still inhabited as late as the 9th century AD.

The original **Temple of Amun**, built by Hatshepsut and Tuthmosis III, was later completely overshadowed by the enormous **Mortuary Temple of Ramses III** which is the dominant feature of Medinat Habu. Ramses III was inspired in the construction of his shrine by the Ramesseum of his father. His own temple and the smaller one dedicated to *Amun* are both enclosed within the massive outer walls of the complex. Also just inside, to the left of the gate, are the **Tomb Chapels of the Divine Adorers** which were built for the principal priestesses of *Amun*. Outside the 'east fortified gate', one of only two entrances, was a landing quay for a canal which once connected Medinat Habu with the Nile.

The well preserved **1st Pylon** marks the front of the temple proper and Ramses III is portrayed in its reliefs as the victor in several wars. To the left of the 1st Court are the remains of the pharaoh's palace; the three rooms at the rear were for the Royal Harem. There is a window between the first court and the palace known as the 'Window of Appearances' which allowed the king to show himself to his subjects.

The reliefs of the **2nd Pylon** feature Ramses III presenting prisoners of war to *Amun* and his vulture-goddess wife *Mut*. The **2nd Court** is surrounded by colonnades and reliefs of various religious ceremonies.

Medinat Habu is off the road on your right as you return from the Valley of Queens. After you have finished wandering around the complex treat yourself to a cold Stella beer at the *Habu Hotel* opposite.

The Colossi of Memnon
The massive, unmistakable pair of statues known as the Colossi of Memnon are all that remain of the temple of the hedonistic Amenophis III. Rising about 18 metres from the plain the enthroned, faceless statues of Amenophis have kept a lonely vigil on the changing landscape around them, surviving the rising flood waters of the Nile which gradually, through annual inundation, destroyed the temple buildings behind them. Over the centuries the crumbling rubble of what was believed to have been one of the most splendid of the Theban temples was ploughed into the fertile soil. A stela, now in the Egyptian Museum, describes the temple as being built from 'white sandstone, with gold throughout, a floor

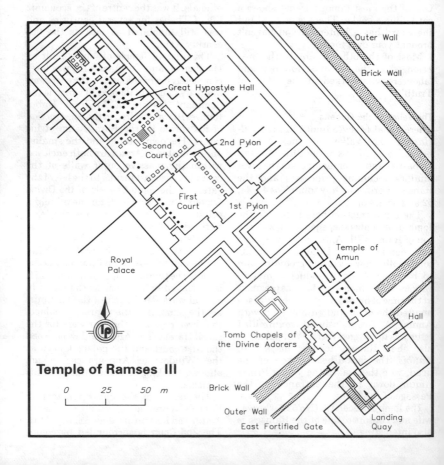

Temple of Ramses III

covered with silver, and doors covered with electrum.' (Electrum was a commonly used alloy of gold and silver.)

The colossi were amongst the great tourist attractions of Egypt during Graeco-Roman times because the Greeks believed they were actually statues of the legendary Memnon, a king of Ethiopia and son of the dawn goddess *Eos*, who was slain by Achilles during the Trojan War. It was the northern statue which attracted most of the attention because at sunrise it would emit a haunting, musical sound which the Greeks believed was the voice of Memnon greeting his mother each day. *Eos* in turn would weep tears of dew for the untimely death of her beautiful son.

Actually the phenomenon of the famous vocal statue was probably the combined effect of a simple change in temperature and the fact that the upper part of the colossus was severely damaged by an earthquake in about 30 BC. As the heat of the morning sun baked the dew-soaked stone, sand particles would break off and resonate inside the cracks in the structure. Certainly, after a well-meaning Roman governor repaired the statue some time in the 2nd century AD, Memnon's plaintive greeting to his mother was heard no more.

The colossi are just off the road, a little north-west of New Qurna – you won't miss them.

Amenophis III had quite a reputation for high and fast living and the ruins of his amazing palace are about one km south of Medinat Habu. The royal residence featured a lake, a banquet hall, private state rooms for Amenophis, a separate residence for his beloved queen Tiy, and quarters for court officials, servants, guests and of course the pharaoh's extensive harem which numbered over 300. Although the palace is badly ruined the remains are quite substantial.

Places to Stay – bottom end

At the bottom of the list (and the barrel) is the *Youth Hostel* on Sharia El Karnak. It is cheap (60 pt to 80 pt), dirty and usually crowded with groups of Egyptian school kids. If you really must stay here it is half-way between Luxor and Karnak temples, near the service taxi station. It's *just* OK for one night and the hours are 7 to 10 am and 3 to 11 pm.

The *El Salam Hotel* on Sharia El Karnak gets rave reviews and has friendly staff and hot showers. The rooms are very clean and range from E£1.50 to E£2 for a double. Everyone gets a free Coke upon arrival and free coffee for the duration of their stay.

The *Grand Hotel*, Sharia Mohammed Farid (turn south on the street parallel to the train tracks, it's the second street on the right) is far from grand but many travellers highly recommend it. It costs E£2.50 per bed or E£4 for a double, with breakfast and hot showers and there's a sundeck/garden on the roof. The managers are very hospitable and sometimes invite the guests to traditional Egyptian weddings.

The *New Karnak*, on Midan El Mahatta, is one of the best at the bottom end with 18 double rooms ranging in price up to E£6. The rooms can also be taken as singles for E£4 per person. You can rent a fan for E£1 per night and there's hot water but bring your own toilet paper. It's not super clean but it's adequate.

The *Horus Hotel* (tel 2165), on Sharia El Karnak facing the Luxor Temple, is comfortable, clean and has friendly staff. Single rooms with/without shower cost E£5/3.40; doubles are E£7.25 with shower and a great view of the Luxor Temple or E£4.50 without. The rooms cost E£1 less in summer. Meals are available and cost E£1 for breakfast, E£2.50 for lunch and E£2.50 for dinner.

The *Pyramids Hotel* (tel 83248), claims to be on Sharia Youssef Hassan but is actually two blocks south on a nameless street (see map). It has singles with bathrooms for E£5, including a fan. There are 20 rooms, a dusty cafeteria and a bar. The young owner, Mr Youssef, is very friendly and is usually willing to negotiate the price of a room. Youssef can also help you arrange just about anything and claims that in the mornings he works as an attorney.

The *St Mark Pensione*, 19 Sharia Michael Boulos (a small street running north-east off Sharia El Mahatta near the Ramoza Hotel), is a tiny tucked-away pension. There are only two rooms, with two single beds or two double beds, the bathroom is clean and there's a hot shower. It costs E£2 per person and you can use the kitchen and sitting room. Breakfast is available; an omelette, bread, cheese, jam and tea costs only E£1. The owner, Mr Atta, will be there or in the lobby of the Ramoza Hotel.

The *Amoun Hotel*, on Sharia El Mahatta has 12 large rooms for E£2 per person including breakfast. There's a television in the lobby and you can use the kitchen and refrigerator. The place is remarkably quiet for a hotel on this street and during summer you can sleep on the rooftop under the stars for free.

The *Hotel Dina* is on Sharia Youssef Hassan about one block from Sharia El Karnak (look for the large sign on top). The rooms are simple but most of them have bathrooms. Doubles are E£6.25 and singles E£5.

The *Four Seasons Hotel* is opposite the Luxor Temple and the views are fantastic. It has 15 rooms all with bathrooms, air conditioning, linen and towels. Doubles cost E£7, singles cost E£6. This place is a great bargain, especially if you get a corner room with a view of the temple. It used to be called the Abu el Haggag.

The *New Palace Hotel* is down the third street on your right as you head south on the street in front of the station. It's clean, has hot water and costs E£3 to E£4 for a double without bath.

On the west bank there are seven hotels, all of which fall into the 'bottom end' price range.

The *Memnon Hotel* is across the road from the Colossi of Memnon. It has hot

1	Museum
2	Windsor Hotel
3	ETAP Hotel
4	Hotel Philippe
5	Bicycle Shop
6	Hotel Savoy
7	Mina Palace
8	Bicycle Shop
9	Hotel Dina
10	Pyramids Hotel
11	The Four Seasons Hotel
12	Mosque of Abu El Haggag
13	Horus Hotel
14	Bus Station
15	Winter Palace, American Express and Telephone Office
16	New Winter Palace
17	Tourist and State Information Office / Tourist Bazaar
18	Luxor Hotel (and Camping)
19	Post Office
20	Juice Stand
21	Mensa Restaurant
22	Bicycle Shop
23	St. Mark's Pensione
24	Ramoza Hotel
25	Amoun Hotel
26	New Karnak Hotel
27	Salt and Bread Cafe

water and dark, dingy rooms which cost E£2 per person including breakfast. The 2nd floor has newer, less drab rooms with balconies overlooking Medinat Habu. Mahmoud Hassan Ali, the owner, is a nice guy.

The *Mersam Hotel* (tel 82403), is home to Sheikh Ali Abdul Rasul a cantankerous old guy with a bone-cracking handshake and an aggressive sense of hospitality that keeps you riveted to your seat, whether you like it or not. This place, also known as the *Ali Abd el Raasul Hotel* or the *Sheik Ali Hotel*, is opposite the Antiquities Office. During winter, rooms cost E£4 per person including breakfast

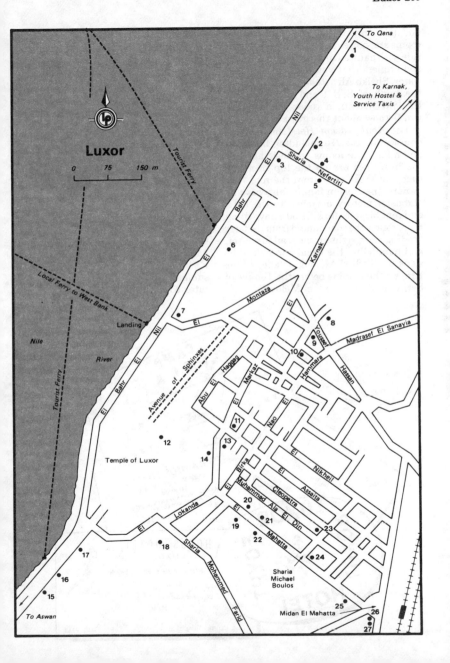

Luxor

0   75   150 m

To Qena

To Karnak,
Youth Hostel &
Service Taxis

Nil
El
Bahr
El

Sharia

Nefertiti

Karnak
El

Montaza

Madrasef El Sanayia

Yousef
El

Hassen

Hammara
El

Tourist Ferry

Local Ferry to West Bank

Nile

River

Landing

El
Bahr
El

Nil
El

Avenue   of   Sphinxes

Abu   El   Haggag

Markaz
El

Nao
El

Temple of Luxor

Birka
El

Nikheil
El

Assalta

Cleopatra

Muhammad Ala El Din

Lokanda
El

Sharia   Mohammed   Farid

Mahatta

Sharia
Michael
Boulos

Midan El Mahatta

To Aswan

and in summer they cost E£2.50. The rooms are, however, a bit on the primitive side with painted mud walls and Turkish-style toilets that you flush with cups of water. Sheikh Ali actually helped discover the tomb of Seti I and if you've read Richard Critchfield's book *Shahatt*, then you'll know about this guy already.

The *Abul Kasem Hotel* has singles/doubles for E£7/10 including breakfast and a fan. The rooms are basic but OK, the best ones are on the top floor and there's a great view from the roof. The owners, the Kasem family, also have an alabaster factory attached to the hotel and rent bicycles for E£1.50 a day. To get there follow the road inland from the ferry landing, turn right on the road just after, and parallel to, the canal and follow the signs to 'Wadi el Melouk' (Valley of the Kings); the hotel is before the Temple of Seti I on Sharia Wadi el Melouk.

The rooms of the *Wadi el Melouk Hotel* (tel 82798) are a bit on the dirty side but the place has a good rooftop restaurant with terrific views. Don't accept packages from the owner or his family for Cairo, unless you're allowed to inspect the contents. To get there, follow the directions for the Abdul Kasem Hotel but turn right and cross back over the canal before you reach Sharia Wadi el Melouk (see map).

The other three hotels are the *Lucky Hotel*, *Titi House* and the *Habu Hotel* but no one recommends them.

Places to Stay – middle

The *Mina Palace* is on the Corniche near the landing for local ferries to the west bank. In winter most of the rooms cost E£19 to E£21 for a single or double. In summer, or when the hotel isn't full, room rates cost up to 50% less and you may

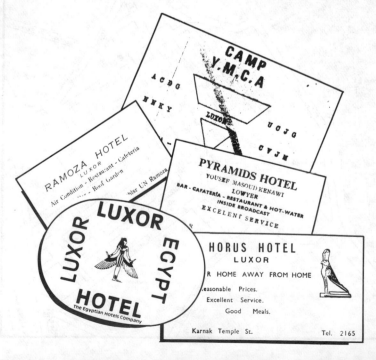

even get a double for E£8 – after bargaining. Rooms include private showers and toilets, air-con, breakfast and use of a refrigerator.

The *Windsor Hotel* is in a small alley just off Sharia Nefertiti between the Corniche and the Hotel Philippe. It's an excellent place with 72 rooms, each with a telephone, air-con and breakfast included. Prices are E£19.30 a single, E£21.96 a double plus taxes and service. This place is popular with European tour groups.

The *Ramoza Hotel* (tel 82270), on Sharia El Mahatta, has been renovated so that it no longer looks as old as its namesake, an 18th dynasty noble. It costs E£15 a double and E£14 a single. There's hot water and a rooftop restaurant with good views.

The *Savoy Hotel* is on the Corniche two blocks north of Luxor Temple. In the main building double rooms with/without bath cost E£12/9.52; and singles with/without bath cost E£9.52/7.70. The rooms are a bit dark but some have balconies facing the Nile. The Savoy also has some garden bungalows which cost E£24 for a double and E£19 for a single.

The *Hotel Philippe* is on Sharia Nefertiti. Room prices are E£12/15 for a single/double. Air-con whether you want it or not, costs an extra E£1.50 and the E£1.25 breakfast is compulsory.

Places to Stay - top end

The hotels in this price range start at about E£30 for a single.

The *Movenpick Jolie Ville* is on Crocodile Island four km from town. It's quite a deluxe place with a swimming pool, tennis courts and sailboats. The pool is open to the public for E£2.50. A shuttle bus runs between the Movenpick and the Winter Palace.

The *Etap Hotel* (tel 82011), is a four star place managed by a French-Egyptian company. The lobby is a nice cool place to hang out. Non-guests can go to the disco for E£5 including drinks; and use the swimming pool for E£5. Single rooms cost E£42 and doubles are E£56 including breakfast.

The *Winter Palace & New Winter Palace* (tel 82222) on Sharia El Bahr, are attached. The new side is not nearly as interesting and romantic as the old which was built to attract the aristocracy of Europe. It costs E£41.35 a double and E£33 a single and there's a swimming pool, ping pong tables and tennis court. Anyone can use the pool for E£2.

The *Luxor Hotel*, on Sharia El Karnak, faces Luxor Temple. It costs E£32.72/26.18 a double/single and all rooms have air-con. Breakfast is compulsory.

Camping You can camp for free in the garden in front of the Luxor Hotel. 'Bowab' Mohammed watches your gear like a hawk. Give him some *baksheesh* and he will gladly dig his talons into any threatening predator.

The *YMCA* (tel 82425), on Sharia El Karnak allows camping on its grounds for E£2 per night, including use of its mouldy showers.

Places to Eat

The *Mina Palace* has a good restaurant which serves cheap grilled fish, rice pilaf, chicken and spaghetti. A full meal will cost about E£3.

The *Savoy Hotel* also has a restaurant. You can sit on the outside terrace overlooking the garden and the Nile and have a delicious meal of Egyptian goulash (I'm not quite sure what it's supposed to be!), fish or chicken for E£5.

The *Amoun Restaurant* serves Oriental kebab, chicken, fish and various rice and vegetable dishes for E£2 per meal.

The *Mensa Restaurant*, on Sharia El Mahatta, has cheap basic food. Dishes include chicken, pigeon stuffed with rice, sandwiches and chicken with French fries and mixed vegetables.

The *ETAP Hotel Coffee Shop* is a pleasant, cool place to retreat for lunch. You can get spaghetti and salad for E£3, sandwiches for E£1 to E£2.30, omelettes for E£2.75 and ice cream for E£1.20.

The *New Karnak Restaurant*, where the food is good and cheap though the portions are small, is next to the New

Karnak Hotel. You can eat chicken for 85 pt, rice and salads for 20 pt, or spaghetti with a tablespoon of sauce for 20 pt – all to the sounds of '50s and '60s American rock 'n roll music. Try the Turkish coffee.

The *Limpy* gives you more food for almost the same prices as the New Karnak. A three course meal costs about E£1.50 and the menu includes good onion soup, fish and salad. It faces the train station; you'll see the sign.

The *Marhaba Restaurant*, an Oriental style dining room on the roof of the Tourist Bazaar building, serves E£4 entrees of kufta, kebab, pigeon and Nile perch, with great views of the river.

The Salt & Bread Cafeteria is on your left as you leave the train station. They serve many entrees including kebab, pigeon and chicken. A full meal costs about E£2.

The juice stand on Sharia El Mahatta opposite the post office has great freshly squeezed drinks.

Entertainment

The best thing to do in Luxor in the late afternoon and early evening is to relax aboard a *felucca*. Local *feluccas* cruise the river throughout the day and cost from around E£1 per person per hour or E£4 per boat per hour. An enjoyable outing is the trip upriver to **Banana Island**. The tiny isle, dotted with palms, is about five km from Luxor and the trip takes two to three hours. Try to work it that you arrive back in time to watch a brilliant Nile sunset from the boat.

If you're after a little more action the *Movenpick Jolie Ville* presents a quite extravagant floor show. For E£25 per person they will dress you up in a *galabiyya* – the traditional flowing cotton gown, take you for a *felucca* ride at sunset, introduce you to 'peasants' and then feed and entertain you in a tent by the Nile.

The *Etap, Winter Palace* and the *Isis* hotels all have folkloric and belly dance performances and discos.

Getting There

Air EgyptAir flies between Cairo, Luxor and Aswan everyday. A one-way ticket to Luxor from Cairo costs E£51 and flights depart at 10.45 am, noon and 3.45, 5.45 and 8.45 pm.

From Luxor to Aswan a one-way ticket costs E£21.75 and flights depart at 8.15 and 11.50 am, and 1.50 and 3.50 pm.

A one-way ticket from Luxor to the Western Oases in the New Valley costs E£44. Flights depart on Sundays and Wednesdays at 6.50 am.

The airport (tel 82306), is seven km east of Luxor and the official price for a taxi between there and town is E£3 per car load. The EgyptAir office is next to the entrance of the (old) Winter Palace Hotel on Sharia El Bahr.

Train Sleeper cars between Cairo, Luxor and Aswan range from the luxurious Wagon-Lits cars to the standard, but still adequate, regular sleepers. The 'Wagon-Lits' fare between Cairo and Luxor is E£39 per person for a two-person compartment, each of which has a sink with hot running water, piped-in music, a small clothes closet and adequate lighting. Dinner and breakfast are served directly to your compartment. If you're craving a bit of comfort, then this is an extremely civilised way to travel. There are daily departures from Cairo at 7 and 7.35 pm; and from Aswan at 2 and 5.45 pm. Refer to the Getting Around chapter for the detailed timetable.

Ordinary overnight trains – some with sleepers – depart Cairo daily at 6.45, 7.20, 8 and 8.30 pm and reach Luxor at 5.40, 7.30, 8.10 and 9.15 am. The sleeper fare is E£17.50 for one way in a single compartment, E£9.50 per person in a double; and E£12.55 for an ordinary 1st class seat. Refer to the Cairo 'Getting There' section for more details.

From Luxor to Aswan there are several trains everyday. The fares are E£1.90 for a 2nd class student ticket in an air-con car; and 35 pt in 3rd class.

Bus From Cairo buses for Luxor depart from Midan Ahmed Hilmi, behind Ramses train station. The fare for a basic air-con bus is E£9, or E£7 for students. The trip takes about 11 hours. The super-deluxe bus costs E£20 and departs Cairo at 5.30 am.

In Luxor the intercity buses leave from in front of the Horus Hotel on Sharia El Karnak.

From Luxor the E£9 air-con buses to Cairo leave at 5 am and 4 pm. They're luxury buses so they don't get crowded and they also stop half way for tea and sandwiches. Some travellers claim they're better than the train as long as you don't sit under the speakers.

From Luxor to Hurghada, on the Red Sea coast, there are air-con buses at 6 am and noon. The four-hour trip costs E£4, or E£2 for students.

From Luxor to Aswan there are buses at 6, 8 and 10 am, noon, 1 and 2 pm. The trip takes four hours and costs E£3.50.

The bus from Luxor to Abu Simbel leaves at 6 am on Saturdays, Mondays and Thursdays and costs E£10.

Service Taxis The taxi station is on Sharia El Karnak, one block inland from the Luxor Museum.

A service taxi to Aswan costs E£3 and takes three hours; to Esna it costs 85 pt and takes 1½ hours; to Edfu it costs E£2 for the two-hour trip; and to Kom Ombo it costs E£2.50 and takes 2½ hours.

You can hire a special taxi for a total of E£36 to take you and seven others to Aswan with stops en route at Esna, Edfu and Kom Ombo.

Boat More than 55 boats offer Nile cruises between Luxor and Aswan, lasting for three to five nights. There are also 11 different night cruises to Luxor which start in Cairo.

The average rates in the high season, from October to April, are: US$70 to US$120 per day on a four-star boat; and US$150 to US$200 per day on a five-star boat. In the low season, May to September, the rates are: US$50 to US$70 for a four-star boat; and US$100 to US$120 for a five-star boat.

The *Hilton, Sheraton, Club Med* and *Marriott* all have luxurious floating hotels which travel the Nile. As a sample, the *Sheraton* Nile Cruise prices for four/seven days are: 1 to 18 October – US$740/1165; 4 June to 5 March – US$930/1460; 1 to 20 December – US$540/860; 5 to 24 January – US$680/1070; 4 May to 5 September – US$820/1290.

Getting Around

Bicycle *Boulos' Bicycles*, 52 Sharia el Mahatta next to a shoe store, charges E£1.50 per day. You must leave your passport or student identification.

Two other places to rent bicycles (refer to the map) are from *Ahmed Kamel Amin* on Sharia Youssef Hassan, near the Hotel Dina, and from the bicycle shop on Sharia Nefertiti near the Hotel Philippe.

Hantour For about E£3 per hour you can get around town by horse and carriage. It's the most common means of transportation in Luxor and the tourist office will have details of the latest rates.

Boat There are, of course, a multitude of *feluccas* to take you on short trips or day tours from Luxor. They leave from various points all along the riverside.

To cross over to the Theban necropolis on Luxor's west bank there are three ferries. The boat landing near Luxor Temple is for the local ferry, which costs only 10 pt. It takes you to the west bank town landing where there are plenty of service taxis and minibuses, but no tickets to the monuments.

The other two ferries are 'tourist' boats which drop you off at the 'tourist' landing, about one km north of the town landing. The tourist ferries cost 25 pt but they're quicker and take you to the ticket kiosk. The tourist ferry landings are in front of the Savoy and the Winter Palace hotels.

A Felucca Down the Nile

A trip to Egypt would not be complete without a ride in a *felucca* – the traditional lateen-rigged boats that ply the waters of the Nile. Once upon a time they were the most important form of transport and communication in the country and were used for ferrying produce and goods up and down the river. They still carry a certain amount of local product but these days the most lucrative cargo is tourists out to experience a bit of life on the river.

The ideal trip is the four-day journey from Aswan to Luxor. We foolishly, however, tried to do it in the opposite direction. After four consecutive days of light winds that died out by 11 am, *and* with the current against us, we had covered less than half the distance to Aswan. If you're travelling downstream from Aswan to Luxor then you can still make progress even if the wind dies out.

A quick check around the travellers' hangouts will usually turn up plenty of people wanting to make the trip so getting a group together should be no problem. Obviously the more people there are the cheaper it's going to be. Remember though that conditions on the *feluccas* are fairly cramped so with any more than about six people you'll spend more time

trying to keep out of each other's way than you will enjoying the ride.

There is no shortage of boats ready to take you – the cries of 'Hello, boat?' from the water's edge will follow you as you walk along the waterfront. Find a boat and haggle ruthlessly – E£40 per day for the boat and E£4 per person per day for food is a fair deal. Get firm answers from the owner as to what you are getting. Make sure he has plenty of blankets, as the nights are freezing, and that he will only be using bottled water for cooking. If you can arrange to visit a few small villages en route so much the better – he may well invite you to his own village to meet his family and have a meal.

Once you finally get out on the water, sit back, relax and enjoy the quiet side of Egypt as you drift slowly past mud brick villages, young girls tending flocks of sheep on the banks and women washing clothes and collecting water in enormous earthenware pots (the men will be off somewhere else, busily drinking tea and talking). All the while, as you sail peacefully along, the barren hills of the desert beyond the water's edge and the cultivated fields are a reminder of how much these people of upper Egypt depend on the Nile for their livelihood.

– **Hugh Finlay**

Esna to Abu Simbel

Following the death of Alexander the Great his huge empire was divided between his Macedonian generals. For 300 years the Greek-speaking Ptolemies ruled Egypt in the guise of pharaohs, respecting the traditions and religion of the Egyptians and setting an example for the Romans that succeeded them.

While their centre of power tied them to Alexandria and the coast they also pushed their way south, extending Graeco-Roman power into Nubia, through their politically sensible policy of assimilation rather than subjugation.

In Upper Egypt they raised temples in honour of the local gods, building them in grand pharaonic style to appease the priesthood and earn the trust of the people. Somehow though these archaic imitations lost something in the translation; in many ways they were stilted, unimaginative edifices lacking the artistic brilliance that marked the truly Egyptian constructions they copied.

In southern Upper Egypt, south of Luxor, the major Graeco-Roman works were a series of riverside temples at Esna, Edfu, Kom Ombo and Philae, admirable as much for their location as their actual artistic or architectural merit.

Beyond Edfu the ribbon of cultivation on the east bank gives way to the Arabian Desert and at Silsileh, 145 km south of Luxor, the Nile passes through a gorge, once thought to mark a cataract. In this area there are Early Dynastic and New Kingdom ruins, including Elephantine and Abu Simbel, and there's the city of Aswan, the great high dam and Lake Nasser which mark the end of Egypt proper, for beyond them lie the forbidding, infertile desert lands of Nubia and the border with Sudan.

ESNA
The Graeco-Roman **Temple of Khnum** is the main attraction of Esna, a small busy farming town on the west bank of the Nile 54 km south of Luxor. All that actually remains of the temple is the well-preserved **Great Hypostyle Hall** built during the reign of the Emperor Claudius and this sits, rather incongruously, in its huge excavation pit amongst the houses and narrow alleyways in the middle of town.

Dedicated to *Khnum*, the ram-headed creator god who fashioned man on his potter's wheel, the temple was begun by Ptolemy VI and built over the ruins of earlier temples. The later built hall, as it stands today, was itself excavated from the silt that had accumulated through centuries of annual Nile floods and is about nine metres below the modern street level.

Khnum

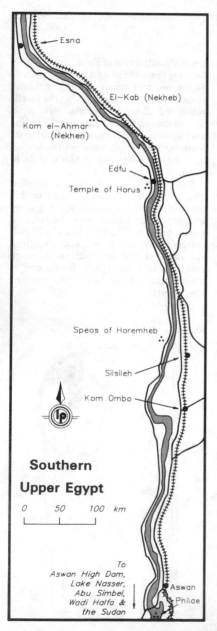

Esna

El-Kab (Nekheb)

Kom el-Ahmar
(Nekhen)

Edfu
Temple of Horus

Speos of Horemheb

Silsileh
Kom Ombo

**Southern
Upper Egypt**

0   50   100 km

To
Aswan High Dam,
Lake Nasser,
Abu Simbel,
Wadi Halfa &
the Sudan

Aswan
Philae

The intact roof of the hall is supported by 24 columns decorated with a series of texts recording hymns to *Khnum* and relating the annual sacred festivals of Esna. The texts also refer to other temples in the area and one from the same era has in fact been recently excavated at Kom Mer, 12 km south of Esna. The west wall of the Roman-built hall is also the only remaining part of the original Ptolemaic temple and features reliefs of Ptolemy VI, Philometor and Euergetes II.

The temple is a couple of blocks east of Esna's main street, about five minutes walk south of the service taxi station. From the Nile the temple is about half a km south of the bridge, which connects Esna with the east bank, and about 200 metres in from the river. The original quay, once connected to the temple by a processional way, is still in use. The temple is open from 7 am to 6 pm and admission costs E£1, or 50 pt for students.

The people of Esna are very friendly and there's a small tourist bazaar but there are no places to stay. A day trip from Luxor is the best way to see the temple as trains, buses and service taxis run frequently between the two towns. The best alternative is a taxi which takes 45 minutes and costs only 75 pt. *Feluccas* will stop at Esna en route between Aswan and Luxor.

EL-KAB & KOM EL-AHMAR

Between Esna and Edfu are the scattered ruins of two settlements dating from Pre-Dynastic to Late Dynastic times. The earliest remains in the area now known as El-Kab, on the east bank of the Nile, are about 6000 years old. Much of what is visible though dates from later than that when the ancient settlement of **Nekheb** was capital of the nome. The local deity was the vulture-goddess *Nekhbet* who was regarded not only as the greatest of the Upper Egyptian goddesses but, along with *Edjo* the cobra goddess of Lower

Egypt, she was guardian of the pharaohs and one of the deities associated with royal and divine births.

The town of Nekheb was enclosed by massive mud-brick walls and still contains the remains of a Roman temple, a sacred lake and cemeteries and the ruins of the main temple of *Nekhbet* with its several pylons, hypostyle hall and birth house. The temple was probably begun before 2700 BC but was enlarged considerably by 18th to 30 Dynasty pharaohs including Tuthmosis III, Amenophis II and the Ramessids.

A few km east of the town enclosure are three desert temples. At the entrance to Wadi Hellal is the rock-hewn, Ptolemaic **Sanctuary of Sheshmetet**. To the south-east of that is a chapel started during the reign of Ramses II, restored under the Ptolemies and dedicated to a number of deities. About 3½ km from Nekheb is the **Temple of Hathor and Nekhbet** which was built by Tuthmosis IV and Amenophis III. North of Nekheb are a number of rock-cut tombs with fine reliefs.

On the opposite side of the river, the remains of the ancient town of **Nekhen**, which pre-dated Nekheb as capital of the nome, stretch for about three km along the edge of the desert. Now known as Kom El-Ahmar, or 'The Red Mound', the area features the ruins of Pre-Dynastic settlements and cemeteries and in the nearby wadis there are several Middle and New Kingdom tombs. The local god was *Nekheny*, a falcon with two long plumes on his head, who was later associated with *Horus*.

El-Kab and Kom El-Ahmar are 26 km south of Esna and north of Edfu.

EDFU

The largest and most completely preserved pharaonic, albeit Greek-built, temple in Egypt is the extraordinary **Temple of Horus** at Edfu. One of the last great Egyptian attempts at monument building on a grand scale, the structure dominates this west bank riverside town, 53 km south of Esna. The town and temple were established on a rise, above the broad river valley around them, and so escaped the annual Nile inundation which contributed to the ruination of so many other buildings of antiquity. Edfu, a sugar and pottery centre, is also a very friendly place even though it seems that no one in town, except the pharmacist, speaks English.

The Temple of Horus

Construction of the huge complex began under Ptolemy III Euergetes I in 237 BC and was completed nearly 200 years later during the reign of Ptolemy XIII (the father of Cleopatra) in the 1st century BC. In conception and design it follows the traditions of authentic pharaonic architecture with the same general plan, scale and ornamentation, right down to the 'Egyptian' attire worn by the Greek kings depicted in the temple's reliefs. Though it is much younger than the temples of Karnak, Luxor and Abydos its excellent state of preservation fills in a lot of historical gaps because it is, in effect, a 2000-year-old replica of an architectural style that was already archaic during Ptolemaic times.

As a copy though it lacks the artistic spontaneity of truly creative minds, in particular the unfettered imagination of the ancient Egyptian craftsmen whose architectural achievements it imitates. Where the Greek influence does penetrate, however, it produces a strangely graceful effect which is most obvious in the fine line of the columns.

Dedicated to *Horus*, the falcon-headed son of *Osiris*, who avenged his father's murder by slaying his uncle *Seth*, the temple was built on the site where, according to legend, the two gods met in deadly combat. Ancient festivals at Edfu celebrated the divine birth of *Horus* and the living king, as all pharaohs were believed to be incarnations of the falcon-god, as well as the victory of *Horus* over *Seth* and the yearly conjugal visit of the

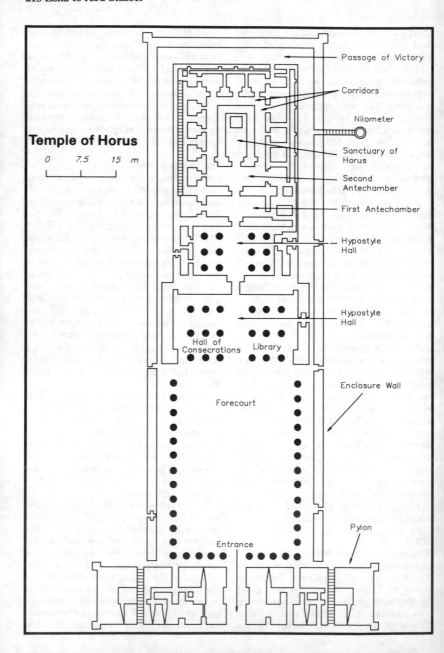

Temple of Horus

0   7.5   15   m

Passage of Victory

Corridors

Nilometer

Sanctuary of Horus

Second Antechamber

First Antechamber

Hypostyle Hall

Hypostyle Hall

Hall of Consecrations

Library

Enclosure Wall

Forecourt

Pylon

Entrance

goddess *Hathor*. Another ritual was the annual re-coronation of the pharaoh to symbolise his oneness with *Horus*. During the proceedings a live falcon was taken from the sacred aviary, crowned in the central court and placed in an inner chamber where it 'reigned' in the dark for a year as the living symbol of *Horus*. As with *Hathor* at Dendara, an image of the god was also taken each year to the roof of the temple for a rejuvenating sun bath.

Excavation of the temple, from beneath sand, rubble and part of the village of Edfu, which had been built on its roof, was started by Auguste Mariette in the mid 19th century. The entrance to the temple is through a massive 36-metre-high pylon guarded by a huge and splendid granite falcon and decorated with colossal reliefs of Pharaoh Ptolemy XIII pulling the hair of his enemies while *Horus* and *Hathor* look on. Beyond the pylon is a court surrounded on three sides by a colonnade of 32 columns covered in reliefs.

Before you enter the temple proper, through the 12 enormous columns of the first of two hypostyle halls, check out the areas on either side. On your left is the **Hall of Consecrations** where, according to the wall inscriptions, *Horus* pours sacred water on the king; and on your right is the so-called **Library** which features a list of books and a relief of *Seshat*, the goddess of writing. On either side of the second hall are doorways leading into the narrow **Passage of Victory** which runs between the temple and its massive protective enclosure walls.

Once through the magnificent **Great Hypostyle Hall** there are two antechambers, the first of which has a staircase, of 242 steps, leading up to the rooftop and a commanding view of the Nile and surrounding fields. You may have to pay the guard a bit of *baksheesh* if you want to go up because the stairs are usually closed.

Through the second chamber, which is wonderfully decorated with a variety of scenes, you come to the **Sanctuary of Horus** where the live falcon, the god and his wife reigned and received offerings. Around the sanctuary there are a number of smaller chambers with fine reliefs and nearby, off the Passage of Victory, a staircase leads down and passes under the outer wall of the temple to a **Nilometer**. The Temple of Horus is open from 7 am to 6 pm and admission costs E£2, or E£1 for students.

Places to Stay & Eat

The *El Medina Hotel*, just off the main square, costs E£4 a double. There is no hot water and the cold water is turned off after 9 pm though you can ask the owner or his family, who live on the 1st floor, to turn it back on. From the top floor you can see something different everyday as most of the houses in town don't seem to have roofs, just lots of baskets. Breakfast costs 25 pt and the owner will gladly serve tea and biscuits in your room.

For meals you can buy canned goods, fruit and vegetables in the *souk*, or town market. The only place to get a Stella beer in town is at the train station across the river.

Horus

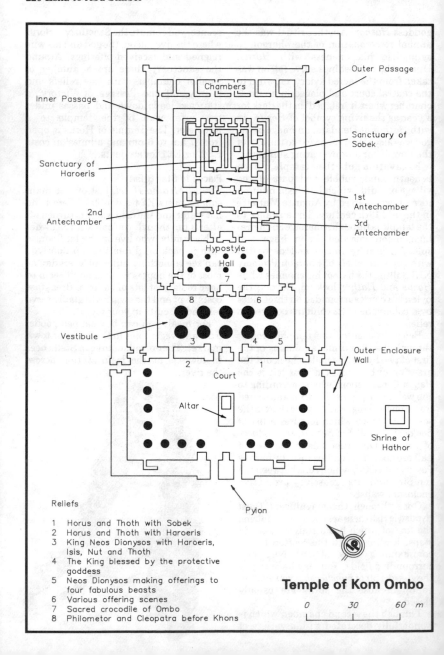

Outer Passage

Chambers

Inner Passage

Sanctuary of
Sobek

Sanctuary of
Haroeris

1st
Antechamber

2nd
Antechamber

3rd
Antechamber

Hypostyle
Hall

Vestibule

Outer Enclosure
Wall

Court

Altar

Shrine of
Hathor

Pylon

Reliefs

1   Horus and Thoth with Sobek
2   Horus and Thoth with Haroeris
3   King Neos Dionysos with Haroeris,
    Isis, Nut and Thoth
4   The King blessed by the protective
    goddess
5   Neos Dionysos making offerings to
    four fabulous beasts
6   Various offering scenes
7   Sacred crocodile of Ombo
8   Philometor and Cleopatra before Khons

Temple of Kom Ombo

0   30   60   m

Getting There

Trains, buses and service taxis stop frequently in Edfu. However the train station is on the east bank of the Nile, about four km from town, and the buses which travel between Luxor and Aswan are usually so crowded by the time they get to Edfu that they're not worth the effort. Service taxis are again the best option. From Esna the trip takes about an hour and costs E£1; while direct taxis from Luxor take about two hours and cost E£2. *Feluccas* will also stop at Edfu on their way north or south.

SILSILEH

At Silsileh, about 42 km south of Edfu, the Nile narrows considerably to pass between steep sandstone cliffs which are cluttered with ancient rock stelae and graffiti. Known in pharaonic times as Khenu, which means 'the Place of Rowing', the gorge also marks the change in the bedrock of Egypt, from limestone to sandstone. The local Silsileh quarries were worked by thousands of men throughout the New Kingdom and Graeco-Roman period to provide the sandstone used in temple building.

On the west bank of the river is the **Speos of Horemheb**, a rock-hewn chapel dedicated to Pharaoh Horemheb and seven deities including the local god *Sobek*.

KOM OMBO

The fertile, irrigated sugar cane and corn fields around Kom Ombo, 60 km south of Edfu, support not only the original community of *fellahin* but also a large population of Nubians displaced from their own lands by the encroaching waters of Lake Nasser. It's a pleasant little place easily accessible en route between Aswan and Luxor but possibly best visited on a day trip from Aswan, which is 40 km to the south.

In ancient times Kom Ombo was strategically important as a trading town on the great caravan route from Nubia and was the meeting place of the routes from the gold mines of the Eastern Desert and the Red Sea. During the Ptolemaic period it served as the capital of the Ombite nome and elephants were brought up from Africa to Kom Ombo to train with the armies to defend the region. The main attraction these days though is the unique riverside temple of Kom Ombo, about four km from the centre of town.

The Temple of Kom Ombo

Kom Ombo, or more precisely, the dual **Temple of Sobek and Haroeris**, stands on a promontory at a bend in the Nile, where in ancient times sacred crocodiles basked in the sun on the riverbank. Although substantially ruined by the changing tides of the river and by later builders who used many of its stones for new buildings, Kom Ombo is nevertheless a stunning sight.

It is also unusual in that, architecturally, everything is doubled and perfectly symmetrical along the main axis of the temple. There are twin entrances, twin courts, twin colonnades, twin hypostyle halls, twin sanctuaries and in keeping with the dual nature of the temple there was probably a twin priesthood.

The left side of the temple was dedicated to *Haroeris*, or *Horus – the Elder*, the falcon-headed sky god; and the right half to *Sobek*, the local crocodile, or crocodile-headed, god who was also worshipped in the Faiyum.

The Graeco-Roman structure faces the Nile, where the entrance **Pylon**, the outer enclosure wall and part of the **Court**, all built by Augustus after 30 BC, have been either mostly destroyed by pilfering stone masons or eroded by the river. The temple proper was actually begun by Ptolemy VI Philometor in the early 2nd century BC; Ptolemy XIII (also known as Neos Dionysos) built the **Vestibule** and **Hypostyle Hall**; and other Ptolemies and later Romans contributed to the relief decoration.

South of the main temple is the Roman **Chapel of Hathor**, dedicated to the wife of *Horus*, which is used to store a large collection of mummified crocodiles dug up from a nearby sacred animal cemetery.

The temple is open from 6 am to 6 pm and admission costs E£1, or 50 pt for students.

Getting There

A service taxi from Aswan to the town of Kom Ombo takes about 30 minutes and costs 50 pt; and to or from Edfu takes about 45 minutes and costs 70 pt. Trains and buses also frequently stop in the town but they are less convenient.

A covered truck runs regularly between the town and the temple, though it actually drops you about one km north of the river complex. The truck costs 10 pt and leaves from behind the mosque, which is on the main street. A private taxi should cost about E£2 for the return trip; and *feluccas* travelling between Luxor and Aswan can stop at the temple itself.

Aswan

Over the centuries, Aswan, Egypt's southern-most city, has been a garrison town and frontier city, the gateway to Africa and the now inundated Land of Nubia, a prosperous market place at the crossroads of the ancient caravan routes and more recently a popular winter resort.

In ancient times the area was known as Sunt; the Ptolemaic town of Syene stood to the south-west of the present city. The Copts called the place Souan, which means 'trade' and it's from this that the Arabic name 'Aswan' was derived.

The main town and temple area of Sunt was actually on the southern end of the island called Yebu, which means both 'elephant' and 'ivory', and which the Greeks later re-named Elephantine Island. A natural fortress, protected as it was by the turbulent river, Aswan was then capital of the first Upper Egyptian nome and a base for military expeditions

Horus & Sobek

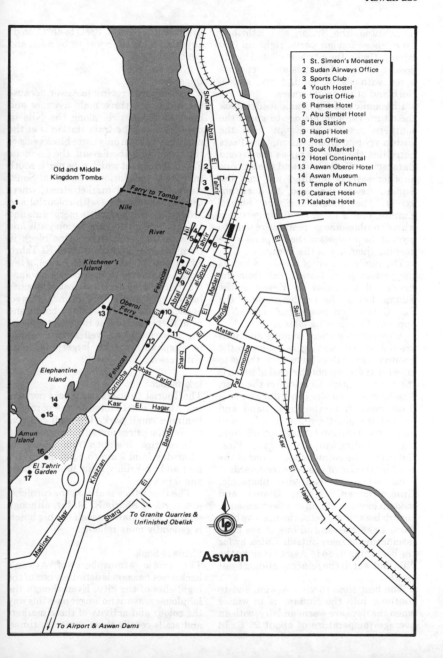

1 St. Simeon's Monastery
2 Sudan Airways Office
3 Sports Club
4 Youth Hostel
5 Tourist Office
6 Ramses Hotel
7 Abu Simbel Hotel
8 Bus Station
9 Happi Hotel
10 Post Office
11 Souk (Market)
12 Hotel Continental
13 Aswan Oberoi Hotel
14 Aswan Museum
15 Temple of Khnum
16 Cataract Hotel
17 Kalabsha Hotel

Aswan

To Granite Quarries &
Unfinished Obelisk

To Airport & Aswan Dams

into Nubia, the Sudan and Ethiopia. From those foreign parts, right up into Islamic times, the city was visited by the great caravans of camels and elephants laden with slaves, gold, ivory, spices, cloth and other exotic wares.

Pharaonic and Ptolemaic leaders took their turn through history to guard the southern reaches of Egypt from the customary routes of invasion, their fleets patrolling the river as far as the Second Cataract at Wadi Halfa and their troops another several hundred km into the Sudan. Aswan was also, to a certain extent, the 'Siberia' of the Roman Empire, one of those far-flung garrisons where troublesome generals were sent, to protect the interests of the Emperor while keeping them out of the Forum.

The modern town of Aswan, which is the perfect place for a break from the rigours of travelling in Egypt or the Sudan, lies at the northern end of the First Cataract on the east bank of the Nile opposite Elephantine Island.

Although its ancient temples and ruins are not as outstanding as others in the country Aswan does have a few things to offer the traveller, not the least of which is the town's superb location on the river. The Nile is magically beautiful here as it flows down from the great dams and around the giant granite boulders and palm-studded islands that protrude from the cascading rapids of the First Cataract. The corniche too, is one of the most attractive of the Nile boulevards.

So, while you can visit pharaonic, Graeco-Roman, Coptic, Islamic and modern monuments, an excellent museum, superb botanic gardens, the massive high dam, Lake Nasser and one of the most fascinating bazaars outside Cairo, by far the best thing to do in Aswan is sit by the Nile and watch the *feluccas* gliding by at sunset.

The best time to visit Aswan, and to continue into the Sudan, is in winter when the days are warm and dry, with an average temperature of about 26°C. In summer it is too hot, 38°C to 45°C, to do anything other than just sit by a fan and swat flies.

Orientation

It takes effort to get lost in Aswan because there are only three main avenues and most of the city is along the Nile or parallel to it. The train station is at the north end of town only three blocks east of the river and its boulevard, the Corniche El Nil. The street which runs north-south in front of the station is Sharia al-Souk, Aswan's splendid market street, where the bazaars overflow with colourful and aromatic wares and where merchants and traders from all over the region jostle and bargain with each other. One block in from the Nile is Sharia Abtal El Tahrir where you'll find the youth hostel, a few hotels and some pricey tourist bazaars. On the corniche itself are most of Aswan's banks, government buildings, travel agencies, restaurants and top hotels and from there you can see the rock tombs on the west bank, as well as the islands of Elephantine (the larger one) and Kitchener.

Information

The Tourist Office is two blocks north of the Abu Simbel Hotel on the corniche, behind a small park. The staff can give you official prices for taxis, *hantours* and *felucca* trips. It's open from Sunday to Thursday from 9 am to 2 pm and 6 to 8 pm; and on Friday from 10 am to noon and 6 to 8 pm.

The Post Office is also on the corniche, just north of Sharia El Matar, although sending your mail through the big hotels is generally more reliable.

Sharia al-Souk

The exotic atmosphere of Aswan's backstreet bazaars is definitely one of the highlights of the city. Even though the fabulous caravans no longer pass this way the colour and activity of these markets and stalls recalls those romantic times.

Top: Washing clothes in the Nile, near Luxor (HF)
Bottom: The main street, Luxor (HF)

Top: Temple of Philae, Aswan (SW)
Bottom: Elephantine Island, Aswan (SW)

Just wander through the small, narrow alleyways off this street and you'll see, hear, smell and, if you want, taste life as it has been for many centuries in these parts. Best of all, you probably won't be hassled by merchants hungry for the tourist buck because most of the market is for the locals.

Fatimid Cemetery
Just south of the city's public gardens is a collection of low stone buildings with domed roofs topped by crescents. Some of these early Islamic tombs also feature figures of local holy people or the more universally revered Sayyida Zeinab, granddaughter of the Prophet.

The Unfinished Obelisk
In the desert south of the Aswan train station are the northern quarries, which supplied the ancient Egyptians with most of the hard stone used in pyramids and temples, and a huge discarded obelisk. Three sides of the shaft, which measures nearly 42 metres long, were completed except for the inscriptions and it would have been the largest single piece of stone ever handled if a flaw had not appeared in the granite. So it lies there, where the disappointed stonemasons abandoned it, still partly attached to the parent rock and with no indication of what it was intended for.

The quarries are about one km from town past the Fatimid Cemetery.

Elephantine Island
Perhaps elephants once roamed the banks of the Nile here, they certainly passed through in the great caravans or with various armies, but it is more likely that Aswan's longest inhabited area was named Yebu after the numerous giant grey granite boulders, in the river around the island, which resemble a herd of elephants bathing.

Apart from being Egypt's frontier town, where the island officials were known as 'Keepers of the Gate of the South', Elephantine also produced most of the pharaohs of the 5th Dynasty and was the centre of the cult of the ram-headed *Khnum*, god of the cataracts and creator of mankind, and his companion goddesses *Anukis* and *Satis*.

Excavation of the ancient town, which began at the start of this century, is still going on and the jumbled remains of the fortress and three temples are visible. There's also a small 3rd Dynasty step pyramid; a tiny chapel reconstructed from the Temple of Kalabsha, which is just south of the High Dam; and, taking up the entire northern end of the island, the deluxe and incongruous Aswan Oberoi Hotel which, most sensibly, has its own private ferry and a three metre fence around it to keep the rich tourists in, and away from the local Nubians.

The inhabitants of the three colourful Nubian villages on the west side of Elephantine are friendly and the alleyways are worth exploring.

The Aswan Museum On the south-east end of the island, overlooking the ruins of the original town and surrounded by an attractive garden, this modest little museum houses a collection of antiquities discovered in Aswan and Nubia. Most of the Nubian artefacts were found and rescued before the construction of the old Aswan Dam. The weapons, pottery, utensils, statues and mummies date from Pre-Dynastic to late Roman times and everything is labelled in Arabic and English. The sarcophagus and mummy of a sacred ram, the animal associated with *Khnum*, is just inside the entrance.

The museum is open in winter from Sunday to Thursday between 9 am and 5 pm and on Fridays from 9 am to 1 pm; and in summer on the same days but only from 8.30 am to 1.30 pm. Admission to the museum and the ruins outside costs E£1, or 50pt for students.

The Nilometer Heavenly portents and priestly prophecies aside, the only sure indication in ancient times of the likelihood of a bountiful harvest was that given by the Nilometer. Descending to the water's edge, from beneath a sycamore tree near the museum, the rock-hewn shaft of the ancient Nilometer measured the height of the Nile. Although it dates from pharaonic times, and bears inscriptions and cartouches from the reigns of Amenophis III and Psammetichus II, it was rebuilt by the Romans and restored last century.

When the Nilometer recorded that the level of the river was high it would mean the approaching annual flood would be heavy and therefore sufficient for the irrigation vital to a good harvest. It also affected the taxation system, for the higher the river, the better the crop season and the more prosperous the *fellahin* and merchants – and therefore the higher the taxes.

You can enter the Nilometer from the river or down steps from above or just view it from a *felucca* on the water.

The Temple of Khnum Amongst the ruins of the ancient town are the remains of a large temple built by Nectanebo, a 4th century BC pharaoh, and dedicated to *Khnum*, the patron of Elephantine and the god who created man on his potter's wheel. At the gateway to the temple Ptolemy XI Alexander II, who ruled around 80 BC, is shown worshipping the ram god. A team of German archaeologists has been excavating and restoring the temple.

Nearby there is a little left of the **Temple of Satis** dedicated to *Khnum's* goddess daughter; and the **Temple of Heqaib**, an interesting stone shrine honouring a prince of the nome. A 6th Dynasty official, Heqaib was deified after his death and remained a cult figure for many centuries. A small **Ptolemaic temple** discovered on the tip of the island has been restored.

To get to Elephantine Island you can take a *felucca*, for 10 pt, from the landing just north of the Cataract Hotel; or catch the Oberoi ferry, though you may never get out of the compound!

Kitchener's Island

One of the most delightful places in Aswan, this island to the west of Elephantine was given to Lord Horatio Kitchener in the 1890s when he was Consul-General of Egypt and commander of the Egyptian army. Indulging his passion for beautiful flowers, Kitchener turned the entire island into a botanical garden, importing plants from the Far East, Africa and India. The gardens, which are perfect for a peaceful stroll, attract an amazing variety of colourfully exotic birds. The hundreds of white ducks in the small out-of-bounds cove at the southern end of the island, however, belong to a biological research station.

There are no ferry services to Kitchener's Island but it's easy enough to hire a *felucca* for a return trip or incorporate the gardens on a river tour. It should cost about E£5 for a visit to the islands of Elephantine and Kitchener and the Mausoleum of Agha Khan.

THE WEST BANK
Tombs of the Nobles

The high cliffs opposite Aswan, a little north of Kitchener's Island, are honey-combed with the tombs of the princes, governors, 'Keepers of the Gate of the South' and other dignitaries of ancient Yebu. They date from the Old and Middle Kingdoms and although most of them are in a sorry state of repair, there are a few worth visiting.

Nos 25 & 26 *The Tombs of Mekhu & Sabni* are of rough 6th Dynasty construction but the reliefs in No 26 record a tale of tragedy and triumph. Mekhu, one of the 'Gate Keepers', was murdered on an expedition into Africa so his son Sabni led the army into Nubia to punish the tribe responsible. Sabni recovered his father's body and sent a messenger to the pharaoh in Memphis to inform him that the enemy had been taught a lesson. On his return to Aswan he was met by priests, professional mourners and some of the royal embalmers, all sent by the pharaoh himself to show the importance that was attached to the keepers of the kingdom's southern frontier.

No 31 *The Tomb of Prince Sarenput II* dates from the 12th Dynasty and is one of the best preserved. There are statues of the prince and wall paintings depicting Sarenput and his son hunting and fishing.

No 36 *The Tomb of Prince Sarenput I* also dates from the 12th Dynasty although it's older than No 31. On the rear wall of a columned court, to the left of the door, the prince is shown being followed by his dogs and sandal-bearer, and there are other scenes of his three sons and women bearing flowers.

No 35 *The Tomb of Heqaib*, the deified official whose temple stood on Elephantine, has a columned facade and some fine reliefs showing fighting bulls and hunting scenes.

If you climb up to **Kubbet al-Hawa**, a small tomb constructed for a local sheikh at the top of the hill, you'll be rewarded with fantastic views of the Nile and surrounding area. From there you can also try to rent a donkey or camel for the trek across the desert to the Monastery of St Simeon.

To get to the west bank tombs, you can either take the ferry from in front of the Tourist Office on the east bank corniche or include them on an *felucca* tour of the river. Admission to the tombs costs E£1, or 50 pt for students.

The Mausoleum of the Agha Khan
Aswan was the favourite wintering place of Mohammed Shah Agha Khan, the 48th Imam, or leader, of the Ismaili sect of Islam. When he died in 1957 his wife, the Begum, oversaw the construction of his domed granite and sandstone mausoleum, which is part-way up the hill on the west bank opposite Elephantine Island. Modelled on the Fatimid tombs of Cairo, the interior, which incorporates a small mosque, is more impressive than the exterior at first suggests. The sarcophagus, of Carrara marble, is inscribed with texts from the Qur'an and stands in a vaulted chamber in the interior courtyard.

The Begum still lives for part of the year in the white villa, below her husband's mausoleum, that was their winter retreat and every day she places a red rose on his sarcophagus; a ritual that is carried on during the summer by her gardener.

The tomb is open from 9 am to 4 pm and admission is free (the guards are not supposed to accept *baksheesh*), but remember to remove your shoes. There is a *felucca* dock just below the mausoleum.

The Monastery of St Simeon
Deir Amba Samaan is a 6th century monastery which, although it hasn't been used for more than 700 years, is one of the best preserved of the original Christian strongholds in Egypt. It is not known who St Simeon was exactly but his monastery survived until the monks were driven out or murdered by Arabs in the 14th century.

Surrounded by desert sands, except for a glimpse of the fertile belt around Aswan in the distance, the monastery bears more resemblance to a fortress than a religious sanctuary and once provided accommodation for about 300 resident monks plus another 100 or so pilgrims. Built on two levels, the lower of stone and the upper of mud-brick, it was surrounded by 10-metre-high walls and contained a church, stores, bakeries, offices, a kitchen, dormitories, stables and workshops.

If you don't fancy a camel or donkey ride from the Noble's Tombs then there is a paved pathway to the monastery from the Agha Khan's Mausoleum. The monastery is open from 9 am to 6 pm and admission costs E£1.

AROUND ASWAN
The Aswan Dam
When the British constructed the Aswan Dam above the First Cataract at the turn of the century it was the largest of its kind in the world. The growing population of Egypt had made it imperative to put more land under cultivation and the only way to achieve this was to regulate the flow of the Nile. Measuring 2140 metres across, the dam was built almost entirely of local Aswan granite between 1898 and 1902. Although its height had to be raised twice to meet the demand, it not only greatly increased the area of cultivable land but provided the country with most of its hydroelectric power. Now completely surpassed in function, and as a tourist attraction, by the more spectacular High Dam six km upstream, it is worth a brief visit as the area around the First Cataract below it is extremely fertile and picturesque.

Sehel Island
Sehel, the large island north of the old Aswan Dam, was sacred to the goddess *Anukis* and her husband *Khnum*. As a destination for an extended *felucca* trip on this part of the Nile, Sehel Island is a good choice, although there isn't much to see apart from a friendly Nubian village and a great many rock inscriptions, dating from the Middle Kingdom to Graeco-Roman times.

One Ptolemaic inscription, on the south-eastern side of the island, records the story of a seven-year famine that plagued Egypt during the much earlier time of Pharaoh Zoser. It seems *Khnum*, god of the cataracts, had withheld the inundation of the Nile for all those years and Zoser finally travelled to Aswan to ask the local priests why the god was punishing the Egyptians. Apparently some land belonging to *Khnum's* traditional estates had been confiscated so as soon as Zoser returned the land and raised a temple to *Khnum* on Sehel, the Nile rose to its accepted flood level.

Philae
The romantic and majestic aura surrounding the temple complex of *Isis* on the island of Philae has been luring pilgrims for thousands of years and during the 19th century the ruins were one of Egypt's most legendary tourist attractions. Even when it seemed they were destined to be lost forever beneath the rising waters of the Nile, travellers still came, taking to row boats to glide amongst the partly submerged columns and peer down through the translucent green to the wondrous sanctuaries of the mighty gods below.

From the turn of this century Philae and its temples became swamped for six months of every year by the high waters of the reservoir created by the construction of the old Aswan Dam. In the 1960s, when the approaching completion of the High Dam threatened to submerge the island completely and forever, the massive complex was disassembled and removed stone by stone from Philae in an incredible rescue organised by UNESCO. The temples were reconstructed on nearby Agilka Island, which was even landscaped to resemble the sacred isle of *Isis*, in positions corresponding as closely as possible to their original layout.

The oldest part of Philae dates from the 4th century BC but most of the existing structures were built by the Ptolemies and the Romans up to the 3rd century AD. The early Christians also added their bit to the island, by transforming the main temple's hypostyle hall into a chapel, building a couple of churches and of course defacing the pagan reliefs; though their inscriptions were in turn vandalised by the early Muslims.

In the beginning though, it was the cults of *Isis, Osiris* and *Horus*, and the

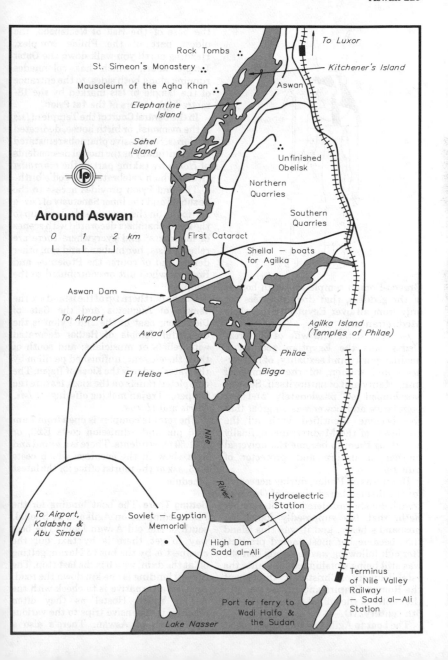

To Luxor

Rock Tombs

St. Simeon's Monastery

Kitchener's Island

Mausoleum of the Agha Khan

Aswan

Elephantine Island

Sehel Island

Unfinished Obelisk

Around Aswan

0   1   2 km

Northern Quarries

Southern Quarries

First Cataract

Shellal — boats for Agilka

Aswan Dam

To Airport

Agilka Island (Temples of Philae)

Awad

Philae

El Heisa

Bigga

Nile River

To Airport, Kalabsha & Abu Simbel

Soviet — Egyptian Memorial

Hydroelectric Station

High Dam Sadd al-Ali

Terminus of Nile Valley Railway — Sadd al-Ali Station

Port for ferry to Wadi Halfa & the Sudan

Lake Nasser

Isis

Graeco-Roman temple raised in honour of the goddess, that drew devotees not only from all over Egypt but the whole Mediterranean.

Isis, the sister and wife of the great *Osiris*, was the Egyptian goddess of healing, purity and sexuality, of motherhood and women, of the promise of immortality and of nature itself. She was worshipped so passionately and her popularity and power was so great that she became identified with all the goddesses of the Mediterranean, finally absorbing them to become the universal mother of nature and protector of humans.

But it was on Philae, during her search for the dismembered pieces of *Osiris*, so treacherously murdered by his brother *Seth*, that *Isis* supposedly found her husband's heart, and it was this island that became her most sacred precinct. Her cult following was so strong that she was still being worshipped long after the establishment of Christianity throughout the Roman Empire and Philae was still the centre of the cult of *Isis* as late as the 6th century AD.

The boat to Agilka Island leaves you at the base of the **Hall of Nectanebo**, the oldest part of the Philae complex. Heading north you walk down the **Outer Temple Court**, which has colonnades running along both sides, to the entrance of the **Temple of Isis** marked by the 18-metre-high towers of the **1st Pylon**.

In the **Central Court** of the Temple of *Isis* is the **mammisi**, or birth house, dedicated to *Horus*. Successive pharaohs reinstated their legitimacy as the mortal descendents of *Horus* by taking part in the *mammisi* rituals which celebrated the god's birth.

The **2nd Pylon** provides access to the **Vestibule** and the **Inner Sanctuary** of *Isis*; a staircase, on the western side, leads up to the **Osiris chambers** decorated with scenes of mourners; and everywhere there are reliefs of *Isis*, her husband and son, other deities and of course the Ptolemies and Romans who built or contributed to the temple.

On the northern tip of the island are the **Temple of Augustus** and the **Gate of Diocletian**; east of the 2nd Pylon is the delightful **Temple of Hathor** decorated with reliefs of musicians; and south of that, the elegant, unfinished pavilion by the water's edge is the **Kiosk of Trajan**. The completed reliefs on the kiosk feature the Emperor Trajan making offerings to *Isis*, *Osiris* and *Horus*.

The temple complex is open from 7 am to 6 pm and admission costs E£3, or E£1.50 for students. There is a sound and light show in the evenings which costs E£5, ask at the tourist office for the latest schedule.

Getting There The boat landing for the Philae complex on Agilka is at Shellal, south of the old Aswan Dam. The best way to get there is by taxi but the cheapest is by the bus to Hazan, getting off at the dam, which is the last stop. The Shellal landing is one km down the road. Another alternative is to check with the Aswan Youth Hostel as they often organise inexpensive trips to the various sites south of Aswan. There's also a motorboat which will take you to the island for about E£4 return, but don't pay until the end of your trip or they may not wait while you explore the island, as they are supposed to.

The High Dam

Egypt's contemporary example of building on a monumental scale contains 18 times the amount of material used in the Great Pyramid of Cheops. The controversial **Sadd al-Ali**, the High Dam, is just over four km wide and 115 metres high. The water contained by the dam has backed up nearly 500 km, taking it deep into the Sudan and creating Lake Nasser, the world's largest artificial lake. The rising level of this incredible reservoir has inundated the land of Nubia with waters as deep as 200 metres, forced the relocation of thousands of Nubians and Sudanese and washed away 45 villages along the banks of the Nile south of Aswan.

While the old Aswan dam successfully regulated the flow of the Nile during the course of a year it was realised, as early as the 1940s, that a much bigger dam was needed to counter the unpredictable annual flooding of the great river. However, it wasn't until Nasser came to power in 1952 that plans were drawn up for a new dam six km south of the British-built one.

The proposed construction created international political tension and focused world-wide attention on the antiquities that would be lost by the creation of a huge lake behind the dam.

In 1956, after the United States, Great Britain and the World Bank suddenly refused the financial backing they had offered for the project, Nasser ordered the nationalisation of the Suez Canal as a means of raising the capital. This move precipitated the Suez Crisis in which France, Britain and Israel took over the canal region and threatened to invade Egypt but were restrained by the United Nations. The Soviet Union then offered

the necessary funding and expertise and work began on the High Dam in 1960 and was completed in 1971.

While the old dam simply controlled the flow of the Nile the High Dam collects and stores water over a number of years so a high or low annual flood can be regulated at all times. The area of Egypt's cultivable land was increased by 30%, the High Dam's hydroelectric station doubled the country's power supply and a rise in the Sahara's water table has been recorded as far away as Algeria.

On the other hand, artificial fertilisers now have to be used because the dam hinders the flow of silt that was critical to the Nile Valley's fertility and it's estimated that in the next 40 years or so that silt will have filled the lake. In recent years the extremely high rate of evaporation from the lake, coupled with low annual floods, has reduced the water level in the reservoir forcing a reduction in the amount of water released for irrigation and power generation. The greatest fear is that should the dam ever break or be sabotaged most of Egypt would be swept into the Mediterranean.

Another consequence of the dam's construction was the fact that a great many valuable and irreplaceable ancient monuments were doomed to be drowned by the waters of Lake Nasser.

Teams from the Egyptian Department of Antiquities and archaeological missions from many countries descended on Nubia to set in motion the UNESCO organised projects aimed at rescuing as many of the threatened treasures as possible. Necropoli were excavated, all portable artefacts and relics were removed to museums and, while some temples disappeared beneath the lake, 14 were salvaged and moved to safety. Ten of these monuments, including the temple complexes of Philae, Kalabsha and Abu Simbel, were dismantled stone by stone and rebuilt on higher ground in Egypt. The other four were donated to the countries which contributed to the rescue effort and include the splendid Temple of

Dendur which has been reconstructed in a glass building in the Metropolitan Museum of Art in New York.

The **Visitors Pavilion**, on the east side of the dam, has exhibits detailing the construction of the High Dam and the dismantling of Abu Simbel. It's open from 7 am to 2 pm and 3 to 6 pm and admission is free. On the west side there is a stone monument honouring Russian-Egyptian friendship and cooperation; and the view from the top of Sadd al-Ali is spectacular.

Getting There The cheapest way to get to the High Dam, 13 km south of Aswan, is by train to Sadd al-Ali station, which is the end of the Cairo-Aswan line. The station is near the docks for the boat to the Sudan and from there you can either take a long walk or a shared taxi to the dam.

If you're planning to take a taxi across the top of the dam, then you might also consider continuing on to the Temple of Kalabsha which is another 10 km south, on the west side of Lake Nasser. If you get a group together it should only cost about E£10 to E£15 for four or five hours.

Kalabsha, Beit al-Wali & Kertassi

As part of the massive UNESCO effort to rescue the doomed monuments of Nubia, these three temples were transplanted from a now submerged site about 60 km south of Aswan. The new site, on the west bank of Lake Nasser a little upriver from the dam, is considered a military area so you need special permission to visit these monuments.

The **Temple of Kalabsha** was erected during the reign of Emperor Augustus, between 30 BC and 14 AD, and was dedicated to the Nubian god *Mandulis*. *Isis* and *Osiris* were also worshipped there and during the Christian era the temple was used as a church.

The West German government financed the transfer and reconstruction of the 13,000 blocks of the temple, from the Nubian village of Kalabsha, and was

presented with the temple's west pylon, which is now in the Berlin Museum. During the rescue operation evidence was found of even older structures, dating from the times of Amenophis II and Ptolemy IX.

An impressive stone causeway leads from the lake up to the **1st Pylon** of the temple, beyond which are the colonnaded **Court** and the **Hypostyle Hall** which has 12 columns. Inscriptions on the walls show various emperors and pharaohs cavorting with the gods and goddesses. Just beyond the hall are three chambers, with stairs leading from one up to the roof. The view of Lake Nasser and the High Dam, across the capitals of the hall and court, is fantastic. An inner passage, between the temple and the encircling wall, leads to a well-preserved **Nilometer**.

The **Temple of Beit al-Wali**, which means 'House of the Holy Man', was rebuilt with assistance from the US government and placed just north-west of Kalabsha. Most of the temple, which was carved from the rocks, was built during the reign of Ramses II. On the walls of the first chamber are several interesting reliefs depicting various events including scenes of the pharaoh's victory over the Kushites and his wars against the Libyans and Syrians. Ramses is shown pulling the hair of his enemies while women plead for mercy.

Just north of Kalabsha are the remains of the **Temple of Kertassi**. Two *Hathor* (cow-headed) columns, a massive architrave and four columns with intricate capitals are the only pieces which were salvaged from Lake Nasser.

Anyone can visit the Kalabsha site but a bit of advance planning is required. The procedure for obtaining permission is simple but can take an hour or so.

You first buy, from the Aswan post office, two 25 pt taxi stamps for each person going to Kalabsha, including your driver if you're going by taxi.

Write a carbon-copied statement, indicating that you would like to visit the area as a tourist to see the Temple of Kalabsha, include your name, nationality and passport number and put the stamps on the back of the letter.

Go to the police station on Atlas St (ask directions at the post office) with all this paperwork and your passport and wait for final permission. The police station is open from 8 am to 2 pm and 7 to 9 pm.

The government price for the taxi to Kalabsha is E£8 but you should double-check with the tourist office for the latest information.

Places to Stay – bottom end

The *Hotel Continental* (tel 22311), is still one of the most popular places to stay in Aswan despite continual reports of hungry cockroaches and slimy toilets. The main redeeming feature is its simple and clean rooms, with commanding views of the Nile, for the rock-bottom price of E£2.50 per double. The hotel is a 20 minute walk from the train station on the corniche and the café downstairs is a great place to meet other travellers and to arrange *felucca* trips down the Nile or taxis to Abu Simbel.

The *Molla Hotel*, on a sidestreet near the bazaar, has been highly recommended. Each room has a sink with hot water and there are hot showers just off the hall. Doubles cost E£3 and breakfast, tea and coffee are available.

The *Youth Hostel* (tel 22313), is on Sharia Abtal El Tahrir not far from the train station. It's not in the greatest shape with dirt, noise and crowded rooms its 'special' features but it is cheap – 60 pt for members and 70 pt for non-members.

The *Rosewan Hotel* (tel 24497) has clean doubles for E£6.50 and the large rooms all have fans. Turn right as you leave the train station, take the first street on the left after a petrol station, and the hotel is in the middle of the next block.

The *Hotel El Safa* is a very dirty deal next to the Rosewan. Doubles cost E£4 and there are sinks in each room.

Places to Stay – middle

The *Ramses Hotel* (tel 24119), on Sharia Abtal El Tahrir, is a good deal and according to some travellers is the best place to stay in Aswan. Doubles with showers and toilets cost about E£10, air-con and TVs are available, and most rooms have Nile views. Breakfast costs about E£1, lunch E£3 and dinner E£3.50. During summer the rooms are discounted by as much as 50%.

The *Happi Hotel*, on Sharia Abtal El Tahrir, has clean doubles with bathrooms for E£18. It's very popular with European tourists and the food is quite decent at E£5 for a three course dinner.

The *Mena House* has doubles with bathrooms for E£15. It's on the right as you come out of the train station.

The *Abu Simbel Hotel* is on the corniche not far from the Tourist Office. It has singles for E£14 and doubles for E£22, with showers and breakfast included. The view of the Nile from the balcony of each room is fantastic.

Places to Stay – top end

The *Cataract Hotel* is an impressive Moorish-style building surrounded by gardens on a rise above the river, with splendid views of the Nile and across the southern tip of Elephantine Island to the Agha Khan's tomb. A double room there costs about E£53 but the hotel is worth visiting just to enjoy a cool Stella or a cocktail on the veranda. The hotel's exterior was used in the movie of Agatha Christie's *Death on the Nile*. The *New Cataract Hotel* is next door.

The *Kalabsha Hotel* nearby is another high class affair with a commanding view of the First Cataract. Its costs E£23.67 a single and E£31.70 a double, including taxes; breakfast is E£2.30, lunch E£7 and dinner E£8.50.

The *Aswan Oberoi* on Elephantine Island has two hotel launches that ferry guests and visitors from the east bank. The views from the Oberoi tower are magnificent and the gardens are a pleasant place to hang around and watch the *feluccas*. Rooms there, however, start at E£100.

Swimming Pools The Oberoi and New

Cataract hotel pools are open to the public for about E£3 per day.

Camping There's a camping site opposite the Ramses Hotel that costs 12 pt a night. There's also an official, but rudimentary, campground near the Unfinished Obelisk, which is not at all a good location.

Places to Eat

The *Monalisa Restaurant*, on the corniche has good and cheap but basic food. You can have breakfast or a main meal of fish and kebab, on the stone terrace overlooking the Nile, for about E£2.

The *Aswan Moon Restaurant*, next to the Monalisa, offers big meals for two people for about E£6.

The *Restaurant el Nil* is on the corniche a few doors down from the Hotel Continental. A full meal with fish or meat, rice, salad, tahina and bread should cost about E£2.

There are several *fuul* and *taamiyya* stands and cheap cafés/restaurants near the train station. The *Gomhoriyya Restaurant* has been recommended.

Getting There

Air EgyptAir flies from Cairo to Aswan daily. The flight takes 2½ hours and costs about E£70.

The return flight to Abu Simbel costs about E£65.

Sudan Airways flies from Aswan to Khartoum every Tuesday at about 4 am for E£170. They share an office in Aswan with Emeco Travel, three blocks north of the Ramses Hotel, and are open from 9 am to 4 pm daily except Fridays.

Train In the following schedule the express train No 85, from Aswan to Luxor to Cairo to Alexandria, has air-con, sleepers and a restaurant. Express No 87, which also stops at Qena, has sleepers and a restaurant. Train No 981 has 1st and 2nd class, air-con and a restaurant; and No 89 has sleepers, air-con, a restaurant and a buffet. The trip from Aswan to Cairo takes about 16 hours and costs from E£1.80 in 3rd class to E£15.50 in 1st.

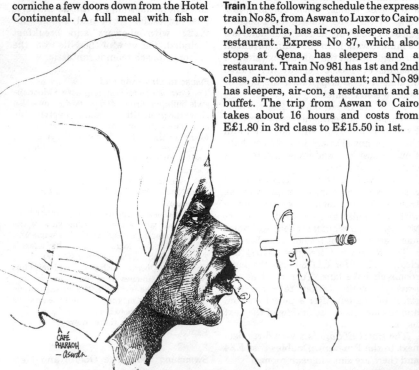

A CAFÉ
PHARAOH
— Aswan

	No 981	No 85	No 89	No 87
Aswan	5.15 am	2.45 pm	4.50 pm	5.45 pm
Kom Ombo	6.15		5.52	
Edfu	7.31		7.07	
Esna	8.49		8.04	
Luxor				
... arr	9.54	6.31	9.07	9.35
... dep	10.14	7.30	9.24	10.22
Qena	11.26		10.46	11.36
Sohag				
... arr	2.10 pm		1.54 am	
... dep	2.24		2.10	
Asyut				
... arr	3.29		3.25	
... dep	3.45			
Mallawi			4.47	
El Minya				
... arr	5.18		5.24	
... dep	5.28		5.35	
Beni Suef	7.03		7.22	
Cairo	8.55	6.45 am	9.20	9.50 am
Alexandria	5.35 am	10.05	1.45 pm	1.43 pm

Bus The bus station is behind the Abu Simbel Hotel. The bus to Abu Simbel costs E£16 return and leaves at 8 am daily.

There are at least five buses per day from Aswan to Kom Ombo, Edfu, Esna and Luxor between 6 am and 6 pm.

Taxi The service taxi station is near the bus station and the Ramses Hotel. Taxis frequently travel south to Abu Simbel and north to most major destinations.

Boat The Sudanese Maritime Office is near the Tourist Office on the corniche and is the place to buy tickets to Wadi Halfa. The steamer leaves from the Aswan docks, near the Sadd al-Ali train station south of the High Dam, anytime between 11 am and 3 pm on a Thursday, Saturday or Monday.

The trip takes about 20 hours and costs E£26 for 2nd class and E£50 for 1st class. There is no longer any deck class. Take plenty of food with you and as soon as you board try to find a space to stretch out on the deck rather than worrying about your seat inside. The wooden seats are uncomfortable, impossible to sleep on

and it's hot, crowded and stuffy. It may also be crowded outside but the scenery is better and you'll get a cool breeze.

I have yet to meet a traveller who didn't like this trip. Although the steamer doesn't make any stops before Wadi Halfa, except once overnight so the captain can sleep, it's a relaxing journey that takes you past Abu Simbel.

As the Thursday steamer arrives in Wadi Halfa on Friday morning and Sudanese offices are closed all day Friday, you cannot disembark until Saturday morning.

In Cairo you can buy steamer tickets at the Sudanese Maritime Office (also called the Nile Navigation Office) at Ramses station. The price of the ticket includes eight cups of tea.

Getting Around
Apart from a few buses, taxis and horse-drawn carriages, *feluccas* are the most common form of transportation to the attractions around Aswan. There is an official government price for hiring *feluccas* (check with the Tourist office) but with a bit of bargaining you should be able to hire an entire boat for five or six hours for about E£6.

The most popular Nile trip, of course, is the four-day journey from Aswan to Luxor. After bargaining, the price for the whole *felucca*, regardless of the number of people in your group, should be about E£40 per day; with food another E£4 per passenger, per day. (See also the end of the Luxor chapter). There's a bit of paperwork to go through before departure but your *felucca* captain should take you through the process as part of the agreed fee.

ABU SIMBEL
While the fate of his colossal statue and Ramesseum in Luxor no doubt niggles at the spirit of Ramses II, and certainly prompted poets to make fun of the dead king's mighty boasts, the mere existence,

Statues of Ramses II at Abu Simbel

in the 20th century AD, of his Great Temple at Abu Simbel must make him shake with laughter and shout 'I told you so!'

Threatened to be swallowed forever beneath the rising water and silt of Lake Nasser, the preservation of the two temples of Abu Simbel, 280 km south of Aswan, must rank as the greatest achievement of the UNESCO rescue operation. And, hewn as they were out of solid rock, the modern technology involved in cutting, moving and rebuilding the incredible temples and statues at least paralleled the skill of the ancient craftsmen who chiselled them out of the cliff face in the first place.

In the 1960s, as work progressed on the High Dam, UNESCO launched a world-wide appeal for the vital funding and expertise needed to salvage the Abu Simbel monuments. The response was immediately forthcoming and a variety of conservation schemes were put forward. Finally in 1964 a cofferdam was built to hold back the already encroaching water of the new lake, while Egyptian, Italian, Swedish, German and French archaeological teams began to move the massive structure.

At a cost of about US$40 million the temples were cut into more than 2000 huge blocks, weighing from 10 to 40 tons each, and reconstructed inside a specially built mountain 210 metres away from the water and 65 metres higher than the original site. The temples were carefully oriented to face the correct direction and the landscape of their original environment was recreated on and around the concrete dome-shaped mountain.

The project took just over four years and the temples of Abu Simbel were officially reopened in 1968, while the sacred site they had occupied for over 3000 years disappeared beneath Lake Nasser.

The **Great Temple of Ramses II** was dedicated to the gods *Ra-Herakhty, Amun* and *Ptah*, and of course, to the deified pharáoh himself; while the smaller **Temple of Hathor** was dedicated to the cow-headed goddess of love and built in honour of Ramses' favourite wife Queen Nefertari. They were carved out of the mountain on the west bank of the Nile between 1290 BC and 1224 BC. By the mid 1800s the sandstone cliff face and temples were all but covered in sand and although they were partially cleared many times it wasn't until the British began excavating, around the turn of this century, that their full glory was revealed.

From the Great Temple's forecourt, a short flight of steps leads up to the terrace before the massive rock-cut facade which is about 30 metres high and 35 metres wide. Guarding the entrance, the four famous colossal statues of Ramses II sit majestically, staring out across the desert as if looking through time itself. Each statue is over 20 metres high and is accompanied by smaller, though much larger than life-size, standing statues of the king's mother Queen Tuya, his wife Nefertari and some of their children.

Above the entrance to the **Great Hypostyle Hall**, between the central throned colossi, is the figure of the falcon-headed sun god *Ra-Herakhty*. The roof of the hall is supported by eight columns, each fronted by a 10-metre-high statue of Ramses; the roof is decorated with vultures representing *Osiris*; and the reliefs on the walls depict the pharaoh in various battles, victorious as usual. In the next hall, the four-columned **Vestibule**, Ramses and Nefertari are shown before the gods and the solar barques that carry the dead to the underworld.

The innermost chamber is the sacred **Sanctuary** where the four gods of the Great Temple sit on their thrones carved in the back wall and wait for the dawn. The temple is aligned in such a way that on February 22 and October 22 every year, the first rays of the rising sun reach across the Nile, penetrate the temple entrance, move along the Hall, through the

Vestibule and into the Sanctuary where they illuminate the somewhat mutilated figures of Ramses II, *Ra-Herakhty*, *Amun* and *Ptah*. (Until the temples were moved, this phenomenon happened one day earlier.)

The secondary complex of Abu Simbel is the rock-cut **Temple of Hathor** which is fronted by six massive standing statues, about 10 metres high. Four of them represent Ramses, the other two are his beloved Queen Nefertari and they are all flanked by the smaller figures of the Ramessid princes and princesses.

The six pillars of the **Hypostyle Hall** are crowned with *Hathor* capitals and its walls are adorned with scenes of Nefertari before *Hathor* and *Mut*; of the queen honouring her husband; and of Ramses, yet again, being valiant and victorious. In the **Vestibule** and adjoining chambers there are scenes of the goddess and her sacred barque and in the **Sanctuary** there is the striking statue of a cow, the sacred symbol of *Hathor*, emerging from the wall.

The admission fee for both temples is E£6, or E£4.50 for students.

A Place to Stay

There is only one hotel at Abu Simbel, the *Nefertari Hotel*, which has doubles for E£40 and singles for E£27.

Getting There

Until July 1985, when the road between Aswan and Abu Simbel was officially opened, the only way to visit the temples of Ramses II and *Hathor* was by flying in. (See Aswan Getting There section.) These days the 280 km can be covered in a variety of ways.

Air-con buses leave for Abu Simbel from the Aswan bus station every day at 8 am. Tickets cost E£16 return and the trip takes about 3½ hours one-way. It leaves Abu Simbel from the Nefertari Hotel at 2.30 pm. You should buy your ticket at least one day in advance.

An even cheaper alternative is to get a

group together and hire a taxi or minibus for a tour of the temples at Philae and Kalabsha, as well as the Aswan Dam and Abu Simbel. A minibus should cost about E£10 per person.

Abu Simbel is 50 km north of the Sudanese border but overland travel between the Sudan and Egypt is still only possible if you have your own transportation. The last section of road between the two countries, however, is due to open soon.

Suez Canal & the Red Sea

The Suez Canal is the culmination of centuries of effort to enhance trade and expand the empires of Egypt by connecting the Red Sea and the Mediterranean. Although the modern canal was by no means the first project of its kind, it was the only one to bypass the Nile, as a means of connecting the two seas, and excavate across the Isthmus of Suez to provide a major shipping route between Europe and Asia.

The first recorded canal was begun by Pharaoh Necho, between 610 BC and 595 BC, and stretched from the Nile Delta town of Bubastis, near present-day Zagazig, to the Red Sea via the Bitter Lakes. Despite the prophecies of his oracle, that the canal would be of more use to invading barbarians than to the Egyptians, Necho persevered with the project until, having caused the death of more than 100,000 workers, he was forced to abandon the idea.

That canal, however, was completed about a century later under Darius, one of Egypt's Persian rulers, and was maintained by the Ptolemies. Cleopatra, in a bid to save what was left of her fleet after the Egyptian defeat at Atrium, attempted to pass up the canal to the Red Sea, failing only because of the low flood level of the Nile that year.

The canal was improved by the Romans under Trajan but over the next several centuries it was either neglected and left to silt up or was dredged for limited use by various rulers, depending on their available resources.

In 649 AD it was restored by Amr, the Arab conqueror of Egypt, in order to facilitate the export of corn to Arabia. Twenty years later, however, it was actually filled in by another caliph, to stop the supply of grain to Mecca and Medina, so he could starve the people with whom he was waging war.

Following the French invasion in 1798 the importance of some sort of sea route south to Asia was again recognised. For the first time the digging of a canal directly from the Mediterranean to the Red Sea, across the comparatively narrow Isthmus of Suez, was considered. The idea was abandoned, however, because Napoleon's engineers mistakenly calculated that there was a 10 metre difference between the two sea levels.

British reports corrected that mistake several years later but it was actually the French consul to Egypt, Ferdinand de Lessups, who ultimately pursued the Suez canal idea through to its conclusion.

In 1854 de Lessups presented his proposal to the Khedive of Egypt, Said Pasha, who authorised him to excavate the canal but, although de Lessups had financial backing from private investors, the project was initially hindered by the British and French governments. Finally, in 1855, the scheme was approved and the Suez Canal Company, headed by Ferdinand de Lessups, was formed and began issuing shares to raise the necessary revenue. Said Pasha granted the Company a concession to operate the canal, to last 99 years from its opening, and from which the Egyptian Government would receive 15% of the annual profits.

Construction began in 1859 but it was not an easy project. At one stage, following an outbreak of cholera, all de Lessups' workers ran away. There was also the major problem of fresh water, or rather the lack of it. Until the company built a freshwater canal to service the construction works, 3000 camels were used to carry fresh water from the Nile.

In 1863 Said was succeeded as Khedive of Egypt by Pasha Ismail who quickened the pace of construction because the American Civil War had disrupted the

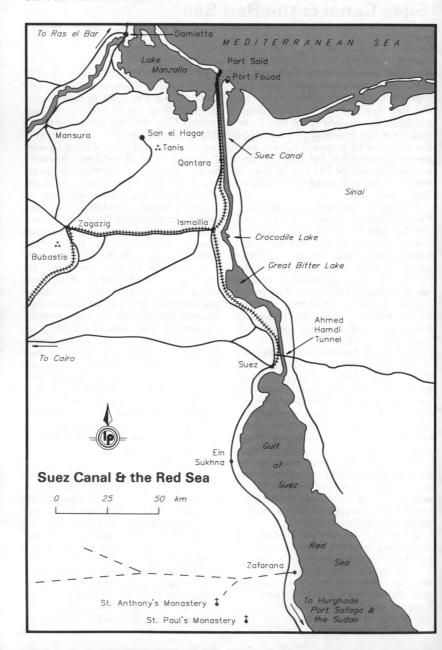

MEDITERRANEAN SEA

To Ras el Bar
Damietta
Port Said
Port Fouad
Lake Manzalla
Mansura
San el Hagar
∴ Tanis
Qantara
Suez Canal
Sinai
Zagazig
Ismailia
∴
Bubastis
Crocodile Lake
Great Bitter Lake
To Cairo
Ahmed Hamdi Tunnel
Suez

Suez Canal & the Red Sea

0   25   50 km

Ein Sukhna
Gulf of Suez

Zafarana
Red Sea

St. Anthony's Monastery ‡
St. Paul's Monastery ‡

To Hurghada Port Safaga & the Sudan

Top: Entrance to the Suez Canal, Port Said (SW)
Bottom: Waiting for fuel on the Qena-Hurghada road (HF)

Top: The Mediterranean at Marsa Matruh (SW)
Left: Saad Zaghloul Square, Alexandria (SW)
Right: The British War Cemetery, El Alamein (SW)

The Suez Canal. Bird's eye view on the Suez Canal

1 Port Said
2 Lake Menzaleh
3 Railway to Jerusalem
4 El Kantara
5 Ismailia
6 Lake Timsah
7 Railway to Cairo
8 Turks attacking Canal during Great War
9 The Biblical Land of Goshen
9a Moses camp before crossing Red Sea
10 Bitter Lakes
11 Track of Israelites crossing Red Sea
12 Sweet Water Canal
13 Railway from Suez to Cairo
14 Suez
15 Port Tewfik

Postcard from the 1890s

world cotton markets. There was increased demand for Egyptian cotton and the completion of the canal would facilitate its export.

The canal was completed amidst much fanfare and celebration in 1869, having cost the lives of thousands of labourers and incurring several million pounds of unanticipated debt to European finance houses. A large part of that debt was due to the extravagant festivities which Ismail had planned for the opening of the canal.

In his desire to establish Egypt as a major world power Ismail sought to impress the kings, queens and various potentates of Europe with a four day party to mark the completion of the new sea route between Europe and Asia.

The inauguration ceremony on 16 November 1869 was a grand affair. When two small fleets, one originating in Port Said and the other in Suez, met at the new town of Ismailia the Suez Canal was declared open and Africa was officially severed from Asia.

In Cairo, Ismail built the Opera House and Sharia al-Ahram, the road from the city to Giza. The latter was constructed so that his *most* special guest, the French Empress Eugenie, could travel to the great pyramids in her carriage. In Ismailia he built a new palace for the occasion; and all along the canal various special events were held. In Port Said, fireworks, feasts and the official opening ball for 6000 guests, were just the start of weeks of lavish hospitality offered to the visiting dignitaries.

The celebration and resulting debts nearly finished Pasha Ismail. By 1875 he had to sell almost half his shares of the Suez Canal Company to the British government. This appeased the creditors but ushered in a period of British control over Egypt which lasted until Nasser overthrew King Farouk in the 1952 revolution.

In 1956 Nasser nationalised the Suez Canal to raise money for the construction of the Aswan High Dam. The US, Britain and France had withdrawn financial backing for the project because of Nasser's willingness to deal with both the Soviet countries and the west. By halting the flow of revenue from the canal to French, British and other foreign shareholders, Nasser was also making a statement about western control in the affairs of Egypt. His move precipitated an invasion of the canal area by France, Britain and Israel but with world opinion against them and no support from the UN, all three countries were forced to withdraw.

The canal was closed for about eight years following the Six Day War in 1967, when Israel returned to the area after Egypt tried to block the Straits of Tiran, the former's only outlet to the Red Sea.

The Israelis entrenched themselves along the eastern bank of the canal by building a line of fortifications called the 'Bar Lev Line'. In 1973 Egypt tried but failed to take the Sinai and Suez Canal back from Israel by blasting the Bar Lev Line with water cannons. By this time the canal was full of sunken ships and sea traffic remained paralysed until 1975, when Sadat reopened the canal.

Since the 1978 Camp David Agreement and the 1979 peace treaty signed between Egypt and Israel, the Suez Canal has been filled with a constant flow of ship traffic. It is 163 km long but is still not wide enough to accommodate modern ships sailing in both directions. There are plans to widen the canal but, for now, ships sailing in opposite directions can pass at only two points – the Bitter Lakes and Al-Ballah.

PORT SAID

The main attraction of Port Said, and the reason for its establishment on the Mediterranean, is the Suez Canal. Its status as a duty free port also makes it the most flourishing of the canal cities. There are some mediocre beaches along the Mediterranean which are good for swimming and, along some of the original city streets, there are some fine old buildings with wooden balconies.

The spectacle of the huge ships and tankers lining up to pass through the northern entrance of the canal is certainly something to be seen but there's not really all that much else to do.

Port Said was founded by its namesake, the Khedive Said Pasha, in 1859 as excavation for the Suez Canal began. Much of the city is an island which was created by filling in part of Lake Manzalla, to the west, with sand from the canal site. The city continued to grow until 1956 when much of it was bombed during the Suez Crisis. It suffered again during the 1967 and '73 wars with Israel. Damage can still be seen but most of the city has been rebuilt.

Today, Port Said has 257,000 people and is connected to the mainland by a bridge to the south and a causeway to the west. There is a ferry across Lake Manzalla to Matariyya and another between Port Said and its sister town, Port Fouad, on the other side of the canal.

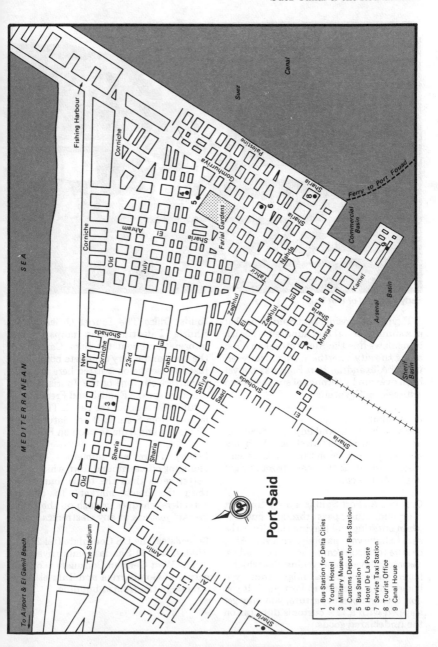

Port Said

1 Bus Station for Delta Cities
2 Youth Hostel
3 Military Museum
4 Customs Depot for Bus Station
5 Bus Station
6 Hotel De La Poste
7 Service Taxi Station
8 Tourist Office
9 Canal House

Early postcard of Port Said

Egyptians consider Port Said somewhat of a summer resort and hundreds of beach bungalows line the Mediterranean coast along the city's northern edge. However, unlike Alexandria, Port Said has not yet been overrun by throngs of sun, sand and sea seeking Egyptians.

Information

Most of the banks and important services are either on Sharia Palestine, which runs along the canal, or on the New Corniche, which runs along the beach front at right angles to the canal.

Customs As Port Said is a duty-free port everyone must pass through customs when entering and leaving the city, so be sure to have your passport with you. Also, be sure to declare cameras, lenses, radios, cassette players or anything else which a bored customs official might think you bought at a discount in Port Said. If you don't, then upon departure, you may get slapped with a 12% customs duty tax on the undeclared goods.

Tourist Office The Tourist Office, at 43 Sharia Palestine, has maps, some information about the Suez Canal and the port, and a very complete hotel list – just in case the ones listed here are full. Zenatte Nour, one of the Tourist Office officials, speaks English and French and is full of facts about the canal. The office is open from 8 am to 2 pm Saturday to Thursday and 8 am to noon on Friday.

Money There are numerous money-changing offices around town which offer better rates than the banks but worse than the black market. To change travellers' cheques or cash on the black market just ask at any electronics store.

Consulates The US Consulate (tel 22154, 23886), is at 11 Sharia Gomhurriya.

The West German Consulate is on the corner of Gomhurriya and Tahr el Bahr streets, in the *Hamza* building.

Post & Telephone The Central Post Office is opposite Farial Gardens, one block from Sharia Gomhurriya.

The telephone and telegraph office is on Sharia Palestine, two blocks north of the Tourist Office. Three minute calls cost about E£11.85 to the US; E£13.35 to Canada; E£17.85 to Australia/New Zealand; and E£10.80 to the UK.

The Canal House
One of the best views of the canal used to be from the large white-columned building south of the ferry terminal and Tourist Office. The dome of the Canal House is now off-limits because, according to the gate guards, it 'contains great secrets'. Even a promise to keep my eyes shut as I passed by the 'secret' offices to the dome didn't get me in. You might try to talk your way in, however, as security at the front gate seems arbitrary.

Port Fouad
This suburb of civil servants was founded, across the canal from Port Said, in 1925. The yacht club in Port Fouad is the place to go to find passage or work on a vessel through the canal as the captains are often looking for crew members. The free ferry from Port Said to Port Fouad, which offers a great view of the canal, leaves about every 10 minutes from a terminal one block south of the Tourist Office.

Military Museum
The small military museum on Sharia 23rd July has some interesting relics from the 1967 and '73 wars with Israel. There are captured American tanks with freshly painted Stars of David, a couple of unexploded bombs and various other unpleasant reminders of recent wars, plus exhibits of ancient pharaonic and Islamic conflicts. The museum costs E£1 to get in and is open from 9 am to 2 pm and occasionally from 5 to 8 pm.

Farial Gardens
If you get tired of watching ships cruise in and out of the canal, Farial Gardens offers a pleasant refuge for a stroll or a picnic. They're in the centre of town next to the bus station.

Things to Buy
Almost anything can be bought in Port Said, from the latest western fashions to Sony walkmen and VCRs, at duty free prices. The best deals can be found along Sharia Gomhurriya, one of the main shopping drags.

Places to Stay – bottom end
The *Youth Hostel*, near the stadium, is the cheapest place to stay in Port Said but, as far as hostels go, it's not such a good deal. It's 80 pt per night, with an IYHF card, and E£1 a night, without; and I've no idea what the rooms are like. When I dropped in at 4.30 pm and asked to see the rooms, the manager stuttered and said, 'No, the *shababs* and *shaba-bettes* (hostelers and hostelerettes) were sleeping'. Sleeping! At 4.30 in the afternoon? Let me know if you stay there.

The *Akry Hotel* and the *El Ghazal Hotel* are a couple of the best deals in town. The Greek-owned *Akry* (tel 21013), at 24 Sharia Gomhurriya has clean singles and doubles without bath for about E£4; and doubles with bath for E£5.50. The *El Ghazal*, at 23 Sharia 23rd July has doubles for E£5.46 with bath or E£4.60 without.

Places to Stay – middle
The *Hotel de la Poste*, on Sharia Gomhurriya, has a fading elegance which the management is attempting to salvage through careful renovation. Doubles with bath cost from E£6.50 to E£12.50 per night and some rooms have TVs and refrigerators. There's a restaurant, bar and patisserie downstairs. It's worth

having a chat with the hotel manager, Mr Salem Sakra, if you can catch him in the evenings. One of the 'Heroes of Port Said', he fought off invading Britons in the 1956 war and later became City Manager and Governor of Sohag Province.

The *Vendome Hotel* (tel 20802), at 37 Sharia Gomhurriya, has clean, simple rooms at E£6/4 for a single with/without bath; or E£9/7.25 a double with/without bath; and all prices include breakfast.

The *Regent Hotel*, a few doors down from the Vendome, has large, charming rooms with hardwood floors, armoires and balconies. They cost E£10 a double without bath or E£11 with.

The *Abu Simbel Hotel*, 15 Sharia Gomhurriya is a modern, almost European-style establishment with showers, toilets, TVs, fans and refrigerators in all rooms There is supposed to be hot water but the 'new' Italian water heaters in each room don't seem to work. At E£13 for a double and E£10.75 for a single (including breakfast), it's slightly overpriced.

Places to stay – top end
The *Holiday*, on Sharia Gomhurriya opposite the Hotel de la Poste, has doubles for E£27 and singles for E£22, including taxes and breakfast. The *ETAP*, on the beach front, gets a four-star rating from the Tourist Office, mostly because of the views. Singles are E£20 and doubles are E£24, plus a 14% tax and E£1.75 for breakfast. You must show official exchange receipts for payment.

Places to Eat
Not surprisingly, there are plenty of fish restaurants in Port Said. One of the best and cheapest is *Galal* on the corner of Gomhurriya and Gaberti streets, one block from the Hotel de la Poste. Fish costs E£3, complete with head and bulging eyes, and a couple of Egyptian salads.

The *Geanola* next door to the Abu Simbel Hotel has big meals of fish, meat, salad and chips etc, for about E£4.50. The owner is Italian, the menu is in French and the waiters are probably from the local convalescent home.

In front of the Hotel de la Poste there's a bar, a café and a restaurant. The latter has cheap hamburgers, sandwiches, salads and, supposedly, pizza.

Opposite the *ETAP* there's the *Hati al Medina* restaurant which serves the best and cheapest kufta, kebab and salads in town.

For a splurge try the *Maxim*, the best restaurant in town, where you can get a full fish dinner for E£10. It's on the corner of Old Corniche and Sharia Gomhurriya and has a splendid view of the ships entering the canal.

Getting There
Bus The bus terminal is on a small street next to the Farial Gardens. Remember to get there early because you must first pass through customs. Inside the terminal, you pass to the left if you have nothing to declare.

Buses to Cairo leave every hour from 7 am to 6 pm. Tickets with the Superjet Company cost E£5 and with the Deluxe Company cost E£3. The Delta bus company charges E£3.50 for a bumpy ordinary bus; E£4 for a bumpy ordinary bus with air-con; or E£6 for the Express which gets to Cairo in 2½ hours, 30 minutes faster than the others.

The Deluxe Company's Cairo-bound buses are the only ones which stop in Ismailia. The trip there takes 1½ hours and they will also stop at Qantara.

Delta buses are the only ones which go to Alexandria. The E£6 Express and the E£5 air-con buses leave at 8 and 10 am and noon. The ordinary Delta bus costs E£4 and leaves at 2.30 pm.

Delta buses leave for Suez at 1 and 4 pm and cost E£2.50 for the 3½ hour trip.

Buses to the Nile Delta towns of Mansur, Damietta, Tanta and Zagazig leave from a bus station on Sharia Stalingrad, just past the Salah Salim mosque.

Service Taxi Service taxis to all the previously mentioned destinations leave from the old railway station square on Sharia Al Amin. The fares are: Qantara – 75 pt; Cairo – E£3; Ismailia – E£1.50; Suez – E£3; and Zagazig – E£2.50.

Train Trains to Ismailia and Cairo leave at 12.45 and 4.45 pm and 5 am. Tickets cost E£1.20 in 2nd class and 60 pt in 3rd class. There is no 1st class. The trip to Cairo takes four hours.

Ship Unless you are a merchant sailor, getting passage on a ship going through the canal is nearly impossible. However, you may be able to get passage or work on a private yacht from Port Fouad.

Getting Around
Hantours The horse-drawn carriages are the best and most enjoyable way to tour Port Said, especially around sunset. The carriage and driver can be hired for about E£3 to E£4 per hour.

QANTARA
The only reason to visit the town of Qantara, which is 80 km south of Port Said, is so that you can cross to the east side of the canal and leave again as quickly as possible. The service taxis, which cross the Sinai to the Egypt-Israel border, leave from the east bank.

Most of Qantara was destroyed during the 1973 war with Israel and the town's buildings are still pocked with bullet holes. A free boat ferries passengers from one side of the canal to the other. Be prepared to join a stampede of people, chickens, and donkeys for a space on the boat. It can be fun if your sense of humour is still intact after trying to talk a donkey out of your seat.

ISMAILIA
Ismailia was founded by and named after Pasha Ismail, the ruler of Egypt during the construction of the Suez Canal in the 1860s. Ferdinand de Lessups, the director of the Suez Canal Company lived in the city until the canal was completed.

Ismailia is perhaps the most picturesque of the new canal towns yet it has been developing quickly, or rather devolving, into an urban mess. The city, of 500,000 people, is divided in two by the railway line and these tracks virtually mark a boundary between well tended streets on one side and a veritable disaster area on the other.

The streets and squares on the eastern side of the city are lined with trees and dotted with malls and parks. The Sweetwater Canal, named for its fresh-water connection with the Nile, weaves through this half of Ismailia, around lush thickets of trees to **Lake Timsah**, or Crocodile Lake, which is the smallest of the Bitter Lakes.

On the other side of the tracks you'll find the main bus and service taxi station, the condition of which is a microcosm of the surrounding neighbourhood – muddy pot-holed streets, horn-honking maniacs and smoking piles of garbage.

Registration
You must register with the police if you intend to stay in Ismailia for more than 24 hours.

Information
Ismailia's main street runs diagonally from the station, around the gardens of Midan El Gomhurriya, to Mohammed Ali Quay, the street which runs beside the Sweetwater Canal.

The Tourist Office is at the end of a 1st floor hall, in the Ismailia Governorate building on Mohammed Ali Quay. It is open from 8 am to 2 pm daily except Fridays and, apart from being somewhat of an educational experience, is next to useless. The slack hours give the sluggish bureaucrats who work there plenty of time to read their newspapers and watch the faded tourist posters peel off the walls. If you really want a lesson in Egyptian bureaucracy, try asking for a street map of Ismailia; I tried and the following happened:

An official from the State Information Office had taken me downstairs to the Tourist Office after unsuccessfully searching for a map himself by opening and closing a lot of drawers. I saw a colourful wall map, just outside the door, as we entered the Tourist Office but realised all the street names were in Arabic. There were two women in the office so I asked for a smaller version of the wall map. They briefly looked up from their newspapers and bare desktops, sighed and shrugged their shoulders.

I looked to the official for help. He also shrugged, so I went back to the wall map outside and started drawing it. The official hovered behind me watching.

Me: What's the name of this street?
Official: Hmmm, do you have a car?
Me: No. What's the name of this square?
Official: Well, if you had a car then I could show you around Ismailia.

He sounded really disappointed. As a final test I pointed to another street on the map – the street right in front of the Governorate building. He didn't know so I asked if he knew someone in the building from Ismailia.

Official: I'm from Ismailia.

Another man appeared and the official asked him for a map. We followed the second official into the Tourist Office. He opened a drawer and pulled out a beautifully drawn map of the city. I asked if they had a photocopy machine so that a copy could be made.

Official: No.
Me: Ok, I'll trace it then. Do you have a sheet of paper?
Official: No.

I didn't believe him. After all, this was a government office. No paper, ha! I remembered that I had some so I started tracing the map myself.

Official: Why are you doing that?
Me: Because you said that you didn't have a copy machine.
Official: We have a copy machine upstairs.

He disappeared with the map but returned after a few minutes without copies.

Official: The map was too big.

I'm not sure what finally prompted her, but one of the women with her nose in a newspaper suddenly opened a drawer and handed me a dusty tourist map of Ismailia. I dashed out of the office with the official closely following me.

Official: Are you sure that you don't have a car?

Money Even the police in Ismailia will offer to change money for you, however it's best to try one of the shops on Sharia Sultan Hussein.

Post & Telephone The Post Office and telephone offices are on the south-west corner of Midan El Gomhurriya.

The Ismailia Museum
This small but interesting museum on Mohammed Ali Quay, a couple of blocks down from the Governorate building, has more than 4000 objects from Pharaonic and Graeco-Roman times. There are statues, scarabs and stelae and details of the completion of the first canal, between the Bitter Lakes and Bubastis, by Darius. The 4th century AD mosaics are the highlight of the collection.

Garden of the Stelae
Near the museum is a garden containing sphinxes from the time of Ramses II. You need permission from the museum to visit the garden.

House of Ferdinand de Lessups
The residence of the one-time French consul to Egypt, used to be open to the public but now you can only see the interior if you're a VIP of some sort. If you really want to see the outside of the house where Ferdinand lived while directing the construction of the Suez Canal, then it's on Mohammed Ali Quay near the corner of Sharia Ahmed Orabi.

Beaches
There are several good beaches around Lake Timsah but using them involves paying to get into one of the resort clubs that dot the shore. Entrance fees vary, as

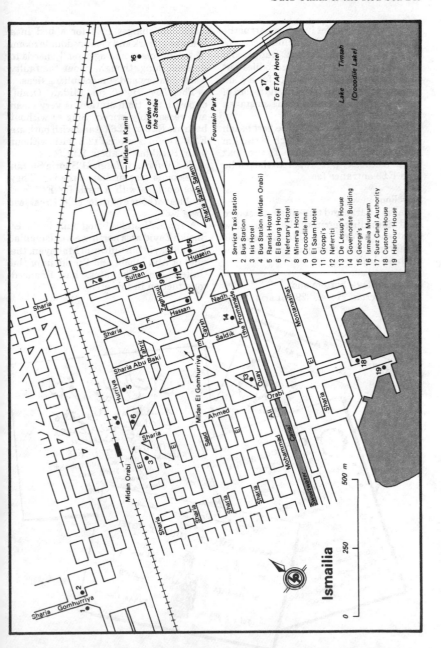

1 Service Taxi Station
2 Bus Station
3 Isis Hotel
4 Bus Station (Midan Orabi)
5 Ramsis Hotel
6 El Bourg Hotel
7 Nefertary Hotel
8 Minerva Hotel
9 Crocodile Inn
10 El Salam Hotel
11 Groppi's
12 Nefertiti
13 De Lessup's House
14 Governorate Building
15 George's
16 Ismailia Museum
17 Suez Canal Authority
18 Customs House
19 Harbour House

Ismailia

Lake Timsah
(Crocodile Lake)

To ETAP Hotel

Fountain Park

Garden of
the Stelae

Midan M Kamil

Sharia Salah Salem

Hussein

Sultan

Zaghloul

F. Hassan

Nadh

Cayish

Saldik

Sharia Abu Baki

Hurriya

Sharia

Sharia Tahrir

Midan El Gomhurriya

Montanasihat

the Promenade

El

El Quay

Orabi

Ali

Sharia

El Ahmed

El Saad

Midan Orabi

Sharia

Sharia Gomhurriya

Mohammed

Canal

Sweetwater

Sharia

0   250   500 m

some include a buffet lunch as part of the admission price, but all include access to a private swimming beach. Supposedly the lake was once full of crocodiles but there have been no sightings for a good many centuries and certainly no record of any swimming tourists being mistaken for lunch.

According to the locals, the best beach is **Le Jardin des Enfants** which is two km north of Ismailia. It belongs to the Suez Canal Authority but is open to the public for a E£3 entrance fee.

Bicycling

Ismailia's parks and tree-lined streets are good bike riding territory. There are a few bike shops on the side streets off Mohammed Ali Quay, just ask around for the best deal.

Places to Stay – bottom end

The *Minerva Hotel*, 29 Sharia Saad Zaghloul, charges E£4 for a bed in a somewhat dark and gloomy double room. The benevolent manager really needs to do something, though, about the faulty water heaters and somersaulting fleas.

The *Isis Hotel* on Midan Orabi, opposite the train station, is very clean and reasonably priced. Singles without bath are E£5 or E£6.50 and with bath are E£9. Doubles are E£12/8 with/without bath. Breakfast is about E£1.50.

The *Nefertary Hotel*, 41 Sharia Sultan Hussein, is very similar to the Isis. They have doubles with a bath for E£7 and doubles without a bath for E£6. Breakfast costs E£1.

A *Youth Hostel* is being built in the El Sheikh Zayid area north-west of Ismailia. Sheikh Zayid bin Sultan al Mahayan, the ruler of Abu Dhabi and President of the United Arab Emirates, has financed construction in this area.

Places to Stay – middle

The *Ramsis Hotel* is on Sharia El Hurriya about two blocks to your left as you leave the train station. It has very clean doubles, with TVs, telephones and air-con in every room, for E£10 per night. Breakfast is, according to the manager, 'almost whatever you want' and costs E£1.20.

The *El Salam Hotel*, on Sharia El Gaysh, has clean singles and doubles with baths for E£15 and E£20 respectively.

The *El Bourg Hotel*, on Midan Orabi, is replacing the *New Palace Hotel* (which is anything but new). According to the owner there will be 27 suites each with colour TVs, bathrooms and air-con. Rooms will cost E£15 to E£20 per night.

Places to Stay – top end

The *Crocodile Inn*, on the corner of Saad Zaghloul and Sultan Hussein streets, seems to have everything except crocodiles. There are various lounges and restaurants including a 24 hour coffee shop. Singles are E£17 and doubles E£22.

The *ETAP*, right on the lake at Gezira el Fursan, has all the amenities of an expensive hotel. For E£5 you can use their swimming pool and beach, and for E£10, on Fridays and Sundays, you can make a pig of yourself at their buffets.

Camping

There are no official camping grounds in the Ismailia area, however it is possible to camp on the beach around Lake Timsah.

Places to Eat

The *Social Club* is a garden restaurant and cafeteria in Milaha Garden, run by the Ismailia Governorate, where you can get good, inexpensive meals.

George's and the *Nefertiti*, both on Sharia Sultan Hussein, serve fish and meat dishes for about E£4 to E£5.

Groppi's is across the street from George's. It's a smaller version of the Cairo Groppi's but with just as good a selection of pastries and ice cream.

Getting There

Bus Buses for Cairo and Port Said depart from Midan Orabi every 30 to 45 minutes. Express buses leave for Cairo at 1.30, 3, 5 and 6 pm. No ticket should cost more than E£2.50.

Buses for Suez, Alexandria and El Arish depart from the Sharia Gomhurriya terminal just west of the train tracks. Buses to Suez cost from 75 pt to E£1 and leave hourly; to Alexandria they cost E£3 or E£3.50, take five hours and leave at 7 am and 2.30 pm; and to El Arish they cost E£2.25, take three hours and leave at 8 and 11.30 am and 1 pm.

Service Taxi Taxis depart frequently from the Sharia Gomhurriya terminal for Cairo – E£2, Port Said – E£1.25 and Suez – E£1.25.

Train Everyday there are eight trains to Cairo, four to Port Said and nine to Suez. At E£3.53, a 1st class ticket on the noon train to Cairo is the most expensive, while the cheapest is the 25 pt 3rd class fare to Port Said. You get what you pay for. Travelling for 25 pt is tantamount to riding in a messy cattle car and 2nd class is not much better.

SUEZ

Suez is a city going through a metamorphosis. It was all but completely destroyed during the 1967 and '73 wars with Israel and traces of the devastation are still visible. The revamped main streets are basically a facade hiding a sordid mess of back street slums, though they are a sign that things are gradually changing for the better. The bombed-out hulls of buildings, some occupied by squatters, walls peppered with bullet holes and streets littered with debris remain amongst the reconstruction works, while three US-made Israeli tanks squat on the Corniche as a memorial to the victories of war.

Suez sprawls around the shores of the gulf where the Red Sea meets the

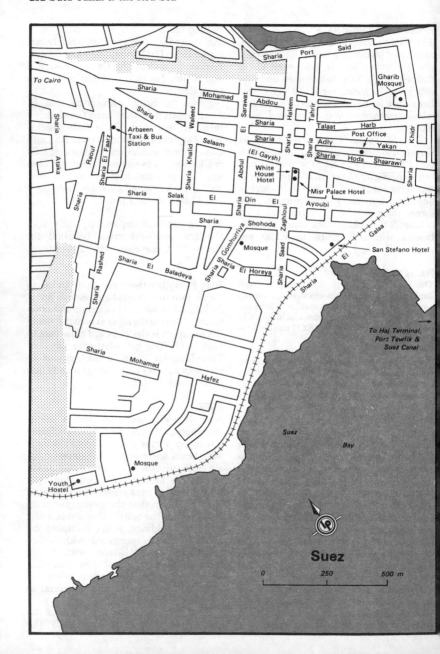

To Cairo

Sharia

Sharia

Sharia

Sharia

Sharia

Sharia

Sharia

Sharia

Sharia

Ataka

Raouf

Rashed

Sharia El Faarz

Sharia Khalid

Salaam

Salak

Abdul

El

Gomhuriya

Baladeya

Mohamed

Hafez

Mosque

Youth Hostel

Port   Said

Sharia

Mohamed

Waleed

El Sarawat

Abdou

Haleem

Tahrir

Sharia

Sharia

Sharia (El Gaysh)

Din   El

Shohoda

Mosque

Sharia El Horeya

Talaat

Adly

Sharia

Harb

Post Office

Hoda

Yakan

Shaarawi

Khidr

Sharia

Galaa

San Stefano Hotel

El

Sharia

To Haj Terminal, Port Tewfik & Suez Canal

Suez   Bay

Suez

0   250   500 m

Arbaeen Taxi & Bus Station

White House Hotel

Misr Palace Hotel

Ayoubi

Saad   Zaghloul

southern entrance of the Suez Canal. There is nothing much to do there, except take in the best view of the ships passing in or out of the canal, and very little in the way of tourist facilities. It's basically just a transit point, not only for the great tankers, cargo vessels and private yachts en route to or from the Mediterranean, but for travellers and the Muslim faithful as well. The Gulf of Suez is one of the departure points for the *Haj*, or pilgrimage to Mecca, and most other people just pass through Suez on their way to the Sinai or the Red Sea beaches.

Information
Tourist Office The staff at the new Tourist Office at Port Tewfik, on the eastern shore of Suez Bay, are helpful almost to the point of being obsequious. They are more than eager to provide information about the city, canal and surrounding sites. The office is open from 8.30 am to 2.30 pm daily except Fridays.

Post & Telephone The Post Office is on Sharia Hoda Shaarawi. The telephone office is on Sharia Salaam between Abdul el Sarawat and Haleem streets.

Money There are plenty of money changing offices in Suez, especially at Port Tewfik. For black market exchanges try the video cassette stores.

Places to Stay - bottom end
The *Youth Hostel*, on Sharia Tariq El Horreya facing the stadium, is often full of stampeding kids. Only stay at this corral, which is a long walk from the bus station, as a last resort. If you're desperate, it costs 80 pt per night for members or E£1.20 for non-members.

The similar but more civilised *Haj Terminal*, on the north shore of Suez Bay, is a good deal for E£1 a night. It's on the corniche street, Sharia El Galaa, between the city and Port Tewfik and is basically four large rooms, each with 150 beds. The showers are clean and there's a cafeteria.

The *Misr Palace Hotel*, 2 Sharia Saad Zaghloul, has 101 beds in single and double rooms of varying prices, standards and degrees of cleanliness. Singles/doubles without showers are E£4.40/7.65; and with showers are E£5.52/10.50. Check the room they offer before you decide to stay.

Places to Stay - middle
The *Hotel Beau Rivage*, 44 Sharia Saad Zaghloul, has singles with showers from E£7.25 to E£8.35 and doubles with showers from E£9.15 to E£10.95. Breakfast is an additional E£1.35.

The *White House Hotel*, 322 Sharia Salaam, is a very clean, respectable and popular place. Singles with showers range from E£20 to E£27, or without are E£14.85; doubles with/without bath are E£24.66/19.25; and they charge you E£1.65 for air-con even when it's cold outside. The hotel restaurant serves a variety of filling meals for E£4 to E£6.

The *Bel Air Hotel* on Sharia Saad Zaghloul, opposite the Misr Palace, has also been recommended. It costs E£9 for a double with bath and the hotel also has a good restaurant.

Places to Stay - top end
The *Red Sea Hotel*, 13 Sharia Riad, Port Tewfik, claims to be one of the best in town although foreigners who have stayed both there and at the White House Hotel might dispute that. Singles/doubles with bath are E£23.25/29.15.

Places to Eat
El Magharbel Restaurant, next door to the White House Hotel, is one of the few restaurants in town. It serves reasonably good meals for about E£4.

You might also try the sandwich shops for cheap meat sandwiches with side orders of pickled vegetables.

The *Social Club* on the Corniche has inexpensive fish as well as hazy views, during the day, of the Gulf of Suez and the surrounding mountains.

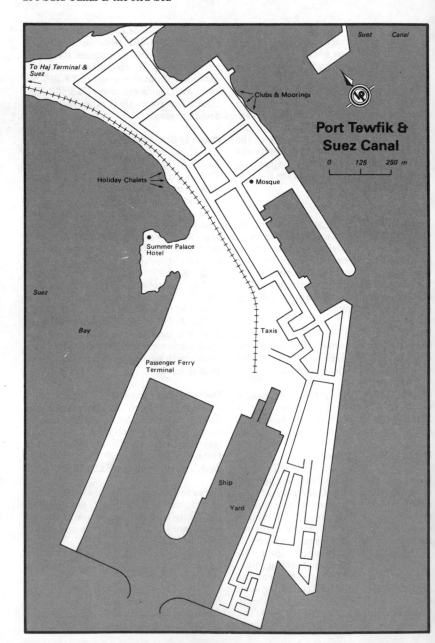

To Haj Terminal & Suez

Suez Canal

Clubs & Moorings

**Port Tewfik &
Suez Canal**

0   125   250 m

Holiday Chalets

● Mosque

Summer Palace
Hotel

Suez

Bay

Taxis

Passenger Ferry
Terminal

Ship

Yard

Getting There

Bus All buses to Cairo, Ismailia, the Red Sea beaches and the Sinai leave from Arbaeen Station on Sharia El Faarz, near the centre of town.

Buses to Cairo (E£2) and Ismailia (E£1) leave every half hour between 7 am and 5 pm. The trip to Cairo takes two hours.

Buses to Ein Sukhna (50 pt) depart at 6 and 10 am and noon.

Air-con buses to Zafarana (E£2), Ras Gharib (E£4) and Hurghada (E£4.50) leave at 6 and 6.30 am. The trip to Hurghada takes five hours.

Buses to Oyun Musa (75 pt), Ras el Sudr (E£1), Hamman Fara'un (E£1.50) and El Tor (E£5.50) leave at 10 am, noon, 1 and 2 pm. The trip takes one hour, 1½ hours and 2½ hours respectively.

Buses to Sharm el Shaykh (E£7) leave at 7 and 10 am and 2 pm and take six hours.

Buses to Wadi Feran (E£5) and St Catherine's (E£5.50) depart at 9.30 and 11 am and take three and four hours.

Buses to Nuweiba (E£6.50) leave at 9.30 and 10 am and the bus to Taba (E£8) leaves at 9.30 am.

Buses to the Sinai go via the Ahmad Hamdi tunnel which goes under the Suez Canal 17 km north of the city. An expatriate in Suez suggested that travellers heading for the Sinai should go to the entrance of the tunnel and wait for the faster, more comfortable Sinai bus from Cairo. The only problem with this is that you must either pay E£10 for a taxi from Suez or talk the driver on the Suez-Ismailia bus into dropping you off at the road junction. The Cairo bus has to pass through the junction but the driver may not stop for you there. Hitching might be possible.

Train Trains to Cairo leave at 5.50 and 9.40 am, 2.50 and 7.15 pm. All trains stop at Qubba Palace. The trip takes approximately 3½ hours.

There are also four daily trains to Ismailia where you can connect with other trains going to Cairo or Port Said. Refer to the Ismailia Getting There section.

Service Taxi Taxis go to all the destinations serviced by buses and trains. They take seven passengers, are faster than buses over long distances and the fares are usually about the same.

Steamer The Egyptian Navigation Company has two ships – the *Algeria* and the *Syria* – which sail between Suez, Jeddah and Port Sudan. The schedule is a bit erratic but there are about four departures a month. Their office is on Sharia El Nabi Mousa and the company also has branches in Cairo and Alexandria.

Getting Around

There are regular microbus services along Sharia Salaam from the Arbaeen bus station to Port Tewfik. They stop to pick up or drop off wherever you want along the route and cost 25 pt.

The Red Sea Coast

WARNING: Much of the coastline is mined. Use only designated beaches and roads and if you're unsure ask the local military authorities.

EIN SUKHNA

Ein Sukhna, which means 'hot eyes', is the site of springs which originate from within Mt Ataka, the highest mountain on the Red Sea coast. There's not much to Ein Sukhna, except a wonderfully deserted beach and the hot springs, but the area is gradually being developed as a resort.

There are buses from Suez every hour from 6 am to 4 pm, so it's possible to visit Ein Sukhna on a day trip from the canal city, which is 55 km north.

If you want to stay longer there is the

Ein Sukhna Hotel which has 80 rooms and 30 bungalows ranging in price from E£30 to E£45 a double.

ZAFARANA

This town, 62 km south of Ein Sukhna and 150 km west of Beni Suef on the Nile, is little more than a way stop for visits to the isolated Coptic Monasteries of St Anthony and St Paul in the mountains which overlook the Gulf of Suez.

The monasteries are open for day trips between 9 am and 5 pm but if you wish to stay overnight you need to obtain permission from the Coptic Patriarch in Cairo (222 Sharia Ramses, Abbassiya). St Anthony's guesthouse is for men only. St Paul's has accommodation for men and women but the monks won't take any visitors at all during Lent.

The Monastery of St Anthony

Hidden away in the barren cliffs of the Eastern Desert, the fortified religious community of St Anthony's, and St Paul's 82 km away, represented the beginning of the Christian monastic tradition. Built in the 4th century AD by the disciples of St Anthony, the walled village at the foot of Mt Kalalah is the largest of the Coptic monasteries.

This founding monastic order sprang up around the son of a merchant who had given up his worldly possessions to devote his life to God. Anthony actually retreated into the desert, in about 294 AD, to escape the disciples he had attracted to his hermit's cave by the Nile. While his followers adopted an austere communal life at the foot of the mountain, Anthony took himself off to a cave, high above the developing monastery village, where he lived to the ripe old age of 105.

Despite its isolation the monastery endured bedouin raids in the 8th and 9th centuries, attacks from irate Muslims in the 11th century and a 15th century revolt by blood-thirsty servants which resulted in the massacre of the monks.

Following the example set by St Anthony, St Paul and their followers 16 centuries ago, the 25 monks and five novices who live at St Anthony's today have dedicated their lives to poverty, chastity, obedience and prayer.

St Anthony's has several churches, chapels, dormitories, a bakery, vegetable garden and a spring. The oldest part of the monastery is the **Church of St Anthony**, built over the saint's tomb. There's also a guesthouse but it's only for men.

If you're hiking in from the main road make sure you're properly equipped, especially with water, as it's a long, hot and dry walk. If you do get this far you should also hike up to the **Cave of St Anthony** which is north-east of the monastery. The medieval graffiti on the walls is fascinating and the view of the hills and valley below is breathtaking.

The Monastery of St Paul

The most fascinating part of this large complex, in the cliffs of the Gebel Galala el Qibliya, is the **Church of St Paul**, cluttered with altars, candles, ostrich eggs (the symbol of the Resurrection) and colourful murals. It was built in and around the cave where Paul lived for nearly 90 years, during the 4th century, after founding the monastery as a show of devotion to St Anthony. The **fortress**, above the church, was where the monks retreated during bedouin raids.

Visitors are more than welcome and a couple of the monks, who speak excellent English, give guided tours. St Paul's has two guesthouses, one inside the monastery for men and one outside for women. Food and lodging are provided free of charge so don't abuse the monks' hospitality.

Getting There

Direct access to the monasteries is limited to private vehicles, tour buses from Cairo or your own two feet.

St Anthony's is 45 km inland from the Red Sea. To get there you follow the rather rough road which runs between Zafarana and Beni Suef. The turn-off to the monastery is about 35 km from Zafarana and from there it's a 10 km walk south through the desert to St Anthony's. Buses occasionally travel from Cairo to the Red Sea via this route across the Eastern Desert but it's really more suited to four-wheel drive vehicles.

To get to St Paul's you can take one of the buses that run between Suez and Hurghada and get off after Zafarana at the turn-off to the monastery. The buses that run between Qena, north of Luxor on the Nile, and Suez go via Port Safaga and Hurghada and can also drop you at the turn-off, which is south of the Zafarana lighthouse. It's then a 13 km hike through the desert.

Another alternative is to get a group together and take a service taxi from Suez or Hurghada.

HURGHADA (GHARDAKA)

The only attractions of this one-time isolated and modest fishing village are the warm and brilliant turquoise waters of the Red Sea, the amazing colours of the splendid coral and exotic creatures of the deep and the soft and deserted white sand beaches backed up by the mountains of the Eastern Desert. There are no ancient tombs and no pharaonic temples or crumbling monasteries, just mother nature at her best.

While the crystal clear waters and fascinating reefs have made Hurghada, or Ghardaka as the Egyptians call it, a popular destination amongst diving enthusiasts the world over, if you're not into beaches, swimming or snorkelling then this developing resort town probably has little to offer.

You can't actually swim at any of the beaches near town because they're too polluted with rubbish and sewerage and with oil from nearby derricks, but there are some good beaches near the Sheraton Hotel, seven km south of Hurghada. There's also, of course, good swimming and excellent diving around the coral reefs and offshore islands and plenty of

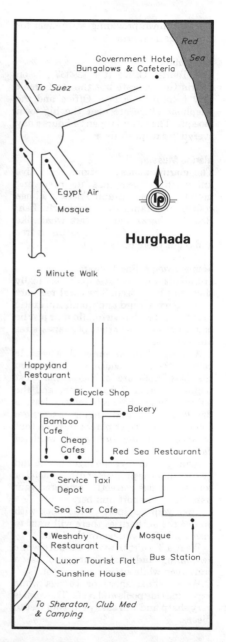

places in town providing equipment for most aquatic sports.

Information
The Tourist Office (tel 439337), is on Sharia Governorate but the staff aren't very helpful. The Post Office and the telephone office are near the big town mosque. The latter is open 24 hours a day everyday except Fridays.

Marine Museum
The marine biology station, about five km north of town, has an interesting museum and aquarium. There is a huge collection of fantastically colourful fish, Red Sea sharks and the rare whale-like manatees. Entry to the museum is free and a bus there costs 15 pt.

Scuba Diving & Snorkelling
Hurghada's underwater paradise really shouldn't be missed. The coral reefs are teeming with weird and wonderful exotic marine beings that swim, float or just lie on the bottom in a variety of shapes, sizes and colours.

Although there is some easily accessible coral at the beach south of the Sheraton the best reefs are offshore, the most popular around **Geftun Island**, and the only way to see them is to take, at least, a day-long boat and diving excursion. There are plenty of places in town that organise trips but first a few words of caution.

Arrange your dive the night before and be sure that the proprietor of your hotel or tourist flat has correctly registered your name and passport number.

Take your passport to the dock with you as the authorities there will want to check it before you board the boat.

Wear a T-shirt to avoid sunburn while swimming and make sure you use a sunscreen while sitting in the boat.

Wear tennis shoes or thongs while exploring tide pools and reefs. The coral is very sharp and will easily cut your feet to pieces.

As pretty as they seem to be, there are quite a few creatures that should be avoided, especially sea urchins, blow fish, fire coral, feathery lionfish, moray eels, turkeyfish, stonefish, parrot fish and, needless to say, sharks.

Snorkelling A day trip, for a minimum of 15 people, which includes transport to and from the harbour, visits to two diving sites, snorkels, masks and a barbecue lunch on Geftun Island costs E£10 per person. The boat leaves at 9.30 am and returns at 5 pm.

A day trip to the 'House of Sharks' costs E£3 per person (E£2 if you bring your own mask) for a minimum of 10 people. No food is included. The boat departs at 10 am and returns at 4 pm.

An overnight trip, for a minimum of 15 people, which includes three meals, snorkels, masks, transport and a night on Geftun Island, costs E£20 per person. Bring your own sleeping bag. The boat leaves at noon and returns at 5 pm the following day.

For information and bookings go to Saleem's, near the bus station, or see Mohammed Yoneas, the manager of the Luxor Tourist Flat. Flippers cost E£1 extra for all of the trips.

There is also a four-day/three-night trip to several distant islands, for a minimum of five people, which includes food, snorkels, masks and drinks. The cost is E£60 per person. A tent is also available for rent but take your own sleeping bag. Talk to Ali at the Red Sea Restaurant for more information.

Scuba Diving A day trip can be arranged at Saleem's for E£40 per person including equipment rental and food.

The Hurghada Sheraton Hotel and Club Med also arrange diving trips. Both have reliable scuba and snorkelling gear. For E£18 per person Club Med will provide two snorkel dives, equipment and a fantastic buffet.

Independent Trips Diving and snorkelling equipment can be rented at Saleem's, Club Med and the Sheraton. Prices are about E£1 for a mask and snorkel; and E£1 for flippers.

Places to stay – bottom end

The *Moon Valley Hotel* is one of the best deals in Hurghada. It is run by the very kind Abd el Zaher family who rent individual huts with private bathrooms for E£7 and E£10, depending on whether you want water all day or just in the mornings and evenings. The price includes breakfast and dinner and the food, cooked by the father of the family, is some of the best in town. Tea and cold drinks are available all day. The hotel is 10 minutes south of town on the road to the Sheraton. To get there, ask any bus or taxi driver to take you to the Doctor's place; he's the owner and everyone in town knows him.

The *Luxor Tourist Flat* has received mixed reviews. Some say it's dirty, others say it's clean but whichever way you look at it, it's definitely cheap. It costs E£2 per person for a bed and access to hot showers and a kitchen. It's on the main road through town, opposite the street to the bus station.

The *Sunshine House*, next door, has rooms and hot showers for E£2 per person.

The *Shakespeare Hotel*, on the same road, costs E£4 per person for a bed. There have, however, been a few complaints from travellers about being overcharged there, so watch out.

Captain Mohammed's *Happy House* on Midan El Dar Mosque used to be the first place travellers checked out. Now, however, the house is only a souvenir shop though it's still worthwhile to at least stop by and chat with Captain Mohammed.

If you arrive by bus you'll be greeted by touts from the many other fairly cheap tourist flats in town, so you'll have no trouble finding a place.

Places to Stay – middle

The *Government Hotel*, on the polluted beach 10 minutes walk north of town, has several two-room bungalows, each with their own kitchen. They cost E£10 a night for as many people as you care to squeeze in. Rooms in the actual hotel cost E£2 in a shared room, or E£4 in a private room. There's also a cafeteria.

Places to Stay – top end

The *Sheraton Hotel*, seven km south of town, charges E£43 for a double and E£35 for a single. If you use the Sheraton beach you'll have to pay E£5 for the privilege.

Club Med run a tourist village, at Maguawish near the Sheraton, and charge E£95 a double per day. This price includes all meals, boat trips, lessons and equipment.

Camping

Free camping is possible on two beaches but neither have facilities of any sort so you need to take your own water and supplies. The camping area next to the government bungalows is polluted with oil. The other beach, near the Sheraton, is much cleaner and closer to the coral reefs but harder to get to. A taxi there will cost E£3 but will take up to seven people; or you could rent a bicycle for E£1 per day.

Places to Eat

The *Weshahy Restaurant*, opposite the Luxor Tourist Flat, is one of the best deals in town and the service is fast and friendly. A breakfast of bread, butter, marmalade, a cheese omelette and coffee costs E£1; or a tasty fish dinner costs E£1.80. They close at 9 pm.

The *Sea Star Café*, about a block north of the Luxor Tourist Flat on the main road, serves a good breakfast of an egg, bread, marmalade and tea for 90 pt.

Down the street opposite the Sea Star Café there are a number of inexpensive restaurants and cafés. These include the *Bamboo Café*, opposite the service taxi depot and the *Red Sea Restaurant*, further east along the street.

The *Bamboo Café* serves a decent three course fish, chicken or calamari dinner for E£1.75.

The *Red Sea Restaurant* is highly recommended. Breakfast is the same as Weshahy's but try their *fatha* – an excellent concoction of rice, chicken or meat, bread and yoghurt served in a ceramic bowl. They also serve wine and beer and are open until 1 am. Lunches cost E£3.45, dinner is about E£2.95, beer is E£1.80, soft drinks are 35 pt and chocolate pudding is 50 pt – not including 12% service.

Further north on the main road the *Happyland Restaurant* serves good but slightly more expensive meals and there's a supermarket, called *Stopshop*, which has a good selection of food.

The meals in the *Government Hotel* cafeteria are also reasonably good value.

Getting There

Air The flight from Cairo to Hurghada, daily at 7 am, costs about E£45 one way. The twice weekly flight from Luxor costs about E£20.

There are flights from Hurghada to Sharm el Shaykh and St Catherine's in the Sinai on Mondays and Fridays at 7 am for E£50 one way.

Bus There are two buses to Cairo which leave between 4 and 5 am everyday. Only one has air-con and a toilet – definitely recommended. Book your tickets at least one day in advance and be present 30 minutes before departure. (See the end of this chapter.) The fare is E£7 and the trip takes eight hours.

There are buses to Suez at 9 am and 10.30 am. The fare is E£4.50 and the trip takes seven hours because the bus is old and makes a lot of stops.

Buses leave for Qena, in the Nile Valley, at 6 and 8 am and 12.30 pm. The fare is E£3 and the trip takes four hours.

Buses leave for Luxor at 6 am and noon.

The fare is E£4 and the journey takes about five hours.

Service Taxi Service taxis go to all the same places as the buses but seven people are needed to get a good price.

Boat Mohammed, at the Luxor Tourist Flat, might be able to arrange passage on a boat from Hurghada to Sharm el Shaykh. It should cost about E£17.50.

Getting Around

It's a bit of a hike south from town to the prime on-shore diving spots and the good beach near the Sheraton. Hurghada's public transport services leave a little to be desired but there are a few ways to get around.

Bicycles Bicycles can be rented in town for E£1 per day.

Hitching It's sometimes possible to hitch around town or out to the beaches but the locals seem accustomed to receiving payment from travellers.

Taxis The fare from town to the Sheraton is an expensive E£3 but the taxis do take up to seven people for that price.

PORT SAFAGA

Port Safaga, 53 km south of Hurghada, is first and foremost a port for the export of phosphates from local mines. Secondly, it's a small resort with a pricey hotel. Free camping is possible at the beach. If you are headed south along the coastal road to the Sudan, you must complete customs formalities in Port Safaga.

The Road to Sudan

Very few travellers seem to venture south of Port Safaga, so if you do make it past the port you'll be journeying through a seldom visited part of Egypt.

QUSEIR

Quseir, a medieval port town of 4000 inhabitants, is 85 km south of Port Safaga and about 160 km east of Qift on the Nile. Until the 10th century it was one of the most important exit points for pilgrims travelling to Mecca and was also a thriving centre of trade and export between the Nile Valley and the Red Sea. The Suez Canal put an end to all that. There's an old fort and a small *souk* worth checking out and excellent snorkelling areas from the beach about five km north of town.

Places to Stay

It's possible to stay at *Samia's* for about E£1.50 per night. Samia is a very helpful guy who's building a few bungalows with cooking facilities, a little north of town.

Getting There

There are daily buses to and from Cairo, via Hurghada, and service taxis travel west to Qift and north to Port Safaga.

MARSA ALAM

Marsa Alam is a fishing village 145 km south of Quseir. A road also connects the village with Idfu, 230 km across the desert to the west.

BERENICE

The military centre and small port of Berenice, 145 km south of Marsa Alam, was founded in 275 BC by Ptolemy II Euergetes I and was an important trading post until the 5th century AD. Near the town, the ruins of the **Temple of Seramis** are still extant. The US Navy occasionally brings its aircraft carriers here. Supposedly, this is one of the staging areas for the US Rapid Deployment Forces.

BIR SHALATAYN

This tiny village 75 km south of Berenice is ostensibly the border post between Egypt and the Sudan. If you get this far, let us know what's there.

Hurghada to Cairo By Bus – maybe

My friend and I were told the day before we planned to leave Hurghada that we didn't need reservations for either of the Cairo buses. The next day we trudged over to the bus station at 4.30 am and half an hour later a gleaming, new bus pulled into the lot. Everything about it spelled comfort and as we had ridden throughout Egypt crammed like sardines on 3rd class trains and local buses this was certainly a welcome sight! We boarded the bus, flopped into a couple of cushy seats and promptly closed our eyes. But it was all too good to be true.

Hey, you're in my seat. Someone was poking my shoulder and I looked up to see a ballooning black gown filled by an Egyptian woman who was large enough to fill both seats. She started shoving plastic shopping bags under my legs.

What do you mean? I asked. *These are our seats.*

No, she hissed and showed me her ticket.

My friend and I tumbled out of our seats and off the bus – it was full. Another bus was supposed to arrive in a half hour so while my friend went across the lot to get a couple of glasses of tea, I stormed into the bus office to buy reserved places for the next bus.

Impossible, they said.

No, it is possible. Sell me two tickets, I squawked.

I think they sold me the tickets just to shut me up. I walked back to the centre of the lot proudly clutching two tickets for reserved seats to Cairo, or so I thought. In the next few moments I discovered otherwise.

As my friend walked out of the café with two glasses of tea on a tray, a windowless bus rumbled into the lot. People converged on the doors like vultures and mothers shoved their kids, along with plastic shopping bags and aluminium pots, through the windows. I yelled to my friend to watch our packs, so he dropped the tray and ran over as I jumped through a window – and belly-flopped right onto the laps of a couple of soldiers. It was too late. The bus was full before it had even stopped.

My friend and I stood over the engine at the back for seven hours. Except for the man who puked on my foot, all the Egyptians around us were friendly. They kept smiling and saying *Welcome in Egypt.*

The Preparation for Life Eternal

It was death, of course, that prompted the construction of the Egyptian pyramids but the incredible amount of resources, effort and time that went into them was indicative of many aspects of life in those days. The tombs served a variety of purposes, not the least of which was the final resting place of the owner and a repository for his worldly possessions.

The size and grandeur of the tomb was designed to enhance the owner's greatness in the eyes of his people during his life but it was also a place of worship for them after his death.

The pyramids were also a symbol of life and death, of life over death and of life after death, serving to preserve the pharaoh in the memory of his people and to ensure his continued existence in the afterlife. It was not a fear of death, or even an obsession with it that guided them, it was rather a belief in life eternal and the desire to be one with the gods that took the Egyptians to such lengths.

The pyramid was seen as an indestructible sanctum for the preservation of the pharaoh's *ka*. This spirit, or life-force from the gods, was the 'double' of a living person but gained its own identity with the death of that person. The pharaoh's *ka* would either continue to exist in his tomb, hence the need for all his belongings, or would journey off to join the gods. The survival of the *ka*, however, depended on the continued existence of the body so the process of mummification developed alongside the technology of tomb building.

In earlier times the dead were buried in shallow graves on the edge of the desert and covered with sand. Due to the dry atmosphere and hot sand this often caused the bodies to dehydrate before the tissues decomposed. As the ancient Egyptians changed their burial rituals and introduced coffins, the technique of mummification was developed to preserve artificially the dead bodies of those who could afford the process, as well as an incredible number of sacred birds, reptiles and animals.

For humans the mummification process took 70 days. The most important aspect was the removal of the vital organs and the drying of the body with a dehydrating agent called natron (hydrated sodium carbonate). The actual wrapping of the body in bandages played no role in the preservation of the corpse.

The main stages were:

The extraction of the brain, which was broken up and removed through the nose.

The removal of the viscera (except for the heart and kidneys) through an incision in the lower left abdomen. The intestines, stomach, liver and lungs were dehydrated with natron, treated with resin and stored separately in canopic jars.

The body was sterilised and the internal cavities were packed with natron and fragrant resins.

The body then underwent the main preservative treatment when it was covered with natron for about 35 days.

The temporary packing was then removed; the limbs were packed, under the skin, with clay; and the body cavities were permanently packed with linen soaked in resin, bags of cinnamon and myrrh, and sawdust.

The body was then annointed with fragrant oils and ointments, the abdominal incision was covered with an amulet of the *Eye of Horus*, and the skin was treated with molten resin.

Finally the body was wrapped, with pieces of jewellery and protective amulets being placed among the bandages.

Alexandria & the Mediterranean Coast

On the north coast of Egypt, west of where the Rosetta branch of the Nile leaves the delta and where the relentless desert meets the sparkling waters of the Mediterranean, there is the charming, somewhat jaded city of Alexandria, once the shining gem of the Hellenistic world. Also there are the Mediterranean resorts of Sidi Abdel Rahman and Marsa Matruh and the famous town of El Alamein, where the tide of WW II turned in favour of the Allies. But apart from Egypt's chief port and the overgrown resorts, this is a sparsely populated region and the road westward to the Libyan border passes along an almost deserted coast that greets the sea with craggy cliffs or smooth sandy beaches.

Under the Ptolemies, who inherited Egypt from Alexander, his city developed into a major port on the trade routes between Europe and Asia. The city's library once contained 500,000 volumes and its research institute, the *Mouseion*, produced some of the most scholarly works of the age. The Pharos lighthouse, built on the island just offshore, was recognised as one of the Seven Wonders of the World.

During the reign of Cleopatra, the last of her line, Alexandria rivalled Rome in everything but sheer force. After a brief fling with Julius Caesar, Cleopatra married her lover Marc Antony, who was high on the list to replace the assassinated

Alexandria

Having conquered Greece, the Macedonian general who became known as Alexander the Great set his sights on Egypt and the Persian Empire. After leading his victorious troops south to Memphis in 332 BC, the general later followed the Nile back to the Mediterranean, choosing a fishing village as the site of his own capital.

Alexander designed the city carefully for he envisioned it as a naval base, a great trading port and the political and cultural centre of his empire. Though he is buried there, Alexander never actually saw the gift he gave the classical world nor probably ever really imagined the greatness it would achieve. Architecturally it was as impressive as Rome or Athens and in the last three centuries BC it attracted some of the finest artists and scholars of the time, becoming a renowned centre of scientific, philosophical and literary thought and learning.

Alexander the Great

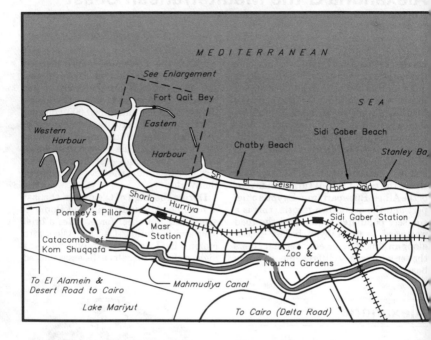

statesman as leader of the Roman Empire. But the union of the Egyptian queen and the Roman general did not go down at all well in Rome, especially with Caesar's nephew Octavian whose sister was already married to Antony.

In the ensuing power struggle the Egyptian fleet of Antony and Cleopatra was defeated at Actium by the superior forces of Octavian, who later renamed himself Augustus and Emperor of Rome. As Octavian led his forces towards Egypt Cleopatra, rather than face capture, put an asp to her breast and ended the Ptolemaic dynasty.

Alexandria was the most powerful and prosperous provincial capital of the Roman Empire and remained the capital of Egypt for the next 600 years under Roman and Byzantine control. Although the original great library had been burned when the Romans under Caesar, had first tried to conquer Alexandria, Cleopatra

had begun a new collection in a new building alongside the famed Serapeum. The city was still regarded as the most learned place on earth.

During the 4th century AD, however, Alexandria's populace was ravaged by civil war, famine and disease and even with the advent of Christianity and Alexandria's rise as a centre of the new religion, the city never regained its former glory. In fact at the end of the century the city's cultural importance was all but wiped out with the destruction, by the Christians, of the library and the *Mouseion*.

The conquering Muslims abandoned Alexandria in the 7th century and established their new capital further south on the Nile. By the time the French arrived in the 19th century Cairo had long since replaced Alexandria in all matters and the Mediterranean port was little more than a fishing village again.

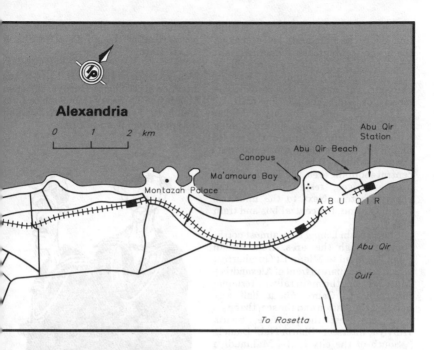

Napoleon's invasion, however, reinstated Alexandria's strategic importance and it underwent a revival during the reign of Mohammed Ali when a canal linking the city with the Nile, new docks and an arsenal were built. The stage was set for Alexandria's return as a vital Mediterranean trade centre and with the completion of the Suez Canal in 1869, its position as a major modern port was assured.

The city also took on quite a cosmopolitan air, attracting large numbers of Europeans, Turks and wealthy Egyptians. That era provided the inspiration for Lawrence Durrell's *The Alexandria Quartet*. During WW II the city was a post for the Allied forces and part of the pivotal Battle of El Alamein was planned by Allied intelligence from Alexandria's Hotel Cecil.

Today Alexandria, the largest port in Egypt and a major industrial centre, is also the country's unofficial summer capital. Every year the perfect Mediterranean climate, the city's relaxed atmosphere and its reputation for the best food in the country draws thousands of holiday makers, especially Cairenes, to its waterfront cafés and beautiful beaches.

More than 5000 ships call at Alexandria annually and the port handles about 80% of Egypt's import and export trade. With a population of more than three million, it is cleaner and less congested than Cairo and although it thrives, to a certain extent, on the romantic reputation of its past it is still a warm and welcoming city.

Orientation

Alexandria is a true waterfront city, nearly 20 km long from east to west and only two km wide. The corniche street, Sharia 26th July, sweeps from the tip of the promontory that was once Pharos

Island (before a causeway and landfill linked it to the mainland), and east along the beach to Montazah Palace. Alexandria's main port is on the western side of the promontory, while the Eastern Harbour, in front of the corniche, is mostly for fishing and pleasure craft.

The focal point of the city is Midan Saad Zaghloul, the large square running onto the waterfront. Around the square and in the streets to the south and west, towards Midan Tahrir, you'll find the central shopping area, the Tourist Office, airline offices, restaurants and the cheaper hotels. Next to the midan is Ramli Station, the central bus and tram depot.

Sharia Nabi Daniel runs almost north-south through this area, from Midan Saad Zaghloul to Midan El Gumhurriya which is the square in front of Alexandria's Masr Station, the main railway terminal for trains to Cairo. About half way between the station and the sea, the city's main east-west thoroughfare, Sharia Hurriya, intersects Sharia Nabi Daniel.

South of the city is the Mahmudiya Canal, linking Alexandria with the Nile, and to the south-west is Lake Mariyut.

Information
Tourist Office At the main Tourist Office, on Midan Saad Zaghloul, you can pick up a free copy of *Alexandria by Day & Night*. The information about restaurants and nightclubs is a bit sketchy, but it's generally not a bad publication. The staff there can give you some information about transport in and out of Alexandria. The office is open from 8.30 am to 6 pm; or 9 am to 4 pm during Ramadan. There are other branches at the train station and the port.

Passport Office If Alexandria is your first port of call in Egypt, remember you have to register your passport within seven days of arrival. It is not necessary to actually go through the process yourself if you're staying in a hotel as the management will register for you. If you do need the passport office though it's at 28 Sharia Talaat Harb.

Money American Express (tel 30084), has an office at 26 Sharia Hurriya. It's open Monday to Thursday from 9 am to 1 pm and 5 to 7 pm; and on Friday and Saturday from 9 am to 1 pm.

IN ALEXANDRIA, EGYPT'S MAIN SEA PORT AN ARRAY OF THINGS NAUTICAL — FISH MARTS BOAT BUILDERS AND SAILORS HOLDING HANDS.

Post & Telephone Office Post Restante is in the main post office on Sharia al-Sahafa, which is left off Sharia Saad Zaghloul as you head west from Sharia Nabi Daniel. It's open from 9 am to 3 pm. There are branch offices at Ramli Station, open from 8 am to 2 pm; and Masr Station, open from 8 am to 5 pm.

The telephone office in Ramli Station is open 24 hours a day.

Books & Bookstores The *Guide to Alexandrian Monuments* describes the prime attractions and details the city's history. It's available from the Graeco-Roman Museum and costs E£1.

The *Newcomers' Guide to Alexandria* was written by resident Americans to help new arrivals cope with the practicalities of life in the city. It's available at some bookstores and from the American Cultural Centre.

E M Forster's *Alexandria: A History & a Guide*, written during WW I, is still regarded as the best historical guide to the city. In a collection of short essays, Forster recreates the 2250 years of Alexandria's existence and then takes the visitor on a guided tour of the city's attractions as they were in 1922. An annotated edition of the book, recently published by Michael Haag Ltd, brings the guide up to date for the modern traveller.

Lawrence Durrell's book *The Alexandria Quartet* offers a fascinating insight into the cosmopolitan community of Alexandria prior to and during WW II.

The best available map of the city is published by Lehnert & Landrock.

You should be able to find these publications in Alexandria from English language bookstores such as *Library Mustakabal*, 32 Sharia Safia Zaghloul; *El Ahram Library*, Sharia Hurriya; or *Dar el Marif* on Midan Saad Zaghloul.

Consulates
Greece
   63 Sharia Iskandar el Akhbar (tel 38454)

Israel
   453 Sharia Hurriya, Rushi District (tel 40933)
Italy
   25 Midan Saad Zaghloul (tel 27292)
Sudan
   99 Gamal Abdel Nasser Road (tel 804258)
Turkey
   11 Sharia Selvago (tel 26879)
UK
   3 Sharia Mena, Rushi District (tel 47166); hours: 8 am to 1 pm, Monday to Friday.
USA
   110 Sharia Hurriya (tel 801911); hours: 9 am to noon, Monday to Friday.
West Germany
   5 Sharia Mena, Rushi District
Yugoslavia
   Sharia Pharaon (tel 806536)

Cultural Centres
The British Council, 9 Sharia Ptolemy (tel 800199)
The French Cultural Centre, 30 Sharia Nabi Daniel (tel 809870)
American Cultural Centre, 3 Sharia Pharaon, behind the consulate; hours: 8 am to 4 pm, Monday to Friday.

Police The Police and Tourist Police can be found in the same building as the Tourist Office on Midan Saad Zaghloul.

Sports Equipment Wet suits, diving equipment, windsurfers and other supplies for water sports, are available from *G Marina*, 193 Sharia Ahmed Shawki, Bulkeley.

Things to See
There is little left of ancient Alexandria. The modern metropolis is built over or amongst the scant ruins of the great classical city. A few sites, often discovered accidentally, have been excavated and preserved but for the most part it is simply an odd column or two or a gateway that marks the spot or possible location of legendary Ptolemaic or Roman edifices.

Much of the romance of Alexandria lies in what was, not what is and it's often a case of simply using your imagination. If you stand on the intersection of Sharia Nabi Daniel and Sharia Hurriya, for instance, you are also at the crossroads of the ancient city, then acclaimed as one of the most glorious places in the world. In those days Sharia Hurriya was known as the **Canopic Way** and it extended from the city's eastern *Gate of the Sun* to the western *Gate of the Moon* and, according to a 5th century bishop, 'a range of columns went from one end of it to the other'.

Just south of this intersection, on Sharia Nabi Daniel you will find what is believed to be the site of the renowned *Mouseion* and library, where the greatest philosophers, writers and scientists of ancient times exchanged ideas.

Nearby, the modern fairly uninteresting Mosque of Nabi Daniel is built on the site of Alexander's tomb and rumour has it that the great Macedonian still lies, wrapped in gold in his coffin of glass, somewhere in the unexplored cellars below.

The Graeco-Roman Museum

The 21 rooms of Alexandria's excellent Graeco-Roman museum contain about 40,000 valuable relics dating from as early as the 3rd century BC. The museum's own guide book gives little indication of where to find anything except for the rooms and *some* exhibits which are numbered. The collection includes many statues of *Serapis* – the fusion of *Osiris* and *Zeus* who was much revered in Alexandria, as well as busts and statues of various Greeks and Romans and a splendid black granite *Apis* bull. There are also mummies and sarcophagi, pottery, tiny terracotta figures, bas reliefs, jewellery, coins and tapestries.

The museum is at 5 Sharia al-Mathaf al-Romani which is the third street on your left as you head east along Sharia Hurriya from Sharia Nabi Daniel. It's open from 9 am to 4 pm daily, except Fridays when it closes at 11.30 am. Admission costs E£1, 50 pt for students.

The Roman Amphitheatre

The 13 white marble terraces of the only Roman theatre in Egypt were discovered only recently, when the foundations for a new apartment building were being dug. Arranged in a semi-circle around the arena, the terraces are excellently preserved and the site is still being excavated.

The amphitheatre is on Sharia Youseff, east of Nabi Daniel and south of Sharia Hurriya. It's open from 9 am to 4 pm and admission costs 50 pt, or 25 pt for students. It will also cost you E£10 to take photographs.

Pompey's Pillar

The massive, yet unimpressive 30 metre-high pink granite column which the Crusaders mistakenly credited to Pompey, because as usual they didn't know any better, rises out of the disappointing remains of the far more splendid and acclaimed **Serapeum**. What was once built up as an acropolis, topped by the Temple of *Serapis* and surrounded by subsidiary shrines and buildings, including Cleopatra's library, now merely features excavated subterranean galleries, the ruins of the **Temple of Isis**, a few sphinxes and Pompey's Pillar.

The latter, which has a circumference of nine metres, was erected amidst the Serapeum complex but at a much later date, around 297 AD, and for Diocletian not Pompey. In the final assault on the so-called 'pagan' intellectuals of Alexandria, in about 391 AD, the Christians destroyed the Serapeum and the Library leaving only Diocletian's monument.

To get to the pillar and the ruins of the Serapeum, which are to the south-west of the city near the Mahmudiya Canal you take bus No 209 from Midan Saad Zaghloul. The site is open from 9 am to 4 pm and admission costs E£1, or 50 pt for students. This ticket also admits you to the nearby Roman catacombs.

Catacombs of Kom el Shuqqafa

The largest known Roman burial site in Egypt, these catacombs are comprised of three tiers of tombs and chambers cut into the rock to a depth of about 35 metres. They were constructed in the 2nd century AD and it's believed they began as a family crypt but were eventually expanded to accommodate more than 300 corpses.

The eerie nature of the catacombs, there is even a banquet hall where grieving relatives paid their last respects with a funeral feast, is accentuated by the weird blend of Egyptian and Roman features in the sculptures and reliefs.

They were discovered accidentally in 1900, when a donkey cart fell through a part of the roof, and have been excavated although the bottom level is usually flooded and inaccessible.

Kom el Shuqqafa is about 10 minutes walk south of Pompey's Pillar or you can take bus No 209 from Midan Saad Zaghloul. The catacombs are open from 9 am to 4 pm and admission costs 50 pt, or 25 pt for students, or you can use the Pompey's Pillar ticket.

Fort Qait Bey

Built on the foundations of the Pharos lighthouse, one of the acclaimed wonders of the ancient world, this 15th century medieval fort guards the entrance to the Eastern Harbour.

The Pharos, Alexandria's original sentinel, reportedly stood 150 metres high, had 300 rooms in the square lower storey and a double spiral staircase leading up through the octagonal-shaped 2nd storey and the circular 3rd storey to the lantern room, which was topped by a statue of Poseidon. It was built on what was then, before the construction of the causeway dividing the two harbours, the island of Pharos during the reign of Ptolemy Philadelphus in about 279 BC.

It is not known exactly what reflected the firelight out to sea, to guide and warn approaching ships, but writings of the time suggest it was a mysterious mirror or even a lens through which the Pharos keeper could even detect ships not seen by the naked eye. If the scientists of ancient Alexandria had discovered the lens then its secret was lost when the two upper storeys were wrecked by a greedy Egyptian caliph. Legend has it that the Byzantine Emperor could not attack Alexandria because of the magic light, so he instructed his agents in the city to spread rumours that the Pharos sat on top of the treasure of Alexander the Great. Before the Alexandrians could do anything to stop him, the caliph had demolished the top half of the lighthouse, sending the 'magic mirror' into the sea.

Although several Muslim leaders attempted its restoration, the Pharos was eventually completely destroyed by an earthquake in the 14th century and left to ruin.

In about 1480 the Mameluke Sultan Qait Bey fortified the peninsula, using the foundations and debris of the Pharos to build his fort, incorporating a castle and mosque within the walls. Mohammed Ali modernised the fort's defences in the 19th century but the minaret and castle were severely damaged by the British bombardment in 1882.

Today, the three floors of the fort house a small naval museum with model ships, paintings and recreations of historic naval scenes. The views of the city from the fort are great. Admission costs 50 pt and to get to Fort Qait Bey and the nearby aquarium, take tram No 15 from Sharia Ramli. To take photographs costs E£10.

Institute of Oceanography

This poor excuse for a marine life museum and aquarium is along the causeway to Fort Qait Bey. The institute has a large variety of stuffed and lacquered fish as well as a few live specimens. A whale skeleton, sponges and coral are also on display. It's open from 9 am to 2 pm and admission costs E£1, or 50 pt for students.

Ras el Tin Palace
The palace buildings, on the western side of the peninsula, are closed to the public but the surrounding gardens are open. Up until 1952 Ras el Tin, which was built by Mohammed Ali, belonged to King Farouk. The 300 rooms of the palace have been kept as they were in the '50s and are used for state guests and other VIPs.

The Mosque of Abu el Abbas Mursi
Dominating the main square on Sharia Tatwig, about one km south of the fort, this is one of the best examples of Islamic architecture in Alexandria. The mosque,

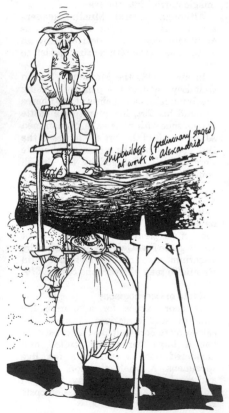

Shipbuilders (preliminary stages) at work in Alexandria

with its four domes and high minarets, was built by Algerians in 1767 over the tomb of a 13th century Muslim saint. It's worth visiting but don't enter during official prayer times. Tram No 15 stops nearby.

The Synagogue
Built just over 100 years ago, this last vestige of what was once a thriving Jewish community now serves only about 70 people. Before the wars with Israel there were about 15,000 Alexandrian Jews who could trace their ancestry back to the founding of the city by Alexander the Great. The synagogue, a fabulous Italian-built structure with pink marble pillars, and the Jewish Community of Alexandria (tel 26189), is at 69 Sharia Nabi Daniel. It's open from 8 to 10 am on Saturdays and from 10 am to 1 pm on other days.

Fine Arts Museum
A limited but interesting collection of modern Egyptian art, and Alexandria's public library, are housed in this museum east of Masr Station. It's on Sharia Mahmoud Bey Salama, which runs along the southern side of the railway tracks, and is open daily, except Friday, from 8 am to 2 pm; on Wednesdays it's also open from 7 to 9 pm. Admission is free.

The Bazaar
The long, mysterious passageways of Alexandria's bazaar, near Midan Manesha, wind through crowded arcades and by colourful stands of jewellery and household items. It's quite interesting and doesn't have the tourist trappings and traps of Cairo's Khan el Khalili.

The Zoo
The surprisingly clean Alexandria zoo, on a small hill surrounded by the gardens of Nouzha and Antoniadis, is a pleasant place to spend a couple of hours. It's about 30 minutes walk from Midan Saad Zaghloul and has a large outdoor café which offers light meals and refreshments.

Al Montazah Palace

The one-time summer residence of the royal family, prior to the 1952 revolution and King Farouk's abdication, Al Montazah Palace is at the eastern end of the corniche. The palace was built by Khedive Abbas II, as was the adjacent Salamlek Hotel which he designed in the style of a chalet to please his Austrian mistress.

The magnificent gardens and groves and the semi-private beach make this an ideal place to spend a relaxing day, although the palace and its museum are apparently no longer open to the public. The grounds, which once featured a menagerie of lions, tigers and bears, now includes the rather tasteless but high class Palestine Hotel, which is a little west of the Salamlek.

Admission to the palace grounds costs 75 pt, or E£1 on holidays, Sundays and Mondays; and 50 pt for students. Bus Nos 120, 220 or 320 from anywhere along the Corniche will get you there.

The Beaches

There are a number of public or semi-private beaches along Alexandria's waterfront, although most of the ones between the Eastern Harbour and Al Montazah are usually crowded and grubby. The best of these include **Sidi Gaber, Mandarra** and **Al Montazah**. At most places you can rent chairs and umbrellas for about E£1 per day.

Ma'amoura Beach, about one km east of Montazah Palace, is considered to be one of the best and even has a few small waves rolling in. You can get there on bus No 220.

The beaches at **Agami** and **Hanoville**, about 17 km west of central Alexandria, are the best though, as they're cleaner and less crowded. Bus Nos 500 and 600 go to both beaches.

ABU QIR

This coastal town, 24 km east of Alexandria, is renowned these days for its excellent seafood restaurants and is important, historically, for two major 18th century battles between the French and English.

During the Battle of the Nile in 1798, Nelson surprised and destroyed the French fleet in the bay at Abu Qir and although Napoleon still controlled Egypt his contact with France by sea was effectively severed. In 1799 the British landed 15,000 Turkish soldiers at Abu Qir but the French force of 10,000 men, mostly cavalry led personally by Napoleon, forced the Turks back into the sea, drowning at least 5000 of them.

On Ma'amoura Bay, near Abu Qir, is the site of ancient **Canopus** which was famous, in Greek legend at least, long before the founding of Alexandria. The settlement, at the end of the limestone ridge which extends from the Libyan Desert, overlooked the *Canopic* mouth of the Nile (which has long since dried up), and was for a time a noted religious centre. Herodotus, in 450 BC, claimed to have seen a temple to Hercules and was informed that Paris and Helen had sought refuge at Canopus during their escape to Troy. Another Greek legend claims the district was named after a pilot of Menelaus' fleet who died there by the Nile on the Greeks' return journey from the Trojan war. Egyptian mythology, however, claims *Canopus* was a god whose body was an earthenware jar!

There are plenty of buses from central Alexandria to Abu Qir every day. It's best to go during the week to avoid the crowds of Alexandrians who flock there on the weekends. If you're into seafood this is definitely the place to go. (See the Places to Eat section following).

Places to Stay - bottom end

The *Hotel Piccadilly* (tel 34802) is on the 8th floor, 11 Sharia Hurriya, three blocks north of Masr Station. Rooms cost E£5 for a single or E£12 for a large double with bath. Some rooms have balconies and breakfast is included.

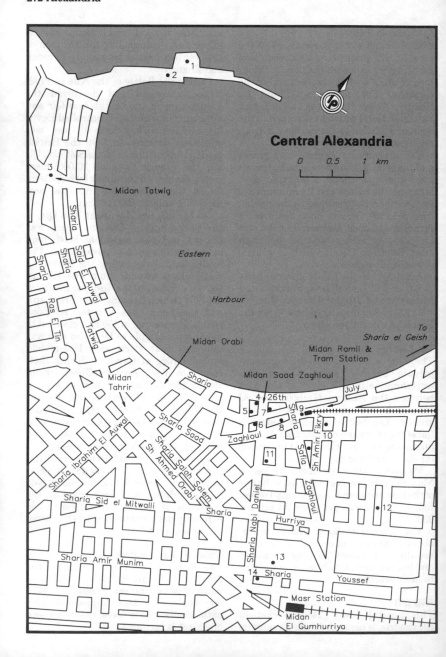

Central Alexandria

0   0.5   1   km

Midan Tatwig

Eastern

Harbour

To
Sharia el Geish

Midan Orabi

Midan Ramli &
Tram Station

Midan Saad Zaghloul

Midan
Tahrir

Sharia

26th

July

Sh Amin Fikry

Zaghloul

Sharia Saad

Sharia Salah Salem

Sh Ahmed Orabi

Sharia Ibrahim El Auwal

Sharia Sid el Mitwalli

Sharia

Zaghloul

Safia

Hurriya

Sharia Nabi Daniel

Sharia Amir Munim

Youssef

Masr Station

Midan
El Gumhurriya

```
 1  Fort Qait Bey
 2  Aquarium
 3  Mosque of Abu el Abbas Mursi
 4  Cecil Hotel
 5  Hotel Acropole
 6  Tourist Office
 7  Buses to Cairo
 8  Metro Hotel
 9  Post and Telephone Office
10  Hotel Ailema / Hyde Park House
11  The Synagogue
12  Graeco-Roman Museum
13  Roman Amphitheatre
14  Bus Station
```

The *Youth Hostel* (tel 75459), 32 Sharia el Geish (Sharia Port Said) costs 80 pt for members or E£1 for non-members. To get there, take tram No 2 from Ramli Station to Chatby Beach. It's open from 7 to 10 am and 2 to 11 pm.

The *Hotel Acropole* (tel 805980), 4th floor, 1 Sharia Gamal al Din Yassin, is one of the best deals in Alexandria. It's clean, pleasant and centrally located, one block west of Sharia Saad Zaghloul. Some rooms have great views of the Mediterranean. It costs E£2.50 to E£4 for a single room; E£7 for a double room; or E£5 for one person in a double room. Taxes and breakfast are included in these prices.

The *Hotel Ailema*, 7th floor, 21 Sharia Amin Fikry just south of Ramli station, is associated with the Hotel des Roses and Pension Oxford in Cairo. The rooms and bathrooms are clean and some have views of the sea. A single room costs E£4 to E£6.65; a double costs E£5.75 to E£9.60; or singles/doubles, with bath, cost E£7.50/10.80. There's a television room and restaurant and it's quite a decent place for the price.

The *Hyde Park House* (tel 35666) is one flight up from the Ailema. The rooms are clean, but a bit dark. Singles/doubles, without bathrooms are E£4.10/7.50; doubles with bath are E£9.50. A

continental breakfast with egg costs E£1.10.

The *Hotel Leroy* (tel 809099), 25 Talaat Harb, is opposite the Passport Office on the top floor of an office building. Most of the rooms are clean and have balconies. Singles/doubles cost E£8.50/16.50 for half-board; or E£4.25/8.90 just for bed and breakfast.

The *New Capri Hotel*, is on 8th floor, 23 Sharia El Mina el Sharkiya. Singles, with/without bath, cost E£7.80/12; and doubles cost from E£11 to E£12.20. Prices include breakfast and taxes.

Places to Stay – middle

The *Admiral Hotel* (tel 32388 & 31493), 24 Sharia Amin Fikry, is just off Midan Ramli. The rooms are clean, but the bathrooms are a bit grimy. Singles with/without bathrooms cost E£10.50/8.30; doubles with/without are E£15/13.50. All prices include breakfast.

The *Salamlek Hotel*, in the grounds of the Montazah Palace, once served as the guest palace for King Farouk's visitors but these days you don't have to be a VIP to get in. Singles cost E£13 and doubles are E£14. The place has air-con, though being so close to the beach and sea breezes, it's really not necessary.

The *Agami Palace Hotel* at Agami Beach, 17 km west of Alexandria, has small, dark rooms that cost E£7 for a single and E£11 for a double.

The *Hanoville Hotel*, at Hanoville Beach, is a little further west of and double the price of the Agami Palace. It's also a bit nicer.

Places to Stay – top end

The *Cecil Hotel* (tel 807055), which overlooks Midan Saad Zaghloul, is a grand and elegant place and something of an institution in Alexandria. Its history is one of romance and intrigue, its guests over the years have included Somerset Maugham, Lawrence Durrell and Winston Churchill and during WW II it was the headquarters of the British Secret

Service. These days a double costs E£22.50, singles are E£18 and many rooms have splendid views of the Eastern Harbour. There's a charming tea lounge, a bar and a casino and you can get breakfast, lunch and dinner for around E£2.20, E£6.60 and E£8.10. Not included are the 17% service charge and tax.

The *Metro Hotel* (tel 4921465), 52 Sharia Saad Zaghloul, is a deluxe place where some rooms have fantastic views and all have telephones and TVs. Doubles/ singles with bath cost E£24/20; or without bath are E£21/16. Meals are served downstairs in the hotel restaurant and cost E£2 for breakfast; E£5.25 for lunch; and E£5.75 for dinner. None of these prices include the 17% tax and service charge.

Places to Eat

The *Santa Lucia*, 40 Sharia Saad Zaghloul, is one of Alexandria's best restaurants. A full seafood meal costs under E£10.

The *East Air Port Piche Restaurant*, on the Corniche near the Eastern Harbour Yacht Club, has sidewalk tables and an upstairs dining room all with good views of the boats and the sea. Their fish costs E£7 per kg including salad and bread and their shrimp costs E£16 per kg.

Fuul Mohammed Ahmed, is one block south of Midan Saad Zaghloul and a street east of Sharia Nabi Daniel and although the sign is in Arabic it's easy to find. All the food is typically Egyptian and very cheap; meals cost piastres, not pounds. *Fuul* dishes come with a green salad, tahina and hummus with olive oil. Try their desserts, especially the *mahalabiya* and creme caramel. They're open from 6 am to midnight.

Al-Ekhlaas, 49 Sharia Safia Zaghloul, serves very good Egyptian food. Kebab and kufta cost about E£4; there's a variety of meat dishes with oriental rice and salad for E£6; and their tahina is excellent. They serve a full dinner special for four people for E£18.

The Greek restaurant *Elite*, 43 Sharia Safia Zaghloul next to the Cinema Metro, has class and culture at reasonable prices. The walls are decorated with prints by Chagall, Picasso and Toulouse-Lautrec and originals by famous Egyptian artists such as Seif Wanly and Ahmed Moustafa. The restaurant is popular with artists, performers and journalists and the menu includes a long list of Greek, French and Egyptian dishes ranging in price from E£4 to E£12. They serve pizza, espresso and moussaka and feature a special dessert called the *Rock and Roll*, which is ice cream blended with jelly and slices of banana and orange, topped with whipped cream.

Cafeteria Asteria, on Sharia Safia Zaghloul opposite the Elite, serves good light meals, including small tasty pizzas for E£2. Sandwiches cost 46 pt, salads are 40 pt and they also serve ice cream, espresso and hot chocolate.

Lourantos, 44 Sharia Safia Zaghloul serves kufta, roast beef, kibda and chicken sandwiches for 30 pt and full meals for E£6.

The *Sandwich Shop* opposite the Hotel Piccadilly in Sharia Hurriya has good sandwiches for 25 pt.

Pastroudis Cafe, 39 Sharia Hurriya, is the place to go to watch the passing parade while drinking Turkish coffee or fresh lemonade.

Chez Gaby, 22 Sharia Hurriya, is open from 8 pm to midnight. The menu includes pizza, lamb cutlets, sauteed scampi and grilled fish with prices ranging from E£2 to E£5.

Restaurant Denis at 1 Sharia Ibn Basaam, three blocks east of Ramli Station, serves fresh seafood by weight. Prices range from E£3 to E£7 for various types of fish, E£30 a kg for shrimp, E£12 a kg for fish, 50 pt for salad.

Taverna Diamantakis, opposite the Ramli Station tram stop, serves fried or grilled fish, squid or shellfish and offer a fairly good Greek salad.

La Pizzeria, 14 Sharia Hurriya, has

pizza and other cheap dishes, including spaghetti for E£1.60; and steak with chips and fresh vegetables for E£3.

The *San Giovanni Restaurant*, jutting out over the sea at 205 Sharia El Geish, Stanley Beach, is one of the best eating places in Alexandria. A full seafood meal costs about E£10. The restaurant is open from 1.30 to 4 pm and 8.30 to 11 pm and features an after-dinner nightclub with live music.

The *Delta Hotel* (tel 29820), 14 Sharia Champollion, Mazarita, has excellent reasonably priced French-style food. Coquille St Jacques costs E£3.50, fish soup is E£2.50, steak with bernaise sauce is E£6.50 and shrimp provencal costs E£10. The Delta is open from noon to 4 pm and from 7.30 to 11.00 pm.

The *Tikka Grill*, on the waterfront near the Abu el Abbas Mosque, has great views. Meals cost from E£5 to E£10 and you can pile your plate up with extras from the salad bar.

Alexander's Restaurant (tel 866111), in the Ramada Renaissance Hotel, 544 Sharia El Geish, Sidi Bishr, is a comparatively expensive but elegant restaurant. Their specialties include smoked salmon, crab and cheese souffle, and grilled fish kebab. Prices range from E£4 to E£15.

El Bardy Coffeeshop, in the same hotel, is a sort of a garden café and is much cheaper than Alexander's. The menu includes milkshakes, cannelloni, tahina and hamburgers and prices for a meal range from E£2 to E£10.

The *New China Restaurant* in the Hotel Corail, 802 Sharia El Geish, Mandarra Bay, (near Al Montazah Palace) serves Chinese food and has splendid views of the Mediterranean. Dinner costs less than E£10 and the restaurant is open from noon to 4 pm and 6 to 11 pm.

Wimpys . . . well, it speaks for itself. There are three in Alexandria – in Montazah, Ma'amoura and Roushdy.

The *Xephyrion* in Abu Qir is quite probably one of the best restaurants in Egypt. Its location alone warrants that honour. Xephyrion is Greek for 'breeze of the sea' and this restaurant, on a magnificent terrace overlooking the ocean with waves breaking below, certainly has that. The menu features Greek-style fish, giant shrimp, shrimp with lemon and oil, fried squid and beer or wine. To order you go to the cashier, choose the fish yourself and tell them how you want it cooked. A tremendous meal costs under E£10, plus a 10% service charge.

Abu Qir Coffeeshop (tel 867850), in the Landmark Hotel, Midan San Stefano, serves meals of ravioli, seafood, chicken and other dishes for about E£1.50 to E£4.50. They are open 24 hours a day.

Ras El Tin Restaurant, also in the Landmark Hotel, is managed by Britons and has international food at fair prices. A plate of hummus, tahina, baba ghanough, olives and pickles goes for about E£3. A complete dinner costs just under E£9.

Entertainment

Most of Alexandria's major hotels have nightclubs and discos, and live music is a feature of the many clubs along the corniche. The most popular include the *Crazy Horse* and the small Greek venue the *Athineos*.

If you don't have anything better to do with your money, there are casinos in the Cecil and Palestine hotels.

For one week every September, Alexandria hosts an International Film Festival of uncensored films from at least 10 countries. The Tourist Office will have the latest details.

Getting There

Air Alexandria's international airport is about seven km from the city centre. A number of airlines fly in and out of Alexandria, mostly connecting Egypt with destinations in north Africa and southern Europe. The one-way flight between Alexandria and Morocco, for instance, costs E£100 with Tunis Air or Royal Air Maroc. The airport also now receives direct charter flights from Germany and Greece.

Train Cairo-bound trains leave Alexandria at least hourly, nearly 24 hours a day, from Masr Station. The trip, via Damanhur and Tanta, takes about three hours and costs E£5.05 in 1st class (E£3.50 for students), or 65 pt in 3rd class.

The train from Alexandria to Marsa Matruh, which is as far west along the coast as foreigners are permitted to travel, takes an uncomfortably long eight hours. The bus service on this route is faster and more comfortable.

Bus Two main bus companies, Delta Bus and the Golden Rocket Deluxe Bus Service, operate services between Alexandria and Cairo. On average there are two buses, in each direction, every half hour between 5.30 am and 8.30 pm. Buses for Cairo leave from Midan Saad Zaghloul and the ticket offices are opposite the Cecil Hotel.

Delta buses travel on both the desert and delta roads to Cairo, so if you have a preference you need to say so when buying your ticket. The trip takes about 3½ hours and costs from E£2.75 to E£4.25 depending on the route, and E£6 if you wish to continue to Cairo airport.

The Golden Rocket Deluxe Bus Service definitely merits five stars; they even serve light refreshments on board during the three hour trip. Tickets cost E£6, or E£10 if you want to go to the Cairo airport.

There are several daily buses between Alexandria and Marsa Matruh that stop in El Alamein and Sidi Abdel Rahman. The trip takes about four hours, costs E£3.50 and buses depart hourly between 8 am and 1 pm.

Buses to Rosetta/Rashid leave every hour from Masr Station. Some are faster than others so if you're in a hurry ask for the *otobis sareeha*, the fast bus.

Buses to Damietta depart at 8 am, noon and 3.30 pm from Midan Saad Zaghloul. The trip takes four hours and costs E£4.

Service Taxi The taxi depot is opposite Masr Station and it costs about E£4 to Cairo and the same to Marsa Matruh. Service taxis to Damietta leave from Midan Tahrir and also cost E£4.

Boat There are regular ferry services between Alexandria and Iraklion, Piraeus, Venice (fares following) and other destinations around the Mediterranean. The ferries usually offer a choice of two or three-berth cabins, either inside or outside and with or without private showers and toilets. The ticket prices vary according to the cabin you choose and the time of year. There are also special youth and student fares and Eurail Pass holders are entitled to a 30% discount.

The approximate fares given here are in US dollars and are representative of *Adriatica's* cheapest and most expensive berths.

From Alexandria to Iraklion, the fares range from $95 to $195 in the low season; and from $105 to $215 in the high season.

To Piraeus the low season fares range from $135 to $260; and the high season fares from $150 to $290.

To Venice it costs from $240 to $495 in the low season; and from $265 to $550 in the high season.

You must confirm your reservation at least 48 hours in advance at the shipping agencies in Cairo or Alexandria and report to the maritime station at least three hours before the ship's departure.

Adriatica's shipping agents in Alexandria are De Castro & Co (tel 35770), 33 Sharia Salah Salem; and Menatours, (tel 809676), Midan Saad Zaghloul. Menatours also represent other shipping lines and have an office in Cairo, at 14 Sharia Talaat Harb.

The Tourist Office can provide information on other shipping lines and destinations.

Getting Around

Most of Alexandria's municipal trams and buses leave from Ramli Station and services operate between 5.30 am and 1 am. Some services also leave from Midan Orabi.

The most important routes are serviced by the following buses: Nos 120, 220 and 320 – up and down the corniche as far as Montazah Palace; No 129 – between Midan Orabi, Montazah Palace and Abu Qir; No 500 – between Ramli Station, Midan Orabi and Agami; and No 17 – between Midan Saad Zaghloul and Agami.

Tram No 15 runs between Ramli Station and Fort Qait Bey; and No 16 runs between Midan Orabi and Pompey's Pillar.

RASHID/ROSETTA

The ancient city of Rosetta, or modern-day Rashid, is 65 km east of Alexandria where the western, Rosetta, branch of the Nile leaves the coastal delta and joins the Mediterranean. Founded in the 9th century, Rosetta is most famous for an inscribed stone that was unearthed by Napoleon's soldiers in 1799. Dubbed the *Rosetta Stone* the basalt slab, which dates to the reign of Ptolemy V (about 196 BC), was carved with inscription in Egyptian hieroglyphs and Greek. The demotic characters, a simplified form of ancient Egyptian hieroglyphs used by the ordinary literate class not the priesthood, enabled the Frenchman Champollion to finally decipher the ancient pharaonic language.

Rosetta prospered as one of the most important ports in Egypt when Alexandria's fortunes declined between the 8th and 19th centuries. It reached its height in the 17th and 18th centuries but as modern Alexandria began to emerge from its long hibernation Rosetta became a virtual backwater.

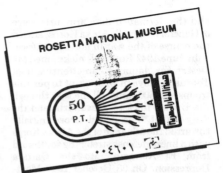

These days Rashid has a certain charm, though its beautiful palm groves tend to shelter a city besmirched with alleyways of garbage and manure. The main attraction is its fine old buildings with colourful facades and superbly intricate *mashrabiyya* screens. The best of these include **Bait Qili** which has been turned into an interesting museum, **Al Amaciali** and the **House of Ali al Fatairi**. The **Mosque of Zaghloul** at the bottom of the main street was founded in 1600 AD and the **Mosque of Mohammed al Abbas**, near the Nile, was built in 1809.

Getting There

Although buses and trains operate between Alexandria and Rashid, the easiest way to get there is by car, either a hire car or service taxi. The latter should cost about E£3.

You can catch a train from Sidi Gaber station in Alexandria to Ma'amoura, just east of Montazah Palace, and then another train from there to Rashid.

Buses leave Alexandria every hour for Rashid, from the Midan Orabi station.

EL ALAMEIN

The small coastal village of El Alamein, 106 km west of Alexandria, is most famous as the scene of a decisive Allied victory over the Axis powers during WW II. The massive battle of El Alamein, between the Allied tank divisions under the command of Field Marshall Montgomery and the German-Italian armoured force of General Rommel's Afrika Korps, altered the course of the war in northern Africa.

In June 1942 Rommel, nicknamed *the Desert Fox*, launched an offensive from Tobruk in Libya in an attempt to push his troops and 500 tanks all the way through the British lines to Alexandria and the Suez Canal. The Allied forces initially thwarted the advance of the Afrika Korps with a line of defense stretching southward from El Alamein into the Qattara Depression. On 23 October 1942 Montgomery's 8th Army swooped down from Alexandria with 1000 tanks and within two weeks had routed the German and Italian forces, driving Rommel and what was left of his Afrika Korps back to Tunis.

More than 80,000 men were killed or wounded at El Alamein and the subsequent battles for control of northern Africa. The thousands of graves in the town's three huge war cemeteries, while being the area's main tourist attraction, are also a bleak and moving reminder of the absolute futility of war.

El Alamein today is a busy construction area. An oil pipeline and new port facilities for shipping Egypt's oil from throughout the country are being built and plans are on the drawing board for a canal across the Qattara Depression from the Nile. The idea of the Qattara Basin Project is to open up new areas of cultivable land to accommodate Egypt's expanding population. Construction of the canal, however, is being delayed by the many Western Desert mine fields left over from WW II. These unexploded mines also present a hazard to wandering travellers, so stick to the beaten tracks.

Things to See

The **War Museum**, on the west side of town, features detailed displays of the El Alamein battles, profiles on Rommel and Montgomery, and various tanks, heavy artillery and other implements of destruction. One section of the museum is dedicated to Egypt's victories in the 1973

war with Israel and the smashing of the Bar Lev line. The museum is open from 9 am to 1 pm and admission costs 50 pt.

The **British Military Cemetery**, on the east side of town, is a haunting, almost beautiful place where more than 7000 tombstones cover a slope overlooking the desert battlefield of El Alamein. The plaques on the walls of the entrance building honour the soldiers of the units from Great Britain, Australia, New Zealand, France, Greece, South Africa, east and west Africa, Malaysia and India that fought for the Allied cause. The cemetery is maintained by the War Graves Commission and admission is free.

The **Italian War Memorial** is about six km west of El Alamein and the **German War Memorial** is another four km, on a hill overlooking the Mediterranean. They are both as chillingly interesting as the Allied cemetery.

Places to Stay & Eat

The *El Alamein Rest House* has singles for E£5 and doubles for E£6.50. Meals at the Rest House's restaurant cost from E£3 to E£4 and, quoting the menu, you can get things like 'spagetti with sauce of sea fruits, fried of grilled shrimps, gelly with fruits and home made cacke'. There is also a cafeteria at the bus stop.

Getting There

To get to El Alamein you can take a train, service taxi or bus from Alexandria's Masr Station or Midan Saad Zaghloul (refer to the Alexandria Getting There section). The train takes twice as long as a bus or taxi and the El Alamein station is inconveniently located across the desert from the town. Getting off the Marsa Matruh bound bus in El Alamein should be no problem as most of the coastal buses from Alexandria and Cairo stop at the Rest House but getting on it in the first place is another thing altogether as they're nearly always full. A service taxi is probably the best option though you may have to pay the full fare to Marsa Matruh.

Whichever alternative you choose it will only cost about E£3 or E£4. Hitching may be possible as the volume of traffic along the coast road is increasing.

From Cairo the buses leave from next to the telephone office on Midan Tahrir and service taxis leave from Ramses station and from in front of the Nile Hilton.

SIDI ABDEL RAHMAN

The fine, white sandy beach and the sparkling blue and green of the Mediterranean make this stunning little resort, 23 km west of El Alamein, one of the most beautiful stretches of coastline you're ever likely to visit.

There is also a small village, about three km inland, which is interesting for the Bedouins who occasionally congregate there. They belong to the Awlad Ali tribe who came into the region several hundred years ago from Libyan Cyrenaica and subdued the smaller, local tribes of the Morabiteen. There are now five main tribes sub-divided into clans each with several thousand members. The Egyptian government has been attempting to settle these nomads, so these days most of the Bedouin have forsaken their tents and now herd their sheep and goats from the immobility of government-built stone houses.

Apart from the spectacular beach, the Bedouin village and the expensive hotel and camping ground there is not much else to Sidi Abdel Rahman.

Places to Stay & Eat

The *Sidi Abd el Rahman Hotel*, a semi-deluxe place right on the beach, costs E£30/37.50 for singles/doubles, plus 17.5% taxes and an extra E£2.30 for breakfast. The seven-person villas attached to the hotel cost E£145 per day.

You can hire a tent at the hotel for E£13.25 for one person or E£16.50 for a two, plus 17.5% taxes and service charges. There are 23 tents, 12 of which are equipped for overnight stays.

The only place to eat in the area is the hotel's restaurant, where lunch costs E£8.10 and dinner E£9.95, so unless you plan to catch and cook your own fish it's a good idea to bring food and water with you.

Getting There

There are buses twice a day between Alexandria and Sidi Abdel Rahman. Tickets cost E£3.50 and the trip takes about three hours.

MARSA MATRUH

The large waterfront town of Marsa Matruh, built around a charming bay of clear Mediterranean waters and clean white sand beaches, is the Egyptian equivalent of the French Riviera. It's a relaxing place, a little less expensive than the other north coast resorts, and quite popular with holidaying Egyptians. Few foreign tourists seem to get this far west but if you have the time it's the perfect spot to take a break from the busy cities and ancient monuments.

There is a strong military presence in the area due to the towns' proximity to Libya and although it's probably not a good idea to go there when tensions with that country are on the rise it is quite safe and hassle free most of the time.

Information

There are really only two streets in Marsa Matruh that you need to know – the Corniche which runs right round the waterfront; and Sharia Alexandria which runs perpendicular to the Corniche, back to the hill behind the town.

The relatively new Tourist Office, on the ground floor of the governorate building on the corner of Sharia Alexandria and the Corniche, is open from 8 am to 2 pm daily, except Fridays when it's open from 4 to 8 pm. The staff are anxious to help the relatively few visitors they receive and can help make the necessary arrangements for visiting the coastline near Libya or the oasis of Siwa.

Most of the hotels are on the Corniche and the restaurants and shops are on or around Sharia Alexandria.

The Rommel Museum

Built into the caves that Rommel used as his headquarters, this museum details the exploits of the famous, or infamous, *Desert Fox* during his WW II campaigns in northern Africa.

The museum, which is east along the Corniche from Sharia Alexandria, is open daily except Fridays from 10 am to 4 pm in summer only. Although it's officially closed during winter you might be able to visit by making special arrangements with the Tourist Office.

A little east of the museum is **Rommel's Beach** which was supposedly where the German field marshall took time off from his tanks and troops to take a daily swim.

The Beaches

As well as the beautiful bay beaches of Marsa Matruh there are also several splendid and unspoilt beaches to the east and west of the town. Some of the more secluded beaches can only be reached by paddle board or surf kayak and these can be rented from a few of the hotels in town. Offshore there is also the wreck of a German submarine and supposedly, in the deeper waters off the eastern beaches there are sunken Roman galleys. Again you'll need a paddle board to get to them.

About 10 km west of Marsa Matruh is **Obayyid Beach**, which is a developing resort with overpriced tent accommodation (see Places to Stay).

The **Beach of Lovers**, *Shatit el Gharam*, a little way from town can only, but easily, be reached by paddleboard across the bay. The large rock formations at this beach are definitely worth seeing.

About 16 km from town, on the ocean

side of the bay, is **Cleopatra's Beach** and nearby, **Cleopatra's Bath**, where the great queen and her Roman lover Marc Antony supposedly fooled around.

In English *agiiba* means 'miraculous' or ' a miracle of nature' and **Agiiba Beach**, about 20 km west of Marsa Matruh, is just that. Accessible only by a path leading down from the clifftop, it is a small but spectacular beach. There is a café nearby where you can get light refreshments.

Places to Stay

The *Arous el Bahr Hotel*, or Bride of the Sea, is on the Corniche facing the water. Singles and doubles, with bath and breakfast, cost E£14 and most of the rooms have balconies overlooking the bay. The staff are extremely helpful, especially about arranging transportation. I must admit though, I was a little taken aback when one of the desk clerks told me that breakfast included 'eggs, bread, tea and shit'. Thinking I had misheard, I asked her again and she repeated 'eggs, bread, tea and shit'. I then asked her if she knew what shit was, and she replied 'Yes, it is *gibna*' (which means cheese). Through my own laughter I managed to explain her mistake, while her face turned various shades of red.

The waterfront *Hotel Beau Site* has received rave reviews even though it looks a bit rundown and weather-beaten. It costs E£12.35/16 for a single/double with bath; or E£9.30/12.35 for a single/double without. It is closed during winter.

The *Hotel des Roses*, which is run by a Greek family, has clean singles and doubles for E£5 and E£6.50; and breakfast for E£1.20. It is also closed during winter.

The *Matruh Hotel* (or Hamada Hotel) is a standard dusty dive on the main drag of town with no hot water or breakfast. Rooms cost a ridiculous E£10 a double, so stay there only as a last resort.

The *New Lido Hotel* is an OK but decrepit place which is also closed in the winter. Some rooms overlook the sea and

it costs E£3 a single or E£6 for a double.

The 60-room *Rommel House Hotel* is a clean place where singles cost E£13.70 and doubles are E£18.25, plus 14% taxes and service charges. All rooms have bathrooms, TVs and (in summer only) refrigerators; some have air-con and, for what it's worth, most are decorated with photo-posters of scantily clad Japanese girls. Breakfast costs E£1.20 and there's a cafeteria.

The *Hotel Rio*, near the centre of town, has singles for E£3.50 and doubles for E£5.60.

The *Hotel Ghazal* is a clean place which costs E£1.50 for a bed – and that's about all you get.

The recently renovated *Hotel Negresco*, behind the Sidi Alwan Mosque on the Corniche, also has a night club and disco. During summer full board costs E£42/60 for a single/double, plus 14% taxes and service; and in winter it costs E£15/20 for a single/double.

If you want to rough it a little the tents on the shore at Obayyid Beach, 10 km west of town, cost E£8 per person per night, including three meals and access to showers and toilets.

Places to Eat

The *Alexandria Tourist Restaurant* serves complete meals of fish, salad and rice for E£2.50; and great tahina for only 25 pt.

The *Restaurant Panayotis Greece* is opposite the Alexandria and according to the 'chef' everything is good. Try the scotalia which is a fantastic Greek salad. A meal of fish, bread and salad costs E£3.

The *Beau Site Restaurant* is part of the hotel and is fairly good but, like the hotel, is closed in winter.

The *Camona Restaurant* on Sharia Galaa serves a kilo of kebab and kofta for E£8 to E£10 – enough for a big meal for at least four people.

Getting There

Train There are several daily trains between Alexandria and Marsa Matruh, but it's a long and tedious trip. It costs about E£4 and can take anything up to eight hours.

Bus Buses to Marsa Matruh, from Alexandria's Midan Saad Zaghloul, cost about E£4 and take four or five hours. They depart hourly between 8 am and 1 pm.

From Cairo there is only one bus per day to Marsa Matruh and it usually leaves at 8 am from a small street on Midan Tahrir directly in front of the Nile Hilton. The Marsa Matruh bus stops under the trees opposite the Alexandria bus stops. You should buy your ticket at least one day in advance from the ticket office which is next to the telephone office on the east side of the Midan. The trip takes eight hours and costs E£10.

From Marsa Matruh there are two daily buses to Siwa Oasis, at 7 am and 3 pm; only the latter bus has air-con. The trip takes about eight hours and costs E£5. To visit Siwa Oasis you need a permit.

Service Taxi This is probably the most convenient way to get to get to Marsa Matruh, especially if you can get a group together. Service taxis frequently leave Alexandria from a stand in the park in front of Masr Station. They take about the same time as the buses and cost E£4.

If you're coming from Cairo the taxi goes via Alexandria, adding about five hours to the trip, and will probably cost about E£7. Taxis leave from Ramses station and from in front of the Nile Hilton.

Hitching It shouldn't be too difficult to get a lift from Alexandria to Marsa Matruh but bring plenty of water and be careful about your exposure to the sun.

Getting Around

Caretas, or donkey carts, are the most common form of transport around the streets of Marsa Matruh. Some are like little covered wagons with colourfully designed canvas covers. A ride around town should cost from 50 pt to 75 pt.

Private taxis can be hired for the day for E£10 to E£20 but you must negotiate and bargain aggressively.

During the summer there are regular bus services from town to Cleopatra, Obayyid and Agiiba beaches. They supposedly leave every 15 minutes from 8 am until sunset.

SIWA OASIS

The lush and productive Western Desert oasis of Siwa, famous throughout the country today for its dates and olives, is 300 km south-west of Marsa Matruh and about 550 km west of Cairo, near the Libyan border.

The original settlers, many centuries ago, were Berbers who were attracted to this island of green in a desolate sea of sand when they discovered several fresh water springs in the area. Although Islam and Arabic eventually reached this far into the desert, Siwa's solitary position has allowed the present-day, predominantly Berber-speaking inhabitants to preserve many of their ancient traditions and customs.

There is now a desert road into the Siwa area but visiting the oasis is still an adventure that very few modern travellers undertake. In fact Siwa's history has been one of such isolation that, apart from the desert caravans of ancient times or the occasional pilgrim who journeyed there to visit the famed Temple of *Amun*, very few outsiders have ever ventured this far into the unknown.

The most illustrious of Siwa's few visitors over the centuries was the young conqueror Alexander, who led a small party on an eight day trek through the desert in 331 BC to seek out the Oracle of the Temple of *Amun*. The temple, the well-preserved remains of which still stand to the east of Siwa, was dedicated to

Ammon, a ram-headed Libyan deity closely associated with Egypt's sun god *Amun* and the king of the Greek gods *Zeus*. Alexander's goal, and apparently he succeeded, was to seek confirmation that he was the son of *Zeus*, and also to uphold the traditional belief that, as the new pharaoh of Egypt, he was also the son of *Amun*.

Apart from a Greek traveller who visited in 160 AD, the people of Siwa did not see another European until 1792.

It takes about eight hours to get to Siwa Oasis from Marsa Matruh, which is quite an improvement on Alexander's journey from the coast, but there's enough red tape involved these days to make your trip just as difficult as his.

Permits

Because of its proximity to Libya you must have written permission from the military to visit the oasis. This procedure could take anything up to 10 days and, depending on the political situation with Libya at the time, permission may or may not be granted.

You must write a letter to the National Security Office, giving your name, passport number, address and reason for wanting to visit Siwa. You will also need to include two passport photos. You will then be given instructions on the next step of the procedure. Things are slowly changing in this area as the Egyptian government is trying to encourage tourists to visit Siwa, so it's probably best to check with the main Tourist Office in Cairo for the latest details. The National Security Office in Marsa Matruh is behind the post office and the Tourist Office in town can also help with arrangements.

Things to See

Siwa's greatest attraction is the oasis itself which boasts more than 200,000 palm trees, 50,000 olive trees and a great many fruit orchards. The vegetation is sustained by more than 300 fresh water springs and streams and the area attracts an amazing variety of bird life including quails and falcons.

On the hill of Aghurmi, to the east of the township of Siwa, are the ruins of the 26th Dynasty **Temple of Amun**. It was built sometime between 663 BC and 525 BC and although there's not much left, what there is has been well-preserved.

The **Gebel al-Mawta**, or Mount of the Dead, is an interesting site 15 km north of the town. There are several tombs in the area, many of which have not yet been excavated and explored. Most of the tombs date from Ptolemaic and Roman times and there seem to be pieces of mummies and mummy cloth scattered all over the place.

Places to Stay

Two hotels are being built to accommodate the gradually increasing number of visitors and camping is possible near the **Baths of Cleopatra**, one of Siwa's most spectacular springs, just outside the township.

Getting There

To reach Siwa, you can either go by bus or in a rented Land-Rover. The latter could cost as much as E£50 per day.

There are two daily buses to Siwa Oasis from Marsa Matruh, at 7 am and at 3 pm. The latter has air-con and the trip takes about eight hours and costs E£5. From Siwa to Marsa Matruh the buses leave at 7 am and 2 pm.

Sinai

A region of awesome and incredible beauty the Sinai has been a place of refuge, conflict and curiosity for thousands of years. Wedged between Africa and Asia its northern coast is bordered by the Mediterranean Sea and its southern peninsula is surrounded by the Red Sea gulfs of Aqaba and Suez. Row upon row of barren and jagged red-brown mountains fill the southern interior, surrounded by relentlessly dry yet colourful desert plains. From the palm-lined coast, dunes and swamps of the north to the white sand beaches and superb coral reefs of the Red Sea, the Sinai is full of contrasts.

In pharaonic times the Sinai's quarries provided enormous quantities of turquoise, gold and copper. Also due to its great strategic importance, the *Land of Turquoise* became the goal of empire builders and was the setting for countless wars.

The Sinai is also a land of miracles and holy places and has been traversed by some of the most famous and influential people in history. Elijah, Jacob and Abraham, the prophets of Judaism, Christianity and Islam, wandered through its hills and deserts. It was there that God first spoke to Moses from a burning bush and later, with the celebrated parting of the Red Sea, He delivered the Israelites from the Egyptian army.

'And Moses stretched out his hand over the sea; and the Lord caused the sea to go back .... And the children of Israel went into the midst of the sea upon the dry ground: and the waters were a wall unto them on their right hand, and on their left. And the Egyptians pursued ... and the Lord overthrew the Egyptians in the midst of the sea. And the waters returned and covered the chariots, and the horsemen, and all the host of Pharaoh that came into the sea after them; there remained not so much as one of them ... Thus the Lord saved Israel that day out of the hand of the Egyptians; and Israel saw the Egyptians dead upon the sea shore.' (Exodus 14: 21-30)

The Sinai was the 'great and terrible wilderness' of the Bible which the Israelites journeyed across in search of the Promised Land and it was from the summit of Mt Sinai that God delivered his Ten Commandments to Moses:

'tell the children of Israel; Ye have seen what I did unto the Egyptians ... If ye will obey my voice and keep my covenant, then ye shall be a peculiar treasure unto me above all people: for all the earth is mine. And ye shall be unto me a kingdom of priests, and a holy nation.'
'... And mount Sinai was altogether in smoke, because the Lord descended upon it in fire; and the whole mount quaked greatly ... And the Lord came down upon mount Sinai ... and called Moses up to the top of the mount ... And God spoke all these words, saying, I am the Lord thy God, which have brought thee out of the land of Egypt, out of the house of bondage. Thou shalt have no other gods before me ...' (Exodus 19,20)

In the 16th century BC the soldiers of the Egyptian army, under Pharaoh Tuthmosis III, were much more lucky than their biblical ancestors when they successfully crossed the Red Sea and the Sinai to conquer Palestine and Syria. Alexander the Great marched across in 332 BC to conquer Egypt; in 48 BC the opposing armies of Cleopatra and her brother Ptolemy battled for the Egyptian throne, just east of present-day Port Said; and throughout the Sinai, holy places mark the spots where Mary, Joseph and Jesus supposedly rested when they fled into the Sinai to escape King Herod.

The Arab general Amr led his forces across the Sinai in 639 AD to conquer Egypt and bring Islam to Africa. In 1160 Salah al-Din built a fortress at Ras el Gindi to protect Muslim pilgrims and guard Egypt against the invading Crusaders. In the 16th century the Ottomans roared across the Sinai to make Egypt part of their empire.

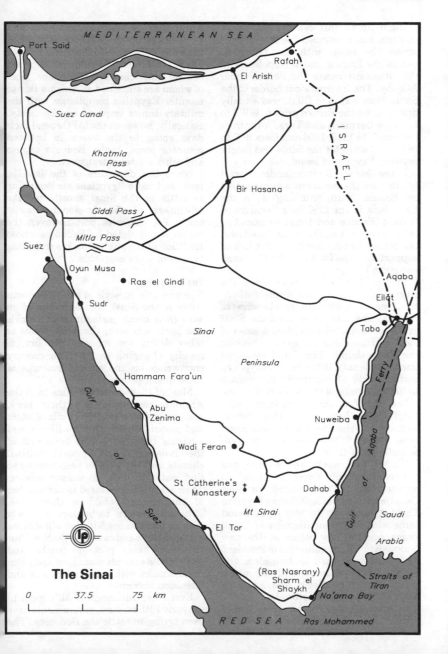

MEDITERRANEAN SEA

Port Said

Rafah

El Arish

ISRAEL

Suez Canal

Khatmia
Pass

Bir Hasana

Giddi Pass

Mitla Pass

Suez

Oyun Musa

Ras el Gindi

Aqaba

Eilat

Sudr

Taba

Sinai

Ferry

Peninsula

Gulf of Aqaba

Gulf of Suez

Hammam Fara'un

Abu
Zenima

Nuweiba

Wadi Feran

St Catherine's
Monastery

Dahab

Saudi

Mt Sinai

Arabia

El Tor

Straits of
Tiran

The Sinai

(Ras Nasrany)
Sharm el
Shaykh

0   37.5   75 km

Na'ama Bay

RED SEA   Ras Mohammed

Right up to this century the power struggle has continued back and forth across the Sinai with the Ottomans versus the French under Napoleon and the Ottomans versus the British under Allenby. The international border of the Sinai, from Rafah to Eilat, was actually drawn up by the British prior to WW I to keep the Germans and Turks away from the canal. In 1948, 1956 and from 1967 to 1979 the battle for the Sinai was fought between Egypt and Israel.

In the 1948 war for independence Israel briefly took the Sinai but was pressured, by Britain, into returning it to the Egyptians. In the 1956 Suez Canal crisis, Britain, France and Israel conspired to take the canal and the Sinai. Israel held the region for four months but a lack of support from the USA and the UN forced its return to Egypt.

In 1967 President Nasser closed the strategic Straits of Tiran, at the southern tip of the Sinai, blocking Israel's access to the sea. The Israelis grabbed the Sinai again and kept it by building a series of fortifications along the eastern bank of the Suez Canal. The Sinai remained impregnable until 1973 when the Egyptians under President Sadat used water cannons to blast the sand dune barriers of the so-called Bar Lev line. Egyptians today continue to brag about their 'secret weapon' and the great victory over Israel even though their celebrations were actually short-lived.

Within two weeks the Israelis had mustered enough forces to launch a counterattack. They crossed the Suez Canal, encircled the 30,000-man Egyptian Third Army, took the city of Suez and came within striking distance of Cairo. Peace negotiations began at the now famous Km 101, culminating in President Sadat's historic visit to Jerusalem, the Camp David Accords and the peace treaty signed by Begin and Sadat in March 1979 in Washington, DC.

In accordance with the treaty, Israel completely withdrew from the Sinai by 25 April, 1982. A Multinational Force and Observers group, the MFO, was established to ensure adherence to the treaty by both Egypt and Israel. The group is comprised of 1500 Americans and 60 Italians, most of whom are stationed at Na'ama Bay to monitor Egyptian compliance with the military limits imposed by the treaty. Basically, however, the MFO spend their days going to the beach in between counting jeeps, tanks, Bedouin camels and other modes of transport.

Since the departure of the Israelis, more and more Egyptians are beginning to settle in the Sinai, mostly to take advantage of the developing tourist trade. For the most part however, the region is populated by Bedouins whose tradition of hospitality makes travelling here even more enjoyable.

The Bedouins

The nomadic lifestyle of the 14 Bedouin tribes of the Sinai, who once moved on with their black goatskin tents, camels and goats whenever the wells, wadis or other desert watercourses ran dry, is rapidly changing as the 20th century encroaches on the age-old customs of these desert people.

Most of their ancestors came from the Arabian peninsula but their laws, customs, religion (which is a mix of Islam and pagan beliefs), their resilience and amazing hospitality were borne out of their isolation, the harshness of the Sinai climate and the need to keep moving to find water in order to simply survive. Their wealth is measured in the number of camels and children they have, although western technology is slowly making its presence felt. You will still see goatskin tents and camels in the Sinai but there are also pick-up trucks and settlements of crude stone huts and palm frond shacks with corrugated roofs and television antennae.

Ever since Mohammed Ali's reign in the early 19th century, governments have been trying to settle the Bedouins. The

Egyptians followed in the path of the Israelis by building schools, medical clinics and social centres for the Bedouins and have also strategically placed hundreds of 55 gallon barrels of water at points where they wish to create stable settlements. Many of the 50,000 Bedouins who inhabit the Sinai now harvest dates, cultivate grain, grow vegetables and cater to the tourists.

General Information
Remember that it gets mighty hot in the Sinai so make sure you always carry water, wear sensible clothes to avoid sun burn (a T-shirt while snorkelling is advisable), and a hat or scarf. While summer temperatures can reach as much as 49°C (120°F), it also gets very cold at night in winter when you'll need a sleeping bag.

The few paved roads through the desert and hills connect only the permanent settlements so, although hitching is possible, the most practical way of getting around is by bus.

Changing money in the Sinai can be awkward so it's best to take as much as possible with you. The banks in Sharm el Shaykh, Taba and El Arish will change any sort of travellers' cheques but US$ cash is the only currency that will be bought anywhere else.

Don't let the undeniably beautiful waters and coral reefs around the Red Sea coast fool you completely as they do have their share of hazards. Always wear sandshoes or fins when you're exploring the reefs as the coral is extremely sharp and the creatures that live there have a tendency to sting if unceremoniously disturbed. There are sharks in the Red Sea but don't panic if you see one – there's nothing that attracts sharks more, than a terror-stricken human flailing about in their territory.

Visas
If you're entering Egypt by way of the Sinai from Israel you of course need an Egyptian visa, which can only be obtained before you get to the border. You must also change the mandatory US$150 at the border and register with the police within seven days.

Special Sinai-only visas are issued at the Taba border, or the Egyptian consulates in Israel, and are valid for seven days. This exempts you from the compulsory currency exchange but travel within the Sinai is limited to the Aqaba coast and St Catherine's. For more information on entering Egypt from Israel refer to the Getting There chapter at the beginning of the book.

OYUN MUSA
Oyun Musa, or the Springs of Moses, is supposedly the place where Moses took the advice of God, on discovering the water there was too bitter to drink, and threw a special tree into the springs which miraculously sweetened the water.

Seven of the 12 original springs still exist and a small settlement has grown up around them. The palm trees are a bit unusual though, as most have had their crowns blown off in various Sinai wars and haven't quite returned to their previous state.

Oyun Musa is about 40 km south of the Ahmed Hamdi tunnel, which goes under the Suez Canal near Suez. Camping is possible but there is no drinkable water as the spring water is too brackish – and there's no sign of the special tree that Moses used.

The daily buses from Cairo to Sharm el Shaykh, at 7.30 and 10.30 am, go via Oyun Musa. They leave from the Sinai Terminal at Midan Abbassiya.

The buses from Suez to El Tor travel through Oyun Musa. They leave Suez at 10 am, noon, 1 and 2 pm, cost 75 pt to Oyun Musa and take one hour.

RAS EL GINDI
The 800-year-old **Fortress of Salah al-Din** at Ras el Gindi is 80 km south-east of the Ahmed Hamdi tunnel. In the 12th

century AD Muslims from Africa and the Mediterranean streamed across the Sinai on their way to Mecca. They followed three caravan routes which all converged at Ras el Gindi, so Salah al-Din built a fortress to protect the pilgrims making their Haj. He also planned to use the fort as a base to launch attacks on the Crusaders who had advanced as far as Jerusalem, though he actually managed to kick them out of the Holy City before the fortress was even finished.

Ras el Gindi is definitely off the beaten track and because it is rarely visited most of the fortress is still standing. There is no public transport there however, so you must either have your own vehicle or hire a taxi.

SUDR

For some strange reason the Egyptians decided to build a tourist resort in this town which developed around one of the country's biggest oil refineries. The *Sudr Tourist Village* has furnished apartments and chalets near the refinery and on the beach which cost E£40 per night. On the main road outside town there's a painted mug shot of President Mubarak next to a sign welcoming you to the tourist village. Mubarak isn't smiling either!

Sudr, or Ras el Sudr, is about 60 km south of the Ahmed Hamdi tunnel. The buses from Suez to El Tor via Sudr, leave at 10 am, noon, 1 and 2 pm. It costs E£1 to Sudr and takes 1½ hours. The Cairo to Sharm bus also goes through Sudr.

HAMMAM FARA'UN

The Egyptians who travel to Hammam Fara'un, or the Pharaoh's Bath, to relax in the hot springs and streams and lie on the beautiful isolated beach, rant and rave about the place. Alas, this splendid isolation won't last much longer as plans are underway for the development of a resort and treatment centre for rheumatism.

The Sinai bus from Cairo can drop you off at the turn-off to Hammam Fara'un, which is 55 km south of Sudr. The beach is not too far from the main road. There are also buses from Suez to Hammam Fara'un at 10 am, noon, 1 and 2 pm that cost E£1.50 and take 2½ hours.

FROM ABU ZENIMA TO EL TOR

Many of Egypt's Sinai development schemes are being implemented along this 90 km stretch of coastline beside the Gulf of Suez. Most of the projects are related to the off-shore oil fields so consequently the area is marred by jumbled masses of pipes, derricks and machinery.

El Tor, the administrative capital of southern Sinai, is a bit of boom town with a broad, clean avenue up the centre bordered by new apartment buildings. There are a couple of hotels in town.

The Sinai bus from Cairo to Sharm el Shaykh goes via El Tor. The 10 am, noon, 1 and 2 pm buses from Suez to El Tor take 4½ hours and cost E£5.50.

NA'AMA BAY & SHARM EL SHAYKH

The southern coast of the Gulf of Aqaba, between Tiran Island in the straits and Ras Mohammed at the tip of the Sinai, features some of the world's most brilliant and amazing underwater scenery. The crystal clear water, the rare and lovely reefs and the incredible variety of exotic fish darting in and out of the colourful coral, have made this a snorkelling and scuba diving paradise, attracting divers from all over the globe.

If you've never had the chance to explore the living treasures of the deep then this is the place to do it because the reefs are accessible and you'll find all the necessary diving equipment as well as accommodation, restaurants, bars and public services around Na'ama Bay and in nearby Sharm el Shaykh.

As a place to stay Na'ama Bay is the better of the two as there isn't really all that much to Sharm el Shaykh (recently renamed Ras Nasrany), which was initially developed by the Israelis during their occupation of the peninsula.

Top: A camel headed for the market, Na'ama Bay (SW)
Left: Red Sea coast near Sharm el Shaykh (SW)
Right: St Catherine's Monastery, Sinai (SW)

Top: Mt Sinai (SW)
Bottom: Camels in the Sinai (SW)

Information

Sharm el Shaykh is about six km south of Na'ama Bay, where the road from the Egypt-Israel border town of Taba meets the main road to the west coast and Cairo.

Most of the public services, such as the post office, telephone office, the Tourist Police, bus station and banks are in Sharm, while the three main dive shops and the best supermarket in the Sinai are at Na'ama Bay.

If you've just arrived in Egypt you can register at the main police station near the port, which is about one km from Sharm el Shaykh.

Things to See & Do

Diving Obviously the main attractions here are underwater and they are best seen with a mask and snorkel or tanks, although there are a few glass bottom boats for those who don't want to get their feet wet.

Na'ama itself has no reefs but the stunning **Near Gardens** and the even more incredible **Far Gardens** are an easy walk from the bay. The Near Gardens are about 45 minutes north of Na'ama, near the point at the end of the bay, and the Far Gardens are another half hour along the coast. Take plenty of drinking water.

Ras Omassid, near Sharm el Shaykh, is easily accessible as prime diving is a three minute walk from the Clifftop Hotel and a simple wade from the beach to the right of the small military outpost.

The other, more spectacular, diving sites in the area require a little more organisation and also cost more as you need to go with one of the dive clubs.

Ras Mohammed, the southernmost point of the Sinai, is without doubt one of the best diving sites in the world. The splendid coral gardens and fish of every imaginable shape, size and brilliant colour provide a stunning visual feast that almost cannot be believed. There is also a shipwreck, a shark observatory and fantastic views, from the beach, of Africa to the south-west and Asia to the east. Fortunately, for its own sake, Ras Mohammed is practically inaccessible. There is no public transport there so the only way to reach it is by car/boat excursions from Sharma el Shaykh and Na'ama Bay.

Tiran Island, in the Straits of Tiran, is also an excellent site, once again accessible only by boat.

Less expensive boat trips can be made to the reefs at **Ras Masrani** and **Ras Umm Sidd**.

Dive Shops

There are three dive shops at Na'ama Bay, all owned by the Sinai Hotels & Diving Clubs company but each providing different services.

The Red Sea Divers' Club, opposite the Marina Sharm Hotel, is the only one of the three clubs, that is run solely by Egyptians.

The Sharm Dive Club (or the Aquanaut) is the most popular club and the manager, Petra Rolf, has been in the Sinai since 1977.

The Aquamarine Diving Centre, next to the Aquamarine Hotel, is managed by a Belgian and an Egyptian. In addition to diving trips, the centre also organises camel safaris into the Sinai. Claude Antoine, the Belgian, is the person to see about these trips.

The prices for equipment rental and diving services are the same at all three shops and are quoted here in US dollars.

1 Full day diving package – $35, including a guide, two dives, weightbelt, a tank with unlimited air and land or local sea transportation.
2 Full day to Ras Mohammed or Tiran Island – $45, including the same provisions as No 1.
3 Introductory dive, with guide – $40.
4 Ten day package deal – $300, including

20 dives and the same provisions as No 1.
5 Five day package deal – $165, including 10 dives, and the same deal as No 1.
6 Five day diving course – $150. You need a minimum of four divers.

The clubs also offer daily rental of their equipment. It costs $1.50 for masks, $1 for snorkels, $2.50 for fins, $4.50 for regulators and 12-litre tanks and $5 for 15-litre tanks.

Windsurfing costs $6 an hour, $25 a day or $10 for a one hour lesson.

There are also two diving boats, the *Corona II* and the *Lady Jenny*, which bring groups down from Eilat and there are two diving clubs in Cairo which can give advice and organise lessons.

The Cairo Diving Club organises monthly trips, rents equipment and offers plenty of information on the dive sites. They meet the first Monday of each month in the Arusa room of the Nile Hilton. Dues are E£25 a year and PADI instruction is available.

The British Sub-Aqua Club offer BSAC and PADI certification and instruction. They meet the third Monday of each month at 7.30 pm in the recreational centre of the British Petroleum building, 31 Lebanon St, Mohandiseen.

Places to Stay

Na'ama Bay There are two official campgrounds on the bay. One has second-rate tents and toilets and is near the beach north of the Aquamarine Hotel. It costs E£3 per person.

The *Shamandura Campgrounds* are right next to the supermarket. Ali el Dib, the big-bellied guy with the undersized Che Guevara T-shirt and bikini shorts, charges happy campers E£1 a night if you have your own tent, E£2 per person if you don't. There are two mattresses per tent and three tents per palm frond hut. The toilets occasionally get clogged and smelly, but with showers, the supermarket, a snackbar and the beach nearby, this is probably one of the best deals in the Sinai.

The *Aquamarine Hotel* has 24 bungalows without bathrooms and 30 new bungalows with bathrooms and the prices are E£16 a single, E£27 a double and E£39 a triple, all including breakfast.

The *Marina Sharm Hotel* is the 90-room remnant of an Israeli resort hotel. The complex includes three restaurants, two cafeterias, a bakery and a ping pong room.

The *Youth Hostel* seems to have been taken over by the University of Suez for use as an Environmental School. They are supposedly doing research but all I could see was a pile of rotting fish on a table.

Sharm el Shaykh The *Youth Hostel*, next to the Clifftop Hotel, costs 80 pt per night. It's OK if you can stand meeting a lot of noisy Egyptian teenagers who insist on having their picture taken with you. It's open from 6 to 10 am and 2 to 8 pm. Alcohol and card playing are banned!

The best deal in Sharm is to rent one of the five tents in the Clifftop's yard. Each has three beds and costs E£10 or E£3.50 per person including access to showers and toilets.

The *Clifftop Village Hotel* is the best place to stay. At about E£17 a single and E£38 a double, it's a bit out of the budget range but it's a good, comfortable place if you can afford it. The management and staff are extremely helpful and will help you organise diving trips.

If you've got your own tent or sleeping bag then it's possible to camp on the beach at Ras Omassid near the Clifftop. Just be discreet and go down the hill to the beach.

Places to Eat
Na'ama Bay The *Snackbar* at the Shamandura campgrounds serves a variety of things at very cheap prices. You can get omelettes for E£1.25, spaghetti for E£1.50, cornflakes for 75 pt and excellent iced mango juice for 75 pt.

The restaurant at the Aquamarine Hotel serves lunch for E£5 and dinner for E£7.

The *Wrecker's Den*, next door, serves similar food a la carte.

The Marina Sharm also runs a few restaurants. The *Red Sea* serves a la carte fish dishes for E£5 to E£7. The *White House* is a barbecue restaurant where Sadat and Begin met while the Israeli airforce bombed a nuclear power plant in Iraq. (The meeting was considered an embarrassment to Sadat.) The *Sultan Pizzeria & Disco* serve decent plate-sized pizzas for E£3 and ravioli and spaghetti for E£1.50. The *Oriental Court Café* in front of the Sultan is a great place where you can plop down on pseudo-Oriental cushions and sip tea or kakaday, suck on a *sheesha* pipe and slurp Stella beers.

Sharm el Shaykh The *Atfed El Misk* is a fairly decent tea house on the right side of the warehouse-like building in the main street. There's not much else in Sharm in the way of eating places except for a few sub-standard cafés.

Getting There
Bus There are two daily buses from Cairo to Sharm el Shaykh and Na'ama Bay, at 7.30 and 10 am. They leave from Midan Abbassiya, take seven hours and cost E£9.50. From Sharm to Cairo the buses leave at 6 and 10 am and 1 pm. There's also a midnight bus which costs E£12.

The bus to Sharm from Taba on the Israel-Egypt border, leaves at 3 pm and costs E£7. Buses from Sharm to Taba via Na'ama Bay, Dahab and Nuweiba leave at 9 am; and to Nuweiba at 5 pm.

The 11 am bus from Sharm to St Catherine's goes via Dahab and costs about E£4.

The buses arrive and leave from in front of the bus ticket office in Sharm el Shaykh and in front of the Marina Sharm Hotel in Na'ama Bay.

Getting Around

The public transport between Sharm and Na'ama Bay basically comes down to a yellow, open-sided *tof-tof* which supposedly runs hourly until 7 pm. If you happen to see it, just flag it down for the 25 pt ride between the two towns. The easiest way to travel around the area, however, is to hitch as there's usually plenty of traffic. Don't expect any of the MFO vehicles to pick you up though as they're not allowed to carry civilians.

DAHAB

The village/beach resort of Dahab, which means 'gold' in Arabic, is 85 km north of Sharm el Shaykh on the Gulf of Aqaba. The Bedouins named the beach after the glimmering sands that resemble gold dust.

The main part of Dahab is the interesting Bedouin village of palm trees, thatched huts, goats and chickens which is actually three km from the Dahab bus stop and tourist resort.

Things to See & Do

Diving This is, of course, the most popular activity in Dahab. The best sites are just north and south of the resort motel. Either look for the waves breaking on the off-shore coral or check the map at the dive shop.

The **Blue Hole** is a popular 70-metre dive recommended only for experienced divers.

There is an International Diving Centre in Dahab where you can rent a snorkel and mask for E£2.50 and fins for an extra E£2. Windsurfers and paddle boards are also available.

Camel Treks Many of the local Bedouins organise camel trips to the interior of the Sinai. One day trips cost E£15 and the best trek is to **Wadi Nay** where there's a small oasis and Bedouin village.

Places to Stay

Camping is possible, either with your own gear on the beach or at one of the official Egyptian camp grounds near the motel. The latter offer three-person tents for E£5 per person. The only shower is on the beach.

The *Dahab Holiday Motel* is owned and operated by the Sinai Hotels & Diving Clubs company. It costs E£28 for a double with half board. The motel's toilets and showers are available for public use for 50 pt per visit.

Another place to try for accommodation is the Bedouin village of Dahab. You can stay in a thatched hut for E£1 per person but it's basically just an air mattress under you and a roof over your head. There is no water and the village has no toilets but the friendly Bedouins try to be as accommodating as possible.

Places to Eat

There is a *Cafeteria/Kiosk* on the beach which sells canned fish, fruit, mineral water and sometimes bread.

The restaurant at the Holiday Motel serves breakfast for E£1 between 7 and 9 am; and lunch and dinner for E£6 per meal between 1 and 3 pm and 8 and 10 pm.

The cheapest and best places to eat are the Bedouin restaurants in the village; some of them are quite a treat. You can sit on the floor, around a fire in the middle, and eats lots of excellent fish for E£1.

The *Bob Marley Restaurant* plays reggae music and sells cheap hash, as part of the menu.

Tota's is one of the best of the Bedouin places. You can get spaghetti for E£1, pizza for 75 pt, salad and feta cheese for 50 pt, soup for 50 pt and sometimes felafel and fuul.

There are about nine other restaurants nearby, just walk along the beach and take your pick.

Getting There & Around

The regular daily buses, in either direction, between Sharm el Shaykh and Taba go via Dahab and Nuweiba. The buses from Sharm to Dahab leave at about 9 am and 5 pm; and from Dahab to Sharm and Na'ama Bay at 8 am and 4 pm. The trip takes 1½ hours and costs E£3.

Buses from Dahab to Nuweiba and Taba leave at 10.30 am and cost E£2; and another to Nuweiba leaves at 6.30 pm.

A taxi from the Dahab bus stop to the Bedouin village costs 50 pt.

NUWEIBA

During the Israeli occupation Nuweiba, which is 87 km north of Dahab, was the site of a major *moshav* (farming settlement), and beach resort. The resort remained, but the moshav has been converted into a residence for Egyptian government officials.

Despite being one of the most popular of the Sinai beaches, Nuweiba is certainly not the most attractive. There is not much in town, just a holiday village, a kiosk, a police station behind the kiosk, the bus stop next to the kiosk, a couple of restaurants and a dive shop. The mountain scenery, however, is reasonably stunning and the coral reefs are certainly spectacular.

Things to See & Do

Once again underwater delights are the feature attraction and scuba diving and snorkelling the prime activities, although camel expeditions from Nuweiba are also a popular diversion.

Diving The Diving Centre offers the necessary equipment for much the same prices as in Na'ama Bay. They also rent out, by the hour, windsurfers for E£6 (or E£10 for a lesson), kayaks for E£3 and pedal boats for E£4. If you can get 10 people together you can rent a glass bottom boat for E£3 per person, per half hour.

Camel Treks Khalid Shaker Ali, the manager of the Diving Centre, arranges and leads camel trips. The shortest trek is to **Ein Furtaga** which takes eight hours for

the round trip, costs E£30 and includes an English speaking guide and lunch.

There are also overnight treks to the Bedouin encampment at **Ein Machmed** for E£45 per day; and to the **Coloured Canyon.** The latter is also known as the Blue Valley because a few years ago a Swiss man painted the whole valley blue. According to the locals, it's a pretty 'spacey' place.

Other camel trips can be arranged by going to the village of **Tarabin**, two km from Nuweiba, and talking to Aish Sliman or other members of his family.

Places to Stay

Camping at the official grounds costs E£10 per tent for a three or four-person tent. You can also camp on the beach near the tents for E£1, but it can get quite windy at night. Bathroom and shower facilities are nearby and cost 25 pt for three visits.

You can also take your sleeping bag south down the beach and sleep under the palm trees for free.

The *Nuweiba Holiday Village* has 90 bungalows with air-con and there's also a bar, private beach, tennis courts and a VCR. The bungalows cost about E£27 per person.

Places to Eat

There are two or three Bedouin restaurants and cafés along the beach south of the Holiday Village, offering cheap, delicious fish with salad and yogurt for E£2 or E£3.

The café closest to the camp grounds is run by a Bedouin who is quite anxious to please his customers. When I asked for fish he jumped into his pick-up, disappeared over a sand dune and returned 45 minutes later with a big fish on the end of a spear. A camel and another Bedouin decided to join me for dinner. The camel didn't like fish, but his owner did and he didn't hesitate to share mine. The camel, which was tied to our table, kept leaning over to sneak the tomatoes from my plate when he thought I wasn't looking. As the sun sank below the mountains behind me, doing amazing things to the colour of the Saudi hills across the water, the table collapsed – the camel had tried to eat the plate as well as the rest of the tomatoes. The fish, the scenery and the company cost E£2.50.

The *Hotel Restaurant* is less romantic and more expensive, although the food is very good. It costs E£7 for a three course meal.

Getting There

Bus The two daily buses, in both directions, between Sharm el Shaykh and Taba stop in Nuweiba. The 10.30 am bus from Dahab also stops in Nuweiba, en route to Taba.

The 11 am and the 11 pm buses from Nuweiba to Cairo go via St Catherine's. The morning bus costs E£15 and the night bus, which leaves from the port, costs E£20.

There are two daily buses from Nuweiba to Suez. They both leave at 7 am but one goes via Sharm and the other via St Catherine's.

The Taba bound buses leave Nuweiba at noon and 3 pm.

Boat

There are two daily ferries from Nuweiba to Aqaba in Jordan. The boat leaves at 10 am and 3 pm, although some travellers have said they leave at 11 am and 4 pm, so check the times. The morning ferry is usually crowded and you have to queue for tickets, so get there early. Some locals spend the night at the dock to be first in line. The three hour trip costs E£37 (with bank receipts) in 3rd class.

Don't buy a return ticket in Egypt as it's cheaper to buy two one-way tickets. The 3rd class ticket from Aqaba to Nuweiba costs JD7.500, or approximately US$21. In Jordan you can also get Egyptians pounds for US dollars at a better rate than in Egypt.

TABA

Some Egyptians claim that a few hundred metres of beach, a luxury hotel and a coffee shop named *Nelson* at a place on the border called Taba are preventing the normalisation of relations between Egypt and Israel. The Israelis want to keep all these things while the Egyptians want the land back with or without the hotel and coffee shop. The conflicting claims seem to be on the verge of being resolved. Meanwhile, Taba, which is on the north-west coast of the Gulf of Aqaba opposite Eilat, serves as one of the border crossings between Egypt and Israel.

The special Sinai-only visa, available from Egyptian consulates in Israel, including the one in Eilat, is also available at Taba and costs US$6.

The bus to Sharm el Shaykh and destinations in between leaves Taba at 3 pm and costs E£7 all the way to Sharm. The bus to St Catherine's Monastery and Cairo leaves at 10 am.

ST CATHERINE'S MONASTERY

Fifteen Greek Orthodox monks reside in this ancient monastery at the foot of Mt Sinai. The monastic order was founded in the 4th century AD by the Byzantine Empress Helena, who had a small chapel built beside what was believed to be the burning bush from which God spoke to Moses.

The chapel was dedicated to St Catherine, the legendary martyr of Alexandria who was tortured on a spiked wheel and then beheaded for her belief in Christianity. Her body was supposedly transported by angels to Mt Catherine, the highest mountain in Egypt which is about six km south of Mt Sinai, where it was 'found' about 300 years later by monks from the monastery.

In the 6th century Emperor Justinian ordered the building of a fortress, with a basilica and monastery as well as the original chapel, to serve as a secure home for the monks of St Catherine's and a refuge for the Christians of the southern Sinai.

Despite the isolated setting, the monastery and Mt Sinai attract a great many tourists and pilgrims. Remember that it is still a functioning monastery, not just a museum piece, so keep that in mind when you visit. Only the chapel, part of the monastery's splendid collection of icons and jewelled crosses, and a rather macabre room full of the bones of deceased monks are open to the public. The monastery is only open to visitors from 9.30 am to 12.30 pm. It is closed on Fridays, Sundays and holidays.

MT SINAI
Although archaeologists or historians may dispute its biblical claim to fame Jews, Christians and Muslims alike revere Mt Sinai and believe that it was from its summit that God delivered his Ten Commandments to Moses.

At a height of 2285 metres, the Mount towers over St Catherine's Monastery. It is easy to climb, as there are two well-defined routes, and the summit is the most popular place in the area to sleep. It's suggested you climb up in time for the sunset, spend the night and return with the sunrise. It is a magnificent experience.

Ask one of the monks for directions if you're not sure where to start. If you go by the camel path it will take about 2½ hours for the ascent and 1½ for the descent. The alternative way is by the taxing 3000 **Steps of Repentance**, which were laid by one monk as a form of penance. If you want to take both routes, it's best to take the path up and the steps down. During summer you should begin your hike at 2 or 3 am to avoid the heat. If you plan to spend the night on the summit however, make sure you have food, water, warm clothes and a sleeping bag (there is no space for a tent), as it gets cold there even in summer.

Just below the summit is **Elijah's Hollow**, a small plateau dominated by a 500-year-old Cypress tree which marks the spot where the prophet Elijah heard the voice of God. On the summit itself, though they'll probably be locked, is a Greek Orthodox chapel, containing beautiful paintings and ornaments, and a small mosque. The views of the surrounding bare and jagged mountains and plunging valleys are spectacular. Throughout the day the colours of the rocks and cliffs change like stone chameleons.

Places to Stay
There is a hostel next to, and run by, the monastery. It's open every day and check-in time is between 5 and 7 pm. It's clean, comfortable, has cooking facilities and cold-water showers and costs E£5 per night. Even if you don't stay there you can use their showers and leave baggage in one of the rooms while you hike up Mt Sinai.

There is supposedly a tourist camp in the village, which is about two km from the monastery, however the very basic but clean hotel in town will probably be easier to find. It costs about E£3 per night.

There is a campsite, about four km west of the monastery, which has ready-erected tents and access to showers for E£3 per night.

The luxury hotel at the airstrip, which is 20 km from the monastery, costs E£47 per night.

Places to Eat
There is a small bakery and a restaurant in the village, near the bus stop, where the food is OK and very cheap. There's also a supermarket where you can buy your own food supplies.

Getting There
Air Air Sinai has regular flights from Cairo to St Catherine's Monastery for about US$60 one way.

Bus The two daily buses from Cairo to St Catherine's leave from the Sinai Terminal near Midan Abbassiya and cost E£7. If you want to go straight to the monastery ask the driver to drop you off at the turn-off, otherwise you'll end up in the village. The most convenient one to take is the

Boarding Pass

سيناء للطيران
AIR SINAI

Boarding Pass

سيناء للطيران
AIR SINAI

10 am bus which drops you off at the turn-off at about 4.30 pm. From St Catherine's Monastery to Cairo there are two buses a day, at 6 am and 1 pm, except on Saturdays when there is no afternoon bus. You can catch them, earlier, from the bus depot in the village.

There are daily buses from Suez to St Catherine's which leave at 11 am and cost E£5.50. One of the 7 am buses from Nuweiba to Suez goes via St Catherine's and takes 2½ hours. The bus to Nuweiba leaves the St Catherine's village at 1 pm.

There's a daily bus to St Catherine's from Sharm el Shaykh. It leaves at 11 am, goes via Dahab and costs about E£4.

Service Taxi Taxis travel in and out of the village irregularly and infrequently. If you're lucky, you might be able to find a taxi willing to take you all the way to Cairo for about E£40 (with three other people).

WADI FERAN
The Bedouin outpost of Wadi Feran is a lush oasis of date palms between the west coast of the Sinai and St Catherine's Monastery. After several km of rough barren desert and harsh rocky hills, this place is certainly a refreshing sight.

The bus between Suez and Wadi Feran costs E£5 and takes three hours.

EL ARISH
El Arish is the capital of the Sinai peninsula on the northern coast. It is a city of 35,000 inhabitants which is trying desperately to become a beach resort even though it is seldom visited because there's not much of interest there.

Information
The police station and hospital are on Sharia 23 July just off the main shore road.

The post office, which is open from Saturday to Thursday between 9 am and

3 pm, and the telephone and telegraph office (open 24 hours a day), are in the same building near the hospital.

Things to See
The Museum One of the few attractions of El Arish, the museum was established a couple of years ago to inform people about life, human and animal, in the Sinai. Displays include stuffed birds and Bedouin handicrafts and clothing. The museum is on the outskirts of town along the road to Rafah.

The *souk* is held every Wednesday when the Bedouins come in from the desert with their camels. The veiled women come in to sell embroidered dresses and the men to sell camel saddles.

There is also of course the palm-lined beach, though this gets very crowded in summer when a makeshift city of tents is erected.

Places to Stay
You can camp on the beach at the official El Arish camping grounds, which are seven km west of the city. It costs E£5 for a tent with two beds and lights or E£2 if you have your own gear.

The *Moon Light Hotel*, near the beach in town, has rooms without bath for E£4 per person or with bath for E£6.

The *El Salaam Hotel* on Sharia 23 July, above the Aziz restaurant on Midan Baladiya, has rooms for E£8 to E£10 per person.

The *Sinai Beach Hotel* is a little more up-market and costs E£20 for a double with bath.

The *Oberoi El Arish* is a relatively recent four star addition to the growing El Arish resort accommodation scene. It's a mere E£40/50 for a single/double with bath, plus 20% taxes and services.

Places to Eat
Good cheap meals of fuul and taamiyya are available at the *Aziz Restaurant* on Sharia 23 July.

The Sammar Restaurant, also on Sharia 23 July, serve kebab and kofta.

A couple of other decent restaurants are the *Sinai Rose Cafeteria* and the *Mashribiyya Cafeteria*. Both are right on the beach and have bars and serve good salads and fish.

Getting There & Around
The Sinai bus from Cairo to the Israeli border at Rafah goes via El Arish and takes about five hours. Service taxis also make the trip from Cairo. For more information on crossing the Rafah border into Israel see the Getting There chapter at the beginning of the book.

A taxi from the El Arish bus station to the beach costs 50 pt.

SUDAN

Introduction

The Sudan is only for the hardiest and most adventurous travellers. There is war in the south, famine in the west and refugees in the east, west and south. The government is practically powerless and the economy is collapsing. Most of the country is as hot as hell from March to September and the rainy season turns roads and tracks, where they exist, into thick streams of mud. It is no wonder that Sudanese Arabs are uncertain if, as an age-old proverb reads, Allah laughed or cried when he created the Sudan.

Yet having painted such an inhospitable picture, the Sudan is an adventurous and fascinating country to visit. It is Africa's largest country – approximately 1/3 the size of the USA. There are only 23¼ million people in this vast area but they comprise more than 300 tribes and speak more than 100 languages and dialects. Most have managed to preserve much of their culture and traditions. In Khartoum, the capital, and other towns this is colourfully evident in the dress, speech and facial scars of the people.

Much of the adventure in the vast expanses of the Sudan lies in getting from place to place. Some buses and trains function but the most common mode of transport is hunching and huddling in the back of a rugged Bedford truck. They travel wherever there are people who have something to buy or sell. The Bedfords almost always get through, unless swirling sandstorms blind the driver or choke the engine, or the roads turn to gooey mud. Even if you are temporarily stranded in some village on the edge of the world, Sudanese hospitality is such that you will always be offered food and shelter.

In the past, it was power and great hidden treasures which made the Sudan the object of numerous invasions and explorations throughout its long jumbled history. Today, much of the Sudan still remains to be explored. It is one of the world's last frontiers.

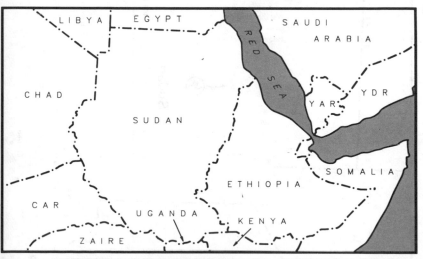

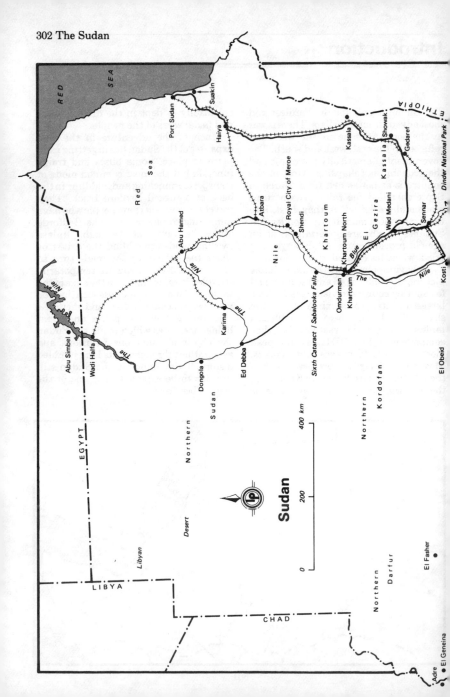

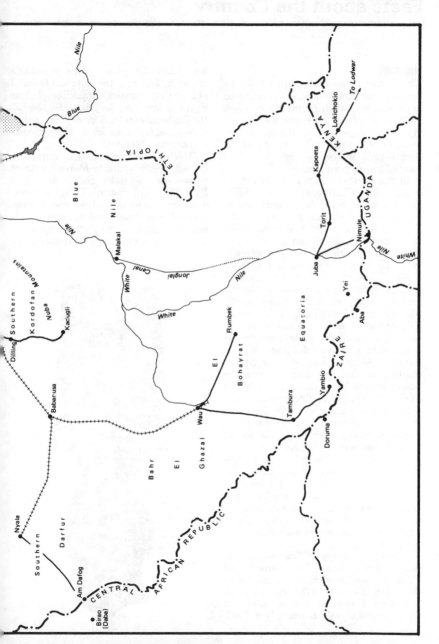

Facts about the Country

HISTORY

The history of the Sudan can roughly be divided into three regions, each comprised of loosely defined kingdoms or sultanates delineated by the Nile, the mountains, the wide expanses of desert or the swamps. Most of what is known of the Sudan prior to the 15th century AD is related to northern Sudan.

In the northern part of Sudan, from present-day Khartoum to Wadi Halfa, knowledge of Sudan's ancient origins comes from Egyptian sources. To the Egyptians of the Old Kingdom period (2600-2100 BC) the Sudan was known as the *Land of Cush* and was the source of ivory, incense, ebony, gold and slaves.

As Egyptian trading and raiding parties increased their forays into the Sudan, the imperialist designs of Egypt's Middle and New Kingdom (2050-1085 BC) pharaohs also increased. Like 20th century imperialists of European ilk, the conquering pharaohs did their best to Egyptianise the Sudanese. Egyptian political control saw dominance in the language, art forms and religion of the Sudan. Signs of this influence can still be seen in the ruins of many Egyptian structures and temples along the Nile in northern Sudan, such as the Temple of Barkal near present-day Karima.

However, as has happened many times throughout history since then, the colonies that powerful kingdoms or countries create often become big headaches as they turn on their creators, or invaders, and sometimes conquer them. That is what happened with Egypt and the Land of Cush.

By the 8th century BC Cush was a great power. Under the ruler Piankhi, the Cushites conquered Egypt, establishing the 25th Dynasty (712-663 BC). In Egyptian historical terms, however, Cush control was short-lived. In 671 BC, less than 50 years after Piankhi's triumph, Taharqa, the last ruler to build at Luxor's celebrated Karnak Temple, lost Egypt to invading Assyrians. By 654 BC the Cushites were back in their old capital of Napata, far to the south of Egypt, near present-day Merowe.

Over the next century the capital was moved from Napata to Meroe (north of present-day Shendi) and a new, less Egyptian kingdom arose. Temples, tombs and pyramids influenced by Greek, Roman and Indian architectural styles were built at Naqa and Musawwarat and a cursive Meriotic script replaced Egyptian hiero-

Cush

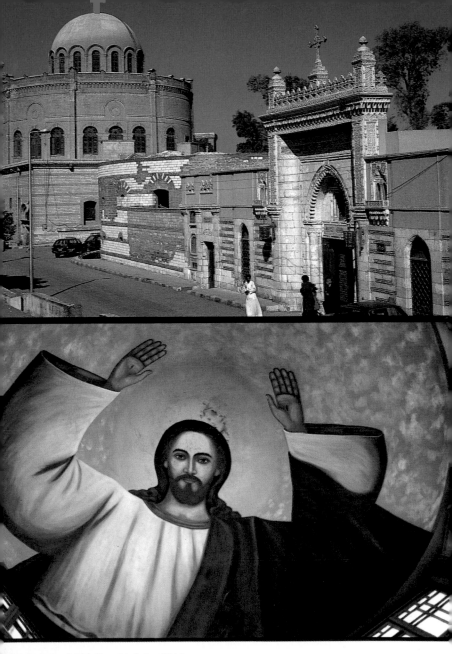

Top: A view of Old (Coptic) Cairo (SW)
Bottom: Deir el-Muharraq, near El Qusiya (SW)

glyphics. However, because this writing remains undeciphered much of the history of Meroe is still a mystery.

It is known that marauding Romans came down from Egypt in 23 BC, sacked Napata and weakened the Meriotic empire. The nomadic Blemmya people, ancestors of the Beja tribe, then moved in like vultures and gradually picked away at the empire until an invasion in 350 AD by the Axumite Kingdom of Ethiopia ensured the demise of Meroe.

By the 4th century AD most of the inhabitants of northern Sudan were Christian; the language spoken was Nubian, the origin of which continues to baffle linguists; and the writing was Coptic script, which is still read by Egyptian Coptic priests. Small Christian kingdoms eventually superseded the Axumites and ruled until the 7th century AD when the followers of the Prophet Mohammed swept into Africa on a conversion rampage.

Over the next several centuries northern Sudan came under Arab influence. By the 16th century Arab tribes were in control, most of the population were Muslim and Islam had spread to the western Sudan regions of the Kordofan and Darfur.

In Darfur the Arab-African Fur people were in control. The exact origins of this tribe, who possessed the darker skin of the Africans and the thin-lipped faces of the Arabs, is unknown as their history before conversion to Islam is somewhat of a mystery.

For centuries the vast desert of the Kordofan isolated the Fur from the political whims and follies of the Nile kingdoms and dynasties. Even with conversion to Islam, they remained isolated, and as late as the 16th century they established an independent sultanate which lasted until 1916. Today, vestiges of this sultanate can be seen in the old Fur capital of El Fasher and, in the town of El Geneina to the west of El Fasher, there is still a man who claims to be Sultan.

Around the same time, another sultanate emerged under the Fung people whose kingdom stretched from the 6th Nile cataract, north of Khartoum, southward to Sennar. Their moments of glory however, were short-lived. They reached their pinnacle of power in the 18th century after repulsing a Shilluk invasion from the south and scoring victories in wars against the Abyssinians (former name of the Ethiopians) and the Fur.

A French doctor named Poncet who visited Sennar in 1699 gave the following description of the Fung:

' ... they were a crafty, suspicious and deceitful people ... A good deal of the Fung's wealth was said to come from the fabulous gold mines at Fazughli, on the Ethiopian border, and the king kept up considerable state. Once every week he would ride out to one of his country houses, accompanied by three or four hundred horsemen and footmen, who sang his praises and played the *tabor* (a small drum) while they marched ... the king, who never appeared in public without a piece of coloured gauze over his face, presided at his court of law with the authority of a Roman governor. Criminals, on being convicted, were thrown to the ground and beaten to death with clubs.'

By the end of the 18th century the Fung empire was fragmented and ripe for pillage and plunder by the Ottoman ruler of Egypt, Mohammed Ali.

Mohammed Ali was a ruthless and power hungry army officer who had gained control of Egypt with the help of the Mamelukes, a mercenary military class who were originally Turkish slaves. Later, when the Mamelukes themselves posed a threat to Mohammed's power, he promptly eliminated the Mameluke leaders in one fell swoop by inviting them all to dinner and murdering them afterwards. Then to quell the understandable disquiet in the Mameluke ranks, and to furbish his coffers, he sent them to the Sudan to bring back gold and 40,000 black Sudanese slaves to build a new army.

Led by Ismail, Mohammed's 25-year-old son, the ragtag army of 10,000 soldiers penetrated the swamps of the Sudd, which had long been a natural barrier to Arab expansion. With the promise of 50 pt each for every human ear they won in war, Mohammed's determined troops managed to open up the south; for the Sudan the results were disastrous.

Three thousand ears were sent back to Mohammed. Ismail also sent his father 30,000 slaves, mostly women and children, though only half of them survived the trip to Cairo. When no gold was found however, Ismail started for home but got only as far as Shendi with his band of not-so-merry mercenaries who had, of course, been taking more than just ears from the Sudanese people. Ismail died a fiery death in a tent set alight by the locals who had had enough of being raped, pillaged and plundered.

When Mohammed heard about his son's death, he too wanted more than ears. By 1823, 50,000 Sudanese had been killed and Mohammed Ali had control of the Sudan.

Egypt remained in control for the next 50 years, until the time of Khedive Ismail who ruled Egypt from 1863 to 1879. Britain and France became increasingly interested in the region, especially with the completion of the Suez Canal in 1869. This expensive project placed Egypt in heavy debt to many foreign powers and initiated European intervention in the affairs of Egypt and the Sudan.

The British were the predominant European power in both countries and in 1873 General Charles Gordon was appointed governor of Equatoria province. In 1877 he became governor general of all the Sudan but resigned three years later in the wake of Khedive Ismail's demise.

In the meantime, a local military leader named Mohammed Ahmad was gaining influence in the nascent world of Sudanese politics. In 1881 he joined forces with Abdullahi ibn Mohammed, of southern Darfur, and declared himself

Mahdi. Traditionally, the Mahdi is a messiah, selected by Allah to lead the *jihad* or holy war in defence of Islam. The Mahdi and his followers called for a return to the fundamental tenets of early Islam, and this formed the foundation of the Mahdiyya movement, which continues to influence Sudanese politics today.

The Mahdi made the Kordofan town of El Obeid his political centre by surrounding the town and starving the population into submission. In the process, the British colonel William Hicks was killed and his Egyptian Army overwhelmed. The Mahdi went on to take the Darfur and imprisoned the Austrian governor of Darfur, Rudolph Slatin.

General Gordon was sent back to Khartoum in early 1884, before the Mahdi laid siege to Khartoum. Once the siege began, Gordon immediately requested reinforcements from Prime Minister Gladstone. The British relief force arrived on 25 January 1885 – three days too late. The Mahdi had already taken Khartoum and Gordon had been decapitated, his head mounted on top of a pole to greet the arriving British troops.

The Mahdi kept control of the Sudan for another 10 years until Rudolph Slatin escaped from prison. Slatin wrote a book about his captivity, titled *Fire & Sword in the Sudan*, and fired up British public opinion. By this time most of Africa had been carved up amongst the European colonial powers, so the British willingly pursued a campaign against the Mahdists.

Under General Herbert Kitchener, the British Army marched all the way to Omdurman meeting little resistance. They arrived on 1 September 1898. The Mahdists attacked the next day with a force of 60,000 men, many of whom were cloaked in suits of mail and long flowing gowns, and armed with sabers and shields. The dead numbered 11,000 Mahdists and only 48 British. On 19 January 1899 the Anglo-Egyptian Condominium Agreement was signed 'with the consent of Her

Britannic Majesty's Government'. The British remained in control of the Sudan until 1952. On 1 January 1956 the Sudanese declared their independence from Great Britain.

The new Republic of the Sudan was immediately faced with problems which were both avoided and created by British control. For the sake of stability, the British had followed a policy of isolating the predominantly African southern part of Sudan from the predominantly Arab northern part. A civil war between the north and the south began even before independence was declared.

By 1958 it was apparent that the parliamentary government of the Sudan was too disunited to cope with the escalating civil war. General Ibrahim Abboud lead a military coup d'etat and overthrew the government, however he too was unable to neutralise the south. An election in 1964 saw Shadek al Mahdi, great grandson of the Mahdi, elected as Prime Minister. But it wasn't until 1969 when Colonel Jafaar Nimeiri lead another coup d'etat, that the southern situation began to change.

Nimeiri established a new government based on 'democracy, socialism and non-alignment' and signed the Addis Ababa Agreement in 1972 which supposedly ended the north-south war. He granted the south a measure of autonomy and for almost a decade northerners and southerners stopped killing each other. The situation changed for the worse, though, as Nimeiri's various economic development projects failed. He had wanted to make the Sudan the 'bread-basket of the Middle East' by encouraging Arab and western investment in projects such as the Gezira Scheme and the Jonglei Canal.

The Gezira is a 25,000 square km marshy region south of Khartoum between the White and Blue Niles. Much of the region is devoted to cotton but it's far from being a bread-basket. The purpose of the Jonglei Canal was to divert a 560-km stretch of the White Nile that

would otherwise flow into the wide marsh south of the Gezira. The additional Nile water could have then been used for further irrigation and cultivation of the Gezira. But Nimeiri invested too heavily, too quickly and in the process amassed a mountain of external debts.

The International Monetary Fund and the United States government then pressured him into increasing the prices of commodities such as bread, sugar and petrol. In the early 1980s he began to turn to Muslim fundamentalists for support, much to the chagrin of the predominantly Christian and animist southerners. For them the last straw was Nimeiri's symbolic declaration of *sharia* – Islamic Law. In September 1983, a month all Nile perch will remember with drunken delight, Nimeiri dumped the capital's entire liquor stocks into the Nile.

The disaffected south again took up arms and a rebel leader named John Garang went into hiding to reactivate the Sudanese Peoples' Liberation Movement, or SPLM. Within a few months the government virtually lost control of the south and Nimeiri declared a state of emergency and suspended the constitution.

Less than two years later in April 1985, Nimeiri was deposed in a coup d'etat engineered by the Sudanese Army. A Transitional Military Government under General Abdul-Rahman Swareddahab took power. He set about purging the extremist Islamic fundamentalists and promised elections within 12 months.

The April '86 elections, the first in 20 years, saw the return of the former prime minister deposed by Nimeiri in 1969. Shadek al Mahdi promised to return Sudan to a democratic and pluralist society, but while political parties and unions now enjoy a freedom rare in Africa, he has put off repealing *sharia* because of pressure from Islamic fundamentalists. Consequently, the civil war is still raging in the south and al Madhi's popularity has declined because of his inability to end the war.

THE SUDAN TODAY

The Sudan today is a nation fraught with political turmoil, economic chaos, civil war, drought, famine, disease and refugee crises.

Politics & Economics

In theory, the Sudan has a British type of parliamentary system. In practice, the system breaks down. There are too many groups with different interests, ethnic backgrounds and cultural traditions. Occasionally coalitions form which temporarily overlook their differences, but they quickly crumble with the slightest disagreement. In the latest elections over 30 political parties originally campaigned for support, but only a few survived the campaign trail. The reasons for this messy political situation stem from more than just divergent interests.

Sudan's economy can be equally blamed, as it is both a cause and an effect of the political situation. Without a strong economy, the Sudanese find it difficult to create a base for a stable government. However, with a per capita income of less than US$400 a year and an external debt of more than US$9,000 million, neither a stable government nor a stable economy seems possible in the near future.

The weak economy in turn, cannot be blamed entirely on political instability. The Sudan is predominantly an agricultural country, its main crops being cotton and sorghum, but with low world commodity prices export revenue has slumped. Due to a surplus of cotton on the world market, the price has plummeted and as a result, thousands of bales of cotton have wasted away in the overflowing warehouses of Port Sudan.

Civil War

The war between the SPLM and the Sudanese government was sparked by Nimeiri's declaration of *sharia*, or Islamic Law, the body of doctrines that regulates the lives of all those who profess Islam. The southerners interpreted this as an abrogation of the Addis Ababa agreement. John Garang, an Iowa State University alumnus and member of the southern Dinka tribe, went into self-imposed exile to lead a revolt against the government. He founded the SPLM with plenty of support from disgruntled southerners and the Ethiopian government across the border.

Most of Garang's arms and supplies come from Ethiopia (or in other words, Gorbachev and Castro), although recently he has also been over-running government army convoys. While the government is hesitant even to acknowledge these raids, Garang himself describes these victories in great detail on his daily radio broadcasts over the *Voice of the Sudanese People's Liberation Movement*. In one broadcast Garang went so far as to recite the serial numbers of the army trucks and blood types of the officers captured. If you want to find out where Garang's troops are currently fighting, and presumably scoring victories against the Sudanese government, tune in to the Voice of the SPLM on the shortwave frequency of approximately 9500 kHz. He broadcasts in English almost everyday from about 2.30 to 3 pm.

Garang claims to have advanced his troops as far as the southern base of the Nuba mountains and to the middle of a marsh, east of the Nile town of Malakal. He has declared any river and air traffic fair game for target practice and has also mined roads to the west, south-west and north of the southern Sudan city of Juba. Consequently, the Nile steamer no longer operates and overland traffic has almost completely stopped (as of 1986).

Drought, Famine & Disease

In 1985/86 the western Sudan regions of the Kordofan and Darfur and part of the eastern region near Kassala and Gedaref experienced severe drought and, subsequently, widespread famine. Six to seven million people were threatened with starvation or severe malnourishment. In the Kordofan 400,000 Sudanese were forced to leave their villages to go in search of food. The United Nations, as well as the United States Agency for International Development and other world aid agencies, rushed food and supplies to as many parts of the country as possible. During the summer months the efforts of the aid agencies themselves, were hindered by temperatures as high as 48°C and ferocious *haboobs*, or sandstorms. The famine also worsened the Sudan's already terrible health situation.

The latest statistics indicate that there are only about 4000 doctors in the Sudan, which means there is approximately one for every 6000 people. To make matters worse, most of these trained medical practitioners are concentrated in or near Khartoum, so the situation in southern Sudan is even more critical. In the south there is one doctor for every 83,000 people.

The supply of medicine is pathetic in all but the large towns and more established refugee camps, so it is no wonder that Sudan's doctors and hospitals are ill-equipped to cope with the assortment of diseases afflicting most Sudanese. The number and types of ailments reads like a litany of woes. There is malaria of various strains, tuberculosis, meningitis, hepatitis, trachoma, glaucoma, bilharzia, measles, dysentery . . . The list goes on and on.

For travellers' preventive health measures refer to the health section in the Egypt Facts for the Visitor chapter. In short though, if you take all the usual health precautions and just use common sense, then you probably won't get anything worse than a bit of *Mahdi's Revenge* (diarrhoea), or dysentery.

Pharmacies in Khartoum, Kassala, Port Sudan and Juba are generally well-stocked. Outside of these places it is a good idea to carry a small kit of medical supplies.

The Refugee Crises

The rock concerts have come and gone, raising millions of dollars for refugee relief supplies in the Sudan and the media blitz harking for more help has subsided, yet there are still more than one million refugees in need throughout the Sudan. Many of these people continue to suffer from malnutrition and disease.

If you are concerned about the situation and are seriously interested in helping, then it's possible to volunteer for a three to six month stint as a relief worker. Doctors, nurses, medical technicians, mechanics and administrators, preferably with experience in the third world, are desperately needed. The following are non-profit organisations which have been helping the refugees in the Sudan.

The American Refugee Committee

Objectives: the improvement of the general health conditions of refugee settlements and camps in eastern Sudan. One of their largest assistance programmes is in the settlement of Wad Sherifa where they operate a medical clinic and feeding centre for 60,000 Ethiopian refugees. They hire doctors, nurses and mechanics for three to six month stints.

LALMBA Association

Objectives: to operate and maintain a medical unit, three village clinics and dispensaries and four feeding centres for malnourished people. Their main centre is in the eastern Sudan town of Showak. The village clinics and feeding centres are to the east near the Ethiopian border. They are based in Golden, Colorado, USA.

Lutheran World Federation

PO Box 40870, Nairobi, Kenya

CARE

Objectives: to provide food and medical assistance to 150,000 Chadian refugees and 400,000 displaced Sudanese in western Sudan and to facilitate the transport of aid from Port Sudan. They are based in New York.

Médecins Sans Frontières

Objectives: to provide emergency medical assistance to refugees. Their address is 68 Boulevard Saint Marcel, 75005 Paris, France.

Catholic Relief Services

Objectives: to provide food and medical assistance and oversee development projects.

OXFAM

Objectives: to provide assistance in the form of food, such as the famous OXFAM 'Energy Biscuits'; clothing and transportation. OXFAM is based in the UK but they also have offices in the USA and Australia.

Save the Children Fund

They are based in the UK and the USA and their involvement in refugee problems in the Sudan is extensive.

AUSTCARE

Objectives: to provide food and medical assistance to refugees in the Sudan, Ethiopia, Somalia and Chad. Their address is GPO Box 9820, Melbourne, Victoria 3001, Australia.

These are only some of the organisations providing assistance in the Sudan. If you are interested in getting involved, keep in mind that previous experience with refugee problems is highly desired by most of these groups. Working in the refugee camps of Sudan is not recommended for the uninitiated.

POPULATION & PEOPLE

The Sudan's population numbers only about 23¼ million, yet there are more than 300 distinct tribes from more than 150 ethnic groups speaking more than 100 languages and dialects. The groups range from the predominantly Muslim Arabs, Nubians and Fur in the north and west, to the more Christian and animist African peoples in the south. It is interesting to travel from north to south to see the transition from Arab to African cultures.

In the north, adherence to Islamic strictures such as *sharia* (Islamic law) is strong. Alcohol and pork are outlawed and clothing is conservative. The men wear long flowing gowns called *galabiyyas* and loosely wrapped turbans called *emmas*. The women wear *tobes* which are nothing more than several metres of sheer, brightly coloured material wrapped around their heads and upper bodies and usually worn over a gown.

In Khartoum, women office workers wear only white *tobes* because, as one woman told me, 'We don't want a carnival atmosphere in our offices'.

In eastern Sudan, the women tend to wear brown or black *tobes* and some, such as the Rashaida women, also wear the ever-mysterious veil revealing only their dark, piercing eyes and curly, black bangs.

As you travel south, the people become darker-skinned, culturally more African and generally less conservative than the northern Muslims. They usually wear less clothing and some tribes, such as the Nuba in the Kordofan province in the Nuba mountains, wear no clothing at all. South of El Obeid you will also find a forlorn pork chop or two and a few varieties of bootleg spirits – things which are definitely in short supply to the north.

Although northerners and southerners are often culturally distinct, some are very similar in appearance as there has been much intermarriage between Arabs and Africans in the Sudan. Consequently, it is often possible to meet a person who looks African yet professes to be Arab. This is also due, in part, to the prevalence of decorative facial scarring.

This practice is common among both African and Arab men and women. The purposes and meanings of different scar patterns vary from group to group though it is usually a sign of tribal identification or, for some women, a sign of beauty.

Another practice which crosses ethnic groups and tribes is female circumcision. Westerners find this barbaric and incomprehensible but for many Sudanese it is still an accepted part of their culture, although the government and many parents supposedly try to discourage it. They are, however, fighting an age-old tradition. An elderly woman in each village is usually assigned the role of circumcising girls when they reach the age of five. Despite the controversy surrounding this practice, many Sudanese women proudly regard their circumcision as a sign of womanhood and a means of pleasing their husbands.

The Sudanese are some of the poorest, yet most generous and hospitable people in Africa. As you travel through the country they will welcome you into their homes to sip tea, break bread, chat and sometimes to stay for a few days. On buses, trains, ferries and even camel caravans, people will share whatever food and drink they have.

On a bus from Khartoum to Kassala, I sat opposite a Sudanese woman and her two young sons. She made a small lunch of cheese sandwiches and olives and, without a word, wrapped a sandwich and a couple of olives in paper and placed it on my lap.

GEOGRAPHY

The Sudan, the largest country in Africa, is bordered by Egypt, Libya, Chad, the Central African Republic, Zaire, Uganda, Kenya and Ethiopia. A country of contrasts, it stretches from the deserts of Nubia to the equatorial rainforests and swamps of the Sudd, just north of the great lakes and the source of the Nile.

In the north, the Nile slices through seemingly endless and lifeless desert plains. In some places the desert comes right up to the banks of the river, while in others a narrow band of vegetation separates the water from the barren sands.

In Khartoum, the two sources of the mighty Nile River become one. The Blue Nile flows down from Lake Tana, through the highlands of Ethiopia and via the Sudanese towns of Er Roseires and Wad Medani before joining the much longer White Nile, which starts from Lake Victoria on the Kenya-Uganda-Tanzania border.

There are several mountain ranges in the Sudan. In the far west is the Jebel Marra range – the highest in the country

and a favourite hiking area among travellers. Closer to Khartoum are the Nuba Mountains – home to the intriguing and long-isolated tribes of the Nuba people. In the east are the Red Sea Hills and the mountain resort of Erkowit, that dates from British colonial days. In the south are the beautiful mountain ranges of Matong and Dongotona. Mt Kinyeti in the Immatong mountains is the highest peak in the Sudan at 3170 metres.

In the northern and western regions, most of the country is sparsely populated desert.

CLIMATE

The climate and weather vary greatly from north to south. The northern two-thirds of the Sudan is hot and dry most of the year. South of Khartoum, the temperatures tend to be lower but the humidity and rainfall are greater.

The best time to visit the Sudan is between November and March, before the rains and after the heat. If you decide that you must go there at any other time, then be prepared for very hot weather. Temperatures of 48°C (118°F) are not unusual in the north and even in the cooler south the maximum temperature is up around 37°C (96°C). In winter, from November to March, it is still hot but it usually gets no higher than the mid-30s.

Throughout the year you will encounter the infamous *haboob*, or *chamseen*, in all but the mountains and tropical regions. During these sandstorms of monstrous proportions, the sun disappears from the sky as a thick curtain of sand falls over the land and the winds begin howling. Everything and everyone in its path gets coated with fine grains of dust.

RELIGION

More than 70% of the population are Muslim, while 20%, or more, adhere to various indigenous religions and 5% are Christian.

Islam

Most Sudanese Muslims, like the Egyptians, belong to the Sunni sect. But, more so than in Egypt, various mystical and political currents of Islam have gained significant followings in the Sudan.

Generally, the mystical side of Islam is referred to as Sufism. Throughout the Sudan various Sufi orders or fraternities follow their own *Tariq*, which is a path or way to God. The members of a Tariq attain a closer relationship with Allah through special spiritual exercises conducted by the sheikh or leader of the Tariq. The exercises vary from simply reciting Qur'anic passages to singing, dancing and whirling oneself into a state of ecstasy. The *Whirling Dervishes* of Omdurman (near Khartoum) are renowned for their weekly whirls.

The more political currents of Islam in the Sudan are not necessarily detached from mainstream Sunni Islam or the various Sufi orders, however, they can be considered as separate groups under the rallying flag of Islam.

One of the most important politico-religious movements in the Sudan is called *Ansar*. It has its roots in the Mahdiyya movement of the late 19th century, the thrust of which has not changed much since then. The members of Ansar believe that a *Mahdi*, a messenger of God and representative of Mohammed, will come to lead the people. The movement has become quite a political force among a variety of tribal groups ranging from the nomadic Baggara Arabs to the sedentary tribes of the White Nile.

A related organisation is the *Ikhwan al Muslimiyya* or Muslim Brotherhood. Essentially, they are a political organisation which seeks religious ends by encouraging the institution of Islamic society and polity based on *sharia*. Their popularity and influence seems to increase as economic conditions worsen. Their developing power was, perhaps, a major reason for Nimeiri's declaration of *sharia* in 1983. The Brotherhood continues to be a major

and, some would say, potentially destabilising influence on Sudanese politics.

Indigenous Religions

At least 20% of the population adheres to some form of indigenous or local religion. The forms vary by ethnic group and tribe but, in general, they relate to certain forces of nature and ancestor worship.

The Dinka, Nuer and other Nilotic tribes of southern Sudan, for example, see human beings as ants in relation to God, though certain men and women among them are sometimes considered to have special god-like powers. They are often accused of being sorcerers or witches, of practising black magic and inflicting illness upon people or animals.

In the north, the notion of the 'evil eye' is prevalent among the Arabs. One who expresses too much interest in the affairs of another can be suspected of deliberately causing harm to that person. To protect against witches, sorcerers and the evil eye, each group has its versions of diviners, witch doctors and exorcists who provide amulets, medicinal concoctions and advice.

Christianity

Only 5% of the population are Christian. Most of them are Roman Catholics but there are some Anglicans. Missionary incursions over the last two centuries, especially in southern Sudan, account for most of the Christian population and missionaries continue to actively 'spread the word' throughout that region.

FESTIVALS & HOLIDAYS

For a rundown of the Islamic holidays and festivals refer to the Egypt Facts about the Country chapter. Other holidays in the Sudan are:

1 January
   Independence Day; commemorates the birth of the independent Republic of the Sudan in 1956. On this day the soldiers who are not fighting civil war battles in

the south get to line up and parade through the streets of Khartoum.

27 March
Unity Day; commemorates the signing of the Addis Ababa Accords which ostensibly unified northern and southern Sudan in 1972.

25 May
May Revolution Day; celebrates Nimeiri's coup d'etat in 1969. Since the overthrow of Nimeiri in 1985, the status of this holiday is in doubt.

25 December
Christmas Day is considered a national holiday.

LANGUAGES
Although there are more than 100 languages and dialects in the Sudan, Arabic is the main language and Dinka is prevalent in southern Sudan. English is spoken throughout the country.

English should suffice for travel in most parts of the Sudan but, as in Egypt, knowledge of even a few words of Arabic brings instant smiles from the locals. Sudanese Arabic is, however, slightly different to Egyptian Arabic.

Pronunciation
The hard **g** sound does not exist. It is pronounced as a **j**. For example, the word *galabiyya* (the long cotton gown worn by men), is pronounced *jalabiyya* in the Sudan.

Secondly, the **sh** sound is generally not used at the end of a verb to negate it. Thus, the Egyptian phrase *mafeesh* – which means 'there is not' or 'there are not' – becomes *mafee* in the Sudan.

Vocabulary
There are also a few differences in vocabulary between the two countries. The following words and phrases are the Sudanese equivalents:

How are you?
- to a man   *Kayf Hallak?*
                    (pron. 'aleck')
- to a woman   *Kayf Hallik?*
                    (pron. 'alick')
Foreigner   *Hawadja*

The word lists in the Egypt section are, for the most part, applicable to the Sudan. *Hawadja* is a word which you will hear often as you travel through the Sudan.

Facts for the Visitor

VISAS

Visas are required by all, but the requirements vary from embassy to embassy and are liable to change at any time. Restrictions relating to South Africa and Israel, however, hold for all applications.

Anyone whose passport contains signs of having visited Israel, such as an Israeli stamp or an Egyptian border stamp, will be denied a Sudanese visa. If you crossed overland to or from Israel, then you are doomed unless you have a second passport. Some embassies will readily issue you a second passport so check with your own government's passport office or embassy. The American Embassy in Cairo, for example, issues second passports in a day or two for US$35. South African nationals cannot obtain Sudanese visas.

Visas must be obtained from a Sudanese consulate or embassy. They cannot be obtained at Sudanese border-posts, airports or ports.

However, at Aswan in Egypt a Dutch traveller and I put on suits and ties and tried to get temporary Sudanese visas from the local Sudanese Trade Representative. We did not get them but we almost got letters supposedly granting us permission to enter the Sudan. According to expatriates in the Sudan, emergency visas used to be issued upon arrival at the airport, so you never know, it may just depend on the mood of the government or the official at the time.

Generally, the requirements for 90-day tourist visas are: US$10 in cash or money order; three passport-size photographs, two copies of the application form; a letter of recommendation from your embassy; and proof of a return air ticket or the means to buy one, this can be a credit card or letter from your bank.

Bear in mind that these requirements can change and are not absolute!

According to some travellers, the Sudanese Embassy in London (tel 8398080), Cleveland Row, SW1, grants visas in 24 hours.

The embassy in Washington, 2210 Massachusetts Avenue, NW, Washington, DC 20008, grants visas in two to three weeks, though it has been known to take as long as two months.

The latest reports about the embassy in Cairo are good. With a letter of recommendation from your embassy it could take as little as two or three hours to get the visa, though in the past there have been waits of up to 21 days.

Americans can get their letters of recommendation from window No 9 in the consular section of the US Embassy in Cairo. The French embassy in Cairo will not issue letters of recommendation for French nationals and Sudanese visas should be applied for in France.

Proof of cholera and yellow fever vaccinations is required for passengers arriving from infected areas. African countries south of latitude 12°N are considered infected areas.

Registration & Visa Extensions

All visitors are required to register within three days of arrival in the country, at the Aliens' Office in Khartoum.

You must also register with the police within 24 hours of your arrival in other towns and cities. According to travellers' reports, though, Kassala seemed to be the only town where the police abided by this rule.

Visa extensions can also be obtained in one day at the Aliens' Office for S£10.

Travel Permits

Travel permits are required for travel anywhere outside Khartoum. They can be obtained for S£5, with two passport-size photographs, in three hours from the

Aliens' Office. To allow for flexibility in your travels through the Sudan, indicate your destinations as regions or provinces rather than individual cities or towns.

MONEY

US$1	=	S£2.45
A$1	=	S£1.65
UK£1	=	S£3.70
C$1	=	S£1.82
DM1	=	S£1.34

Sudanese currency is divided into pounds (S£) and piastres; 100 piastres = S£1.

Theoretically, you are supposed to declare the amount of foreign currency that you bring into the Sudan. However, I have heard no reports of anyone ever being asked for a currency declaration form or official exchange receipts. It is, therefore, hardly surprising that the black market for foreign currency, especially US dollars and British pounds, is flourishing in the Sudan.

At some hotels, however, bank receipts showing that you changed money officially must be presented if you want to pay your bill in Sudanese pounds. Most of the hotels which require this though, are so outrageously priced that they're out of the average traveller's budget anyway. Airlines also require bank receipts for international ticket purchases.

There are three exchange rates in the Sudan. Hotels have the worst rates – US$1 = S£2.20; banks are a bit better – US$1 = S£2.45; and the black market, of course, is the best – US$1 = S£3.70 for travellers' cheques or S£4.20 for US$1 cash. In the information on each town, I have tried to indicate the best places for changing money.

If you're coming overland from Egypt, you can buy Sudanese pounds in the Aswan bazaars, from the stalls, curio shops and camel traders. The rate is less than the black market rate in the Sudan but better than the bank rate.

Transferring Money

The best way to have money sent to you in Khartoum is through Citibank. Call home or send a telex to your bank and give them your passport number. To claim your money in Khartoum you will need to show an onward air ticket and your passport, and pay a commission of US$11.

American Express has an office in Khartoum but they do not offer any financial services such as cashing cheques or money transfers.

GENERAL INFORMATION

Post

The Post Office in Khartoum is open from 7.30 am to 1 pm and 5.30 to 6.30 pm. Mail to the USA takes about two weeks but from the US can take up to a month.

There is a Poste Restante service in the Central Post Office of every major town and city.

Electricity

The electric current is 240 volts AC.

Time

There is only one time zone in the Sudan and that is two hours ahead of Greenwich Mean Time. So, when it's 12 noon in Khartoum it is: 10 am in London; 5 am in New York and Montreal; 2 am in Los Angeles; 1 pm in Moscow; and 8 pm in Melbourne and Sydney.

Business Hours

Most shops are open from 8 am to 2 pm and 6 to 8 pm. Government offices are officially open from 8 am to 2.30 pm. If you must visit a government office, however, it's better to show up after 9 am to give the busy bureaucrats enough time to have tea and read the newspaper.

Banks are open from Saturday to Thursday between 8.30 am and noon.

Fridays are holidays for Muslims; and Sundays are holidays for Christians.

MEDIA

Newspapers & Magazines

Five to six-day-old copies of *The International Herald Tribune*, and week-old editions of *Time, Newsweek* and *The Economist* can be bought at the Meridien and the Hilton in Khartoum.

One of the best sources of current information on the Sudan is the English-language magazine *Sudanow* published in Khartoum by the Ministry of Culture & Information. Although it is a government publication, it is surprisingly frank and critical of the government. Recent articles have included discussions of 'Sudan's paraplegic economy', the problems of Sudan Railways and why southern Sudan is rebelling.

Radio & Television

The Sudan has one television station and a few radio stations. The TV news in English is at 7.25 pm and there are occasionally also English-language programmes.

For the latest radio news in English tune into the Voice of America or the British Broadcasting Corporation. Both operate on several short wave frequencies and a couple of medium wave frequencies at various times throughout the day and night.

HEALTH

Vaccinations

You must have yellow fever and cholera vaccinations if you have come from an infected area, which includes most African countries south of the Sudan. Other recommended vaccinations include typhoid and tetanus and you should also consider gamma globulin for protection against infectious hepatitis.

Health Precautions, Medical Kit & Insurance

Refer to the Health section in the Egypt Facts for the Visitor chapter for detailed information on the more common ailments and diseases in this part of the world and how to avoid or treat them; the suggested items for a first aid kit; and advice on how sensible it is to have travel insurance.

Medical

There is a severe shortage of adequately trained medical personnel and medical equipment in the Sudan and most of the country's doctors and facilities are in Khartoum. There are doctors and hospitals in most towns but the level of medical care is a far cry from western standards.

If you become seriously ill, first try to see a doctor from one of the relief agencies. If that doesn't work and you need to be hospitalised, try to leave the country. I realise this sounds a bit alarmist, but after seeing a few wards and hearing a couple of horror stories about hospital conditions from expatriate teachers and doctors, I believe it is sound advice.

An expatriate teacher who was hospitalised for a knife wound (he was stabbed in the arm one night in Khartoum) told me that they allowed him to stay in the hospital as long as he wanted because most of the ward was being emptied out. The patients who had been there were being moved to the tuberculosis ward because they had all contracted TB after entering the hospital for other, unrelated ailments. The teacher left the hospital as quickly as possible.

Another possibility for medical treatment is through the International Association for Medical Assistance to Travellers (IAMAT). Check with the US or British embassies for further information.

Food & Water

Unless your stomach has already been introduced to the revengeful cuisine of other third world locales, then the chances are that diarrhoea will strike. Once again refer to the Health section in the Egypt Facts for the Visitor chapter for info on how to cope.

Tap water in Khartoum and Kassala is generally safe to drink, however in other parts of the country you should boil the water or use water purification tablets or iodine. Sometimes the water may be so cloudy that it may be a good idea to filter it through a handkerchief or piece of cloth.

FILM & PHOTOGRAPHY

Permits are required for photography in the Sudan and can be obtained free from the Sudanese Tourism Corporation office. The permit is merely a formality as you will rarely, if ever, be asked to produce it.

It is still, of course, a good idea to exercise discretion when taking photographs in the Sudan. Do not point your camera at anything which might be considered to be related to the military or of high security. This includes air fields, bridges, soldiers and government buildings. When taking photographs of the locals it is always better to ask first, as some people simply don't like being photographed and others are offended by it.

Film is expensive in the Sudan so stock up before you arrive. Processing, on the other hand, is relatively cheap. Expatriate residents in Khartoum recommend the *Fantastic Colour Lab*, which is on the ground floor of the building which houses the French Cultural Centre, around the corner from the Taysir Bus Company. They can process a 36 colour print film in two hours for about S£30.

ACCOMMODATION
Youth Hostels

There are two youth hostels in the Sudan – one in Khartoum and the other in Port Sudan. At S£1.50 per night (slightly less with a Youth Hostel Card), they are the cheapest places to stay though conditions are very basic. They have lots of bunk beds crammed in a room and bathrooms are dirty, but if you are on an extremely tight budget, then you may not mind getting what you pay for.

Lakondas

The most common form of accommodation in the Sudan, the lakondas usually consist of a series of basic rooms around an open courtyard. Beds tend to be closely woven rope nets stretched over a wooden frame. When it is hot – which is often – the beds are put in the courtyard. They are simple, but cheap and comfortable places to stay. Prices are usually less than S£15 per night.

Government Rest Houses

These are also common throughout the Sudan. They are one step above the lakondas and sometimes even cheaper. Outside of Khartoum, Kassala and Port Sudan, these are some of the best places to stay. Prices and arrangements for accommodation vary from town to town.

Hotels

Khartoum has its fair share of luxury hotels, such as the Hilton and the Meridien, and like luxury hotels in any country they are comfortable but expensive.

The cheaper hotels in the Sudan are usually run by Greeks or Sudanese and do not require bank receipts proving that you changed your money officially. They have most of the amenities of semi-decent hotels, such as bugless beds, running water, maybe even a sink *and* a bathroom in the room and occasional meals. They usually have a big fan whirling over the bed or an air-cooler which drips and moves the air with a lot of noise. Room prices tend to range from S£20 to S£70.

FOOD

Sudanese food is very simple. Few spices are used and most dishes are seasoned with only lemon juice, salt, pepper and broth. Following are some of the most common dishes.

Vegetables

Fuul is stewed beans served in a variety of ways – sometimes with a sprinkling of cheese and mixed with salad. It is eaten by first mashing the beans with the salad and scooping the result into your mouth with a piece of pita bread.

Fassoulia is a dish of smaller, stewed beans which taste a bit like Heinz baked beans without the sauce.

Bit-tatas are boiled potatoes.

Salata is a salad of tomatoes, green leaf lettuce, onions, green peppers, and lime juice dressing.

Sherifa is a green vegetable similar in texture to spinach.

Addis is the ever-popular yellow lentil, one of the most common vegetables in the Sudan.

Bamiyya, also known as ladies' fingers or okra, is a long green vegetable with red tips often used in soups and stews.

Mashay are tomatoes or aubergines stuffed with rice and minced lamb.

Many vegetable dishes are served with one lump of meat, a splash of oil and a watery broth.

Meat Dishes

Kebab is stewed or skewered meat, usually lamb.

Kalawi is chopped kidney, usually served with a bit of bread and a dash of lemon juice.

Kibda is stewed or skewered liver.

Shia is strips of beef or lamb, cooked on a bed of coals and served with salad.

Lahma is a large, almost indistinguishable lump of beef or lamb served in soup.

Gammonia is stewed sheep's stomach, often served with tomatoes and onions.

Fish & Chicken

Nile Perch is a speciality of Khartoum and Omdurman and is served with a coating of fried batter and red peppers. It is usually available only in the mornings.

Chicken is usually stewed and served in a soup or broth.

Breads

Kisera is a thin, unleavened bread made from *durra*, which is a type of maize.

Gurassa is a thick, unleavened bread not often found in Khartoum but common elsewhere.

Dessert

Hoshab is a cold, red cocktail made from chopped bananas, figs and raisins. It is the only dessert I know of and it's superb.

DRINKS

A variety of freshly squeezed juices is available throughout the Sudan. Some of the best include *kakaday* – a drink made from the hibiscus plant, *limoon* – lemonade, *burtuaan* – orange juice, *manga* – mango juice, guava juice and grapefruit juice.

Hot Drinks

Laban, which is hot sweetened milk, is very popular with the Sudanese but is served only in the evenings.

Shai saada is a sweet tea, served in small glasses without milk and sometimes spiced with cloves, mint or cinnamon.

Shai bi-laban is sweet tea with milk, usually only served in the early morning or early evenings.

Shai bi-nana is a sweet, mint-flavoured tea.

Ahwa Fransawi literally means 'French coffee' but it generally refers to western-style instant coffee, such as Nescafe.

Ahwa Turki is very strong Turkish coffee, served in very small coffee cups.

Jebbana is very strong coffee served from a tin or earthenware container with a conical spout. It is drunk from small china bowls and often spiced with cinnamon, ginger or other spices. *Jebbana* refers to the name of the container.

Alcoholic Drinks

Alcohol is officially banned under Islamic law, however, it is still possible to find a few bootleg concoctions.

Aragi is a clear, strong drink made from dates. It tastes a bit like Bacardi rum and can easily knock you off your feet.

Merissa is a beer made from sorghum which looks gross but tastes unique.

Tedj is the name for a variety of wines made from dates or honey, some of which isn't too bad.

BOOKS

Not many books have been written about the Sudan but there are a few which are highly recommended.

Nick Worrall's *Sudan* (London Times Press), is an excellent summary, in words and photographs, of the diversity of cultures in contemporary Sudan.

Alan Moorehead's classics, *The Blue Nile* and *The White Nile* (New English Library, 1982 and Penguin Books), should be read by anyone planning a trip to Egypt or the Sudan. Both books are certain to whet your appetite for exploration and adventure.

Mike Asher's book *In Search of the 40 Days Road* recounts his search for the trail which Sudanese camel-traders follow when taking their camels north to Aswan. It was published in 1984 by Longman Publishers and is a bit difficult to find.

The Sudan, A Country Handbook is the best general reference on the Sudan. It is published by the American University Press in Washington, DC and is updated every three to five years.

The London Times publication *With Geldof in Africa* recounts Bob Geldof's 1985 BANDAID trips to refugee camps. The photographs are a superb and very moving presentation of the peoples of Sudan.

Leni Riefenstahl's book, *The People of Kau* (Collins Publishers, 1976), is also recommended for its photographs. Her book caused a bit of controversy a few years ago because it drew a lot of attention to the Nuba people. The Sudanese government was embarrassed by the nakedness and 'primitive ways' of the Nuba people. The development-conscious government did not want the Sudan presented to the world as a country of naked tribesmen who paint themselves with red mud, wrestle and hunt with spears. Yet it is the ability of these people to continue their traditional way of life that is one of the beautiful things about the Sudan.

Al-Tayyib Salih's books are also recommended. He writes fictionalised literary accounts of life in the Sudan and one can learn much from his books. Some of the titles include *The Wedding of Zein & Other Stories* and *The Season of Migration to the North* (3 Continents Press, Washington DC, 1978).

MAPS

Michelin Map No 154 of North-East Africa is excellent for the Sudan but lousy for Egypt. The Land Survey office near the Government Palace in Khartoum sells some of the best maps on the Sudan.

THINGS TO BUY

On the streets of Khartoum and Kassala men and boys cloaked in gowns and turbans will rush up to you clutching swords, daggers and knives. Each weapon is sheathed in stained leather and ready for use – or rather sale. As many Sudanese still often wear daggers and swords at their sides as part of their dress, although as a form of protection they have been superseded by modern weaponry, these little demonstrations are a bit scary.

When I arrived in Khartoum I didn't realise that these sword-bearing characters merely wanted to sell me their wares so I ran away down the street the first time

one of them waved his sword in my face. However, if you're a budding Lawrence of Arabia or Mata Hari or you've just always wanted an exotic blade, then this is definitely the place to buy it.

In the Omdurman *souk* you can buy some beautiful pieces of ivory jewellery for half the price you'd pay in Europe or the US – that is if you don't object to contributing to the decline of the elephant population. Other ideologically unsound artefacts include stuffed crocodiles or wallets and purses made from crocodile skin; the World Wildlife Fund would have a fit here.

Many places in the *souk* also sell beautiful ebony carvings.

WHAT TO BRING

Since it is warm in the Sudan throughout the year, bring light clothing. If you are planning a trek into the cooler climes of Jebel Marra or the isolated Red Sea Hills resort of Erkowit, then bring a sweater.

During the rainy season you must have a poncho or cool, loose-fitting rain jacket, though it is still warm even when it rains.

It is also a good idea to have a bandana (the large, usually chequered handkerchief often seen on the bad guys in westerns), to cover your mouth and nose during sandstorms or wild rides on the backs of lorries.

Other suggested accessories include: sunglasses, a hat, a big plastic rubbish bag to cover your pack during rain and sand storms, insect repellent, a mosquito net, a bed sheet (sleeping bags are useful only as something to sleep on) and nylon cord to string up your mosquito net and use as a laundry line.

Most toiletries and first aid supplies are readily available in Khartoum and Port Sudan.

Getting There

AIR

Flying is the most expensive way to get to the Sudan. Ironically, it costs only a bit less for a one-way flight to Khartoum from Nairobi or Cairo than it does to buy a return ticket from London. That is due, in part, to the currency exchange regulations in Egypt and Kenya.

On the other hand because of the troubles in southern Sudan, which makes travelling overland through there almost impossible, flying is really the only way to enter the country from any of the southern African countries.

If you buy airline tickets in the Sudan you must produce bank receipts to prove you changed the money officially, which makes the tickets quite expensive.

For more detailed general information on the types of tickets and the best places to buy them, refer to the Getting There chapter in the Egypt section at the start of the book.

From the UK

Several airlines fly from London to Khartoum, including EgyptAir, British Airways, Aeroflot (via Moscow, but they are not the cheapest), Balkan Air (via Sofia, Bulgaria), Kenyan Airways, and Sudan Airways. The best deals on flights to Khartoum can be found in the London magazines *Time Out*, *LAM* or *The News & Travel Magazine (TNT)*. The approximate return fare, through one of London's 'bucket shop' travel agencies is US$320.

From Europe

Amsterdam Some of the best fares in Amsterdam are through the student travel bureau *NBBS Reiswinkels* (tel 020 237686), Dam No 17. KLM has reasonably priced return flights to Khartoum which the NBBS can arrange.

KLM also fly from Khartoum to Kilimanjaro (about US$390) and Dar es Salaam (about US$430) in Tanzania. They sometimes offer student discounts of 25%.

Switzerland In Zurich, check with the Air Ticket Service AG (tel 01-2526464) at Seilergraben 49. They are especially good at arranging unique around-the-world fares.

From Africa

Sudan Airways, Kenyan Airways, Air Ethiopia Tunis Air, British Airways and KLM are some of the airlines which provide services between the Sudan and other African countries.

One-way flights between Nairobi and Khartoum cost about US$300; and from Entebbe to Khartoum they're about US$270. If you buy your ticket in the Sudan to fly from Khartoum to Nairobi or Entebbe these tickets will cost considerably more because of the currency regulations.

From Egypt

A one-way flight from Cairo to Khartoum costs about US$300.

A unique way to fly from Egypt to the Sudan is with Sudan Airways from Aswan to Khartoum. Sudan Airways has been dubbed *Insha'allah* Airways and it won't take you long to work out why it has earned this nickname. *Insha'allah* means 'if God wills it'.

The flight leaves Aswan every Tuesday at the Allah-forsaken hour of 4.30 am, or earlier if the plane fills up before, and costs about US$200. I arrived at the Aswan airport at 3 am and watched as a group of men in long flowing robes and turbans dragged pig-sized aluminum pots and huge bundles wrapped in blankets through the door. They had to open their bundles and pots for security and check their daggers in at the ticket counter.

In the waiting lounge I could see one other westerner – a young man in a white linen jacket and straw hat with a portable typewriter and plastic shopping bag in one hand, and a silver-headed walking cane in the other. His name was Willy and he set off the alarms when he went through the metal detector because one of his legs was prosthetic. The Egyptian security guard took the leg off and searched it.

Willy and I boarded after most of the caravan had clambered to their seats and what greeted us was certainly a sight to be seen. Our travelling companions were all men who could have been right off the movie set of *Lawrence of Arabia* – and they all looked petrified. As the plane began to move down the runway, I understood their fear. It groaned and creaked as it accelerated and took an agonisingly long time to take off. It did however, get us safely to Khartoum and the caravan got their daggers back.

BOAT
There is ferry-service four times a month between Port Sudan and Suez but the schedule is a bit erratic. For more information, see the Port Sudan getting there section.

The most common overland route from Egypt to the Sudan is the Nile steamer from Aswan to Wadi Halfa. It leaves from the docks south of the High Dam between 11 am and 3 pm on Mondays and Thursdays. The journey takes about 20 hours and costs E£26 for 2nd class and E£50 for 1st class. The steamer ride can be hot and uncomfortable but it is an interesting way to enter the country. For more details see the Aswan Getting There section.

OVERLAND
It is currently possible to safely enter the Sudan from only three of the eight countries on its borders: Egypt, Chad and the Central African Republic. Conditions on most borders, except Egypt's, are apt to change for the worse because civil war in southern Sudan, Uganda and Chad has made travel by land extremely difficult or impossible.

We have, however, received some recent reports from a traveller who hitch-hiked into Chad from the Sudan. He received lifts with European Community trucks guarded by armed escorts, and lived to write us a letter about it.

There were trucks travelling from Kenya, Uganda and Zaire but it's not possible to take this route because of the strife in southern Sudan.

The only way to enter Sudan overland from Kenya or Uganda at the moment is to do the long circuit through Zaire to the Central African Republic, and into the Sudan at Nyala in the west. It's an arduous journey, taking at least four weeks from Kenya. Reports also indicate that there are trucks going from Bangui in the CAR to Nyala in the Sudan, almost everyday for about US$35. The price is probably subject to bargaining though.

The most common overland route is from Egypt and, depending on how adventurous you are, there are a few alternatives. The easiest and most popular is the Nile steamer up Lake Nasser between Wadi Halfa and Aswan; if you have your own vehicle it's possible to drive along the Red Sea coast; or you can try and join the camel herders on 'The 40 Day Road' from western Sudan, through the Sahara to Aswan.

For more information refer to the Egypt Getting There chapter and the Aswan Getting There section.

Getting Around

Whichever route you take through the Sudan, you'll end up having to use an interesting collection of trucks, riverboats, trains, international agency jeeps, mail vans, camels, donkeys and even the occasional free flight, as baggage, in a light plane. Apart from flights, all travel is slow and many routes are impassable during the rainy season from June to September, so allow plenty of time to get through this country. It isn't just road transport which takes time though, even the trains are notoriously slow and subject to long delays.

AIR

Sudan *Insha'allah* Airways is the only airline which makes internal flights and, theoretically, they fly to all of the Sudan's major cities. Check the latest issue of *Sudanow* for up to date flight information.

It is difficult, if not impossible, to make reservations for any internal flights from Sudan Airways offices in other countries.

Waiting lists for most flights can be as long as three weeks. In Khartoum I met a United Nations Development programme official who waited two weeks before he got on a flight to El Obeid, which is only about 340 km as the crow, or plane, flies.

Some travellers have managed to hitch rides around the country with cargo planes but the chances of this are fairly slim and depend entirely on the whims of the pilots themselves.

Although it's not recommended with the current political situation, we have heard of some people hopping cargo planes from Khartoum to Juba. The *only* reason to go to Juba at the moment would be the very unlikely possibility that you could get another free or cheap cargo plane out of the Sudan. It's not advisable to go to Juba just for the hell of it. The government still holds the town but the rebels have it surrounded and the whole region is under their control.

The following information, however, was sent to us by Lias Olsen (USA) who

travelled through the Sudan in late 1985. It may be useful if the situation in the south changes for the better.

Try cargo flights – go to the airport manager's office and tell him your problem. He will direct you to Banjari Air, a subsidiary of Trans-Arabian. Their office is out on the runway, a long hot walk over the tarmac. They fly to Juba daily, but at various unscheduled times, and will let you fly as cargo for nothing. However, if they direct you to their town office (near the Kenyan Embassy), the officials there will tell you that you need a special permission paper to fly as cargo from the Department of Civil Aviation. The special permission means that you agree to accept all responsibility for your flight, in case you die aboard or are injured. It takes a few hours to get this, but one can receive it easily if you just say that Sudan Airways flights are booked weeks in advance so you need to fly as soon as possible.

TRAIN
Sudan Railways runs an extensive but somewhat rundown collection of trains. The system dates back to General Kitchener's rush to clobber the Mahdi in the late 1890s. He laid track from Wadi Halfa to Abu Hamed across 370 km of harsh Nubian desert in 1897 at the rate of half a km a day. For details of this line's schedule today and other train services see the Getting There sections of the relevant towns.

There are three classes on Sudanese trains – 1st, 2nd and 3rd. First class compartments carry six passengers but 2nd and 3rd class compartments seem to have no limit to the number of passengers. The 2nd and 3rd classes also have sub-classes called *mumtaz* which translates as 'excellent'. So, presumably, 2nd class *mumtaz* is better than regular 2nd class. The differences are usually barely noticeable though.

It is also possible to ride on top of the trains for free although this is not officially condoned because people have been known to fall off. It is often difficult to plant yourself firmly on top and it can get quite hot and dusty, so protect yourself from the elements and tie your pack down.

Student discounts of 50% to 75% are available for those under 26 years-old. Permission can be obtained from the Ministry of Youth in Khartoum or the Area Controllers' office in other towns. Travellers report, however, that the discounts are not available on the train from Wadi Halfa.

BUS
Travelling by bus is very common throughout the Sudan even though only 2% of the country's roads are paved. The most common type of bus is built a bit like a raised tank with an open frame and several rows of slatted benches. The sides have canvas flaps which fold down to keep the dust out. There are also 'luxury' buses but these only run between Khartoum, Kassala and Port Sudan. A couple of the luxury bus lines have air-con or semi-air-con buses, comfortable seats and shock absorbers. This is luxury indeed if you're going to be spending eight to 10 hours on a bus.

TRUCK
Souk lorries, which are big Bedford market trucks, transport goods and people between almost every town and village in the Sudan. For a minimal amount of money you get to share the back of a truck with as many as 40 people, sacks of grain, live goats, bags of sugar and bundles of cotton or whatever else needs to be transported and sold. Some travellers I met in the Sudan swear by this economical form of travel but you never know what might be in that large, putrescent bundle next to you. My travel companions on one truck trip were a pile of dead, desiccated goats with eyes bulging and mouths agape. All 10 goats stared at me from Showak to Kassala, where I thankfully got off.

If you do travel by truck, there are a few things to keep in mind. Take plenty of water for desert trips (you can buy large, plastic Thermos jugs in Khartoum), and it's a good idea to take something to eat as well. Food could be a problem along the way, depending on your destination, although bread is usually available in most villages. Make sure you have a hat or something to cover your head during the day and the nights can be cold, so be prepared. A torch (flashlight) is useful and lastly, you must be in fairly decent physical shape to endure travel by truck.

BOAT

As of mid-1986, the civil war hostilities have stopped the Nile steamers and most other Nile boat traffic, except the steamer from Aswan to Wadi Halfa. Garang has threatened to shoot at any boats moving south of Kosti.

CAMELS

In western and northern Sudan camels are also a common beast of burden and transport. Most of them are bred in western Sudan, so it is there that you will probably get the best deal on a camel –approximately US$150 for the latest model. But be warned if you have never ridden a camel – they can be noisome, temperamental and very difficult to handle.

DONKEYS

These contrary, sometimes adorable, critters are used throughout the Sudan as a mode of transport. *Souks* in most towns and villages sell them quite cheaply so you can even own-your-own donkey and travel at will, if you can get it to go where *you* want.

LOCAL TRANSPORT
Bus

Buses and 'boxes' are common transport in most cities. 'Boxes' are small pick-up trucks with two benches and a canvas covering over the back. They usually travel prescribed routes and are much cheaper than taxis.

Taxis

Taxis are prevalent in Khartoum, Omdurman, Kassala, Port Sudan and Wadi Halfa. Fares are subject to the whims of the drivers and the bargaining abilities of the passengers. Flagging down a taxi is simple – just stick your arm out and wave.

BICYCLES

Bicycles are not used much in the Sudan because most of the roads are so bad. However, in 1984 a couple of British cyclists built a contraption which allowed them to ride their bikes on the railway tracks and they travelled all the way from Wadi Halfa to Khartoum.

HITCHING

Hitching rides for free is uncommon in the Sudan as most drivers will ask for some sort of compensation.

Khartoum

The sun was rising as I hopped in a taxi at the Khartoum airport terminal and asked the driver to take me 'downtown'. Ten minutes later he stopped on a dirt street cluttered with trash and lined on one side with small two-storey buildings and on the other with a low white wall topped by shards of glass.

'We're here,' the driver said.

'Where?' I asked.

'Downtown, downtown Khartoum. *Ahlan wa Sahlan*,' he replied, which means welcome.

Actually, the 'real' downtown was just around the corner on El Gamhuriyya Avenue. But, although the buildings were taller, the street was paved and there was almost enough traffic to merit traffic lights, my first impressions stuck; it is a quiet city.

Khartoum lacks the congestion and squalor of other third world capitals and the streets near the river are lined with trees, which make it a very peaceful place to stroll. The population of only four to five million is spread between Khartoum and its sister cities, Omdurman and North Khartoum, across the Nile.

Khartoum was established as a military outpost in 1821 by Ismail, Mohammed Ali's son, who chose the site at the confluence of the Blue and White Niles on a jut of land which resembled a *khartoum*, or elephant's trunk. The city grew and prospered, especially between 1825 and 1880 when many of the inhabitants made their fortunes through the roaring slave trade. The slaves were captured from regions south of Khartoum and sold to traders in Egypt, Turkey and other northern countries.

Khartoum became the capital of the Sudan in 1834 and was used as a base by many European explorers of Africa. During the latter part of the 19th century however, its prosperity declined and it

was ransacked twice – first by the Mahdi to get rid of Gordon and then by Kitchener to get rid of the Mahdi.

Cook's *Traveller's Handbook for Egypt & the Sudan*, published in 1929, had the following to say about Gordon's defeat:

In 1884 General Gordon went to Khartûm to withdraw the Egyptian garrison, but very soon after the city was besieged by the Mahdi and his followers, and Gordon's position became desperate; famine, too, stared him in the face, for he distributed daily among the destitute in the city the supplies which would have been ample for the garrison . . . During the whole of January Gordon continued to feed all the people in Khartûm; 'for that he had, no doubt, God's reward, but he thereby ruined himself and his valuable men' . . . On the night of 25th January (1885) Gordon ordered a display of fireworks in the town to distract the people's attention, and in the early dawn of the 26th the Mahdists crossed the river, and, swarming up the bank of the White Nile where the fortifications had not been finished, conquered the Egyptian soldiers, who made but feeble resistance, and entered the town. Numbers of Egyptians were massacred, but the remainder laid down their arms and, when the Mahdists had opened the gates, marched out to the enemy's camp. The Dervishes rushed to the palace, where Gordon stood on the top of the steps . . . and in answer to his question, 'Where is your master, the Mahdi?' their leader plunged a huge spear into his body. He fell forward, was dragged down the steps, and his head having been cut off was sent over to the Mahdi in Omdurmân. The fanatics then rushed forward and dipped their spears and swords in his blood, and in a short time the body became 'a heap of mangled flesh'.

The Mahdi professed regret at Gordon's death, saying that he wished he had been taken alive, for he wanted to convert him . . . Khartûm was given up to such a scene of massacre and rapine as has rarely been witnessed even in the Sudan.

Thirteen years later Sir Herbert Kitchener and his troops took back the city, raising the British and Egyptian flags 'amid cheers for Her Majesty Queen Victoria, and the strains of the Khedival Hymn'. Kitchener began rebuilding Khartoum in 1898 and designed the streets along the lines of the Union Jack so that the city would be easier to defend. North Khartoum, on the other side of the Blue Nile, was developed as an industrial area at about the same time.

Before his defeat, the Mahdi had established the sister city of Omdurman across the confluence of the two Niles. Designed in a more traditional fashion with many small narrow streets, mud-brick buildings and a huge *souk*, this area has managed to resist many of the changes of the 20th century and retain its Islamic character.

It's not difficult to imagine how life in Khartoum may have been at the turn of the century, as the arcaded sidewalks and colonial-style architecture of some of the government buildings are still reminiscent of the Empire at her height. In typical British Imperialist fashion however, the description in Cooks *Traveller's Handbook* of 1929 is perhaps a little over the top:

The rebuilding of the city began immediately after the arrival of the British, and the visitor can judge for himself of the progress made in this respect during the twenty-three years of peace which have followed its occupation by a civilised power. (!!)

Orientation

The city centre lies on the south bank of the Blue Nile, and the British put their indelible mark on Khartoum by laying the streets out in the shape of the British flag. There you'll find the cheap hotels, restaurants and government offices.

South of the centre, across the railway line, is the New Extension which contains most of the embassies, the expatriates' clubs and the airport.

The city of Omdurman is north across the White Nile and Khartoum North is on the other side of the Blue Nile.

Information
Registration

Everyone is required to register with the Aliens' Registration Office in Khartoum within three days of arrival. The office is on the left side of El Khalifa Avenue down the street from the Central Post Office and towards the Nile.

Tourist Office

The Tourist Information Office (tel 74664) is on the corner of El Huriyya St and El Baladaya Avenue in the Sudan Tourist & Hotels Corporation building. It's open from 8.30 am to 2.30 pm. Photo permits are issued free there and also available is a colourful map of the Sudan.

Post & Telecommunications

Postal, telegraph and telephone services are all in the same building on the corner of El Gamaa and El Khalifa avenues.

The Post Office is open daily, except Fridays, from 8.30 am to 1 pm. It costs 75 pt for ordinary international letters. Poste Restante is located there.

The Telephone Office is open daily, except Fridays, from 8.30 am to 8 pm. Calls should be booked several hours or even a day in advance.

The Telegraph & Telex Office is open 24 hours a day, seven days a week including holidays. Telex numbers in Khartoum have become five-digit, so any previous three-digit numbers are now prefixed by 22.

American Express

The American Express Office is opposite the British Airways Office on a small side street just off El Gamhuriyya Avenue, between El Taiyar Morad and El Khalifa avenues. The office is upstairs, above the KLM office, and is open daily, except Fridays and Sunday evenings, from 8.30 am to 1.30 pm and 5.30 to 7.30 pm. Financial services, such as cheque cashing or cash exchange, are not available at this office.

The mail pick-up box is on the front counter and access to the box is

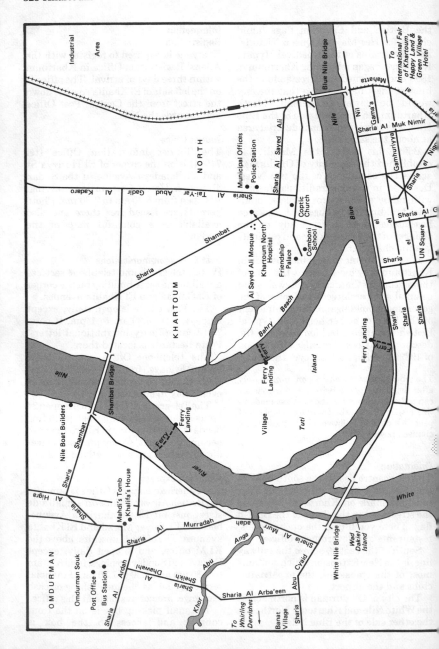

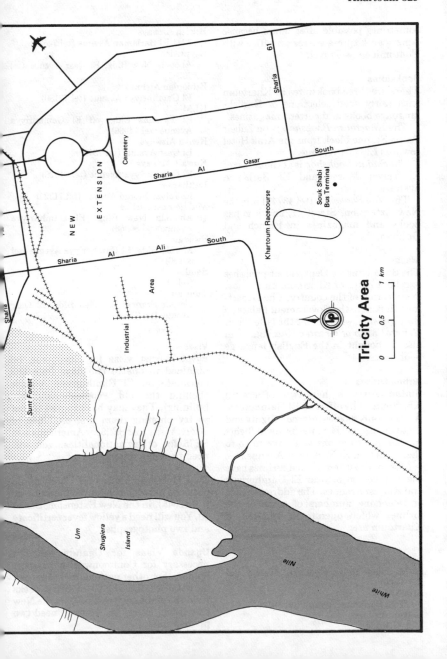

Tri-city Area

0   0.5   1 km

Sunt Forest

NEW EXTENSION

Cemetery

Sharia 61

Sharia Al Gasar South

Sharia Al Ali South

Industrial Area

Khartoum Racecourse

Souk Shabi Bus Terminal

Sharia

Um Shugiera Island

Nile

White Nile

sometimes possible after hours because American Express shares an office with Contomichalos Travel.

Bookstores

There are three bookstores in Khartoum with fairly good selections of English-language books and current magazines.

The *Khartoum Bookshop* is on Zubeir Pasha St, one block from the Arak Hotel towards El Qasr Avenue.

The *Sudan Bookshop* is at the corner of El Taiyar Morad and El Barlaman avenues.

The *Nile Bookshop* (tel 43749) is in the New Extension, Street 41, and also has books and magazines in French and German.

Maps

The Sudan Survey Department publishes excellent maps of Khartoum and almost every corner of the country. The Department is next to the Government Palace on the right side, when facing the Nile. Their *General Map of Greater Khartoum* can also be bought in the English-language bookstores.

Airline Offices

Sudan Airways has two offices in Khartoum. The office on El Gamhuriyya Avenue only books internal flights and flights to Egypt. For international flights to other destinations you have to go to their office on El Barlaman Avenue.

Most of the international airlines have their offices on or near El Gamhuriyya and El Qasr avenues. The addresses and/or telephone numbers of some of the airlines which operate in and out of Khartoum are:

Air France
    Meridien Bldg, El Qasr Avenue (tel 76606)
Alitalia
    87 El Barlaman Avenue (tel 80526)
Balkan Airlines
    (tel 76234)

British Airways
    3241 El Barlaman Avenue (tel 74577)
EgyptAir
    Abouela New Bldg, El Qasr Avenue (tel 70259)
Ethiopian Airlines
    El Gamhuriyya Avenue (tel 77180)
KLM
    El Fayehaa Bldg, off El Gamhuriyya Avenue (tel 74066)
Kenya Airways
    El Qasr Avenue (tel 73429)
Kuwait Airways
    El Gamhuriyya Avenue (tel 81826)
Lufthansa
    El Taiyar Morad Avenue (tel 71322)
Middle East Airlines
    Abouela New Bldg, El Gamhuriyya Avenue (tel 80968)
Swissair
    Morhig Bldg, El Gamhuriyya Avenue (tel 80196)
Saudia
    (tel 71633
Tunisair
    c/o Air France, Meridien Bldg, El Qasr Avenue (tel 75726)

Visas

Egypt Tourist visas for Egypt can be obtained in one to two days from the consulate on El Gamhuriyya Avenue (behind the old Peoples' Assembly building). They may have moved offices so try phoning them first on 77646 or 70291. Visas cost S£26 for Americans and S£75 for other nationalities. You will need two photographs.

Chad One-month visas for Chad can be obtained in half an hour from the embassy (tel 42545), in the New Extension, Street 19. You will need a yellow fever certificate and two photographs.

Uganda Visas for Uganda are not necessary for Commonwealth passport holders. For other nationalities visas can be obtained for S£2.60 in three weeks from the embassy (tel 43049), in the New Extension, Street 35. You will need two photographs.

Zaire The embassy (tel 42451) is in the New Extension between 21st and 23rd streets. The embassy issues multiple entry visas but will not accept Sudanese pounds. It costs US$27 for one month, US$53 for two months and US$66 for three months. You need three passport photos and it can take from a couple of days to a few weeks for the visa to be issued.

CAR The embassy of the Central African Republic (tel 44167) is in the New Extension near 35th St. A 10-day visa costs S£70 and you need three passport photos. Some travellers have got their visas in a day, but it can take up to two weeks.

Embassies

The telephone numbers of some of the other embassies in Khartoum are:

Austria	77170
Belgium	75564
China	73651
Denmark	80489
France	77619
West Germany	77990
Greece	73155
India	80341
Italy	45270
Japan	44549
Jordan	45893
Netherlands	47271
Niger	78420
North Yemen	43918
Pakistan	42434
Saudi Arabia	41938
Somalia	44800
South Yemen	44947
Sweden	76308
Switzerland	71161
Turkey	73894
UK	70760
USA	74611

Cultural Centres

Cultural centres are great places to catch up on the latest news and to learn more about the Sudan. Most have libraries, show films and sponsor various cultural events.

The British Council has two centres. The Khartoum centre (tel 80269), is a block west of the British Embassy on Zubeir Pasha St. The Omdurman centre (tel 53281), is near the stadium. The green bus in front of the Arak Hotel goes directly there. Both are open Saturdays to Thursdays from 8.30 am to 12.30 pm and 5.30 to 8.30 pm.

The American Center (tel 40876), is one block from the Kenyan Embassy in the New Extension, Khartoum 2, El Ammarat. It's open Sunday to Friday from 9 am to 1 pm and Sunday to Wednesday from 5 to 8 pm. Films are shown every Monday at 6 pm and video programmes, including the ABC's *World News*, are shown Wednesdays at 6 pm, Fridays at 10 am, and Sundays at 6 pm. The English Teaching Program at the centre occasionally needs part-time English teachers.

The Goethe Institute (tel 77833), is on Mek Nimir Avenue and is open Monday to Friday from 5.30 to 8.30 pm.

The French Cultural Centre (tel 72837), is on El Qasr Avenue opposite UN Square and is open Saturdays to Thursdays from 9 am to 1 pm and 6 to 8 pm.

The Soviet Cultural Centre (tel 81258), is not publicised much but it does exist and is open Saturdays to Thursdays from 9 am to 2 pm and 5.30 to 9 pm.

Khartoum's Clubs

Various ethnic, religious and national clubs form the backbone of social life in Khartoum, especially for the city's expatriate residents. Although all require membership, it is sometimes possible to obtain temporary membership or enter with a member. The clubs' activities vary from music, film presentations and athletics, to serving food, conducting tours and providing accommodation.

The American Club US passport-holders can obtain a one-day membership for

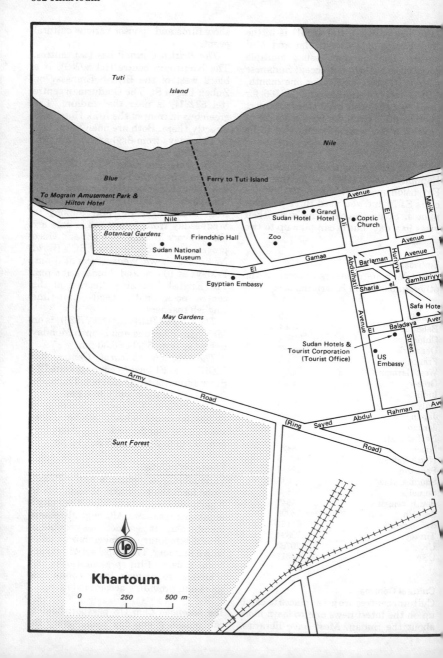

Tuti Island

Nile

Blue

Nile

Ferry to Tuti Island

To Mograin Amusement Park & Hilton Hotel

Nile

Avenue

El

Malik

Botanical Gardens

Friendship Hall

Sudan National Museum

Egyptian Embassy

Sudan Hotel

Grand Hotel

Zoo

Coptic Church

Ali

El

Avenue

Gamaa

Abdulhati

Barlaman

Huriyya

Avenue

Avenue

Gamhuriyya

Sharia el

El

Avenue

May Gardens

Baladaya

Safa Hotel

Ave

Sudan Hotels & Tourist Corporation (Tourist Office)

US Embassy

Street

Army

Road

(Ring   Sayed   Abdul   Rahman

Road)

Ave

Sunt Forest

Khartoum

0   250   500 m

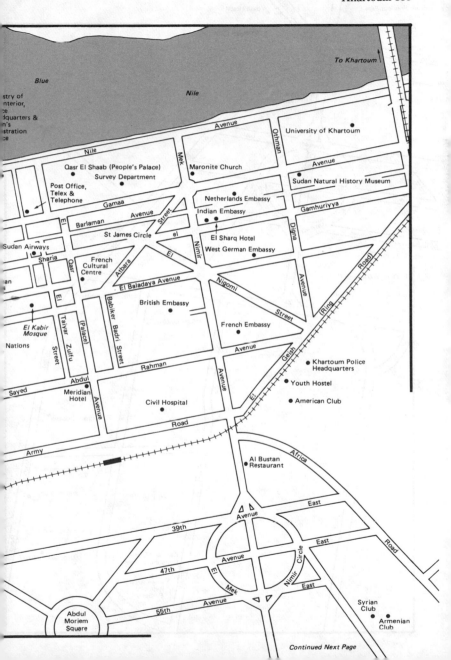

To Khartoum

Blue

Nile

Ministry of
Interior,
Police
Headquarters &
Women's
Registration
Office

Nile

Qasr El Shaab (People's Palace)

Survey Department

Post Office,
Telex &
Telephone

Gamaa

Barlaman   Avenue

St James Circle

Sudan Airways

Sharia

el

Qasr

el

French
Cultural
Centre

El Baladaya Avenue

El Kabir
Mosque

Nations

Taiyar   Zulfu   (Palace)

Babiker Badri Street

Atbara

El

Nimir

St James Circle

Street

Mek

Maronite Church

Netherlands Embassy

Indian Embassy

El Sharq Hotel

West German Embassy

Nigomi

British Embassy

French Embassy

Rahman

Abdul

Meridian
Hotel

Civil Hospital

Road

Sayed

Army

Avenue

Avenue

Street

University of Khartoum

Avenue

Sudan Natural History Museum

Gamhuriyya

Digna   Avenue

Avenue

Geish

El

Khartoum Police
Headquarters

Youth Hostel

American Club

(Ring   Road)

Al Bustan
Restaurant

Africa

East

39th

Avenue

Avenue

47th

Avenue

Mek

55th   Avenue

Nimir Circle

East

East

East

Syrian
Club

Armenian
Club

Abdul
Moriem
Square

Continued Next Page

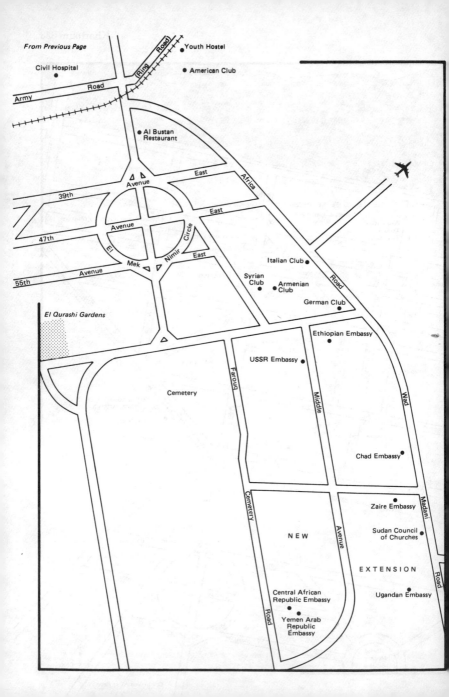

S£5. Anyone can enter with a member. There's a restaurant/snack bar, swimming pool and a couple of tennis courts. A few expatriates claim, however, that the drinking water in the club has made them sick.

The club (tel 70114), is around the corner from the Youth Hostel near the train tracks (refer to the Khartoum map).

The Sudan Club This is actually the Commonwealth Club and official membership is absolutely required for entrance, accommodation and use of their swimming pool and squash courts. Exceptions are occasionally made for members of the British East India Club, the Turf Club of Cairo and similar establishments around the old empire. Commonwealth passport-holders are also sometimes granted entrance for S£5 a day. If you don't fall into the right category, you should forget it unless you know a member and are willing to pay S£3 for a morning visit, S£3 for the afternoon and S£3 again for the evening. They obviously want to discourage undesirable elements - such as this Yankee writer.

Nevertheless, even if you are without the proper connections it is worth visiting the club just to check out the information boards inside the gate. Occasionally there are movies, lectures, cultural events and tours given by old retired officers - to places such as Colonel Hick's last battleground, which are sometimes open to the public.

The Sudan Club (tel 72044) is on the corner of El Barlaman Avenue and Contomichalos St. The manager's office - a terribly bureaucratic place - opens at 8.30 am.

The Syrian & Armenian Clubs These two clubs, which are opposite each other in the New Extension area of Khartoum, both serve delicious Middle Eastern food and have music on Thursday nights. They are a cross between a hotel lounge and a student pub without the alcohol. Refer to the Khartoum map or call the Syrian Club (tel 42660) or the Armenian Club (tel 43165) for more info. Boxes from UN Square pass near the clubs.

Other Clubs If you're an inveterate socialiser, there's also the German Club (tel 42438), the Hellenic Club (tel 43757) and the Italian Club (tel 42322).

National Museum

The National Museum is the best of Khartoum's four museums. The 1st floor exhibits feature artefacts and antiquities from pre-historic Sudan and later periods including the Kingdoms of Cush and Napata. On the 2nd floor there are colourful frescoes and mosaics from the ruins of ancient churches in northern Sudan.

In the garden outside there are the reconstructed temples of Buhen and Semna which were salvaged from parts of Nubia that were flooded by Lake Nasser.

The **Temple of Buhen** was built by Egypt's Queen Hatshepsut in about 1490 BC and contains some very colourful hieroglyphs and interesting graffiti left by passing Greeks in the 3rd century BC.

The **Semna West Temple** was built by Hatshepsut's successor Pharaoh Tuthmosis III and dedicated to the god *Dedwen*, one of the least known gods of ancient Egypt.

The museum is open Tuesday to Sunday from 8.30 am to 8.30 pm and on Fridays from 8.30 am to noon and 3.30 to 8.30 pm. The green buses in front of the Arak Hotel stop in front of the museum which is west of the city centre near the Botanical Gardens.

The Ethnographical Museum

This museum has a small, but interesting collection of items relating to village life in the Sudan. Clothing, musical instruments and hunting, cooking and fishing implements are on display. The museum is on El Gamaa Avenue and is open Saturday to Thursday from 8.30 am to 1.30 pm and on Fridays from 8.30 am to 12.30 pm.

The Natural History Museum
This museum features collections of stuffed birds and model replicas of crocodiles, snakes and other reptiles. It's also on El Gamaa Avenue and open the same hours as the Ethnographical Museum.

Graphic Museum
Frankly, I had difficulty finding this museum. However, if models and displays about diseases and infections in the Sudan interest you, this is the place to go. You'll have to ask the Tourist Office for directions.

The College of Fine & Applied Arts
The students occasionally hold public exhibitions of their work, which provides a unique opportunity to gain an insight into other aspects of Sudanese culture and society. The College is part of the University of Khartoum.

Mograin Amusement Park
This is Khartoum's mini-Disneyland and features a roller coaster, a carousel, a ferris wheel and a few other typical amusement park attractions. It's near the tip of the 'elephant trunk' peninsula, a short distance from the National Museum and is open daily until 9 pm. The entrance fee is S£1.50 and rides are S£1 each. You can get there on a green bus from in front of the Arak Hotel.

Khartoum Zoo
The zoo is near the amusement park and National Museum. There are a few healthy-looking animals but it's fairly depressing and not a place for animal lovers. Take the green bus, again from in front of the Arak Hotel.

Tuti Island
The inhabitants of this island, at the confluence of the Blue and White Niles, are descendants of the Mahas people from northern Sudan. One of the most interesting aspects about visiting the island however, is the ferry ride across the Blue Nile.

The ferry leaves from in front of the cinema just down from the National Museum and the landing procedure, as the ferry hits the shore, is quite an amusing spectacle. Men, boys and donkeys always scramble off first while the women wait until they're absolutely certain that the ferry's metal gang-way is firmly planted in the mud on the bank before they tip-toe off the boat.

I waited on board while all this happened and one of the crew said hello, shook my hand and then disappeared up the landing. He returned a couple of minutes later with a glass of sweetly spiced tea for me. When I offered him some money for the tea and the boat ride, he adamantly refused and nearly threw me and the money into the Nile.

At the Tuti Island landing a bus picks up passengers for the trip to the small brickhouse village in the centre of the island. There is nothing much of interest there though.

From the village it's a 10-minute walk to the landing for the small, leaky sailboat which takes you across the other branch of the Blue Nile to Bahry Beach in North Khartoum not far from the Friendship Palace Hotel. Ask someone in the village for directions.

Two boys work on the boat and while one paddles with a big stick, the other furiously tries to scoop the water out faster than it seeps in through cracks patched with bits of rag. If you happen to fall into the Blue Nile, you neeedn't worry about bilharzia. There might be crocodiles – but bilharzia is confined to the White Nile.

If you survive the boat trip, and most people do, then the beach in front of the Friendship Palace Hotel is a good place to go swimming.

Top: Fruit market, Khartoum (SW)
Left: Tomb of the Mahdi, Omdurman (SW)
Right: A White Nile 'ferry', Khartoum (SW)

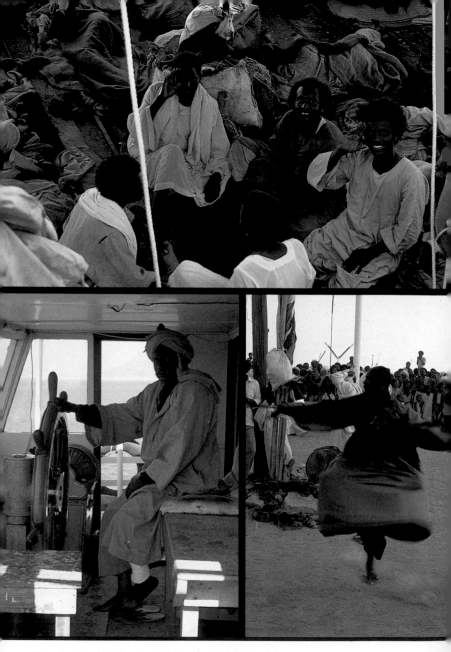

Top: Passing the time on the ferry, Lake Nasser (HF)
Left: Mohammed the ferry driver, Lake Nasser (HF)
Right: A whirling Dervish, Omdurman (HF)

The Race Track

Khartoum's race track is south of the city near Souk Shaby. There are races on Fridays and Sundays from 4 pm and polo matches on Wednesdays and Saturdays at 4 pm. Boxes for Souk Shaby and the race track leave from El Taiyar Zulfa St near UN Square.

Verona Fathers

The Verona Fathers are an Italian-based Jesuit missionary order who have been working in the Sudan for several years. They operate a unique secondary school in Khartoum, on El Qasr Avenue near the Meridien Hotel, and also help run a refugee camp on the outskirts of the city.

The school has no walled classrooms; the students simply sit in groups, around the large interior courtyard, with their teacher and a blackboard.

The Fathers don't mind having visitors and often present BBC video shows on various aspects of the Sudan such as the construction of the Jonglei Canal.

Omdurman

Khartoum's sister city, across the confluence of the two Niles, is a world apart from the capital. At first Omdurman has the appearance of a large, diffused village. There is no skyline of gleaming high-rise offices, most of the buildings are mud constructions, the streets are mostly narrow and dusty alleys and goats wander between the houses. Little seems to have changed since the Mahdi made this his capital after decapitating General Gordon and defeating the British in 1885.

The Souk

The Omdurman Souk is the Sudan's largest market and attracts people from all over the country to sell an amazing variety of wares. In the shops and stalls, craftsmen carve and shape pieces of ebony and ivory into candlesticks and statuettes; goldsmiths and silversmiths crouch over glimmering bits of metal, pounding and cutting out jewellery; and other merchants hang shrivelled crocodiles and zebra heads in their store windows. Some of the jewellery is nice but, frankly, Cairo's Khan el Khalili bazaar is more extensive. The green buses in front of the Arak Hotel end their routes at the souk.

The Whirling Dervishes

Every Friday afternoon, approximately an hour before sunset, a group of dervishes, dressed in *galabiyyas* and brightly coloured patchwork gowns, gather in front of the Hamed al Niel Mosque in Omdurman. These men come together to venerate, in a most unusual way, a 19th century sheikh who was the head of their *tariqa*, or 'path' of Islam.

The *tariqs* had their origins in 16th-century Sufism and the members of these various groups follow an ascetic, more mystical form of Islam. The sheikh of each *tariqa* teaches his members his own particular path to Allah, which may involve simply studying the Qur'an or taking part in a frenzied ceremony called a *dhikr*. As most Sudanese Muslims today, belong to an order of some sort you may see quite a variety of *dhikrs* as you travel through the Sudan.

The whirling dervishes of Omdurman follow the teachings of the late Sheikh Hamed al Niel, who is venerated as a saint because it is believed that he was, and is still, able to perform miracles and act as an intermediary between the members of the *tariqa* and Allah.

As a show of respect for the sheikh, some of the men who have gathered at the mosque begin beating steadily on big drums. This signals the dervishes to begin their march across the field to the mosque. They enter the circle of observers which forms in front of the mosque and begin chanting and walking slowly around a pole. As the drum beat and chanting speed up they, and whoever else wants to join them, attempt to whirl themselves into a detached state of mind. The object of this *dhikr*, is 'oneness with Allah' and it lasts until sunset or complete dizziness – whichever comes first.

Dervishes begin their initiation into the ways of the *tariqa* at the age of 10, so outside the circle of whirling men there are usually a few young boys mimicking their elders.

To get to the Hamed al Niel Mosque, take a green bus from in front of the Arak Hotel and get off at the Al Murradah Stadium on El Arbein Avenue (pronounced arba'een). Walk straight past the stadium and through the village to a field, from where it's only a 10-minute walk to the mosque on the other side. You can sometimes hitch a ride across the field.

The Mahdi's Tomb

The Mahdi and his army of 50,000 men were responsible for instigating the first uprising against the British in the 1880s. After capturing Khartoum from the British in 1885 however, the Mahdi apparently retired to a life of amazing decadence and grew tremendously fat as his harem of 30 women attended to his every whim. The only interruptions he allowed were the occasional councils of war.

The Mahdi died on 22 June 1885, only five months after General Gordon was beheaded, and was entombed inside a mosque with a shiny silver dome. The Khalifa Abdullahi, who had taken over the Mahdi's residence after his death, declared that Omdurman was the 'sacred city of the Mahdi' and that a pilgrimage to the Mahdi's tomb was an obligation of Sudanese Muslims, in place of the Haj to Mecca which was prohibited.

General Kitchener destroyed the mosque when he recaptured Khartoum in 1898. Cook's 1929 *Traveller's Handbook to Egypt & the Sudan* described the desecration as 'necessary'.

The tomb was badly injured in the bombardment of Omdurmân on the 22nd, and after the capture of the town it was destroyed by the British, the Mahdi's body being burnt in the furnace of one of the steamers and his ashes thrown into the river. This was considered to be necessary as the building had become a symbol of rebellion and fanaticism, the goal of pilgrimages and the centre of fraudulent miracles.

The mosque and tomb were rebuilt in 1947 by the Mahdi's son. Foreigners are not permitted to enter. The green bus from the Arak Hotel passes near the mosque and the Khalifa's house nearby. The Mahdi's Tomb is the building with the more conical shaped dome.

The Khalifa's House Museum

Beit el Khalifa was built in 1887 as the home of the Mahdi's successor. The mud and brick building has changed little from the time when the Khalifa Abdullahi lived there, before his defeat by General Kitchener's forces in the 1898 Battle of Omdurman.

The house is now a museum, featuring relics from the Mahdi's various battles and the British occupation of the Sudan. The steel boat which French General Marchand used to 'occupy' Fashoda in 1897 and the Arrol Motor car used by Sir Wingate, who was the Governor of Sudan in 1902, are on display in the courtyard. There is also a 'water room', where there were even facilities for hot baths, and interesting suits of mail from the Battle of Atbara in 1898 and numerous Mahdiya war banners and guns.

The Khalifa's House is opposite the Mahdi's Tomb so you can take the same bus. It's open Tuesday to Sunday from 8.30 am to 8.30 pm and on Fridays from 8.30 am to noon and 3.30 to 8.30 pm. The entrance fee is 22 pt.

Nile Cruises

Most of the major hotels offer two to three-hour cruises for about S£30 and they are highly recommended by all who have taken them. The Acropole Hotel offers a cruise every Friday at 10 am but you need to book, at least one day in advance, with George. The Hilton Hotel does a sunrise cruise every Friday and Saturday and the Grand Hotel also offers a cruise. Check with them for their latest schedules.

Nile Boat Builders

On the Omdurman side of the Nile just north of the Shambat Bridge, a group of men can be seen sawing and hacking at long planks of wood. They are building the broad-sailed boats which are seen up and down the Nile.

Places to Stay - bottom end

The *Youth Hostel*, or Student House, which is across the railway line from El Geish Rd (refer to the Khartoum map), is one of the cheapest places to stay in Khartoum. But although it costs only S£1.80 for a bunk bed, in a room of about 10 beds, it is not really recommended because of the high incidence of thefts. One traveller reported that not only were all his belongings stolen, but also US$100 he had in the safe! This place is only for the desperate.

The *Port Sudan Hotel* on Kulliyat el Tibb St, about five minutes walk from the train station, offers beds in a courtyard for S£1.75 each and a room to lock-up your gear. They also have clean and airy rooms for S£2.

The *Bahr el Ghazal Hotel*, near Souk Arabi off Malik Avenue (the sign is in Arabic), is also cheap but don't expect much from this place. It costs S£2.50 a night for a bed in a four to five-bed room. The windowless rooms are a bit dark and gloomy but as the showers and toilets are combined in the same stall they at least, by default, are kept fairly clean. During the summer you can sleep on the roof. If you are just looking for a place to sleep, this is certainly one of the cheapest.

The *El Khalil Hotel*, opposite the bus station on El Baladaya Avenue near UN Square, costs S£3 a single and S£5.50 a double.

The *El Nowyi Hotel* on El Isbitalya St is a good deal. Doubles are S£14 to S£20 for two or S£7 to S£10 for one. There are a couple of singles with attached bathrooms and the rooms are cleaned every day.

The *Asia Hotel* is popular with travellers and costs S£12 per night for a dusty single. The rooms on the roof are the best and have good views of UN Square. It is next to the Safa Hotel on El Baladaya Avenue, around the corner from the Tourist Office.

Places to Stay - middle

The *Nakiel Hotel* is an excellent deal and is especially popular with Sudanese honeymooners. It's centrally located, opposite the Souk Arabi and a couple of blocks from UN Square. The sign is in Arabic but it's easy to find, just go up the lane next to the *Mubkhar* (incense seller) that is marked on the Khartoum map. Rooms cost S£28.60 for a single, S£40 for a double. The place has been renovated and all rooms have air-con, overhead fans and typically dungeon-like toilet-stalls. The lobby has a television and fuzzy sofas.

The *El Sawahli Hotel* has 24 clean, simply furnished rooms with air-coolers and overhead fans. Showers and toilets are shared on each floor and it costs S£28 a double and S£42 a triple. It's on Zubeir Pasha St, about a block north-east of UN Square.

The *Safa Hotel* on El Baladaya Avenue near the Tourist Office is popular with travellers. It costs S£20 for a single with an overhead fan and air-cooler and the rooms are clean and simply furnished but a bit dark. If you get claustrophobic, seek refuge in the lobby among the potted plants and cushioned chairs.

The *El Sharq Hotel* is a place of last resort; it costs S£33 for a single in a dark, grimy room with peeling walls, stained sheets, a sink and an overhead fan. The

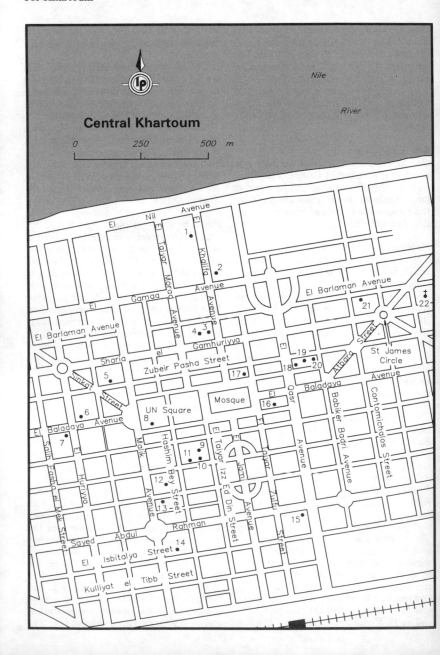

Central Khartoum

Nile River

1 Alien's Registration Office
2 Post Office
3 British Airways
4 American Express / KLM Airlines
5 El Sawahli Hotel
6 Safa Hotel
7 Tourist Office
8 Bus to Sanghat
9 Nakiel Hotel
10 Mubkhar (Incense Seller)
11 Hotel Nilein
12 Souk Arabi-buses to Souk Shabi
13 Bahr el Ghazal Hotel
14 El Nowyi Hotel
15 Meridien Hotel
16 Boxes to Souk Shabi
17 Arak Hotel & buses to Omdurman
18 French Cultural Centre
19 Metropole Hotel
20 Acropole Hotel
21 Sudan Club
22 Greek Church

smaller front rooms share a common bathroom where it's a good idea to wear shoes or sandals. The rooms surrounding the courtyard at the rear each have bathrooms which resemble medieval torture chambers, but the doors do have locks. Be insistent if you have a masochistic preference for one of these rooms.

The *Metropole Hotel* (tel 71166), 4 Zubeir Pasha St, has a certain mystique about it. Like the higher priced Acropole two doors down, the Metropole is a favourite among expatriates and seems to attract an odd assortment of characters fit for a spy novel, including journalists, Bombay pipe salesmen, mysterious Belgian-Turkish businessmen with cases full of money, Sudanese entrepreneurs and ex-politicians. Rooms are S£47 a single, S£60 for one person in a double or S£80 for a double, including three meals, and all have big whirling overhead fans. Most rooms also have a sink, an air-cooler, a desk and a dresser. The meals are almost

the same every day – bread, tea and eggs for breakfast; murky soup, bread, salad and meat for lunch; and usually cold left-overs from lunch for dinner.

The *Sudan Club* has limited accommodation available for members or associate members (see the Khartoum Clubs section). It costs S£51 a night for a single or a bed in a double room. The rooms are clean, cool and comfortable. Meals are also available.

Places to Stay – top end
The *Acropole Hotel* is run by a Greek guy named George who always smiles when you meet him. He must be happy, his hotel is almost always full of expatriates as it's the unofficial hang-out for many of the development aid and refugee relief workers. George has greatly assisted several international agencies in expediting communications and providing information. Rooms cost S£121 a single and S£160 a double, including full board. Rates are official so bank receipts showing official money exchange must be presented. If you are not staying there, it's at least worth stopping by for tea and a chat with some of the guests. Everybody there seems to have an interesting story to tell about some part of the Sudan. You can ring George on 72680 (night calls tel 72026), or telex 22190 ACROP SD.

There are five international category hotels in Khartoum: the *Hilton*, the *Meridien*, the *Grand*, the *Friendship Palace* and the *Arak*. All have similar high standards and the rates range from US$110 to US$130 a single or US$130 to US$150 a double. The Friendship Palace is renowned for its concerts and fantastic views of the Blue and White Niles from the roof. Once again, official exchange receipts must be shown if you're paying in Sudanese pounds.

Places to Eat
Most of Khartoum's restaurants are simple, nameless places which serve a single dish or small variety of dishes. The

system for eating in these places is to first buy tokens for the dishes you want from the cash register. Then take the tokens to the kitchen window and hand them to the 'cooks'. There are no utensils. The Sudanese use bread to scoop up their food.

Eritrean restaurants are also plentiful in Khartoum and are mostly run by refugees from the northern Ethiopian province of Eritrea. However, most of these disappear as quickly as they appear and they don't advertise, so you must ask Eritreans to show you the way. Most of the restaurants are small rooms hidden behind unmarked metal doors. They usually serve *Ngira* – a spicy vegetable and meat concoction served with soft, flat bread.

Cheap Restaurants
The numbers in the following list of eating places and tea houses relate to the Khartoum food and drink map.
1 A *juice stand* which serves good freshly squeezed orange juice.
2 A *restaurant* which serves mainly grilled Nile Perch in the mornings.
3 A *juice stand* which serves both orange and lemon juice.
4 Another *juice stand* which specialises in lemon drinks.
5 A stand which serves hot sweetened milk mostly in the evenings.
6 *Maxim's Burgers* is Sudan's first attempt at western-style fast food. The hamburgers are meagre, but tasty if you drown the meat in ketchup.
7 This is a café which specialises in *Hoshab* – a Sudanese fruit cocktail. It's directly opposite the shop with the Arabic Coca-Cola signs.
8 Excellent *spiced tea* is available here. They are very busy from 9 to 10 am.
9 The *Garden Restaurant*, in front of the El Kabani Hotel, is a popular place although the 'garden' is small with only a couple of trees.
10 This is a great place for fresh milk and yogurt and a stand in front sells fried fish in the evenings.

11 The entrance of this *Eritrean tea house* is the last unmarked blue metal door on your left. Specially spiced Eritrean tea is served from 7 am. You sit on rope beds under a thatched bamboo

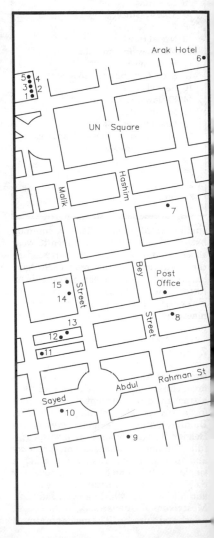

awning and watch squawking chickens scramble away from the woman stirring a big pot in the corner.

12 Freshly baked bread is available here at night and in the morning.

13 This place is great for those on a shoestring budget who want a taste of typical Sudanese cuisine. As with all Sudanese eating places, there are no knives and forks. They serve fuul, addis, kebab and kalawi. It's the place with the bright purple doors and a Michael Jackson photograph on the wall.

14 A chewing tobacco shop. It's interesting to watch how eagerly the Sudanese men buy the tobacco. The men selling this sludge-like stuff can hardly cram it into little plastic bags fast enough to meet demand.

15 A typical Sudanese bakery.

16 This fish place, opposite the Bulgarian Trade Mission, serves fresh fish, with cucumbers and yogurt, every morning.

17 The *Casa Blanka* serves decent omelettes and great ice cream. Try the mango ice cream.

Hotel Restaurants

There are some more western-style restaurants in the big hotels.

At the *Grand Hotel* the chicken and roast beef sandwiches are renowned among some expatriates. Breakfast is overpriced, though, and served in a large, mysteriously quiet dining room.

At the *Hilton Hotel*, the Ivory Room's S£27 all-you-can-eat buffet on Fridays is one of the best deals in town. The regular restaurant serves carefully prepared three course meals with delicious European and Sudanese dishes ranging in price from S£30 to S£40.

The *Friendship Palace Hotel* serves club sandwiches and tuna fish sandwiches in the Tuti Café. There is also a S£28 buffet every night in the restaurant.

Other Restaurants

There is a *Chinese Restaurant* in the New Extension on Street 15 near the airport. It costs about S£30 to S£40 for a full meal of typical Chinese food.

There is a *Korean Restaurant* nearby; it's in the Africa Hotel, just past the entrance to the airport road and near the exit to Street 30. Look for the hotel sign and red lantern. They serve traditional Korean food including octopus.

Meals are also served at the *Sudan Club* at 7 am, 1 pm and 6 pm. The Nubian cook makes a mean but delicious beef curry with bananas, vegetables and peanuts for S£8. See the Khartoum's Clubs section for details about the club.

Getting There

Air For information on flights into, around and out of the Sudan, refer to the Getting There and Getting Around chapters at the start of the Sudan section.

If you're arriving in Khartoum on an international flight the entry procedure is easy. You have to fill out two arrival registration forms before going through passport control. The forms are on the side counters next to the tourist information booth. The booth sometimes has maps and information about Khartoum.

The Sudan is a 'dry' country. The customs people are strict about liquor and will confiscate any that you have.

After customs there is a bank window on your right where you can change money if you can't wait until you get into town.

Everyone flying out of Khartoum airport is required to pay a departure tax of S£15 for internal flights and S£30 for external flights.

For flights to Cairo a *location certificate* must be obtained from the agency or airline office where you bought the ticket or confirmed your reservation.

Going North

Train There are four trains a week going north. The train to Wadi Halfa departs at 6.40 am on Sundays and Wednesdays. It stops at Abu Hamed and then continues across the Nubian Desert to Wadi Halfa.

The other train goes to Karima. It departs at 10.45 am on Sundays and Wednesdays and takes seven to nine hours.

You have to book a day in advance and the fares, in Sudanese pounds, to those destinations, are:

Class	Atbara	Wadi Halfa	Karima
1st	17.05	50.05	45.28
2nd mumtaz	13.95	40.95	36.23
2nd	11.50	33.70	29.70
3rd mumtaz	7.75	22.75	20.13
3rd	5.90	17.30	15.30

Bus There is a bus to Karima, which leaves from behind the central post office in Omdurman every Saturday and Tuesday at 10 am. The journey takes 24 hours, across the desert and through oases, with stops at Shendi, Atbara and Abu Hamed. The fare to Karima is S£15 for a seat in the front and S£11 for a seat towards the back.

You usually need to book bus tickets at least a day in advance.

Truck Trucks for Karima and Dongola also leave from Post Office Square in Omdurman. The trip to Dongola takes more than a day.

Going East & North-East
Train There is a train from Khartoum via Sennar to Gedaref and points beyond but the trip is agonisingly slow.

Bus Travelling by bus is the most common way to go to Wad Medani, Gedaref, Kassala and Port Sudan.

The buses leave from Souk Shabi in south Khartoum daily between 6 and 7.30 am. You must book your ticket at least one day in advance. The companies with the best buses are Sugipto, Arrow, and Taysir as their vehicles have comfortable seats, occasional air-con and complimentary tea. Bring your own cup for the tea, unless you want to share the 'public' cup with

what I am sure will be at least one TB carrier. Fares range from S£15 to S£22.

Taysir's tickets can be bought from the company's city office which is in the same building as the French Cultural Centre on El Qasr Avenue. The other companies have their offices at Souk Shabi.

All buses to Kassala stop at Wad Medani, Gedaref and Showak. The journey to Kassala takes from seven to nine hours depending on the number of police checkpoints along the way. There are no buses which go all the way to Port Sudan on the same day.

Truck Trucks to all the east and north-east destinations also leave from Souk Shabi.

Going West
Trains and buses make the trip to El Obeid. From El Obeid the train continues on to Nyala. Trucks also go from Omdurman all the way to Nyala.

Train The train goes via Kosti and supposedly leaves on Tuesdays at 5.15 pm for El Obeid and on Mondays at 10.30 am for Nyala.

The trip to El Obeid usually takes 31 hours but during the rainy season, from May to September, it can take as long as 63 hours. Check with the Khartoum station master for the latest details. The train to Wau has stopped running.

Fares from Khartoum are:

Class	El Obeid	Nyala
1st	37.30	72.60
2nd mumtaz	30.06	59.40
2nd	25.16	43.05
3rd mumtaz	17.00	33.00
3rd	12.92	25.10

Bus Buses for El Obeid leave from the Omdurman Souk five days a week, except during the rainy season. The bus can't be driven at night because the road is nothing more than a track in the desert so the trip can take 24 hours if the bus doesn't get to El Obeid before sunset. Take warm clothing because you may have to camp in the desert with the rest of the passengers.

There are two types of buses which make this trip. Local buses, which are Bedford truck chassis with windowless bodies, travel five days a week. When the sandstorms come, tarps are tied over the sides in a futile attempt to keep the dust out. The second type of bus is run by the Military Transport Corporation, leaves every two days and has real windows. Both buses cost about S£30, depending on fuel shortages.

Trucks Trucks for destinations in western Sudan also leave from the *souk* in Omdurman.

Going South

Travelling from Khartoum to points south of Kosti is practically impossible because of the civil war. John Garang's SPLM forces recently shot down a plane to Juba, so that service has been discontinued.

Bus Buses to Kosti and Sennar leave daily from Souk Shabi in south Khartoum. Sugipto and Taysir companies run the buses. The trip takes 4½ hours and costs S£10.

Getting Around

Airport Transport The airport is 10 to 15 minutes from central Khartoum and taxi fare to the centre is about S£15.

There are also buses to town from the main road; just flag one down. The trip costs 25 pt but the buses are often full by this point because they are coming from the outlying suburbs.

Bus & Box Buses, 'boxes' and taxis are the main ways of getting around Khartoum. Most of the buses and boxes begin and end their trips in and around United Nations Square. I have attempted to indicate as best as possible where the transport in each corner of the square goes. However, as I walked around the square and asked

the drivers their routes, I got some very strange responses. One conversation, in Arabic, went something like this:

The first driver I approached was a young guy in a shaggy *galabiyya* and turban that was falling off his head. He was snoozing over the steering wheel of the bus when I rapped on the door frame.

'Excuse me, where does your bus go?' I asked.

'Where do you want to go?' He was still sort of sleepy.

'I don't want to go anywhere. I just want some information because I'm writing a guidebook to the Sudan.'

'It goes to . . . uh . . . Wait a minute,' he replied. He asked one of the other drivers who had dashed over to see what the *khawaja* (that's me and anyone else with a white face) wanted. 'Hey, where does my bus go?' he whispered.

By this time I was surrounded by four baffled drivers all babbling and arguing about where the bus was supposed to go. And then, a miracle occurred – a passenger appeared. He was a young man, wearing wire frame glasses and carrying books under his arm. I cornered him before he boarded.

'Do you know where this bus goes?' I asked.

'Nowhere, I just came here to read,' he said.

I walked away and then saw why there had been so much confusion. Pieces of the engine lay scattered in the dust next to an open box of tools on the other side of the bus.

My efforts in UN Square were not all for naught though. I scooped up the following information. All buses on El Taiyar Zulfu St, in front of the Arak Hotel go to Omdurman. That includes the big green bus mentioned in previous sections.

Boxes to Omdurman leave from the corner of El Gamhuriyya Avenue and El Huriyya St.

Buses to Souk Shabi in south Khartoum leave from Souk Arabi which is little more than a dirt lot near the Hotel Nilein.

Boxes to Souk Shabi leave from a dirt lot opposite the mosque on El Taiyar Zulfu St.

Boxes to the New Extension and the airport leave from El Jami Avenue.

If you are ever in doubt, ask an intelligent-looking person where to go. If that person doesn't speak English just say *otobees* (for bus) or *box le*, then your destination, shrug your shoulders and look confused. The Sudanese are very helpful and you'll eventually get where you want to go.

Taxi If you are in a hurry (that's a difficult state of mind in the Sudan) or just frustrated, then take one of the battered yellow taxis cruising up and down the boulevard. They are relatively cheap – S£2 to S£3 for a ride across town. The fare to the airport is usually about S£10 to S£15.

Northern Sudan

The 1628-km stretch of Nile between Wadi Halfa and Khartoum is often overlooked by travellers, yet it is along this route that some of the finest ruins of ancient Sudan can be found. The kingdoms of Cush, Meroe and Napata all rose in this region and although the pyramids, temples and palaces they left behind don't rival those of Egypt, they are untouched by the commercialism which has consumed the Egyptian monuments. You are left alone to explore, undisturbed by anxious guides and con artists selling trinkets and camel rides. It is this opportunity to be a solitary explorer which makes these sites all the more appealing and worth visiting.

Northern Sudan is also home to the distinctive people of Nubia and several Arab tribes. As much of Nubia was submerged by the waters of Lake Nasser, which was created by the construction of the Aswan High Dam, the Nubian people are now scattered throughout Upper Egypt and northern Sudan. About 50,000 of them were resettled at Khasham el Girba, on the Atbara River, when the dam was being built. Despite the diaspora the Nubians have retained their unique language and many of their traditional ways.

The two predominant Arab tribes in northern Sudan are the *Shaigia* and the *Gaalyeen*. The town of Shendi is the main centre of the Gaalyeen, who are scattered throughout the region from Atbara to the sixth cataract. The Shaigia are dispersed throughout northern Sudan amongst the Nubians and the Gaalyeen.

To truly experience this part of Sudan you have to forgo the rigours of the train trip for the harshness of truck rides through barren desert plains and meagre oases, where the roads are seldom more than faint tracks in the sand. Between Dongola and Karima, however, you can take a break from bouncing around in the back of a truck to cruise up or down the Nile on an old steamer for a few days.

WADI HALFA

There is not much to Wadi Halfa. Basically, it's a transit point, where the the Lake Nasser steamer from Aswan meets the Sudan Railway's train for Khartoum. Near the dock there is an ice plant and cold storage house built by the People's Republic of China in the 1970s for a then, and still, nascent fishing industry. The Chinese even provided 35 two-tonne fishing boats.

At the quay you will be eagerly met by taxi drivers and money-changers. The latter will happily change your excess Egyptian pounds at a rate of E£1 to S£2.50, while the former will try to take your Egyptian pounds at a poor rate for the ride into town. Try furious bargaining, S£4 is about right for the fare. Otherwise, just start the long, hot walk to town and someone might take pity and give you a free ride. It's a few km, just follow the tracks in the sand. Don't head for the buildings you see ahead and to the left – that's the fish processing plant. You can also change money with the shopkeepers in town.

Places to Stay & Eat

In town there are two basic but clean hotels near the train station. The *Hotel Nile* costs S£5 a night; and the *Hotel Bohaera*, which also serves meals, costs S£7.50. Even if you don't stay there, take time out for a soothing cup of tea (75 pt) in the cool Bohaera lounge.

Before dropping your gear at one of these hotels, however, go to the train station and make your reservation immediately, if you want to travel 1st class.

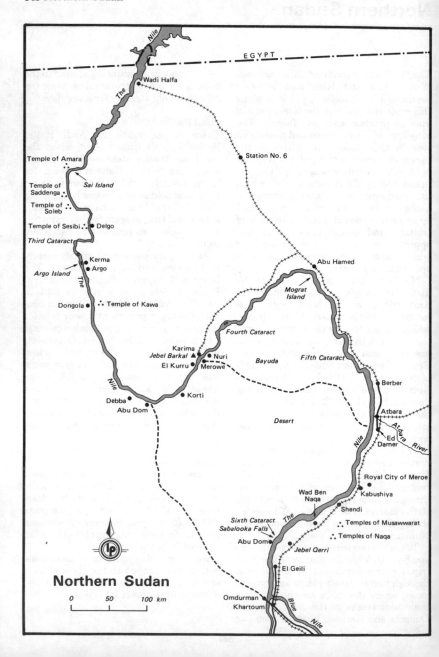

Northern Sudan

0   50   100 km

Getting There

For information on getting to Wadi Halfa from Egypt or Khartoum, refer to the Getting There sections for Aswan and Khartoum.

Train The 1st class fare to Khartoum is S£56. Second and 3rd class are bad but cheap. You can travel on top of the train for free but as one traveller reports: 'You have to jump on out of sight of the conductor when the train is already in motion and there are few hand-holds ... with your stuff it's impossible. That must be left inside for fellow travellers to watch.'

The train usually leaves the day after the steamer arrives, giving visitors a chance to spend money and boost the economy of Wadi Halfa. Boarding begins at 10 am, but hundreds of people crowd around the gate several hours before. When the signal is given the gates open and everyone scrambles for a seat. Even if you get one, you still have to sit for several hours until the train is ready to leave.

The trip to Khartoum takes 32 hours, more or less, even with the five stops a day for Muslim prayers. The train also stops at the 10 numbered stations in the Nubian desert. At Station 6, tea and sometimes food can be purchased. Most compartments do not have windows, there are no lights and sand swirls in, coating everybody with Nubian desert dust. The train also stops frequently to clear sand from the tracks. By nightfall everybody looks ghostly.

Truck Another way south out of Wadi Halfa is by truck to Dongola. Although the road *is* marked on the Michelin map, it really does not exist so the trip is extremely rough. It takes two to three days, costs about S£40 and you need to bring your own food. Along the way you will pass several ancient Egyptian and Napatan era sights.

SAI ISLAND

Sai Island is 190 km south of Wadi Halfa and contains the ruins of a small Egyptian temple built by the Egyptian pharaoh Tuthmosis III in about 1460 BC.

On the east bank of the Nile, opposite Sai Island, is the **Temple of Amara** which superseded a fort built there by Seti I in about 1300 BC. The temple was one of a series commissioned by Ramses II, around 1270 BC, and is one of the most complete constructions surviving from his reign.

SADDENGA & SOLEB

Twenty km further south are the ruins of the **Temple of Saddenga**, built by Pharaoh Amenophis III for his consort Queen Tiy in about 1370 BC. It's a bit difficult to visit because it is on the west bank.

The **Temple of Soleb**, a few km south, is also difficult to visit. It was built also by Amenophis III to commemorate his victories over local tribes.

DELGO

The village of Delgo is a popular truck stop 68 km south of Soleb. There is a rest house in the village. Trucks from Wadi Halfa sometimes end their trips there but other trucks and pick-ups cover the 110-km trip to Dongola.

Across the Nile, there are the subterranean ruins of the **Temple of Sesibi**, built by Amenophis IV (Akhenaten) around 1360 BC.

DONGOLA

Dongola is the heart of ancient Nubia. It is famous for its palm groves, which are a welcome sight after hundreds of km of rough desert. Date harvest time is in September when young boys from the town scale the palms with knives clenched between their teeth and whack off clusters of dates. It's quite a show.

There's a colourful fruit and vegetable market behind the main square and, occasionally, nomads come in from the desert to buy and sell camels, sugar, tea and other goods.

On the east bank there are the ruins of the **Temple of Kawa**, which was the repository of gifts for the Cushite ruler

Taharqa. Taharqa was king of the Land of Cush from 688 BC to 663 BC and was also the last pharaoh of Egypt's 25th Dynasty, until he lost the country to invading Assyrians. A ferry takes you across the river.

Places to Stay & Eat

There is a rest house and a couple of *lakondas* near the hospital in town. The pleasant *Hotel El Mana* costs S£5 a night, there are fans in the rooms and clean cold showers. You can also camp along the banks of the Nile.

There are tea houses on every corner, cheap food in the cafés opposite the daily market and a well-stocked pharmacy.

Getting There

The schedule for the steamer to Karima is erratic and it may not run at all from March to June when the level of the Nile is low. If you do get on it though, the four-day journey to Karima is calm and perfect for recuperating from the truck trip. On the other hand if there's no sign of the steamer and you don't feel like hanging around Dongola, you could always hop on another truck. The one-day trip through the desert to Karima costs about S£10.

There are also country buses and a 'luxury' bus to Khartoum via Ed Debba.

KARIMA

Karima is a busy market town with a population of over 15,000. The market is held twice a week and attracts people from the surrounding villages. But apart from the *souk* and a couple of Coca-Cola stores offering a brief respite from midday summer temperatures of 50°C, there is little of interest in the town itself. Outside of town however, there are several important archaeological sites dating from the ancient Egyptian and Napatan kingdoms.

Jebel Barkal

Two km south of the town is Jebel Barkal, a 100-metre-high hill, which the 18th-

Dynasty Egyptians considered sacred. In the 13th century BC, Tuthmosis III and Amenophis II built the **Temple of Amun** at the foot of the hill, and it remained a religious centre for the next 1000 years.

Pyramid Tombs

South of the temple are the pyramid tombs of Kurru built by the Napatan King Piankhi long after pyramid construction stopped in Egypt. The pyramids are much smaller than the Egyptian ones and have suffered terribly from looting.

There are other pyramids opposite Karima in the village of Nuri, although the pyramidal section of these tombs has crumbled. Ferries cross the Nile regularly from Karima and the tombs are 10 km upstream and two km inland. There are usually boxes available to get you there.

Places to Stay & Eat

Accommodation is limited in Karima. There is a *rest house* at the local canning company; the basic *Taharqa Hotel* in town; and the *El Nassar Hotel* which has dorm beds for S£4. The restaurant on the main square has good food.

Getting There

Buses and trucks leave for Khartoum a few times a week. The one-day journey takes you through the Bayuda Desert.

There's a 3rd class, 12-hour train trip twice a week to Abu Hamed to meet the Wadi Halfa-Khartoum train.

Lastly, there's a steamer from Karima to Dongola which stops at the ruins of Old Dongola on the way.

ABU HAMED

Abu Hamed is a railroad junction town and the only reason to stay there is if you miss the train to Khartoum or Wadi Halfa. Next to the railway station there's a *government rest house* with a huge verandah and showers. To stay there, you first need permission from the police station near the mosque.

It's an interesting sight when the train

arrives each night. A market, illuminated by little kerosene lanterns, suddenly materialises out of nowhere around the train. You can usually buy fruit, vegetables and bread.

There is also an hourly ferry to the former Christian stronghold of Mograt Island, which is the largest island in the Nile.

ATBARA

The Atbara River, which flows down from the Ethiopian highlands, meets the Nile at this city which has a population of 75,000. Atbara is also the junction of two of Sudan's major train routes, the Khartoum to Wadi Halfa and the Atbara to Port Sudan lines.

The railway dominates life in the city, so it's not surprising that this is a major centre for the Sudanese railway unions. It was also the scene of an attempted coup by pro-communist army officers in 1971.

The city also figured prominently in Sudan's colonial history. The Battle of Atbara in 1898, was the first major battle between the British and the Mahdists since the defeat of Gordon. In April of that year the Mahdist army marched down the Nile, as far as Atbara, to meet Kitchener's Anglo-Egyptian expedition. The Arabs were completely routed and 2000 Mahdists were killed when Kitchener and his army attacked with superior modern artillery and the rousing music of Scottish pipes and English flutes, drums and brass instruments. The young Winston Churchill witnessed the battle as a war correspondent and later wrote a book about his experiences called *The River War*.

After the victory, Kitchener marched on to take Khartoum while British officials settled into Atbara. They expanded the railway and built several large colonial-style houses which can still be seen. There is also an Anglican Church in Atbara, which is one of the few in northern Sudan.

Atbara is especially interesting for railway buffs because it's a graveyard, of sorts, for the steam locomotives that died during Nimeiri's rule. He supposedly ignored the railways, the railway unions and the city itself because the Communist Party was, and still is, very strong there.

There are ferries from town across the confluence of the Atbara and Nile rivers and there's also an interesting camel and crafts market on Saturdays at nearby Ed Damer. To get to the latter you can take a box from Atbara.

Places to Stay

There aren't too many places to stay in Atbara as the popular Hotel Astoria burned down in 1984. There is a small hotel next to the site of the former Astoria which costs 50 pt per night.

The *Hotel Atbara*, next to the Watania Cinema, is recommended. The *Youth Hostel* is nearby but it's rundown and dirty. A more up-market place is the colonial-style *rest house* on Main Avenue, 10 minutes from the train station.

Getting There

Train The extremely crowded train to Khartoum takes 12 hours and costs S£18 for 1st class, S£12 for 2nd, and S£8 for 3rd.

There is also a train to Port Sudan from Atbara which takes 18 hours to cover the 474 km distance. It has not been recommended. If you want to skip Port Sudan, you could get off the train at Haiya junction, but it might be difficult to catch a bus from there.

Bus There is a very bumpy daily bus to Khartoum for S£13. It takes eight hours.

THE ROYAL CITY OF MEROE

About 100 km south of Atbara are the ruins of the capital of the ancient Kingdom of Meroe. The kings of Meroe resided here from 592 BC to 350 AD and gained fame in the Graeco-Roman world for their prosperous iron industry and agricultural development. Their architecture was highly developed and reflected extensive Egyptian influence. Hieroglyphic inscriptions on the ruins of pyramids, palaces and temples in the area show that the Meroites worshipped Egyptian deities. The Meroites also developed their own script which has been only partly deciphered.

The Kingdom of Meroe ended in 350 AD with the rise of King Ezana, of the Kingdom of Axum in Abyssinia, and the subsequent invasion of Meroe by his armies.

In the 1820s an Italian explorer named Ferlini arrived in what was left of the royal city, with the Turko-Egyptian forces of Mohammed Ali. Ferlini was specifically looking for treasure, but managed to find only a single cache of gold, in pyramid number six, which he smuggled back to Milan for auction. In his greedy search however, he hacked the tops off 40 pyramid tombs. Although his vandalism can still be seen, these pyramids are in better shape than those at Nuri and Kurru.

Between the Nile and the train tracks stands the **Temple of Amun** as well as traces of the royal palaces and swimming pool that were nearby. About 1½ km to the east are the ruins of another temple. The royal pyramids, where the Meroites buried their dead, are in the desert five km to the east.

Getting There To get to the ruins take the train to Kabushiya from where you can get local transportation to Bagrawiya, the village near the site. There is a rest house nearby.

SHENDI
The town of Shendi, 70 km south of the Royal City of Meroe, is the starting point for visiting the Meroitic Temples of Musawwarat and Naqa. Local transport goes to both places from Shendi and from a village to the south called Wad Ben Naqa. There is a cheap hotel at Shendi and transportation to and from Khartoum is frequent.

Temple of Musawwarat
The site of the Temple of Musawwarat, about 20 km south of Shendi, features a reconstructed temple complex and the remains of a palace. There are also statues of elephants and lions scattered in the sand near the *hafirs*, which were reservoirs that the Meroites dug to provide the area with water.

Temple of Naqa
The Temple of Naqa is 40 km east of the Nile and 55 km south-west of Shendi. A kiosk at the temple reflects the extent of Roman influence in the Sudan. On the back wall of the temple, carvings show that the Meroites worshipped a lion god named *Apedemek*.

SABALOOKA FALLS
These beautiful but seldom visited waterfalls are at the Sixth Cataract of the Nile, about 50 km north of Khartoum. If you're into kayaking, and just happen to have a kayak with you, then this place is recommended. A British expatriate kayaker in Khartoum visits Sabalooka regularly and somehow has avoided getting bilharzia. To get there, you get off the bus at Jebel Qerri or Abu Dom and persuade a local to take you the rest of the way.

Western Sudan

Travel through western Sudan is rough and tough, but fascinating. It is a diverse region covering an area of 549,579 square km, from the deserts and plains of Kordofan to the mountains and hills of Darfur. There are more than six million people living in this region from as many as 23 tribes and ethnic groups, including the Arab Baggara tribes of Northern Kordofan, the African Nuba people of the Nuba mountains and the black Saharan nomads of the Zaghawa tribe of Northern Darfur.

Most of the land is harsh desert pocked with the tiny thorns of *heskanit* grass and sharp acacia bushes. The heskanit sticks to your skin and clothes and is brutal to extract. In the midst of this apparent bleakness however, there are beautiful lakes, mountains, hills and lush groves of palms and prickly trees.

The history of the provinces of Kordofan and Darfur is simpler to summarise than the land and its people. Not much is known of the early history of this region as there are no ruins of ancient palaces and temples from bygone kingdoms and dynasties.

Until Islam entered the region in the 16th century, most of the scattered tribes and groups were isolated from each other. By 1596 the dynasty of Sultan Suleiman Solong had established itself in Darfur and had Islamised and united the Fur people. For the next 320 years the Fur Sultanate thrived and fended off challenges from the Fung Sultanate and Abyssinians in the east. The Sultanate ended in 1916 when it was overthrown by Anglo-Egyptian forces after Kitchener's initial victory over the Mahdists in 1898.

El Obeid, the capital of Kordofan, had been the Mahdi's first political centre. It was there that he decimated the weaker, less numerous forces of Colonel Hicks in 1883 and consolidated his political power and military forces before marching to Khartoum.

Today, the towns and villages of Kordofan and Darfur are still strongholds for Mahdiyism. The Umma Party, one of Sudan's foremost political parties, is headed by the great-grandson of the Mahdi, the present Prime Minister Sadek al Mahdi, and has a big following in western Sudan.

Over the last few years drought and famine in Kordofan and Darfur provinces, and in neighbouring Chad, have displaced or killed hundreds of thousands of people. The United Nations estimated that over 400,000 Sudanese had to leave their villages in search of food and water. At the same time, thousands of Chadians swarmed into Sudan to escape war and hunger in their own country. In 1985 and '86 food and medical aid was rushed into the area from all over the world.

Although the problems persist, stories abound from travellers and expatriate relief workers of the incredible hospitality and friendliness of the Sudanese. Even in this region, faced with such adversity, the people share whatever food and drink they have with visitors. Do not abuse the privilege of experiencing Sudanese hospitality. A token of thanks such as a small gift means a lot. The gesture alone is worth 1000 camels.

EL OBEID

El Obeid is a city of 200,000 people surrounded by inhospitable desert. Apart from having once been the Mahdi's capital, El Obeid is also famous as the 'gum arabic capital of the world' and has the second and third best football teams in the Sudan.

For those yearning to know, gum arabic is used in the manufacture of ink and food thickeners. It's also one of the ingredients in the soluble capsules of some pain killers

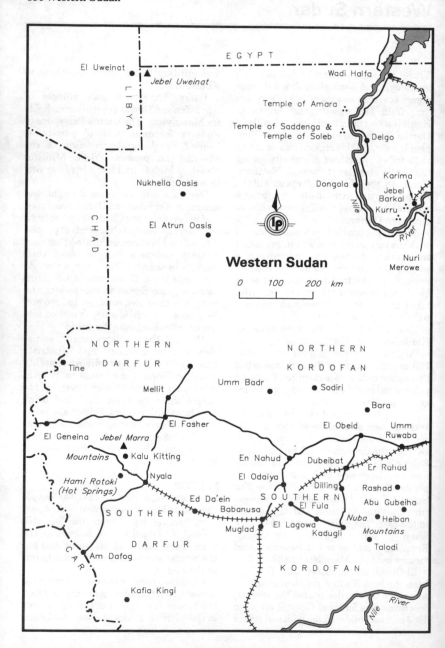

EGYPT

El Uweinat

LIBYA

Jebel Uweinat

Wadi Halfa

Temple of Amara

Temple of Saddenga &
Temple of Soleb

Delgo

Nukheila Oasis

CHAD

Dongola

Karima
Jebel
Barkal
Kurru

El Atrun Oasis

Nile

River

Nuri
Merowe

Western Sudan

0   100   200 km

NORTHERN
DARFUR

NORTHERN
KORDOFAN

Tine

Mellit

Umm Badr

Sodiri

Bara

El Geneina

El Fasher

El Obeid

Umm
Ruwaba

Jebel Marra

Mountains

Kalu Kitting

En Nahud

Dubeibat

Er Rahad

Hami Rotoki
(Hot Springs)

Nyala

El Odaiya

Dilling

Rashad

Ed Da'ein

Babanusa

SOUTHERN

El Fula

Abu Gubeiha
Nuba   Heiban

SOUTHERN

Muglad

El Lagowa

Kadugli

Mountains

C.A.R.

DARFUR

Talodi

Am Dafog

KORDOFAN

Kafia Kingi

Nile

River

and other drugs. The gum arabic is extracted from little balls hanging from the branches of acacia trees.

Information

The British Council runs a small library which is open daily, except Fridays, from 8.30 am to 12.30 pm and 4.30 to 6.30 pm. They occasionally show films.

The city has no electricity except that provided by private generators.

The water supply in El Obeid fluctuates. When it dries up completely water has to be trucked in.

For those travellers who cannot make-do without television, the Syrian and Coptic Clubs have sets and generators.

Things to See

There is a small museum in town which has displays on Sudan's ancient history and Colonel Hicks' defeat at the hands of the Mahdi's forces. Outside of town there's a monument to Hicks, which marks the site of the battlefield, but it's definitely off the beaten track and you'll need a guide if you really want to see it.

El Obeid also has one of the largest cathedrals in Africa - the result of extensive missionary efforts in the area. El Obeid has a large African Catholic community and the drum and xylophone music which accompanies Sunday services has a distinctly African beat. It is worth 'going to church' just to hear the music.

There are two *souks* in El Obeid. One market is predominantly for meat and vegetables, although cloth and clothing are also sold and you can have a shirt or pair of pants made there in a day. The market is older, prices for produce tend to be lower and some local crafts are available.

Places to Stay

There are not many places to stay in El Obeid. Try the *John Hotel*, near the *souk*, which is a basic, lakonda-style place with four beds to a room. It costs S£5 per night per person.

The *Government Rest House* near the governor's office is a pleasant place to stay. Single rooms cost S£7 per night.

Other places which have been recommended by travellers include the *International*, the *Arous* and the *Shikan*.

Places to Eat

There are several good cafés and tea stalls near the *souks*. There's a take-away fish and chicken restaurant and an old ice cream shop which also sells beef burgers. The best place to eat Sudanese food is the *Banker's Club*.

Getting There

Train There are three trains a week to El Obeid from Khartoum - on Saturdays, Thursdays and Fridays. The schedule is a bit erratic though, especially during the rainy season, which often means there is only one train a week from El Obeid to Khartoum - on Thursdays. The 1st class fare is S£45.

Trains from El Obeid to Nyala leave on Saturdays and Fridays and take three to four days.

Bus There are daily buses to El Obeid from Omdurman (refer to the Khartoum Getting There section for details). There are also daily buses from El Obeid's main *souk* to Omdurman.

There is a daily bus south to the railway junction villages of Dubeibat, Dilling and Kadugli. The trip costs S£15 to S£20, takes from four to seven hours to get to Kadugli and the road is paved most of the way.

Truck Souk lorries travel in and out of El Obeid every day. Most of the trucks leave from the main *souk* and go to virtually every town and village in the area. Their destinations, and the duration of the journey, include: El Fasher, two to three days; Nyala, three to five days; Khartoum, 24 hours; and Umm Ruwaba, three hours. All of these trips are unscheduled and subject to frequent fuel shortages.

Fuel was a problem in El Obeid for a

couple of elderly Britons who had driven their beaten-up Land Rover all the way from South Africa. Their ages were difficult to ascertain because they looked as worn and rugged as their vehicle. They told me that when they arrived in El Obeid:

We had to change money at the bank in order to buy diesel fuel for the Land Rover, but then there wasn't any fuel so two of the bank managers took a rubber tube and sucked fuel out of the bank's supply for us. They were in suits and ties and pretty jovial about the whole thing.

After travelling through Africa we're not keen on people but these people are really friendly. When we were camping out the lorry drivers would stop, toot their hooters and ask 'Are you OK?'

UMM RUWABA

The small town of Umm Ruwaba is 135 km east of El Obeid along a terrible road. There is a small but interesting camel market where members of the Arab *Baza'a* tribe sell their camels. The town is also home to some of the more African *Jawa'ama* tribe. The two groups seem to stay away from each other. The town can also be reached by train from Khartoum.

Southern Kordofan

THE NUBA MOUNTAINS

Everyone who has travelled in this region raves about the beautiful scenery and fascinating ways of the Nuba people. The Nuba are dispersed throughout villages in the mountains where they practise terrace farming. They remained isolated from the modern world until quite recently and have managed to retain most of their traditional ways. Body painting and scarring, female circumcision and bloody wrestling matches are common.

A photo-journalist named Leni Riefenstahl assembled a beautifully photographed account of the Nuba called *The People of Kau*. Her photographs of the naked Nuba and their wrestling matches and courting dances piqued the curiosity of many travellers and accelerated the Nuba's exposure to the outside world.

The Sudanese government, ever so mindful of its development and modernisation efforts, was embarrassed by this display of native traditionalism. They attempted to impede visits to the Nuba Mountains by insisting that foreigners obtain travel permits and leave their cameras in Kadugli. They have also undertaken a programme to clothe the Nuba. I have met several travellers however, who 'forgot' their permits and had no problems travelling there.

There are a few obvious points to take into consideration though if you're visiting this region, the most important of which is to show respect for the traditional ways of these people. This is a rather contentious issue for travellers because the influx of inquisitive westerners is already having an effect. These days, much to the displeasure of the Nuba elders, the younger men paint themselves and perform their dances for dollars with little regard for Nuba tradition.

If you wish to take photographs, it is always better to ask first and keep in mind that the Nuba are people, not museum pieces or circus performers, so do not gawk at them.

Er Rahad

The town of Er Rahad, although comparatively commercialised and not particularly noteworthy, is a good starting point for treks into the Nuba Mountains. The best part of town is the lake where you can buy wonderful eel steaks and eat them by the water.

There is a lakonda-style hotel in town. There are daily souk lorries from El Obeid to Er Rahad and the trip costs S£5.

A common truck route in this region is from Er Rahad south through part of the Nuba Mountains to Sidra, Karling, Rashad, Abu Gubeiha, Kologi, Tosi and

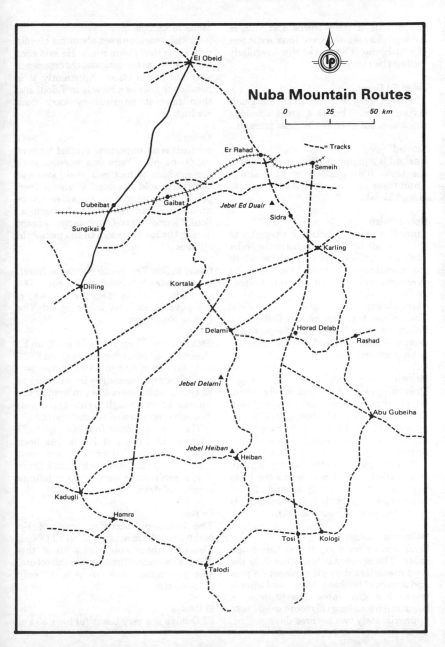

Nuba Mountain Routes

0   25   50 km

- - - = Tracks

El Obeid

Er Rahad

Semeih

Dubeibat

Gaibat

Jebel Ed Duair

Sidra

Sungikai

Karling

Dilling

Kortala

Delami

Horad Delab

Rashad

Jebel Delami

Abu Gubeiha

Jebel Heiban

Heiban

Kadugli

Hamra

Tosi

Kologi

Talodi

Talodi. All of these towns and villages have good *souks* and most have some sort of rest house. The trucks run irregularly during the rainy season

Jebel Ed Duair

The souk lorry will pass Jebel Ed Duair before Sidra. This is a great climbing mountain but only for the most intrepid.

Rashad

Rashad is a gorgeous place so if you have the time, it's definitely worth visiting. From there you can catch a souk lorry to Horad Delab.

Horad Delab

From this village junction it's possible to get lorry rides to most villages in the Nuba Mountains. Check out the lush palm tree grove while you are there. You can sleep overnight on a rope net bed in the cafés.

Abu Gubeiha

The unique highlight of Abu Gubeiha, a village south of Rashad, is the pervasive aroma of mangoes and guavas from the nearby groves.

Heiban

This village is at the base of Jebel Heiban, the third highest mountain in the Sudan (Mt Kinyeti is the highest). It is at the centre of the Nuba Mountain range and, supposedly, the coldest place in the country.

The village is predominantly African and Christian, which explains the large number of pigs running around. If you haven't seen a pork chop in a while, this is your chance to pig-out (sorry!).

Heiban to Kadugli

Souk lorries regularly travel this rough route. The scenery is magnificent as the road meanders through a mountain pass and groves of baobabs, palms and prickly trees. For the more adventurous, a beautiful hike along this route would take approximately two to three days.

Talodi to Kadugli

A British teacher raved about his bicycle ride along this 75-km route. He said that the scenery was fantastic and the experience well worth the effort. Apparently it is possible to borrow a bicycle in Talodi and then have it returned by lorry from Kadugli.

Kadugli

Kadugli is an important market town of 30,000 people. There is a popular *souk* there, where many traditional foods and spices are sold. Kadugli is also a good point from which to begin walks or excursions into the Nuba Mountains. Souk lorries travel regularly, except during the rainy season, to the mountain villages.

Places to Stay *The South Kordofan Hotel*, is a lakonda-style hotel, which costs S£5 per night. The only other place to stay is the government rest house called *The Palace Resthouse*.

Getting There There's a daily bus from El Obeid to Kadugli, which costs about S£20 and takes from four to seven hours.

There are two buses a day from Kadugli to El Obeid which leave from in front of the cinema. From Kadugli to Dilling you pass through sorghum and sesame country.

The souk lorry route from Kadugli to El Lagowa, El Fula and Nyala has been highly recommended for the magnificent scenery. You can catch the train at El Fula if you don't mind waiting an indefinite number of days.

En Nahud

The Southern Kordofan town of En Nahud is 215 km south-west of El Obeid. The only thing noteworthy about this place is its unique limestone architecture. The government *rest house* is the only place to stay.

El Odaiya

El Odaiya is a very beautiful town 83 km

south of En Nahud. There are lots of trees and green hills, especially after the rains. The 145-km lorry ride to Babanusa has been recommended for its scenery.

Babanusa

Babanusa is a railway junction village where you can catch trains to Nyala, Er Rahad and Khartoum.

Muglad

Muglad is a Texas-style boom town a few km south of Babanusa. It's basically an oil exploration base, complete with an airstrip and a large compound full of foreigners.

NORTHERN KORDOFAN

Bara

There is not much to this oasis town, which is just north of El Obeid, except a lot of vegetable gardens. Buses going between Khartoum and El Obeid stop there though.

Sodiri

Sodiri is a very bleak place in the middle of the desert 167 km north-west of Bara. There used to be a large camel market there but it and the people of Sodiri suffered greatly during the famine of 1985.

Umm Badr

This mere dot on the map, seemingly in the middle of nothing but desert, is apparently quite a surprising little place. One intrepid traveller who ventured there described it as 'a very beautiful, very green lake area where a lot of camel nomads hang out'. It is a two to three-day lorry trip from El Obeid.

Southern Darfur

Ed Da'ein

This is a railroad village almost 200 km west of Babanusa. It is the 'capital' of the nomadic Rizeigaat tribe and the people there are very friendly and hospitable. It's a very laid back place with a lakonda-style hotel.

NYALA

Nyala was capital of the Fur Sultanate from the time of its establishment in the late 16th century. The Fur people became united under the banner of Islam and the sultanate thrived and prospered for over 300 years partly because of Nyala's isolation from the rest of Sudan. Despite the modern railroad connection to Khartoum, the town is still an isolated outpost on the edge of the desert at the base of a mountain range dominated by the Sudan's second highest mountain, Jebel Marra.

Information

The staff at the government Tourist Office in town can help you plan a trek to Jebel Marra, including the purchase of a donkey, camel or horse from the *souk*.

Another good source of information about treks to Jebel Marra are the British English teachers in Nyala.

The tourist and registration offices are just past the radio mast.

Nyala has three *souks* but because of the drought and famine in the region, the main market is now only a quarter the size it was in 1985. On the other side of the wadi, however, two wild sort of *souks* have sprung up which the locals have dubbed 'Texas' and 'Korea'. Most of the souk lorries leave from the Texas *souk*.

Places to Stay

The Government Rest House, opposite the main *souk*, is a good place to stay if you can get permission. The rooms surround a garden courtyard and all have wash basins. You can cook in the guest house kitchen if you bring your own food.

The Darfur Hotel is a cheap, basic place that costs S£1.50 for a mattress on rusty springs. It's difficult to store your gear there though.

A few other hotels which have been recommended by travellers include the *Deenobee Hotel, Hotel Zaire* and the *Andafusu Hotel*.

Camping There are two unofficial camping sites in Nyala. Although the land is privately owned, it is sometimes possible to camp along **Wadi Nyala** among the mango trees and monkeys. The other site is under the mango trees of the **Kondua Forest**, about four km further down the wadi.

Places to Eat
The *Camp David* near the Darfur Hotel tops the list of eating places. They serve delicious cakes, tea and milk.

Another place is the 'hole-in-the-wall', near the mosque in the centre of town, where you can get veal cutlets.

Fresh food is readily available in the *souk* and tinned food is also available in town but it's expensive.

Getting There
Nyala is the rail terminus and the tedious trip back to Khartoum could take as long as five days. For fare information refer to the Khartoum section.

There are no buses.

Souk lorries leave from the all three markets, although the majority depart from the Texas *souk*. They travel to practically every destination imaginable, including the Central African Republic, Khartoum, the villages near Jebel Marra, El Fasher and El Geneina. The trip to El Fasher takes 1½ days and is a popular route.

Hami Rotoki
On the way to the village of Kass near Jebel Marra, you might consider making a stop at the medicinal hot springs of Hami Rotoki. The locals claim the water there is hot enough to make tea with, yet not so hot that you can't take a dip.

JEBEL MARRA MOUNTAINS
This is a high and beautiful region of rivers, orchards and fine, hilly walking country. No two people's experiences here are the same, but travellers agree that the hospitality in these mountains is second to none.

Nyala is the starting point for a visit to Jebel Marra, an extinct volcanic crater which, at 3071 metres, is the second highest mountain in the country and the feature attraction of this area.

Food and water are no problem and you can't really get lost because the local people are always pointing you in the right direction. The locals will also insist that you visit their houses and fill your arms with fruit.

To get to Jebel Marra you take a truck from Nyala to Nyatiti, from where you begin your walk – just head towards the mountains. Halfway to Quaila, just past the first village, there is an excellent waterfall and pool where you can camp and swim. The schoolteacher in Quaila may be able to find accommodation for you and point you in the right direction for the crater. From Quaila you walk to the hot springs, then up to the crater of Jebel Marra. Once at the top, you go halfway round the rim before heading down again, to the crater floor. From there you walk out through the canyon to Taratonga, where there is a weekly truck to Nyala.

From Taratonga you can visit some of the nearby villages if you have the time. Sunni, in the north, or Gandator and Kalu Kitting, in the south-west, are three worth visiting. From Kalu Kitting you can get back onto the main road between Nyala and Nyatiti, at a place called Nyama, where there's a camp for the German construction gang who have been building the road. They often have transport going to Nyala and some travellers said they were allowed to use the camp swimming pool.

It is also possible to trek to Jebel Marra in the opposite direction. The exact route you take will naturally depend on your objectives and time, but the following is one possible route.

Jebel Marra Trek

First, take a truck from Nyala to Menawashi (S£4), which is basically just a truck stop with several people selling food. There's no rest house there but the locals will probably offer you accommodation in their huts.

From Menawashi it's a two-hour walk over flat, scrubby land to Marshing. There's usually an empty hut or two there, so just ask the village schoolteacher where you can sleep. There's also a café in Marshing, where you can get soup and bread for S£1 and tea for 25 pt, and a market on Wednesday and Sunday.

A five-hour walk from Marshing brings you to the beautiful village of Melemm. There is a *rest house* next to the police station and the police there are very friendly and will probably supply you with firewood, water and other necessities. There is a market in Melemm on Mondays and Fridays.

The all-night truck ride from Melemm to Deribat costs about S£5 and takes you through beautiful hills, some of which are so steep it may be necessary to winch the truck up. There's no rest house in Deribat but there are several tea houses, a café and a Monday market.

A two-hour walk from Deribat will take you to Jawa, where you can stay in the huge new hospital which is not occupied yet. The market day in Jawa is Thursday.

About 1½ hours away is Sunni, one of the Jebel Marra's most scenic settlements. The large old *rest house* there has four beds which cost S£1.50 each. There's no *souk*, but a small shop sells rice, nuts, dates, cigarettes and the occasional chicken. Don't miss the 35-metre-high waterfall behind the power station.

From Sunni it's a five-hour walk/scramble to Lugi. The views en route are beautiful but it gets very cold, especially at night, and there are only a few huts in the fields along the way. There's no rest

house or market at Lugi but there is a small store with basic supplies.

The next leg is the 2¼-hour walk to Taratonga through a landscape of conifers and heather very similar to the Scottish highlands. Taratonga itself is a picturesque little village, set on wooded, grassy slopes. There's a market on Saturday and a shop which sells basic supplies. The *rest house* is in disrepair so if you're there during the rainy season it's better to look for an empty hut, or try the schoolhouse. The village teacher speaks English and can arrange guides to the crater for you.

It's a good idea to get a guide up to the crater or the walk could take you a lot longer than necessary. It usually takes three hours with a guide but could take five to eight hours if you go it alone. The same applies between the crater and the next village of Kronga (also known as Kuela), which takes about five hours with a guide but much longer if you get lost.

From Kronga it's a 1½ hour walk to the village of Khartoum, where there's a Saturday market; and then another 3½ hours to Nyatiti, with its well-stocked market, cafés, *rest house* and transport back to Nyala.

If you don't fancy walking or you don't have camping equipment, it's possible to buy donkeys and sell them again when you're ready to leave.

Dagu Jebels

The Dagu Jebels are a two-day hike from Nyala. Prehistoric rock paintings are an interesting feature of these hills. This is beautiful walking country, especially after the rains, but watch out for the heskanit burrs which are very thick and sticky in this area.

Kafia Kingi

This village, in the south-west corner of Southern Darfur, is most interesting for the people who live in the area. The Fallata Umboro, members of a non-Arab nomadic group, are descended from the Fulani people of West Africa and are famous for their *fakis*. A *faki* is usually a teacher but the Fallata give their teachers the status of magicians. These *fakis* travel around, for one month each year, collecting roots and herbs. When they return, people come to them for spells and secret potions. The *fakis'* love potions are popular, especially among old women. The women pour the potion into the tea of the men whose attention they are trying to attract.

The Sudanese government recently declared the area around Kafia Kingi a national park. The park is still nameless and barely accessible but souk lorries occasionally travel into the region.

NORTHERN DARFUR
El Fasher
El Fasher first gained prominence in the early part of the 18th century as a principal centre of the Fur Sultanate. It was also the starting point for one of Africa's most famous caravan routes, the *Darb al Arba'een* or the '40 Day Road'. Incredibly wealthy camel caravans laden with ebony, spices, ivory and beautiful cloth, as well as hundreds of slaves captured from other parts of Africa, regularly made the long trip across the desert to the great bazaars of Aswan and Asyut in Egypt.

In the early 19th century, as if slavery itself wasn't horror enough, Mohammed Ali commissioned two Coptic priests in Asyut to carry out castrations on most of the young male slaves who survived the arduous journey.

Although Mohammed had managed to extend his military might into other parts of the Sudan, his ambition to conquer El Fasher and gain control of the Darfur and the great caravan route, was never realised. It was not until 1874, long after his death, that Darfur became a province of Egyptian Sudan. This control lasted until the time of the Mahdi and the subsequent downfall of the Khalifa in 1898. A religious zealot named Ali Dinar

then established an autonomous sultanate based in El Fasher. The sultanate lasted until 1916 when, on 6 November, a couple of British planes flew in and shot Sultan Ali Dinar dead from the air. The locals of El Fasher revere the sultan as a martyr.

During WW II El Fasher was a small, but important US airbase for C-47 cargo planes. It was basically a refuelling stop for planes flying the Miami to North Africa supply route.

Places to Stay & Eat *The Government Rest House*, which was once the British Commissioner's residence, is a good place to stay. It's in the building next to the palace.

Buji's, one of the few restaurants in town, is on Palace Rd and serves decent roast beef and chips. Opposite Buji's is the only place in El Fasher to get ice cream.

Getting There There are souk lorries and a few buses travelling to most destinations near El Fasher. There is a weekly bus to Mellit; a twice weekly bus to Kutum; and daily buses and lorries to Nyala.

Mellit
This village, north of El Fasher, is home to a large number of camel breeders and salt traders from the semi-nomadic Zaghawa tribe who, until recently, spoke only their own Saharan languages. They have now been Arabised and most Zaghawa also speak some form of Arabic and profess Islam.

The salt traders of Mellit travel 140 km north by camel through the Tabago Hills to the village of Malha, where they meet the salt miners who come down from the Meidob Hills. The salt is then taken back to Mellit and on to El Fasher.

The camel traders of Mellit take a much more difficult route. They travel for 27 days from Mellit, north through the Tabago and Meidob hills, then across the Sahara Desert to the oases of El Atrun and Nukheila and finally on to Jabal al Awaynat on the Libyan border where they sell their camels. If you dare, you may accompany the Zaghawa on this trek but they usually tend to lose camels and a few people along the way.

El Geneina

The Sudan's westernmost town is basically a principal border post for crossing into Chad. El Geneina was once the centre of a powerful sultanate but is now the seat of the 'powerless' Sultan of Massalit, the son of a ruler installed by the British in the first half of this century. Although his kingdom is split between Chad and the Sudan, the Sultan still holds court everyday in a courtyard at the base of his palace. With a bit of diplomacy you might be able to talk your way into the palace for an official audience.

There is a *Government Rest House* in town. Souk lorries regularly travel to Chad from El Fasher.

Tine

The village of Tine is a two-day lorry ride north of El Geneina. It was possible to cross into Chad from there but the war in Chad may have put an end to that. The strife there has also caused increased banditry in the Sudan. To combat this, the Sudanese government formed a Camel Corps of armed nomads, who have been quite effective in tracking down these bandits. Their presence has added a sort of Wild West atmosphere to the place.

TO/FROM CENTRAL AFRICAN REPUBLIC

Occasionally, there are trucks from the Texas *souk* in Nyala which go all the way to Bangui in the CAR. Depending on the driver, the trip will cost you anything from S£120 to S£250. The route is via the Sudanese village of Am Dafog and the CAR border town of Birao. The journey can take from four to 17 days as the truck

drivers often spend a couple of days selling their wares in *souks* along the way.

Between August and December there are no trucks between Nyala and Bangui and the police refuse to grant travel permits to head west at that time because of the rains. This doesn't mean that you can't make it though. If you choose to ignore the permit regulations, there are trucks as far as Rahad el Berdi from Nyala. The trip costs around S£15 and takes about 12 hours. You can stay at the police station in Rahad.

Once there, you can ask around for a guide and animal transport to Am Dafog. Camel trains are the usual means of transport and should cost about S£5 for your bags and S£30 if you also want to ride. The 160-km trail goes through a tough course of shallow swamps and coarse grass, but you shouldn't take longer than five days. Donkeys and guides are also available in Rahad for about S£50.

At Am Dafog you can stay at the police station and food is available at a café. There's an interesting *souk* which straddles the border between the CAR and the Sudan; and a lake which has water even at the end of the dry season.

The journey from Am Dafog to Birao (the Sudanese often refer to this town as Daba) takes another 1½ days. You can hire camels in Am Dafog; two camels and a guide should cost S£25 per person. Along the way you will ford at least five deep wadis and stay with nomads while they herd their cattle. The nomads are usually very hospitable and helpful. You eat with them – prime steak, fresh milk and yogurt – and if you're lucky, they may treat you to some of their music.

I met a British couple who had driven this route in the opposite direction. They saw no other vehicles for three days and their only comment about the trip was: 'What a horrible track of sand'.

Eastern Sudan

Eastern Sudan is one of the most accessible regions of the country. The 1200-km stretch of good tarmac road linking Khartoum to Kassala and Port Sudan, travels through terrain that is basically flat, except for around the Red Sea Hills area south of Port Sudan. The road, which was completed in 1980, has greatly facilitated the transport of goods and people and was built in this region because much of the Sudan's sorghum, an important staple, is grown there.

Over the past few years, however, drought and pestilence has resulted in poor crops and has increased the great hardship faced by the locals and the thousands of refugees that have crowded into the region.

There is a great diversity of people in eastern Sudan. In the Red Sea Hills there are the nomadic Beja people who speak Bedawiya, a language without script, and bear a close resemblance (according to some experts), to the ancient Egyptians. Near Kassala are the Rashaida people, nomadic camel and goat breeders who live in goat skin tents and drive Toyota pick-up trucks; in the Gedaref area the predominant people are the Shukriya Arabs; and throughout the region there are also Eritrean and Tigréan refugees who have fled drought, famine and war in Ethiopia.

The refugee crisis is one of the most urgent problems in eastern Sudan. There are more than 300,000 refugees in camps and settlements along the 439-km stretch of road from Wad Medani to Kassala. However, you cannot really see from the road how bad conditions are in the camps. As many as 20% of the refugees, mainly women and children, are malnourished; disease is rife and there are shortages of shelter, adequate water supplies and clothing.

If you have an opportunity to visit a camp, it is worth doing so to increase your awareness of the desperate problems of these refugees. Don't make a visit merely for the sake of sightseeing though; the refugees need your help, any help at all. So spread the word and do what you can!

WAD MEDANI
Wad Medani is a city of 145,000 people on the Blue Nile. It's the first major city south of Khartoum along the road to Port Sudan, but there's not much of interest for the visitor there.

Opposite Wad Medani, on the other side of the Blue Nile (which is supposedly free of bilharzia) there's a good swimming beach. You can take a box for 50 pt from the Wad Medani vegetable *souk* to the village of **Hantub** which is just near the beach.

The *Gulinar Restaurant* near the central post office serves good Ethiopian 'curries', chicken & chips, yogurt and salads. Each table is painted with the name of a different African country.

There are a couple of good bookshops near the Gulinar which sell English-language books and you can buy interesting wedding drums in the *souk*.

Most of the numerous buses and lorries that operate between Khartoum, Kassala and Port Sudan stop in Wad Medani. For more info see the Getting There sections for those cities.

EL FAU
There are numerous refugee camps and settlements along the road between Wad Medani and Gedaref. Several new settlements have sprung up around El Fau and the Sudanese government has been attempting to transfer refugees from other camps to these settlements.

GEDAREF
With a population of 30,000, Gedaref is a

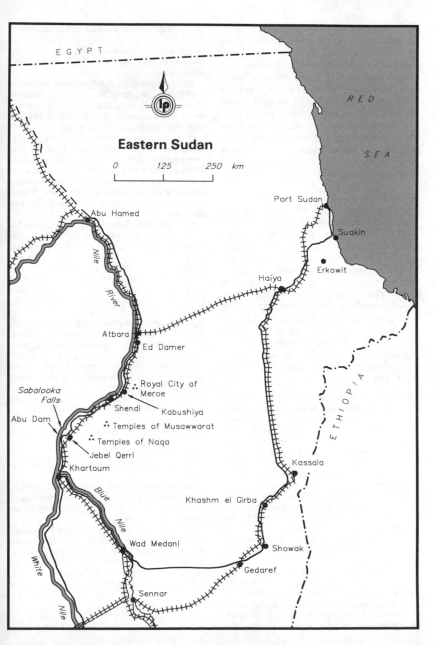

EGYPT

RED

SEA

Eastern Sudan

0   125   250   km

Port Sudan

Suakin

Abu Hamed

Erkowit

Nile

Haiya

River

Atbara

Ed Damer

Royal City of
Meroe

Sabalooka
Falls

Shendi   Kabushiya

Abu Dam

Temples of Musawwarat

Temples of Naqa

Jebel Qerri

Khartoum

Kassala

ETHIOPIA

Blue

Khashm el Girba

Nile

Showak

Wad Medani

White

Gedaref

Nile

Sennar

dirty, semi-industrial city renowned only for its sesame seeds, huge quantities of which are auctioned daily.

If you somehow get stuck in this sesame centre and need a place to stay, then check out the *Amir Hotel* or approach an expatriate. The *souk* and grocery stores are well stocked so you won't go hungry.

Gedaref is along the main road, so there are frequent lorry and bus connections in both directions, to Khartoum or Kassala and Port Sudan. The main road is a short distance from town but it's easy to hitch.

SHOWAK

The small town of Showak is the eastern Sudan headquarters for the United Nations High Commission for Refugees and a Colorado-based charity called LALMBA (pronounced la-lum-ba). LALMBA operates a medical clinic, feeding centre for malnourished people and workshop for prosthetic limbs. They also run small medical clinics and feeding centres in the villages of Abuda, Um Ali and Wad Hileau which are to the east of town near the Ethiopian border. To give you some idea of life in a refugee camp, the following is an account of a day in Wad Hileau:

Sister Bridget Haase, a nun from Crystal City Missouri in the US, is one of the people responsible for seeing that the malnourished kids of the Wad Hileau settlement get fed. She exudes an incredible enthusiasm for her work as, every morning, she marches across the field from the LALMBA compound to the mud rondavels, canvas tents and grass mat huts of the refugees.

'These we call the defecation fields,' she told me, pointing around her at the flat and barren fields that were devoid of life except for a few people squatting in the distance.

'There are latrines,' she explained, 'but they are too far and too few for many of the refugees.'

Water is also a problem in Wad Hileau. The only source of water is a tank one mile from the huts and tents on the camp's periphery. The camp grew faster than the water supply could be extended and many of the refugees, especially the women and children, have neither the containers nor the energy to fetch it. With so little water available, many of the refugees cannot wash regularly, consequently diseases of every sort are rife throughout the settlement.

Tuberculosis is the most common disease in Wad Hileau, as in most refugee camps, because of the cramped living quarters and the lack of water and sanitation. Coughing and spitting keep the vicious cycle of TB going.

In one tent designed for two or three people, there were four women, one of whom was pregnant, and kids of all sizes sitting in the dirt. Wisps of smoke from a tin can charcoal stove in front seemed to do nothing to deter the swarm of flies inside; and the flies clung to everything, including the mouths and eyes of the children.

A couple of the kids – a tiny baby boy and a thin, scraggly four-year-old girl – wore the numbered plastic bracelets LALMBA had given them to indicate they were registered with the feeding centre. They were just two of the settlement's hundreds of severly malnourished kids. About 5% of the children at Wadi Hileau are in this category, although a year ago the statistics were much worse.

At the feeding centre, which was just a flat grass-roofed enclosure with mat walls, there was a line of children waiting to be weighed. Clusters of women and children sat off to the side sipping cups of porridge, while opposite, in a roped-off section, the severely malnourished kids were trying to eat.

At the settlement's medical clinic, Ashagrie Kindie, one of the medical examiners, told me about another problem which they must contend with – the cultural medicine of the refugees.

'Parents burn their children with hot nails because they think disease can be burnt out,' he said.

'And when someone has malaria or hepatitis they cut 44 places on his body. I tell them that it is bad because the bleeding will make them worse. It's a difficult job.'

Ashagrie is typical of many of the Ethiopian political refugees. He fled his country because one day the army came to his town of Gonder.

'They gathered all the students from little to big in front of the school and started shooting them. I saved my life by running.'

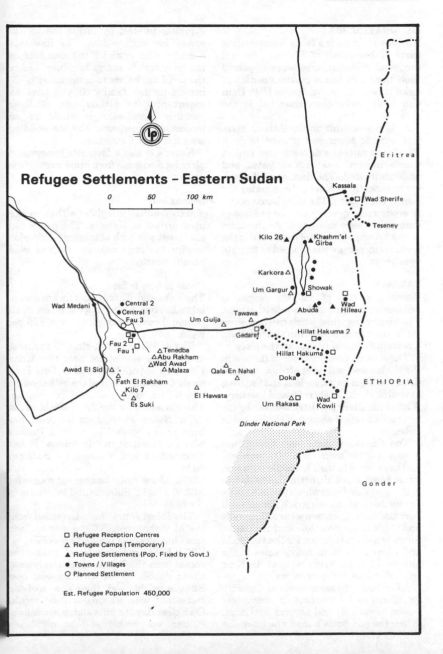

Refugee Settlements – Eastern Sudan

0   50   100 km

Eritrea

Kassala
Wad Sherife

Teseney

Kilo 26 ▲   Khashm'el Girba ▲

Karkora △

Um Gargur △   Showak

Central 2 ●
Central 1 ●
Fau 3 ○

Wad Medani

Tawawa △

Um Gulja △

Gedaref □

Abuda ●   Wad Hileau ▲

Fau 2 □
Fau 1 □

△ Tenedba
△ Abu Rakham
△ Wad Awad
△ Malaza

Awad El Sid △

Fath El Rakham △
Kilo 7 △
Es Suki △

Qala En Nahal △

El Hawata △

Hillat Hakuma 2 □

Hillat Hakuma □

Doka ●

Um Rakasa △

Wad Kowli □

ETHIOPIA

Dinder National Park

Gonder

□ Refugee Reception Centres
△ Refugee Camps (Temporary)
▲ Refugee Settlements (Pop. Fixed by Govt.)
● Towns / Villages
○ Planned Settlement

Est. Refugee Population 450,000

KHASHM EL GIRBA

Khashm el Girba is a fairly uninteresting town 62 km north of Showak. Several thousand Nubians, who were displaced from their own lands by the creation of Lake Nasser when the Aswan High Dam was built, have been resettled in the area.

A dam was built on the Atbara River just outside town and proved to be a classic example of a development project whose impact was miscalculated and underestimated. The dam caused severe environmental problems by altering the flow of the Atbara. The river banks began to erode more quickly and large areas of date palms were destroyed. As the dates were a principal source of livelihood in the area, many people were forced to migrate to other towns.

KASSALA

Kassala, a city of 150,000 people, is famous for its fruit and its *jebels*, or hills. The bizarre sugarloaf jebels can be seen on the horizon from several km away and add a certain mystical beauty to the place.

The *souk* is considered one of the best in the Sudan and sells grapefruits, oranges, dates, pomegranates, melons and bananas, as well as cloth, local crafts and jewellery. A lot of the silver jewellery is made by the mysterious veiled women of the Rashaida tribe.

The Rashaida came over from Saudi Arabia a little more than 150 years ago and have clung to their nomadic ways ever since. Most, if not all, of the Rashaida live in the goat skin tents which you will see by the roadside as you approach Kassala and Port Sudan. The women wear unique veils and thick silver bracelets and necklaces. Silver is a status symbol for the Rashaida and some store it in heavy safes in the middle of their tents – next to their television sets and generators.

A Rashaida girl announces her eligibility for marriage by wearing an intricately woven silver veil and several necklaces. When the girl finds a man she likes, she expresses interest by lifting the veil to expose her chin to him. The Rashaida consider chins erotic! If the man accepts the invitation to marry her, then, before the wedding, he has to come up with 100 camels for her family. If you have an opportunity to attend one of their wedding ceremonies, it would be an interesting experience. The big wedding season is after Ramadan.

Kassala is also a favourite honeymoon place for Sudanese from other parts of the country.

Information

You are required to register with the police upon arrival in Kassala. The police can also assist you with obtaining permission to visit the huge refugee camp of Wad Sherifa nearby.

Places to Stay & Eat

The *Taka* and *Watania* hotels are cheap, lakonda-style places opposite the Shell station. Beds in both places cost S£5 per night.

The *Al Waha Hotel*, close to the *souk* and down a side street near the Africa Hotel, is also popular with travellers. It's a clean, dormitory-style place with showers and toilets. Beds cost S£4 per person. There is a safe for keeping valuables.

The *Salam Hotel*, near the *souk*, has been recommended by several Britons who are teaching in the Sudan. It has clean rooms and showers for S£6 per night.

The *Africa Hotel* has decent rooms for S£3.50 a night. Showers and toilets are in the halls.

The *Toteel Hotel*, down the street from the Al Waha, costs S£30 a single. Each room has a ceiling fan and air-cooler.

The *El Sharq Palace Hotel*, around the corner from the Toteel, is relatively new. Clean double rooms with showers cost S£44 a night and there's a roof-top restaurant with reasonably good meals. On a clear day the hills and mountains of Eritrea are visible and at night it's

Top: The jebels of Kassala (SW)
Bottom: A cattle drive in eastern Sudan (SW)

Top: A camel yard in eastern Sudan (SW)
Left: Ruins of a coral building, Suakin (SW)
Right: Medical clinic in a refugee camp in eastern Sudan (SW)

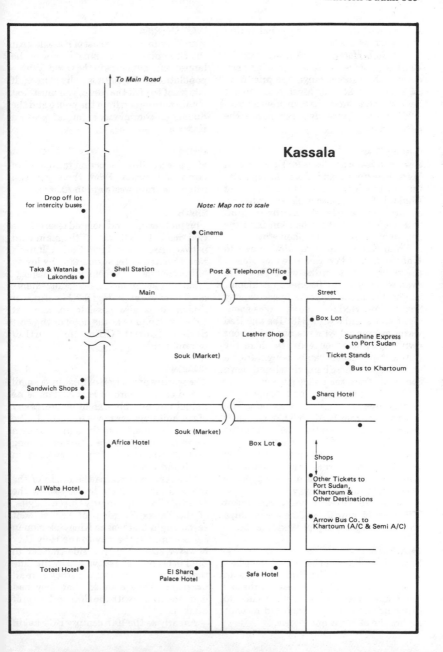

sometimes possible to see the battle fireworks across the border in Ethiopia.

The *Safa Hotel*, a block away from the El Sharq Palace, is a new, sparkling clean hotel with 35 rooms ranging in price from S£13.60 to S£52.50. Most rooms don't have showers but all have overhead fans.

There are a few sandwich shops near the Africa Hotel.

Getting There

Several buses a day leave for Kassala from both Khartoum and Port Sudan. The buses from Khartoum also stop at Wad Medani, Gedaref, Showak and Khashm al Girba. In Kassala the buses drop you off in a parking lot about one km from the centre of town near the Shell station.

From Kassala there are daily buses to Khartoum and Port Sudan which stop at the major towns on the way. There are even some buses to Teseney in Ethiopia.

The Sunshine Express bus company goes to Port Sudan, the trip takes about eight hours and costs S£18. Tea and iced water are served en route but bring your own cup unless you want to share the public cup. Tickets can be bought from a shed behind the Sharq Hotel and down the street from the police station.

The Sugipto, Taysir and Arrow companies have daily buses to Khartoum. The fares range from S£15 to S£22 and their ticket offices are near the *souk* (refer to the map of Kassala). Arrow is the best as they have big, air-con vehicles with shaded windows. The journey takes seven to 10 hours, depending on the number of police checkpoints along the way.

There are boxes opposite the ticket offices which go to the village of Khatmiya and the refugee camp of Wad Sherifa.

KHATMIYA

From this village at the base of the jebels you can begin a climb up into the hills. In the early evening bats appear in the sky and baboons come down from the hills to drink from the village well. On moonlit nights the effect is quite eerie.

WAD SHERIFA

Wad Sherifa, which is east of Kassala near the Ethiopian border, must be one of the largest refugee camps in the world. With a population of 150,000 it is a city in itself. If you want to visit the camp, you must first obtain permission from the police and the Sudanese commissioner of refugees in Kassala.

HAIYA

Haiya is a railroad junction town 351 km north of Kassala. From there you can catch the train westward to Atbara.

ERKOWIT

This picturesque and isolated resort in the Red Sea Hills is 30 km off the main road between Kassala and Port Sudan. It has a rarely visited hotel surrounded by lovely hills, streams and vegetation. Transportation and accommodation arrangements must be made at the Red Sea Hotel in Port Sudan. It is also possible to camp at Erkowit. Enquire at the hotel or the Port Sudan Tourist Office for further information.

SUAKIN

The feature attraction of Suakin, a small island 58 km south of Port Sudan, is its unique but crumbling architecture. Many of the buildings are made from coral. The island is connected to the mainland by a short causeway. Once a major trading centre, Suakin's history is cloaked in myth and legend.

One legend concerns the origin of the name Suakin which translates as the *Land of Ginn*. Apparently Queen Balgies, of the Sabaa Kingdom of Yemen, sent seven virgin maidens to King Solomon in Jerusalem. On the way to the Holy City however, the ship was side-tracked to Suakin because of a storm and by the time the girls arrived in Jerusalem they were all pregnant. They claimed that they had had intercourse with the *Ginn*, a demon of Suakin.

As early as the 10th century BC Suakin

was an important centre and was used by Ramses III as a port for trade with people across the Red Sea. Over the next several hundred years it declined in importance and it was not until the 19th century during Ottoman rule that Suakin became a prosperous slave-trading centre. In 1881 the Mahdi restored the coral buildings which today are crumbling again. When Port Sudan was established in 1905 Suakin was deserted.

It may no longer be possible to stay overnight at Kitchener's old headquarters on Suakin Island, however you can stay at the police station in the village of El Geif on the mainland. Supposedly you need to first get permission from the Red Sea Province headquarters in Port Sudan, but I seriously doubt the necessity of this. The headquarters is full of somnolent bureaucrats who will keep you waiting for hours and then tell you that 'today' a permit is not necessary. The same goes for registration. Check with them first though, just in case someone in the permit office wakes up momentarily.

There are frequent boxes and minibuses between Port Sudan and Suakin. It's also possible to hitch and can easily be visited in a day trip from Port Sudan.

PORT SUDAN

Port Sudan is a sea port and harbour city with a population of more than 200,000. It was established by the British in 1905 to facilitate the export of raw commodities such as cotton, sorghum and sesame. The city has fallen into disrepair and decay but the beautiful lattice woodwork on the windows of many of the older buildings, and the carefully planned but defoliated parks are signs of a more elegant past. The main attractions in and around Port Sudan are the trip to Suakin, the possibility of Red Sea diving and great chocolate milkshakes.

Information

There is a Tourist Office with very helpful staff near the Red Sea Hotel. The registration and permit offices are at the Red Sea Province Headquarters nearby.

Diving

There are four travel agencies which can help arrange diving trips in the area. They are the Hamido Travel Agency; Red Sea Enterprise (run by Captain Halim); the Al Somkari Travel Agency; and Juju Safari and Tourism Agency.

Another diving possibility is to go to the yacht basin at the end of Suakin St and ask for Angelo Della Valle or Captain Abdul Nabi, of the yacht *Felicidad*. Angelo and the captain take groups diving for very reasonable rates and also give basic diving instruction. Some of the diving sites they take you to include:
The wreck of the Italian cargo ship *Umbria* which was purposely sunk in 1940 because it contained 3000 tons of bombs and the crew didn't want to surrender to the British.
Shaabrumi reef where Jacques Cousteau conducted his 'Precontinent II' experiments. He left behind a giant, pod-like underwater hangar and several shark cages.
Turtle Island and the beautiful Dolphins' Reef.

Places to Stay - bottom end

The 50-bed *Youth Hostel* is a basic place with several dorm rooms, cooking facilities and a refrigerator. It's in the Salabona part of town, north of the port and its position on the Red Sea is picturesque – if you ignore the garbage on the beach and the sludge in the water. It costs S£1.50 a night with a youth hostel card and S£2 without. To get there take a red bus from the central market bus lot.

The *Africa Hotel* is a cheap dive which is often full. It's down the street from the Sudan Shipping Line building and costs S£1.50 a night.

Two other cheapies which have been recommended are the *Zahran Hotel* and the *Friendship Hotel*.

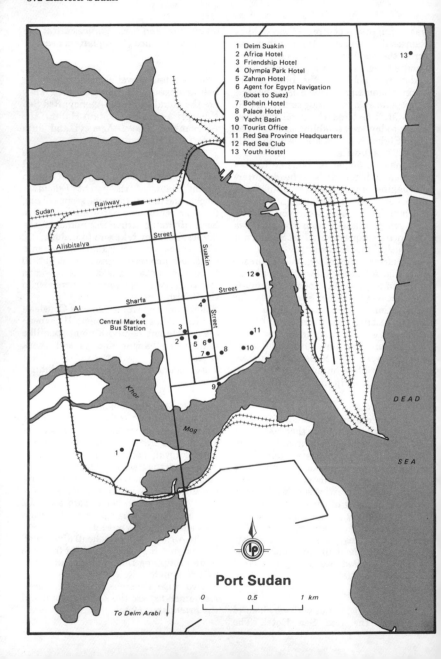

1 Deim Suakin
2 Africa Hotel
3 Friendship Hotel
4 Olympia Park Hotel
5 Zahran Hotel
6 Agent for Egypt Navigation
  (boat to Suez)
7 Bohein Hotel
8 Palace Hotel
9 Yacht Basin
10 Tourist Office
11 Red Sea Province Headquarters
12 Red Sea Club
13 Youth Hostel

Sudan   Railway

Alisbitalya   Street

Suakin

Al   Sharfa   Street

Central Market
Bus Station

Street

12

11

4

3

2   5   6

7   8   10

9

K'hor

Mog

1

DEAD

SEA

Port Sudan

0   0.5   1 km

To Deim Arabi

Places to Stay - middle
The *Bohein Hotel* is one of the best deals in town. It is clean, well maintained and singles/doubles cost S£34/55 without showers or S£40.50/61 with. Breakfast is included and all the rooms have fans and air-coolers.

The *Palace Hotel* is a nice place but it's fairly expensive and you have to show bank receipts when paying. It costs S£59.40 a night for a single with shower and air-con. They show free video movies every night, usually in English.

The *Red Sea Hotel* has similar rates and also requires bank receipts.

The *Olympia Park Hotel* is a decent, but overpriced place across the street from the statue of Osman Digna at the corner of Al Sharfa and Suakin streets. Rooms cost more than the Bohein and aren't as clean.

Places to Eat
The restaurant at the Palace Hotel serves beef burgers and tasty milkshakes. Service is horrendous and don't be surprised when they tack an extra 30% on your bill for service and taxes. Nevertheless, it is still not a bad deal.

There is a nameless place near the yacht basin which serves very good shish kebab in the evenings.

The only other place to eat in town, apart from the local cafés scattered throughout the city, is the *Red Sea Club*. Temporary membership costs S£3 and entitles you to use the swimming pool and snooker tables and eat whatever the cook feels like serving. This is also a good place to meet divers and perhaps arrange a diving trip.

Getting There
Air There is a daily Sudan Airways flight between Port Sudan and Khartoum which is fairly easy to get on. The Sudan Airways office in Port Sudan is around the corner from the Zahran Hotel.

Train The 'Superexpress' leaves on Mondays at 8 pm and only stops at Atbara and Shendi. The connecting train to Wadi Halfa from Khartoum supposedly arrives in Atbara on Wednesdays.

The fares to Khartoum are: sleeping car with full board, S£90; 1st class, S£65; 2nd class, S£55; and 3rd class, S£45. You must make reservations at least a day or two in advance. This is Sudan's 'nice' train.

The regular train leaves on Saturdays at 6 pm, however, it is not unusual to wait up to 12 hours before the train actually departs. The trip to Atbara takes 18 hours. The 1st class fare is S£26 and 2nd class is almost always packed to the hilt. It meets up with the northbound train in Atbara on Sunday.

Bus There are daily buses from Kassala to Port Sudan. Buses from Khartoum to Port Sudan take two days. For more details on these buses refer to the Kassala and Khartoum Getting There sections.

All buses from Port Sudan to Kassala and Suakin leave daily from Deim Suakin (refer to the map). Buses depart at 6, 6.30 and 7 am. The Sunshine Bus Company is one of the better companies. but you need to make reservations at least one to two days in advance. Tickets to Kassala cost about S£17.

Truck The souk lorry parks are in Deim Arabi and just south of the city's outskirts. You can hitch there from town.

Steamer The Egyptian Navigation Company company operates two ships, the *Syria* and the *Algeria*, to Jedda and Suez. The agent's office is in the Sudan Shipping Line building and tickets can also be bought in Khartoum at Sabra Travel and the Reservations Agency (tel 75349 and 77083). All foreigners must show bank receipts to buy the tickets. There are approximately four trips a month but be wary of the departure times which Sabra give you.

There are five classes with different facilities. The fares to Suez range from S£133 in deck class (no bed) to S£234 in

1st class A (double cabin, with toilet and shower). Fares to Jedda range from S£120 in deck class to S£198 in 1st class A.

AROUS

Arous is an overpriced resort 50 km north of Port Sudan. The bad, bumpy road practically makes the place inaccessible but if you do manage to get there, you'll find excellent diving offshore in the colourful coral reefs.

You can camp near the resort hotel but bring your own food if you don't want to pay the outrageous prices at the hotel. Inquire at the Tourist Office in Port Sudan about transportation. There are sometimes souk lorries heading in this direction. Diving equipment can be rented at the hotel.

Southern Sudan

WARNING: SOUTHERN SUDAN IS CONSIDERED A WAR ZONE. TRAVEL IN THIS REGION AT YOUR OWN RISK.

In 1987 travel south along the White Nile from Kosti to Juba, either overland or by steamer, was impossible for foreigners. The SPLM *Anya-nya 2* rebels have been waging a guerilla war against the government since 1983 when rebel leader John Garang went into hiding to reactivate the Sudanese Peoples' Liberation Movement.

The main reason for the rebellion in the south was Nimeiri's declaration of *sharia*, which made Islamic Law applicable to the entire country. The SPLM, representing the predominantly Christian and animist southerners, kept up the hostilities even after the 1985 coup d'etat, which ousted Nimeiri and brought in the one-year rule by the Transitional Military Council. The rebels are continuing their fight against the new government, led by Shadek al Mahdi, because although the Prime Minister regularly announces the 'imminent abrogation of *sharia*' he has not yet done so.

The central government lost control of the south when the railway from Babanusa to Wau was sabotaged, the Kosti-Juba Nile steamer was blown up (in February 1984), and roads throughout the region were mined. Oil exploration projects sponsored by Chevron in the area of Bentiu were abandoned due to rebel attacks and the French engineers building the Jonglei Canal were also forced to stop.

Despite all the trouble, a few travellers have reported that travel is possible, but quite difficult and, of course, risky. The only way to travel to Juba overland is the western route via Wau, Tambura, Yambio, Maridi and Yei. There are flights from Khartoum to Juba (and vice versa) but these are usually booked several weeks in advance and the latest reports indicate the service may have been discontinued as one of these planes was shot down by the rebels. You might be able to hitch a ride with a charter company (refer to the Getting There sections for the Sudan and Khartoum).

Travel to Kosti and beyond to Sennar, Dinder, Dinder National Park, Ed Damazin and Er Roseires is possible.

KOSTI
Kosti, a relatively small city along the White Nile, was named after a Greek shopkeeper. There's not much of interest there except, maybe, the Kenana sugar plant which is a significant development project for the Sudan. It's a half hour from town.

Places to Stay
The *Tabidi Hotel*, a lakonda-style hotel built around a courtyard, has been recommended by travellers. There are three beds to a room and it costs S£12 for the entire room whether you need it or not. Ten metres from the hotel is an open field leading to the Nile.

The *Abu Zayd Hotel* is very clean and costs S£5 per person and there's also a colonial-style *Government Rest House*.

Getting There
There are frequent buses to Sennar and Khartoum that leave from near the railroad tracks. It costs S£3 to Sennar in a bus with padded seats.

SENNAR
Sennar is a convenient transit point with easy lorry connections to Suki and the village of Dinder.

The *Hotel Tourism*, behind the market and opposite the cinema, costs S£4 and is very clean but it's not the cheapest in town.

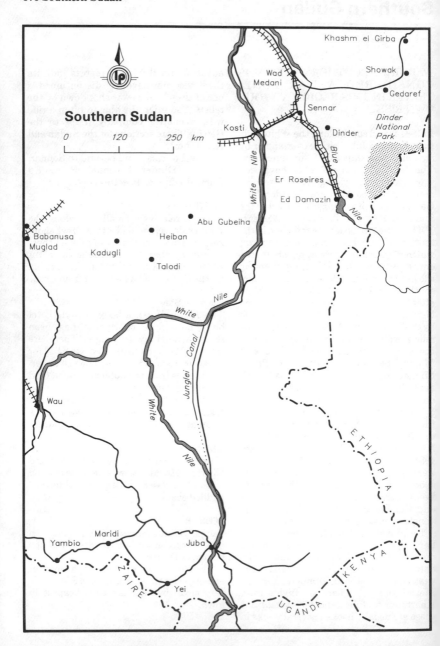

DINDER

The main attraction of this dusty little village is the extremely friendly and hospitable people. You will constantly be followed by a parade of kids who want to shake hands with you. The villagers will also overwhelm you with invitations to share food and drink with them in their homes. This is a good base for visiting the Dinder National Park.

Places to Stay

There's a *rest house* for the national park rangers where you can stay if there's room. To get there, walk a short distance out of the village, up the street past the mosque and huts and you'll see the yellow buildings of the rest house on your left. There are three beds to a room and it costs S£5 per person. Warm water showers are available and there's also a refrigerator and crockery. It's a very peaceful, quiet place and the walk from the rest house, through the forest to the Nile is beautiful.

DINDER NATIONAL PARK

One of the Sudan's 14 game reserves, this park features many animals including giraffes, lions, buffaloes, kudus, waterbucks, baboons, monkeys and crocodiles. The best time to visit is between December and May when you'll usually have the place to yourself.

Very few people manage to visit the park at any time though, and no wonder as the fees you must pay, per person, include: park fee – S£8; car entry fee – S£15; game scout fee, per day – S£3; photo permit – S£10; accommodation, per night – S£15; and tours inside the park, per day – S£30.

Getting There

If you don't have your own transport, hitching is the only way to get to the park. You might be able to hitch a ride from the rest house in Dinder, as all vehicles going to the park stop there first.

ER ROSEIRES

The town of Er Roseires is at the head of a lake created by the Er Roseires dam. It's a beautiful place with lots of trees, green hills and tall savannah grasses. Swimming is possible down river from the dam, but you will get your bag searched when you cross the bridge down from the dam.

There's a *youth hostel* in town.

TRAVELLING FURTHER SOUTH

Just in case the political situation in this region improves, the following is some slightly out-dated information about the Kosti-Juba Nile steamer, from before the civil war flared up again. It will probably change but this should give you a good idea of what to expect.

It is not recommended to make this journey, or the following overland trip south from Juba, while the civil war hostilities continue.

Kosti to Juba

The old steamer was sunk by SPLM rebels in February 1984, but there are two new boats, the *Juba* and *Nimule*. They only have 1st and 2nd class, but they do the journey in far less time than the old boat used to.

Travelling upstream should take six to eight days and downstream only about four days. There are departures two or three times a week in either direction and the fares were S£55 in 1st class and S£40 in 2nd class. If you want a berth then you must book in advance as there won't be any spare berths on the day of sailing.

Meals can be bought on the boat but they are not cheap – S£1.65 for lunch and S£1.75 for dinner. If you want to keep costs down, take some food of your own and a portable stove. Putting your own food together also helps pass the time. Water comes straight from the Nile and is not boiled. The toilets get sluiced down once a day but they don't stay that way for long. You will also need insect repellent.

If you're heading north from Juba, it's worth hanging around the harbour for a while to talk to the crew members of boats docked there. Some travellers have managed to get free lifts as far north as Malakal. You can save a lot of money this way, as boats from Malakal to Kosti cost S£15 in 2nd class or S£19 in 1st class.

Depending on how you take to slow boats, this journey can be interesting – as there are plenty of tribal villages and wildlife en route – or boring. If it turns out to be the latter, you could always pass some time by writing us a letter and telling us about the latest developments. Be careful about taking photographs of tribespeople on the river banks. The boat crew are especially sensitive and many travellers have had their film ripped from their cameras.

South from Juba

Going south from Juba, you have a choice of crossing into Uganda or Kenya. Until Idi Amin was deposed in Uganda, the main route south went directly into Kenya via Torit, Kapoeta, Lokichoggio and Lodwar. It's still possible to go this way if you're looking for a rugged trip, but you should allow at least a week for the journey. It's not possible during the rainy season. The Lodwar-Kapoeta section was being upgraded but the civil war has probably put an end to this.

Most travellers these days take the road into Uganda via Nimule. To do this trip you need a permit, which is obtained in Juba. There are trucks most days from Malakia, two km from Juba, which go to Kenya via Uganda. They cost Kenyan Sh300 or S£20. The drivers prefer Kenyan shillings but they will also accept US$ and UK£.

The journey takes about 1½ days and there are many army/police checkpoints en route where you will be thoroughly searched. Ugandan army and police will pressure you into giving them certain items of your baggage. A polite but firm refusal and a little humour may do the trick, otherwise leave something in the top of your pack that you can do without.

They seem to be particularly fond of medical supplies and may take these and leave the rest of your pack alone. It's best to go through in the morning, as they're more likely to be sober then. There are also daily buses between Juba and Nimule which cost S£3.05 and take about six hours.

From Wau to Juba there is really only one route. What appears to be the direct route on the maps, Wau-Rumbek-Juba, is almost impassable these days and there's virtually no traffic along it. Apart from that, it goes too close to the fighting, and the *Anya-nya 2* guerillas have warned that they will kill all white people on sight.

The road that you must take is Wau-Tambura-Yambio-Maridi-Yei-Juba. You'll need to get rides on trucks from Wau to Yei, but from Yei to Juba you have the choice of truck or bus. There are daily buses in either direction between Yei and Juba, which depart Juba between 6 and 7 am. The total cost of the lifts from Wau to Juba shouldn't be much more than S£20.

The Wau to Tambura stretch is pretty bad, but the Germans have been busy building a new road from Juba to Yambio so this section is much better. There are incredible views into the Nile and Zaire river basins along the Maridi-Yei section.

The best people to approach for lifts along this route are the international aid agencies like UNICEF and FAO (the UN's Food & Agriculture Organisation), Sudanese government departments and the Sudanese Council of Churches, but keep in mind that their priorities are to assist local inhabitants first. If you find yourself stuck in Wau, there is a mail truck which leaves every Monday for Juba and takes three to five days – but there's a lot of competition for seats.

JUBA

The government still holds this town but the SPLM have the surrounding region under their control. Though many travellers do grow to like Juba, it is definitely a 'one-horse town' and there's no reason, at the moment to go there.

You must register with the police on arrival in Juba; this costs 10 pt for a revenue stamp. If you're heading south, you must get an exit permit before you leave. These permits are obtainable from the Immigration Office, which is in the same building as the police, and cost 25 pt. Get this permit before you start looking for a lift. Photography permits can be obtained from the Ministry of Information, but they have to be counter-signed by the police.

Malakia

This traditional village is where much of the life of Juba actually takes place. The market is well worth visiting, especially if you're about to take the boat north to Kosti (if you can). Among other things, you can buy portable stoves for S£1 to S£2 and charcoal for 25 pt.

Malakia is two km from Juba. The main Juba souk lorry truck park is near the *souk*.

The Imetong Mountains

Dominated by the Sudan's highest mountain, Mt Kinyeti (3170 metres) the Imetong Mountains were developed as a hill station resort by the British colonial authorities.

If you have time for a detour, this region east of Juba and south of Torit is worth visiting. Make your way to the *Gilo Guest House* in **Gilo** which, although it was looted in the civil war, still retains a lot of old world charm. There are no mosquitoes or tsetse flies in these hills and it's wonderfully cool. You can forget about this place in the rainy season, however, as the road is impassable.

Places to Stay

For many years the most popular hotel in Juba has been the *Hotel Africa*. It costs S£1.25 per bed or 50 pt to sleep on the floor. Because of its popularity, however, it is often full and the management have become slack and allowed the place to run down. It was recently described by one traveller as 'no better than the boat'. Another traveller drew attention to the 'cholera-style toilets'. The hotel serves food which is good but certainly not the cheapest in town.

If you don't like the Africa or can't get in, try the *MTC* (Multi-Service Training Centre or Medical Training Centre), behind the football stadium, which has 10 beds for S£1.50 each, or floor space for 50 pt.

If you need something more comfortable, try the *Juba Hotel*, which costs S£30.

You may also be able to stay on the verandah of the Immigration Office free of charge.

Places to Eat

For food, go to the *People's Restaurant* or the *Greek Club*. Another popular place is *Unity Garden* on May St.

Most of the tap water in Juba comes straight from the Nile and is not filtered. If you drink it you'll get sick.

WAU

You can sleep free in the Wau police station yard as long as you don't mind bedding down in the dust along with the mosquitoes and a bunch of interesting criminals.

If you don't fancy that try the *Catholic Mission*, which sometimes dispenses a little Christian charity; or the *Youth Hostel*, which costs S£1.50 per night.

For relatively cheap accommodation try *El Nilein Hotel* or the *Riverside Hotel*.

You can get good meals for S£4 at the *Unity Restaurant*.

YAMBIO

You can stay at the beautifully located *Protestant Mission* for S£2 per night. From Yambio you can cross the border into Zaire via the market village of Gongura. From the latter place trucks are available to Isorio.

Egyptian Gods & Goddesses

Ammon – ram-headed Libyan god worshipped in the Siwa region of Egypt. He was identified with the Egyptian, Greek and Roman gods *Amun, Zeus* and *Jupiter.*

Amun – one of the deities of creation and the patron god of Thebes. *Amun*, his wife *Mut* and their son *Khons* formed the Theban triad.

Amun-Ra – king of the gods and the fusion of *Amun* and the sun god *Ra.*

Anubis – jackal-headed god of embalming and of the dead.

Anukis – wife of *Khnum*; wears a white crown flanked by two gazelle horns.

Aten – god of the sun disk, worshipped as the sole deity by Pharaoh Akhenaten and Queen Nefertiti.

Atum – god of the rising sun, identified with *Ra.*

Bastet – cat goddess; local deity of Bubastis in the Nile Delta.

Edjo – cobra-goddess of Lower Egypt; she was the protector of the pharaoh and was represented on his crown as a uraeus.

Geb – god of the earth and husband of *Nut.*

Haroeris – *Horus* the Elder, a form of *Horus* the falcon-god.

Hathor – goddess of pleasure and love. Represented as a cow, a woman with a cow's head, or a woman with a headdress of a sun disk fixed between the horns of a cow. She was the wet-nurse and lover of *Horus*, and the local deity of Dendara in the Nile Valley.

Horus – the falcon god; the offspring of *Isis* and *Osiris.* Identified with the living pharaoh.

Ihy – the youthful aspect of the creator gods.

Isis – the powerful goddess of healing, purity, sexuality, motherhood and women. The sister and wife of *Osiris* and mother of *Horus*, she was also the divine mourner of the dead. She was worshipped so passionately that she became identified with all the goddesses of the Mediterranean and finally became the universal mother of nature and protector of humans.

Khnum – ram-headed god of the Nile cataracts and local god of Elephantine Island. He was often shown as creator, molding humanity on his potter's wheel.

Khons – god of the moon and time; son of *Amun* and *Mut.*

Maat – goddess of truth and the personification of cosmic order.

Min – ithyphallic god of the harvest and fertility; local god of Achmim and patron deity of desert travellers.

Montu – falcon-headed warrior god and the original patron deity of Thebes.

Mut – vulture or lioness-headed war goddess; wife of *Amun.*

Neith – goddess of war and hunting, and protector of embalmed bodies.

Nekhbet – vulture-goddess of Nekheb; guardian of the pharaohs (with *Edjo*) and a deity associated with royal and divine births.

Nekheny – local falcon god of ancient Nekhen, later associated with *Horus.*

Nepthys – guardian deity and sister of *Isis.*

Nut – sky goddess, often depicted as a woman or a cow stretched across the ceilings of tombs, swallowing the sun and creating night. Each morning, she would give birth to the sun.

Opet – hippopotamus goddess; the mother of *Osiris.*

Osiris – ruler of the Underworld. Osiris was murdered by his brother *Seth* and brought back to life by his sister *Isis* to rule as the judge of the dead.

Ptah – creator god who formed the world with words from his tongue and heart. Local deity of ancient Memphis.

Ra – the great sun god. He was creator and ruler of other deified elements of nature and was often linked with other gods.

Ra-Harakhty – a falcon-headed god, the fusion of *Ra* and *Horus.*

Satis – the daughter of *Khnum* and *Anukis*; this family was the triad of the First Cataract and was worshipped at Elephantine Island (Aswan).

Sekhmet – a lioness-headed goddess; the 'spreader of terror' and wife of *Ptah.*

Serapis – Graeco-Egyptian god; the fusion of *Osiris* and *Zeus.*

Seshat – goddess of writing.

Seth – evil brother and murderer of *Osiris.*

Shu – the god of air, separating *Nut* from *Shu.*

Sobek – crocodile or crocodile-headed god; local deity of the Faiyum and Kom Ombo.

Thoth – ibis-headed god of wisdom, healing and writing; local god of ancient Hermopolis in the Nile Valley.

Wepwawet – wolf god and avenger of *Osiris* and the local god of Asyut in the Nile Valley.

Glossary

Bab – gate.

Book of the Dead – the ancient theological compositions, or hymns, that were the subject of most of the colourful paintings and reliefs on tomb walls. Extracts from these so-called books were believed to assist the deceased person safely into the afterlife via the Kingdom of the Dead. The texts were sometimes also painted on a roll of papyrus and buried with the dead.

Canopic Jars – pottery jars which held the embalmed internal organs and viscera – liver, stomach, lungs, intestines – of the mummified pharaoh. They were placed in the burial chamber near the sarcophagus.

Capitals – in pharaonic and Graeco-Roman architecture the top, or capital, of a column was decorated with plant forms, such as the papyrus, palm or lotus, or other motifs like the human face and cow's ears of the goddess *Hathor*.

Caravanserai – a large inn enclosing a courtyard used for accommodation of caravans.

Caretas – donkey cart.

Cartouche – oblong figure enclosing the hieroglyphs of royal or divine names.

Cenotaph – a symbolic tomb, temple or place of cult worship that was additional to the pharaoh's actual burial place.

Electrum – an alloy of gold and silver used for jewellery, ornaments and decorating buildings.

Fellahin – the peasant farmers or agricultural workers who make up the majority of Egypt's population.

False Door – a fake, seemingly half-open *ka* door in a tomb wall which enabled the pharaoh's spirit, or life force, to come and go at will.

Galabiyya – a full-length robe worn by men.

Haj – The pilgrimage to Mecca that all Muslims should make at least once in their lifetime.

Hantours – horse-drawn carriages.

Heb-Sed Festival – a five-day jubilee of royal rejuvenation, celebrated after 30 years of a pharaoh's reign and then every three years thereafter.

Heb-Sed Race – the traditional re-enactment, during the festival, of a pharaoh's coronation. The king sat first on the throne of Upper Egypt and then on the throne of Lower Egypt to symbolise the unification of the country and the renewal of his reign.

Hieroglyphs – the ancient Egyptian form of writing which used pictures and symbols to represent objects, words or sounds.

Hypostyle Hall – a columned hall, usually where the roof is supported by pillars.

Iconostasis – a screen with doors and icons set in tiers, used in eastern Christian churches.

Ithyphallic – denoting the erect phallus of a pharaoh or god (most often in reference to the god *Min*); a sign of fertility.

Ka – the spirit, or 'double', of a living person which gained its own identity with the death of that person. The survival of the *ka*, however, required the continued existence of the body, hence mummification. The *ka* was also the vital force emanating from a god and transferred through the pharaoh to his people.

Khedive – Egyptian viceroys (governors) under Ottoman suzerainty (1867-1914).

Kiosk – an open-sided pavilion.

Kuttab – a Qur'anic school for boys.

Liwan – a vaulted hall, opening into a central court, in the *madrassa* of a mosque.

Lotus – a white lily, regarded as sacred by the ancient Egyptians who likened their land to the lotus – the Delta was the flower, the Faiyum the bud, and the Nile and its valley the stem. The lotus was specifically identified with Upper Egypt.

Madrassa – a theological college that is part of a non-congregational mosque.

Mammisi – a birth house. In these small chapels or temples, the rituals of the divine birth of the living king were performed. All pharaohs were believed to be incarnations of the falcon god *Horus*.

Mashrabiyya – ornate carved wooden panel or screen; a feature of Islamic architecture.

Mastaba – the Arabic word for 'bench'; a mud brick superstructure above tombs from which the pyramids were developed.

Midan – town or city square.

Mihrab – the niche in the wall of a mosque, indicating the direction of Mecca.

Minbar – the pulpit in a mosque.

Mortuary Complex – a pharaoh's last resting place usually comprised: a pyramid which was the king's tomb and the repository for all his household goods, clothes and treasure; a funerary temple on the east side of the pyramid which served as a cult temple for worship of the dead pharaoh; pits for the *solar barques*; a valley temple on the banks of the Nile, where the mummification process was carried out; and a massive causeway from the river to the pyramid.

Muezzin – Muslim crier.

Natron – a whitish mineral of hydrated sodium carbonate that occurs in saline deposits and salt lakes and acts as a natural preservative. It was used in ancient Egypt to pack and dry out the body during mummification.

Nilometer – a staircase descending into the Nile and marked with registrations, above low water, to measure and record the levels of the river especially during the inundation.

Nome – administrative division or province of ancient Egypt.

Obelisk – monolithic stone pillar with square sides tapering to a pyramidal top and used as a monument in ancient Egypt. They were usually carved from pink granite and set up in pairs at the entrance to a tomb or temple. A single obelisk was sometimes the object of cult worship.

Opet Festival – celebration held in Luxor (Thebes) during the Nile inundation season, when statues of the Theban triad – *Amun, Mut* and *Khons* – would be transported down river from Karnak Temple to Luxor Temple to join in the festivities.

Papyrus – the plant identified with Lower Egypt; writing material made from the pith of this plant; or a document written on this paper.

Pylon – a monumental gateway at the entrance to a temple.

Pyramid Texts – paintings and reliefs on the walls of the internal rooms and burial chamber of pyramids and often on the sarcophagus itself. The texts recorded the pharaoh's burial ceremonies, associated temple rituals, the hymns vital to his passage into the afterlife and, sometimes, major events in his life.

Sabil – a covered, public drinking fountain.

Sarcophagus – the huge stone or marble coffin, encasing other wooden coffins and the mummy of the pharaoh or queen.

Scarab – a dung beetle regarded as sacred in ancient Egypt and represented on amulets or in hieroglyphs as a symbol of the sun god *Ra*.

Serapeum – network of subterranean galleries constructed as tombs for the mummified sacred *Apis* bulls (Saqqara); the most important temple of the Graeco-Egyptian god *Serapis*.

Serdab – a hidden cellar in a tomb or a stone room in front of some pyramids containing a coffin with a life-size, lifelike painted statue of the dead king. Serdabs were designed so the pharaoh's *ka* could communicate with the outside world.

Sharia – Islamic law, the body of doctrines that regulates the lives of Muslims. Arabic for 'road' or 'way'.

Solar Barque – wooden boat placed in or around the pharaoh's tomb. It was the symbolic vessel of transport for his journey over the sea of death to the Kingdom of the Dead, for judgement before *Osiris*, and final passage to the eternal afterlife.

Souk – market.

Speos – rock cut tomb or chapel.

Stele/stelae – stone or wooden commemorative slab or column decorated with inscriptions or figures.

Ulama – group of Muslim scholars or religious leaders; a member of this group.

Uraeus – a rearing cobra with inflated hood, associated with the goddess *Edjo*. It was the most characteristic symbol of Egyptian royalty and was worn on the pharaoh's forehead or crown. The sacred, fire spitting serpent was an agent of destruction and protector of the king.

Wakala – an inn for travelling merchants built around a courtyard, with living quarters above the warehouses and stables.

Index

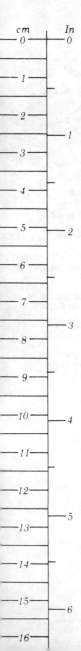

Temperature

To convert °C to °F multipy by 1.8 and add 32

To convert °F to °C subtract 32 and multipy by 5/9

Length, Distance & Area

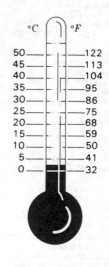

	multipy by
inches to centimetres	2.54
centimetres to inches	0.39
feet to metres	0.30
metres to feet	3.28
yards to metres	0.91
metres to yards	1.09
miles to kilometres	1.61
kilometres to miles	0.62
acres to hectares	0.40
hectares to acres	2.47

Weight

	multipy by
ounces to grams	28.35
grams to ounces	0.035
pounds to kilograms	0.45
kilograms to pounds	2.21
British tons to kilograms	1016
US tons to kilograms	907

A British ton is 2240 lbs, a US ton is 2000 lbs

Volume

	multipy by
Iiperial gallons to litres	4.55
litres to imperial gallons	0.22
US gallons to litres	3.79
litres to US gallons	0.26

5 imperial gallons equals 6 US gallons
a litre is slightly more than a US quart, slightly less
than a British one

Lonely Planet

Lonely Planet published its first book in 1973. Tony and Maureen Wheeler had made a lengthy overland trip from England to Australia and, in response to numerous 'how do you do it?' questions, Tony wrote and they published *Across Asia on the Cheap*. It became an instant local best-seller and inspired thoughts of a second travel guide. A year and a half in South-East Asia resulted in their second book, *South-East Asia on a Shoestring*, which they put together in a backstreet Chinese hotel in Singapore in 1975. The 'yellow book', as it quickly became known, soon became *the* guide to the region and has now gone through five editions, always with its familiar yellow cover.

Soon other writers started to come to them with ideas for similar books – books that went off the beaten track and took an adventurous approach to travel, books that 'assumed you knew how to get your luggage off the carousel,' as one reviewer described them. Lonely Planet soon grew from a kitchen table operation to a spare room and then to its own office. It also started to develop an international reputation as the Lonely Planet logo began to appear in more and more countries. Always the emphasis has been on travel for travellers and Tony and Maureen still manage to fit in a number of trips each year and play a very active part in the writing and updating of Lonely Planet's guides.

Today over 20 people work at the Lonely Planet office in Melbourne, Australia and there are another half dozen at the company's US office in Oakland, California. Keeping guidebooks up to date is a constant battle and although the basic element in that struggle is still an ear to the ground and lots of walking, modern technology also plays its part. All Lonely Planet guidebooks are now stored and updated on computer. In some cases authors take lap-top computers into the field with them. Lonely Planet is also using computers to draw maps and eventually many of the maps will also be stored on disk.

At first Lonely Planet specialised extensively in the Asia region but these days it is also developing major ranges of guidebooks to the Pacific region, to South America and to Africa. The list of walking guides is also growing and Lonely Planet is producing a unique series of phrasebooks to 'unusual' languages. In 1982 the company's *India – a travel survival kit* won the Thomas Cook Guidebook of the Year award, the major international award for travel guidebooks and the company's business achievements have been recognised by twice winning Australian Export Achievement Awards, in 1982 and 1986.

The people at Lonely Planet strongly feel that travellers can make a positive contribution to the countries they visit both by better appreciation of cultures and by the money they spend. In addition the company tries to make a direct contribution to the countries and regions it covers. Since 1986 a percentage of the income from each book has gone to aid groups and associations. This has included donations to famine relief in Africa, to aid projects in India, to agricultural projects in Nicaragua and other Central American countries and to Greenpeace's efforts to halt French nuclear testing in the Pacific. In 1987 $30,000 was donated by Lonely Planet to these projects.

Guides to the Middle East

Israel - a travel survival kit

This is a comprehensive guidebook to a small, fascinating country that is packed with things to see and do. This guide will help you unravel its political and religious significance – and enjoy your stay.

Jordan & Syria - a travel survival kit

Roman cities, ancient Petra, Crusader castles – these sights, amongst many others, combine with Arab hospitality to make this undiscovered region a fascinating and enjoyable destination.

Yemen - a travel survival kit

The fertile mountains and plateaus of the Arabian Peninsula have preserved a treasure trove for adventurous travellers – superb architecture, dramatic countryside and friendly people.

West Asia on a shoestring

A complete guide to the overland trip from Bangladesh to Turkey. Information for budget travellers to Afghanistan, Bangladesh, Bhutan, India, Iran, Maldives, Nepal, Pakistan, Sri Lanka, Turkey and the Middle East.

Turkey - a travel survival kit

Unspoilt by tourism, Turkey is a travellers' paradise, whether you want to lie on a beach or explore the ancient cities that are the legacy of a rich and varied past. This acclaimed guide will help you to make the most of your stay.

Lonely Planet Newsletter

We collect an enormous amount of information here at Lonely Planet. Apart from our research there's a steady stream of letters from people out on the road. To make the most of all this info we produce a quarterly Newsletter (approx Feb, May, Aug, and Nov).

The Newsletter is packed with down-to-earth information from the pens of hundreds of travellers who write from first-hand experience. Whether you want the latest facts, travel stories, or simply to reminisce, the Newsletter will keep you in touch with what is going on.

Where else could you find out:
• about boat trips on the Yalu River?
• where to stay if you want to live in a typical Thai village?
• how long it takes to get a Nepalese trekking permit?
• that Israeli youth hostel stamps will get you deported from Syria?

One year's subscription is $10.00 (that's US$ in the USA or A$ in Australia), payable by cheque, money order, Amex, Visa, Bankcard or MasterCard.

Order Form

Please send me four issues of the Lonely Planet Newsletter. (Subscription starts with next issue. 1987 price – subject to change.)

Name and address (print) ....

....

....

Tick one

☐ Cheque enclosed (payable to Lonely Planet Publications)
☐ Money Order enclosed (payable to Lonely Planet Publications)
Charge my ☐ Amex, ☐ Visa, ☐ Bankcard, ☐ MasterCard for the amount of $......................

Card No ....   Expiry Date ....

Cardholder's Name (print) ....

Signature ....   Date ....

Return this form to:

Lonely Planet Publications	or	Lonely Planet Publications
PO Box 2001A		PO Box 88
Berkeley		South Yarra
CA 94702		Victoria 3141
USA		Australia

Lonely Planet travel survival kits

Alaska
Australia
Bali & Lombok
Bangladesh
Burma
Canada
China
Chile & Easter Island
East Africa
Ecuador & the Galapagos Islands
Egypt & the Sudan
Fiji
Hong Kong, Macau & Canton
India
Indonesia
Japan
Jordan & Syria
Kashmir, Ladakh & Zanskar
Kathmandu & the Kingdom of Nepal
Korea & Taiwan
Malaysia, Singapore & Brunei
Mexico
New Zealand
Pakistan
Papua New Guinea
Peru
Philippines
Raratonga & the Cook Islands
Sri Lanka
Tahiti
Thailand
Tibet
Turkey

Lonely Planet Shoestring Guides

Africa on a Shoestring
North-East Asia on a Shoestring
South America on a Shoestring
South-East Asia on a Shoestring
West Asia on a Shoestring

Lonely Planet Trekking & Walking Guides

Bushwalking in Papua New Guinea
Tramping in New Zealand
Trekking in the Indian Himalaya
Trekking in the Nepal Himalaya

Lonely Planet Phrasebooks

Indonesia Phrasebook
China Phrasebook
Nepal Phrasebook
Papua New Guinea Phrasebook
Sri Lanka Phrasebook
Thailand Phrasebook
Tibet Phrasebook

And Also

Travel with Children
Travellers Tales

Lonely Planet Distribution

Lonely Planet travel guides are available round the world. If you can't find them, ask your bookshop to order them from one of the distributors listed below. For countries not listed, or if you would like a free copy of our latest booklist, write to Lonely Planet in Australia.

Lonely Planet Distributors

Australia
Lonely Planet Publications, PO Box 88, South Yarra, Victoria 3141.
Canada
Raincoast Books, 112 East 3rd Avenue, Vancouver, British Columbia V5T 1C8.
Denmark, France & Norway
Scanvil Books aps, Store Kongensgade 59 A, DK-1264 Copenhagen K.
Hong Kong
The Book Society, GPO Box 7804.
India & Nepal
UBS Distributors, 5 Ansari Rd, New Delhi – 110002
Israel
Geographical Tours Ltd, 8 Tverya St, Tel Aviv 63144.
Japan
Intercontinental Marketing Corp, IPO Box 5056, Tokyo 100-31.
Netherlands
Nilsson & Lamm bv, Postbus 195, Pampuslaan 212, 1380 AD Weesp.
New Zealand
Roulston Greene Publishing Associates Ltd, Private Bag, Takapuna, Auckland 9.
Papua New Guinea see Australia
Singapore & Malaysia
MPH Distributors, 601 Sims Drive, £03-21, Singapore 1438.
Spain
Altair, Balmes 69, 08007 Barcelona.
Sweden
Esselte Kartcentrum AB, Vasagatan 1u, S-111 20 Stockholm.
Thailand
Chalermnit, 108 Sukhumvit 53, Bangkok 10110.
UK
Roger Lascelles, 47 York Rd, Brentford, Middlesex, TW8 0QP
USA
Lonely Planet Publications, PO Box 2001A, Berkeley, CA 94702.
West Germany
Buchvertrieb Gerda Schettler, Postfach 64, D3415 Hattorf a H.